Jane Smith
'47

THE BEST PLAYS OF 1946-47

EDITED BY

BURNS MANTLE

The Best Plays of 1899-1909
(*With Garrison P. Sherwood*)
The Best Plays of 1909-19
(*With Garrison P. Sherwood*)
The Best Plays of 1919-20
The Best Plays of 1920-21
The Best Plays of 1921-22
The Best Plays of 1922-23
The Best Plays of 1923-24
The Best Plays of 1924-25
The Best Plays of 1925-26
The Best Plays of 1926-27
The Best Plays of 1927-28
The Best Plays of 1928-29
The Best Plays of 1929-30
The Best Plays of 1930-31
The Best Plays of 1931-32
The Best Plays of 1932-33
The Best Plays of 1933-34
The Best Plays of 1934-35
The Best Plays of 1935-36
The Best Plays of 1936-37
The Best Plays of 1937-38
The Best Plays of 1938-39
The Best Plays of 1939-40
The Best Plays of 1940-41
The Best Plays of 1941-42
The Best Plays of 1942-43
The Best Plays of 1943-44
The Best Plays of 1944-45
The Best Plays of 1945-46
The Best Plays of 1946-47
Contemporary American
Playwrights (1938)

THE BEST PLAYS
OF 1946-47

AND THE
YEAR BOOK OF THE DRAMA
IN AMERICA

EDITED BY
BURNS MANTLE

With Illustrations

DODD, MEAD AND COMPANY
NEW YORK   -   -   -   1947

INTRODUCTION

THE theatre staggered a little this last season. It was recovering slowly from a post-war hangover that made its advancing steps uncertain—a hangover the likes of which it had not known since the boom days of the nineteen-twenties, just before the crash. Remember?

The theatre's mental processes, too, were a bit on the foggy side. Its established dramatists, as well as those in search of a hearing, were still reeling slightly from their impact with a wartime conditioning, or reconditioning, that included the hysterical struggle of a dazed and unhappy world trying to right itself with the help of an untried United Nations gyroscope.

Small wonder the theatre proceeded unsteadily from start to finish the season of 1946-47. Great wonder that it did so well. Admittedly it wasn't easy to find ten worthily representative scripts for this annual record. But those we did find, all written by American dramatists, do their writers and sponsors full credit.

It was a season of revivals, as its reviewers are quick to protest. But they were fine revivals, and they stood up amazingly, despite their age and previous degrees of service and local fame.

As worthily representative plays I have taken, first, the professional critics' choice, Arthur Miller's "All My Sons." A year or two belated as an exposure and criticism of wartime cheaters and cheating, you may say, but I doubt if it could have been written or produced sooner than it was. I like it, both because it is a thoughtful work and because its acceptance does credit to the talent of a new writer who was a little unkindly treated when his "The Man Who Had All the Luck" was lightly brushed off the season before.

Eugene O'Neill's delayed return to a theatre he long had honored was an event of outstanding importance. His "The Iceman Cometh" is strong meat and not suited to sensitive stomachs—or to sensitive souls, especially those sensitive souls who, quite honestly, have no use for the theatre except as a home of cheerful entertainment. But the season would have been notably weakened in output and quality if we had not had a chance to see and to weigh this work of America's first dramatist.

It is possible to argue that Maxwell Anderson's "Joan of Lorraine" would not have been the magnificent success it proved if it had been denied the performance of the radiant Ingrid Bergman. I take polite issue with that belief. Miss Bergman did add greatly to the impressiveness of "Joan," but if you will keep close watch of future theatre records you will, I'm sure, read of a succession of other notable and highly successful performances of this heroine's role. No one is likely to top the Bergman achievement, but a score or more are quite likely to approach it closely and with equal felicity.

By similar reasoning it can be rightfully claimed that no dramatist of major standing could possibly retell the story of Joan the Maid without producing impressively holding drama—just as the story of Jesus Christ, in any intelligent and honest retelling, will inevitably inspire both awe and reverence. A moving dramatic power is inherent in each. But Maxwell Anderson did evolve a new and fascinating dramatic pattern for his "Joan" by relating the story as the adventure of an essentially commonplace theatrical stock company, a treatment for which he deserves full credit and wide reading.

In Lillian Hellman's "Another Part of the Forest" you will also find a gifted dramatist's skill impressively employed. In going back to the people with whom she lived so long, respected so little and yet recognized as being so honestly average in the writing of "The Little Foxes," I have a feeling Miss Hellman has set a precedent a host of her fellow writers may be quick to follow, though, we can hope, not to imitate.

Ruth Gordon's "Years Ago" is a simple domestic comedy made important, to this season at least, by the understanding and technically skillful performances of Fredric March and Florence Eldridge. With these two serving as a personal and professional anchor, young Patricia Kirkland added another promising ingénue to that class of ambitious youngsters from which the acting profession largely grows.

There wasn't much fun in this season's dramas. It was good, therefore, that Norman Krasna came along with "John Loves Mary." He gave this editor a grand opportunity to leaven the Best Plays list with a little fun. This is a comedy even more trivial, it may be, than was the same author's "Dear Ruth." And yet, accepting its premise, the playgoer is pretty sure to find himself having a fine time in the theatre. "John Loves Mary" is one of those farcical comedies that depends quite frankly on extravagant situations rather than recognizable characters. The "could happen" type. Could, but probably wouldn't.

George Kelly swings lightly, and with the left hand, at the divorce problem in "The Fatal Weakness." His greater contribution to the season, however, was in providing a heroine with a sense of proportion as well as one of humor that suited Ina Claire so well it lured her from a temporary retirement. This romance-ruled lady is able to cover her acquirement of marital freedom with a conventional claim of injured pride, but she still retains sufficient curiosity to take her to her philandering partner's second marriage—a new idea for divorcees.

"The Story of Mary Surratt" was one of the season's earlier failures. This may have been because Broadway playgoers and their visiting cousins, and the newspaper reviewers before them, did not enjoy being reminded of one of the less convincing episodes in American history. It may be because we were too close to the last war to care for another story based on wartime miseries. But "Mary Surratt" is well written by John Patrick and represents a vast and careful research. It was well acted, particularly by Dorothy Gish and Kent Smith. By the time my choice was narrowed to "Mary Surratt," or the Mabley-Mins "Temper the Wind," or Jean-Paul Sartre's "No Exit," I was considerably puzzled. I finally decided on "Surratt," because I think it was one of the better plays of the year, and a little because of its complete American background. This, after all, is an American year book. If you harbor an urge to make something of that, go ahead.

Moss Hart's "Christopher Blake" is, admittedly, one of his lesser achievements representing one of his better ideas. In a country in which the divorce record is the greatest in the world and in history, what more pathetically worthy of serious discussion than the fate of the divorce orphan, especially from the viewpoint of an imaginative victim? The defense rests.

Now another question arose that we had to thresh out. It happens that for the first time in we don't know when this season saw the play with music come into a new prominence, as is more fully indicated in the chapter devoted to The Season in New York. Fantasy was underscored. I felt that some notice should be taken of this trend. Therefore I decided to try the experiment of making the libretto of a music play stand on its own feet, without, as is customary, depending on the usual supports, the musical score and the dance arrangements. The result is not too happy, but there it is. Of the two novelties, I voted with the Critics' Circle for the Lerner-Loewe "Brigadoon" as the best musical play of the season.

John Chapman has again served me as a representative at the front, keeping an eye on Broadway if I happened to be away. Mr.

Chapman also wrote the digests of three of the plays included in this volume—those of "The Iceman Cometh," "Years Ago" and "The Fatal Weakness." His is a valued assistance.

This volume of the "Best Plays" is the thirtieth of the series, including the two Mantle-Sherwood volumes covering the double decade between 1899 and 1919. These were added after the Mantle volumes were begun the season of 1919-20.

For the thirtieth time, then, the editor's most appreciative thanks to you, his consistently faithful and most loyal public of Best Play supporters.

B. M.

Forest Hills, L. I., 1947

CONTENTS

THE BEST PLAYS OF 1946-47

THE BEST PLAYS OF 1946-47

THE SEASON IN NEW YORK

THIS has been a year of revivals, but not one of revival, in the theatre. Of eighty-seven major productions, old and new, I count nineteen that were brought back from other years. The fact that six of them can be numbered with the major successes of the season is fairly remarkable. It is a testimony, not only to the quality of dramatic writing in other years, but also to the acting ability of those present-day players who were able to bring again to life characters associated in the main with other personalities frequently of greater theatre fame.

The poised and handsome Cornelia Otis Skinner elected to play the effective role of Mrs. Erlynne to the Mrs. Windermere of Penelope Ward, one of London's favored beauties. These two, properly, even handsomely supported, sartorially and scenically, carried Oscar Wilde's "Lady Windermere's Fan" through a total of 228 performances.

José Ferrer, an actor of versatile talent and a gift for characterization, offered a youngish Cyrano de Bergerac in contrast to those of Richard Mansfield and Walter Hampden of earlier theatre periods. He repeated the Rostand classic 192 times.

John Gielgud, a leader of the London theatre, brought to Broadway a perfectly staged and cast revival of the aforementioned Mr. Wilde's "The Importance of Being Earnest." Booked for a limited run, Mr. Gielgud was induced to extend this for additional weeks before he turned to a second classical resurrection, that of Congreve's "Love for Love."

Theatre Inc. followed its successful revival of Bernard Shaw's "Pygmalion" (with Gertrude Lawrence) of last season with Synge's "The Playboy of the Western World" this season. Again pains were taken by Richard Aldrich and his associates to stage a revival worthy of the Abbey Theatre and the Irish Players, who first brought the "Playboy" to America. Burgess Meredith came on from Hollywood to play the boastful Christopher Mahon and Eithne Dunne came from Dublin to play the heroine. A ten-week run was the reward.

3

Judith Evelyn, who had scored a personal success of propor-
tions in the melodrama "Angel Street" two years before, agreed to
play the heroine in a revival of that former Pulitzer prize winner,
George Kelly's "Craig's Wife." This, too, was a performance
critically and popularly well received. It helped to keep Mrs.
Craig active for an additional nine weeks.

Bert Lahr, who once knew the old-time "Burlesque Wheel" as
well as he did his own home, and maybe better, was happily chosen
for a revival of the Arthur Hopkins-George Watters "Burlesque,"
which Hal Skelly and Barbara Stanwyck played for the better part
of a year back in 1927-28. Lahr's revival of his old-time burlesque
routine, plus definitely helpful support from Jean Parker of the
cinema, kept "Burlesque" playing from the holidays through the
remainder of the season.

Others ranged from a quick failure for an all-Negro experiment
with "Lysistrata" to a friendly success for Eva Le Gallienne and
Florida Friebus' "Alice in Wonderland." "Alice" helped to save
the day for the American Repertory's season, as later more fully
reported.

The Hecht-MacArthur "The Front Page" did reasonably well
for ten weeks but the American Repertory sponsors were disap-
pointed by a lack of playgoer interest in Barrie's "What Every
Woman Knows" and Sidney Howard's "Yellow Jack." Good old
"Chocolate Soldier" was brought back in March and hung on till
May, with a couple of talented young people, Keith Andes and
Frances McCann, in the Bummerli and Nadina roles.

The American Repertory Company started its season with high
hopes and a great confidence crowding each other in the hearts of
Margaret Webster, Cheryl Crawford and Eva Le Gallienne. They
had subscriptions in bank for $300,000 and a company of estab-
lished players in rehearsal. They were to offer a revival of "Henry
VIII," with Walter Hampden playing Wolsey; Barrie's "What
Every Woman Knows," with June Duprez in the role that Maude
Adams and Helen Hayes had made memorable, and Ibsen's "John
Gabriel Borkman," which can always be depended upon to draw
forth the considerable Eva Le Gallienne following.

Reviewers were kind to all three of the opening week's offerings,
and quite enthusiastic about "Androcles and the Lion," which was
later added to the repertory. Ernest Truex played the name part
originally done by O. P. Heggie. But it was soon apparent that
the repertory idea as such had not stimulated the interest of the
company's well-wishers as much as hoped for. It was decided in
the circumstances to put aside temporarily the ordered change of

bill, and concentrate on developing a run for "Androcles." When this interest began to slip, a further compromise was made. The version of "Alice in Wonderland" which had been prepared by Miss Le Gallienne and Florida Friebus for production at the Civic Repertory Theatre fifteen years ago was put in rehearsal in association wth Rita Hassan, who had had the foresight to acquire a proprietary interest in the script. Again public response was friendly and immediate and "Alice," running into the late Spring, did much to revive the spirits of all those who had had anything to do with the repertory enterprise.

The revival of "Alice" served to top a series of fantasies that notably punctuated this unusual season. First had come "Finian's Rainbow," the fantastic story of a leprechaun who came from Ireland to bury a pot of gold in America's Fort Knox territory in the confident expectation that its contents would increase and multiply. E. Y. Harburg and Fred Saidy were responsible for this story, and Burton Lane wrote an attractive score to go with it, the popular "How Are Things in Glocca Morra?" being the production hit.

Later came the "Brigadoon" that has been included in this record to represent the musical novelties of the year. Alan Jay Lerner wrote the story of "Brigadoon" and Frederick Loewe composed the score. Both were in the nature of superlative jobs. "Brigadoon" did as much for the stimulation of interest in the music drama as any of the plays had done for the spoken drama. The Messrs. Lerner and Loewe had made their debut with "The Day Before Spring" the season of 1945-46.

Finally there were two short operas, written and composed by Gian-Carlo Menotti, one called "The Telephone" and the other "The Medium," the first short and humorous, the second longer and with thrills added. Produced in the late Spring, these added another novelty to the list. It was Mr. Menotti's request that his little works of art should be judged by the drama reporters rather than the music critics. The editorial bosses agreed, and the drama men proved beautifully responsive.

This was also the season that Maurice Chevalier came back to entertain and to explain a little unpleasantness stemming from the charge that he really didn't have to be quite as friendly as he seemed to be with the enemy Nazis the time they were occupying Paris in the war years. Maurice explained by declaring the report untrue. That a lot of people over here believed him, or didn't care too much, was indicated by the fact that he began his season of intimate song recitals to a pack-jammed theatre ($9.60 a seat being the cost of an orchestra stall opening night), and continued it thereafter for six weeks (the top prices dropping to $4.80 for mid-week places and $6 for week-ends). The generally accepted verdict was that the engaging Frenchman had not changed much, if any, in the 15 years since he was here before.

Our English-speaking allies were neither as generous nor as successful visitors to our theatre this year as they were last year. Laurence Olivier, leader of the Old Vic troupe and voted the best actor in Wendell Willkie's one world in 1945, was represented only by the picture "Henry V," in which he played Henry and which he directed. Garlands of superlatives were again festooned about the Olivier neck by the reviewers.

John Gielgud, a stage graduate of the same group that has brought us Maurice Evans, Olivier and Ralph Richardson, scored both a personal and directorial success with his productions of Wilde's "The Importance of Being Earnest" and Congreve's "Love for Love," as previously noted.

But Donald Wolfit, a minor actor-manager who has built up a considerable provincial following in England by touring a repertory of Shakespearean drama, had an unhappy time on his first visit to America. Unwisely, it seems to this reporter, he selected "King Lear" as an opening bill. A difficult and none too popular tragedy, even when included in the repertory of an established and popular Shakespearean star, "Lear" offers additional handicaps for a stranger. Wolfit took a beating from the critics with good grace and went on to "As You Like It," in which Iden Payne's daughter Rosalind played her namesake; "The Merchant of Venice," in which Wolfit proved an acceptable Shylock; "Volpone," a revival of the bawdy Ben Jonson farce that caught the fancy of a goodly crowd, and "Hamlet," in which the star again gave a conventional but honest account of himself and his art.

It is possible, even probable, that theatre historians of other years will refer to this season as that in which a number of well-intentioned experimental theatre enterprises were launched in New York. In addition to the American Repertory above referred to, the Equity-Library Theatre, which had its first good start the season of 1945-46, made definite strides. John Golden increased his sponsor interest and Sam Jaffee his most active interest in organization, as more fully appears in George Freedley's chapter devoted to these experimental enterprises elsewhere in these pages. Mr. Freedley likewise reports on the first year of an Experimental Theatre proper, which had the endorsement of a still abortive but entirely earnest and hopeful National Theatre movement, blessed by Congress and helped on at least one occasion by the American Theatre Wing, that noble war-time emergency organization that did so much for our own and visiting service men during the war years.

It was to the work of the Theatre Wing, incidentally, that the late Antoinette Perry devoted practically all her time during the war, and it was in memory of this splendid service that the Wing established the annual Antoinette Perry Awards, which it is expected will eventually take their place in importance with those of the Motion Picture Academy Awards of Hollywood. In Hollywood the awards are called "Oscars." On Broadway the Perry awards are known as "Tonys."

The fanciest of the experimental theatre schemes was that thought up by a gentleman named H. G. Lengsfelder. He organized one known as "Your Theatre, Incorporated." All those who bought seats for a Your Theatre, Inc., production prior to production became automatically shareholders in the company. No one was permitted to buy more than twenty-four shares, or tickets, however, and that not only discouraged speculators but also encouraged the democratic way of life. Your Theatre, Inc., collected something like 3,000 subscribers for its first production, that of a farce comedy called "Heads or Tails." The income served to finance the production of the play, which was blasted by the reviewers as impossible, but Your Theatre, Inc., was not too discouraged. It proceeded to organize its own staff of critics, who wrote a series of favorable reviews, and these were printed as advertisements.

The Summer months were, as usual, dull stretches in the New York theatre, for all there were five productions made in June and July. The first of these was a Shakespeare comedy to which Ruth Chatterton had taken a fancy. "Second Best Bed" was the title, and Ruth played the role of the heroine, Anne Hathaway Shakespeare. Having been practically deserted by her Will, who was in London carving out a success as playwright and producer, Anne had about made up her mind to divorce Will and marry a Stratford-on-Avon native named Poggs. About this time Will arrives from London for a visit and, such is still his charm, Anne has soon forgotten Poggs. N. Richard Nash was the author.

The second June entry was one called "The Dancer," written by Milton Lewis and Julian Funt. This had to do with alleged episodes from the life of a famed ballet dancer whose mind gave way. Living under the protection of a wealthy dilettante, the dancer devotes his off time to murdering village prostitutes, puzzling the local gendarmerie greatly. Pursued also by his wife, who wants his supposedly hidden fortune, and his daughter, who would like to be sure that his madness is not hereditary, the dancer's life is not a happy one. The law finally catches up with him.

Sonja Henie, star skater and shrewd producer of skating extravaganza, with her partner, Arthur M. Wirtz, brought "Icetime" to the Center Theatre, with Freddie Trenkler, Joan Hyldoft, the Brandt Sisters, Fritz Dietl and the Bruises featured. The reception was, as usual, highly popular.

The farcical "Maid in the Ozarks," which had run for weeks and weeks in Chicago and was frankly advertised as "the worst play in the world," was forced through a ten-week run on Broadway, still advertised as "the worst." There was neither gain nor gaiety in the adventure.

September struggled to take its traditionally rightful place as the opening month of a new theatre season, but the struggle was in vain. There was a revival of the Hecht-MacArthur "The Front Page" which did pretty well for ten weeks, and Ben Hecht obliged with a propaganda spectacle drama for the Palestinian Jews called "A Flag Is Born." This worthy effort started with Paul Muni as a kind of guest star and acquired Luther Adler when Muni was forced to return to other chores. A tour followed 120 Broadway performances.

Richard Tauber, a popular Continental tenor who had been singing Lehar's "Yours Is My Heart Alone" for an uncounted number of years, finally got to New York with that musical comedy, now pretty well dated. There was some enthusiasm for a few weeks, but when the Tauber larynx gave out, after 36 performances, the engagement was ended.

Henry Myers tried to assemble a new opera out of a combination of Victor Herbert's "The Fortune Teller" and "The Serenade," but as "Gypsy Lady" it could get no more than 80 performances. Even an Agatha Christie mystery, "Hidden Horizon," was through in two weeks.

As frequently happens, there were a number of little stinkers produced the next several weeks, but also a few of the season's better things also made an appearance. Eugene O'Neill's "The Iceman Cometh," for one. Long awaited, this four-hour drama, starting originally in the late afternoon, calling time for dinner at 7 o'clock and then continuing from 8:15 to 11, was an immediate critical and box-office sensation.

As noted, José Ferrer came close to his heart's desire with a revival of "Cyrano de Bergerac" and Cornelia Otis Skinner had a grand time with a revival of Oscar Wilde's "Lady Windermere's Fan." Elisabeth Bergner suffered a minor shock when her usually devoted following refused to take a revival of John Webster's "The Duchess of Malfi." Burgess Meredith was happy playing "The Playboy of the Western World" to the satisfaction of most of his critics, including the Irish. Clifton Webb was a little less happy than usual substituting for Noel Coward in the latter's newest comedy, "Present Laughter," and Helen Hayes fairly knocked them off their seats playing as Anita Loos' slightly alcoholic heroine in "Happy Birthday." A teetotaler is Helen, but she had fun pretending to be a Newark schoolteacher who, in the cause of a romantic experimentalism, captured her man.

The only interesting failure during these weeks was a new adaptation of Louis Verneuil's one-act, two-character play called "Jealousy" when Eugene Walter adapted it for A. H. Woods in 1928. "Obsession" was the new title, and Basil Rathbone and Eugenie Leontovich were the players. An all-colored version of "Lysistrata" was withdrawn after 4 performances. John Golden made a star of Donald Cook for the production of a comedy called "Made in Heaven," by Hagar Wilde, but even with Donald's aid it was through after 100 performances.

To practically everyone's surprise, the experienced and gifted George Kaufman and the less experienced but also gifted Nunnally Johnston, not to mention the lyrical Ira Gershwin and the musical Arthur Schwartz, failed expensively with a musical comedy called "Park Avenue." It had to do satirically with the rich marrying set, but was never very amusing.

Three top lady showmen, Cheryl Crawford, Margaret Webster and Eva Le Gallienne, with a subscribed capital of $300,000, brought the American Repertory Theatre, Inc., into existence, as previously mentioned. They started with Shakespeare's "Henry VIII," followed with Barrie's "What Every Woman Knows," Ibsen's "John Gabriel Borkman" and Shaw's "Androcles and the Lion." "Androcles" proved the hit of this group. Later "Yellow Jack" was added.

Maxwell Anderson, who had failed rather unhappily with a post-war problem play, "Truckline Café," came back cheerily and dramatically in November with "Joan of Lorraine" and Ingrid Bergman. Reviewers who had chastised this dramatist brutally the season before, now wrote glowingly of his dramatist's gifts as revealed anew with "Joan." Miss Bergman became the personality success of the new season, and everything was lovely in that section.

Also Ina Claire, who had been living quietly in her California home for a period of years, decided to give George Kelly's "The Fatal Weakness" the aid of her agreeable presence and her smart high comedy playing—which was a good thing for "The Fatal Weakness" as well as for Miss Claire.

Lillian Hellman, having become deeply interested in the characters she had created for "The Little Foxes" some seasons back, decided to use them in another drama that should go back to their lives twenty years before "The Little Foxes" and, in a way, show how they got the way they did. "Another Part of the Forest" was her selected title, and her success with the throwback drama can be judged by the digest contained in this record.

An early importation was Jean-Paul Sartre's study of a scene in Hell called "No Exit." This proved an intelligently controversial drama. It set the critics by the ears, but interested the playgoing public only slightly. It may be that, having heard M. Sartre was the leader of a new group classified in Paris as Existentialists, playgoers accepted that information as a warning.

Moss Hart's "Christopher Blake" and Ruth Gordon's "Years Ago" were late November and early December Broadway entries. Neither was received with the rapture playwrights hope for, but they both did their authors credit, as more fully appears in other pages of this volume.

Jean Dalrymple's revival of "Burlesque," which Arthur Hopkins and George Manker Watters wrote in 1927, and in which both Barbara Stanwyck and Hal Skelly scored personal hits, gave Bert Lahr a fine chance to revive his burlesque-wheel past, and Jean Parker an equally good chance to get away from Hollywood, where she had been a picture star without a Broadway background. They both scored personal hits.

There was considerable surprise expressed when the stage version of "Here Comes Mr. Jordan," Harry Segall's outstanding screen success of the early nineteen forties, did not satisfy its "legitimate" public. Sidney Blackmer and Donald Murphy played the leads and Philip Loeb scored personally as the prize-fight manager. When playgoers did not respond the play was withdrawn after nine performances.

That popular sustaining playgoing public, the Irish and the Jews, did a good deal for "Toplitsky of Notre Dame." The reviews were lukewarm, but audience reaction was definitely favorable. A modernized version of John Gay's "Beggar's Opera," done over with a New York gangster background as "Beggar's

Holiday," also found a public of which several of the reviewers were doubtful.

A serious post-war drama, the best of the line up to the time of its production at Christmas holiday time, was "Temper the Wind," written by Edward Mabley and Leonard Mins. It came upon that war-play weariness freely confessed by playgoers, however, and never got really started. It had to do with American occupational forces in Bavaria, but never approached the similarly motivated "Bell of Adano" of the previous season. The play was withdrawn after 35 performances. This, however, was a much better record than that earned by Martha Gellhorn and Virginia Cowles' comedy, "Love Goes to Press," which lasted but 5 performances. This one told of more or less actual experiences encountered by the authors, who were war correspondents in Italy. The press boys seemed inclined to question the credibility of the witnesses.

A gratifying surprise success was scored by a musicalized version of Elmer Rice's "Street Scene." Kurt Weil furnished what reviewers delight to refer to as a "distinguished score," Mr. Rice preserved both the sanity and dramatic value of his original story, and three singers of operatic gifts and ambitions, Polyna Stoska, Anne Jeffreys and Norman Cordon, gave weight and balance to an exceptional cast. Out-of-town audiences were reported as being apathetic, but the New York crowds promptly and irrevocably reversed this attitude.

"Finian's Rainbow" was revealed as the first out-and-out novelty of the season, coming to Broadway in January and delighting its first audiences to demonstrations of enthusiastic approval. The story, written by E. Y. Harburg and Fred Saidy, was pleasantly fantastic; the music, by Burton Lane, was heavy with melody, the comedy was fresh (occasionally a bit too fresh), and business was wonderful.

Hugh White was unable to interest folk in his "Little A." Jessie Royce Landis, as pleasant a human as ever graced the American theatre, suddenly blossomed forth as a terrible woman, and that wasn't easy for her public to take, though she loved the novelty of being evil for a change. She played a scheming and avaricious person who, as a house servant, had trapped "Little A" into a loveless marriage, bore a son which his own father, "Big A," had fathered, and thereafter nagged "Little A" until he turned on her. He missed the bullet she sent after him and got a measure of revenge when that same bullet found the heart of the wicked one's illegitimate offspring. Ten minutes of exciting drama before the last curtain helped the drama, but couldn't save it.

Bobby Clark, deeply disappointed at being forced back from his attack upon the classics in a roughly hewn version of Molière's "Would-Be Gentleman" the season before, took a chance trying to save a revised version of Victor Herbert and Henry Blossom's "Sweethearts," a Christy McDonald hit of happier years. Bobby wound up this adventure by parking the show in one of his capacious comedy pockets and walking away with it.

John Patrick, whose well-loved "The Hasty Heart" had been a success of the season of 1944-45, lost the time spent in a year's research when a dramatic tragedy of his called "The Story of Mary Surratt" failed of popular approval. The reviewers were kind, and a capable cast headed by Kent Smith and Dorothy Gish gave an excellent reading of the play, but playgoers evidently did not want to be reminded of a probable miscarriage of justice so close to their own history. Mary Surratt was the Washington boarding house keeper sentenced to death as a co-conspirator concerned with the assassination of Abraham Lincoln.

Another of those not-quite-good-enough comedies was William McCleery's "Parlor Story." It told amusingly of an honest editor's effort to get away from a school of journalism and have himself appointed president of a state university. He was foiled by the political plottings of the owner of his paper, who wanted to hold him, and the bold defiance of one of his students, who writes an editorial on marriage for the school paper that is alleged to have communistic overtones.

Tallulah Bankhead made a sorry choice of a play called "The Eagle Has Two Heads," which Ronald Duncan adapted from the French of Jean Cocteau. Even the usually loyal Bankhead public was discouraged. After 29 performances the piece was withdrawn.

There was considerable excitement stirred up by the approach of James Mason, an English actor who had achieved wide popularity in the cinema drama on both sides of the Atlantic. By his own choice Mr. Mason decided to make his American stage debut in "Bathsheba," a Biblical drama written by Jacques Deval, the French playwright and author of "Tovarich." While the play was approaching Broadway a division of opinion arose between Mr. Mason and Mr. Deval as to whether "Bathsheba" should be played as a tragedy or a comedy. The actor, hearing an audience dominated by Princeton students laugh in the wrong places, plumped for comedy; the author held out for tragedy. Apparently what New York saw was a compromise, and rather a weak compromise at that. Broadway was also inclined to laugh at the play, and wasn't entirely straight-faced in its acceptance of the over-sold picture star. As a result "Bathsheba" was a four-week failure.

Boastfully insisting that the Russians could laugh as well as mope, Thelma Schnee, actress, made an adaptation of a Russian comedy written by Konstantine Simonov and translated as "The Whole World Over." It turned out to be a modest little domestic comedy having to do with the housing shortage in Moscow. The cast was headed by Joseph Buloff, playing a kind and simple-hearted college professor. The comedy's reception was also kindly, and, with a bit of forcing, ran for 101 performances.

There had not been an old-time George Abbott success since this producer's "Best Foot Forward" in 1941. The enthusiasm attending the first performance of "Barefoot Boy with Cheek" was therefore gratefully acknowledged by all concerned, including the audience. This was another typical combination of youth and satire, telling a fanciful story of a tough comedienne's (Nancy Walker's) effort to organize the campus radicals of the University of Minnesota. Musical comedy fans greatly liked it.

The American Repertory Theatre, after many weeks of discouraging drilling, struck oil finally with a revival of "Alice in Wonderland," which Eva Le Gallienne and Florida Friebus adapted for the old Civic Repertory fifteen years ago. It was not exactly a gusher the discouraged Repertorians brought in, but the response to it was much better than they had known for any of their other plays, save Shaw's "Androcles and the Lion."

Mady Christians and Miriam Hopkins bravely tried a joint starring engagement in an English drama called "Message for Margaret." Nobody could understand just why. The play, written by James Parish, and a success, it is reported, in London, proved completely lifeless and artificial in its Broadway production and was quickly withdrawn.

After that the season drew to an unhurried and unexciting close. A drama with which the exiled Ferenc Molnar of Hungary had been toying during his enforced and, I suspect, unhappy wartime stay in New York was produced by Archer King and Harrison Woodhull. "Miracle in the Mountains" was the title. It was a legend play. In it Julie Haydon played a trusting servant girl who had been betrayed by the mayor of a Carpathian village and later brought to trial for the slaying of her illegitimate son. The mayor, confident of going undetected, is finally driven out of his mind by a visiting attorney who undertakes the girl's defense. A crucial scene is the resurrection of the dead boy by the mysterious attorney, and the excited report of the distraught mayor that has seen the Angel of the Lord in the courtroom.

Three performances and "Miracle in the Mountains" was withdrawn.

A noisy juvenile comedy called "A Young Man's Fancy" was roughly treated by the reviewers, but continued playing into the hot weather. The late-season surprise hit of the two short musical plays written by Gian-Carlo Menotti, "The Telephone" and "The Medium," and John Gielgud's revival of Congreve's "Love for Love" gave a touch of quality to late May.

Michael Todd brought "Up in Central Park" to the City Center for a popular-priced run which didn't come off. Then Sonja Henie and Arthur Wirtz staged another ice show at the Center, with the usual popular results, and the Summer closed in.

THE SEASON IN CHICAGO

By Claudia Cassidy
Drama Editor of the *Chicago Tribune*

ALTHOUGH by the end of the season of 1946-47 Chicago showmen had dusted off the ugly word recession and in some cases were dourly contemplating its hideous relative, depression, the prick in the bubble of prosperity came so late on the shiny scene that while we counted fewer shows and fewer playing weeks than at the peak of wartime expansion a year ago, Chicago and its visitors spent just about the same amount of money enjoying them. *Variety's* tabulators again totted the opulent total of more than $6,000,000, and Brock Pemberton, in a gesture more whimsical than his play, took the lion's share for a rabbit that wasn't there.

For "Harvey" was the season's unquestioned champion. It ran 43 weeks at the Harris and could have kept right on running had Joe E. Brown not departed for vacation with a Hollywood detour. Its intake tilted toward $900,000, and those who mourned not seeing Frank Fay as Harvey's bemused companion were, if not outnumbered, at least outtalked by those who considered Mr. Brown's cozy curtain speech superior to the play. Harvey himself was more elusive in this than in the Pulitzer Prize version—I sometimes thought that, lonely, he had run off to see Mr. Fay—but no complaints were heard about Marion Lorne, a voluble actress rather in the Laura Hope Crews tradition who came home after years in London to make a hit as that other droll of the Dowd clan, Elwood's sister.

Yet though "Harvey" was the season's pet (bounded at both ends of its Harris engagement by "Laura," which held for our town an unrequited affection) the Theatre Guild was perhaps its darling. Subscribers, sometimes a bit morose at the unpredictable results of buying five theatrical pigs in a poke, found themselves beginning the season with the grave and lovely "Lute Song" and ending it with that towering giant, "The Iceman Cometh," and getting that exquisite comedienne, Ina Claire, to boot. Opinion was split on the other offerings, but in the long (sic!) run all was forgiven. "The Magnificent Yankee" still had Louis Calhern, with Sylvia Field a felicitous replacement for Dorothy Gish, and Walter Huston had "Apple of His Eye," though not everyone knew what he wanted with it.

Still, the Theatre Guild was sitting pretty and it decided to consolidate the position. In an unprecedented gesture it confounded subscribers by opening "Carousel" late in May as the first subscription play of the 1947-48 season. Cynics attributed this booking less to altruism than to retaliation. "The Red Mill," booked into the Shubert Theatre, had capriciously transferred its affections to the twice as big Civic Opera House, whereupon the Shubert, local flagship of the Shuberts, reached out for the most formidable rival it could commandeer and opened "Carousel" the next night in opposition. Considering the quality of the Rodgers-Hammerstein musical, the fact that it has sent subscription booming, and the undeniable truth that some of us found "The Red Mill's" corn higher than its tulips, the battle array looked a bit one-sided. But as this was written "Carousel" was selling out the 2,000-seat Shubert and "The Red Mill" was running up what would have been a week's gross elsewhere merely by having prosperous weekends in the 3,600-seat opera house.

How long this would last no one knew at season's end. For the supply of cash customers eager for two of the best was undeniably dwindling. Managers no longer opened the door and dodged, but showed signs of dusting off neglected tokens of hospitality, such as the considerate filling of mail orders, the dawning suspicion that perhaps not all shows are worth $4.80, or even displaying such forthright candor as that of the Studebaker treasurer who told a man in the line for "The Iceman Cometh" that no, the seats were not good, he certainly would not be able to see all the stage, but that they were all that were left except a couple behind a post. The man bought them anyway and was dismayed to find he could see everything except the flowers Cora put on the piano for Harry Hope's party.

Although showfolk feel such things as recessions in their bones —and ticket racks—statisticians can back them up. Charting the curve of our last decade in theatrical flight, we are back just about where we started in number and kind of shows, a hasty descent considering that we struck the peak of the war boom only last season. Note these figures. In 1936-37 Chicago had 36 shows, of which 21 were plays and 15 musicals. In 1946-47 we had 37 shows, of which 23 were plays and 14 musicals. Yet just a year ago, from the first of June, 1945, to the end of May, 1946, we had 42 shows, with 29 plays and 13 musicals. A year ago we had 329 weeks of playgoing in nine theatres. In 1946-47 we had 280 weeks in the same houses. Ballot box stuffers could add 22 weeks for the engagement under Theatre Guild auspices of Laurence Olivier's eye-filling "Henry V."

That ten-year cycle, by the way, dredged up some engaging echoes. As Joe E. Brown was the favorite this time, ten years ago another family style clown, Charlotte Greenwood, held the record. Ina Claire's "The Fatal Weakness" was her first Chicago play since "End of Summer," ten years ago. Katharine Cornell, here at season's start with "Antigone" and "Candida," was using "Candida" a decade ago to bolster "Wingless Victory." Morris Gest was inconsolable that "Lady Precious Stream" was snatched away by booking errors just as Chicago began to love it. This time Michael Myerberg was able to bring "Lute Song" back to thrive on such affection. It ran a total of 20 weeks to an estimated $430,000, and we hope Dolly Haas and Yul Brynner can come again.

Such lusty box-office approval explains why with fewer shows we spent just about the same amount of money as the year before. There is nothing particularly illuminating in the fact that in 1946-47 we split our 23 plays into 13 new ones, 6 return engagements or revivals, and 4 holdovers, and that our 14 musicals divided into 7 new ones, 5 return engagements or revivals, and 2 holdovers. That just means we had fewer new shows than we had a year ago. But aside from the cream already skimmed, those shows held the bravura and bravado of José Ferrer's "Cyrano de Bergerac," the overnight stardom in "Dream Girl" of Richard Widmark and piquant little Judy Parrish, whose illness closed the show. It gave us first look at Bobby Clark as he made "Sweethearts" singular, dubbed Ray Bolger the toast of the dancing town, and sent us a "Call Me Mister" as fleet as the best two-year-old on a fast track.

True, we had Mae West as a G-girl, and a "Follow the Girls" so dismaying the first night audience anticipated the first act curtain with a mass exit which caused bystanders to think the theatre was on fire. And I thought more of Max Wylie's "The Greatest of These" (Eddie Dowling directing Mary Boland, Sam Jaffe, Bramwell Fletcher and Gene Raymond) and of Ben Hecht's "A Flag Is Born" (played here by Jacob Ben-Ami) than the howls of "Propaganda!" that clubbed them into silence. But altogether, all things considered, it wasn't a bad season.

The busiest theatre was the Blackstone. Of its 51 weeks, 32 were devoted to "State of the Union," held over from the previous season, with 38 weeks in all. There also were 3 weeks of "The Student Prince," 13 of "Three to Make Ready," and 3, so far, of "Call Me Mister." The Harris came next with 48 weeks, 1 devoted to the completion of Katharine Cornell's "Antigone" and "Candida" repertory, 4 to an inferior stage version of "Laura," with Miriam Hopkins and Otto Kruger, and 43, of course, to "Harvey." "Laura," undismayed by the earlier rebuff, was back on the doorstep June 1 to begin the 1947-48 season, this time with Mr. Kruger and our "The Voice of the Turtle" pair, K. T. Stevens and Hugh Marlowe, or Mr. and Mrs. Marlowe.

The Shubert (47 weeks) was being called the house of no hits until "Carousel" came along to break the spell. One long-run musical after another rolled in, only to find short shrift. "Up in Central Park" ran 12 weeks, "Bloomer Girl" 7½ weeks, "Follow the Girls" lasted 6, and "Song of Norway" 16, with an estimated gross of $554,000. "Beggar's Holiday" collapsed after 2 weeks, and "Cyrano," which needed a more intimate house, stayed only 3. "Carousel" had just half a week and a rosy future.

The Selwyn's 42 weeks went to "Come On Up, Ring Twice," which ran 8, "Dream Girl," cut short with 13, the Gertrude Lawrence "Pygmalion," with Dennis King an expert Higgins, which ran 8 and hurried off to Mexico, the return of "Springtime for Henry" with 3, "The Greatest of These" with 2, and "The Fatal Weakness" with 8. The Erlanger's 41 weeks held a one-week holdover of "The Merry Wives of Windsor," 4 weeks of "Obsession" (the Eugenie Leontovich-Basil Rathbone remake of "Jealousy"), 10 weeks of the returning "Oklahoma!", 3 of Maurice Evans' GI "Hamlet," 4 of "Apple of His Eye," 5 of "The Magnificent Yankee," and 14, so far, of that expert comedy "Born Yesterday," played here by Richard Rober, Jan Sterling and Laurence Hugo.

The Studebaker ran 33½ weeks, with 20 for "Lute Song's" two engagements, 7 for "I Remember Mama," weakened by cast changes and a bad scenic start, 3½ for "A Flag Is Born," and three for "The Iceman Cometh," a pygmy run for the O'Neill giant, which came here just in time to end its season.

The Civil Theatre's 9 weeks gave 6 to "Anna Lucasta" (its total was 42) and 3 to a dull revival of "The Front Page." The Civic Opera House, usually devoted to opera, ballet and concert, had 8 theatre weeks, 4 for "Sweethearts," 3 for "Blossom Time" and 1, so far, for "The Red Mill." Where is that ninth theatre? When the season started, "Windy City" was slated for one last week at the Great Northern. Midway it was halted when fire laws clamped down after the La Salle Hotel disaster. There is talk of expensive remodeling, and talk, too, of restoring the Auditorium. But that was in boom times. Now—we shall see.

THE SEASON IN SAN FRANCISCO

By Fred Johnson

Drama Editor of the San Francisco *Call-Bulletin*

WHILE showmen still clung to their belief in San Francisco as a "good show town," the customers ended their twelve months of theatre-going with digestions seemingly unimpaired after consuming much of the bad along with the prevailing good.

The impresarios', of course, was a boxoffice view of the year that had seen more than a score of touring attractions come and go, with the prospect of a third legitimate theatre being established by Autumn and dedicated to the better brand of stage fare.

The more discriminating patrons had cause for pondering the current extent of entertainment as compared with the days when a half dozen houses catered to their varied tastes. In that earlier era of class distinction among types of theatres there were playhouses for different showgoing groups, each with its distinguishing admission tariffs. It was the day of moderate railroad and hotel rates and double or treble the present number of road attractions. Broadway musicals came regularly with complete companies and productions—if not always the original. None was shut out, as happened this season to the project of a return engagement of "Carmen Jones."

But for the past dozen or more years the good and bad in entertainment has been served only in two adjoining theatres—the Curran and Geary, under one management—and often with small difference in price scales. That virtual conformity in the cost of amusement has made little difference, however, since—for instance—the two Al Rosens' farce, enigmatically titled "Mary Had a Little," did a healthy five weeks' traffic as compared with the three lean ones of "The Magnificent Yankee."

By the time Louis Calhern, Sylvia Field and their excellent supporting company had ceased wondering about San Francisco's legendary discrimination in theatre fare, even the optimistic student of show business was asking if the Theatre Guild-American Theatre Society's season of five plays had made much west coast history, after all.

But the series, which obviously had come to a bad ending, had done well as a whole between early October and the end of

March. Only one other offering, John Patrick's "The Story of Mary Surratt," had done as badly, although exceeding the run afforded it on Broadway. Pauline Lord in "The Glass Menagerie," which opened the series; "Lute Song"—despite a pre-Christmas lay-off of one week—and Maurice Evans' "Hamlet" made the score three to two as between the season's successes and failures.

Homer Curran, theatre owner and co-producer of "Song of Norway," associated himself with youthful Russell Lewis and Howard Young in the opulent revival of "Lady Windermere's Fan," which later was to intrigue Broadwayans. But the Lewis-Young venture alone with "The Hasty Heart" and "Mary Surratt" was of much less encouragement in their effort to revive production on this coast.

As evidence that the bad and so-so among new plays weren't always as lucky bait as "Mary," Lee Shubert was associated with Lewis J. Deak in a production of "Ten O'Clock Scholar," a new domestic comedy by Joseph Schrank, with Fay Bainter and Thomas Mitchell as the starring team and the latter as director. Its three weeks' run—also a period of rewriting—was forced and unprofitable. It was but little better, though more promising, for Pauline Williams' new comedy, "Accidentally Yours," another home circle charade starring Billie Burke and Grant Mitchell. Later it was to tenant a Chicago theatre.

It was J. J. Shubert's turn to look westward for renewing of his interest in Mae West when again she took the road in "Come on Up," her exhibitionist farce with melodramatic trimmings. This came along with the bad ones, but her fortnight's gratifying business might have been extended. This caused both Miss West and Shubert to wonder why they had shied at San Francisco some months earlier, when she had played the piece in nearby Oakland under the title of "Ring Twice." Shubert also was to commend the larger city's taste and loyalty a few months later when the refurbished "Student Prince" returned once more to meet its usual ready-made audience.

The nostalgia of "Life with Father," however, had lost some of its appeal on the comedy's fourth reappearance, teaming Edwin Maxwell and Viola Frayne. Once a long-run attraction here, its latest stay was materially cut down.

But it was a different story with the arrival of Gertrude Lawrence in "Pygmalion," for a full month's engagement. Then Katharine Cornell returned for a third time in "The Barretts of Wimpole Street" for almost as long, with Sir Cedric Hardwicke replacing the sick Wilfrid Lawson in the final nights, playing the elder Barrett, after Producer Guthrie McClintic had stepped into the role for several previous performances.

Long-run honors—ten weeks—were equally shared by "Anna Lucasta"—counting two engagements—and "State of the Union," co-starring Conrad Nagel and Irene Hervey.

Michael Todd's success with "Hamlet" was far from matched by his "Up in Central Park," with a production expanded for, but not well fitted to, the huge Civic Auditorium's platform. And Jan Kiepura in "The Merry Widow" was again brought into Memorial Opera House for four unexciting performances.

San Francisco Showmen, a semi-professional group, failed in its attempt to establish a permanent theatre with a production of "The Front Page," and Hollywood Actors' Laboratory presented for one week an excellent cast in "Home of the Brave."

San Francisco Civic Light Opera Association's new season had an earlier than usual opening in April with a revival of "Rosalinda" and with Eric Wolfgang Korngold, its co-adapter, as musical director. "Song of Norway" returned after three years of international success, with most of its original cast, playing five weeks instead of the usual three allotted each operetta. It was to be followed by "The Three Musketeers" and "Louisiana Purchase," starring its original trio, William Gaxton, Victor Moore and Vera Zorina.

The year's most promising outlook for a professional repertory theatre came of the formation of San Francisco Theatre Association, following more than a year of survey and preparation. By early Summer the organization had obtained a lease of the Tivoli Theatre, a former legitimate house restricted of late to the films, with plans for production to begin in the early Fall.

Headed by John Jennings, a repertory actor and Yale alumnus, the financially well-supported association's plan was for a staff of three directors and a company of twenty or more professional actors to appear in one production monthly, with a tentative minimum top of $2.50.

Jennings' answer as to why San Francisco should want anything more than or different from the present commercial theatre is his belief that only the New York boxoffice hits are of interest to theatre owners here. He adds that these successes remain on Broadway until receipts are diminished and on taking to the road their companies are of second or third rate or remnants of the original cast.

Curran and the Wobber brothers still had not abandoned their plans for a third modern theatre on Geary Street, to be erected when building conditions are improved.

THE SEASON IN SOUTHERN CALIFORNIA

By Edwin Schallert

Drama Editor of the *Los Angeles Times*

EXCEPT for its beginning and a few weeks toward the end, the 1946-47 theatrical season in Southern California must be regarded as one of "tantalizing unfulfillment." It was a fair and rather full period for the stage in comparison with recent years, but did not live up to the best hopes and prophecies.

It is a curious thing that the brightest native-born developments seemed to concentrate themselves on the edge of Summer. This also happened during the 1945-46 fiscal year. Results were promisingly yielded during the July to September (1946) quarter. It was during that time that the Gryphon Productions at Laguna Beach took the spotlight and accomplished a most commendable series of presentations.

In the Fall, an effort was made to renew this record of success in Hollywood at El Patio Playhouse, where "Twentieth Century," "Blind Alley," "On Borrowed Time" were given as revivals, while "Macbeth" was also seen in streamlined version. The most successful event was "Twentieth Century," with Keenan Wynn, Tamara Geva and Lionel Stander. George Coulouris gained a personal triumph in "Blind Alley." Boris Karloff, Ralph Morgan, Beulah Bondi, Margaret Hamilton, Joseph Crehan and young Tommy Ivo composed the exceptional cast of "On Borrowed Time."

The importance of this effort, which stemmed from the Laguna Beach project, cannot be denied, because it helped to turn the minds of the Hollywood professional group toward the stage, and especially summertime theatre. It had a distant relationship to three different enterprises which saw their inception late in the 1946-47 season, namely, the launching of an important group endeavor at the Coronet Theatre early in June, as well as elaborate plans for reactivating the Gryphon organization, and the institution of yet another Summer enterprise by David O. Selznick actors at La Jolla.

The new Gryphon schedule and the plays centering in La Jolla do not come within the purview of this seasonal review. However, the first offering of the Coronet Theatre organization, "The Skin

of Our Teeth," had unusual luster, with Carol Stone assuming the Tallulah Bankhead role, as she did with Author Thornton Wilder himself in an East Coast Summer production, and such personalities as Jane Wyatt, Keenan Wynn, Hurd Hatfield and Blanche Yurka featured.

John Houseman has been a moving force in this whole undertaking, which will naturally have to be fully judged in the light of its further progress. It is the sort of thing that many people have "talked up" for years. Hollywood actors, it has long been felt, need the transition to the stage, even as the stage can well gain by their presence. Yet they are fearful of risking their fate in a sea of mediocrity.

The Summer theatre, well conducted, is more easily ventured into than that "awful challenge" which seems to lurk in downtown Los Angeles. Coronet, of course, is not a playhouse in a resort area. It is located on La Cienega Boulevard, not far from the Turnabout Theatre. But it is at least away from the main stem, and thus assumes something of the informal community character.

In the domain of Coastal and community efforts the Actor's Laboratory Theatre is again to be commended for endowing its productions of "Home of the Brave" and "To the Living" with quality, as well as its staging of a set of one-act plays.

"Home of the Brave" with Mack Williams, Harlan Warde, Kenneth Patterson, Leo Penn, Don Hanmer, Robert Karnes and others in its cast, had the best run, and made a lasting impression. It was directed by Phil Brown. "To the Living," by Anthony Palma, was also efficiently given, while the one-act plays, three by Tennessee Williams and one by Sean O'Casey, benefited by splendid performances of Jessica Tandy and Vincent Price. Miss Tandy appeared in "Portrait of a Madonna" and Price in "The Last of My Gold Watches," both by Williams. "Mooney's Kids Don't Cry" by the same author and "The End of the Beginning" by O'Casey were on the bill.

The Actors Lab suffered a technical setback when the Las Palmas Theatre, which housed these attractions, was taken over for the showing of foreign films. The Mayan Theatre in downtown Los Angeles is now also cinematic. Such is the advancement—backwards—of the stage in its established haunts!

A new organization, Stage, Inc., made a brief "try" during the year at the Musart Theatre, presenting "Dunnigan's Daughter" with Jay Novello, Mady Correll, John Holland, Warren Ashe and Peggy Wynne, and also "Charley's Aunt," but that was about the extent of this inauguration.

A new play, "George," by John Meredyth Lucas, was tried out during the Gryphon season at Laguna Beach, with Signe Hasso as the feminine lead and Robert Milton as stage director. However, while it invoked a modern technique, it lacked the living quality. What this theatre did of greatest benefit was in casting John Emery, Claire Trevor, Allyn Joslyn, young Guy Madison, Wynn, Miss Geva and others in its popular repertoire, which included "Dark Victory," "Petrified Forest," "Dear Ruth," directed by Mel Ferrer; "Room Service," "Boy Meets Girl," besides some plays already named. Ferrer, for the 1947 Summer season, was engaged to conduct activities at La Jolla.

To such noted stars as Gertrude Lawrence, Katharine Cornell and Maurice Evans in "Hamlet" went the solid box-office conquests. The Cornell glamour seemed especially undiminished, even in the familiar "The Barretts of Wimpole Street." The engagement was rendered notable by the presence of Sir Cedric Hardwicke as Edward Moulton-Barrett, a role which he created in London. He replaced Wilfrid Lawson, who was taken ill during the San Francisco engagement. It was indeed a stellar interpretation. Brian Aherne appeared as Robert Browning.

Hardwicke figures in the 1946-47 chronicle also as the stage director of "Pygmalion," in which Miss Lawrence starred at the revivified Belasco Theatre with Dennis King, Ralph Forbes and Cecil Humphreys. There was some criticism of the eccentricities of the Lawrence portrayal, though Hardwicke, who had been out of touch with the play for a time, was not blamed for this. Miss Lawrence was a popular hit in the George Bernard Shaw comedy, originally seen here more than 30 years ago with Mrs. Patrick Campbell.

Evans brought a fine company in his very modern-type "Hamlet," including Philip Foster, Doris Lloyd, Miles Malleson, Pamela Conroy, and Nelson Leigh, among others. Leigh was also the Christus of the Pilgrimage Play.

Looking back on the early part of the 1946-47 season, the West Coast points with pride to "Lady Windermere's Fan," which had its origination as a revival in San Francisco under the Lewis and Young aegis. The Oscar Wilde comedy, after leaving the Coast, had a happy New York history.

In Los Angeles "Lady Windermere's Fan" was estimated as a beautifully mounted achievement. Henry Daniell, Penelope Ward, John Buckmaster, Estelle Winwood and Rex Evans were in the cast.

"The Glass Menagerie" arrived late in 1946, with Pauline Lord

as the star and Richard Jones, Jeanne Shepperd and Edward Andrews as the other three principals. Oddly enough, this was only a little before the death of Laurette Taylor, who created the part that Miss Lord enacted.

Miss Lord imbued the assignment with great sympathy. The response she aroused from the critical was varied. Yet none could deny the humanness that she brings to a character of this type. Miss Shepperd was definitely appealing, and Jones acceptable, being especially good in his narration.

"State of the Union" twice "checked in" during the season, with Conrad Nagel, Irene Hervey and Henry O'Neill helping to illumine its topical interest. "Anna Lucasta" was also a double time event. It first played the Biltmore and then the Belasco. The company combined New York and Chicago personnel, with Ruby Dee as Anna, Warren Coleman and Alice Childress particularly successful.

"The Hasty Heart" was proffered with Erin O'Brien-Moore, Dean Harens and Whitner Bissell. Louis Calhern, with Sylvia Field, commanded attention with his Justice Oliver Wendell Holmes in "The Magnificent Yankee." Dorothy Gish, who had appeared opposite him in New York, essayed the ill-fated "The Story of Mary Surratt." Billie Burke and Grant Mitchell did not have too joyous a time of it with their testing of "Accidentally Yours" by Pauline Williams. "Lute Song," with Dolly Haas, Yul Brynner and Louis Hector, was moderately liked. "Life with Father" came back again, with Edwin Maxwell and Viola Frayne. "Merry Wives of Windsor," under the Theatre Guild aegis, brought Charles Coburn, Jessie Royce Landis, Romney Brent, Gina Malo, Whitford Kane, David Powell and Charles Francis. Contrastingly, in the bawdy realm, Mae West appeared in "Come on Up," a rather weak melodramatic farce with Westian trimmings.

To the record of plays and productions having their origin in Los Angeles or on the Coast must be added the world premiere of "Father Was President," by Malvin Wald and Walter Doniger. This had Albert Dekker in the Theodore Roosevelt role, and evidenced merit; "The Gentle Approach" by John O'Dea, dealing with the returned soldier's problems, cast including Lilian Fontaine, Marcy McGuire, William Wright, Isabel Jewell, Jacqueline De Wit and Wally Cassell; "Assassin" by Irwin Shaw, "Bachelor's Women" by Robert Sheban, "Trial by Fire" by George H. Dunne, S.J. "Turquoise Matrix" by Ruth Haggin Cole and Gabrielle Winship, "Maryella," prize-winning Utah Centennial

Play, by Nathan and Ruth Hale.

This does not take into account such weird excrescences as "Lady Godiva's Horse," "Shared Wife," and the abomination champion "She Dood It in Dixie."

"Father Was President" had its initiation at the Phoenix Theatre, which revived "The Good Fairy" during the play-giving year, and subsequently faded as a habitat of the spoken drama. Before the transference of the Las Palmas to the cinema, the Actors Lab, already referred to, had done "Inspector General," a repeat of "Volpone" and "Juno and the Paycock," with Sara Allgood and Whitford Kane. The very praiseworthy "Papa Is All," which first saw the light in the little theatre area, attained a more professional unveiling at El Patio.

It could hardly be said that any of the newer plays reached first base in the full sense of that word, and most of them ended their careers ingloriously. There has scarcely ever been such a season where things failed to come off, no matter what the glow surrounding anticipations.

This even reached into the creative sphere of light opera, for the synthesized "Fortune Teller" was scarcely a rival for "Song of Norway." It was seen in New York under the title "Gypsy Love." Despite a lustrous Coastal cast, and the well-loved Victor Herbert melodies, the flimsiness of the story was a detriment.

The Los Angeles Civic Light Opera has a solid audience. They turned out en masse for the homecoming of "Song of Norway," which enjoyed a sensational four weeks in the Spring of 1947. This was followed by "Rosalinda" and "The Three Musketeers." "Louisiana Purchase" was slated for the beginning of the 1947-48 season.

Again it has been a triumphant light opera year. In fact, from beginning to end of the season the urge was on for musical entertainment. All through the Summer, for instance, the Greek Theatre, which had long been closed, displayed such musicals as "The Firefly," with Allan Jones and Irene Manning; "New Moon," with Joe Sullivan, Marion Bell and Pinky Lee; "East Wind" with Allan Jones, "Rosalie," "Two Hearts in Waltz Time," with Kenny Baker and Miss Manning; "Wizard of Oz" and others. Gene Mann was the impresario, and people of the motion picture colony were interested in the project.

September saw Mike Todd following the regular Hollywood Bowl concert season with his presentation of "Up in Central Park," literally transplanting a great Eastern recreation center into the confines of a western. It was probably the most spectacular attempt at entertaining a large public with this type of show in theatrical history. The Bowl does not naturally lend itself to an event of this character, yet "Up in Central Park" did a surprisingly good business, even though it did not afford satisfaction to those who were a hundred yards or so from the stage. Very difficult for the performers, who worked diligently.

"The Merry Widow," with Jan Kiepura and Marta Eggerth, played the Philharmonic Auditorium. The Breden-Savoy Comic Opera Company, as a small Çoast organization, offered Gilbert and Sullivan at El Patio. "Student Prince" made its habitual trip through. "As We Like It," a revue, was an interesting experiment.

The tried and true thrived on. "Drunkard" was in its 15th year as the season ended, Turnabout, holding forth since 1941, Padua Hills remaining a novel perennial attraction.

"The Mission Play" was brought back at San Gabriel, with Pedro de Cordoba as Father Junipero. Adrian Awan was responsible for alterations in the staging. "Ramona" had its second post-war year, but the Pilgrimage Play was absent during the Summer of 1946.

The Pasadena Community Playhouse record continues outstanding. Three premieres were sponsored—"Stairs to the Roof" by Tennessee Williams, reported on by this writer when it was introduced at the Playbox about two years ago; "A Yankee Fable" by Guy Andros, and "O, Susanna!" by Florence Ryerson and Colin Clements.

"Stairs to the Roof" is rich in its imaginative impact. The other two furnished colorful sidelights on the American scene. They held promise.

"For Keeps" by F. Hugh Herbert, "Truckline Café" by Maxwell Anderson, "The Mermaids Singing" by John Van Druten were Coast firsts at the Playhouse. "But Not Goodbye," "The Rich Full Life," "Home of the Brave," "Laura," "Mr. Pickwick," "Ten Little Indians," "The Late George Apley," "The Hasty Heart," "State of the Union," Shakespeare's "As You Like It" were performed. The 1946 Midsummer Drama Festival was dedicated to Clyde Fitch, whose plays in some cases proved to be quaintly charming antiques, although not for this portion of the 20th century.

Unusual among new little theatre efforts was the Circle Players' productions of "The Adding Machine," "Ethan Frome" and "The Time of Your Life." This is a different organization from the one that was in existence a few years ago in Hollywood, though, like its predecessor, it too specializes in central staging. The Charles Chaplin sons, Charles, Jr., and Sydney, and Edward G. Robinson, Jr., are among the interesting personnel.

Call Board Theatre, which has an enviable record of idealistic play-presenting, attained its 100th production during the year. The Geller Workshop and Bliss-Hayden proceed with regularity. Jewel Box, Westwood Village, Conservatory and various others are more or less actively in the little theatre field.

It is an extensive pattern that Southern California offers theatrically, though the devotees of the drama often wish that it was less of a crazy quilt and more definite in design and purpose.

ALL MY SONS

A Drama in Three Acts

By Arthur Miller

AS the story was told at the time of the drama's production (and well told by John Hutchens of the New York *Times*, incidentally), Arthur Miller came by the basic idea for his "All My Sons" drama during a conversation with a somewhat serious-minded Middle Western lady during the war years. She knew of a war profiteer's idealistic daughter, this lady told Mr. Miller, who, though she loved her father devotedly, had had the courage to expose him. After which she left home immediately and for good.

The conversation rambled on after that and came shortly to the theatre and young Mr. Miller's literary ambitions, which included the drama. (He was approaching his currently interesting early thirties at the time, and had already made a promising start as a writer of parts.)

"Where do you get ideas for plays and stories?" the lady asked. "Oh," replied Mr. Miller, quite truthfully, "I just pick them up here and there."

But he did not tell her, even if he knew it at the time, that he had just picked up a corker. It took him something like two years to get down to making it into a drama.

The New York play reviewers were not all of one mind concerning the virtues of "All My Sons," but they were fairly unanimous in admitting that Mr. Miller was now showing even greater promise than he had shown in 1944, when his first play, "The Man Who Had All the Luck," was withdrawn after a single week of bad business. In April the New York Drama Critics' Circle gave "All My Sons" its award as the best play of the season of American authorship.

"With the production of 'All My Sons' the theatre has acquired a genuine new talent," declared Brooks Atkinson in the *Times*, as his opening salute to Mr. Miller, and Louis Kronenberger of *PM* marked up that estimate by adding: "Arthur Miller seems to me to stand easily first among our new generation of playwrights." So much for Mr. Miller. It is always a little thrilling to herald the debut of a newcomer of authentic achievement.

As indicated opinions of the play were varied, but there was general agreement that, as Robert Garland summed it up in the *Journal-American,* "It says something of moment about something of moment; it says it with controlled emotion and impressive skill. Frequently it is indignant, but always about the real and righteous things."

The Joe Kellers live in the outskirts of an American town. We meet them one early Sunday morning in August, the time being "in our era." Joe Keller is sitting in his back yard almost completely surrounded by sections of the Sunday papers.

The back yard is homey and secluded. At one side there is a trellised arbor shaped like a sea shell. Tall poplars fringe the sides of the yard. We face the back porch of a seven-room house.

There is such litter here and there as might have been caused by a lively wind storm the night before, and across the yard from the arbor there is the four-foot stump of a slender apple tree with its fruit-bearing branches toppled beside it.

Joe is not alone with his Sunday papers. In the arbor his neighbor, Jim Bayliss, is also concentrating on a section.

"Keller is nearing sixty. A heavy man of stolid mind and build, a business man these many years, but with the imprint of the machine-shop worker and boss still upon him. When he reads, when he speaks, when he listens, it is with the terrible concentration of the uneducated man for whom there is still wonder in many commonly known things, a man whose judgments must be dredged out of experience and a peasant-like common sense. A man among men. . . . Bayliss is nearing forty. A wry, self-controlled man, an easy talker. . . ."

Presently a second neighbor, Frank Lubey, joins the two. He comes from the house on the right, through a small space between the poplars. "Frank is thirty-two but balding. A pleasant, opinionated man, uncertain of himself, with a tendency toward peevishness when crossed, but always wanting it pleasant and neighborly."

The conversation is casual and fragmentary. Neither Keller nor the doctor is much interested in the papers. All the news is bad, as usual, according to Frank. Keller can find more of real interest in the want ads than in the news.

Frank is interested, however, in the broken tree. "You know, it's funny," says he. "Larry was born in November. He'd been twenty-seven this Fall. And his tree blows down."

Keller is touched. "I'm surprised you remember his birthday, Frank. That's nice."

"Well, I'm working on his horoscope."

"How can you make him a horoscope? That's for the future, ain't it?"

"Well, what I'm doing is this, see. Larry was reported missing on February 9th, right?"

"Yeah?"

"Well, then, we assume that if he was killed it was on February 9th. Now, what Kate wants . . ."

"Oh, Kate asked you to make a horoscope?"

"Yeah, what she wants to find out is whether February 9th was a favorable day for Larry."

"What is that, favorable day?"

"Well, a favorable day for a person is a fortunate day, according to his stars. In other words it would be practically impossible for him to have died on his favorable day."

"Well, was that his favorable day?—February 9th?"

"That's what I'm working on to find out. It takes time! (*With inner excitement.*) See, the point is, if February 9th was his favorable day, then it's completely possible he's alive somewhere, because . . ."

Doctor Jim Bayliss decides to take a part in the conversation, largely because he is convinced from Frank's end of it that that young man's completely out of his mind. What Doctor Jim is really interested in is the beautiful girl who was supposed to be here.

That would be Annie, and, as Keller explains, Annie is even now still asleep upstairs. "We picked her up on the one o'clock train last night," reports Keller. "Wonderful thing. Girl leaves here, a scrawny kid. Couple of years go by, she's a regular woman. Hardly recognized her, and she was running in and out of this yard all her life. That was a very happy family used to live in your house, Jim."

"Like to meet her," cracks Jim. "The block can use a pretty girl. In the whole neighborhood there's not a damned thing to look at. . . . Except my wife, of course." He adds to this hastily, as Sue Bayliss comes from the yard at left. "Sue is rounding forty, an overweight woman who fears it."

Chris Keller has come from the house. "He is thirty-two, like his father solidly built, a listener. A man capable of immense affection and loyalty." Chris' father would interest him in a part of the paper, but Chris doesn't want to see anything but the book section. "I like to keep abreast of my ignorance," he explains. . . .

Keller is worried about the effect on Mother of the broken tree, when she sees it. But she has seen it. Chris had got up when he heard the tree cracking and looked out his window. It was about four in the morning. Mother was standing by the tree. When it cracked she had run into the kitchen and Chris could hear her crying.

This worries Keller. Evidently Mother is walking around at night and dreaming about Larry again—as she did after he died. What's the meaning of that?

Chris doesn't know the meaning, but he does know that they have made a terrible mistake with Mother. "You know Larry's not coming back, and I know it. Why do we allow her to go on thinking that we believe with her?"

"What do you want to do, argue with her?"

"I don't want to argue with her, but it's time she realized that nobody believes Larry is alive any more."

It is Keller's idea that they can't say that to Mother until they're sure; until there is some proof. Having heard nothing from Larry for three years is proof enough to Chris.

"The trouble is the goddam papers," explodes Keller. "Every month some boy turns up from nowhere so the next one is going to be Larry, so . . ."

CHRIS—All right, listen to me. (*Slight pause.*) You know why I asked Annie here, don't you?

KELLER (*he knows, but . . .*)—Why?

CHRIS—You know.

KELLER—Well, I got an idea, but . . . What's the story?

CHRIS—I'm going to ask her to marry me.

KELLER (*after pause—nods*)—Well, that's only your business, Chris.

CHRIS—You know it's not only my business.

KELLER—What do you want me to do? You're old enough to know your own mind.

CHRIS (*annoyed*)—Then it's all right, I'll go ahead with it?

KELLER—Well, you want to be sure Mother isn't going to . . .

CHRIS—Then it isn't just my business.

KELLER—I'm just sayin' . . .

CHRIS—Sometimes you infuriate me, you know that? Isn't it your business too, if I tell this to Mother and she throws a fit about it? You have such a talent for ignoring things.

KELLER—I ignore what I gotta ignore. The girl is Larry's girl. . . .

CHRIS—She's not Larry's girl.

KELLER—From Mother's point of view he is not dead and you have no right to take his girl. (*Pause.*) Now you can go on from there if you know where to go. See? I don't know. Now what can I do for you?

CHRIS (*getting up*)—I don't know why it is, but every time I reach out for something I want, I have to pull back because other people will suffer. My whole bloody life, time after time, after time.

KELLER—You're a considerate fella, there's nothing wrong in that.

CHRIS—To hell with that.

KELLER—Did you ask Annie yet?

CHRIS—I wanted to get this settled first.

KELLER—How do you know she'll marry you? Maybe she feels the same way Mother does.

CHRIS—Well, if she does then that's the end of it. From her letters I think she's forgotten him. I'll find out. And then we'll thrash it out with Mother. Right? Dad, don't avoid me.

KELLER—The trouble is you don't see enough women. You never did.

CHRIS—So what? I'm not fast with women.

KELLER—I don't see why it has to be Annie . . .

CHRIS—Because it is.

KELLER—That's a good answer, but it don't answer anything. You haven't seen her since you went to war. It's five years.

CHRIS—I can't help it. I know her best. I was brought up next door to her. These years when I think of someone for my wife, I think of Annie. What do you want, a diagram?

KELLER—I don't want a diagram . . . I . . . I'm . . . She thinks he's coming back, Chris. You marry that girl and you're pronouncing him dead. Now what's going to happen to Mother? Do you know? I don't.

His father is convinced that Chris should give the matter more thought, but Chris is convinced three years' thought is enough. If he can't marry Annie, have a regular wedding and all that, he will have to get out, marry someone else and live somewhere else—maybe in New York.

But the business? Keller wants to know what's to become of that. If Chris quits the business, what's the good of anything?

What has he (Keller) been working for all these years! Only for Chris. The whole shootin' match is for Chris. . . .

Mother comes from the house to the porch. "She is in her early fifties, a woman of uncontrolled inspirations, and an overwhelming capacity for love."

At the moment Mother is a little peeved. Keller has put a sack of potatoes in the garbage can, thinking it was garbage. If she could only break him of the habit of trying to be helpful—

"That settles you for today," suggests an amused Chris.

"Yeah, I'm in the last place again. I don't know, once upon a time I used to think that when I got money again I would have a maid and my wife would take it easy. Now I got money, and I got a maid, and my wife is workin' for the maid."

Mrs. Keller has made a hasty survey of the yard. The wind had certainly done some job on that place. She moves over toward the garden and picks a few rose petals from the ground—

"No more roses. It's so funny," Mother ruminates; "everything decides to happen at the same time. It'll be his birthday soon; his tree blows down, Annie comes. Everything that happened seems to be coming back. I was just down in the cellar and what do I stumble over? His baseball glove. I haven't seen that baseball glove in a century."

"Don't you think Annie looks well?" Chris asks her.

"Fine. There's no question about it. She's a beauty . . . I still don't know what brought her here. Not that I'm not glad to see her, but . . ."

"I just thought we'd all like to see each other again."

From time to time Mother has pressed her hand to the top of her head. There's a funny pain there, but it's not like a headache. Probably because she had had a terrible night. It's because she doesn't sleep, insists Keller. She's wearing out more bedroom slippers than shoes.

"I never had a night like that," Mother goes on.

"What was it, Mom? Did you dream?" Chris asks.

"More, more than a dream."

"About Larry?"

"I was fast asleep, and . . . Remember the way he used to fly low past the house when he was in training? When we used to see his face in the cockpit going by? That's the way I saw him. Only high up. Way, way up, where the clouds are. He was so real I could reach out and touch him. And suddenly he started to fall. And crying, crying to me. . . . Mom, Mom! I could hear him like he was in the room. Mom!—It was his voice! If

I could touch him I knew I could stop him, if I could only . . . I woke up and it was so funny . . . The wind . . . it was like the roaring of his engine. I came out here . . . I must've still been half asleep. I could hear that roaring like he was going by. The tree snapped right in front of me . . . and I like . . . came awake. (*She suddenly realizes something, turns with a reprimanding finger shaking slightly at* KELLER.) See? We should never have planted that tree. I said so in the first place; it was too soon to plant a tree for him."

Chris is alarmed. "Too soon?" he echoes.

"We rushed into it." Mother's anger is mounting. "Everybody was in such a hurry to bury him. I *said* not to plant it yet. (*To* KELLER.) I *told* you to . . . !"

Chris has gone to her and taken her by the arm protestingly. "The wind blew it down!" he says, firmly. "What significance has that got? What are you talking about . . . Mother, please . . . Don't go through it all again, will you? It's no good, it doesn't accomplish anything. I've been thinking, y'know—maybe we ought to put our minds to forgetting him."

"That's the third time you've said that this week."

"Because it's not right; we never took up our lives again. We're like at a railroad station waiting for a train that never comes in."

Chris thinks they should, the four of them, go out to dinner, have some fun. He'll get his mother the aspirin. She can start with that.

Chris is barely inside the house before Mother turns on Keller. Why did Chris invite Annie there? Why, all of a sudden? He's not going to marry her! She's positive of that. Annie isn't interested in getting married. That's why she has stayed single these last three and a half years. Annie's faithful, faithful as a rock.

"Nobody in this house dast take her faith away, Joe. Strangers might. But not his father, not his brother."

"What do you want me to do? What do you want?"

"I want you to act like he's coming back. Both of you. Don't think I haven't noticed you since Chris invited her. I won't stand for any nonsense."

"But, Kate—"

"Because if he's not coming back, then I'll kill myself! . . ."

They can laugh at her if they like, but they cannot laugh Mother out of the conviction that there is meaning in such a thing as the tree, Larry's memorial, breaking the night Ann goes to sleep in his room. She believes, but someone must believe with her. Joe must believe above all. Why him above all? Keller demands. Mother does not answer that.

Ann and Chris come out on the porch. "Ann is twenty-six, gentle, but despite herself capable of holding fast to what she knows."

There is much admiration for Ann on the part of the Keller family. Chris thinks she is the prettiest gal any of them ever saw. Mother has agreed that she has developed wonderfully, even if she may have added a few pounds. Keller takes count of how nice her legs have turned out.

Ann's spirit is in tune with Jim's. She thinks they should eat at the shore that night and raise a little hell around there, as they used to do before Larry went—

Ann's mention of Larry is a little exciting to Mother. It shows that Ann remembers Larry; that he is still in her thoughts—

"That's a funny thing to say," ventures Ann, wonderingly. "How could I help remembering him?"

She has been a little surprised to find that all the clothes in the closet of her room are Larry's; that his shoes are all shined, just as though—

Mother wants to talk seriously to Ann, but she has some trouble getting through the interruptions of the family. First, about Ann's mother. Is she getting a divorce? No, she isn't. Ann thinks that when her father gets out, he and her mother will live together in New York—

"That's fine," agrees Mrs. Keller. "Because your father is still . . . I mean he's a decent man after all is said and done."

"I don't care. She can take him back if she likes."

"And you? You . . ."

Ann shakes her head negatively, and Mother changes her questioning to include Ann's feeling about Larry. Is Ann waiting for him? No, she is not, Ann is quick to answer. To do that, she thinks, would be a little ridiculous—

MOTHER—I know, dear, but don't say it's ridiculous, because the papers were full of it; I don't know about New York but there was half a page about a man in Detroit missing longer than Larry and he turned up from Burma.

CHRIS—He couldn't have wanted to come home very badly, Mom.

MOTHER—Don't be so smart! Why couldn't he of lost his memory? Or . . . or . . . it could've been a million things.

What is impossible that hasn't already happened in this world?
Who is smart enough to say what can happen?

CHRIS (*going to her with a condescending smile*)—Mother,
you're absolutely . . .

MOTHER (*waving him off*)—Don't be so damned smart! Now
stop it! (*Pause.*) There are just a few things you *don't* know.
All of you. And I'll tell you one of them, Annie. Deep, deep in
your heart you've always been waiting for him.

ANN (*resolutely*)—No, Kate.

MOTHER (*with increasing demand*)—But deep in your heart,
Annie!

CHRIS—She ought to know, shouldn't she?

MOTHER (*looking at* ANN, *pointing at her*)—Don't let them tell
you what to think. Listen to your heart. Only your heart.

ANN (*going to her*)—Why does your heart tell you he's alive?

MOTHER—Because he has to be.

ANN—But why, Kate?

MOTHER—Because certain things have to be, and certain things
can never be. Like the sun has to rise, it has to be. That's why
there's God. Otherwise anything could happen. But there's God,
so certain things can never happen. I would know, Annie—just
like I knew the day he (*Indicates* CHRIS.) went into that terrible
battle. Did he write me? Was it in the papers? No, but that
morning I couldn't raise my head off the pillow. Ask Joe. Suddenly I knew. I knew! And he was nearly killed that day.
Annie, you know I'm right! (*Turns, trembling.*)

ANN—No, Kate!

Frank Lubey is back. He is excited to see Ann again, but he
doesn't help clear the atmosphere any by asking, a little abruptly,
about her father—

"How about it, does Dad expect a parole soon?"

"I really don't know, I . . ."

"I mean because I feel, y'know, that if an intelligent man like
your father is put in prison, there ought to be a law that says
either you execute him, or let him go after a year. Because if you
look at your statistics . . ."

They manage to get rid of Frank, but Ann is left wondering.
Is the neighborhood still talking about her dad? If it is she
doesn't want to meet any more of the neighbors. They try to tell
her that nobody thinks about the case any more. No one, at
least, except Mother. And she is still conscious of it only because
Joe has made it a point to play policeman with the kids—

"Actually what happened," explains Keller, "was that when I got home from the penitentiary the kids got very interested in me. You know kids. I was (*Laughs.*) like the expert on the jail situation. And as time passed they got it confused and . . . I ended up a detective." Keller is still laughing at that.

"Except that *they* don't get it confused," persists Mother. "He hands out police badges from the Post Toasties boxes." They all laugh at this.

ANN (*wondrously at them, happily*)—Gosh, it's wonderful to hear you laughing about it.

CHRIS—Why, what'd you expect?

ANN—The last thing I remember on this block was one word— "Murderers!" Remember that, Kate? . . . Mrs. Hammond standing in front of our house and yelling that word . . . ? She's still around, I suppose.

MOTHER—They're all still around.

KELLER—Don't listen to her. Every Saturday night the whole gang is playing poker in this yard. All the ones who yelled murder taking my money now.

MOTHER—Don't, Joe, she's a sensitive girl, don't fool her. (*To* ANN.) They still remember about Dad. It's different with him— (*Indicates* JOE.)—he was exonerated, your father's still there. That's why I wasn't so enthusiastic about you coming. Honestly, I know how sensitive you are, and I told Chris, I said . . .

KELLER—Listen, you do like I did and you'll be all right. The day I come home, I got out of my car—but not in front of the house . . . on the corner. You should've been here, Annie, and you too, Chris; you'd a seen something. Everybody I knew was getting out that day; the porches were loaded. Picture it now; none of them believed I was really innocent. The story was, I pulled a fast one getting myself exonerated. So I get out of my car, and I walk down the street. But very slow. And with a smile. The beast. I was the beast; the guy who sold cracked cylinder heads to the Army Air Force; the guy who made twenty-one P-40s crash in Australia. Kid, walkin' down the street that day I was guilty as hell. Except I wasn't, and there was a court paper in my pocket to prove I wasn't . . . and I walked . . . past . . . the porches. Result? Fourteen months later I had one of the best shops in the state again, a respected man again; bigger than ever.

CHRIS (*with admiration*)—Joe McGuts!

KELLER (*with great force*)—That's the only way you lick 'em is guts! (*To* ANN.) The worst thing you did was to move away from here. You made it tough for your father when he gets out, and you made it tough for me. Sure, they play poker, but behind their eyes is that dirty thought—Keller, you were very intimate with a murderer. That's why I tell you, I like to see him move back right on this block.

MOTHER (*pained*)—How could they move back?

KELLER—It ain't gonna end till they move back! (*To* ANN.) Till people play cards with him again, and talk with him, and smile with him—you play cards with a man you know he can't be a murderer. And the next time you write him I like you to tell him just what I said. (ANN *simply stares at him.*) You hear me?

Ann is surprised that none of them holds anything against her father. Neither she nor her brother ever writes to him any more. Nor have they written since the news about Larry's crashing came to them. It seemed wrong to pity a man who had knowingly sent out defective parts that would crash an airplane. Twenty-one pilots had died, and who could say Larry was not one of them.

Mother resents that thought. So long as Ann is there let her be careful never again to couple Larry's going with anything her father had done. Larry's not dead. So there's no argument.

Keller would add his bit. The imperfect cylinder heads had gone only into P-40s, and so far as they knew Larry never flew a P-40.

"So who flew those P-40s, pigs?" Chris wants to know.

"The man was a fool, but don't make a murderer out of him," Keller answers. There is a note of growing anxiety, almost of pleading, as he turns to Ann. "You gotta appreciate what was doin' in that shop in the war. It was a madhouse. Every half hour the Major callin' for cylinder heads, and they whippin' us with the telephone. The trucks were hauling them away hot, damn near. I mean just try to see it human, see it human. All of a sudden a batch comes out with a crack. That happens, that's the business. A fine hair-line crack. All right, so . . . so he's a little man, your father, always scared of loud voices. What'll the Major say?—Half a day's production shot. What'll I say? You know what I mean? Human. So he takes out his tools and he . . . covers over the cracks. All right . . . that's bad, it's wrong, but that's what a little man does. If I could've gone in that day I'd a told him—junk 'em, Herb, we can afford it. But alone he was afraid. But I know he meant no harm. He believed they'd hold up a hundred percent. And a lot of them did. That's a mistake, but it ain't murder. You mustn't feel that way about him. You understand me? I don't like to see a girl eating out her heart."

"Joe, let's forget it," suggests Ann. . . .

Keller has gone into the house. Chris and Ann are free for their first confession of love. Chris is afraid that Ann may be sorry she came—after all that has been said. Ann isn't sorry, but she thinks she shouldn't stay. It is rather plain that Mrs. Keller doesn't want her. But Chris does—

"Ann, I love you! I love you a great deal," Chris says, earnestly. "I love you!" She waits for him to go on. "I have no imagination," he says, "that's all I know to tell you. I'm embarrassing you. I didn't want to tell it to you here. I wanted some place with trees around . . . some new place, we'd never been; a place where we'd be brand new to each other. . . ."

ANN (*touching his arm*)—What's the matter?

CHRIS—You feel it's wrong here, don't you? This yard, this chair.

ANN—It's not wrong, Chris.

CHRIS—I don't want to win you away from anything. I want you to be ready for me.

ANN—Oh, Chris, I've been ready a long, long time.

CHRIS—Then he's gone forever. You're sure.

ANN—I almost got married two years ago.

CHRIS— . . . Why didn't you?

ANN—You started to write to me . . .

CHRIS (*after slight pause*)—You felt something that far back?

ANN—M-Hm.

CHRIS—Ann, why didn't you let me know?

ANN—I was waiting for you, Chris. Till then you never wrote. And when you did, what did you say? You sure can be ambiguous, you know.

CHRIS (*looking toward the house, then at her, trembling*)— Give me a kiss, Ann. Give me a . . . (*They kiss.*) God, I kissed you, Annie, I kissed Annie. How long, how long I've been waiting to kiss you.

ANN—I'll never forgive you. Why did you wait all these years? All I've done is sit and wonder if I was crazy for thinking of you.

CHRIS—Annie, we're going to live now! I'm going to make you so happy. (*He kisses her but without their bodies touching.*)

ANN—Not like that you're not.

CHRIS (*laughing*)—Why? I kissed you . . .
ANN—Like Larry's brother. Do it like you, Chris.

Now a new embarrassment has overtaken Chris. He is suddenly conscious and unhappy. He wants to get away from there, to be alone with Ann, as though there was something of which he was ashamed. And there is. Chris can't forget the war. Or the sacrifice men made in the war. He remembers the company of which he had command. He lost most of those men. "They didn't die," he says. "They killed themselves for each other. I mean that exactly. A little more selfish and they'd've been here today. . . ."

Out of the sacrifices it seemed to Chris a new kind of responsibility was being born. Man for man. And then he had come home and there was no consciousness of sacrifice, no meaning in the new responsibility, the whole thing was accepted as a kind of bus accident—

"Like when I went to work with Dad, and that rat race again. I felt . . . ashamed somehow. Because nobody was changed at all. It seemed to make suckers out of a lot of guys. I felt wrong to be alive, to open a bankbook, to drive the new car, to see the new refrigerator. I mean you can take those things out of the war, but when you drive that car you've got to know that it came out of the love a man can have for a man, you've got to be a little better because of that. Otherwise what you have is really loot, and there's blood on it. I didn't want to take any of it. And I guess that included you."

"And you still feel that way . . ."

"No . . ."

"Because you mustn't feel that way any more."

"I want you now, Annie."

"Because you have a right to whatever you have. Everything, Chris, understand that?"

"I'm glad you feel that way."

"To me too . . . And the money, there's nothing wrong in your money. Joe put hundreds of planes in the air, you should be proud. A man should be paid for that . . ."

"Oh, Annie, Annie . . . I'm going to make a fortune for you!"

"What'll I do with a fortune . . ." Ann is laughing softly, and he kisses her. . . .

Keller has come to call Ann. Her brother George is on long distance, calling from Columbus. When Ann goes to answer the call, Chris explains to his father the rather ardent kissing scene he had broken in upon. Chris and Ann are getting married.

Keller is still a little too distracted by Ann's long distance call to pay much attention to the marriage news. Ann's brother is calling from Columbus. Why? All these years George doesn't go near his father. Suddenly he does go—and Ann comes to visit them—

"It's crazy, but it comes to my mind. She don't hold nothin' against me, does she?" Keller is worried.

"I don't know what you're talking about."

"I'm just talkin'. To his last day in court the man blamed it all on me; and this is his daughter. I mean if she was sent here to find out something—"

Chris is angry. "Why? What is there to find out?"

Ann's voice can be heard from the house. She is trying to learn what it is that has excited her brother.

Keller glances at the house. "I mean if they want to open up the case again, for the nuisance value, to hurt us."

"Dad . . . how could you think that of her."

It's Chris that Keller is thinking of—Chris and his future. He wants Chris to spread out. He doesn't want anything to happen that will interfere with a new sign, "Christopher Keller, Inc.," going up over the Keller plant. He wants to build Chris a house, with a driveway from the road. He doesn't want Chris to be ashamed of the Keller money. It's good money—

"Oh, you're going to have a life, Chris!" promises Keller, exultantly, grabbing his son playfully by the throat. "We'll get Mother so drunk tonight we'll all get married! . . . There's gonna be a wedding, Kid, like there never was seen! Champagne, tuxedos . . . !"

Again Ann can be heard at the phone. "Well, what did he tell you, for God's sake? All right, come then. Yes, they'll all be here, nobody's running away from you! And try to get hold of yourself, will you? All right, all right, good-by!"

When Ann comes from the house she is "somber with nervousness." George will be in on the seven o'clock. No, she assures them, there's nothing wrong. She could think it's something stupid, knowing her brother. Anyway, she'd like to go for a drive or something . . .

Chris approves that idea. As they start out the driveway Mother comes quickly to Keller, her eyes fixed on him—

KELLER—What happened? What does George want?

MOTHER—He's been in Columbus since this morning with Herb. He's gotta see Annie right away, he says.

KELLER—What for?

MOTHER—I don't know. (*With warning.*) He's a lawyer now, Joe. George is a lawyer.

KELLER—So what?

MOTHER—All these years he wouldn't even send a postcard to Herb. Since he got back from the war, not a postcard.

KELLER (*angering*)—So what?

MOTHER (*her tension breaking*)—Suddenly he takes an airplane from New York to see him. An airplane!

KELLER—Well? So?

MOTHER (*trembling*)—Why?

KELLER—I don't read minds. Do you?

MOTHER—Why, Joe? What has Herb suddenly got to tell him that he takes an airplane to see him?

KELLER—What do I care what Herb's got to tell him?

MOTHER—You're sure, Joe?

KELLER (*frightened, but angry*)—Yes, I'm sure.

MOTHER (*sitting stiffly in chair*)—Be smart now, Joe. The boy is coming. Be smart.

KELLER (*desperately*)—Once and for all, did you hear what I said? I said I'm sure!

MOTHER (*nodding weakly*)—All right, Joe. (*As he straightens up.*) Just . . . be smart.

"Keller, in hopeless fury, looks at her, turns around, goes up to the porch and into the house slamming the screen door violently behind him. Mother sits stiffly, staring, seeing."

The curtain falls.

ACT II

It is early evening of the same day. Chris has just got around to taking the branches of the broken tree out into the street. His mother has made a pitcher of grape juice for the expected Georgie. She remembers that he always liked grape juice.

But, try though she does, to accept normally the situation about to be complicated by George Deever's arrival, Mother is worried. So is Dad. That's why Dad is asleep. He always sleeps a lot when he's worried—

"We're dumb, Chris. Dad and I are stupid people. We don't know anything. You've got to protect us."

"You're silly! What's there to be afraid of?"

"To his last day in court Herb never gave up the idea that Dad made him do it. If he's coming to reopen the case I won't live through it. We can't go through that thing again."

"George is just a damned fool, Mother, how can you take him so seriously?"

"That family hates us. Maybe even Annie . . ."

"Oh, now, Mother . . ."

"You think just because you like everybody, they like you! You don't realize how people can hate. Chris, we've got a nice life here, everything was going so nice. Why do you bring them into it? We struggled all our lives for a little something, and now . . ."

"All right, stop working yourself up. Just leave everything to me."

Chris and his mother have gone to dress when Sue Bayliss finds Ann in the yard. Doctor Jim has gone to the station to pick up George. Sue is in a gossipy mood, but there is one serious thought troubling her. She hopes after Chris and Ann are married that they will move away from there. Her husband is unhappy when Chris is around. Why?

". . . I like Chris," Sue would explain. "If I didn't I'd let him know, I don't butter people. But there's something about him that makes people want to be better than it's possible to be. He does that to people."

"Why is that bad?"

"My husband has a family, dear. Every time he has a session with Chris he feels as though he's compromising himself by not giving up everything for research. As though Chris or anybody else isn't compromising. It happens with Jim every couple of years. He meets a man and makes a statue out of him."

Ann is not surprised. She'd never think of Chris as a statue, but— And then Sue's real reason for feeling as she does is revealed. She resents the Kellers going on as they have been when they must know how people feel about them. Chris continues working with his father, doesn't he? And taking money out of the Keller firm? And Chris must know—

Ann's anger is mounting. She resents Sue's aspersions. She resents everything Sue has said—

"You know what I resent, dear?" Sue demands. "I resent living next door to the Holy Family. It makes me look like a bum, you understand?"

"I can't do anything about that."

"Who is he to ruin a man's life? Everybody knows Joe pulled a fast one to get out of jail."

"That's not true."

"Then why don't you go out and talk to people? Go on, talk to them. There's not a person on the block who doesn't know the truth."

"That's a lie. They're on the best terms with the block. People come here all the time for cards and . . ."

"So what? They give him credit for being smart. I do too. I've got nothing against Joe. But if Chris wants people to put on the hair shirt let him take off his broadcloth. He's driving my husband crazy with that phony idealism of his and I'm at the end of my rope on it!"

Chris has come from the house. He would have Sue go in and quiet his mother. Sue is an interesting woman, he reminds Ann after Sue has gone into the house. Interesting—and a great nurse, too.

Ann can't quite take that. She is remembering Sue's gossip, and the duplicity suggested. Doesn't Chris know that Sue despises him? And why didn't he tell her that all the block thinks Joe Keller is guilty? Why should Chris take the trouble to deny it?

For one reason, Chris didn't want to do anything that would discourage Ann's visit. For another, it doesn't matter who may think of his father as being guilty, he, Chris, knows he is not. "Do you think I could forgive him if he'd done that thing?" he demands.

"George is coming from my father, and I don't think it is with a blessing," says Ann.

"You've got nothing to fear from George," Chris assures her, taking her hands. "The man is innocent, Ann. I know he seems afraid, but he was falsely accused once and it put him through hell. How would you behave if you were faced with the same thing again? Believe me, Ann, there's nothing wrong for you here! Believe me, Kid!"

Keller has come from the house. He has something on his mind. He has been thinking of Ann's brother, George. If George isn't well, as Ann says, why should he stay on in New York? Why shouldn't he come there and let Keller use his local influence to get him set up?

Frankly, Keller admits, he is making the suggestion selfishly. Chris is his father's greatest and only accomplishment—

". . . What I want to know, Annie, is no matter what happens, my son is my son. That there's nothin' going to come between me and him. You follow me?"

"No. Why do you say that?"

"Because . . . face the facts, facts is facts . . . your father hates me. I don't have to tell you to his last day in court he blamed the whole thing on me, that I put him there . . . and the rest of it. You know that."

ANN—Well, he'll say anything.

KELLER—Right. He'll say anything. But let's face it, a year, eighteen months, he'll be a free man. Who is he going to come to, Annie? His baby. You. He'll come old, mad, into your house.

ANN—That can't matter any more, Joe.

KELLER—*Now* you say that, but believe me, Annie, blood is blood. A man harps long enough in your ears and you're going to listen. And . . . my son is in your house and . . . What I'm drivin' at, I don't want that hate to come between us. (*Gestures between* CHRIS *and himself.*)

ANN—I can only tell you that that could never happen.

KELLER—You're in love now, Annie, but believe me, I'm older than you; a daughter is a daughter, and a father is a father. And it could happen. (*Slight pause.*) What I like to see you do, is this. Your father wouldn't talk to me. But he'll talk to you and he'll talk to your brother. I like you both to go to him in prison and tell him . . . "Dad, Joe wants to bring you into the business when you get out."

ANN (*surprised, even shocked*)—You'd have him as a partner?

KELLER—No, no partner. A good job. (*He sees she is a little mystified. He gets up, speaks more nervously.*) I want him to know, Annie . . . while he's sitting there I want him to know that when he gets out he's got a place waitin' for him. It'll take his bitterness away. To know you got a place . . . it sweetens you.

ANN (*with an edge of fear, but the stress upon the reprimand*) —Joe, you owe him nothing.

KELLER—No, no . . . I owe him a good kick in the teeth, but . . .

CHRIS—Then kick him in the teeth. I don't want him in the plant, so that's that. And don't talk like that about him—people misunderstand you.

Keller would go on with the discussion. He still can't understand why Ann should want to crucify her father. They finally prevail upon him to go in and finish dressing.

Chris and Ann are alone when Dr. Jim comes hurriedly through the driveway. He has left George in the car. It is his advice that they don't see George there. Kate is not too well, and it would be

better if they were to save her a scene. The truth is George has
come back with blood in his eye. It will be much better if
Chris would drive him to some place and talk to him alone.

Chris will have none of that. No one there is afraid of George.
Let him come in. With this he starts for the driveway and meets
George. "George is Chris' age, but a paler man, now on the edge
of his self-restraint. . . . An instant's hesitation and Chris steps
up to him, hand extended, smiling."

"Helluva way to do; what're you sitting out there for?" demands Chris, with an attempt at heartiness.

"Doctor said your mother isn't well, I . . .'"

"So what? She'd want to see you, wouldn't she? We've been
waiting for you all afternoon."

Ann's greeting is more casual. She is a little disgusted to find
George sloppily dressed, and his shirt collar soiled. George takes
a few minutes to adjust himself to the familiar but definitely
changed scene. He is surprised to find the poplars as thick as
they are. He is touched that good old Kate should remember his
fondness for grape juice. The sight of the broken tree stirs his
curiosity. It is Larry's tree they tell him. Had they planted it
for fear they would forget Larry? he asks. Chris bridles a bit at
that.

Ann notices that George is wearing a hat. When did he start
that? Only today. Doesn't she recognize it? It's her father's
hat. Father had asked him to wear it—

"How is he?" Ann's query is dutiful but fearful.

"He got smaller," reports George, laughing "with his lips
shut."

"Smaller?"

"Yeah, little." He holds out his hand to measure. "He's a
little man. That's what happens to suckers, you know. It's good
I went to him in time—another year and there'd be nothing left
but his smell."

"What's the trouble with George?" Chris would know. "The
trouble is when you make suckers out of people once you shouldn't
try to do it twice," George answers bitterly.

George has come for Ann. Ann isn't married yet and she isn't
going to get married—not to Chris, anyway. Why? Because
Chris' father had destroyed her family!

Chris refuses to argue so silly a statement. George doesn't want
to be the voice of God, does he? George's trouble always has
been that he dives into things. Let him remember he's a big boy
now— Is he going to talk like a grown man or isn't he? Ann

senses the outbreak that is coming. Quickly she urges George to control his anger; to sit down and answer Chris calmly.

"Now, what happened?" she asks, quietly. "You kissed me when I left, now you . . ."

GEORGE (*breathlessly*)—My life turned upside down since then. I couldn't go back to work when you left. I wanted to go to Dad and tell him you were going to be married. It seemed impossible not to tell him. He loved you so much. (*Slight pause.*) Annie . . . we did a terrible thing. We can never be forgiven. Not even to send him a card at Christmas. I didn't see him once since I got home from the war! Annie, you don't know what was done to that man. You don't know what happened.

ANN (*afraid*)—Of course I know.

GEORGE—You can't know, you wouldn't be here. Dad came to work that day. The night foreman came to him and showed him the cylinder heads . . . they were coming out of the process with defects. There was something wrong with the process. So Dad went directly to the phone and called here and told Joe to come down right away. But the morning passed. No sign of Joe. So Dad called again. By this time he had over a hundred defectives. The Army was screaming for stuff and Dad didn't have anything to ship. So Joe told him . . . on the phone he told him to weld, cover up the cracks in any way he could, and ship them out.

CHRIS—Are you through now?

GEORGE—I'm not through now! (*To* ANN.) Dad was afraid. He didn't know if they'd hold up in the air. Or maybe an Army inspector would catch him. . . . But Joe told him they'd hold up, and swore to him . . . swore to him on the phone, Annie, that if anything happened he would take the whole responsibility. But Dad still wanted him there if he was going to do it. But he can't come down . . . he's sick. Sick! He suddenly gets the flu! Suddenly! But he promised to take responsibility. Do you understand what I'm saying? On the telephone you can't *have* responsibility! In a court you can always deny a phone call and that's exactly what he did. They knew he was a liar the first time, but in the appeal they believed that rotten lie and now Joe is a big shot and your father is the patsy. (*He gets up.*) Now what're you going to do? Answer me, what're you going to do; eat his food, sleep in his bed? You didn't even send your own father a card at Christmas, now what're you going to do?

CHRIS—What are *you* going to do, George?

GEORGE—He's too smart for me; I can't prove a phone call.

CHRIS—Then how dare you come in here with that rot?

ANN—George, the court . . .

GEORGE—The court didn't know your father! But you know him. You know in your heart Joe did it.

CHRIS—Lower your voice or I'll throw you out of here!

ANN—George, I know everything you've said. Dad told that whole thing in court and they . . .

GEORGE (*almost weeping*)—The court did not know him. Annie! (*To* CHRIS.) I'll ask you something, and look me in the eye when you answer me.

CHRIS (*defiantly*)—I'll look you in the eye.

GEORGE—You know your father . . .

CHRIS (*with growing fear, and therefore anger*)—I know him well.

GEORGE—And he's the kind of boss to let a hundred and twenty-one cylinder heads be repaired and shipped out of his shop without even knowing about it?

CHRIS—He's that kind of boss.

GEORGE—And that's the same Joe Keller who never left his shop without first going around to see that all the lights were out?

CHRIS (*with growing fury*)—The same Joe Keller.

GEORGE—The same man who knows how many minutes a day his workers spend in the toilet.

CHRIS—The same man.

GEORGE—And my father, that frightened mouse who'd never buy a shirt without somebody along—that man would dare do such a thing on his own?

CHRIS—On his own. And because he's a frightened mouse this is another thing he'd do: throw the blame on somebody else because he's not man enough to take it himself. This is *exactly* what he'd do. He tried it in court but it didn't work, but with a fool like you it works!

GEORGE—Oh, Chris, you're a liar to yourself.

ANN (*deeply shaken*)—Don't talk like that.

CHRIS—Tell me, George. What happened? The court record was good enough for you all these years, why isn't it good now? Why did you believe it all these years?

GEORGE—I had no reason not to believe it. And besides—I thought you believed it. That meant something too, you know. But today I heard it from his own mouth. From his mouth it's altogether different from the record. Anyone who knows him, and knows your father, will believe it from his mouth. Your father tricked him. He took everything we have. I can't beat that. But this I can. She's one item he's not going to grab. (*Turns to* ANN.) Get your things. Everything they have is covered with blood. You're not the kind of girl who can live with that.

Ann, mystified and wondering, doesn't want to believe what George is saying. George would force the truth upon her. There is plenty of evidence to convict Joe Keller. There are plenty of signs to indicate that Chris knows the truth and is deliberately denying it, even to himself. The Keller business doesn't belong to Chris now, but it will one day.

If Chris will let George talk ten minutes with Joe Keller he will have his answer, if he isn't afraid to hear it.

"I'm not afraid of the answer," Chris insists. "I know the answer. But my mother isn't well and I don't want a fight here now, and all you're going to do is fight with him."

That, to George, is proof that Chris is afraid to hear the truth, and a final reason why Ann should go with him, now. Again Ann would make her own decision, but later. Now she hears Mother Keller coming. She quickly adds her demand to that of Chris that George will not start anything now.

Mother's greeting of George is maternal and affectionate. She would cup his face in her hands and pity him because they have made an old man of him. Georgie looks starved to Mother. That shouldn't be. She would start right now feeding him, even if he hasn't any appetite—

"Honest to God, it breaks my heart to see what happened to all the children," says Mother. "How we worked and planned for you, and you end up no better than us."

"You . . . you haven't changed, you know that, Kate?" declares George, with deep feeling.

"None of us changed, Georgie. We all love you. Joe was just talking about the day you were born and the water got shut off. People were carrying basins from a block away—(*Laughs.*)—a stranger would think the whole neighborhood was on fire!"

George is not to be diverted from his determination to leave on the eight-thirty. He again insists that Ann shall come with him, and they try to dissuade him.

"If you want to go, I'll drive you to the station now," says Chris, "but if you're staying, no arguments while you're here."

"Why should he argue?" demands Mother. "Georgie and us have no argument. How could we have an argument, Georgie? We all got hit by the same lightning, how can you . . . ? Did you see what happened to Larry's tree, Georgie? (*She has taken his*

arm, and unwillingly he moves across toward the tree with her.)
Imagine? While I was dreaming of him in the middle of the night,
the wind came along and . . ."

Lydia Lubey is the last of the neighbors to greet George. She
is the girl, Mother insists, George should have married, but didn't.
George went away to fight Fascism and Frank Lubey stayed home,
kept just ahead of the draft, married Lydia, fathered three children
and kept up all the payments on his house. George, remembering,
looks a little longingly after Lydia. She has greatly softened his
mood. In a lot of ways it is good to be back, he admits. Mother
would press the idea home—

"I'm smarter than any of you, and now you're going to listen to
me, George," she says with authority. "You had big principles,
Eagle Scouts the three of you; so now I got a tree, and this one—
(*Of* CHRIS.)—when the weather gets bad he can't stand on his
feet. (*Indicates* LYDIA's *house.*) And that big dope next door
who never reads anything but Andy Gump has three children and
his house paid off. Stop being a philosopher. Look after *yourself.*
Like Joe was just saying—you move back here, he'll help you get
set, and I'll find you a girl and put a smile on your face."

"Joe? Joe wants me here?" George's surprise is genuine.

"He asked me to tell you, and I think it's a good idea," adds
Ann, eagerly.

"Certainly," Mother goes on. "Why must you make believe
you hate us? Is that another principle—that you have to hate
us? You don't hate us, George, not in your heart. I know you,
you can't fool me, I diapered you."

They are all laughing when Keller comes from the house. He
greets George with a nervous friendliness. He would have George
come to dinner with them; is disappointed that he can't. Keller is
pleased to tell George of the changes he has made in the Keller
plant, and of the success that has followed. He inquires sympathetically after George's father, and is sorry to hear that he is not
well—

"That's the way they do, George. A little man makes a mistake and they hang him by the thumbs; the big ones become
ambassadors. I wish you'd a told me you were going to see Dad."

GEORGE (*studying him*)—I didn't know you were interested.

KELLER—In a way, I am. I would like him to know, George,
that as far as I'm concerned, any time he wants he's got a place
with me. I would like him to know that.

GEORGE (*looking at* MOTHER)—He hates your guts, Joe. Don't you know that?

KELLER—I . . . imagined it. But that can change, too.

MOTHER—Herb was never like that.

GEORGE—He's like that now. He'd like to take every man who made money in the war and put him up against a wall.

KELLER—He'll need a lot of bullets.

GEORGE—And he'd better not get any.

KELLER—That's a sad thing to hear.

GEORGE (*now with his bitterness dominant*)—Why? What'd you expect him to think of you?

KELLER (*the force of his nature rising, but under control*)—A thing can be sad even if you expect it. I expected it because I know your father. And I'm sad to see he hasn't changed. As long as I know him, twenty-five years, that part of him made me sad. The man never learned how to take the blame. You know that, George.

GEORGE—Well, I . . .

KELLER—But you do know it. Because the way you come in here you don't look like you remember it. I mean like in 1937 when we had the shop on Flood Street. And he damn near blew us all up with that heater he left burning for two days without water. He wouldn't admit that was his fault either. I had to fire a mechanic to save his face. You remember that.

GEORGE—Yes, but . . .

KELLER—I'm just mentioning it, George. Because this is just another one of a lot of things. Like when he gave Frank that money to invest in oil stock.

GEORGE (*distressed*)—I know that, I . . .

KELLER (*driving in, but restrained*)—But it's good to remember those things, kid. The way he cursed Frank because the stock went down. Was that Frank's fault? To listen to him Frank was a swindler. And all the man did was give him a bad tip.

GEORGE—I know those things . . .

KELLER—Then remember them, remember them. There are certain men in the world who rather see everybody hung before they'll take blame. (*They stand facing each other*, GEORGE *trying to judge him.*)

They urge George to stay over, at least long enough to have dinner with them. Then he can catch the midnight if he insists. Their pleading is so eager and sincere that George is quite moved. "I never felt at home . . . anywhere but here . . ." he says, looking around at them. "I feel so . . . Kate, you look so young, you know? You didn't change at all. It . . . rings an old bell." He has turned to Keller. "You, too, Joe, you're amazingly the same. The whole atmosphere is."

"Say, I ain't got time to get sick," boasts Joe.

"He hasn't been laid up in fifteen years . . ." adds Mother.

"Except my 'flu during the war," Keller quickly corrects her. "Heh?"

"My 'flu, when I was sick during . . ."

Mother is quick to catch his meaning. "Well, sure . . ." she adds, nervously turning to George; "except for that 'flu, I mean. . . . I just forgot it, George . . . I mean, he's so rarely sick it slipped my mind. I thought he had pneumonia. He couldn't get off the bed."

"Why did you say he's never . . . ?"

"I know how you feel, kid, but I couldn't help it." Keller is trying desperately to cover. "I'll never forgive myself, because if I could've gone in that day I'd never allow Dad to touch those heads."

"She said you've never been sick."

"I said he *was* sick."

George turns to Ann. "Didn't you hear her say . . . ?"

"Do you remember every time you were sick?" Mother demands.

"I'd remember pneumonia . . ."

"Now, George!" Ann is anxious.

"Especially if I got it on the day my partner was going to patch up cylinder heads! What happened that day, Joe?"

Before Joe can answer, Frank Lubey appears. Mother is quick to take advantage of the break. Frank has brought Larry's horoscope. Nobody except Mother is interested. George stands staring at Keller. Ann is troubled about George. Chris comes from the house and is puzzled about what has happened.

There is good news in Larry's horoscope, Frank has found. Larry was reported missing on February 9, and February 9 was his "favorable" day; the odds are a million to one that a man will not die on his favorable day. That's known. Therefore, Frank reasons, somewhere in the world Larry is alive.

If that is true, as Mother would like to believe, she thinks Ann and Chris had better alter their plans. Chris will have none of this nonsense, nor permit his mother to interfere. Nor will Ann, despite George's urging.

"I packed your bag," Mother says to Ann; "all you have to do is to close it."

Ann is on the verge of tears. "I'm not closing anything," she says, indicating Chris. "He asked me here and I'm staying till he tells me to go. Till he tells me."

"That's all," Chris bursts out suddenly. "Nothing more till Christ comes, about the case or Larry; not another word as long as I'm here."

The horn of George's taxi is heard in the street. Ann would gently urge her brother toward the driveway. Now they have disappeared and Chris has turned a little savagely on his mother. What did she mean, packing Ann's bag?

"She doesn't belong here," weakly answers Mother.

"Then I don't belong here," snaps Chris.

"She's Larry's girl; she's Larry's girl!"

"And I'm his brother and he's dead, and I'm marrying his girl."

"Never, never in this world!"

It is when Joe Keller would also interfere that Mother becomes emotionally hysterical. When he accuses her of talking like a maniac she strikes him across the face. For a moment everything stops. The silence is broken by Mother's trembling, hysterical whispers predicting the coming of Larry to continue his plan of marrying Ann. Till that happens everybody must wait. If they will not, if Chris insists on letting Larry go, he may as well let his father go, too. So long as any of them shall live, Larry must live, too. Let them understand that.

"She's out of her mind," mutters Keller, as Mother sobbingly runs into the house.

"Then . . . you did it?" Chris has turned on his father. His voice is tense and broken.

KELLER (*the beginning of plea in his voice*)—He never flew a P-40.

CHRIS—But the others.

KELLER (*insistently*)—She's out of her mind.

CHRIS (*unyielding*)—Dad . . . you did it?

KELLER—He never flew a P-40, what's the matter with you?

CHRIS—Then you did it. To the others.

KELLER—What's the matter with you? (*Seeing wildness in his eyes.*) What the hell is the matter with you?

CHRIS (*incredulously*)—How . . . how could you do that?

KELLER (*lost*)—What's the matter with you?

CHRIS—Dad . . . Dad, you killed twenty-one men.

KELLER—What, killed?

CHRIS—You killed them, you murdered them.

KELLER—How could I kill anybody?

CHRIS—Dad! Dad!

KELLER (*trying to hush him*)—I didn't kill anybody!

CHRIS—Then explain it to me. What did you do? Explain it to me or I'll tear you to pieces! What did you do then? What did you do? Now tell me what you did. What did you do?

KELLER (*horrified*)—Don't, Chris, don't . . .

CHRIS—I want to know what you did, now what did you do? You had a hundred and twenty-one cracked engine heads, now what did you do?

KELLER—If you're going to hang me then I—

CHRIS—I'm listening, God almighty, I'm listening!

KELLER—You're a boy, what could I do? I'm in business, a man is in business; a hundred and twenty-one cracked, you're out of business; you got a process, the process don't work, you're out of business; you don't know how to operate, your stuff is no good; they close you up, they tear up your contracts, what the hell's it to them? You lay forty years into a business and they knock you out in five minutes, what could I do, let them take forty years, let them take my life away? (*His voice cracking.*) I never thought they'd install them. I swear to God. I thought they'd stop them before anybody took off.

CHRIS—Then why'd you ship them out?

KELLER—By the time they could spot them I thought I'd have the process going again, and I could show them they needed me and they'd let it go by. But weeks passed and I got no kick-back, so I was going to tell them.

CHRIS—Then why didn't you tell them?

KELLER—It was too late. The paper, it was all over the front page, twenty-one went down, it was too late. They came with handcuffs into the shop, what could I do? (*Weeping, he approaches* CHRIS.) Chris . . . Chris, I did it for you, it was a chance and I took it for you. I'm sixty-one years old, when would I have another chance to make something for you? Sixty-one years old you don't get another chance, do ya?

CHRIS—You even knew they wouldn't hold up in the air.

KELLER—I didn't say that. . . .

CHRIS—But you were going to warn them not to use them . . .

KELLER—But that don't mean . . .

CHRIS—It means you knew they'd crash.

KELLER—I don't mean that.

CHRIS—Then you *thought* they'd crash.

KELLER—I was afraid maybe . . .

CHRIS—You were afraid maybe! Almighty God in heaven, what kind of a man are you? Kids were hanging in the air by those heads. You knew that!

KELLER—For you, a business for you!

CHRIS (*with burning fury*)—For me! Where do you live, where have you come from? For me!—I was dying every day and you were killing my boys and you did it for me? I was so proud you were helping us win and you did it for me? What the hell do you think I was thinking of, the goddam business? Is that as far as your mind can see, the business? What is that, the world—the business? What are you made of, dollar bills? What the hell do you mean, you did it for me? Don't you have a country? Don't you live in the world? What the hell are you? You're not even an animal, no animal kills his own, what are you? What must I do to you? I ought to tear the tongue out of your mouth, what must I do? (*He is weeping and with his fist he begins to pound down upon his father's shoulder, and* KELLER *stands there and weeps.*) What? What! What! What! (*He stumbles away, covering his face as he weeps.*) What must I do, Jesus God, what must I do? (*He falls into a chair and cries.*)

KELLER (*raising a hand weakly and coming toward him weeping*)—Chris . . . My Chris . . .

The curtain falls.

ACT III

It is two o'clock that night. The moon casts a bluish light over the Keller yard. The light shows from Ann's room but the lower floor windows are dark. Mother is discovered "rocking ceaselessly in a chair, staring at her thoughts." Keller is inside the house, peering through the screen door.

Presently Dr. Jim Bayliss comes from next door. He has just returned from an emergency call. "Somebody had a headache and thought he was dying," Jim explains to Mother. "Half of my patients are quite mad."

He would have Mother go to bed. She shouldn't be sitting up this way. But Mother is waiting for Chris and refuses to be moved. Chris had had an argument with his father and then driven away.

What had Chris and his father argued about? Had Keller told Chris? Kate need not be afraid of telling him, Jim says. He's known for a long time. And he's been wondering how Chris would take it when he knew. He's quite sure that Chris will come back—

"... We all come back, Kate," Jim declares. "These private little revolutions always die. The compromise is always made. In a peculiar way. Frank is right—every man does have a star. The star of one's honesty. And you spend your life groping for it, but once it's out it never lights again. I don't think he went very far. He probably just wanted to be alone to watch his star go out."

"Just as long as he comes back."

"I wish he wouldn't, Kate. One year I simply took off, went to New Orleans; for two months I lived on bananas and milk, and studied a certain disease. It was beautiful. And then she came, and she cried. And I went back home with her. And now I live in the usual darkness; I can't find myself; it's even hard sometimes to remember the kind of man I wanted to be. I'm a good husband; Chris is a good son—he'll come back."

Jim has gone to have a look around the park for Chris. Keller, coming from the house, is looking for an answer to his worries. He thinks maybe he should have a talk with Ann who hasn't left her room since Chris drove away. But mostly Keller needs Mother's advice. What should he do when Chris comes back?

Mother isn't sure, but she has an idea. "I think if you sit him down and you . . . explain yourself. I mean you ought to make it clear to him that you *know* you did a terrible thing. (*Not looking into his eyes.*) I mean if he saw that you realize what you did. You see?"

"What ice does that cut?"

"I mean if you told him that you want to pay for what you did."

"How can I pay?"

"Tell him . . . you're willing to go to prison." Then, as she notices his rising anger, and the expression of amazement on his face, Mother quickly continues: "You wouldn't go! He wouldn't ask you to go. But if you told him you wanted to, if he could feel that you wanted to pay, maybe he would forgive you."

"He would forgive me! For what?"

"Joe, you know what I mean!"

Joe doesn't know, or says he doesn't. What had he done? They wanted money, and he made money. He had spoiled them both. He should have turned Chris out to make his own dollars. What Keller had done he had done for the family. There's nothing bigger to a man than his family. That's what Mother should tell Chris.

"I'm his father and he's my son, and if there's something bigger than that I'll put a bullet in my head! . . . Now you know what to tell him. . . . Goddam, if Larry was alive he wouldn't act like this. He understood the way the world is made. He listened to me. To him the world had a forty-foot front, it ended at the building line. This one, everything bothers him. You make a deal, overcharge two cents and his hair falls out. He don't understand money. Too easy, it came too easy. Yes, sir. Larry. That was a boy we lost. Larry. Larry. Where the hell is he?" His voice has risen to an impatient cry.

"Joe! Joe, please! . . . you'll be all right; nothing is going to happen. . . ."

"For you, Kate! For both of you! That's all I ever lived for!"

"I know, darling, I know . . ."

Ann comes from the house. She wants to have a talk with Mother. Ann has no idea of doing anything about Joe, but she is insistent that Mother shall set her right with Chris. "I'd like you to tell him that Larry is dead and that you know it." When that situation is cleared up Ann will be ready to go away with Chris and leave the Kellers alone.

"My dear, if the boy was dead, it wouldn't depend on my words to make Chris know it," Mother protests. "The night he gets into your bed, his heart will dry up. Because he knows and you know. To his dying day he'll wait for his brother! No, my dear, no such thing. You're going in the morning, and you're going alone. That's your life, that's your lonely life!"

Ann is not impressed. "Larry is dead, Kate!" she says, her voice level and calm. "He crashed off the coast of China, February 9th. His engine didn't fail him but he died. I know."

Mother will not believe that. Excitedly she demands a more convincing statement—

"First you've got to understand," Ann goes on. "When I came, I didn't have any idea that Joe . . . I had nothing against him or you. I came to get married. I hoped . . . (*She brings out a letter from her pocket.*) So I didn't bring this to hurt you. I thought I'd show it to you only if there was no other way to settle Larry in your mind."

"What is that?"

"He wrote me a letter just before he . . ."

"Larry?"

"I'm not trying to hurt you, Kate." Mother is reading the letter. "You're making me do this, now remember you're . . . Remember!" A long low groan escapes Mother's throat as she reads. "Oh, my God . . ."

"Oh, Kate dear! I'm so sorry . . ." There is pity—and fear —in Ann's voice.

Chris comes down the driveway. He seems exhausted. Ann goes to him. His mother does not move. Where had he been? Just driving around. He thought Ann would be gone. Now let them both sit down. He'll say what there is to say—

Mother has come to Chris and taken his hand. "Chris, you look so . . ." Her voice is anxious. "You smashed your watch?"

CHRIS—Against the steering wheel. I had a little accident. It's nothing, just a fender . . . I wasn't looking, Mother . . . I'm going away. For good. (*To* ANN *alone.*) I know what you're thinking, Annie. It's true. I'm yellow. I was made yellow here. In this house. Because I suspected my father and I did nothing about it. If I knew the night I came home what I know now, he'd be in the district attorney's office by this time, and I'd have brought him there. Now if I look at him, all I'm able to do is cry.

MOTHER—What are you talking about? What else can you do?

CHRIS—I could jail him. I tell it to you with your teary eyes. I could jail him, if I were human any more. But I'm like everybody else now. I'm practical now. You made me practical.

MOTHER—But you have to be.

CHRIS—The cats in that alley are practical, the bums who ran away when we were fighting were practical. Only the dead weren't practical. But now I'm practical, and I spit on myself. I'm going away. I'm going now.

ANN—I'm coming with you . . .

CHRIS—No, Ann, I can't make that.

ANN—I don't ask you to do anything about Joe. I swear I never will!

CHRIS—Yes, you do. In your heart you always will.

ANN—Take me with you. No one will understand why you're . . .

CHRIS—Maybe a few . . . in some hospital somewhere, there's a few will understand.

ANN—Then do what you have to do!

CHRIS—Do what? What is there to do? I've looked all night for a reason to make him suffer . . .

ANN—There is reason!

CHRIS—What? Do I raise the dead when I put him behind bars? Then what'll I do it for? We used to shoot a man who acted like a dog, but honor was real there, you were protecting something. But here? This is a land of the great *big* dogs, you don't love a man here, you eat him. *That's* the principle; the only one we really live by— It just happened to kill a few people this time, that's all. The world's that way, how can I take it out on him? What sense does that make? This is a˙zoo, a zoo!

ANN (*to* MOTHER)—Why are you standing there? *You* know what he's got to do!—Tell him.

MOTHER (*clutching the letter tighter*)—Let him go.

ANN—I won't let him go, you'll tell him . . . !

MOTHER (*warning*)—Annie . . . !

ANN—Then I will!

Keller comes from the house. When Chris would pass, his father stops him. He would talk with Chris. "Exactly what's the matter?" Keller demands, excitedly. "Without the philosophy involved? What's the matter? You got too much money? Is that what bothers you?"

"It bothers me." There is an edge of sarcasm in Chris' tone.

If it's the money that bothers him, Keller goes on, let Chris take it and give it to charity. Or throw it in the sewer. If it's dirty money, burn it. Let Chris say what he wants to do—

"It's not what I want to do. It's what you want to do!" Chris is trembling when he answers.

"What should I want to do? . . . Jail? . . . You want me to go to jail?" Chris' eyes have filled. "What're you crying for? If you want me to go say so! Don't cry! Is that where I belong?—Then tell me so! What's the matter, why can't you tell me? (*Furiously.*) You say everything else to me, say that! I'll tell you why you can't say it. Because you know I don't belong there. Because you know! If my money's dirty there ain't a clean nickel in the United States. Who worked for nothin' in that war? When they work for nothin' I'll work for nothin'. Did they ship a gun or a truck outa Detroit before they got their price? Is that clean? Nothin's clean. It's dollars and cents, nickels and dimes; war and peace, it's nickels and dimes, what's clean? The whole goddam country is gotta go if I go! That's why you can't tell me."

"That's exactly why."

"Then . . . why am I bad?"

"I don't call you bad. I know you're no worse than most, but I thought you were better. I never saw you as a man. I saw you as my father. (*Almost breaking.*) I can't look at you this way, and I can't look at myself!"

Ann has moved quickly over to Mother and snatched the letter from her hand. The next minute she has thrust it in Chris' hand, despite Mother's wild attempt to retrieve it. As Chris unlocks his mother's hands from his wrists and starts to read the letter the agony of her plea is increased. It is Keller she is thinking of now. "Don't tell him . . ." she pleads piteously.

Chris has turned on his father. "Three and one-half years . . . he says with quiet, deadly earnestness. Talking; talking. Now you tell me what you must do . . . This is how he died, now tell me where you belong."

KELLER (*in deadly fear*)—Chris, a man can't be a Jesus in this world.

CHRIS—I know all about the world. I know the whole crap story. Now listen to this, and tell me what a man's got to be! (*He reads.*) "My dear Ann." (*To* KELLER.) You listening? He wrote this the day he died. Listen, don't cry . . . listen! . . . "My dear Ann: It is impossible to put down the things I feel but I've got to tell you something. Yesterday they flew in a load of papers from the States and I read about Dad and your father being convicted. I can't express myself; I can't tell you what I feel, I can't bear to live any more. Last night I circled the base for twenty minutes before I could bring myself in. How could he have done that? Every day three or four men never return and he sits back there doing business. I don't know how to tell you what I feel. I can't face anybody. I'm going out on a mission in a few minutes. They'll probably report me missing. If they do, I want you to know that you mustn't wait for me. I tell you, Ann, if I had him here now I could kill him . . ." (KELLER *grabs the letter from him*)—Now blame the world. . . . Do you understand that letter?

KELLER (*looking up slowly*)—I think so . . . Get the car . . . I'll put on my jacket.

MOTHER—Why are you going? You'll sleep. Why are you going?

KELLER—I can't sleep here. I feel better if I go now.

MOTHER—You're so foolish; Larry was your son too, wasn't he? You know he'd never tell you to do this!

KELLER (*with absolute conviction of letter*)—What is this if it isn't telling me? Sure, he was my son. But I think to him they were all my sons. And I guess they were, kid . . . I guess they were . . . I'll be down in a minute.

MOTHER (*to* CHRIS)—You're not going to take him.

CHRIS—I'm taking him!

MOTHER—It's up to you, if you tell him to stay he'll stay. Go and tell him!

CHRIS—Nobody could stop him now!

MOTHER—You'll stop him! How long will he live in prison? Are you trying to kill him?

CHRIS (*of the letter*)—I thought you read that!

MOTHER—The war is over! Didn't you hear? . . . It's over!

CHRIS—Then what was Larry to you? A stone that fell into the water? It's not enough to be sorry; Larry didn't kill himself to make you and Dad sorry!

MOTHER—What more can we be!

CHRIS—You can be better! Once and for all you can know there's a universe of people outside and you're responsible to it, and unless you know that you threw your son away, because that's why he died! (*A shot is heard from the house. They stand frozen for a brief second.* CHRIS *starts for the porch.*) Find Jim! (*He goes into the house.*)

MOTHER (*over and over*)—Joe . . . Joe . . . Joe . . .

CHRIS (*coming from the house and going to her arms*)—Mother . . .

MOTHER—Ssshh! Ssshh!

CHRIS—I didn't mean that he . . .

MOTHER—Ssshh! Ssshh . . . Don't, don't dear; you mustn't take it on yourself. Forget now, live now.

She moves from him and as she mounts the porch steps he hears the growing sound of her weeping. She goes inside. Alone, he comes erect, moves away from the sound; does not turn to it, as

THE CURTAIN FALLS

THE ICEMAN COMETH

A Drama in Four Acts

BY EUGENE O'NEILL

(Digest by John Chapman)

THE afternoon of October 9, 1946, was the event of the New York season—perhaps of a dozen seasons, for the first play by Eugene O'Neill in twelve years was about to have its first performance. At that, "The Iceman Cometh" was not a new drama, the freshest product of the author's small, precise handwriting. O'Neill had written it in 1939 and had made several other plays, including "Moon for the Misbegotten," since.

Various factors had held up "The Iceman." First was O'Neill's determination to complete a cycle of American dramas, taking many years in the writing, before offering any of them for production. Second was the state of his health, which was worrisome. Third was the beginning of World War II. This cataclysm profoundly disturbed the dramatist, making him feel that nothing much else, including his own plays, was important. It did not matter that "The Iceman Cometh" was ready; O'Neill felt that the public, with greater things on its mind, was *not* ready.

The locale of "The Iceman Cometh" and many of the characters in it come from O'Neill's memory of his own footloose days in New York. It is Harry Hope's saloon before dawn on a Summer day in 1912. Hope's place is not unlike what historians recall as Jimmy-the-Priest's, a dive of that era in the part of the West Side known as Hell's Kitchen. It is a Raines Law hotel, for there are rooms above, and restrictions on the serving of liquor are gentler.

The saloon itself consists of a barroom in front, with doors swinging out on the street, and, partitioned by a curtain, a back room crammed with chairs and round tables. One door in the back room opens on a hallway leading to the rooms upstairs; another to a toilet with a sign, "This is it!" The walls are splotched, peeled and stained, and dusty grime has opaqued the windows.

In the hard light from a pair of wall brackets ten men are revealed in various states of consciousness or unconsciousness. All but one of them are shabbily clad bums; some, heads on tables, are asleep; others sit staring at nothing. Only one, Larry Slade, seems wide awake. He is about 60, with a week's beard and a mystic's meditative eyes. He is wide enough awake to catch the "Sst" of Rocky, the night bartender, as Rocky comes through the curtain from the bar carrying a bottle and a glass.

Slade, checking to see if Harry Hope, the boss, is asleep at a nearby table, nods, and Rocky comes over. "Make it fast," he urges in a low voice, and Larry pours and gulps down a drink.

"Don't want de Boss to get wise when he's got one of his tight-wad buns on," explains Rocky. "Ain't de old bastard a riot when he starts dat bull about turnin' over a new leaf? 'Not a damned drink on de house,' he tells me, 'and all dese bums got to pay up deir room rent. Beginnin' tomorrow,' he says." Rocky is and looks like a tough guy, a Neapolitan-American, but he is senti-mental and good-natured.

As Rocky takes a chair alongside, Larry grins, "I'll be glad to pay up—tomorrow. And I know my fellow inmates will promise the same. They've all a touching credulity concerning tomor-rows." He is half drunk, and mocking. "It'll be a great day for them, tomorrow—the Feast of All Fools, with brass bands play-ing! Their ships will come in, loaded to the gunwales with can-celed regrets and promises fulfilled and clean slates and new leases on life."

"Yeah," grunts Rocky cynically, "and a ton of hop!"

LARRY (*leans toward him, a comical intensity in his low voice*) —Don't mock the faith! Have you no respect for religion, you unregenerate Wop? What's it matter if the truth is that their favoring breeze has the stink of nickel whiskey on its breath, and their sea is a growler of lager and ale, and their ships are long since looted and scuttled and sunk on the bottom? To hell with the truth! As the history of the world proves, the truth has no bearing on anything. The lie of a pipe dream is what gives life to the whole misbegotten mad lot of us, drunk or sober. And that's enough philosophic wisdom to give you for one drink of rot-gut.

ROCKY (*grins kiddingly*)—De old Foolosopher, like Hickey calls yuh, ain't yuh? I s'pose you don't fall for no pipe dream?

LARRY (*a bit stiffly*)—I don't, no. Mine are all dead and buried behind me.

ROCKY—Yeah, just hangin' around hopin' you'll croak, ain't

yuh? De old anarchist wise guy dat knows all de answers! Dat's
you, huh?

LARRY (*frowns*)—Forget the anarchist part of it. I'm through
with the Movement long since. I saw men didn't want to be saved
from themselves, for that would mean they'd have to give up greed,
and they'll never pay that price for liberty. So I said to the world,
God bless all here, and may the best man win and die of gluttony!
And I took a seat in the grandstand of philosophical detachment
to fall asleep observing the cannibals do their death dance. (*He
chuckles at his own fancy—reaches over and shakes* HUGO's
shoulder.) Ain't I telling him the truth, Comrade Hugo?

ROCKY—Aw, fer Chris' sake, don't get dat bughouse bum
started!

HUGO (*raises his head and peers at* ROCKY *blearily through his
thick spectacles—in a guttural declamatory tone*)—Capitalist
swine! Bourgeois stool pigeons! Have the slaves no right to sleep
even? (*Then he grins at* ROCKY *and his manner changes to a
giggling, wheedling playfulness, as though he were talking to a
child.*) Hello, leedle Rocky! Leedle monkey-face! Vere is your
leedle slave girls? (*With an abrupt change to a bullying tone.*)
Don't be a fool! Loan me a dollar! Damned bourgeois Wop!
The great Malatesta is my good friend! Buy me a trink! (*He
seems to run down, and is overcome by drowsiness. His head
sinks to the table again and he is at once fast asleep.*)

ROCKY—Thank Christ he's out again. (*More exasperated than
angry.*) He's lucky no one don't take his cracks serious.

LARRY (*regarding* HUGO *with pity*)—No. No one takes him
seriously. That's his epitaph. Not even the comrades any more.
If I've been through with the Movement long since, it's been
through with him, and, thanks to whiskey, he's the only one
doesn't know it.

ROCKY—He's goin' to pull dat slave-girl stuff on me once too
often. (*His manner changes to defensive argument.*) Hell, yuh'd
tink I wuz a pimp or somethin'. Everybody knows me knows I
ain't. I'm a bartender. Dem tarts, Margie and Poil, dey're just
a side line to pick up some extra dough. Strictly business, like dey
was fighters and I was deir manager, see? Hell, dey'd be on de
Island most of de time if it wasn't fer me. I treat dem fine. Dey
like me. What if I do take deir dough? Dey'd on'y trow it away.
But I'm a bartender and I work hard for my livin'. You know
dat, Larry.

LARRY (*with inner sardonic amusement—flatteringly*)—A
shrewd business man, who doesn't miss any opportunity to get on

in the world. That's what I'd call you.

ROCKY (*pleased*)—Sure ting. Dat's me. Grab another ball, Larry. (LARRY *pours a drink from the bottle on* WILLIE'S *table and gulps it down.* ROCKY *glances around the room.*) Jees, yuh'd never tink all dese bums had a good bed upstairs to go to. Scared if dey hit the hay dey wouldn't be here when Hickey showed up, and dey'd miss a coupla drinks. Dat's what kept you up too, ain't it?

LARRY—Not so much the hope of booze, if you can believe that. I've got the blues and Hickey's a great one to make a joke of everything and cheer you up.

ROCKY—Yeah, some kidder! Remember how he woiks up dat gag about his wife, when he's cockeyed, cryin' over her picture and den springin' it on yuh all of a sudden dat he left her in de hay wid de iceman? (*He laughs.*) I wonder what's happened to him. Yuh could set your watch by his periodicals before dis. Always got here a coupla days before Harry's birthday party, and now he's on'y got till tonight to make it. I hope he shows soon. Dis dump is like de morgue wid all dese bums passed out. (WILLIE OBAN *jerks and twitches in his sleep and begins to mumble. They watch him.*)

WILLIE (*blurts from his dream*)—It's a lie! (*Miserably.*) Papa! Papa!

LARRY—Poor devil. (*Then angry with himself.*) But to hell with pity! It does no good. I'm through with it!

ROCKY—Dreamin' about his old man. From what de old-timers say, de old gent made a pile of dough in de bucket-shop game before de cops got him. (*He considers* WILLIE *frowningly.*) Jees, I've seen him bad before but never dis bad. Look at dat get-up! Been playin' de old reliever game. Sold his suit and shoes at Solly's two days ago. Solly give him two bucks and a bum outfit. Yesterday he sells de bum one back to Solly for four bits and gets dese rags to put on. Now he's through. Dat's Solly's final edition he wouldn't take back for nuttin'. Willie sure is on de bottom.

LARRY (*sardonically*)—It's a great game, the pursuit of happiness.

WILLIE (*suddenly yells in his nightmare*)—It's a God-damned lie! (*He begins to sob.*) Oh, Papa! Jesus! (*All the occupants of the room stir on their chairs but none of them wakes up except* HOPE.)

ROCKY (*grabs his shoulder and shakes him*)—Hey, you! Nix! Cut out de noise! (WILLIE *opens his eyes to stare around him with a bewildered horror.*)

HOPE (*opens one eye to peer over his spectacles—drowsily*)—
Who's that yelling?

ROCKY—Willie, Boss. De Brooklyn boys is after him.

HOPE (*querulously*)—Well, why don't you give the poor feller
a drink and keep him quiet? Bejeeses, can't I get a wink of sleep
in my own back room?

ROCKY (*indignantly to* LARRY)—Listen to that blind-eyed,
deaf old bastard, will yuh? He give me strict orders not to let
Willie hang up no more drinks, no matter—

HOPE (*mechanically puts a hand to his ear in the gesture of
deafness*)—What's that? I can't hear you. (*Then drowsily iras-
cible.*) You're a cockeyed liar. Never refused a drink to anyone
needed it bad in my life! Told you to use your judgment. Ought
to know better. You're too busy thinking up ways to cheat me.
Oh, I ain't as blind as you think. I can still see a cash register,
bejeeses!

ROCKY (*grins at him affectionately now—flatteringly*)—Sure,
Boss. Swell chance of foolin' you!

HOPE—I'm wise to you and your sidekick, Chuck. Bejeeses,
you're burglars, not barkeeps! Blind-eyed, deaf old bastard, am
I? Oh, I heard you! Heard you often when you didn't think.
You and Chuck laughing behind my back, telling people you
throw the money up in the air and whatever sticks to the ceiling is my share!

ROCKY (*winks at* LARRY)—Aw, Harry, me and Chuck was
on'y kiddin'.

HOPE (*more drowsily*)—I'll fire both of you. No one ever
played Harry Hope for a sucker! (*His eyes shut again—mutters.*) Least you could do—keep things quiet— (*He falls asleep.*)

Another inmate, Willie, begs a drink from Rocky, taking it
right from the bottle in big swallows. Another of the sleepers,
Joe Mott, a Negro, struggles awake and queries, "Where's
Hickey? I was dreamin' Hickey come in de door, crackin' one
of dem drummer jokes, wavin' a big bankroll and we was all
goin' to be drunk for two weeks."

But Hickey is just a dream and Joe wants liquor. "I got
idea," he proposes. "Say, Larry, how 'bout dat young guy,
Parritt, came to look you up last night and rented a room?"
Larry thinks Parritt is broke, is surprised and resentful when
Joe tells him he saw the newcomer flash a roll when he paid his
rent. Anyhow Parritt is no friend, Larry says.

"His mother and I were friends years ago," he explains. "You've read in the papers about that bombing on the Coast when several people got killed? Well, the one woman they pinched, Rosa Parritt, is his mother. She'll get life, I think."

Soon Parritt himself comes downstairs—a boy of 18 with good looks which have something unpleasant about them. His clothes are new and sporty and his manner is that of a poolroom hanger-on. Larry invites him to a seat—and pointedly invites him to buy. Parritt pleads that he's broke, then grudgingly offers to buy from a small wad of dollar bills—all he's got to live on till he gets a job. Joe Mott takes a drink, the bartender says he will have a cigar and Larry says he is on the wagon—total damage, 15 cents.

Rocky withdraws to the bar for a wink of sleep, Joe falls asleep again after asking to be waked up if Hickey comes.

"Who's Hickey?" asks Parritt.

"A hardware drummer," Larry explains. "An old friend of Harry Hope's and all the gang. He's a grand guy. He comes here twice a year regularly on a periodical drunk and blows in all his money."

"What kind of joint is this, anyway?"

"It's Bedrock Bar, the End of the Line Café, the Bottom of the Salt Sea Rathskeller, the Last Harbor! No one here has to worry about what they're going to do next, because there is no farther they can go. It's a great comfort to them. Although even here they keep up the appearances of life with a few harmless pipe dreams about their yesterdays and tomorrows."

Hesitantly, not quite frankly, young Parritt tells Larry something of himself. Obviously, he is in flight and hiding—and lonely. He has been looking for Larry as the only one who would understand—the only friend of his mother's who ever paid any attention to him when he was a boy.

Larry remembers; remembers the lad as a serious, lonely little shaver of 7. He remembers his mother, too, now jailed. "The Burns dicks knew every move before it was made," the son explains, "and someone inside the Movement must have sold out and tipped them off."

They talk of Rosa Parritt, of her devotion to the Movement and of Larry's reasons for abandoning it to take refuge in Harry Hope's place. After thirty years in the Cause, Larry has to admit he wasn't made for it. "I was born," he explains, "condemned to be one of those who has to see all sides of a question."

Young Parritt keeps steering the conversation back to his mother and how fond Larry must have been of her. There is something puzzling about the boy—something, Larry feels, that isn't right. Larry finds himself moved by pity and sympathy; he is disturbed, and resentful at being disturbed.

Old Hugo, still another of the drowsers, aroused from his usual stupor, breaks into the conversation by declaiming: " 'The days grow hot, O Babylon! 'Tis cool beneath thy willow trees!' " He peers muzzily at the boy, then, without recognition, exclaims in a tone of denunciation, "Gottamned stool pigeon!"

The effect on young Parritt is remarkable. Momentarily he stammers a "What the hell do you mean?" Then, furiously, he draws back his fist to hit Hugo.

Ignoring the threat and now recognizing Parritt, Hugo giggles, "Hello, leedle Don! Leedle monkey-face. I did not recognize you. How is your mother? Where you come from?" Then, bullyingly, he demands a dollar and a drink—and without waiting for either plunges his head down on his arms and is again asleep.

Parritt is curious about the other sleepers in the back room. What do they do for a living?

"As little as possible," explains Larry. "Once in a while one of them makes a successful touch somewhere, and some of them get a few dollars a month from connections at home who pay it on condition that they never come back. For the rest, they live on free lunch and their old friend, Harry Hope, and get drunk every day."

Willie Oban lifts his head and ramblingly offers his own life story—a Harvard man, son of the late world famous Bill Oban, King of the Bucket Shops. His father thought it a good idea to have a lawyer in the family—"but," says Willie, "I discovered the loophole of whiskey and escaped his jurisdiction." And, speaking of whiskey, he tries to cadge a drink from Parritt and fails. "Let us," he suggests, "join in prayer that Hickey, the Great Salesman, will soon arrive bringing the blessed bourgeois long green! . . . Meanwhile, I'll sing a song." In a boisterous baritone he begins a chantey which rouses the sleepers to grumbling wakefulness and brings Rocky in from the bar. Hope, furious, demands of Rocky, "Can't you keep that crazy bastard quiet?"

Rocky moves in, shaking Willie roughly. "Piano!" he warns. "What d'yuh tink dis dump is, a dump?"

HOPE—Give him the bum's rush upstairs! Lock him in his room!

ROCKY (*yanks* WILLIE *by the arm*)—Come on, Bum.

WILLIE (*dissolves into pitiable terror*)—No! Please, Rocky! I'll go crazy up in that room alone! It's haunted! I— (*He calls to* HOPE.) Please, Harry! I'll be quiet.

HOPE (*immediately relents—indignantly*)—What the hell you doing to him, Rocky? I didn't tell you to beat up the poor guy. Leave him alone, long as he's quiet. (ROCKY *lets go of* WILLIE *disgustedly and goes back to his chair in the bar.*)

WILLIE (*huskily*)—Thanks, Harry. You're a good scout. (*He closes his eyes and sinks back in his chair exhaustedly, twitching and quivering again.*)

HOPE (*addressing* MCGLOIN *and* MOSHER, *who are sleepily awake—accusingly*)—Always the way. Can't trust nobody. Leave it to that Dago to keep order and it's like bedlam in a hooker shop, singing and everything. And you two big barflies are a hell of a help to me, ain't you? Eat and sleep and get drunk! All you're good for, bejeeses! Well, you can take that "I'll-have-the-same" look off your maps. There ain't going to be no more drinks on the house till hell freezes over! (*Neither of the two is impressed either by his insults or his threats. They grin hangover grins of tolerant affection at him and wink at each other.* HARRY *fumes.*) Yeah, grin! Wink, bejeeses! Fine pair of sons of bitches to have glued on me for life! (*But he can't get a rise out of them and he subsides into a fuming mumble. Meanwhile, at the middle table,* CAPTAIN LEWIS *and* GENERAL WETJOEN *are as wide awake as heavy hangovers permit.* JIMMY TOMORROW *nods, his eyes blinking.* LEWIS *is gazing across the table at* JOE MOTT, *who is still chuckling to himself over* WILLIE'S *song. The expression on* LEWIS'S *face is that of one who can't believe his eyes.*)

LEWIS (*aloud to himself, with a muzzy wonder*)—Good God! Have I been drinking at the same table with a bloody Kaffir?

JOE (*grinning*)—Hello, Captain. You comin' up for air? Kaffir? Who's he?

WETJOEN (*blurrily*)—Kaffir, dot's a nigger, Joe. (JOE *stiffens and his eyes narrow.* WETJOEN *goes on with heavy jocosity.*) Dot's a joke on him, Joe. He don't know you. He's still plind drunk, the ploody Limey chentleman! A great mistake I missed him at the pattle of Modder River. Vit mine rifle I shoot damn fool Limey officers py the dozen, but him I miss. De pity of it! (*He chuckles and slaps* LEWIS *on his bare shoulder.*) Hey, wake up, Cecil, you ploody fool! Don't you know your old friend, Joe? He's no damned Kaffir! He's white, Joe is!

LEWIS (*light dawning—contritely*)—My profound apologies,

Joseph, old chum. Eyesight a trifle blurry, I'm afraid. Proud to call you my friend. No hard feelings, what? (*He holds out his hand.*)

JOE (*at once grins good-naturedly and shakes his hand*)—No, Captain, I know it's mistake. Youse regular, if you is a Limey. (*Then his face hardening.*) But I don't stand for "nigger" from nobody. Never did. In de old days, people calls me "nigger" wakes up in de hospital. I was de leader ob de Dirty Half-Dozen Gang. All six of us colored boys, we was tough and I was de toughest.

WETJOEN (*inspired to boastful reminiscence*)—Me, in old days in Transvaal, I vas so tough and strong I grab axle of ox wagon mit full load and lift like feather.

LEWIS (*smiling amiable*)—As for you, my balmy Boer that walks like a man, I say again it was a grave error in our foreign policy ever to set you free, once we nabbed you and your commando with Cronje. We should have taken you to the London zoo and incarcerated you in the baboons' cage. With a sign: "Spectators may distinguish the true baboon by his blue behind." (JIMMY TOMORROW *blinks benignantly from one to the other with a gentle drunken smile.*)

JIMMY (*sentimentally*)—Now, come, Cecil, Piet! We must forget the War. Boer and Briton, each fought fairly and played the game till the better man won and then we shook hands. We are all brothers within the Empire united beneath the flag on which the sun never sets. (*Tears come to his eyes. He quotes with great sentiment, if with slight application.*) "Ship me somewhere east of Suez—"

.LARRY (*breaks in sardonically*)—Be God, you're there already, Jimmy. Worst is best here, and East is West, and tomorrow is yesterday. What more do you want?

JIMMY (*with bleary benevolence, shaking his head in mild rebuke*)—No, Larry, old friend, you can't deceive me. You pretend a bitter, cynic philosophy, but in your heart you are the kindest man among us.

LARRY (*disconcerted—irritably*)—The hell you say!

PARRITT (*leans toward him—confidentially*)—Christ! What a bunch of cuckoos!

JIMMY (*as if reminded of something—with a pathetic attempt at a brisk, no-more-nonsense air*)—Tomorrow, yes. It's high time I straightened out and got down to business again. (*He brushes his sleeve fastidiously.*) I must have this suit cleaned and pressed. I can't look like a tramp when I—

JOE (*who has been brooding—interrupts*)—Yes, suh, white folks always said I was white. In de days when I was flush, Joe Mott's de only colored man dey allows in de white gamblin' houses. "You're all right, Joe, you're white," dey says. (*He chuckles.*) Wouldn't let me play craps, dough. "Any odder game and any limit you like, Joe," dey says. Man, de money I lost! (*He chuckles—then with an underlying defensiveness.*) Look at de Big Chief in dem days. He knew I was white. I'd saved my dough so I could start my own gamblin' house. Folks in de know tells me, git Harry Hope give you a letter to de Chief. And Harry does. Don't you, Harry?

HOPE (*preoccupied with his own thoughts*)—Eh? Sure. Big Bill was a good friend of mine. I had plenty of friends high up in those days. Sure, I gave you a letter. I said you was white. What the hell of it?

JOE (*to* CAPTAIN LEWIS, *who has relapsed into a sleepy daze and is listening to him with an absurd strained attention without comprehending a word*)—You see, Captain. I went to see de Chief, shakin' in my boots, and dere he is sittin' behind a big desk. He keeps me waitin' and waitin'. Den he says slow and quiet like dere wasn't no harm in him, "You want to open a gamblin' joint, does you, Joe?" But he don't give me no time to answer. He jumps up, lookin' as big as a freight train, and he pounds his fist like a ham on de desk, and he shouts, "You black son of a bitch, Harry says you're white and you better be white or dere's a little iron room up de river waitin' for you!" Den he sits down and says quiet again, "All right. You can open. Git de hell outa here!" So I opens, and he finds out I'se white, sure 'nuff, 'cause I run wide open for years and pays my sugar on de dot, and de cops and I is friends. (*He chuckles with pride.*) Dem old days! Many's de night I come in here. Dis was a first-class hangout for sports in dem days. Good whiskey, fifteen cents, two for two bits. I t'rows down a fifty-dollar bill like it was trash paper and says, "Drink it up, boys, I don't want no change." Ain't dat right, Harry?

HOPE (*caustically*)—Yes, and bejeeses if I ever seen you throw fifty cents on the bar now, I'd know I had delirium tremens!

JOE (*chuckling*)—Gittin' drunk every day for twenty years ain't give you de Brooklyn boys. You needn't be scared of me!

LEWIS (*suddenly turns and beams on* HOPE)—Thank you, Harry, old chum. I will have a drink, now you mention it, seeing it's so near your birthday. (*The others laugh.*)

Hope (*puts his hand to his ear—angrily*)—What's that? I can't hear you.

Lewis (*sadly*)—No, I fancied you wouldn't.

Hope—I don't have to hear. Booze is the only thing you ever talk about!

Lewis (*sadly*)—True. Yet there was a time when my conversation was more comprehensive. But as I became burdened with years, it seemed rather pointless to discuss my other subject.

Hope—You can't joke with me! How much room rent do you owe me, tell me that?

Lewis—Sorry. Adding has always baffled me. Subtraction is my forte.

Hope (*snarling*)—Arrh! Think you're funny! Captain, bejeeses! Showing off your wounds! Put on your clothes, for Christ's sake! This ain't no Turkish bath! Lousy Limey army! Took 'em years to lick a gang of Dutch hayseeds!

Wetjoen—Dot's right, Harry. Gif him hell!

Hope—No lip out of you, neither, you Dutch spinach! General, hell! Coxey's Army, that's what you'd ought t'been General in! Bragging what a hell of a shot you were, and you missed him! And he missed you, that's just as bad! And now the two of you bum on me! (*Threateningly.*) But you've broke the camel's back this time. You pay up tomorrow or out you go!

Lewis (*earnestly*)—My dear fellow, I give you my word of honor as an officer and a gentleman, you shall be paid tomorrow.

Wetjoen—Ve swear it, Harry! Tomorrow vidout fail!

McGloin (*a twinkle in his eye*)—There you are, Harry. Sure, what could be fairer?

Mosher (*with a wink at McGloin*)—Yes, you can't ask more than that, Harry. A promise is a promise—as I've often discovered.

Hope (*turns on them*)—I mean the both of you, too! An old grafting flatfoot and a circus bunco steerer! Fine company for me, bejeeses! Couple of con men living in my flat since Christ knows when! Getting fat as hogs, too! And you ain't even got the decency to get me upstairs where I got a good bed!

McGloin—Ed and I did our damnedest to get you up, didn't we, Ed?

Mosher—We did. But you said you couldn't bear the flat because it was one of those nights when memory brought poor old Bessie back to you.

Hope (*his face instantly becoming long and sad and sentimen-*

tal—mournfully)—Yes, that's right, boys. I remember now. I could almost see her in every room just as she used to be—and it's twenty years since she— (*His throat and eyes fill up. A suitable sentimental hush falls on the room.*)

McGLOIN (*with a huge sentimental sigh—and a calculating look at* HOPE)—Poor old Bessie! You don't find her like in these days. A sweeter woman never drew breath.

MOSHER (*in a similar calculating mood*)—Good old Bess. A man couldn't want a better sister than she was to me.

HOPE (*mournfully*)—Twenty years, and I've never set foot out of this house since the day I buried her. Once she'd gone, I didn't give a damn for anything. I lost all my ambition. You remember, Ed, you too, Mac—the boys was going to nominate me for Alderman. But when she was taken, I told them, "No, boys, I can't do it. I simply haven't the heart. I'm through." I would have won the election easy. (*He says this a bit defiantly.*) Oh, I know there was jealous wise guys said the boys was giving me the nomination because they knew they couldn't win that year in this ward. But that's a damned lie! I'd have been elected easy.

McGLOIN—It was a sure thing.

MOSHER—A dead cinch, Harry. Everyone knows that.

HOPE—Sure they do. But after Bessie died, I didn't have the heart. Still I know while she'd appreciate my grief, she wouldn't want it to keep me cooped up in here all my life. So I've made up my mind I'll go out soon. Take a walk around the ward, see all the friends I used to know, get together with the boys and maybe tell 'em deal me a hand in their game again. Yes, bejeeses, I'll do it. My birthday, tomorrow, that'd be the right time to turn over a new leaf. Sixty. That ain't too old.

Awake now, the men are dreaming their dreams aloud. Jimmy is going to get his things from the laundry and get back his job running "the publicity department." Jimmy Tomorrow, he is called, but his name is James Cameron. He is small and clean and wears threadbare black. His eyes, though bloodshot, are friendly and guileless; his speech is educated and his manners are those of a gentleman.

Another dreamer, Cecil Lewis, is obviously British, obviously a former army officer. He has white hair, a military mustache and the complexion of a turkey. He is stripped to the waist, having used his coat, shirt, undershirt, collar and tie as a rolled-up pillow. Now he addresses a table companion, Piet Wetjoen. They

are going to England, he assures Piet, as soon as his estate is
settled. He wants Piet to see how beautiful England is.

"Ja," agrees Wetjoen, "I know how beautiful it must be." But
he longs for the Veldt, for he is a Boer—a huge, Dutch farmer
type not much younger than Lewis.

Joe Mott, the Negro, has his own plans. He'll make his stake
and open a new gambling house before the boys leave, and he'll
stake them to any game they want to buck.

"Bejeeses," observes Hope with condescending pity, "Jimmy's
started them off smoking the same hop."

And indeed Jimmy has. There is another pair, for instance—
Ed Mosher and Pat McGloin, who are sitting on either side of
Hope. Pat's old occupation of policeman is stamped all over him,
and it would not be hard to guess, from his flashy clothes, phony
rings and brass watch chain, that Ed Mosher once was a circus
man.

McGloin, adding his dream to the others, is going to have his
case reopened and prove that he was not a grafter. Mosher, on
the other hand, is going back to his career of expert thievery—
short-changing customers at a circus ticket window. Chucklingly,
Ed remembers how once he short-changed his own sister, the late
Mrs. Harry Hope, on a ten-dollar bill.

But the time has been passing and still there is no sign of
Hickey. "Say, Ed, what the hell do you think's happened?"
asks Harry. "Bejeeses, I hope he'll turn up. Always got a million funny stories. You and the other bums have begun to give
me the graveyard fantods. I'd like a good laugh with old Hickey.
Remember the gag he always pulls about his wife and the iceman?"

It is daylight by now—opening time. Rocky switches off the
lights and the back room becomes drabber and dingier than ever
in the gray illumination filtering through grimy windows. A door
is heard slamming, then a low murmur, then a laugh.

"Somebody's coming now," says Hope.

"Aw, dat's only my two pigs," Rocky informs him. "It's about
time dey showed."

Everybody except Larry and Parritt goes back to dozing, and
even Parritt has his eyes closed. Rock's two "pigs" appear—
typical dollar streetwalkers in tawdry finery. Pearl seems to be
of Italian extraction, and Margie is a typical slum girl. Each
retains some youthful freshness, although the game is beginning
to give them hard, worn expressions.

"Jees, Poil, it's de Morgue wid all de stiffs on deck," observes

Margie. Sighting Parritt, the newcomer, she offers him a professional invitation but the boy fails to react.

"You dumb broads cut the loud talk," warns Hope, and Rocky suggests that they sit down before he knocks them down. "Well," asks the bartender, "how'd you tramps do?"

They did pretty good—found two drunks on Sixth Avenue, took them to a real hotel and hoped the drunks would let them alone and allow them a night's sleep on good mattresses. But the gentlemen argued and quarreled over politics and sang "School Days" until the house detective came up and told everybody to get dressed and take the air.

At Rocky's urging the girls take rolls of bills from their stocking-tops and hand them over. "You dumb baby dolls gimme a pain," he observes. "What would you do wid money if I wasn't around? Give it all to some pimp."

Teasingly, Pearl begins, "Jees, what's the difference?" Then, hastily placating, "Aw, I don't mean dat, Rocky." The girls were only kidding. "We know yuh got a regular job," soothes Margie. "Dat's why we like yuh, see? Yuh don't live offa us. Yuh're a bartender." Rocky's hurt feelings vanish and he becomes genial again.

"Anyway, we wouldn't keep no pimp, like we was reg'lar old whores," says Margie. "We ain't dat bad." To which Pearl agrees: "No, we're tarts, but dat's all."

Another tart, Cora, appears with her man—Chuck, the day bartender. Cora still has a trace of prettiness, but is older and more worn than the other girls. Chuck, husky and tough, has on a straw hat with a vivid band, a loud suit, tie and shirt, and yellow shoes. Cora greets everybody with a cheerful, "Hello, bums." She has dragged Chuck out of bed to celebrate because her night's work has been easy—picking the pocket of a drunken sailor for $12. She orders Rocky to set up the drinks.

In spite of Cora's profession and Buck's business relationship with her, the two are in love. Their dream is to get married and have a farm—a matter for vast amusement among the denizens of Harry Hope's place.

Cora perks up the crowd by announcing that she and Chuck have seen Hickey—right on the next corner. "He says, 'Tell de gang I'll be along in a minute. I'm just finishin' figurin' out de best way to save dem and bring dem peace.'" This brings a chuckle from Hope. "Yeah, Harry, he was only kiddin'. But he was funny, too, somehow," says Cora. "He was different, or somethin'."

"Sure, he was sober, Baby," says Chuck. Hickey, sober, is a puzzle to Harry—but maybe it's just some new gag he's pulling.

"Here is the old son of a bitch," announces Rocky, and the long-awaited Theodore Hickman makes a jovial appearance. He is about 50, and his expression is fixed in a salesman's winning smile of self-confident affability and hearty good fellowship. His clothes are those of a successful small town drummer. Hickey starts a rousing, "Hail, hail, the gang's all here" and the others join vociferously.

Rocky gives him the key to his regular room and brings a bottle of whiskey and a couple of glasses—one with a chaser of water. At Hickey's invitation to drink hearty they all drink, but he takes only the water. "I'm off the stuff. For keeps," he tells his amazed friends. "I don't need it any more." They all stare, hoping it's a gag; but he has made them vaguely uneasy.

If anybody wants to get drunk it is all right with him, Hickey says reassuringly. But as for himself— "Well, I finally had the guts to throw overboard that damned lying pipe dream that'd been making me miserable, and then all at once I found I was at peace with myself and I didn't need booze any more. . . . But what the hell! Don't let me be a wet blanket. Set 'em up again, Rocky." He peels a ten-dollar bill off a big roll. "Keep the balls coming until this is killed. Then ask for more."

A relieved Harry Hope remarks, "That sounds more like you, Hickey. That water-wagon bull— Cut out the act and have a drink, for Christ's sake."

HICKEY—It's no act, Governor. It don't mean I'm a teetotal grouch and can't be in the party. Hell, why d'you suppose I'm here except to have a party, same as I've always done, and help celebrate your birthday tonight? You've all been good pals to me, the best friends I've ever had. I've been thinking about you ever since I left the house—all the time I was walking over here—

HOPE—Walking? Bejeeses, do you mean to say you walked?

HICKEY—I sure did. All the way from the wilds of darkest Astoria. Didn't mind it a bit, either. I'm a bit tired and sleepy but otherwise I feel great. (*Kiddingly.*) That ought to encourage you, Governor—show you a little walk around the ward is nothing to be so scared about. (*He winks at the others.* HOPE *stiffens resentfully for a second.* HICKEY *goes on.*) I didn't make such bad time either for an old guy, considering it's a hell of a ways, and I sat in the park a while thinking. I'd been standing on the corner some time before Cora and Chuck came along. Of course, I was only kidding Cora with that stuff about saving you. (*Then seriously.*) No, I wasn't either. But I meant save you from pipe dreams. I know now, from my experience, they're the things that really poison and ruin a guy's life and keep him from finding any peace. And the cure for them is so damned simple, once you have the nerve. Just stop lying about yourself and kidding yourself about tomorrows. (*He is staring ahead of him now as if he were talking aloud to himself as much as to them. Their eyes are fixed on him with uneasy resentment. Taking on a salesman's persuasiveness.*) Now listen, boys and girls, don't look at me as if I was trying to sell you a goldbrick. Nothing up my sleeve, honest. Let's take an example. Any one of you. Take you, Governor. That walk around the ward you never take—

HOPE (*defensively sharp*)—What about it?

HICKEY (*grinning affectionately*)—Why, you know as well as I do, Harry. Everything about it.

HOPE (*defiantly*)—Bejeeses, I'm going to take it!

HICKEY—Sure, you're going to—this time. Because I'm going to help you. I know it's the thing you've got to do before you'll ever know what real peace means. (*He looks at* JIMMY TOMORROW.) Same thing with you, Jimmy. You've got to try and get your old job back. And no tomorrow about it! (*As* JIMMY *stiffens with a pathetic attempt at dignity—placatingly.*) No, don't tell me, Jimmy. I know all about tomorrow. I'm the guy that wrote the book.

JIMMY—I don't understand you. I admit I've foolishly delayed, but as it happens, I'd just made up my mind that as soon as I could get straightened out—

HICKEY—Fine! That's the spirit! And I'm going to help you. You've been damned kind to me, Jimmy, and I want to prove how grateful I am. (*He looks around at the others.*) And all the rest of you, ladies included, are in the same boat, one way or another.

LARRY (*who has been listening with sardonic appreciation—in his comically intense, crazy whisper*)—Be God, you've hit the nail on the head, Hickey! This dump is the Palace of Pipe Dreams!

HICKEY (*grins at him with affectionate kidding*)—Well, well! The Old Grandstand Foolosopher speaks! You think you're the big exception, eh? You're retired from the circus. You're just waiting impatiently for the end—the good old Long Sleep! (*He chuckles.*) Well, I think a lot of you, Larry, you old bastard.

I'll try and make an honest man of you, too!

LARRY (*stung*)—What the devil are you hinting at, anyway?

HICKEY—You don't have to ask me, do you, a wise old guy like you? Just ask yourself. I'll bet you know.

PARRITT (*watching* LARRY'S *face with a curious sneering satisfaction*)—He's got your number all right, Larry! (*He turns to* HICKEY.) That's the stuff, Hickey. Show the old faker up! He's got no right to sneak out of everything.

HICKEY (*regards him with surprise at first, then with a puzzled interest*)—Hello. A stranger in our midst. I didn't notice you before, Brother.

PARRITT (*embarrassed, his eyes shifting away*)—My name's Parritt. I'm an old friend of Larry's. (*His eyes come back to* HICKEY *to find him still sizing him up—defensively.*) Well? What the hell are you staring at?

HICKEY (*continuing to stare—puzzledly*)—No offense, Brother. I was trying to figure— Haven't we met before some place?

PARRITT (*reassured*)—No. First time I've ever been East.

HICKEY—No, you're right. I know that's not it. In my game, to be a shark at it, you teach yourself never to forget a name or a face. But still I know damned well I recognized something about you. We're members of the same lodge—in some way.

PARRITT (*uneasy again*)—What are you talking about? You're nuts.

HICKEY (*dryly*)—Don't try to kid me, Little Boy. I'm a good salesman—so damned good the firm was glad to take me back after every drunk—and what made me good was I could size up anyone. (*Frowningly puzzled again.*) But I don't see— (*Suddenly breezily good-natured.*) Never mind. I can tell you're having trouble with yourself and I'll be glad to do anything I can to help a friend of Larry's.

LARRY—Mind your own business, Hickey. He's nothing to you—or to me, either. (HICKEY *gives him a keen inquisitive glance.* LARRY *looks away and goes on sarcastically.*) You're keeping us all in suspense. Tell us more about how you're going to save us.

HICKEY (*good-naturedly but seeming a little hurt*)—Hell, don't get sore, Larry. Not at me. We've always been good pals, haven't we? I know I've always liked you a lot.

LARRY (*a bit shamefaced*)—Well, so have I liked you. Forget it, Hickey.

HICKEY (*beaming*)—Fine! That's the spirit! (*Looking around at the others, who have forgotten their drinks.*) What's the matter, everybody? What is this, a funeral?. Come on and drink up! A little action! (*They all drink.*) Have another. Hell, I don't want to be a pain in the neck. (*He yawns with growing drowsiness and his voice grows a bit muffled.*) Christ, I'm sleepy all of a sudden. That long walk is beginning to get me. I better go upstairs. Hell of a trick to go dead on you like this. (*He starts to get up but relaxes again. His eyes blink as he tries to keep them open.*) No, boys and girls, I've never known what real peace was until now. (*His eyes close.*) You can let go of yourself at last. Let yourself sink down to the bottom of the sea. Rest in peace. Not a single damned hope or dream left to nag you. (*He pauses—mumbles.*) Excuse—all in —got to grab forty winks— Drink up, everybody—on me— (*The sleep of complete exhaustion overpowers him. His chin sags to his chest. They stare at him with puzzled uneasy fascination.*)

HOPE (*forcing a tone of irritation*)—Bejeeses, that's a fine stunt, to go to sleep on us! (*Then fumingly to the crowd.*) Well, what the hell's the matter with you bums? You're always crying for booze, and now you've got it under your nose, you sit like dummies! (*They start and gulp down their whiskies and pour another.* HOPE *stares at* HICKEY.) I can't figure Hickey. I still say he's kidding us. Kid his own grandmother, Hickey would. What d'you think, Jimmy?

JIMMY (*unconvincingly*)—It must be another of his jokes, Harry, although— Well, he does appear changed. But he'll probably be his natural self again tomorrow— (*Hastily.*) I mean, when he wakes up.

LARRY (*staring at* HICKEY *frowningly—more aloud to himself than to them*)—You'll make a mistake if you think he's only kidding.

PARRITT (*in a low confidential voice*)—I don't like that guy, Larry. He's too damned nosy. I'm going to steer clear of him. (*LARRY gives him a suspicious glance, then looks hastily away.*)

JIMMY (*with an attempt at open-minded reasonableness*)—Still, Harry, I have to admit there was some sense in his nonsense. It is time I got my job back—although I hardly need him to remind me.

HOPE (*with an air of frankness*)—Yes, and I ought to take a walk around the ward. But I don't need no Hickey to tell me, seeing I got it all set for my birthday tomorrow.

LARRY (*sardonically*)—Ha! (*Then in his comically intense, crazy whisper.*) Be God, it looks like he's going to make two sales of his peace at least. But you'd better make sure first it's the real McCoy and not poison.

Hope (*disturbed—angrily*)—Bejeeses, you bughouse I-Won't-Work harp, who asked you to shove in an oar? What the hell d'you mean, poison? Just because he has your number— (*He immediately feels ashamed of this taunt and adds apologetically.*) Bejeeses, Larry, you're always croaking about something to do with death. It gets my nanny. Come on, fellers, let's drink up. (*They drink,* Hope's *eyes are fixed on* Hickey *again.*) Stone cold sober and dead to the world! Spilling that business about pipe dreams! (*He bursts out again in angry complaint.*) He ain't like the old Hickey! He'll be a fine wet blanket to have around at my birthday party! I wish to hell he'd never turned up!

Mosher (*who has been the least impressed by* Hickey's *talk and is the first to recover and feel the effect of the drinks on top of his hangover—genially*)—Give him time, Harry, and he'll come out of it. I've watched many cases of almost fatal teetotalism, but they all came out of it completely cured and as drunk as ever. My opinion is the poor sap is temporarily bughouse from overwork. (*Musingly.*) You can't be too careful about work. It's the deadliest habit known to science, a great physician once told me. He practiced on street corners under a torchlight. He was positively the only doctor in the world who claimed that rattlesnake oil, rubbed on the prat, would cure heart failure in three days. I remember well his saying to me, "You are naturally delicate, Ed, but if you drink a pint of bad whiskey before breakfast every evening, and never work if you can help it, you may live to a ripe old age. It's staying sober and working that cuts men off in their prime." (*While he is talking, they turn to him with eager grins. They are longing to laugh, and as he finishes they roar. Even* Parritt *laughs.* Hickey *sleeps on like a dead man, but* Hugo, *who had passed into his customary coma again, head on table, looks up through his thick spectacles and giggles foolishly.*)

Hugo (*blinking around at them. As the laughter dies he speaks in his giggling, wheedling manner, as if he were playfully teasing children*)—Laugh, leedle bourgeois monkey-faces! Laugh like fools, leedle stupid peoples! (*His tone suddenly changes to one of guttural soapbox denunciation and he pounds on the table with a small fist.*) I vill laugh, too! But I vill laugh last! I vill laugh at you! (*He declaims his favorite quotation.*) "The days grow hot, O Babylon! 'Tis cool beneath thy villow trees!" (*They all hoot him down in a chorus of amused jeering.* Hugo *is not of-fended. This is evidently their customary reaction. He giggles good-naturedly.* Hickey *sleeps on. They have all forgotten their uneasiness about him now and ignore him.*)

Lewis (*tipsily*)—Well, now that our little Robespierre has got the daily bit of guillotining off his chest, tell me more about your doctor friend, Ed. He strikes me as the only bloody sensible medico I ever heard of. I think we should appoint him house physician here without a moment's delay. (*They all laughingly assent.*)

Mosher (*warming to his subject, shakes his head sadly*)—Too late! The old Doc has passed on to his Maker. A victim of over-work, too. He didn't follow his own advice. Kept his nose to the grindstone and sold one bottle of snake oil too many. Only eighty years old when he was taken. The saddest part was that he knew he was doomed. The last time we got paralyzed together he told me: "This game will get me yet, Ed. You see before you a broken man, a martyr to medical science. If I had any nerves I'd have a nervous breakdown. You wouldn't believe me, but this last year there was actually one night I had so many patients, I didn't even have time to get drunk." Poor old Doc! When he said this he started crying. "I hate to go before my task is completed, Ed," he sobbed. "I'd hoped I'd live to see the day when, thanks to my miraculous cure, there wouldn't be a single vacant cemetery lot left in this glorious country." (*There is a roar of laughter. It penetrates* Hickey's *exhausted slumber. He stirs on his chair, trying to wake up, managing to raise his head a little and force his eyes half open. He speaks with a drowsy, affectionately en-couraging smile. At once the laughter stops abruptly and they turn to him startledly.*)

Hickey—That's the spirit—don't let me be a wet blanket—all I want is to see you happy— (*He slips back into heavy sleep again. They all stare at him, their faces again puzzled, resentful and uneasy.*)

The curtain falls.

ACT II

It is getting on toward midnight of the day Hickey arrived. The scene now is deeper into the back room, so that the black curtain dividing it from the bar forms the right wall. The room has been prepared for Harry Hope's birthday party. Four of the round tables have been pushed together to make one long one, and this uneven, improvised banquet board has been covered with old tablecloths borrowed from a neighborhood beanery; it is laid with plates, glasses and cutlery and behind it and at the ends are seventeen chairs. Bottles of bar whiskey are within reach of any sitter. At the far end of the room, away from the bar, is an upright piano. The light brackets are hung with red ribbon. On a separate table are a birthday cake with six candles and several packages tied with ribbon.

Cora, Chuck, Margie, Pearl and Rocky are busy with preparations. The girls and the two bartenders have dressed up. Larry is drinking meditatively, and Hugo, as usual, has passed out with his head on the banquet table.

They have all had plenty to drink and those who are awake are trying to act in the spirit of the occasion, but there is something forced about their manner. When Cora asks Chuck what he thinks of a bouquet she has arranged in a beer schooner, Chuck inquires grumpily what the hell does he know about flowers? Pearl asks Rocky when it will be time to light the candles on the cake.

Rocky, equally grumpy, replies, "Ask dat bughouse Hickey. . . . Just before Harry comes down, he says." Hickey, indeed, is getting Rocky's goat, with his telling everybody where they get off.

"I told him dat's aw right for de bums in dis dump," he growls. "I hope he makes dem wake up. I'm sick of listenin' to dem hop demselves up. But it don't go wid me, see? I don't kid myself wid no pipe dream"—at which remark Pearl and Margie take on a derisive look which is not lost on Rocky.

"Don't let Hickey put no ideas in your nuts if you wanta stay healthy," he warns. (*Then angrily.*) "I wish de louse never showed up! I hope he don't come back from de delicatessen. He's ridin' someone every minute. He's got Harry and Jimmy Tomorrow run ragged, and de rest is hidin' in deir rooms. Dey're all actin' cagey wid de booze too, like dey was scared if dey get too drunk, dey might spill deir guts or somethin'. And everybody's gettin' a prize grouch on."

Cora agrees, "Yeah, he's been hintin' 'round to me and Chuck, too. Yuh'd tink he suspected me and Chuck hadn't no real intention of gettin' married. We're goin' to get married tomorrow. Ain't we, honey?"

CHUCK—You bet, Baby.

ROCKY (*disgusted*)—Christ, Chuck, are yuh lettin' dat bughouse louse Hickey kid yuh into—

Cora (*turns on him angrily*)—Nobody's kiddin' him into it, nor me neider! And Hickey's right. If dis big tramp's goin' to marry me, he ought to do it, and not just shoot off his old bazoo about it.

Rocky (*ignoring her*)—Yuh can't be dat dumb, Chuck.

Cora—You keep outa dis! And don't start beefin' about crickets on de farm drivin' us nuts. You and your crickets! Yuh'd tink dey was elephants!

Margie (*coming to* Rocky's *defense—sneeringly*)—Don't notice dat broad, Rocky. Yuh heard her say "tomorrow," didn't yuh? It's de same old crap.

Cora (*glares at her*)—Is dat so?

Pearl (*lines up with* Margie—*sneeringly*)—Imagine Cora a bride! Dat's a hot one! Jees, Cora, if all de guys you've stayed wid was side by side, yuh could walk on 'em from here to Texas!

Cora (*starts moving toward her threateningly*)—Yuh can't talk like dat to me, yuh Dago hooker! I may be a tart, but I ain't a cheap whore like you!

Pearl (*furiously*)—I'll show yuh who's a whore! (Chuck *and* Rocky *grab them from behind.*)

Chuck (*forcing* Cora *into a chair*)—Sit down and cool off, Baby.

Rocky—Nix on de rough stuff, Poil.

Margie (*glaring at* Cora)—Why don't you leave Poil alone, Rocky? She'll fix dat clock! Or if she don't, I will!

Rocky—Shut up, you! (*Disgustedly.*) Jees, what dames! D'yuh wanta gum Harry's party?

Pearl (*a bit shamefaced—sulkily*)—Who wants to? But nobody can't call me—

Rocky (*exasperatedly*)—Aw, bury it! What are you, a voigin? (Pearl *stares at him, her face growing hard and bitter. So does* Margie.)

Pearl—Yuh mean you tink I'm a whore, too, huh?

Margie—Yeah, and me?

Rocky—Now don't start nuttin'.

Pearl—I suppose it'd tickle you if me and Margie did what dat louse, Hickey, was hintin' and come right out and admitted we was whores.

Rocky—Aw right! What of it? It's de truth, ain't it?

Cora (*lining up with* Pearl *and* Margie—*indignantly*)—Jees, Rocky, dat's a fine ting to say to two goils dat's been as good to yuh as Poil and Margie! (*To* Pearl.) I didn't mean to call yuh dat, Poil. I was on'y mad.

Pearl (*accepts the apology gratefully*)—Sure, I was mad, too,

Cora. No hard feelin's.

ROCKY (*relieved*)—Dere. Dat fixes everytin, don't it?

PEARL (*turns on him—hard and bitter*)—Aw right, Rocky. We're whores. You know what dat makes you, don't you?

ROCKY (*angrily*)—Look out, now!

MARGIE—A lousy little pimp, dat's what!

ROCKY—I'll loin yuh! (*He gives her a slap on the side of the face.*)

PEARL—A dirty little Ginny pimp, dat's what!

ROCKY (*gives her a slap, too*)—And dat'll loin you! (*But they only stare at him with hard sneering eyes.*)

MARGIE—He's provin' it to us, Poil.

PEARL—Yeah! Hickey's convoited him. He's give up his pipe dream!

ROCKY (*furious and at the same time bewildered by their defiance*)—Lay off me or I'll beat de hell—

CHUCK (*growls*)—Aw, lay off dem. Harry's party ain't no time to beat up your stable.

ROCKY (*turns to him*)—Whose stable? Who d'yuh tink yuh're talkin' to? I ain't never beat dem up! I just give dem a slap, like any guy would his wife, if she got too gabby. Why don't yuh tell dem to lay off me?

MARGIE (*a victorious gleam in her eye—tauntingly*)—Aw right, den, yuh poor little Ginny. I'll lay off yuh till de party's over if Poil will.

PEARL (*tauntingly*)—For Harry's sake, not yours, yuh little Wop!

ROCKY (*stung*)—Say, listen, youse! Don't get no wrong idea— (*But an interruption comes from* LARRY *who bursts into a sardonic laugh. They all jump startledly and look at him with unanimous hostility.* ROCKY *transfers his anger to him.*) Who de hell yuh laughin' at, yuh half-dead old stew bum?

LARRY (*ignoring them, turns to* HUGO *and shakes him by the shoulder—in his comically intense, crazy whisper*)—Wake up, Comrade! Here's the Revolution starting on all sides of you and you're sleeping through it! Be God, it's not to Bakunin's ghost you ought to pray in your dreams, but to the great Nihilist, Hickey! He's started a movement that'll blow up the world!

Cora remembers that Hickey hasn't pulled the iceman gag this time. "D'yuh suppose dat he did catch his wife cheatin'?" she wonders.

"Aw, dat's de bunk," assures Rocky. "He ain't pulled dat joke or showed her photo around because he ain't drunk. And it he'd caught her cheatin' he'd be drunk, wouldn't he? He'd have beat her up and den gone on de woist drunk he'd ever staged. Like any other guy'd do."

Joe, the Negro, comes in from the hallway and there is a noticeable change about him—a tough swagger. He announces that he's through being doorman outside, telling people the place is closed for the night on account of the party.

At Chuck's suggestion Joe has a drink—on Hickey. "All right," says Joe, defiantly gulping a big drink, "I'se earned all de drinks on him I could drink in a year for listenin' to his crazy bull. I drinks on him but I don't drink wid him."

Larry, talking more to himself than to the others, has an idea about Hickey. "I have a feeling he's dying to tell us, inside him, and yet he's afraid," he says. "He's like that damned kid. If he's afraid, it explains why he's off booze. Afraid if he got drunk he'd tell—"

But what it is Larry thinks Hickey might tell goes unspoken, for Hickey himself appears, booming, jovial and loaded with bundles, which Margie and Pearl take from him and put on the table. Hickey has heard Larry.

"You've got me all wrong," he advises good-naturedly. "I'm not afraid of anything now—not even myself. You better stick to the part of Old Cemetery, the Barker for the Big Sleep—that is, if you can still let yourself get away with it!"

Hickey dispatches Chuck and Rocky to fetch still another package he has left in the hall. It is a basket piled with quarts of champagne—so munificent a gift that a spirit of festivity seizes everybody. There being no champagne glasses, they decide they will drink from beer schooners.

"Ve vill trink vine beneath the villow trees," giggles Hugo.

HICKEY (*grins at him*)—That's the spirit, Brother—and let the lousy slaves drink vinegar! (HUGO *blinks at him startledly, then looks away.*)

HUGO (*mutters*)—Gottamned liar! (*He puts his head back on his arms and closes his eyes, but this time his habitual pass-out has a quality of hiding.*)

LARRY (*gives* HUGO *a pitying glance—in a low tone of anger*)— Leave Hugo be! He rotted ten years in prison for his faith! He's earned his dream! Have you no decency or pity?

HICKEY (*quizzically*)—Hello, what's this? I thought you were in the grandstand. (*Then with a simple earnestness, taking a*

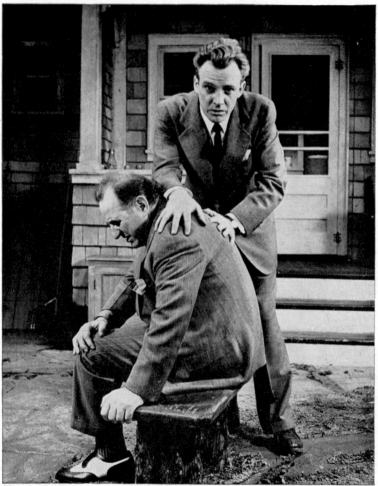

"ALL MY SONS"

Chris— . . . For me! I was dying every day and you were killing my boys and you did it for me? . . . What the hell do you think I was thinking of—the goddam business? What is that, the world, the business? What are you made of, dollar bills?

(*Edward Begley, Arthur Kennedy*)

"THE ICEMAN COMETH"

The four featured players of Mr. O'Neill's drama take time out at rehearsal to sample a new batch of cold tea, of which they consume quarts and quarts at every performance, pretending it is the choicest rotgut whiskey.

(*Carl Benton Reid, James Barton, Dudley Digges, Nicholas Joy*)

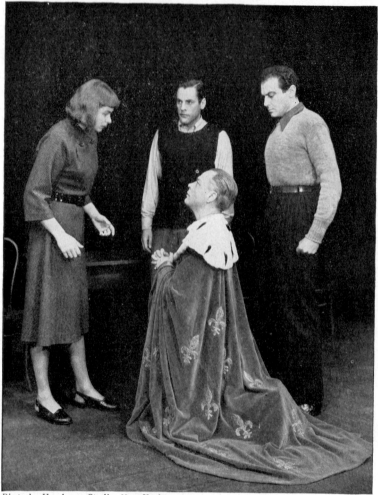

"JOAN OF LORRAINE"

Being a play within a play, the staged rehearsals of "Joan of Lorraine" were conducted with such costumes and properties as were available. In this scene the Dauphin of France is giving his royal robes a workout.

(Ingrid Bergman, Kevin McCarthy, Romney Brent, Martin Rudy)

"ANOTHER PART OF THE FOREST"

Marcus—No, no! I don't mean you knew it was a lie. But let me see it, and then tell me.

Lavinia—Let him see it, of course.

Ben—Oh, tell him to come down and look at it. I'll put it here, under the gun.

(*Wesley Addy, Mildred Dunnock, Percy Waram*)

"YEARS AGO"

Mrs. Jones—You know I been thinking, Clinton, everybody else has got one and we ought to have a telephone.

Clint Jones—Wouldn't have one if you gave it to me!

(Florence Eldridge, Fredric March)

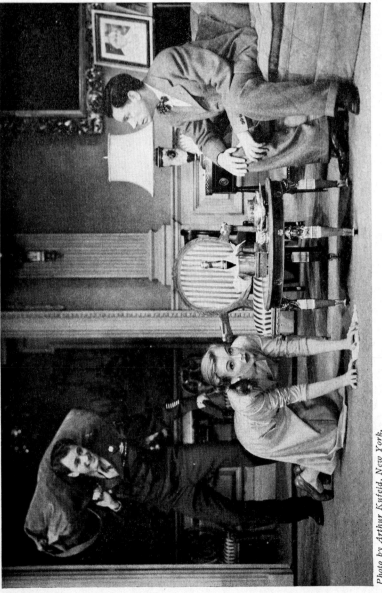

Photo by Arthur Kufeld, New York.

"JOHN LOVES MARY"

John—Mary!!
Mary—Oh, no! You get out! You turn right around and leave! . . . I planned for three years how you were going to see me, and it wasn't going to be like this.

"THE FATAL WEAKNESS"

Mrs. Espenshade—He's being watched.

(Ina Claire, Howard St. John, Margaret Douglass)

"THE STORY OF MARY SURRATT"

"A large, square room on the third floor of the Old Penitentiary Building has been converted, for the purposes of this trial, into a crudely arranged courtroom. . . . Mary Surratt is called to the stand."

(Kent Smith, Dorothy Gish, Richard Sanders)

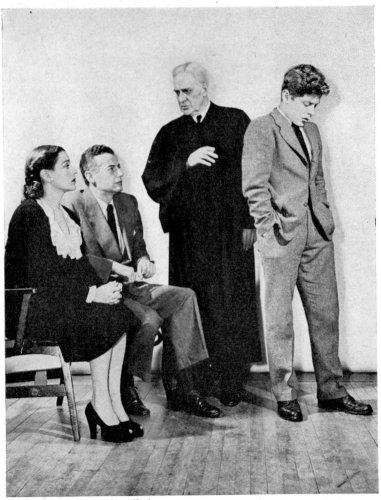

"CHRISTOPHER BLAKE"

The trouble that people have with marriage, the Judge explains, has been going on as long as marriage has existed. "Lots of people come before me, and I don't always try to bring them together. Sometimes I do, because I feel that if they can get over that one jam they're in they've a good chance to make it work, and they ought to try."

(Martha Sleeper, Shepperd Strudwick, Robert Harrison, Richard Tyler)

Photo by Vandamm Studio, New York.

"BRIGADOON"

Mr. Lundie—Tommy lad! Ye? My, my! Ye mus' really love her! Come, lad! Ye shouldna be too surprised, lad. I told ye when ye love someone deeply anythin' is possible. Even miracles!

(George Keane, David Brooks, William Hansen)

chair by LARRY, *and putting a hand on his shoulder*.) Listen, Larry, you're getting me all wrong. Of course, I have pity. But now I've seen the light, it isn't my old kind of pity—the kind yours is. It isn't the kind that let's itself off easy by encouraging some poor guy to go on kidding himself with a lie—the kind that leaves the poor slob worse off because it makes him feel guiltier than ever—the kind that makes his lying hopes nag at him and reproach him until he's a rotten skunk in his own eyes. I know all about that kind of pity. I've had a bellyful of it in my time, and it's all wrong! (*With a salesman's persuasiveness*.) No, sir. The kind of pity I feel now is after final results that will really save the poor guy, and make him contented with what he is, and quit battling himself, and find peace for the rest of his life. Oh, I know how you resent the way I have to show you up to yourself. I don't blame you. I know from my own experience it's bitter medicine, facing yourself in the mirror with the old false whiskers off. But you forget that, once you're cured. You'll be grateful to me when all at once you find you're able to admit, without feeling ashamed, that all the grandstand foolosopher bunk and the waiting for the Big Sleep stuff is a pipe dream. Then you'll know what real peace means, Larry, because you won't be scared of either life or death any more. You simply won't give a damn! Any more than I do!

LARRY (*has been staring into his eyes with a fascinated wondering dread*)—Be God, if I'm not beginning to think you've gone mad! (*With a rush of anger*.) You're a liar!

HICKEY (*injuredly*)—Now, listen, that's no way to talk to an old pal who's trying to help you. Hell, if you really wanted to die, you'd just take a hop off your fire escape, wouldn't you? And if you really were in the grandstand, you wouldn't be pitying everyone. (LARRY *again is staring at him fascinatedly*. HICKEY *grins*.) As for my being bughouse, you can't crawl out of it that way. Hell, I'm too damned sane. I can size up guys. Even where they're strangers like that Parritt kid. He's licked, Larry. I think there is only one possible way out you can help him to take. That is, if you have the right kind of pity for him.

LARRY (*uneasily*)—What do you mean? (*Attempting indifference*.) I'm not advising him, except to leave me out of his troubles.

HICKEY (*shakes his head*)—You'll find he won't agree to that. He'll keep after you until he makes you help him. Because he has to be punished, so he can forgive himself. He's lost all his guts. He can't manage it alone, and you're the only one he can turn to.

LARRY—For the love of God, mind your own business! (*With forced scorn.*) A lot you know about him! He's hardly spoken to you!

HICKEY—No. But I do know a lot about him just the same. I've had hell inside me. I can spot it in others. (*Frowning.*) Maybe that's what gives me the feeling there's something familiar about him, something between us. (*He shakes his head.*) No, it's more than that. I can't figure it. Tell me about him. For instance, I don't imagine he's married, is he?

LARRY—No.

HICKEY—Hasn't he been mixed up with some woman? I don't mean trollops. I mean the old real love stuff that crucifies you.

LARRY (*with a calculating relieved look at him—encouraging him along this line*)—Maybe you're right. I wouldn't be surprised.

HICKEY (*grins at him quizzically*)—I see. You think I'm on the wrong track and you're glad I am. Because then I won't suspect whatever he did about the Great Cause. That's another lie you tell yourself, Larry, that the good old Cause means nothing to you any more. (LARRY *is about to burst out in denial but* HICKEY *goes on.*) But you're all wrong about Parritt. That isn't what's got him stopped. It's what's behind that. And it's a woman. I recognize the symptoms.

LARRY (*sneeringly*)—And you're the boy who's never wrong! Don't be a damned fool. His trouble is he was brought up a devout believer in the Cause and now he's lost his faith. It's a shock, but he's young and he'll soon find another dream just as good. (*He adds sardonically.*) Or as bad.

Hickey checks over the party arrangements—cake all set, presents all set. He tells Pearl and Margie to get the grub ready in the bar. "I'll go upstairs now and root everyone out. Harry the last. I'll come back with him. Somebody light the candles on the cake when you hear us coming, and you start playing Harry's favorite tune, Cora."

Cora ousts Joe from the piano stool and gropingly plays "The Sunshine of Paradise Alley." Joe corrects her now and then by humming the melody. Larry, giving a sudden laugh, says, "Be God, it's a second feast of Belshazzar, with Hickey to do the writing on the wall!"

First to join the party is Willie Oban, sober, his eyes sick and haunted. He refuses Cora's offer of a drink. To Larry he says it has been hell up in his room—"but I've got it beat now. By

tomorrow morning I'll be on the wagon. I'll get back my clothes
the first thing. Hickey's loaning me the money. I'm going to do
what I've always said—go to the D. A.'s office. He was a good
friend of my Old Man's. He was only an assistant then. He was
in on the graft, but my Old Man never squealed on him. So he
certainly owes it to me to give me a chance."

Willie is grateful to Hickey for making him wake up to himself—but at the same time he resents the salesman. Larry's advice is for Willie to put the nearest bottle to his mouth until he
doesn't give a damn for Hickey.

Parritt comes down. "Can't you make Hickey mind his own
business?" he asks Larry. "The way he acts, you'd think he had
something on me."

LARRY—I've nothing to say. Except you're a bigger fool than
he is to listen to him.

PARRITT (*with a sneer*)—Is that so? He's no fool where you're
concerned. He's got your number, all right! (LARRY'S *face
tightens but he keeps silent*. PARRITT *changes to a contrite, appealing air*.) I don't mean that. But you keep acting as if you
were sore at me, and that gets my goat. You know what I want
most is to be friends with you, Larry. I haven't a single friend
left in the world. I hoped you— (*Bitterly*.) And you could be,
too, without it hurting you. You ought to, for Mother's sake.
She really loved you. You loved her, too, didn't you?

LARRY (*tensely*)—Leave what's dead in its grave.

PARRITT—I suppose, because I was only a kid, you didn't think
I was wise about you and her. Well, I was. I've been wise, ever
since I can remember, to all the guys she's had, although she'd
tried to kid me along it wasn't so. That was a silly stunt for a
free Anarchist woman, wasn't it, being ashamed of being free?

LARRY—Shut your damned trap!

PARRITT (*guiltily but with a strange undertone of satisfaction*)
—Yes, I know I shouldn't say that now. I keep forgetting she
isn't free any more. (*He pauses*.) . . . But I'm sure she really
must have loved you, Larry. As much as she could love anyone
besides herself. But she wasn't faithful to you, even at that, was
she? That's why you finally walked out on her, isn't it? I remember that last fight you had with her. I was listening. I was
on your side, because you'd been so good to me—like a father. I
remember her putting on her high-and-mighty free-woman stuff,
saying you were still a slave to bourgeois morality and jealousy
and you thought a woman you loved was a piece of private property

you owned. I remember that you got mad and you told her, "I don't like living with a scut, if that's what you mean!"

LARRY (*bursts out*)—You lie! I never called her that!

PARRITT (*goes on as if* LARRY *hadn't spoken*)—I think that's why she still respects you, because it was you who left her. You were the only one to beat her to it. She got sick of the others before they did of her . . . (*He pauses—then with a bitter repulsion.*) It made home a lousy place. I felt like you did about it. I'd get feeling it was like living in a hooker shop—only worse, because she didn't have to make her living—

LARRY—You bastard! She's your mother! Have you no shame?

PARRITT (*bitterly*)—No! She brought me up to believe that family-respect stuff is all bourgeois, property-owning crap. Why should I be ashamed?

LARRY (*making a move to get up*)—I've had enough!

PARRITT (*catches his arm—pleadingly*)—No! I promise I won't mention her again! (LARRY *sinks back in his chair.*) I know this isn't the place to— Why didn't you come up to my room, like I asked you? We could talk everything over there.

LARRY—There's nothing to talk over!

PARRITT—But I've got to talk to you. Or I'll talk to Hickey. I feel he knows, anyway! And I know he'd understand, all right— in his way. But I hate his guts! I'm scared of him, honest. There's something not human behind his damned grinning and kidding.

LARRY (*starts*)—Ah! You feel that, too?

PARRITT (*pleadingly*)—But I can't go on like this. I've got to decide what I've got to do. I've got to tell you, Larry!

LARRY (*again starts up*)—I won't listen!

PARRITT (*again holds him by the arm*)—All right! I won't. Don't go! (LARRY *lets himself be pulled down on his chair.* PARRITT *examines his face and becomes insultingly scornful.*) Who do you think you're kidding? I know damned well you've guessed—

LARRY—I've guessed nothing!

PARRITT—But I want you to guess now! I'm glad you have! I know now, since Hickey's been after me, that I meant you to guess right from the start. That's why I came to you. (*Hurrying on with an attempt at a plausible frank air that makes what he says seem doubly false.*) I want you to understand the reason. You see, I began studying American history. I got admiring Washington and Jefferson and Jackson and Lincoln. I began to feel patriotic and love this country. I saw that all the ideas be-hind the Movement came from a lot of Russians like Bakunin and Kropotkin and were meant for Europe, but we didn't need them here in a democracy where we were free already. And then I saw it was my duty to my country—

LARRY (*nauseated—turns on him*)—You stinking rotten liar! Do you think you can fool me with such hypocrite's cant! (*Then turning away.*) I don't give a damn what you did! It's on your head—whatever it was! I don't want to know—and I won't know!

PARRITT (*as if* LARRY *had never spoken—falteringly*)—But I thought Mother would be caught. Please believe that, Larry. You know I never would have—

LARRY (*his face haggard, drawing a deep breath and closing his eyes—as if he were trying to hammer something into his own brain*)—All I know is I'm sick of life! I'm through! I've for-gotten myself! I'm drowned and contented on the bottom of a bottle. Honor or dishonor, faith or treachery are nothing to me but the opposites of the same stupidity which is ruler and king of life, and in the end they rot into dust in the same grave. All things are the same meaningless joke to me, for they grin at me from the one skull of death. So go away. You're wasting breath. I've forgotten your mother.

There is a scuffle behind the bar curtain and the bartenders ap-pear, one holding Captain Lewis and the other General Wetjoen. The malign influence of Hickey has got even these two fighting. The rest of the crowd calm the men down, and McGloin and Mosher are the next to enter—both drunk and both talking about "that bastard" Hickey and what he has done to Harry Hope. Evidently the salesman has persuaded Harry to take his long-planned walk around the ward tomorrow. And, as a matter of fact, Mosher is clearing out tomorrow, and so is McGloin—one to the circus, the other to get reinstated on the police force.

Hickey bursts in, bustling and excited. "Half a minute to go. Harry's starting down with Jimmy." Margie and Pearl light the candles, Cora gets set at the piano and everybody stands up—even Hugo. As Hope and Jimmy enter they all shout a "Happy Birth-day!" and Cora begins playing and singing "She's the Sunshine of Paradise Alley." Hickey grabs Hope's hand, but Hope jerks it away angrily and snarls:

"Cut out the glad hand, Hickey. D'you think I'm a sucker? I know you, bejeeses, you sneaking, lying drummer! And all you bums! What the hell you trying to do, yelling and raising the roof? Hey, you dumb tart, quit banging that box! Bejeeses, the least you could do is learn the tune!"

The effect on the party is shattering. Even reproachful words from Hickey mollify him only for a moment. "It's that lousy drummer riding me that's got my goat," Harry confides to Margie. He starts to admire his cake, then turns angrily from it. Nor is Jimmy any happier, even when Hickey reminds him of his promise of help. "Only watch out on the booze, Jimmy," the salesman cautions.

Jimmy is mooning about a girl named Marjorie. "Now listen, Jimmy," says Hickey with an amused wink at Hope, "you needn't go on. We've all heard the story about how you came back to Cape Town and found her in the hay with a staff officer. We know you like to believe that was what started you on the booze and ruined your life."

Jimmy objects that his life is not ruined, but Hickey continues, with a kidding grin: "But I'll bet when you admit the truth to yourself you'll confess you were pretty sick of her hating you for getting drunk. I'll bet you were really damned relieved when she gave you such a good excuse."

Jimmy is stricken. Hickey pats him on the back and says, with sincere sympathy, "I know how it is, Jimmy. I—" He stops abruptly and for an instant becomes confused. Larry leaps into the opening.

"Ha! So that's what happened to you, is it?" Larry taunts. "Your iceman joke finally came home to roost, did it?"

But Hickey has recovered himself and is no mark for Larry. "Let's start the party rolling! Bring on the big surprise!" Rocky and Chuck appear from the bar laden with big trays bearing schooners of champagne. Old Hugo grabs a schooner, takes a greedy gulp, then puts it on the table with a grimace of distaste. "Dis vine," he announces, "is unfit to trink. It has not properly been iced."

Hickey proposes a toast to Harry—and takes a drink himself, just to be sociable. There is a chorus of "Here's how, Harry," and "Here's luck." Hope is deeply touched.

HOPE (*lamely*)—Bejeeses, I'm no good at speeches. (*General ad lib. "Aw, come on," etc.*) All I can say is thanks to everybody again for remembering me on my birthday. (*Bitterness coming out.*) Only don't think because I'm sixty I'll be a bigger

damned fool easy mark than ever! No, bejeeses! Like Hickey
says, it's going to be a new day! This dump has got to be run
like other dumps, so I can make some money and not just split
even. People has got to pay what they owe me! I'm not running
a God-damned orphan asylum for bums and crooks! Nor a God-
damned hooker shanty, either! Nor an Old Men's Home for lousy
Anarchist tramps that ought to be in jail! I'm sick of being
played for a sucker! (*They stare at him with stunned, bewildered
hurt. He goes on in a sort of furious desperation, as if he hated
himself for every word he said, and yet couldn't stop.*) And don't
think you're kidding me right now, either! I know damned well
you're giving me the laugh behind my back, thinking to yourselves,
The old, lying, pipe-dreaming faker, we've heard his bull about
taking a walk around the ward for years, he'll never make it! He's
yellow, he ain't got the guts, he's scared he'll find out— (*He
glares around at them almost with hatred.*) But I'll show you,
bejeeses! (*He glares at* HICKEY.) I'll show you, too, you son of
a bitch of a frying-pan-peddling bastard!

HICKEY (*heartily encouraging*)—That's the stuff, Harry! Of
course you'll try to show me! That's what I want you to do!
(HARRY *glances at him with helpless dread—then drops his eyes
and looks furtively around the table. All at once he becomes miserably contrite.*)

HOPE (*his voice catching*)—Listen, all of you! Bejeeses, forgive me. I lost my temper! I ain't feeling well! I got a hell of
a grouch on! Bejeeses, you know you're all as welcome here as
the flowers in May! (*They look at him with eager forgiveness.
ROCKY is the first one who can voice it.*)

ROCKY—Aw, sure, Boss, you're always aces wid us, see?

HICKEY (*rises to his feet again. He addresses them now with
the simple, convincing sincerity of one making a confession of
which he is genuinely ashamed*)—Listen, everybody! I know you
are sick of my gabbing, but I think this is the spot where I owe
it to you to do a little explaining and apologize for some of the
rough stuff I've had to pull on you. I know how it must look to
you. As if I was a damned busybody who was not only interfering in your private business, but even sicking some of you
on to nag at each other. Well, I have to admit that's true,
and I'm damned sorry about it. You know old Hickey. I was
never one to start trouble. But this time I had to—for your own
good! I had to make you help me with each other. I saw I
couldn't do what I was after alone. Not in the time at my dis-

posal. I knew when I came here I wouldn't be able to stay with
you long. I'm slated to leave on a trip. I saw I'd have to hustle
and use every means I could. (*With a joking boastfulness.*)
(*They stare at him, bitter, uneasy and fascinated. His manner
changes to deep earnestness.*) But here's the point to get. I swear
I'd never act like I have if I wasn't absolutely sure it will be worth
it to you in the end, after you're rid of the damned guilt that makes
you lie to yourselves you're something you're not, and the remorse
that nags at you and makes you hide behind lousy pipe dreams
about tomorrow. You'll be in a today where there is no yesterday
or tomorrow to worry you. You won't give a damn what you are
any more. I wouldn't say this unless I knew, Brothers and Sisters. This peace is real! It's a fact! I know! Because I've got
it! Here! Now! Right in front of you! You see the difference
in me! You remember how I used to be! Even when I had two
quarts of rotgut under my belt and joked and sang "Sweet Adeline," I still felt like a guilty skunk. But you can all see that I
don't give a damn about anything now. And I promise you, by
the time this day is over, I'll have every one of you feeling the
same way! (*He pauses. They stare at him fascinatedly. He
adds with a grin.*) I guess that'll be about all from me, boys
and girls—for the present. So let's get on with the party. (*He
starts to sit down.*)

LARRY (*sharply*)—Wait! (*Insistently—with a sneer.*) I think
it would help us poor pipe-dreaming sinners along the sawdust
trail to salvation if you told us now what happened to you that
converted you to this great peace you've found. (*More and more
with a deliberate, provocative taunting.*) I notice you didn't deny
it when I asked you about the iceman. Did this great revelation
of the evil habit of dreaming come after you found your wife was
sick of you? (*While he is speaking the faces of the gang have
lighted up vindictively, as if all at once they saw a chance to revenge themselves. As he finishes, a chorus of sneering taunts begins, punctuated by nasty, jeering laughter.*)

HOPE—Bejeeses, you've hit it, Larry! I've noticed he hasn't
shown her picture around this time!

MOSHER—He hasn't got it! The iceman took it away from
him!

MARGIE—Jees, look at him! Who could blame her?

PEARL—She must be hard up to fall for an iceman!

LEWIS—Come to look at you, Hickey, old chap, you've sprouted
horns like a bloody antelope!

Wetjoen—Pigger, py Gott! Like a water buffalo's!
Willie (*sings to his Sailor Lad tune*)—

"Come up," she cried, "my iceman lad,
And you and I'll agree—"

(*They all join in a jeering chorus, rapping with knuckles or glasses on the table at the indicated spot in the lyric.*)

"And I'll show you the prettiest (Rap, rap, rap)
That ever you did see!"

(*A roar of derisive, dirty laughter. But* Hickey *has remained unmoved by all this taunting. He grins good-naturedly, as if he enjoyed the joke at his expense, and joins in the laughter.*)

Hickey—Well, boys and girls, I'm glad to see you getting in good spirits for Harry's party, even if the joke is on me. I admit I asked for it by always pulling that iceman gag in the old days. So laugh all you like. (*He pauses. They do not laugh now. They are again staring at him with baffled uneasiness. He goes on thoughtfully.*) Well, this forces my hand, I guess, your bringing up the subject of Evelyn. I didn't want to tell you yet. It's hardly an appropriate time. I meant to wait until the party was over. But you're getting the wrong idea about poor Evelyn, and I've got to stop that. (*He pauses again. There is a tense stillness in the room. He bows his head a little and says quietly.*) I'm sorry to tell you my dearly beloved wife is dead. (*A gasp comes from the stunned company. They look away from him, shocked and miserably ashamed of themselves, except* Larry *who continues to stare at him.*)

Larry (*aloud to himself with a superstitious shrinking*)—Be God, I felt he'd brought the touch of death on him! (*Then suddenly he is even more ashamed of himself than the others and stammers.*) Forgive me, Hickey! I'd like to cut my dirty tongue out! (*This releases a chorus of shamefaced mumbles from the crowd. "Sorry, Hickey," "I'm sorry, Hickey." "We're sorry, Hickey."*)

Hickey (*looking around at them—in a kindly, reassuring tone*)—Now look here, everybody. You mustn't let this be a wet blanket on Harry's party. You're still getting me all wrong. There's no reason— You see, I don't feel any grief. (*They gaze at him startledly. He goes on with convincing sincerity.*) I've got to feel glad, for her sake. She's at peace.

The curtain falls.

ACT III

It is a hot mid-morning in Harry Hope's barroom—the morning of Harry's birthday. The back-bar mirror is covered with white mosquito netting. There is a small free lunch counter, and spiggoted barrels of cheap whiskey stand on a shelf. The partitioning curtain has been drawn and one notices that the banquet table has been broken up.

Joe Mott is sullenly sawdusting the floor and Rocky, who has just finished polishing up, is irritable because he is working Chuck's time so Chuck and Cora can get married. Rocky joins Larry, Parritt, and the sleeping Hugo at the barroom table. "Some party last night, huh? Jees, what a funeral! It was jinxed from de start, but his tellin' about his wife croakin' put de K.O. on it."

It had indeed been some party, and this has been some morning, what with the gang sneaking upstairs last night without touching the booze and eats—and what with Hickey hopping from room to room all night long. Hickey has dragged Jimmy out first thing to get his laundry and has given Willie money to get his clothes out of pawn. "And all de rest," informs Rocky, "been brushin' and shavin' demselves wid de shakes."

"He didn't come up to my room! He's afraid I might ask him a few questions," defiantly announces Larry. But Parritt says Hickey couldn't get in because Larry had his door locked. Parritt couldn't get in, either. But now Larry is here and the boy forces himself on him—to talk of Hickey.

"I'm getting more and more scared of him," the youth confesses. "Especially since he told us his wife was dead. . . . I don't know why, but it started me thinking about Mother—as if she was dead. I suppose she might as well be. Inside herself, I mean. It must kill her when she thinks of me. . . . Do you know, Larry, I once had a sneaking suspicion that maybe, if the truth was known, you were my father."

Larry's denial is violent. "I never laid eyes on your mother until after you were born." The boy's continual harping on the subject of his mother is vastly irritating to Larry—but the lad keeps it up. "It must be the final knockout for her if she knows I was the one who sold."

"Shut up, damn you!" warns Larry.

"It'll kill her," pursues Parritt with desperate urgency. "But I never thought the cops would get her! You've got to believe that! . . . But here's the true reason, Larry—the only reason! It was just for money! I got stuck on a tart and wanted dough to blow in on her and have a good time! That's all I did it for! Just money! Honest!" Parritt has the terrible grotesque air of one who gives an excuse which exonerates him from any real guilt.

In fury Larry begins to shake the boy and Rocky breaks it up with a "What's comin' off here?"

"This gabby young punk was talking my ear off," explains Larry, controlling himself. "He's a worse pest than Hickey."

"Yeah, Hickey— Say, listen, what d'yuh mean about him bein' scared you'd ask him questions? What questions?"

"Well, I feel he's hiding something. You notice he didn't say what his wife died of." Larry doesn't know himself what he is getting at—except that he is sure that Hickey has brought death here with him.

Rocky speculates on the possibility of Mrs. Hickman having committed suicide. This would account for Hickey's having gone bughouse—but bughouse or not the salesman has brought trouble to Rocky. Margie and Pearl took a couple of bottles to their room last night, got stinko and had a row with Rocky. Walked out on him, as a matter of fact—went on strike and headed for a day at Coney Island.

Nor is Chuck, the day bartender, any happier than Rocky. He comes in from the hall, dressed in his Sunday best and looking sleepy, uncomfortable and grouchy. Cora, he announces, wants a sherry flip—for her noives. As if a sherry flip were obtainable in such a dive.

"Pipe de bridegroom, Larry," taunts Rocky. "One week on dat farm in Joisey, dat's what I'll give yuh! Yuh'll come runnin' in here some night yellin' for a shot of booze 'cause de crickets is after yuh! Jees, Chuck, dat louse Hickey's coitnly made a prize coupla suckers outa youse."

Off guard, Chuck, agrees—then truculently announces that he and Cora are going through with the marriage. But he wishes Cora would cut out her beefing—and he'd like about a quart of redeye under his belt.

Rocky—Well, why de hell don't yuh?

Chuck (*instantly suspicious and angry*)—Sure! You'd like dat, wouldn't yuh? I'm wise to you! Yuh don't wanta see me get married and settle down like a reg'lar guy! Yuh'd like me to stay paralyzed all de time, so's I'd be like you, a lousy pimp!

Rocky (*springs to his feet, his face hardened viciously*)— Listen! I don't take dat even from you, see!

CHUCK (*puts his drink on the bar and clenches his fists*)—
Yeah? Wanta make sometin' of it? (*Jeeringly.*) Don't make
me laugh! I can lick ten of youse wid one mitt!

ROCKY (*reaching for his hip pocket*)—Not wid lead in your
belly, yuh won't!

JOE (*has stopped cutting when the quarrel started—expostulat-
ing*)—Hey, you, Rocky and Chuck! Cut it out! You's ole
friends! Don't let dat Hickey make you crazy!

CHUCK (*turns on him*)—Keep outa our business, yuh black
bastard!

ROCKY (*like* CHUCK, *turns on* JOE, *as if their own quarrel was
forgotten and they became natural allies against an alien*)—Stay
where yuh belong, yuh doity nigger!

JOE (*snarling with rage, springs from behind the lunch counter
with the bread knife in his hand*)—You white sons of bitches! I'll
rip your guts out! (CHUCK *snatches a whiskey bottle from the
bar and raises it above his head to hurl at* JOE. ROCKY *jerks a
short-barreled, nickel-plated revolver from his hip pocket. At this
moment* LARRY *pounds on the table with his fist and bursts into a
sardonic laugh.*)

LARRY—That's it! Murder each other, you damned loons, with
Hickey's blessing! Didn't I tell you he'd brought death with him?
(*His interruption startles them. They pause to stare at him, their
fighting fury suddenly dies out and they appear deflated and
sheepish.*)

ROCKY (*to* JOE)—Aw right, you. Leggo dat shiv and I'll put
dis gat away. (JOE *sullenly goes back behind the counter and
slaps the knife on top of it.* ROCKY *slips the revolver back in his
pocket.* CHUCK *lowers the bottle to the bar.* HUGO, *who has
awakened and raised his head when* LARRY *pounded on the table,
now giggles foolishly.*)

HUGO—Hello, leedle peoples! Neffer mind! Soon you vill eat
hot dogs beneath the villow trees and trink free vine— *Abruptly in
a haughty fastidious tone.*) The champagne vas not properly
iced. (*With guttural anger.*) Gottamned liar, Hickey! Does
that prove I vant to be aristocrat? I love only the proletariat!
I vill lead them! I vill be like a Gott to them! They vill be my
slaves! (*He stops in bewildered self-amazement—to* LARRY *appealingly.*) I am very trunk, no, Larry? I talk foolishness. I am
so trunk, Larry, old friend, am I not, I don't know vhat I say?

LARRY (*pityingly*)—You're raving drunk, Hugo. I've never
seen you so paralyzed. Lay your head down now and sleep it off.

Hugo (*gratefully*)—Yes. I should sleep. I am too crazy trunk. (*He puts his head on his arms and closes his eyes.*)

Joe (*behind the lunch counter—brooding superstitiously*)— You's right, Larry. Bad luck come in de door when Hickey come. I's an ole gamblin' man and I knows bad luck when I feels it! (*Then defiantly.*) But it's white man's bad luck. He can't jinx me! (*He comes from behind the counter and goes to the bar— addressing* Rocky *stiffly.*) De bread's cut and I's finished my job. Do I get de drink I's earned? (Rocky *gives him a hostile look but shoves a bottle and glass at him.* Joe *pours a brimful drink—sullenly.*) I's finished wid dis dump for keeps. (*He takes a key from his pocket and slaps it on the bar.*) Here's de key to my room. I ain't comin' back. I's goin' to my own folks where I belong. I's sick and tired of messin' round wid white men. (*He gulps down his drink—then looking around defiantly he deliberately throws his whiskey glass on the floor and smashes it.*)

Rocky—Hey! What de hell—!

Joe (*with a sneering dignity*)—I's on'y savin' you de trouble, White Boy. Now you don't have to break it, soon's my back's turned, so's no white man kick about drinkin' from de same glass. (*He walks stiffly to the street door—then turns for a parting shot—boastfully.*) I's tired of loafin' 'round wid a lot of bums. I's a gamblin' man. I's gonna get in a big crap game and win me a big bankroll. Den get de okay to open up my old gamblin' house for colored men. Den maybe I comes back here sometime to see de bums. Maybe I throw a twenty-dollar bill on de bar and say, "Drink it up," and listen when dey all pat me on de back and say, "Joe, you sure is white." But I'll say, "No, I'm black and my dough is black man's dough, and you's proud to drink wid me or you won't get no drink!" Or maybe I just says, "You can all go to hell. I don't lower myself drinkin' wid no white trash!" (*He opens the door to go out—then turns again.*) And dat ain't no pipe dream! I'll git de money for my stake today, somehow, somewheres! If I has to borrow a gun and stick up some white man, I gets it! You wait and see! (*He swaggers out through the swinging doors.*)

The swinging doors which have emitted Joe soon admit Willie Oban, who is shaved and wears an expensive suit, good shoes and clean linen. Willie is sober, but his face is sick and he has the shakes. Rocky offers him a drink, but Willie stifles his yearning and refuses. It wouldn't do to go to the D. A.'s office smelling of booze.

Another of Hickey's miracle men appears—the Britisher Lewis, spruce-looking but beset by katzenjammer. With false bravado he, too, declines a drink. Surprisingly, he turns in his room key, explaining that he can't live under the same roof with that stupid bounder of a Boer. And, speaking of the devil, Wetjoen arrives— outwardly swaggering, sneering at Lewis, and inwardly ill.

Lewis explains his plans. He's going to see a pal at the British Consulate and get some kind of job with the Cunard—a temporary one, until he can save enough for a first-class passage home.

"Dot's biggest pipe dream of all," sneers the Boer. He, Wetjoen, still a powerful man, is going to get a job—any job, because he puts on no gentleman's airs. In Lewis' direction he taunts, "Und *I* can go home to my country!"

Lewis, trembling with repressed anger, observes, "There was a rumor in South Africa, Rocky, that a certain Boer officer—if you call the leaders of a rabble of farmers officers—kept advising Cronje to retreat and not to stand and fight—"

"And," hotly insists Wetjoen, "I was right!" Trying to copy Lewis' manner, he informs the world in general, "I haf also heard rumors of a Limey officer who, after the war, lost all his money gambling vhen he vas tronk. But they found out it vas regiment money, too, he lost—"

The two bartenders keep the Britisher and the Boer from each other's throats. A happy day at Harry Hope's indeed. "By God," laughs Larry, "you can't say Hickey hasn't the miraculous touch to raise the dead, when he can start the Boer War raging again!" This comment acts like a cold douche on the two belligerents, and they subside. Lewis, attempting a return to his jaunty manner, starts for the street door.

"Py Gott, if dot Limey can go I can go!" announces Wetjoen. But the door stops them and they almost collide. Lewis has just happened to think it wouldn't be decent to pop off without saying good-by to good old Harry. And good old Jimmy. Wetjoen allows he'll wait, too.

Chuck remembers he came for a drink for Cora, and takes her some whiskey. Parritt makes a futile try for Larry's attention, but Larry roughly demands to be left in peace. "I've told you you can't make me judge you! . . . Set 'em up, Rocky. I swore I'd have no more drinks on Hickey, if I died of drought, but I've changed my mind! Be God, he owed it to me, and I'd get blind to the world now if it was the Iceman of Death himself treating!" This startling notion brings a look of superstitious awe to Larry's face. "What made me say that, I wonder?" Then, with a sardonic laugh, "Well, be God, it fits, for Death was the Iceman Hickey called to his home!"

Two more reformed characters make their appearance—Mosher and, shortly, McGloin. Their appearance is like the others'—comparatively good outwardly, but nothing inside. They, too, are snarling at each other, and each proposes to get his job back. When Cora arrives she, at least, is drunk—and dressed and rouged in her gaudy best. "Hickey just told us, ain't it time we beat it, if we're really goin'," she explains. With frightened anger she adds, "If I had to listen to any more of Hickey's bunk, I'd brain him. Come on, honey," she says, putting her hand on Chuck's arm, "let's get started before he comes down."

Cora and Chuck, too, are snarling at each other, and another rousing argument is well started when Chuck hears someone upstairs in the hall. Grabbing Cora, he warns, "Here's Hickey comin'! Let's get outa here!" They are the first of all who have gathered in the bar to make a break.

Rocky (*gloomily pronounces an obituary*)—One regular guy and one all-right tart gone to hell! (*Fiercely.*) Dat louse Hickey oughta be croaked! (*There is a muttered growl of assent from most of the gathering. Then* Harry Hope *enters from the hall, followed by* Jimmy Tomorrow, *with* Hickey *on his heels.* Hope *and* Jimmy *are both putting up a front of self-assurance, but* Cora's *description of them was apt. There is a desperate bluff in their manner as they walk in, which suggests the last march of the condemned.* Hope *is dressed in an old black Sunday suit, black tie, shoes, socks, which give him the appearance of being in mourning.* Jimmy's *clothes are pressed, his shoes shined, his white linen immaculate. He has a hangover and his gently appealing dog's eyes have a boiled look.* Hickey's *face is a bit drawn from lack of sleep and his voice is hoarse from continual talking, but his bustling energy appears nervously intensified, and his beaming expression is one of triumphant accomplishment.*)

Hickey—Well, here we are! We've got this far, at least! (*He pats* Jimmy *on the back.*) Good work, Jimmy. I told you you weren't half as sick as you pretended. No excuse whatever for postponing—

Jimmy—I'll thank you to keep your hands off me! I merely mentioned I would feel more fit tomorrow. But it might as well be today, I suppose.

Hickey—Finish it now, so it'll be dead and buried forever, and you can be free! (*He passes him to clap* Hope *encourag-*

ingly on the shoulder.) Cheer up, Harry. You found your rheumatism didn't bother you coming downstairs, didn't you? I told
you it wouldn't. (*He winks around at the others. With the exception of* Hugo *and* Parritt, *all their eyes are fixed on him with
bitter animosity. He gives* Hope *a playful nudge in the ribs.*)
You're the damnedest one for alibis, Governor! As bad as
Jimmy!

Hope (*putting on his deaf manner*)—Eh? I can't hear—
(*Defiantly.*) You're a liar. I've had rheumatism on and off for
twenty years. Ever since Bessie died. Everybody knows that.

Hickey—Yes, we know it's the kind of rheumatism you turn
on and off! We're on to you, you old faker! (*He claps him on
the shoulder again, chuckling.*)

Hope (*looks humiliated and guilty—by way of escape he glares
around at the others*)—What are all you bums hanging round staring at me for? Think you was watching a circus! Why don't
you get the hell out of here and tend to your own business, like
Hickey's told you? (*They look at him reproachfully, their eyes
hurt. They fidget as if trying to move.*)

Hickey—Yes, Harry, I certainly thought they'd have had the
guts to be gone by this time. (*He grins.*) Or maybe I did have
my doubts. (*They glare at him with fear and hatred. They
seem about to curse him, to spring at him. But they remain silent and motionless. His manner changes and he becomes kindly
bullying.*) Come on, boys! Get moving! Who'll start the ball
rolling? You, Captain, and you, General! You're nearest the
door. And besides, you're old war heroes! You ought to lead
the forlorn hope! Come on, now, show us a little of that good
old battle of Modder River spirit we've heard so much about!
You can't hang around all day looking as if you were scared the
street outside would bite you!

Lewis (*turns with humiliated rage—with an attempt at jaunty
casualness*)—Right you are, Mister Bloody Nosey Parker! Time
I pushed off. Was only waiting to say good-by to you, Harry,
old chum.

Hope (*dejectedly*)—Good-by, Captain. Hope you have luck.

Lewis—Oh, I'm bound to, Old Chap, and the same to you.
(*He pushes the swinging doors open and makes a brave exit, turning to his right and marching off outside the window at right of
door.*)

Wetjoen—Py Gott, if dot Limey can, I can! (*He pushes the
door open and lumbers through it like a bull charging an ob-*

*stacle. He turns left and disappears off rear, outside the farthest
window.*)

HICKEY (*exhortingly*)—Next? Come in, Ed. It's a fine summer's day and the call of the old circus lot must be in your
blood! (MOSHER *glares at him, then goes to the door.* MCGLOIN
jumps up from chair and starts moving toward the door. HICKEY
claps him on the back as he passes.) That's the stuff, Mac.

MOSHER—Good-by, Harry. (*He goes out, turning right outside.*)

MCGLOIN (*glowering after him*)—If that crooked grifter has
the guts— (*He goes out, turning left outside.* HICKEY *glances
at* WILLIE *who, before he can speak, jumps from his chair.*)

WILLIE—Good-by, Harry, and thanks for all your kindness.

HICKEY (*claps him on the back*)—That's the way, Willie!
The D. A.'s a busy man. He can't wait all day for you, you
know. (WILLIE *hurries to the door.*)

HOPE (*dully*)—Good luck, Willie. (WILLIE *goes out and
turns right outside. While he is doing so,* JIMMY, *in a sick panic,
sneaks to the bar and furtively reaches for* LARRY'S *glass of
whiskey.*)

HICKEY—And now it's your turn, Jimmy, old pal. (*He sees
what* JIMMY *is at and grabs his arm just as he is about to down
the drink.*) Now, now, Jimmy! You can't do that to yourself.
One drink on top of your hangover and an empty stomach and
you'll be oreyeyed. Then you'll tell yourself you wouldn't stand
a chance if you went up soused to get your old job back.

JIMMY (*pleads abjectly*)—Tomorrow! I will tomorrow! I'll
be in good shape tomorrow! (*Abruptly getting control of himself—with shaken firmness.*) All right. I'm going. Take your
hands off me.

HICKEY—That's the ticket! You'll thank me when it's all
over.

JIMMY (*in a burst of futile fury*)—You dirty swine! (*He
tries to throw the drink in* HICKEY'S *face, but his aim is poor
and it lands on* HICKEY'S *coat.* JIMMY *turns and dashes through
the door, disappearing outside the window at right of door.*)

HICKEY (*brushing the whiskey off his coat—humorously*)—All
set for an alcohol rub! But no hard feelings. I know how he
feels. I wrote the book. (*He turns to* HOPE—*encouragingly.*)
Well, Governor, Jimmy made the grade. It's up to you.

LARRY (*bursts out*)—Leave Harry alone, damn you!

HICKEY (*grins at him*)—I'd make up my mind about myself
if I was you, Larry, and not bother over Harry. He'll come

through all right. I've promised him that. He doesn't need anyone's bum pity. Do you, Governor?

HOPE (*with a pathetic attempt at his old fuming assertiveness*)—
No, bejeeses! Keep your nose out of this, Larry. What's Hickey
got to do with it? I've always been going to take this walk, ain't
I? Bejeeses, you bums want to keep me locked up in here's if I
was in jail! I've stood it long enough! I'm free, white and
twenty-one, and I'll do as I damned please, bejeeses! You keep
your nose out, too, Hickey! You'd think you was boss of this
dump, not me. Sure, I'm all right! Why shouldn't I be? What
the hell's to be scared of, just taking a stroll around my own
ward? (*As he talks he has been moving toward the door. Now
he reaches it.*) What's the weather like outside, Rocky?

ROCKY—Fine day, Boss.

HOPE—What's that? Can't hear you. Don't look fine to me.
Looks's if it'd pour down cats and dogs any minute. My rheumatism— (*He catches himself.*) No, must be my eyes. Half
blind, bejeeses. Makes things look black. I see now it's a fine
day. Too damned hot for a walk, though, if you ask me. Well,
do me good to sweat the booze out of me. But I'll have to watch
out for the damned automobiles. Wasn't none of them around
the last time, twenty years ago. From what I've seen of 'em
through the window, they'd run over you as soon as look at
you. Not that I'm scared of 'em. I can take care of myself.
(*He puts a reluctant hand on the swinging door.*) Well, so long—
(*He stops and looks back—with frightened irascibility.*)
Bejeeses, where are you, Hickey? It's time we got started.

HICKEY (*grins and shakes his head*)—No, Harry. Can't be
done. You've got to keep a date with yourself alone.

HOPE (*with forced fuming*)—Hell of a guy, you are! Thought
you'd be willing to help me across the street, knowing I'm half
blind. Half deaf, too. Can't hear those damned automobiles.
Hell with you! Bejeeses, I've never needed no one's help and I
don't now! (*Egging himself on.*) I'll take a good long walk
now I've started. See all my old friends. Bejeeses, they must
have given me up for dead. Twenty years is a long time. But
they know it was grief over Bessie's death that made me—
(*He puts his hand on the door.*) Well, the sooner I get started—
(*Then he drops his hand—with sentimental melancholy.*) You
know, Hickey, that's what gets me. Can't help thinking the last
time I went out was to Bessie's funeral. After she'd gone, swore
I'd never go out again. (*Pathetically.*) Somehow, I can't feel
it's right for me to go, Hickey, even now. It's like I was doing

wrong to her memory.

HICKEY—Now, Governor, you can't let yourself get away with that one any more!

HOPE (*cupping his hand to his ear*)—What's that? Can't hear you. (*Sentimentally again but with desperation.*) I remember now clear as day the last time before she— It was a fine Sunday morning. We went out to church together. (*His voice breaks on a sob.*)

HICKEY (*amused*)—It's a great act, Governor. But I know better, and so do you. You never did want to go to church or any place else with her. She was always on your neck, making you have ambition and go out and do things, when all you wanted was to get drunk in peace.

HOPE (*falteringly*)—Can't hear a word you're saying. You're a God-damned liar, anyway! (*Then in a sudden fury, his voice trembling with hatred.*) Bejeeses, you son of a bitch, if there was a mad dog outside I'd go and shake hands with it rather than stay here with you! (*The momentum of his fit of rage does it. He pushes the door open and strides blindly out into the street and as blindly past the window behind the free-lunch counter.*)

ROCKY (*in amazement*)—Jees, he made it! I'd give yuh fifty to one he'd never— (*He goes to the end of the bar to look through the window—disgustedly.*) Aw, he's stopped. I'll bet yuh he's comin' back.

HICKEY—Of course, he's coming back. So are all the others. By tonight they'll all be here again. You dumbbell, that's the whole point.

Outside, Hope has gone to the curb and looked fearfully up and down for automobiles—on a street which does not have more than two motor cars an hour. Rocky is watching him excitedly, as though Harry's venture outdoors was a race he had bet on. Larry defiantly turns on Hickey. "And now," he queries, "it's my turn, I suppose?"

"Why," grins Hickey, "we've discussed all that. Just stop lying to yourself—" His bland omniscience infuriates Larry.

Rocky recitedly reports that Hope is starting across the street. "He's goin' to fool yuh, Hickey, yuh bastard!" But Hope stops, right in the middle of the street; then turns back. In a moment he lurches through the swinging doors and gasps, "Bejeeses, give me a drink quick! Scared me out of a year's growth! Bejeeses, that guy ought to be pinched!"

It was an automobile, says Harry—but Rocky, who was watching all the time, is disbelieving. Disgusted, Rocky announces that he, too, is going to get stinko. He thought Harry had some guts. "Automobile, hell! Who d'yuh tink yuh're kiddin'? Dey wasn't no automobile! Yuh just quit cold!"

Hickey lays a soothing hand on Hope's shoulder. "You've faced the test and come through," he reassures. "You're rid of all that nagging dream stuff now."

Hope appeals to Larry. He saw the automobile, didn't he? Larry compassionately assures him, "Sure I saw it, Harry. You had a narrow escape." Hickey indignantly resents this white lie; it is, he tells Larry, the wrong kind of pity. If he'll only wait until the final returns are in he will find that Harry is finally at peace with himself.

"Come now, Governor," Hickey urges Hope. "What's the use of being stubborn, now when it's all over. Give up that ghost automobile."

Hope collapses, spiritually and physically, and reaches for a bottle. Hugo, in one of his periodic moments of consciousness, observes that Harry looks funny—looks dead. Hugo scrambles to another table, next to Parritt, and falls asleep again.

"Another one who's begun to enjoy your peace!" Larry's comment to Hickey is bitterly condemning.

"Oh, I know it's tough on him right now, the same as it is on Harry," admits Hickey. "But that's only the first shock. I promise you they'll both come through all right."

Hope continues to drink, mechanically, complaining that the booze has no kick in it, and Hickey reveals his first trace of underlying uneasiness. "You're all right, aren't you, Harry?" But Harry isn't. He wants to pass out like Hugo.

"It's the peace of death you've brought on him," Larry accuses.

Losing his temper for the first time, Hickey shouts, "That's a lie!" But he soon recovers. Look at himself, he advises. Does he look dead?

"Let's all pass out. Who the hell cares?" grumbles Hope. But there's no life in the booze. And by now Hickey is plainly worried. Something has gone wrong with his plan for Harry. Sensing Hickey's uncertainty, Larry plunges into an attack. "What did your wife die of?"

Hickey reproaches, "You're not very considerate, Larry. But, if you insist on knowing now, there's no reason you shouldn't. It was a bullet through the head that killed Evelyn."

A tense silence follows this statement. Then Larry pursues, "You drove your poor wife to suicide? I knew it!"

"I didn't say poor Evelyn committed suicide. It's the last thing she'd ever have done, as long as I was alive. . . . No, I'm sorry to have to tell you my poor wife was killed."

Larry stares at Hickey with growing horror. Parritt jerks his head up from his hands and looks around frightenedly, as though somebody had spoken of his mother being killed. Rocky's round eyes are popping, but Harry Hope continues to stare dully at his table top and Hugo, as usual, gives no sign of life.

"Moidered? Who done it?" blurts Rocky.

"Don't ask questions, you dumb Wop! It's none of our damned business!" warns Larry. "Leave Hickey alone!"

With an amused and affectionate smile, Hickey addresses Slade. "Still the old grandstand bluff, Larry? Or is it some more bum pity?" To Rocky he explains, "The police don't know who killed her yet. But I expect they will before very long."

Hope, dull and callous, says his bets are on the iceman. Hugo sobs for a drink. Hickey is expressing kindly concern over Hope, for it's time he began to feel happy, as

The curtain falls.

ACT IV

About half past one the next morning the back room is again in operation—if it can be called an operation. Larry, Hugo and young Parritt are at one of the round tables—Hugo with his head on his arms, as usual, but this time he is not asleep. Parritt is looking half pleadingly, half sneeringly, at Larry, but Larry keeps his eyes fixed on the floor. They have a bottle of whiskey. Cora is sitting at another table, and opposite her is Captain Lewis. McGloin, Wetjoen, Willie Oban, Mosher and Jimmy Tomorrow are at other places in the room. In the bar section Joe is sprawled in a chair in sodden slumber. Only Rocky is standing, tired and tough-looking. The atmosphere is oppressive, stagnant.

Rocky is trying to arouse Joe and get him to move into the back room, because it is after hours, when Chuck appears, drunk, sullen and bearing the marks of a brawl. His knuckles are raw, he has a mouse under one eye, his hat is gone and his suit is dirty.

Rocky is fed up with the job. "Yuh say if I'd take your day yuh'd relieve me at six," he accuses Chuck. "Well, yuh're takin' over now, get me, no matter how plastered yuh are!"

"Plastered, hell! I wisht I was. I've lapped up a gallon, but it don't hit me right. And to hell wid de job. I'm goin' to tell Harry I'm quittin'."

"Yeah? Well, I'm quittin', too."

Chuck's marriage is off, and he is through playing sucker for that crummy red-head, Cora. It was her sherry flips. All the way walking to the Jersey ferry she had to stop at every ginmill and have one. "I got tinkin', Christ, what won't she want when she gets de ring on her finger and I'm hooked?" So Chuck has bowed out. But that isn't the way Rocky heard it from Cora. Cora says *she* told Chuck to go to hell. Ignoring this information, Chuck continues:

"I got tinkin', too, Jees, won't I look sweet wid a wife dat de minute your back is toined, she'd be cheatin' wid de iceman or someone. Hickey done me a favor, makin' me wake up. . . . On'y it was fun, kinda, me and Cora kiddin' ourselves."

Suddenly Chuck's face hardens. "Where is dat son of a bitch Hickey? I want one good sock at dat guy—just one!—and de next buttin' in he'll do will be in de morgue! I'll take a chance on goin' to de Chair—!"

"*Piano!*" warns Rocky. "Keep away from him, Chuck! He ain't here now, anyway. He went out to phone, he said. He wouldn't call from here. I got a hunch he's beat it. But if he does come back, yuh don't know him, if anyone asks yuh, get me? I don't know nuttin', see, but it looks like he croaked his wife."

Chuck shows a flash of interest. Rocky explains that Larry is wise, and Rocky has tried to tell the others to stay clear. And if Hickey gets the Hot Seat there will be no mourning by Rocky —not with Harry so licked he can't even get drunk and all the gang licked, too. They all sneaked in, the gang, like pooches with their tails between their legs. Jimmy Tomorrow had been the last to arrive. A cop had found him on a dock looking at the water and crying and had brought him in.

The air of defeat is universal. Joe, after his flash of arrogance, is servile. Waking from his chair in the bar he begs a seat next to Captain Lewis in the back room. "I should feel honored," says Lewis, "that a bloody Kaffir would lower himself to sit beside me."

Chuck demands money of Cora and Cora obediently hands over a small roll of bills. "Jees," she says with a tired wonder at herself, "imagine me kiddin' myself I wanted to marry a drunken pimp."

"Dat's nuttin', Baby," counters Chuck. "Imagine de sap I'da

been, when I can get your dough just as easy widout it!"

Parritt jeeringly observes that Larry is pretending not to notice him—that he'd like to forget the boy is alive. "He kept himself locked in his room until a while ago, but he couldn't make it work! There must have been something there he was even more scared to face than he is Hickey and me! I guess he got looking at the fire escape and thinking now handy it was, if he was really sick of life and only had the nerve to die!"

Larry's face has tautened, but he pretends not to hear as Parritt presses on: "He used to love her, too. So he thinks I ought to take a hop off the fire escape!" Parritt's mood breaks and he begins to plead. "For God's sake, Larry, can't you say something? Hickey's got me all balled up. . . . I've got to know what I ought to do—"

"God damn you," grits Larry in a stifled tone, "are you trying to make me your executioner?"

With false bravado the youth nudges Rocky and observes that Larry is an old, no-good, drunken tramp—and he ought to take a hop off the fire escape.

"Sure," agrees Rocky. "Why don't he? Or you? or me? What de hell's de difference? Who cares?" There is a faint stir from the crowd, as if Rocky's statement has struck a chord in their numbed minds. Like sleepers they mumble, almost in chorus, "The hell with it" and "Who cares?"

Rocky expresses the hope that Hickey won't come back, but Larry grimly pronounces, "He'll come back. He'll keep on talking. He's got to. He's lost his confidence that the peace he's sold us is the real McCoy, and it's made him uneasy about his own."

As Larry is speaking Hickey appears in the doorway; his grin is gone, he no longer is self-assured. As he speaks the crowd shrinks away from him. "That's a damned lie, Larry," Hickey says angrily. Then his tone changes. "Well, well! How are you coming along, everybody? Sorry I had to leave you for a while, but there was something I had to get finally settled."

Hope expresses the wish that Hickey will now settle something about the booze, which is like drinking dishwater. Nobody can pass out. There is a chorus of agreement—"We can't pass out! You promised us peace!"

Hickey is exasperated. By rights they should be contented now, without a single damned hope or lying dream left. It must be their pigheaded stubbornness. Hickey rouses himself to his old brisk manner. There is little time left, for he has made a

date for two o'clock, and they must get busy right away and find
out what's wrong. "Don't you know you're free now to be yourselves, without having to feel remorse or guilt? Can't you see
there is no tomorrow now? . . . Then why the hell don't you
get pie-eyed and celebrate?"

Hickey now acts hurt. They're putting on this half-dead act
to get back at him because they hate his guts. He pleads for
them not to hate him. "It makes me feel you suspect I must
have hated you. But that's a lie! Oh, I know I used to hate
everyone in the world who wasn't as rotten a bastard as I was!
But that was when I was still living in hell—before I faced the
truth and saw the only possible way to free poor Evelyn."

The group in the back room of Harry Hope's saloon stirs with
awakening dread, grows tense. They try to shut Hickey off, but
with an obsessed look on his face he continues:

"The one possible way to make up to her for all I'd made her
go through, and get her rid of me so I couldn't make her suffer
any more, and she wouldn't have to forgive me again! I saw I
couldn't do it by killing myself, like I wanted to for a long time.
That would have been the last straw for her. She'd have died
of a broken heart to think I could do that to her. She'd have
blamed herself for it, too. Or I couldn't just run away from
her. She'd have died of grief and humiliation if I'd done that
to her. She'd have thought I stopped loving her."

Hickey becomes strangely, impressively simple. "You see,
Evelyn loved me," he explains. "And I loved her. That was the
trouble. It would have been easy to find a way out if she hadn't
loved me so much. Or if I hadn't loved her. But as it was,
there was only one possible way. I had to kill her."

There is a gasp from the crowd. Larry tries to halt the recital.
They remember the old days when Hickey brought kindness and
they don't want to know things that will make them help send
him to the Chair. With angry scorn Parritt interrupts, "Ah, shut
up, you yellow faker! Wouldn't I deserve the Chair too, if I'd—"

"God damn you, stop shoving your rotten soul in my lap!"
Larry is furious. Hickey resumes. The reason why he has been
trying to rid the crowd of their pipe dreams is because of what a
pipe dream did to Evelyn and him. In a strange, running narrative manner he begins at the beginning, "You see, even when we
were kids, Evelyn and me—"

There is a chorus of objections—who the hell cares, they want
to pass out. Hope is still complaining about the booze. Jimmy
Tomorrow, looking like a wax figure, talks to himself. It was a

stupid lie, Jimmy's nonsense about tomorrow. Nobody would give him his job back. He was fired for drunkenness and he is much worse now—and it was a pretense, his story that his wife's adultery ruined his life. "I discovered early in life," Jimmy explains to himself more than to anybody else, "that living frightened me when I was sober." When his wife was unfaithful he didn't care—he was glad to be free. "Even grateful to her, I think, for giving me such a good tragic excuse to drink as much as I damned well pleased."

Jimmy stops like a mechanical doll which has run down. Two men come quietly in, and at a peremptory sign from one of them Rocky realizes they are detectives and his expression freezes into a wary blankness. When one of the visitors asks for a guy named Hickman, Rocky wouldn't know.

"Listen, you! This is murder. And don't be a sap. It was Hickman himself phoned in and said we'd find him here around two." Rocky shrugs and points out Hickey, who is insisting that he's got to tell the gang his story because if he got balled up about them how does he know he wasn't balled up about himself?

HICKEY (*his tone again becoming musingly reminiscent*)—You see, even as a kid I was always restless. I had to keep on the go. You've heard the old saying, "Ministers' sons are sons of guns." Well, that was me, and then some. Home was like a jail. I didn't fall for the religious bunk. Listening to my old man whooping up hell fire and scaring those Hoosier suckers into shelling out their dough only handed me a laugh, although I had to hand it to him, the way he sold them nothing for something. I guess I take after him, and that's what made me a good salesman. Well, anyway, as I said, home was like jail, and so was school, and so was that damned hick town. The only place I liked was the pool rooms, where I could smoke Sweet Caporals, and mop up a couple of beers, thinking I was a hell-on-wheels sport. We had one hooker shop in town, and, of course, I liked that, too. Not that I hardly ever had entrance money. My old man was a tight old bastard. But I liked to sit around in the parlor and joke with the girls, and they liked me because I could kid 'em along and make 'em laugh. Well, you know what a small town is. Everyone got wise to me. They all said I was a no-good tramp. I didn't give a damn what they said. I hated everybody in the place. That is, except Evelyn. I loved Evelyn. Even as a kid. And Evelyn loved me. (*He pauses. No one moves or gives any sign except by the dread in their eyes that they have heard him. Except* PARRITT, *who takes his hands from his face to look at* LARRY *pleadingly.*)

PARRITT—I loved Mother, Larry! No matter what she did! I still do! Even though I know she wishes now I was dead! You believe that, don't you? Christ, why can't you say something?

HICKEY (*too absorbed in his story now to notice this—goes on in a tone of fond, sentimental reminiscence*)—Yes, sir, as far back as I can remember, Evelyn and I loved each other. She always stuck up for me. She wouldn't believe the gossip—or she'd pretend she didn't. No one could convince her I was no good. Evelyn was stubborn as all hell once she'd made up her mind. Even when I'd admit things and ask her forgiveness, she'd make excuses for me and defend me against myself. She'd kiss me and say she knew I didn't mean it and I wouldn't do it again. So I'd promise I wouldn't. I'd have to promise, she was so sweet and good, though I knew darned well— (*A touch of strange bitterness comes into his voice for a moment.*) No, sir, you couldn't stop Evelyn. Nothing on earth could shake her faith in me. Even I couldn't. She was a sucker for a pipe dream. (*Then quickly.*) Well, naturally, her family forbid her seeing me. They were one of the town's best, rich for that hick burg. Strict Methodists, too. They hated my guts. But they couldn't stop Evelyn. She'd sneak notes to me and meet me on the sly. I was getting more restless. The town was getting more like a jail. I made up my mind to beat it. I knew exactly what I wanted to be by that time. I'd met a lot of drummers around the hotel and liked 'em. They were always telling jokes. They were sports. They kept moving. I liked their life. And I knew I could kid people and sell things. The hitch was how to get the railroad fare to the Big Town. I told Mollie Arlington my trouble. She was the madame of the cathouse. She liked me. She laughed and said, "Hell, I'll stake you, Kid! I'll bet on you. With that grin of yours and line of bull, you ought to be able to sell skunks for good ratters!" (*He chuckles.*) Mollie was all right. She gave me confidence in myself. I paid her back, the first money I earned. But that's ahead of my story. The night before I left town, I had a date with Evelyn. I told her straight, "You better forget me, Evelyn, for your own sake. I'm no good and never will be. I'm not worthy to wipe your shoes." I broke down and cried. She just said, looking white and scared, "Why, Teddy? Don't you still love me?" I said, "Love you? God, Evelyn, I

love you more than anything in the world. And I always will!"
She said, "Then nothing else matters, Teddy, because nothing but
death could stop my loving you. So I'll wait, and when you're
ready you send for me, and we'll be married. I know I can make
you happy, Teddy, and once you're happy you won't want to do
any of the bad things you've done any more." And I said, "Of
course, I won't, Evelyn!" I meant it, too. I believed it. I loved
her so much she could make me believe anything. (*He sighs.
There is a suspended, waiting silence. Even the two detectives
are drawn into it. Then* HOPE *breaks into dully exasperated,
brutally callous protest.*)

HOPE—Get it over, you long-winded bastard! You married
her, and you caught her cheating with the iceman, and you
croaked her, and who the hell cares? What's she to us? All we
want is to pass out in peace. (*A chorus of dull, resentful protest from all the group. They mumble, like sleepers who curse
a person who keeps awakening them,* "What's it to us? We want
to pass out in peace!" HOPE *drinks and they mechanically follow his example. He pours another and they do the same. He
complains with a stupid, nagging insistence.*)

HICKEY (*goes on as if there had been no interruption*)—So I
beat it to the Big Town. I got a job easy, and it was a cinch
for me to make good. I had the knack. It was like a game,
sizing people up quick, spotting what their pet pipe dreams were,
and then kidding 'em along that line, pretending you believed
what they wanted to believe about themselves. Then they liked
you, they trusted you, they wanted to buy something to show
their gratitude. It was fun. But still, all the while I felt guilty,
as if I had no right to be having such a good time away from
Evelyn. In each letter I'd tell her how I missed her, but I'd keep
warning her, too. I'd tell her all my faults, how I liked my
booze every once in a while, and so on. But there was no shaking Evelyn's belief in me, or her dreams about the future. After
each letter of hers, I'd be as full of faith as she was. So as soon
as I got enough saved to start us off, I sent for her and we got
married. Christ, wasn't I happy for a while! And wasn't she
happy! I don't care what anyone says, I'll bet there wasn't two
people who loved each other more than me and Evelyn. Not
only then but always after, in spite of everything I did— (*He
pauses—then sadly.*) Well, it's all there, at the start, everything
that happened afterwards. I never could learn to handle temptation. I'd want to reform and mean it. I'd promise Evelyn, and
I'd promise myself, and I'd believe it. I'd tell her, it's the last

time. And she'd say, "I know it's the last time, Teddy. You'll never do it again." That's what made it so hard. That's what made me feel such a rotten skunk—her always forgiving me. My playing around with women, for instance. It was only a harmless good time to me. Didn't mean anything. But I'd know what it meant to Evelyn. So I'd say to myself, never again. But you know how it is, traveling around. The damned hotel rooms. I'd get seeing things in the wall paper. I'd get bored as hell. Lonely and homesick. But at the same time sick of home. I'd feel free and I'd want to celebrate a little. I never drank on the job, so it had to be dames. Any tart. What I'd want was some tramp I could be myself with without being ashamed—someone I could tell a dirty joke to and she'd laugh.

CORA (*with a full, weary bitterness*)—Jees, all de lousy jokes I've had to listen to and pretend was funny!

HICKEY (*goes on obliviously*)—Sometimes I'd try some joke I thought was a corker on Evelyn. She'd always make herself laugh. But I could tell she thought it was dirty, not funny. And Evelyn always knew about the tarts I'd been with when I came home from a trip. She'd kiss me and look in my eyes, and she'd know. I'd see in her eyes how she was trying not to know, and then telling herself even if it was true, he couldn't help it, they tempt him, and he's lonely, he hasn't got me, it's only his body, anyway, he doesn't love them, I'm the only one he loves. She was right, too. I never loved anyone else. Couldn't if I wanted to. (*He pauses.*) She forgave me even when it all had to come out in the open. You know how it is when you keep taking chances. You may be lucky for a long time, but you get nicked in the end. I picked up a nail from some tart in Altoona.

CORA (*dully, without resentment*)—Yeah. And she picked it up from some guy. It's all in de game. What de hell of it?

HICKEY—I had to do a lot of lying and stalling when I got home. It didn't do any good. The quack I went to got all my dough and then told me I was cured and I took his word. But I wasn't, and poor Evelyn— But she did her best to make me believe she fell for my lie about how traveling men get things from drinking cups on trains. Anyway, she forgave me every time I'd turn up after a periodical drunk. You all know what I'd be like at the end of one. You've seen me. Like something lying in the gutter that no alley cat would lower itself to drag in—something they threw out of the D.T. ward in Bellevue along with the garbage, something that ought to be dead and isn't! (*His face is convulsed with self-loathing.*) Evelyn wouldn't have heard from

me in a month or more. She'd have been waiting there alone,
with the neighbors shaking their heads and feeling sorry for her
out loud. That was before she got me to move to the outskirts,
where there weren't any next-door neighbors. And then the door
would open and in I'd stumble—looking like what I've said—into
her home, where she kept everything so spotless and clean. And
I'd sworn it would never happen again, and now I'd have to start
swearing again this was the last time. I could see disgust having
a battle in her eyes with love. Love always won. She'd act as if
nothing had happened, as if I'd just come home from a business
trip. She'd never complain or bawl me out. (*He bursts out a
tone of anguish that has anger and hatred beneath it.*) Christ,
can you imagine what a guilty skunk she made me feel! If she'd
only admitted once she didn't believe any more in her pipe dream
that some day I'd behave! But she never would. It was the
same old story, over and over, for years and years. It kept piling
up, inside her and inside me. God, can you picture all I made her
suffer, and all the guilt she made me feel, and how I hated myself! If she only hadn't been so damned good—if she'd been the
same kind of wife I was a husband. God, I used to pray sometimes she'd— I'd even say to her, "Go on, why don't you,
Evelyn? It'd serve me right. I wouldn't mind. I'd forgive
you." Of course, I'd pretend I was kidding—the same way I
used to joke here about her being in the hay with the iceman.
She'd have been so hurt if I'd said it seriously. She'd have
thought I'd stopped loving her. (*He pauses—then looking
around at them.*) I suppose you think I'm a liar, that no woman
could have stood all she stood and still loved me so much. Well,
I'm not lying, and if you'd ever seen her, you'd realize I wasn't.
It was written all over her face, sweetness and love and pity and
forgiveness. (*He reaches mechanically for the inside pocket of
his coat.*) Wait! I'll show you. I always carry her picture.
(*Suddenly he looks startled. He stares before him, his hand falling back—quietly.*) No, I'm forgetting I tore it up—afterwards.
I didn't need it any more. (*He pauses. The silence is like that
in the room of a dying man where people hold their breath, waiting for him to die.*)

   CORA (*with a muffled sob*)—Jees, Hickey! Jees! (*She shiv-
ers and puts her hands over her face.*)

   PARRITT (*to* LARRY *in a low insistent tone*)—I burnt up Mother's picture, Larry. Her eyes followed me all the time. They
seemed to be wishing I was dead!

HICKEY—It kept piling up, like I've said. I got so I thought of it all the time. I hated myself more and more. I got so I'd curse myself for a lousy bastard every time I saw myself in the mirror. I felt such pity for her it drove me crazy. It got so every night I'd wind up hiding my face in her lap, bawling and begging her forgiveness. And, of course, she'd always comfort me and say, "Never mind, Teddy, I know you won't ever again." Christ, I loved her so, but I began to hate that pipe dream! I began to be afraid I was going bughouse, because sometimes I couldn't forgive her for forgiving me. I even caught myself hating her for making me hate myself so much. There's a limit to the guilt you can feel and the forgiveness and the pity you can take! You have to begin blaming someone else, too. I got so sometimes when she'd kiss me it was like she did it on purpose to humiliate me, as if she'd spit in my face! But all the time I saw how crazy and rotten of me that was, and it made me hate myself all the more. You'd never believe I could hate so much, a goodnatured, happy-go-lucky slob like me. And as the time got nearer when I was due to come here for my drunk around Harry's birthday, I got nearly crazy. I kept swearing to her every night that this time I really wouldn't, until I'd made it a real final test to myself—and to her. And she kept encouraging me and saying, "I can see you really mean it now, Teddy. I know you'll conquer it this time, and we'll be so happy, dear." When she'd say that and kiss me, I'd believe it, too. Then she'd go to bed, and I'd stay up alone because I couldn't sleep. I'd get so damned lonely. I'd get thinking how peaceful it was here, sitting around with the old gang, getting drunk and forgetting love, joking and laughing and singing and swapping lies. And finally I knew I'd have to come. And I knew if I came this time, it was the finish. I'd never have the guts to go back and be forgiven again, and that would break Evelyn's heart because to her it would mean I didn't love her any more. (*He pauses.*) That last night I'd driven myself crazy trying to figure some way out for her. I went in the bedroom. I was going to tell her it was the end. But I couldn't do that to her. She was sound asleep. I thought, God, if she'd only never wake up, she'd never know! And then it came to me—the only possible way out, for her sake. I remembered I'd given her a gun for protection while I was away and it was in the bureau drawer. She'd never feel any pain, never wake up from her dream. So I—

HOPE (*tries to ward this off by pounding with his glass on the table—with brutal, callous exasperation*)—For the love of Christ, give us a rest! Who the hell cares? We want to pass out in peace! (*They all, except* PARRITT *and* LARRY, *pound with their glasses and grumble in chorus:* "*Who the hell cares? We want to pass out in peace!*" MORAN, *the detective, moves quietly from the entrance in the curtain across the back of the room to the table where his companion,* LIEB, *is sitting.* ROCKY *notices his leaving and gets up from the table in the rear and goes back to stand and watch in the entrance.* MORAN *exchanges a glance with* LIEB, *motioning him to get up. The latter does so. No one notices them. The clamor of banging glasses dies out as abruptly as it started.* HICKEY *hasn't appeared to hear it.*)

HICKEY (*simply*)—So I killed her. (*There is a moment of dead silence. Even the detectives are caught in it and stand motionless.*)

This confession, so long in coming, produces an exhausted relief in Parritt. "I may as well confess, Larry," he says. "There's no use lying any more. You know anyway. I didn't give a damn about the money. It was because I hated her."

Oblivious to the interruption, Hickey goes on. "And then I saw that was the only possible way to give her peace and free her from the misery of loving me. I saw it meant peace for me, too, knowing she was at peace. I felt as though a ton of guilt was lifted off my mind. I remember I stood by the bed and suddenly I had to laugh. . . . I remember I heard myself speaking to her, as if it was something I'd always wanted to say: 'Well, you know what you can do with your pipe dream now, you damned bitch!' "

With a horrified start, as if shocked out of a nightmare, Hickey stammers a denial of what he has just said. "I couldn't have said that! If I did I'd gone insane! You've known me longer than anyone, Harry. You know I must have been insane, don't you, Governor?"

Harry Hope's first reaction is to utter a "Who the hell cares?" Then his face lights up, as if he were grasping some dawning hope in his mind. "Insane? You mean—you were really insane?"

"Yes, or I couldn't have laughed." The two detectives move in.

"That's enough, Hickman," grates Detective Moran. "You know who we are. You're under arrest." Hickey is handcuffed. Pleadingly, Hickman addresses Harry Hope:

"You know I couldn't say that to Evelyn, don't you, Harry—unless—"

Hope grasps eagerly at the answer. "And you've been crazy

ever since? Everything you've said and done here—"

"Yes, Harry, of course, I've been out of my mind ever since! All the time I've been here! You saw I was insane, didn't you?"

The officers move the protesting Hickey out. The first to speak is Harry Hope. "Poor crazy son of a bitch!" He reaches for a drink, and the others follow suit.

"May the Chair bring him peace at last, the poor tortured bastard," whispers Larry.

"Yes," says Parritt, in a strange insistent voice, "but he isn't the only one who needs peace. He's lucky. It's all decided for him. I wish it was decided for me." Parritt is off again on his one subject—his mother and his sense of guilt about her. Following Hickey's lead in confessing, the boy exclaims, "And I'm not putting up any bluff, either, that I was crazy afterwards when I laughed to myself and thought, 'You know what you can do with your freedom pipe dream now, don't you, you damned old whore!'"

Larry's face is convulsed with detestation and his voice has a condemning command in it: "Go! Get the hell out of life, God damn you, before I choke it out of you! Go up—"

Parritt seems suddenly at peace with himself. Simply and gratefully he says, "Thanks, Larry. I just wanted to be sure." He walks to the door and out with a careless swagger, and Larry waits from now on, listening for the sound he knows will be coming from the back yard outside the window—listening but trying not to listen in an agony of horror.

Old Hugo sounds the keynote—the requiem for Hickey. "I'm glad they take that crazy Hickey avay to asylum—I think I have a trink now."

They all have a drink now. Harry Hope, jubilant, feels the kick of the liquor he has consumed. "It was Hickey kept it from—I know that sounds crazy, but *he* was crazy, and he'd got all of us as bughouse as he was. Bejeeses, it does queer things to you, having to listen day and night to a lunatic's pipe dreams—pretending you believe them, to kid him along and doing any crazy thing he wants to humor him. It's dangerous, too. Look at me pretending to start for a walk just to keep him quiet. I knew damned well it wasn't the right day for it. The sun was broiling and the streets full of automobiles. Bejeeses, I could feel myself getting sunstroke and an automobile damn near ran over me. Ask Rocky."

Tipsily but earnestly Rocky agrees about the automobile. "I thought yuh was a goner," he confirms.

Hope, cackling laughter, is getting drunk and glad of it. Drinks, he advises, are on the house—and all begin to get drunk as rapidly as possible. Larry, however, still is listening.

"Christ! Why don't he—?"

Cora and Chuck are happy that their nonsense about getting married is over with—they ain't even picked out a farm yet! Jimmy Tomorrow has figured Hickey out: Hickey's talk about tomorrow was the fixed idea of the insane. Willie, Lewis and the others are once more content—but still Larry is waiting, listening.

"God damn his yellow soul, if he doesn't soon I'll go up and throw him off!" He has half risen from his chair when from outside the window there comes the noise of something hurtling down. Larry drops back, hiding face in hands. Harry Hope wonders what the noise was. "Aw, nuttin'," reassures Rocky. "Something fell off de fire escape."

But Larry knows. "Poor devil! God rest his soul in peace." Then in self-derision, he continues, "Ah, the damned pity—the wrong kind, as Hickey said! Be God, there's no hope! I'll never be a success in the grandstand—or anywhere else! Life is too much for me! I'll be a weak fool looking with pity at the two sides of everything till the day I die! . . . May that day come soon!"

Startled at himself, surprised, Larry grins sardonically and concludes, "Be God, I'm the only real convert to death Hickey made here. From the bottom of my coward's heart I mean that now!" He moves to the hall door and goes out.

Hope calls effusively—but with no answer—for Larry to come back and get paralyzed. Personally, Harry Hope is oreyeyed and he wants to sing. They all sing, happily and drunkenly.

THE CURTAIN FALLS

JOAN OF LORRAINE

A Drama in Prologue, Two Acts and Epilogue

By Maxwell Anderson

ON her flight from Stockholm, Sweden, to Hollywood, California, Ingrid Bergman paused briefly in New York to play opposite Burgess Meredith in a revival of Ferenc Molnar's "Liliom." That was in 1940. Miss Bergman was politely impressed by New York, including its frequently changing skyline, and was pleasantly received by its drama critics. Following the engagement of "Liliom," which continued for a total of 56 performances, she continued on her way west.

A more pronounced success was there awaiting her as a motion picture actress, in the technique of which she had been well-trained in her native Sweden. Within a few years she became an outstanding favorite of the country's cinema enthusiasts, a winner of Academy awards and a virtual, though modest, dictator of her own terms so far as monetary rewards were concerned. Then, quite naturally, her thought turned again to the legitimate stage and she kept an eye open for the proper role, meaning naturally such a role as would inspire her enthusiasm.

It was in 1944 that Maxwell Anderson, having completed the script of "Joan of Lorraine," decided that, if he could induce her to leave her picture commitments, Miss Bergman was the very actress he would like to have play his heroine. He made a trip to Hollywood just to talk with her about it. He left a manuscript with her. All her life, the actress told him, she had wanted to play Joan the Maid, and she thought this was the appointed time.

However, she had agreed to make a tour of soldier camps in Germany the summer after V-Day, and did. But she took with her the Anderson script and, as a part of her program, read scenes from the play to the soldiers, filling in the interludes and connecting descriptions of scenes.

"It wasn't very good," she afterward told Helen Ormsbee of the New York *Herald Tribune*, "but the soldiers were the kindest audiences. They liked it. I told them always, 'This is from Maxwell Anderson's play that I am going to do sometime. Don't

forget!' It was like those 'trailers' on the screen in movie theatres, showing what is coming. I called that talk my 'trailer.'
Well, ex-soldiers come here now and remind me of what I said."

There has been considerable discussion of the unique form in
which Mr. Anderson has set his study of Joan. His play is
actually the presentation of a rehearsal of a play having to do
with the life of Joan of Arc, in which the actress playing Joan
disagrees frequently with the director about changes the supposed author of the script has insisted upon inserting.

It was feared by some who had read the script that this form
would prove destructive of audience illusion. To the contrary it
came, as Brooks Atkinson wrote in the New York *Times*, "as
further proof of the fact that sincere and earnest plays which
do not depend upon the physical illusion of scenery and costumes
can be remarkably exhilarating. When the occasion is sufficiently genuine, theatre as make-believe is infinitely more evoca-
tive than theatre as realism."

"Joan of Lorraine" reached New York by way of Washington
in mid-November. In Washington both Mr. Anderson and Miss
Bergman challenged the right of the directors of the National
Theatre, in which they played, to bar the attendance of Negroes.
The controversy flared feverishly for days, but was finally re-
solved temporarily in the theatre's favor and the fulfillment of
existing contracts.

We approach the Anderson drama by way of a prologue. The
curtain rises on what is practically an empty stage, though there
is an assortment of chairs and tables scattered about, some to
indicate certain set pieces of scenery for rehearsal purposes. A
chair and a stool represent a fireplace, for example, and two
chairs, set back to back, stand for a doorway.

The stage manager and his assistant, a girl, are sitting at a
small battered table, the script of the play before them. Jimmy
Masters, who is directing the play, is pacing restlessly up and
down, a slouch hat pulled over his eyes against the lights. There
are small groups of actors scattered about the stage, most of
them in nondescript rehearsal clothes. They are waiting for the
rehearsal to start. There is some trouble about the lights. The
stage lights are too bright, but, if the overhead electric lights
are to be turned on, that means an electrician will have to be
hired. Union rules. Okay. Let the electrician be hired—

"We've got twenty-seven backers for this play," snaps Masters, "and they can all go broke before I use a rehearsal light

for a run-through. Are we set up for the first scene, Al?"

"I think we've got everything indicated," reports Al, the stage manager. "This is the fireplace, this is the spinning wheel, this is the outside door. The table is smaller than the one we're going to use, and there won't be room for props. No dishes, for one thing."

"We'll work out the business with the food later. Does everybody know the schedule for today? . . . I'll say it again, just in case someone didn't hear. Listen, folks. We'll begin at the beginning and go straight through, so don't wander away. You'll have to watch your own cues."

The actors move toward their places in the scene, or into the wings offstage, if they are not a part of it.

Mary Grey, leading lady of the troupe, wanders in. She is a quiet, modest little lady with a cheery greeting for Masters. They have evidently been quarreling about certain aspects of this play they are rehearsing, but Mary has forgotten that for the moment. She remembers they are to have lunch together. Perhaps they can continue the quarrel then. She still thinks Masters is completely wrong—but for the present she will go on playing everything the way he wants it—"and, little by little," she adds slyly, "you'll discover that I was right."

"Or that I was," counters Masters. "It's possible!"

Jimmy Masters is a director with convictions. And with theories. So much is made plain when, a moment later, he is explaining to the cast that, personally, he does not believe a play, any play, should be taken too seriously in rehearsal—

"My notion is that the more you kid the play and the actors and everybody concerned the better it is for all of us. If there's anything or anybody that won't stand kidding, now's the time to find it out. . . . We've been running along that way for nearly three weeks, one big brainless family, no holds barred, letting ourselves go and sort of lapsing into our parts. And the method works. Even when we know what's going on it works. We're getting the feeling of this thing. But that's all preparation. What we're all waiting for and working toward is the miracle—the miracle that has to happen with every play that's going to go. Some day we'll start cold as usual, just reading lines, and then that holy fire'll begin to play around one actor—and then another—and then around the whole scene—and then the spirit'll descend on all of us at once—and we'll make a new world about the size of a star and set it down on a bare stage, surrounded by kitchen chairs and mockery and bungling mechanics and directors. And afterward maybe we'll never hit anything as good as that again, but we'll get an echo of it, as much as we can recall—and we'll put that echo into costumes and sets and polish it up, and what the first night audience will be in on."

There are other Masters theories. One is that all the good play-wrights are dead—but if he can't have a dead playwright he'll settle for an absent one. And another is that if an actor is going to be good in a play he must understand it. Let him illustrate—

"When Joan was nineteen years old, after she'd crowned her king and saved France, she was captured by her enemies and put on trial for her life. And they asked her the toughest question ever put to the human race. Why do you believe what you be-lieve? Remember that? It's in the second act. . . . That's right. That's the question we all have to answer. And that's the big scene in anybody's life, when he has to answer that question." . . . "Let's get going."

"Places, please," calls Al. "Act one, scene one! . . . Curtain going up!"

JOAN IN HER HOME

The play begins. Or, at least, this serious rehearsal of the play begins. The scene is the home of Jacques D'Arc. He is head man of the village and he is worried. "Every year the English and the Burgundians draw closer," he is repeating to Isabelle, his wife, "till now they're at our own doorstep, and there's nothing left of France but a little patch, without even a king. And it's not a war now, only bands of robbers riding up and down, taking purses from the rich and food from the poor—caring nothing for which side you're on, or which side they're on. What will it be like for our children—and what must our children think of it, looking out on all of this? It would be small wonder if a child went a little bad."

Cousin Durand Laxart is calling on the D'Arcs. It has been some time since he has been there. There had been a misunder-standing. Durand would like to explain. It was when Jeannette had come to the Laxart home in the Spring and had insisted that her uncle take her with him when he went to buy seed in Vau-couleurs. Then in Vaucouleurs Jeannette had urged that he take her to see the Lord of Beaudricourt "because she had a message for the Dauphin that must be delivered." Durand had protested at first, but finally agreed, remembering all the time that there had been a prophecy that a virgin out of Lorraine should come to the aid of France.

Robert de Baudricourt had received Jeannette, and had listened to her. But after he had listened he had laughed at her and told Durand Laxart to take her home. Durand hopes now that Jacques will understand why he had done what he had done.

Jacques is still firm, but Isabelle D'Arc understands, and she feels that now Durand should be told of the secret they have been keeping to themselves. Two years before, she relates, Jacques had had a dream about soldiers raiding their village. In the dream their daughter Jeannette had of her own will gone away with the soldiers on one side. At first they had thought nothing of it, Jeannette being the good and gentle girl she was, but after the dream had persistently repeated itself Jacques had spoken to Jeannette about it. She had gone very white as she listened and finally she had confessed that there might be truth in such a dream as that—

"And when we asked more about it she said yes, it was true that she was to lead an army. Afterward she said many things like that, but it was only the talk of a child, so we still thought nothing of it. Not till she went with you to Vaucouleurs. Then we began to be afraid that our girl was a little mad—and it seemed that you had encouraged her in her madness."

Jacques is very excited. "I told her that I would drown her in the River Meuse before such a thing should happen! With my own hands!" he bursts out.

But Isabelle is not excited. She thinks Jacques should now forgive Durand. A moment later, when the D'Arc children, Jeannette, Jean and Pierre, have come from the sheep cote, the reconciliation is effected. Her Uncle Durand has come, Jacques explains to Jeannette, hoping to be forgiven for his part in taking her to Vaucouleurs and to the Lord of Baudricourt. He would like her to go home with him for a visit. She can go if she will promise that there will be no more Vaucouleurs foolishness.

Jeannette is contrite. She never expects to go to Vaucouleurs again. With that promise Jacques is content to take Durand's hand and forget the incident. Thus the scene ends.

SHE FINDS A WAY TO SPEAK

While Al is rearranging the furniture to represent a scene in the sheep cote that is to follow, Masters thinks they can try out Joan's celestial voices—

"It's all right to say that Joan heard voices, but to show Joan on the stage listening to those voices—and to let the audience hear them—that will take some doing," admits Jimmy. "It's all got to be just right, or it'll be all wrong."

He calls the players who are to represent the Voices and stations them in the wings, while he goes from the stage to the auditorium to listen. "Try to keep that radio-announcer gravy out of your voice," he advises Quirke, one of the Voices; "that haliveroil with viosterol they spread on the commercials."

Quirke tries, but his reading is still on the sonorous side. " 'Jeannette! Daughter of God, child of France!' " he reads.

"My God, it's the cascara program," explodes Masters. "No, no! Say it, man, just say it in your own natural tone—don't try to sound like an archangel. The radio's cluttered with archangels and Gabriels. Just talk like yourself."

" 'And when these things are finished let nothing deter you,' " reads Miss Reeves as the second of the Voices; " 'for you must crown the Dauphin at Rheims.' "

"Look up that pronunciation, will you, Al? . . . Look up all those pronunciations . . ." advises the director.

The interlude is ended and the second scene is called.

It is in the sheep cote, after Joan has ministered to an ailing lambkin and turned to her prayers. She again hears the Voices. At first they are inclined to take her to task—

"We have spoken to you many times," comes the Voice of St. Catherine. "It's more than four years since you first heard the Voice in your garden. But you have not yet begun what you must do. And this year will soon be gone."

"I know. I think of it."

"You must go again to Robert de Baudricourt, and he will give you escort to the Dauphin." It is St. Margaret who is speaking now. "You must leave Lorraine and ride out into France. You must warn the Dauphin not to despair, for a change will come over the war when you are with him. You will rescue France from the English and crown the Dauphin at Rheims. You are the one prophesied."

"Robert de Baudricourt only laughed."

"He will not laugh at you again."

"I have not even a way to go to Vaucouleurs.—And when I speak to de Baudricourt I blush and forget what I must tell him."

"As to the way to Vaucouleurs, your Uncle Durand will take you."

"Will he quarrel with my father again?"

"He will take you.—And as for your speech with Baudricourt— think carefully what you have to say, for you will see him soon."

"I have all the words in my mind, but when the time comes—"

"Think carefully what you will say, for you will see him soon."

"I will do everything, but tell me, please tell me how to begin.
(*The light begins to fade.*) Don't go without telling me that. I
am only a girl. I know nothing of arms or horsemanship or the
speech of kings and high places. How can I find my way to these
things alone?"

The lights have disappeared and Joan is near to tears when her
brothers, Jean and Pierre, find her. That she has been praying
again they are convinced, and that isn't good. They had heard
their father tell Uncle Durand that she prayed too much and had
become too pious and maybe a little crazy—enough to think perhaps she was the maid from Lorraine that was to save the King.

"I don't know how a virgin from Lorraine, or anywhere, could
go to war and give orders and save France," admits Joan, voicing
her own doubt. "How would a girl from the country know how
to speak in camps or courts? How would she make her way to
the Dauphin? How would she address him? How would she
address her enemies when they appeared before the walls and she
must give a challenge or a reply? If she had grown up in Orleans,
among royalty and courtiers, she might do something with the help
of God. But a maid, here among the border farms, living as we
live—"

No girl could do it, brother Jean is convinced, but a boy might.
A boy would know how to speak to courtiers and soldiers. To
prove it, Jean gives them a sample of the way he would speak up
to the baby King of England, and to the Duke of Bethfort, who
calls himself regent, and the rest of them. It is quite an impressive
performance and Joan listens intently. But Pierre only laughs.

"I am a laborer and a farmer," concludes Jean, forcefully, facing his audience and using his pitchfork as an imaginary pike. "I
don't know A from B in your fine books! But when you are all
dead and cut up into sausage and we have thrown you into the
fosse, it won't matter where I came from, you Duke of Bethfort
and your baby King! Forward, my friends! Keep good heart!
They are frightened! They are falling of themselves! Strike
them when they fall! God with us!"

Now that he has his fork, Pierre thinks Jean might as well come
with him and finish the stable.

"Don't you think I'm good, Jeannette?" pleads Jean.

"You almost make me believe a boy could do it. Or a man,"
muses Joan. And after the boys have left her she stops to look

again at the lamb. Now she has knelt beside it and is speaking
to it—

"Oh, ramkin, ramkin, if I could speak large and round like a
boy, and could stand that way and make my words sound out like
a trumpet,—if I could do that I could do all the things God wants
me to do. But I'm a girl, and my voice is a girl's voice, and my
ways are a girl's ways. If only I were a man! If only I could
shout like a man! But that wouldn't help either, for it wouldn't
fit with the prophecy. (*She stands slowly and walks to where*
JEAN *had stood. She puts a hand on her hip.*) It will be ridiculous, it will sound foolish, but in the name of God I must try it.
(*She speaks in imitation of* JEAN.) You, you baby King of England, here without warrant from God, and you, Duke of Bethfort,
who call yourself regent, go home, go back to your own country.
(*She pauses.*) It's worse than I thought. It sounds wrong for a
girl to say it. And yet it's a way. It's the only way I see. I must
try it, and try it, and try again. (*She takes her stance.*) Sir
Robert de Baudricourt, I am the maid of Lorraine, the one prophesied, and I come to you because I have a message from God for
our Dauphin who should be king. (*She pauses.*) Yes. Yes.
When I have done it many times it may cease to be strange—and
come easily. God help me, it's a kind of play-acting, a thing forbidden, yet if it's the only way it must be God's way. (*She takes
her stance again.*) My Dauphin, my King, I have come to you
with messages from the King of Heaven. It is His will that you
reign in France as His regent—and that Bethfort and the English
be utterly defeated at my hands. And for your private ear I have
more to tell you, a revelation from St. Margaret that will gladden
your heart."

When Durand Laxart approaches the sheep cote, he finds Joan
with her head bowed in thought. He has come, he tells her, to
say farewell and tell her that her father is agreed that she can
come to them in December, when they are expecting a new babe
at their house. But December, Jeannette insists, will be too late.
She must go with him now—

"You are only a poor peasant, Durand Laxart, and I am only a
poor maiden from Lorraine, yet it is given to us two to be the first
to know that Orleans will be rescued, that the armies of the English will be defeated and that France will rise again and be free.
We must take this news to men far greater than any we have ever
seen. We must stand before courts and speak to kings. If you
accept this your name will be coupled with mine and never forgotten. If you refuse me your name and the name of France will

be forgotten together. For I can't go alone. It is God who calls on us both."

For a time Durand Laxart hesitates, but Joan's tone and her prophecy are convincing.

"God help me if I should do wrong," he murmurs. "Your father is a hard man."

"When I have saved France we shall both be forgiven. That I know," promises Joan. Nor will she wait to get her things from the house or to say good-by. "God gives me only one year of victory," she explains. "It must not be wasted. Even an hour. Come!"

"Curtain!" calls the stage manager, as Joan and Durand leave the stage.

Masters is well pleased with his actors for the way they played the last scene. It may be that Cordwell (who is personally convinced that as Jean D'Arc he "stank") was a bit broad in the Duke of Bethfort scene, but that will have to be proved by audience contact—

"Anyway," insists Masters, "it's not bad to hit that Duke of Bethfort stuff pretty hard. Joan has to have something to imitate. You see, she's always been shown on the stage as a sort of Tom Paine in petticoats, a rough, mannish hoyden, with visual delusions, strong common sense, and a rather homo predilection for soldiers' clothes and manners. Even Shaw follows that line, but it doesn't seem to be historically accurate. As far as the evidence goes she was a modest and unassuming village girl who never would have raised her voice anywhere if she hadn't been convinced that she was carrying out God's orders. And if she was this kind of girl, and completely feminine, then her problem was how to make herself heard, how to get her message out to the world. Well, she could have picked up an idea from her brothers as well as not, and we're supposing she did. Her own letters to the English are in this same mock-heroic style—and so I don't think you're far off the way you're doing it now."

There is an interruption from the office. Trouble about the theatre lease. Trouble about the costumes. They're arriving in sections. All right—let the actors wear the sections. Masters wants to see them. Trouble, too, about Mary's getting a chance to explain to Jimmy her objections to the things that are happening to the play in the rewriting the author has been doing—and Jimmy has said that this is the last day they can discuss major revisions in the script—

"I don't like to bring things up this way," Mary admits, "in the middle of rehearsals—"

"Don't waste time apologizing—"

MARY—All right. Well, when I first read the play it was just the story of how Joan was told by her saints what she must do, and how she went out into the world and did her work and was tried by her enemies and executed—

MASTERS—Yes.

MARY—But now it's the story of how she was told by her saints what she must do, and how she finds that she must compromise with the world, and even work with evil men, and allow evil to be done, before she can accomplish her task. I'm sorry. I say it so badly—

MASTERS—No, you say it very well.

MARY—But it seems to me the way the play is now it means that we all have to compromise and work with evil men—and that if you have faith it will come to nothing unless you get some of the forces of evil on your side.

MASTERS—That's right. I don't think I'd call them the forces of evil—but you have to get some of the people who are running things on your side—and they're pretty doubtful characters mostly.

MARY—But is that what we want to say, in a play about Joan of Arc?

MASTERS—It's what I'd like to hear said. And of course you knew there was to be some re-writing. We both knew it.

MARY—But to change what the whole play says—

MASTERS—Changing one word can change what a play says—

MARY—But it's a mistake, Jimmy. It's like a desecration of Joan to treat her that way. We were talking about it last night—

MASTERS—Who?

MARY—Some of the cast. We were having dinner and trying to think what was wrong—

MASTERS—Actors should just have dinner, Mary—they shouldn't try to think.

MARY—But they have to think or they can't act!

MASTERS—Yes, I guess I did say that. Al, right after this next scene, I want everybody on stage. The whole cast.

AL—Yes, sir.

MASTERS—Clear for one-three now.

AL—Yes, sir. Clear the stage for thirteen, please, Mr. Sheppard!

MARY—Must we have them all in on this?

MASTERS—I think they should all hear it.
MARY—All right.

Again the stage is cleared of all actors except those in the action, and the third scene is played.

A POET AT THE COURT OF THE DAUPHIN

Joan, who has donned boy's clothes for the journey, is on her way to the Court of the Dauphin at Chinon. She is accompanied by Jean de Metz and Bertrand de Poulency, and they have just arrived outside the walls of Chinon. Joan would continue into the city, but De Metz protests—

"We've traveled three hundred and fifty miles across France in the worst end of a bad winter, and we've slept on more cold ground than beds, and we've eaten on an average of once a day—and not well—we've run away from Burgundians three times, and now we've arrived—those are the towers of Chinon sticking up over the walls there in the sunset—and we've had no food today, we haven't been off our horses since noon; and you don't want to stop to eat."

"We could eat in Chinon."

"No, Jeannette. I give you my word we can't. Men and horses must pause occasionally. You may be made of metal, but we're not. We can enter Chinon in the morning."

Alain Chartier, a fairly imposing person, has arisen from a resting place alongside the road and faced the group. They would question him as regards their chances of entering Chinon. Chartier is discouraging. Even if they could get within the walls, they would find neither food nor a place to rest. These have all been taken by citizens who have spent the day awaiting the coming of the virgin from Lorraine. It is the same along every road leading to Chinon. Just now, at dinner time, the crowds have given up waiting and stormed the city for food.

Chartier, too, is awaiting the coming of the Maid—but in a special way. He has been sent by the Dauphin to act as a sort of guide and friend, and smuggle the girl in a back entrance. Danger? Well, there is some danger that the Maid might be torn apart by a loving mob. Does Chartier bring a sign from the Dauphin? He has a paper bearing the Dauphin's seal—

"I am Alain Chartier, a poet and hanger-on at the court of the illustrious Charles." Chartier has swept off his hat and is kneeling at the feet of Joan. "He bids me greet the Maid fairly and give her welcome."

"Did he say you were to kneel to me?"

"No."

"I'd rather nobody knelt to me."

"Then nobody will, I assure you." Chartier has arisen and is dusting his knee. "It's not a position one chooses for comfort. Before we proceed further will you tell me why you wish to see the Dauphin, and upon whose authority you come."

"I bring messages of hope and reassurance for the Dauphin from the Lord of Heaven, and if it be God's will I hope I may see him soon, for the time is short."

"His time?"

"No, mine. I have only a little time, so little that I cannot waste nights or days or half-hours. I should be in Chinon to-night."

"Then you will be. . . ."

It is best, agrees Chartier, that they send for their horses and proceed at once. But before they can get away he must continue his supercilious investigation of them and their mission. Some-one among them is a master of strategy. Chartier is willing to concede that; someone is possessed of brains and uses them. "In the history of France I remember no name built up with such suddenness, no enthusiasm so wide-spread, no career advanced under such favorable auspices." But as for this virgin of Lorraine business—they don't have to keep up appearances with him. What is it they want? Also, what are their domestic arrangements? Who sleeps with whom? "For convenience' sake let's get such matters out of the way at once."

"Sir, on the way here, since we had a little money, and traveled through much Burgundian country where we dared not enter the inns, we slept mostly in the open fields. We lay down all three together, the maid between us for warmth and protection, and one blanket above." There is a threat of mounting anger in Poulengy's tone.

"A menage a trois?"

"Sir, if you mean anything against the Maid or doubt our respect for her, I advise you to watch what you say. Jean de Metz here is quick with his hands and hasty of temper, and so is Bertrand Poulengy—that's myself."

As for Joan, she is now convinced that they can do without the services of this Alain Chartier. She cannot believe that he represents the Dauphin. "The Dauphin is a good and honest man, and worthy to be king."

Chartier is quickly put in his place and is deeply puzzled. Can it be that these three simple farm people are real? That the Maid's vision is sincere? If so he would help them. Let them take such money as there is in his purse and turn back to where they came from. This Maid from the frontiers does not deserve what will happen to her in Chinon—

"There is nothing in that court but evil," declares Chartier. "A weak ruler draws evil to him as a dead dog draws buzzards. There's nobody left around Charles save the dead, the dying and the vultures. He's lost nearly all his kingdom, and what's left he's selling, acre by acre, to pay for his cheap little pleasures. . . . They say you have promised to set a crown on Charles' head and raise the siege of Orleans for him— Let me tell you about his crown and his kingdom—a kitchen history of France—while they finish watering the horses. Charles' mother Isabeau says he's a bastard and therefore has no claim on the throne of France. She states this formally in a treaty, and the history of her amours goes far to confirm what she says. So far as I can tell Charles cares very little whether he is a bastard or not, or who governs France— the French, the English, or the Burgundians—so long as he keeps his silly little court together and has the women he wants and enough money to stave off the tradesmen." . . . "There's no honor or decency left around him. None of any kind—in government, or religion—or the arts. Nothing but carrion flesh and the big black birds pulling at it."

"Why would Charles send out to greet me if this were true?" Joan would know.

"You have caused a great stir. With you he might raise an army and frighten Burgundy enough to get some money out of him."

JOAN—If there is an army raised I will stand at the head of it, and the towns of Burgundy will not only be threatened—they will be taken—and when once I have taken them they will not change hands again—

CHARTIER—They will be sold back before the capitulation is signed.

JOAN—It may be that the Dauphin has lost faith in himself and in the kingdom of France. I shall bring his faith back to him, messire, and, with the help of God, I shall bring all France back to him. Behind me, Alain Chartier, in all the towns I have passed

through, men and women are talking of the rescue that I bring to
France. Wherever I have been seen the Burgundians are not safe,
and they know it. Wherever I have slept on the ground a whisper
has gone out among the folk, and the men-at-arms go over to the
Dauphin who is to be king. It is not my doing. I am a poor maid,
and all I have is that I am chosen of God. That is all I have but
it is all that anyone needs, and it will be enough. You see these
two men with me. They were only soldiers. They had no faith—
but now they have. And all of France will have faith. Take me
to the Dauphin who is to be our king.

DE METZ—The horses are ready.

CHARTIER—By God—

JOAN—And do not swear. I will have no swearing in my presence.

CHARTIER—Before God, then—you are neither charlatan nor
fool.

JOAN—As for the first I can't answer, for I don't know what
your word means. If I am a fool, God at least has not held it
against me.

CHARTIER—Maybe I'm the fool—for there's either a brightness
on your face or something that dazzles my eyes. I begin to believe—yes, if there were help possible for France—you might
bring it. If somebody else were Dauphin—I—or Dunois—anybody—there might be some hope. But there's nothing in the man.
He's empty. And if you don't succeed where you're going—then,
girl, you're not likely to live very long afterward.

JOAN—I know very well that I'm to die.

CHARTIER—You know it?

JOAN—But not before I bring hope back to France. Not until
I've taught her how to win.

CHARTIER—I would never have thought it possible, but I begin
to believe—to believe—God knows— You bring even my wry
half-faith back to me.

JOAN—If you are a man of France you shall have your faith
back whole; for all France is to be ours before we are done.

CHARTIER—You know, I've never knelt to a woman for any
reason except that it was the proper thing to do, but I have a
strange desire to kneel to you and kiss your hand—because of
what you have said—(*He kneels.*)—because—well, because there
was mockery in my first greeting—and I'd like to wipe that out.

JOAN (*taking her hand away*)—I'm dirty and weary from long
traveling, and we have no time for these tricks you play at court.
Take me to the Dauphin.

CHARTIER—And may I see his face when he first talks with you?
AL—Curtain.

It is in the third interlude that Mary has a chance to speak her
mind regarding what has been happening to the play they are
rehearsing since the author began to rewrite it. Jimmy Masters
has assembled the entire company on the stage, Voices and all,
that they may hear what is troubling their unhappy star. Mary
has talked with several of them before, and, though she feels that
Masters is now deliberately putting her on the spot, she is quite
willing to restate her convictions. As for that, Masters has his
own explanation—

"We have to discuss this now or not at all," explains Jimmy,
"and the whole company ought to hear it. . . . And if the script's
to be changed, we have to know it today. Tomorrow's just one
day too late."

MARY—All right. I'll say what I said last night—I have always
wanted to play Joan. I have studied her and read about her all
my life. She has a meaning for me— She means that the great
things in this world are all brought about by faith—that all the
leaders who count are dreamers and people who see visions. The
realists and common-sense people can never begin anything. They
can only do what the visionaries plan for them. The scientists can
never lead unless they happen to be dreamers, too.

MASTERS—I go right along in that, Mary. Everybody lives by
faith and dreams. Everybody follows a gleam of some sort, and
nobody can prove his gleam isn't ignis fatuus.

MARY—But I had another reason for wanting to do this play
now. Joan's life means to me—that if you die in a great cause—
for something you believe so deeply you're willing to die for it—
then you're not lost—your sacrifice is not lost—and the world can
be better and different because of your dying.—I guess we all lost
somebody in the war—somebody near to us that we won't see
again. I did. And I wanted to do this play because it could
mean—he's not dead—none of them are dead who gave their lives
for the world we believe in. They saved that world for us—and
kept it for us. They are more alive than we are, for we shall
never change the world much—but they did—

MASTERS—Yes.

MARY—You say yes, but you don't mean yes, because the way
the play's being rewritten it's in favor of compromise and getting
along as well as you can with what you have. You said yesterday

that no faith will bear critical inspection—

MASTERS—Yes, I did say that—

MARY—And I don't believe it!   I don't believe that Joan died in vain, or that those who died in the war died in vain!

MASTERS—No—I don't either.

MARY—But doesn't the play mean that now—doesn't the coronation scene mean that, when she discovers that the Dauphin is dishonest and a fraud and allows him to be crowned anyway.

MASTERS—No. It means just the opposite.

MARY—I wish you'd tell me how.

MASTERS—Mary, dear, the world is run by money-changers and bargainers.   Sometimes a saint or a prophet comes along and gets so much influence with the people that the bargainers and politicians have to pay some attention.   But they don't quit running the earth on that account.   They just shift their bargains enough so that the public conscience is satisfied, and get rid of the saint as fast as they can.   Once in a long while there's a saint who's a bargainer also, like Lincoln or Roosevelt, and he plays ball with crooks and works for the common good at the same time.   But nearly always the crooks are in control and the people and the men of good-will are on the outside with no power except for the fact that they can tip over the whole machine if they don't like the way things are going.

MARY—But what has that got to do with Joan?

MASTERS—Only this—that the bargainers were running the earth when she was alive—and they're running the earth now. And she had to decide whether she'd stay with that small-time crook of a king and try to make him act for the people occasionally or leave him, just as we have to decide whether we'll keep an eye on the United Nations or give up and look the other way. Right now the crooks are bargaining over who's going to own the earth—they're doing it in Paris and at Hunter College and wherever two or three politicians get together—and a lot of people look at those politicians, dividing up empires, and say, "What's the use?   We fought the war to stay free, and a lot of men died, and the brigands are quarreling over the loot again!   It's no use." And they get cynical and give up.   And what I want this play to say is that we should never give up.   We have a faith, and we have to hold those brigands to our faith—to world government or world peace or whatever it is.   Because they're in there making trades all the time, and we'll never get any part of our dream except by trading for it.

MARY—But then why bring in Joan?   Why take the purest,

simplest, most honest person that ever lived and say that she had to take part in the bargaining to get things done?

MASTERS—Because it's true. If she hadn't learned to speak and then gone out into the world, and argued with people and met the king and learned to deal with him—even learned to get along with his crooked, stupid court—she never would have got started. There'd never been no country of France.

MARY—It's not true. I think if she'd ever said one thing she didn't mean, or allowed one dishonest word to pass without denying it, she couldn't have had any influence. Compromise is not a virtue. Once you begin to compromise you're lost.

Masters is ready to argue this point further, but time is short and he thinks they had better get on with the scene—if Mary is willing to let things stand as they are for the present. A little reluctantly Mary agrees and the stage is cleared for the next scene—

JOAN AT ORLEANS

As Al announces the rise of the curtain with twelve verbal "Bongs!" to represent the Cathedral chimes, we find the Dauphin and a recent favorite, Aurore, pretending to be in bed. Aurore would stay there and cuddle, but the Dauphin has appointments. He must get up. When he does so he is revealed as a small, weak-featured young man, on the petulant side as to manners and easily irritated.

"The whole trouble, Aurore, is that I'm a reasonable man," explains the Dauphin to the insistent Aurore; "and a man who'll listen to reason has no chance against unreasonable people. The bishop and the treasurer rush in and make me do something and then Joan and the Bastard rush in and make me take it back—"

"But how can they make you—?"

"They insist. They're not logical about it. Now I'm logical. I know that all human decisions are based on insufficient evidence. A man never really has enough evidence even to prove that he ought to get up in the morning—"

"Then come back. Please."

"I can't—I—"

"I'd better go. I'll be in the way."

"Not if you stay under the covers and don't go traipsing about with nothing on."

"What town did we come to last night?"

"We're in Orleans, right in the front lines. And now that I

think of it I'm very much annoyed about being here. I never should have let them persuade me to come. It's dangerous here. Nobody knows how the battle will go. But Joan was completely unreasonable, as usual."

"Are you afraid?"

"I, afraid? Of course not. Only a king shouldn't be risked in a position of danger. It's bad strategy. Suppose I were taken? Think of the ransom we'd have to pay— And it's all that virgin's fault. Tremoille keeps telling me if I don't go about and show myself she'll run away with all my authority—so—here I am."

"She's no virgin."

"Oh, yes, she's intacta. She's been examined."

"Indeed?"

"By the best possible authorities—a committee of jealous and suspicious women. They say she's intacta. Also she hears prophecies and wins victories. But she's annoying. She annoys nearly everybody. She arrogates power to herself. And we have to stop that."

"I think I'll go to sleep."

The Dauphin has some notion of following Aurore's example, but before he can get back under the covers there is a knock at the door. Three of his councilors have come for a conference. They are Tremoille, Dunois and the Archbishop of Rheims, and they have news of importance to report.

Fighting has been going on since seven, and it is now twelve. The Virgin of Lorraine, who refuses to fight the war with ordinary sense, according to Tremoille, has already taken three more forts. She has acted without consulting anyone. She has refused to give quarter to the nobles and she won't take a cent of ransom money. "The thought of money never occurs to her," wails Tremoille. "We're losing thousands of pounds—thousands!"

And now Joan is about to lead a fourth attack, he reports, and this time against the river gate, which Dunois had ordered closed against the Maid's wishes. This, the Dauphin agrees, was good judgment, seeing the position was impregnable—

"But the heart of the matter is this, Your Highness," protests an excited Dunois; "she must not make another attack without consulting you. She's running away with your royal prerogatives. You must put yourself at the head of your troops."

"Gentlemen, I will do anything that's reasonable, but I will not put myself at the head of my troops. I will not fight a battle. This whole idea of fighting battles was Joan's. It wasn't mine. I don't want to be king as much as all that. If she wants to fight battles let her fight them."

Soon they are protesting excitedly that little by little Joan is taking the kingdom and the army away from them. The Archbishop of Rheims would stimulate the opposition of the Dauphin, who frankly is not interested. Dunois would reassert his authority as the head of the army, in which the Maid is herself serving, but he knows, as Rheims points out to him, that if ever the question of leadership is brought to an issue the army will follow the Maid to the last man.

Tremoille would compromise. If the Dauphin cannot control Joan, let him at least employ her to his own ends. She must not be allowed to approve the killing of nobles who would pay handsome ransoms. All aristocrats must be taken alive and carefully guarded. That is the only way to refill the treasury and re-establish authority.

They are still in argument when Joan, accompanied by La Hire, invades the conference. Their appearance is brusque and military. La Hire is wearing helmet and sword, Joan her silver armor. And they are angered that the river gate should have been closed against their attack of the Tourelles. Even though the Dauphin has agreed with Dunois that it would be unwise to attack the Tourelles, Joan is not impressed—

"Gentle Dauphin, you have been with your council and I have been with mine. My Voices told me to attack the Tourelles boldly and at once. They told me to attack from three sides—from the river, from the city, and from the far bank. And we had set it all in motion." . . . "The gatekeeper and his officer will be torn to pieces if that order stands."

One glance from the window convinces Dunois that it would be better to rescind his order and open the gate to the Maid's army. Briefly Joan then turns her attention to Aurore, ordering her out of the Dauphin's bed and out of the city. Let her follow the four hundred other harlots who have preceded her. Aurore, protesting plaintively that she hasn't had breakfast, finally clutches her clothes about her and leaves.

Now Joan would dictate a letter to Sir William Glasdale, commander of the Tourelles, which the Dauphin volunteers to set down—

"You, Sir William Glasdale—and you, men of England, who have no right to be in this kingdom of France, the King of Heaven commands you through me, Joan the Maid, to abandon your forts and go back where you belong. And if you fail to do this I will make such a hai-hai among you as will be eternally re-

membered. I am warning you for the third and last time. When
I warned you this morning, Sir William Glasdale, you called me
bitch—and other names which you should not have used, for you
will be in the presence of God within an hour."

The letter is to be signed by "Joan the Maid," signed for her,
because she cannot write—and fastened to a cross-bowman's
arrow and thus shot where it will come within Glasdale's notice.
She is not at all moved by the Archbishop's protest against the
sending of "so silly, boastful, illiterate, treasonous and heretical"
a letter—treasonous because the Maid has defied the Dauphin
about taking the nobles prisoner; heretical because she prophesies
Glasdale's death and prophecy is sorcery—

"It's not prophecy," answers the Maid, gently. "It's only that
we shall take the bastion—and in the taking of it he will be
killed." God wishes the letter to be sent and it will be sent.
She will see to that herself. Joan takes the letter and leaves
them, followed by Dunois.

The Dauphin has an idea, which he is entirely frank in confessing to Tremoille. He knows that his kingdom is being sold
out from under him. He knows that Tremoille is the greatest
thief and the most accomplished liar in France, and that what he
has stolen as treasurer he has kept. But it has occurred to the
Dauphin that if Joan continues to win against the British he will
soon be in a position to pay Tremoille all that the kingdom owes
and be rid of him. Then, if Joan should go on and win Paris,
too, it will be possible for him to push the British out of France
and forget all the rest of his debts.

Tremoille is not frightened at the prospect. The Dauphin,
says he, is obviously "counting his ortolans in the egg." These
victories of the virgin the Dauphin pictures might happen, but it
is not at all likely they will. True, Joan has won three forts
without the slightest attention to tactics. She has relied entirely
on her personal prestige and the fanatic enthusiasm of her fol-
lowers, aided by the fear she inspires in her opponents. If she
were willing to stop there all might be well. But she isn't.
"She's like a gambler that doubles the stake with every throw
because he's winning. Sooner or later the dice must fall against
her, if not tomorrow, then soon. But I think today."

"Why?"

"Because her luck has held about as long as luck can hold. I
think she will fail to take the Tourelles. She will be discredited
as a seer and a general. The men will begin to grumble. They
have not been paid. They have been sent to confession like chil-

dren. Their women are taken from them. They'll quit. One defeat and they'll quit. Forget your dream of taking city after city, forget your dream of eating Burgundy and me. It will not come true."

Like an answer to the Tremoille prophecy a great crash is heard. They all rush to the windows. The battle at the river gate is on. The forces of the Maid are again using all the unheard of arts of warfare—including what Tremoille describes as "the same unimaginative frontal attack." Fireboats on the river have set the bridge ablaze—

"The bridge is down!" shouts the excited Dauphin. "That's what that crash was! Oh, you wise crafty councilors, you ancient Satans, her men are fighting in the Tourelles itself!—While you stood here hoping for disaster she has taken it—she has won it! I should be there! I should be helping her—encouraging her!"

"Much help she needs from you, and much encouragement!" ventures the Archbishop.

"This is the end of the siege of Orleans!" shouts the Dauphin. "They are beaten!" And he rushes out to join the victors.

The Archbishop of Rheims and Tremoille decide to retire to the Tremoille apartments to consider the next move.

Presently Joan appears. She carries an arrow in one hand, a kerchief in the other. She has been wounded and is trying to clean a blood stain from her left shoulder. She is sitting on a low stool and, like a little girl, is weeping for the dead—the English dead—for whose death she feels responsible. Nor can an excitedly victorious Dunois comfort her—

"But don't you see that we have won, Joan?" protests Dunois. "Don't you see that my city is free? You have done it; you alone, I think."

"My wound throbs awfully—and I have been the death of many men—and I wish I had never come here. I wish I were home again. I wish I could go home."

"Why, you're a little girl, Joan. Just a little girl."

"Didn't you know it?"

"No."

"The other was all put on. So they'd respect me, and listen to me. But I can't do it any more. I went through so many things, because I looked forward to victory. I thought victory would be beautiful. But it's ugly and bloody and hateful."

"I've never seen anything more beautiful than you as you

stood on the edge of the fosse lifting your standard.—I happened
to glance up just as you leaped, when you were calling on them
to follow. When I think of victory I shall think of you as you
looked then—"

The Dauphin has bustled in, followed by La Hire and two of
the guard. Their excitement over the victory is great. They
are puzzled to find the Maid crying in the face of such a victory.
Especially puzzled to find her crying over the English dead. They
have come, La Hire explains, to see that Joan's wound is taken
care of and to bring her a message from the army—

"We have the Tourelles, and Glasdale's down under water, and
you're wounded but alive, thank God. And from now on it's your
army. I'm an old and wicked soldier, but I've left off swearing
and whoring at your word. We follow you, we follow the Maid.
Pay or no pay, we stay with you."

La Hire, with Dunois, would carry Joan out that the army may
see her, but she has no heart for that honor. She is much depressed by the Archbishop of Rheims, who has returned with
Tremoille, and would warn all who follow the Maid that they
follow a sorceress and a heretic. Her visions are evil and she
will bring evil to France.

"Then I say that you lie," is Joan's answer to this charge.
"My visions are good, and they bring good to France! They
have saved Orleans today for the Dauphin, and they will set a
crown on his head in your own Cathedral at Rheims!" . . . "I
have a heavy weight on my soul today. I think of many men
who died unshriven at my order—and I could turn gladly back
to Domremy. If there are men within your own council who
call me sorceress and heretic I shall have no heart to go further."

"Then I'll get rid of them," promptly promises the Dauphin,
and thereupon issues an official edict that neither the Archbishop
nor Tremoille shall henceforth serve him as councilors, but shall
be replaced by Dunois and La Hire. They, with Joan, shall hereafter be his council.

It is a proper action, Joan agrees. If he is to be worthy to be
king he must have worthy people about him. If he is to be king
his people must believe in him—

"They must believe you honest," Joan warns, "and they won't
believe it unless you are. For the people have a strange instinct
about these things. If you aren't honest, sooner or later they
find it out. To be a king you must be worthy to be a king."

The Dauphin would like to believe that Joan is right; that all he needs is faith in God to win his kingship. But he is still doubtful.

"I'm not a very worthy man, really," confesses the Dauphin. "Are you quite sure God can do anything with me?"

JOAN—He has changed the whole face of France in this one year. He has conquered more than half of your kingdom for you. Can He not change one human heart?

DAUPHIN—That's the question.

JOAN—I have seen Him work in the hearts of many people. He will change you.

DAUPHIN—Well, if you say so. Come—I'm willing to risk it if you are. After all, I'm the only Dauphin there is about. Set me on the throne, and stay by me, Joan, for personally, you know, I have no visions at all. No visions and no faith.

JOAN—God will send you faith.

DAUPHIN—You want me to be king, even if I doubt it?

JOAN—God wants you to be king. You will have faith, and you will believe in yourself, and you will govern France for Him.

DAUPHIN—You're a very strange girl. I almost believe you. What worries me most is—we have no money. They have all the money.

JOAN—We shall not need money, my Dauphin. Or if we need it we shall have it.

DAUPHIN—Now, if I believed that, you know—

JOAN—You may believe it.

DAUPHIN—Give me your hands, you three. (*They clasp hands.*) You are my council now. We shall have whatever we need?

JOAN—As soon as there is faith in your heart, you shall have whatever you need.

DAUPHIN (*dropping their hands*)—I don't know whether I want to do this. I have made some very powerful enemies. (*He looks out after Tremoille and Rheims.*) And if it's all going to depend on my having faith—that's a catch—that's a real catch, you know.

JOAN—Oh, my King, my King, put aside your fears! Be noble as I have dreamed you to be, be as God requires you to be, be as France needs you! Your France, your nation, your people —so helpless without you, but unconquerable as soon as you turn your trust to God!

DUNOIS—My lord, look at her face. Can you look at her and doubt?

DAUPHIN (*looking at* JOAN)—No. I don't doubt it now. Give me your hands again. (*They clasp hands.*)

AL—Curtain.

It is now 1 o'clock and a recess in the rehearsal is called until 2. Let everybody be back promptly. Before he leaves, Masters would like to tell Mary that he is well pleased with the way she has just played the scene on the steps. And he would like her to know, too, that he feels just as she does about the men who died in the war.

As for that, Mary finds it hard to believe him. If he felt as he says he does he would not ask her to play in a play that has been changed definitely from the play that she agreed to play. No, she is not thinking of walking out on him. That would be unfair, too. But she doesn't see why the dialogue cannot be put back the way it was in the beginning. "It's a mere matter of cutting," insists Mary. "The whole new meaning is in that one new stretch of dialogue that could be lifted right out."

Mary is ready to admit that practically every play and every picture finds itself in a similar jam at some time. All that those who have convictions can do is to stick to their convictions. Masters agrees that that is true. But what Mary doesn't realize is the New York theatre situation that every producer faces—

"You heard me saying that the theatre we're supposed to open in turns out to be rented from a man who put through a minor swindle to get the lease on it—and he's in jail, and if we don't cover a bad check of his he'll stay there and lose his lease and we can't open."

"But, Jimmy, it's like going into partnership with thieves! It's like buying in the black market—"

"We're in that already. Every set in the New York theatre is built with black market materials. And I'd hate to ask where some of the investors' money came from—some that came in in thousand dollar bills." . . .

"But where does this end?"

"It doesn't end. The world's like that. It's always been like that. And the theatre's in the world, like everything else. And I still think it's worth while to put on a play about Joan of Arc— in the middle of all this. The human race is a mass of corruption tempered with high ideals.—You can't sacrifice your integrity, but short of that—"

"I will not say it! Oh, now I see it clearly, and I will not say it! You want the play to mean that Joan had to work with dishonest people to put a kingdom together, just as we have to work with dishonest people to put on a play or build a world government! And it's not true! It's never been true! You can refuse to work with thieves!"

"You'll touch dishonesty somewhere as soon as you start to get anything done!"

"I don't believe it and I will not play it that way! She wasn't like that and we don't have to be like that!"

Their tempers have mounted now, and neither is prepared to give way. Mary is firm in declaring that she will not play Joan as the part has been rewritten. Masters thinks she is taking a good deal on herself when she tries to dictate to an author how he should write his play.

Masters is going to lunch. He may come back and he may not. If he doesn't, let Al, the stage manager, take direction from Mary.

Mary is going to lunch, too. And she may not come back either. If she doesn't, Mr. Masters is welcome to have everything his own way.

The stage is deserted.

The curtain falls.

ACT II

An hour later the company is slowly assembling. Neither Masters nor Mary has shown up. Al is posing Tessie as a stand-in for Mary, while the electricians place and mark the lights for the altar during the coronation scene in the Cathedral.

Masters shortly appears. He is disturbed not to find Mary. It may be they will not be needing any lights, or any theatre. However, they can start the coronation scene, if everything is ready. Mary is not in the first of that.

But first it appears that certain members of the troupe, spurred on by the controversy in which Mary and Masters have been indulging, would also like answers to a few problems. For example, Actor Long, who plays Dunois and doubles as the Bastard of Orleans, would like to know—

"Why can't a fellow just live by common-sense, without faith, dreams or religion?"

"What's common-sense?" demands Masters.

Long—Oh, keeping to the right when you go down the street.
Garder—Obeying the traffic laws.
Jeffson—Staying away from strange women.

WARD—Saving your money.

MASTERS—A man may keep to the right-hand side of the street out of common-sense, but common-sense has nothing to do with where he's going. You'd never do anything living by common-sense. Nobody lives sensibly. Let any man try to explain his motives for living the way he does. By all the rules of common-sense he'll sound like an idiot. Why do you marry the girl you get married to? Nobody ever explained that satisfactorily yet.

DOLLNER—Couldn't a man live by science?

MASTERS—Hell, if you live you have to be going somewhere. You have to choose a direction. And science is completely impartial. It doesn't give a damn which way you go. It can invent the atom bomb but it can't tell you whether to use it or not. Science is like—well, it's like a flashlight in a totally dark room measuring two billion light-years across—and with walls that shift away from you as you go toward them. The flash can show you where your feet are on the floor; it can show you the furniture or the people close by; but as for which direction you should take in that endless room it can tell you nothing.

LONG—That puts you in my class, boy. Science is no better than common-sense.

MASTERS—It's the same thing as far as I can see. Common-sense is yesterday's science; or science will be plain common-sense tomorrow.

LONG—But I don't have any faith.

MASTERS—Oh, yes, you do. And you live by it. Everybody has a notion of what the world's like and what he's like in it. My notion of what I'm like has been giving me ulcers for years. But what you think about the world is your faith, and if you begin to doubt it you have to put something in its place quick or you'll fall apart. A man has to have a faith, and a culture has to have one—and an army. An army may move on its belly, but it wouldn't move at all if it didn't believe in something.

JEFFSON—That might go for an army, but not for me.

MASTERS—No? You look hard at yourself, any one of you, and you'll find you're living by something you can't explain—maybe a formal religion, maybe a crazy-quilt philosophy you made up for yourself out of odds and ends, maybe a cause, maybe the S.P.C.A. or the Baconian theory or Freud or scientific research or communism or Christian Science or anti-vivisection, or somebody you're in love with, or an institution that needs cherishing—like our poor old theatre here on Manhattan, driven to the wall by Gresham's Law.

KIPNER—What's Gresham's Law?

MASTERS—Cheap stuff drives good stuff off the market.

KIPNER—Oh!

MRS. BARNES—What's your religion, Mr. Masters?

MASTERS—I guess democracy. I believe in democracy, and I believe the theatre is the temple of democracy. A democratic society needs a church without a creed—where anybody is allowed to talk as long as he can hold an audience—and that's what the theatre is—though it's sort of dwindling down to a side-chapel here, lately.

As for his own faith, Masters is willing to confess that he cannot prove anything that he believes, but he has faith that what he believes is true. "Every faith looks ridiculous to those who don't have it," he concludes, when pressed. ". . . We live by illusions and assumptions and concepts, every one of them as questionable as the Voices Joan of Lorraine heard in the garden. We take on our religions the way we fall in love, and we can't defend one any more than the other." . . . "More and more men are going to realize that it's our destiny to be in the dark and yet go forward—to doubt our religions and yet live by them. To know that our faith can't be proved and yet stick to it."

Mary has not appeared, but Masters decides to go on with the scene and the actors are called to their places. Tessie can stand by to fill in for Mary if necessary.

"Curtain going up," calls Al.

THE CORONATION AT RHEIMS

The actors have taken their places before the altar. The Archbishop and the Dauphin are discussing the proper procedure to be followed previous to the anointing of the new king.

From outside Tremoille brings word that great crowds are gathering. The Cathedral could be filled many times.

"After all, there's been no such event in all our history," the Archbishop reminds the Dauphin. "This triumphal march of yours across France . . . the defeat of the English at Patsy and La Beauce—these things have mounted into something really tremendous, at least in the popular mind."

Nor is the Archbishop willing to admit that Joan, the Maid, has been the responsible agent. "Remember, you've had to restrain and guide her constantly," prompts Rheims. "She receives more credit than is due her, because of your naturally generous disposition. Any other prince in your place would have got rid of her long ago."

The Dauphin considers that point, but is inclined to think it would be unwise for him to let the Maid go before he is rid of the Duke of Burgundy. As for that, Tremoille has a remedy. Burgundy has already made advances. By messenger he has offered the Dauphin a hundred thousand gold crowns for a two weeks' truce.

The Dauphin is impressed. What could they lose by two weeks? Quickly he makes up his mind. "I'll take it. Find the envoy before he leaves," he orders Tremoille.

"Yes, Your Highness. I believe, too, that if you will spare Paris—if you will only hold Joan back from attacking Paris— there's enough money in the wind to set a king up forever."

That, the Dauphin agrees, is also a matter that will bear thinking about.

This is the cue for the entrance of La Hire, Dunois and Joan. They come in, with Tessie carrying Joan's part. But before they can speak more than a few lines Mary Grey appears, wearing Joan's silver armor. She had decided, during her walk, that she would come back and finish out the afternoon anyway. Masters is willing to take his leading lady on that basis and the scene proceeds.

"It's the day we fought for, and waited for," Joan is saying. "And it's come. I think I shall be as happy today as any mortal has ever been in this world. For I shall watch the anointing and the coronation of my king— So much is done that looked impossible."

"It all looked impossible. What's left should be easy," agrees Dunois.

"Well, not easy, but we'll do it," says La Hire.

"We came to one decision this morning, we of the military," Dunois explains to the Dauphin. "We decided to strike while the iron's hot. As soon as your crown is firm on your head we start rolling for Paris." . . . "As the procession comes down the aisle our new king will descend the steps to his horse, and then mount to take his place at the head of the greatest army ever led by a French sovereign. We shall strike at Paris before they can organize a resistance. And that will be the end of Burgundy, and of the English in France."

A startled Dauphin is not prepared to accept these arrangements. They will have to cancel them. He is already negotiating a truce with Burgundy. There has been far too much bloodshed.

"You cannot do this, my Dauphin," protests Joan, in support of Dunois and La Hire. "It would mean that you threw away all the advantage we have fought so hard and given so much blood to win."

But the Dauphin is not to be moved. Whoever has advised him, he will stand by his decision—

"What do you three know of the expedients to which the heads of nations must stoop?" he demands, querulously. "What do you know of statecraft? You are children in such matters. A ruler has to rob, murder, compromise, lie, cheat, steal, and enter into compacts with all sorts of brigands in order to keep going!—"

JOAN—But you did all these things before I came—and they didn't help!

DAUPHIN—And do you think your coming has reformed the methods of government? Men have been governed by corruption since the invention of government. They like it. They don't want to be governed any other way! And if you think a green girl from the country is going to change that by winning some victories you have more delusions than I thought.

JOAN—Men hate corruption! And God hates it!

DAUPHIN—I don't know about God, but men take to it very naturally. You promised me I'd have money when I needed it, remember? Well, I need it very badly, and God does nothing about it.

JOAN—And now I begin to wonder why God wished you to be king.

DAUPHIN—I wondered that myself when you first came to me, but you explained it very convincingly at the time. And now that I'm to be made king, and practically am king, I tell you I shall do as I please. And I please to make a truce with Burgundy, and maybe I shall never march on Paris at all. Maybe I'll decide that it's wiser not to.

DUNOIS—You know how this looks, Your Highness. Like betrayal or stupidity.

LA HIRE—Or both.

DAUPHIN—I never said I was wise. I never said I was honest, I never said I was handsome. But this girl came to me and said I must be king of France. And somehow or other it's come about —I don't think I'm an especially good person to be king. But here I am, and the Archbishop's waiting to crown me, and half of France is waiting outside, and I think it's a little late to do anything about it.

TREMOILLE (*entering*)—They're about to open the doors. You'd better take your places. How many are to stand with the king?

RHEIMS—These three.

DAUPHIN—Not you, Tremoille. It wouldn't look well.

TREMOILLE (*going out*)—Yes, Your Majesty.

DUNOIS—Come, Joan. The rest of us don't matter, kings or nobles. It's you they want to see, the Maid of France in her white armor.

JOAN—If the truce is signed with Burgundy I shall never wear this armor again. I shall dedicate it to God and lay it on His altar—and try no more.

LA HIRE—Nonsense. We'll march on Paris with or without sanction.

DAUPHIN—If you do I'll have the bridges burned, I'll cut off your supplies, I'll—I'll stop you some way—I'll govern my own kingdom—and better than you could! (*He kneels.*)

JOAN—Why does he do this? What has happened?

LA HIRE—He has sold us out, Joan.

DUNOIS—Yes, he has sold us out. And we are pilloried here to look on at his crowning. Stand erect, Maid. The folk will soon be entering. We must stand erect—and take it.

Joan is not content. She must press the Dauphin for an admission that he has, in fact, sold them out. If he has he must not be a king of France. It is not too late to prevent that. She will herself tell the people of Rheims what he has done. She will speak out in the cathedral. Nor can the protesting Archbishop stop her.

The Dauphin is defiant now. He refuses to call back Tremoille and countermand the truce with Burgundy—

"I won't do it!" he declares petulantly. "I'm going to be king, and I'm going to do as I please, and if Joan doesn't agree she can always leave! It might be a very good idea for her to leave! I will not be told what to do all the time! It's too late to stop my coronation—much too late! It can't be done now!"

JOAN—I can tell the people of France what you have done, and how you betray them! If they still want you to be king—

DAUPHIN—Try to tell them, and see what good it does!

JOAN—I shall tell them—and then I shall go.

DUNOIS—Joan?

JOAN—Yes, Dunois.

Dunois—Don't leave him. Stay with him.

Joan—After he has betrayed us all—and his country—and even himself?

Dunois—Yes. You see, if you speak out you may destroy him, and if you do that you'll destroy all you've accomplished—for France will have no king. And if you speak out and he's crowned anyway, and you leave him, what will France have? A government of pure corruption. No saint, no faith, no good angel, no good influence—just corruption. But if you stay with him he will have to think a little of the people of France, and not always of his own bargains, for the people of France will trust you, and he will sometimes have to listen to you.

Joan—But would I be honest to stay—to stand here at his crowning and say nothing about what he has done?

Dunois—Didn't your Voices tell you that you were to set the Dauphin on the throne in the cathedral at Rheims?

Joan—Yes.

Dunois—Well—this is the Dauphin—the only one we have—and this is the cathedral—and the doors are about to be opened. You are doing what God told you to do.

La Hire—It makes a man wonder if God would be wrong.

Joan—No. He could not be wrong. This is the king He chose and He could not be wrong. And yet—

Dunois—Every government is made up of bargainers, Joan. That's to be expected. Even God must be aware of that. And it's a lucky country where the bargainers don't have it all their own way—where there's somebody like you about, making the bargainers behave.

Joan—I've had small success so far.

Dunois—You must not give up. You must try.

Joan—I will let him be crowned. God could not be wrong.

Now Mary steps out of character and walks down to the footlights to face Masters. This is the section of dialogue to which she objects, and these few lines could come out so easily. But—again at Masters' request—she agrees to finish the scene. And does. Then she renews her protest—

"All the rest I can believe," she says, "but I don't see how she can decide so deliberately to give her blessing to corruption."

"The author wants it that way."

"You spoke to him about it?"

"At lunch time. And it's his own decision. Not mine."

"Oh. So that settles that. Your way."

"I guess it does. He's not going to change it."

"I see."

Mary is still undecided as to whether she should go on or not. The announcement that the man Sweeter, from whom they are to lease a theatre if they can get him out of jail, is on the wire does not help. However, she will finish this day's rehearsal at any rate, and that's the most she is prepared to promise.

Al has gone back to setting the stage when Masters calls for the actor who is to play the Inquisitor. That would be Harry, and Harry has been given permission to take the day off to fill a date with the radio—

"Oh, yes," Masters remembers. "The warmsey-woolsey, eatsy-wheatsy hour. God knows I wouldn't keep an actor from a radio job. The radio holds the actors in New York and keeps 'em alive till we need 'em. The radio's bread and butter, and anything they pick up in the theatre is just whore-money."

It also appears that there is no under-study for the Inquisitor. Al had hoped that Masters himself would read the part. Without too much reluctance Masters agrees, but he will need the help of the pronouncing dictionary of place names.

"Tomorrow we're going through and check up on every pronunciation in the script," the director announces. "Some authentic Parisian is likely to come to the opening, and shoot the Archbishop before he gets halfway through that list of French towns." . . .

The rehearsal proceeds.

She Dedicates Her White Armor

Joan, wearing the boy's clothes as before, and carrying the white armor, comes in. She lays the armor on the altar and then kneels—

Joan—King of Heaven, I come to fulfill a vow. The truce with Burgundy is signed, we are at peace, I shall wear this white armor no more. I leave it here on your altar. We are at peace, my King, but not such a peace as we dreamed; no, horribly, evilly in armistice, with much of the war to be fought and our enemies preparing while we dwindle here from town to town, holding court, receiving embassies, and dismissing soldiers. From town to town, from city to city, I have attended, doing the King's bidding, for he asks me to stay beside him—and this is the king of your choosing, Your regent in France. We have feasted in

Compiègne, Senlis and Beauvais, and we must feast in many more, if the plans hold.—But, O King of Heaven, the food is bitter. It is bought with money the King has accepted in payment for provinces and cities. I would rather sleep on the ground again, and chew my handful of beans, and rise to face the rank of English spears. For this way we shall lose all we have won. Even I can see that, and my Voices have said nothing.—If my Voices would speak again—and if they would tell me what I should do—then I could sleep at night and accept what comes to me. But they have not spoken, they are silent. And I ask again and again—may I go into battle, or must I remain with the King and his household, busy with the nothings that fill these days? If my Voices do not answer, if no injunction is laid on me, then I cannot stay here. I must arm again and find the enemy, and fight as before.—Let my Voices speak to me if this is wrong . . . Will St. Michael speak to me, or St. Catherine, or St. Margaret? (*There is no answer.*) Then I go to find Alencon and La Hire and Dunois. And an armor of iron—and the ax and sword of a soldier. Long ago my Voices told me that I would be taken prisoner. Well, when it comes I shall at least have arms in my hands.

(JOAN *rises and turns to go.* AL *calls curtain.*)

Now Masters has come again to the footlights. He would like, as an old admirer, if Mary doesn't mind, to relapse a bit and admire her again. He liked that scene.

Mary is pleased, but she is thinking of something else at the moment. "Do you know what I was thinking?" she says. "There's a scene the play really needs—a transition scene between this one and the next. Because the next time we see her she's been taken prisoner by the English, and it's never explained."

"That's what the author's working on over there now. That's why he's locked in the hotel room. He's promised we'll have it tomorrow."

And so they go on to the first trial scene, with various actors coming in and taking their places.

THE TRIAL—THE QUESTION

Cauchon, the Bishop of Beauvais, is presiding over this division of the ecclesiastical court, which, as he explains, has assembled to put certain questions to the prisoner. This is a case of "alleged heresy, blasphemy and sorcery," but that is not all. If it were, Joan the Maid would have been easily convicted on all three counts. "She has freely admitted enough heretical beliefs and actions to burn all the virgins in Europe," insists Cauchon.

It would be easy for this court to condemn the Maid to death and turn her over to the soldiers to be burned. But— "She has given the people of France a rallying cry and a cause. We must blacken her fame and destroy her name. If we do not she will have beaten us."

"Joan has done two things," Cauchon explains to the Inquisitor, who has refused to take part in the further questioning of the Maid until he is better satisfied with her guilt. "She has put Burgundy and the English in danger. She has also put the church in danger. It happens, my dear Vicar, that this same need to discredit Joan which is felt by the peers of Normandy and England is felt also by the church which you and I represent. For Joan has begun a heresy. She appeals from the church on earth to the church in heaven. She does not recognize the necessity for an agent between the individual soul and its God. And this heresy of hers begins to affect the whole western world."

Joan is led into the court by Father Massieu. It pleases her to stand rather than to sit before them. Yes, she will answer truthfully anything which pertains to this trial and which she is allowed to answer. There are some questions which she has been forbidden by her Voices to answer—

"How can we give you a fair trial when you will not tell us all the truth?" demands Thomas de Courselles, one of her judges.

"How can you give me a fair trial when you are all English or Burgundians, and not one churchman from loyal France among you? I stand here among the enemies of my king, and they pretend to judge me fairly! Why do you desire the English to be in France, when France is not their country?"

INQUISITOR—Let us put this matter aside. It is no part of our process—

JOAN—It is very much a part of your process! It is why I am here! Because you wish to be rid of an enemy!

INQUISITOR—No, Joan. I am interested in one thing only: your soul and your relation to the mother church. I sit here not as a Burgundian, not as your enemy, but as the representative of the Inquisitor of France. If I can save you from evil, I shall save you. If I can find you innocent I shall find you so.

JOAN—Then you are not like him who sits with you, for he believes me guilty now.

CAUCHON—I shall not answer that. I shall return good for evil by telling you what every prisoner wishes to know—news from outside his prison. Do you wish to hear it?

JOAN—If you tell it truly.

CAUCHON—It may sound like a fabrication, for it is all on our side, yet it's true. Your king, the king you set on his throne, has sold Paris to the Duke of Burgundy. And he lives up to that bargain very honestly. He has broken down the bridges leading to Paris—and the Bastard has given up and resigned his command and gone home. There's your Charles the Seventh.

JOAN—I will listen to nothing against my king.

CAUCHON—This is perhaps nothing against him, but it is also true. Your king has abandoned you. He knows that you are a prisoner here, and he has made no offer of ransom.

JOAN—I know nothing of ransoms.

CAUCHON—You know that ransom and exchange of prisoners are common among us. Talbot is still your king's prisoner. He could have offered Talbot for you. He has not done so. He has not offered one sou. Your old friends have given you up very gaily and easily. There is no help coming—no hope for you save in this court.

JOAN—There is no hope here.

COURCELLES—Do you believe yourself to be in a state of grace?

JOAN—If I am not, may God put me there. If I am, may He keep me there.

That, insists Father Massieu, is a good answer. It is ignored by the court. Why, Cauchon next demands, does Joan insist on wearing men's clothes when they are forbidden to women by the church? Because, Joan explains, she had found them more comfortable and more fitting when she rode with soldiers, and because she feels better in men's clothes so long as she is guarded day and night by men jailers of evil minds.

Yes, it is true, she has been told by her Voices that she will be rescued, but she does not know what they mean by rescue, or when it will come. Again her Voices have awakened her to warn her against the evil men who are plotting to harm her. But why must she go on answering the same questions? They know what is happening, they know what has happened to her. For days and nights she has not slept and yet she is brought repeatedly before them—

"Place me in another prison, give me women about me," she pleads. "This is not fair. It is not a trial. I come before you half mad with what I must endure in my cell—and without rest, without rest day or night."

The petty questioning goes on until even the Inquisitor is moved to protest. If he were to state clearly to Joan the case against her it may be that she will find herself on their side, and thus avoid the torture of the fire—

"Here is the case against you: You hear voices, have visions and inspirations, which you say come from God. The church, which is God's representative on earth, does not recognize the possibility of direct inspiration from God to His children. If you have visions we must condemn them as evil and condemn you as evil. Unless—unless—you see, there is a way out—unless you also condemn your visions as evil."

Joan stands firm. She knows her Voices are good. What they led her to do was good. That is proof enough. Can she be sure of her king and the men around him? No. She cannot be sure of them. And that, declares the Inquisitor, is an admission that will yet save her.

But Joan is sorely troubled. Can't they see that all she wants is to do right? Of all the tortures she has suffered that doubt is the greatest. Her Voices had come to her when she was a child. She has always believed in them. But she would give them up instantly if she knew they were evil. But she doesn't know. And the court hasn't told her—

"It's because I wish to do right that I stand out stubbornly through these sleepless nights and try to find God's way in my thinking," protests the Maid. "But I will not be trapped. I will not betray the truth to avoid the fire."

"Never!" agrees the Inquisitor. "I would as soon betray myself! But the way is easy and clear now. You have come to the great question—the one that goes to the root—the one to which all thinking men must come—why do I believe what I believe? Isn't that it?"

"Yes. Then you do know."

"I came to it myself, though not so young as you. I came to it in middle age, and it tortured me as it tortures you now. And I fought my way through to an answer. Do you wish to know what it was?"

"With all my heart."

"It is this: One must believe nothing which cannot be solidly proved. All hopes, all dreams, all aspirations, all imaginings, must be ruthlessly emptied out. The soul must be rinsed to the bottom of all these things—and must hold only to what can be proved."

"But then what is there that can be proved?"

"The doctrine and the teachings of the church. They come down in unbroken succession from the word of God. Nothing else is solid. Nothing else can be proved. Not even that we are here. Not even that the sun rises and sets. Not even that I speak to you. Not the four walls about us. Not the voices of our friends. All these could be appearance, illusions, feverish concepts. We could awake tomorrow and find that we dreamed this trial, dreamed this place and time. How then can you trust your visions? When the church itself, the one thing solid, has said that they are lies?"

"But if I give them up I shall be empty. All my world and my life will have no meaning."

The Executioner, a tall forbidding figure in black, wearing a mask, stands in the door of the cell. He has come at the bidding of Cauchon. He is the man who will put Joan to the fire if she persists in her heresy. But before that he will submit her to the boot and the mercy-wheel in the hope of saving her soul.

"You have heard my confession; you know my heart; what should I do?" Joan has turned pleadingly to Father Massieu.

"There is only one way to save yourself," answers the priest. "You must submit to the judgment of the church. You must renounce your visions."

Between them they have worn down Joan's resistance. "I don't know what is true. I don't know what is good," she cries. "Bring me a dress to wear and leave me alone in my prison. I will do as you say. I will believe no more in my visions. I will let the church decide."

Courcelles presents the papers for her to sign. She draws a circle as her mark. The church receives her as a penitent.

"Take me to my cell and let me sleep," pleads Joan, wearily. "God help me, I may have done wrong, but I must rest."

The scene is ended.

THE TRIAL—JOAN ANSWERS

In her cell next morning Joan is kneeling in prayer. "King of Heaven, the night is over," she prays. "My jailers have worn themselves out with tormenting me, and have gone to sleep. And I should sleep—I could sleep safely now—but the bishop's questions come back to me over and over. What if I were wrong? How do I know that my visions were good? I stare wide awake at the dawn in the window and I cannot find an answer.—So many things they said were true. It is true that the king we crowned at Rheims is not wise nor just nor honest. It is true that his realm is not well governed. It is true that I am alone, that my friends have forgotten me, both the king and the nobles who fought beside me. There is no word from them, no offer of ransom. And I am doubly alone, for I have denied my visions, and they will come to me no more.—I believe my visions to be good. I know them to be good, but I do not know how to defend them. When I am brought into a court, and must prove what I believe, how can I prove that they are good and not evil? —Yes, and I ask myself whether I have been honest always, for when I went among men I acted a part. It was not only that I wore boy's clothes—I stood as my brother stood and spoke heartily as he spoke, and put my challenges in the words he would have spoken. When I spoke with my own voice nobody listened, nobody heard me, yet was it honest to assume ways that were not my own?—I know there's to be no answer. I can expect no answer now, after I have betrayed and denied my saints.—They will not burn me now because I admitted that I could not prove my Voices good—and I submitted to the church. And now, when I am to live, when I have done what they say is right, I am more unhappy than when they said I was wrong, and must die."

A light brightens near her and soon the Voices are heard again. St. Michael assures the Maid that she has not done wrong, that what she has done will set France free. Though her king is not a good king, "a king is not for long," and good will come of his crowning. True, they confuse her with questions that no man can answer. "But the church itself is built on revelations, and these revelations came out of darkness and went back into darkness like your own."

Now it is St. Catherine's voice she hears, advising her to answer her persecutors boldly, as her brother spoke. "Resume your faith. Speak boldly as before. You were not wrong."

And now St. Margaret speaks: "Jeannette, within one year you have changed the whole face of France. If you keep your faith— and if you hold fast to the end—this is only a beginning. Let them fire the scaffold beneath you if they dare. The fire they set will burn down ten thousand tyrannies before it's burnt out. It will run from kingdom to kingdom, from century to century. It is not only the French who will be set free."

"Then—my cause is to win—but there's to be no rescue for me?"

"Are you afraid, daughter of France?"

"I'm afraid of the fire. Only of the fire."

"If it's too difficult, if you cannot bear it, then it's not required of you. You have done what you set out to do. You have saved Orleans and crowned the Dauphin at Rheims. You have had your year, your work is done, and they cannot undo it. Make your peace with them if you must. Even so, you have done well."

"Even if I continue to deny you, still I have done well?"

"Yes. They cannot take from you what you have done. The kingdom of France will never be as it was."

Joan prays that she will be strong, even in the face of the Executioner and the stake. While they are with her she feels strong. She prays that she will not turn against them. But the fire has always frightened her. It may again. If it does, will they be angry with her?

"How could we be angry with you, Jeannette?" answers St. Margaret. "In all France, in all her thousand years, there has been no child such as you."

The light has disappeared.

Father Massieu is horror struck to find that Joan is still in men's garb. Why has she not changed? Because of the guards? He will send them away. Let her hurry, hurry!

"Joan, Joan, they come this morning to make sure you have kept your oath. And you have broken it. A heretic may repent and be forgiven, but a heretic who repents and then falls back into error, for such there is no forgiveness."

It is too late. Cauchon, the Inquisitor, and the others are at the cell door. Cauchon is quick to charge the Maid with having broken her word.

"She meant all that she said," speaks Father Massieu in Joan's defense. "She dealt honestly with us. But we have not dealt honestly with her. The guards were left in this cell last night as before."

"I made no promise about the guards. She has retained the clothes of a man. She has broken her signed abjuration. And she was warned of the penalty."

The Inquisitor has joined with Father Massieu in demanding that Joan be given a chance to keep her promise.

"For the love of the church and of God we must forgive this girl and let her be forgiven," pleads the Inquisitor. "If you have your way, if the soldiers take her and send her spirit up from the fire and cast her body to the winds, we shall never hear the last of this day's work. The winning of a few victories—that could be put aside as a nine days' wonder. But if she dies in this faith of hers—if we make her a martyr and a symbol—why, then her ashes and her words will blow abroad like seeds and take root on deserts and pavements! They will flower in heralds and prophets to spread her fame! This will be her age, her century, and all the rest of us, priests and kings, will be minor figures in her tragedy!" . . . "There is more at hazard than the soul of a child."

"Very well," agrees Cauchon. "Let her put on her dress."

But now they must reckon with a new Joan. "It won't help now to change my clothes," she says. "I've heard my Voices again, and I trust them, and they are good. I'm sorry that I denied them." . . . "It was hard to say, but now that I say it I'm glad again, and happy. Even though it means that I must die."

"We told you yesterday that your voices were evil, and you had no answer."

Mary does not go on. There is something on her mind. Al tosses her the next line—" 'I have an answer now—' " but she does not pick it up. First she must speak to Masters—

"I know! I know now! And I was right!" she calls exultantly. "She will not compromise when her own soul is in question. She will die first! She'd rather die!"

"Yes, that's true, Mary."

"Oh, why didn't you say it?"

"I did say it, Mary. Not as well as Joan, and maybe not well at all, but I did say it."

"I wish I'd understood, because that makes all the difference! She will compromise in little things, in things that don't matter, but when it comes to her Voices and what she believes she will not tell one lie—or live one lie! She'd rather step into the fire—and she does!"

"Right!"

"Then we've found it! Because that is the meaning of her life—and the meaning of the play! I'm sorry—we can go on now—what was the line?"

" 'I have an answer now—' "
The scene continues.

JOAN—I have an answer now. I believe in them in my heart. There is no other authority.

CAUCHON—Do you deny the authority of the church?

JOAN—I believe in the church from my heart. There's no other way to believe.

CAUCHON—The church has called your Voices evil. One or the other you must deny.

JOAN—That's your belief, Bishop Cauchon, but not mine. Each must believe for himself. Each soul chooses for itself. No other can choose for it. In all the world there is no authority for anyone save his own soul.

INQUISITOR—Then you choose death.

JOAN—I know you tried to save me.

INQUISITOR—I have never tried to save you. I have spoken only for the strict and correct application of the canon law. When the law is on your side, I am there also. When you set yourself against the law I must set myself against you. But I still plead with you: do not force us to abandon you. The individual soul cannot choose its own faith, cannot judge for itself!

JOAN—Yet every soul chooses for itself. Who chose your faith for you? Didn't you choose it? Don't you choose to keep it now?

COURCELLES—There's singular logic in this.

CAUCHON—I think not.

JOAN—Yes, you did choose it. You choose to keep it. As I choose to keep mine. And, if I give my life for that choice, I know this too, now: Every man gives his life for what he believes. Every woman gives her life for what she believes. Sometimes people believe in little or nothing, nevertheless they give up their lives to that little or nothing. One life is all we have, and we live it as we believe in living it, and then it's gone. But to surrender what you are, and live without belief—that's more terrible than dying—more terrible than dying young.

INQUISITOR—I came this morning ready to receive you back. I must now join with the Bishop of Beauvais in turning you over to the secular authorities, with the recommendation that you be gently dealt with.

MASSIEU—Before it's too late, do you know what that means, Joan? It means the fire.

JOAN—To live your life without faith is more terrible than the fire.

For a little Joan talks with them—with Father Massieu and with the Inquisitor—and then she is alone. "How sharply I see—how different everything looks—now that I know I'm to die!" she muses. "The window—and the dim cell—and the black dress." She has picked up the dress and is looking at it. "I wanted a black dress when I left Domremy, but I had to wear that old, red patched one.—It seems so long ago. I wonder where my mother and father are. The taxes are remitted on the town of Domremy. Remitted forever, it's said. And I'm to die today. I must face it and play it out. I must stand proudly and speak well. I must not disgrace my visions. They will be with me at the end. I can depend on them as on Father Massieu.—And if it were to do over, I would do it again. I would follow my faith, even to the fire. It cannot take long to die. It will be a little pain, and then it will end, and then I won't know. No, the pain will not be little—but it will end—and up to the end my Voices will speak to me."

The Executioner has come. He manacles the Maid's hands behind her. "I shall not give you any trouble," she says, as she walks before him out the door.

The rehearsal is over.

As we approached "Joan of Lorraine" by way of a prologue, we leave the play by way of an epilogue.

Mary has returned to the stage for an imaginary curtain call. She is met by Jimmy Masters, who takes her hand with considerable enthusiasm. It has been a good rehearsal and several moot points have been settled.

"Do you know what I learned in these last scenes?" Mary asks.

"No."

"It doesn't matter what an author tries to write about her. It doesn't matter what you and I believe about her. She will always win out, and come through, and use us for her purpose."

"And what was her purpose?"

"To say that there's nothing in the world as important as a pure faith, purely followed—that all men have to give way before such a faith—the bargainers and the kings, and the men of power—they all have to give way and follow people like Joan."

"Some of them make a good thing out of it."

"Yes, but they follow."

"Then we were both right."

"Yes—I guess perhaps you were right, too."

"So it's all settled?"

"In these last scenes there were some of her own words. I could feel them turning and moving on my tongue. Like live things— And as for who owns the theatre—or gets rent from it— I don't know who owns any theatre in New York—or gets rent from it. I can't judge among them. Yes, it's all settled."

The company call for the next day is for the same time. The players begin to scatter.

"And we won't quarrel again?" Masters ventures, hopefully.

"Oh, about other things—" Mary isn't sure.

"Till tomorrow, then."

"Tomorrow," answers Mary, gaily, as they go out.

THE CURTAIN FALLS

ANOTHER PART OF THE FOREST

A Drama in Three Acts

By Lillian Hellman

THERE may be other instances in which a playwright has, in effect, written the sequel to a drama before he got around to writing the drama on which the sequel is based, but they are unknown to this editor. Lillian Hellman, an acknowledged leader among American dramatists, wrote the very successful drama called "The Little Foxes" as far back as 1939. It was not until 1946 that she got around to tying that drama in with "Another Part of the Forest," which really furnishes a foundation for the former play.

Naturally, Miss Hellman did not plan this particular sequence deliberately. It just happened. "You can imagine that after living with 'The Little Foxes' for several years I got to be on pretty chatty terms with the Hubbard family," she told Lucius Beebe of the New York *Herald Tribune* in one interview. "I knew them inside out, and while no more tolerant of their rapacity and avarice, I began to feel a mixture of sentiments toward them which in no way derived from anything they themselves represented. I began to dislike the audience hypocrisy by the terms of which people who saw the show seemed to derive a feeling of moral superiority to the Hubbards. . . . This gave me a sort of jolt. It did not change my graveyard affection for the Hubbards, whom I cherish as one would cherish a nest of particularly vicious diamond-back rattlesnakes, but it did make me feel that it was worth while to look into their family background and find out what it was that made them the nasty people they were."

"The Little Foxes," which will be recalled as one of Tallulah Bankhead's most popular starring engagements—she playing the heroine, Regina—told of an adventure of the Hubbards which had its inception in the Spring of 1900. Regina was then 40. "Another Part of the Forest" (a title derived from the notation of scene changes in Shakespeare's "As You Like It") goes back to the year 1880. Father and Mother Hubbard were alive then, Father the completely dominant head of the family, and perhaps the most vicious influence in the lives of his three children, Benjamin, Oscar and Regina.

In 1880 we find the Hubbards living in the Alabama town of Snowden. It is a Summer Sunday morning. The scene is the side portico of the Hubbard house. From the portico, French doors lead into the living room. Under a side stairway that mounts to a balcony on an old wing of the house, from which the bedrooms are reached, there are doors into the dining room and a back door leading into the kitchen. "The main part of the house, built in the 1850s, is Southern Greek. It is not a great mansion but it is a good house built by a man of taste from whom Marcus Hubbard bought it after the Civil War."

It is quite early and the only Hubbard in sight is Regina. She is, at this time, "a handsome girl of 20," who has evidently pinned her hair high in a hurry, and as hurriedly thrown a pretty negligee over her nightgown.

At the moment Regina is in serious conversation with John Bagtry, "a man of 36, with a sad, worn face." John is wearing a shabby riding shirt and Confederate cavalry boots. He glances about apprehensively. He would restrain Regina's not too repressed excitement and the occasionally high tones of her voice. He did not, John admits, expect to encounter Regina this early in the morning, and he feels that if any of her family were to find her there in her wrapper and with him the discovery might cause a pretty scandal.

Nobody's awake, Regina insists, and in any case she doesn't care. Why hadn't John met her the night before? Well, John didn't feel that he could leave his Aunt Clara and his Cousin Birdie, who wanted to talk. They were lonely—

"It's not the first time you didn't come. And you think I shouldn't be angry, and take you back the next day. It would be better if you lied to me where you were. This way it's just insulting to me. Better if you lied."

John doesn't like that accusation. What he has done he would do again. But he is willing to be a little conciliatory. ". . . Look, honey, I did mean to come to meet you. But I've lived on them for fifteen years. They're good to me. They share with me the little they've got, and I don't give back anything to them—"

"I'm getting sick of them," declares Regina, tensely. "They've got to know about you and me some day soon. I think I'm going to sashay right up to that Sacred Plantation grass and tell them

the war's over, the old times are finished, and so are they. I'm
going to tell them to stay out of my way—"

"They've never mentioned you, Regina." John's tone is sharp.

"That's what's called good breeding; to know about something and not talk about it?"

"I don't know about good breeding."

"They think they do. Your cousin Birdie's never done more
than say good morning, in all these years—when she knows full
well who I am and who papa is. Knows full well he could buy
and sell Lionnet on the same morning, its cotton, and its women
with it."

John's voice is stern now, and gently threatening. "I would not
like to hear anybody talk that way again. No, I wouldn't."

Regina's attitude changes quickly. She is sorry. She would
give him her apology. She was angry about last night because
she was eager to tell him of a plan she has evolved; a wonderful
plan she will tell him about if he will meet her late the next night—

John isn't interested. They should stop where they are. He is
no good for her. He's too old. Yes, too old at 36. There is only
one thing he is good for, says John. That's war. He was happy
in the war. He has a plan, too. It is to find another war—in
Brazil, perhaps. That's where Cod Carter is fighting. John has
just had a letter from Cod—

The arrival of Regina's mother, Lavinia Hubbard, "a woman of
about 58 or 60; stooped, thin, delicate-looking," and Coralee, "a
sturdy colored woman of about 45," interrupts John's explanation.
"Lavinia has a sweet, high voice and a distracted nervous way of
speaking." Coralee is holding a parasol over her.

Lavinia and Coralee have been to church, to *their* church, Lavinia explains. "The colored folks said a prayer for me, and a
little song. It's my birthday!" John Bagtry offers his congratulations and good wishes—

"Thank you, sir," Lavinia goes on. "And later I'm going back
to the second service. And I know a secret: they're going to give
me a cake. Ain't that lovely of them, and me undeserving? I
always go to the colored church. I ain't been to a white church
in years. Most people don't like my doing it, I'm sure, but I got
my good reasons—"

"All right, Mama," interposes Regina, quickly. But Lavinia is
not to be stopped—

"I remember you and your cousins the day you left town for
war," she prattles on, to John. "I blew you a kiss. Course we

were living in our little house then, and you didn't know. But I blew you all a kiss."

"I'm glad to know it, ma'am," declares John, pleasantly. "It was a great day. A hot day." . . .

Marcus Hubbard opens the door of his bedroom and comes out on the upper porch. "He is 63, a strong-looking man, with a soft voice of great tone and depth. He speaks slowly, always, as if he put value on the words." He'll be down in a minute, he announces, to have his first cup of coffee with Regina.

At Marcus Hubbard's appearance John moves quickly back into the living room doorway, out of sight from the porch. Lavinia has disappeared into the house. Regina, amused at John's nervousness, wants him to meet her father some day. Not at the Hubbard store. There, at the house.

"I guess no Bagtry ever been inside our house," she says. "But would your Aunt Clara and your Cousin Birdie allow you to come, do you reckon?"

"Allow me? I didn't think that was the way it was. I thought your papa didn't want anybody here—"

"Will you meet me tomorrow night, same place? Darling, darling! Please! Please! (*She pulls him toward her. He hesitates for a second. Then he takes her in his arms.*) Meet me? Please, darling!"

"I always do. No matter what I say or think, I always do."

He starts to kiss her, then runs quickly around the house and disappears. Regina stands for a moment staring after him.

A moment later Ben Hubbard appears, evidently home from a journey. "He is 35, a powerful calm man with a quiet manner." Ben has seen Bagtry, and is surprised. Surprised both that Bagtry should be there and that Regina should receive him on the porch in her wrapper. His criticism makes little impression on Regina. . . .

Marcus has come downstairs. Ben is not pleased at having been ordered back from his trip by his father, who pretends now that he can barely remember why he sent for him. Something to do with the account books at the store, probably. And why didn't Ben want to come back? Because, Ben explains, a little testily, he had hoped to make an investment in Birmingham Coal, Inc. He wanted to invest two thousand dollars. It would be worth fifty thousand some day. He wanted to try and raise the money in Mobile, after his father had refused to loan it to him. Marcus isn't at all interested in this foolish old scheme of Ben's. . . .

Col. Isham is calling. "He is a man of 65. He walks slowly as if his legs were bad." The Colonel has come on a serious matter. Presently he states it—

". . . Now, please listen to me. Two nights ago, Sam Taylor in Roseville was badly beaten up. Last night fourteen people identified the night riders as the Cross boys from over the line, and your son, Oscar. They are angry men up in Roseville."

Marcus has gone to the dining room door. "Benjamin!" he calls. "Rope Oscar and bring him out here immediately." He turns back to Col. Isham. "I told you fifteen years ago you were a damn fool to let your Klansmen ride around, carrying guns—"

ISHAM (*going close to* MARCUS)—Were you frightened of our riding on you? I came here to tell you to make your son quit. He can thank me he's not swinging from a rope this minute. You have good reason to know there's not a man in this country wouldn't like to swing up anybody called Hubbard. . . . I stopped my friends last night but I may not be able to stop them again. Tell him what patriots do is our business. But he's got no right to be riding down on anybody—

OSCAR (*appearing in doorway*)—*Rope* me out! I can stand up. Never felt my Saturday night liquor that bad— Nobody has to rope me out, Papa.

ISHAM (*to* MARCUS)—Taylor is a good man. He's got no money for treatment, got no job now, won't get one again.

MARCUS (*to* OSCAR)—Colonel Isham has just saved you from a lynching party. Should I thank him?

OSCAR (*terrified*)—Lynching! What did—Colonel Isham—I—

ISHAM—I don't want to speak with you.

MARCUS—Who does?

OSCAR—But what did I—

MARCUS—Do I have to tell you that if you ever put those robes on again, or take a gun to any man— (*Takes a roll of money from his pocket—throws it to* BEN.) Count out five hundred dollars, Benjamin.

OSCAR (*very nervous*)—You mean Taylor? I wasn't riding with the Klan boys. No, I wasn't. I was thinking about it, but—

BEN (*counting the money*)—No, he couldn't have been with them. He took me to the Mobile train and the train was late, so we sat talking. He couldn't have got up to Roseville.

ISHAM—You say you're willing to swear to that, Mr. Benjamin? You sure you're willing to go against fourteen people identifying your brother—

BEN—Oh, Oscar looks like anybody.

MARCUS—Give the money to Colonel Isham, Benjamin. (*Waves* OSCAR *away.*) Go away, Oscar. (OSCAR *exits through dining room door.*) Please use the money for Taylor.

ISHAM—We'll take care of him, Hubbard.

MARCUS—You won't take care of him because you can't. Learn to be poor, Isham, it has more dignity. Tell Taylor there will be a check each month. Tell him that my other son, Benjamin, wishes to make amends. Ben has a most charitable nature.

ISHAM—There is no need for so much. A hundred would be more proper.

MARCUS—Good day, Colonel. Don't give me lectures on propriety.

For a second Col. Isham hesitates about taking the money. Then he puts the bills in his pocket and departs toward the street.

Marcus Hubbard's early morning visit with his children is varied and characteristic. He thinks Ben showed more loyalty than sense trying to furnish an alibi for Oscar, but that's all right. As for Oscar, Marcus doesn't wonder that he is in a bad humor, as Regina charges. Oscar owes him an added five hundred dollars now—an announcement that sets Oscar shaking with nervous resentment.

But Marcus has little time for either Oscar or Ben. He is soon concentrating all his attention on Regina. Even his daughter's confession that she has been sending to Mobile for new dresses and other things—including a fur piece and muff that cost three hundred dollars alone—do not disturb him too much. Not until Regina intimates that possibly she might be wanting these new things for a trousseau, does Marcus show signs of irritation.

"A trousseau? So that's what you're buying?" blurts out Ben. "I saw Horace Giddens in Mobile last evening, and he was mighty disappointed you haven't answered his letter about coming up for another visit here."

"Hey, he wouldn't be bad for you, Regina," chimes in Oscar.

"He's in love with you," adds Ben. (*At which point* MARCUS *slams shut the book he has been reading.*) ". . . It's good society, that family, and rich," Ben goes on. "Solid, quiet rich."

"And you'd get to like him," adds Oscar, cheerily. "A lot of people get married not liking each other. Then, after marriage, they still don't like each other much, I guess—"

"Are you still drunk?" demands Ben, giving his brother a slap.

The suggestion of a wedding in the offing has excited Lavinia. She hopes— But Marcus soon puts a stop to her hopes. Marcus wants to know, and from Regina, just what's going on. Nor is he

completely satisfied with Regina's explanation that it's nothing—
nothing more than another of Ben's plans to annoy him. She had
bought the clothes because she wanted to take a little trip. But
if it is going to cause all this fuss she'll send the things back.

Regina has gone to her father and taken him by the arm.
"Spoiling your Sunday," she murmurs, sympathetically. "Come
on, darling. Let's take our lunch and go on a picnic, just you and
me. We haven't done that for a long time."

Lavinia would like to talk with Marcus now. It's her birthday.
Remember? And when she had tried to talk with him her last
birthday he had put her off until this birthday. Now—

But Marcus is still too busy. Let Regina have Bell put them
up a fine picnic lunch. Let her put in a good bottle of wine, too.
". . . I'll bring my Aristotle," he says to Regina. "You'll read in
English, I'll follow you in Greek. Shall we walk or drive?"

"Let's walk. You get the books and I'll get my things." Regina starts to follow Marcus into the house. At the door she turns
and smiles at Ben. "You never going to learn, Ben. Been living
with Papa for thirty-five years, and never going to learn—"

BEN—Learn what, honey?

OSCAR—Papa's sure hard on me. It's unnatural. If a stranger
came in, he'd think Papa didn't like me, his own son.

REGINA (*to* OSCAR)—You want some money? If you had any
sense you'd know how to get it: just tell Papa *Ben* don't want you
to have it. You'll get it. (*To* BEN.) You ain't smart for a man
who wants to get somewhere. You should have figured out long
ago that Papa's going to do just whatever you tell him not to do,
unless I tell him to do it. (*Pats his shoulder*.) Goodness gracious,
that's been working for the whole twenty years I been on earth.

BEN (*to* REGINA)—You are right, and you're smart. You must
give me a full lecture on Papa some day; tell me why he's so good
to you, how you managed, and so on.

REGINA (*laughing*)—I'm busy now, taking him on a picnic.

BEN—Oh, not now. Too hot for lectures. We'll wait for a
winter night. Before the fire. I'll sit opposite you and you talk
and I'll listen. And I'll think many things, like how you used to
be a beauty, but at fifty years your face got worn and sour.
Papa'll still be living, and he'll interrupt us, the way he does even
now: he'll call from upstairs to have you come and put him to bed.
And you'll get up and go, wondering how the years went by—
(*Sharply*.) Because, as you say, he's most devoted to you, and
he's going to keep you right here with him, all his long life.

REGINA (*angrily*)—He's not going to keep me here. And don't you think he is. I'm going away. I'm going to Chicago— (*She catches herself.*) Oh, well, I guess you'd have to know. But I wanted him to promise before you began any interfering—I'm going for a trip, and a nice long trip. So you're wrong, honey.

BEN (*slowly*)—He's consented to the trip?

REGINA (*gaily*)—No. But he will, by the time the picnic's over.

OSCAR—Chicago? You sure got Mama's blood. Little while now, and you're going to be just as crazy as Mama.

REGINA (*to* BEN)—And the trip's going to cost a lot of money. I got books from hotels, and I know. But you'll be working hard in the store and sending it on to me—

BEN—You could always come home occasionally and go on another picnic. This time I don't think so. Papa didn't just get mad about you and Horace Giddens. Papa got mad about you and any man, or any place that ain't near him. I wouldn't like to be in the house, for example, the day he ever hears the gossip about you and Bagtry— (*Sharply.*) Or is Bagtry going to Chicago?

REGINA (*tensely, softly*)—Be still, Ben.

With the added threat that if Ben starts anything he is likely to find himself in trouble, Regina goes upstairs and disappears into her room.

Ben has turned on Oscar. Why had his brother beaten Sam Taylor? Oscar tries to say it was because Taylor was a no-good carpet-bagger, but under pressure he admits it was because Taylor had tried to make evening appointments with Laurette. When Ben would know if Laurette is the "little whore" Oscar has been courting, there's the promise of a scuffle. Ben soon stops that—

"Now listen to me, you clown," he says sharply. "You put away your gun and keep it away. If those fools in your Klan want to beat up niggers and carpet-baggers, you let 'em do it. But you're not going to make this county dangerous to me or dangerous to the business. We had a hard enough time making them forget Papa made too much money out of the war, and I ain't ever been sure they forgot it."

"Course they haven't forgot it. Every time anybody has two drinks, or you call up another loan, there's plenty of talk, and plenty of hints I don't understand. If I had been old enough to fight in the war, you just bet I'd been right there, and not like you, bought off. I'm a Southerner. And when I see an old carpet-bagger or upstart nigger, why, I feel like taking revenge."

"For what? Because Papa made money on them? (*Very sharply*.) Put away that gun, Sonny, and keep it put away, you hear me?"

"All right, all right. I want to thank you. I forgot. For saying that I was talking to you on the train. Thanks, Ben."

"I wasn't lying for you. I was trying to save five hundred dollars."

Miss Birdie Bagtry is calling. The Hubbard brothers are taken by surprise. It has been a long time since she has been in that house. Birdie is "a slight, pretty, faded-looking girl of twenty. Her clothes are seedy; her face is worn and frightened." She apologizes for taking their time especially on "this day of privacy," but she'll be bothering them only a few minutes. She couldn't go to the store to see them, without setting the town talking. And what would her mama and her Cousin John think?

Oscar has left Birdie with Ben and Ben would know what it is Miss Birdie would like to talk to him about. Well, it seems the Bagtrys are having a mighty bad time. That can't go on. Birdie's mama knows that. She has been trying to get help from her kinfolk. Not those in Bowden. Mama had gone all the way to Natchez to keep the Bowden kin from knowing. But the Natchez kin couldn't help, either, much as they'd like to for Papa's dead sake—and Grandpa's—

Ben would bring Birdie back to the subject of her visit. Why did Mama make the trip to Natchez?

"To borrow money on the cotton. Or on the land," confesses Birdie, softly. "Or even to sell the pictures, or the silver. But they said they couldn't: that everybody was raising cotton that nobody else wanted. I don't understand that: I thought people always wanted cotton."

"They will again in fifty years."

"Oh! Fifty years! Well, I guess we can't wait that long. The truth is we can't pay or support our people, Mr. Benjamin, we can't— Well, it's just killing my mama.

What Birdie wants to know is, will Mr. Benjamin, or his father, or both of them, loan money on the Bagtry cotton, or land? If they will, Birdie's mama can do a lot of things with it—pay all her people and give Cousin John money to go away. John is anxious to go somewhere where there's a war. To Brazil, maybe. He could be a general in Brazil and earn a lot of money.

Will Birdie inherit Lionnet? Ben asks. Yes, she will—but Birdie wouldn't want him to think that her mama—

"You don't want your mama to know that you've come here?"
ventures Ben.

"Oh, no, no! She'd never forgive me, rather die—" Birdie is
greatly embarrassed.

"To think you had to come to us?" laughs Ben.

"I didn't mean that. I am so sorry. I didn't—"

"You have not offended me, ma'am. I only ask because as I
understand it you don't own Lionnet, your mama does. But you
don't want her to know about the loan. And so who could sign
for it?"

"I would." Birdie is staring at him. "Oh! You mean you
can't sign for what you don't own? Oh, I see. I hadn't thought
of that. Oh! That's how much of a ninny I am. . . . Forgive
me for bothering you. I shouldn't have. I'm sorry I just ruined
your Sunday morning. Good day, sir."

Before Oscar sulkily accepts the assignment to walk Birdie
home, Ben makes further investigations regarding the Bagtrys'
need of a loan. How much would they want? Five thousand dollars estimates Birdie. They'd need that much to pay the help,
buy seeds, pay their debts, etc.

"You know, of course, that all loans from our company are
made by my father," Ben explains. "I only work for him. Yours
is good cotton and good land. But you don't own it. That makes
it hard. It's very unusual, but perhaps I could think of some way
to accommodate you. A promise from you, in a letter—"

"Oh! Oh! Of course, I'd make the promise."

"I'll tell my father all about it; and you come back this afternoon—"

"Oh, no! I couldn't say all that today again. I just couldn't—
(Softly.) That's silly. Of course I could. What time will I
come?"

"I have a pleasanter idea. Come tomorrow evening. Once a
month my father has a music evening, with musicians from Mobile
to play on the violin, and flatter him. He's always in a good
humor after his music. Come in then, Miss Birdie, and please
invite Captain Bagtry to escort you."

"You really think there's any chance? Your papa would—
And my mama wouldn't ever have to find out?"

"I will do my best for you before you come," promises Ben,
with a bow.

"Thank you very much." For a second Birdie hesitates, then,
with determination, she says: "I will be most pleased to come."

Oscar has lingered to protest his having to attend Birdie, but

Ben is firm about that. He is thinking of doing Oscar a favor. If things work out right for him he would be able to lend Oscar the five hundred to pay Papa back. Why? Because he wants Oscar to be particularly nice to Birdie—"Flatter her, talk nice. She's kind of pretty," suggests Ben.

"Pretty? I can't stand 'em like that."

"I know. Virtue in women offends you. Now go on. Be charming. Five hundred possible dollars charming!"

"All right."

Marcus has come from the living room carrying a book, his hat and a bottle of wine. The picnic mood is upon him, and he is gay. He doesn't approve of Ben's soberness. Or his resentment at his lot. If Ben were to read a little more Aristotle it might take his mind off money.

Ben tells him of his invitation to the Bagtrys'. He thought it would please Marcus to have the quality folk coming to the Hubbards' for a favor. Marcus is suspicious. "You teasing me?" he demands.

BEN—No. The girl just left here. She wants us to lend money on the cotton. Her mama didn't know and mustn't know. But Miss Birdie doesn't own the place—

MARCUS—Then what kind of nonsense is this?

BEN—Maybe it's not nonsense. Take a note from her. If she dies before her mother—

MARCUS—Who said anything about dying? You're very concerned with people dying, aren't you?

BEN (*laughing*)—You hate that word. (*Quickly.*) Her mother could get out of it legally, maybe, but I don't think she would . . . Anyway, the old lady is sick, and it's worth a chance. Make it a short loan, call it in a few years. They've wrecked the place and the money won't do 'em much good. I think the time would come when you'd own the plantation for almost nothing— (*Looks up at* REGINA.) A loan would make them happy and make us money. Make the Bagtrys grateful to us—

REGINA (*softly*)—Course I don't know anything about business, Papa, but could I say something, please? I've been kind of lonely here with nobody nice having much to do with us— I'd sort of like to know people of my own age, a girl of my own age, I mean—

MARCUS (*to* BEN)—How much does she want?

BEN (*after a moment's hesitation*)—Ten thousand dollars.

MARCUS—On Lionnet? Ten thousand is cheap. She's a fool.

BEN (*smiling*)—Yes, I think she's a fool.

MARCUS (*giggling*)—Well, the one thing I never doubted was your making a good business deal. Kind of cute of you to think of their coming here to get it, too. Bagtrys in this house, begging. Might be amusing for an hour.

REGINA—We've got to be nice to them. Otherwise I just wouldn't want to see him come—(*Quickly.*) unless we'd be awful nice and polite.

MARCUS—They'll think we're nice and polite for ten thousand.

REGINA (*laughing in high good humor*)—I guess. But you be pleasant to them—

MARCUS—Why, Regina? Why are you so anxious?

REGINA—Papa, I told you. I been a little lonesome. No people my age ever coming here. I do think people like that sort of want to forgive you, and be nice to us—

MARCUS (*angrily*)—Forgive me?

REGINA (*little girl tearful*)—I'm mighty sorry. What have I done? Just said I'd like to have a few people listen to your old music. Is that so awful to want?

MARCUS (*pleadingly*)—Come on now, honey. It's been a long time since you been willing to spend a Sunday with me. If I was sharp, I'm sorry. Don't you worry. I'll be charming to the visiting gentry.

Ben has thought of something else. Miss Birdie is scared of asking Marcus for the loan. Perhaps it would be better if Papa just gave his consent and he (Ben) were to handle the details. Marcus' mind is back on the picnic. He doesn't want to hear of the woes of Lionnet. Let Ben do what he likes. But—it will be kind of nice owning Lionnet.

Lavinia would stop the departure for the picnic. This is the day—her birthday—that Marcus had promised to talk with her—and he is putting her off again. And after he had sworn on Lavinia's Bible, too. She pleads pathetically that Marcus keep his promise. Even her tears have no effect on him—

"Stop that nonsense," he says, sharply. "Get hold of yourself. I've had enough of that. I want no more."

"I'm not making any trouble," pleads Lavinia. "You know that, Marcus. Just promise me tomorrow."

"Stop it! I've had enough. Try to act like you're not crazy. Get yourself in hand!" And he walks away.

Regina and Coralee would comfort Lavinia, but she can't understand. "He didn't say any of those things," she wails. "He said he would speak with me sure thing— No man breaks a Bible

promise, and you can't tell me they do. You know I got my cor-
respondence with the Reverend. He wants me to come and I got
my mission and my carfare. In his last letter the Reverend said
if I was coming I should come, or should write him and say I
couldn't ever come. 'Couldn't ever come—' Why did he write
that?"

"I don't know."

"Your people are my people. I got to do a little humble service.
I lived in sin these thirty-seven years, Coralee. Such sin I couldn't
even tell you."

"You told me."

"Now I got to finish with the sin. Now I got to do my mission. And I'll be—I'll do it nice, you know I will. I'll gather the
little black children round, and I'll teach them good things. I'll
teach them how to read and write, and sing the music notes and—"

"Oh, Miss Viney," wearily suggests Coralee. "Maybe it's just
as well. Maybe they'd be scared of a white teacher coming among
them."

For a little while Lavinia continues a rambling lament, but
Coralee is able finally to interest her in other things—

"Nice and cool in your room. Want to lie down?" Lavinia
doesn't answer. "Want to play a little on the piano? Nobody's
inside." Again no answer. "All right, if you don't want to. I tell
you what. Come on in the kitchen and rest yourself with us."

This idea catches Lavinia's interest. Coralee takes her arm and
they start out.

The curtain falls.

ACT II

The following evening Marcus Hubbard is entertaining his musician friends. They are in the living room of the Hubbard house—
Harold Penniman, "a tall, fattish man," and Gilbert Jugger, "who
looks like everybody." Marcus, Penniman and Jugger are standing in front of a music stand, looking down at a score. Ben and
Oscar are sitting at a table, each with a glass of brandy and the
brandy decanter in front of them.

The living room is modestly furnished. The furniture is from
the previous owner, but "Marcus has cleared the room of the orna-
ments and the ornamented. . . . A Greek vase, glass enclosed,
stands on a pedestal; a Greek statue sits on the table; Greek battle
scenes are hung on the walls."

The conversation swings between the music score and the
brandy, both of which are approved. Presently Lavinia comes

from the dining room to announce, with some hesitation but considerable eagerness, that a cold collation has been prepared—a cold collation being "what you call food when you have guests."

"There'll be a dish of crabs, of course. And a dish of crawfish boiled in white wine, the way Belle does. And a chicken salad, and a fine strong ham we've been saving— (*Stops.*) Oh! I'm worrying you gentlemen."

"Worrying us?" Penniman has lifted his glass. "You, the honor of Rose county, and the redeemer of this family—"

But Marcus stops him, taking the glass from his hand and carrying it to the table. Marcus wants to discuss music. His music. He is flattered by Penniman's suggestion that this, Marcus' third composition, should be played in Mobile—first at the school and later, maybe—

They decide to try the composition now, with Marcus playing the solo violin part. They move out to the porch, Marcus stopping on the way to compliment Regina on her ravishing appearance in one of her new Chicago dresses. Regina is pleased with the compliment, but she has other things on her mind. First, Mama must go upstairs and let Coralee fix her up for the hightoned guests who are coming. Second, Regina must not forget to see that Papa orders up the best champagne. . . .

Oscar is in trouble. He would like to have his father help him. Oscar has an appointment tonight with a young lady from Roseville, but Ben is trying to press him on the Bagtry girl—

"Ben's figured they're so hard up for money they might even have me," says Oscar. "It all fits in with this mortgage you're giving them, or something. He's got his eye on the cotton— (*Laughs.*) And Ben's eye goes in a lot of directions, mostly around corners. It's true, Papa. He made me take the girl home yesterday. . . ."

Marcus is no more than idly interested. He is still fussing with his music. "The mortgage, and then the girl and you," he mutters. "Interesting man, Benjamin."

Oscar is persistent. He would like to have his father meet Laurette, whom he deeply loves. She is of the lower classes, Oscar admits—but that's no reason for Ben to cry her down. Can Oscar bring Laurette to the concert? It would be a good joke on Ben to have a member of the lower classes sort of mixing with the gentry at the Hubbards'. Oscar is also prepared to defend Laurette's professional standing—

"Oh, maybe she was a little wild before I met her, but— She

was left an orphan, and she didn't know what else to do, starving and cold, friendless."

"Oh, God, shut up!" Marcus shudders at the picture. Then he laughs. "All right, go and get her if you like." Marcus insists, however, that Laurette shall come dressed. He wouldn't like her to appear unrobed, he suggests slyly.

On his way out Oscar meets Regina. When his sister hears that he is going for Laurette, she is far from pleased. She would have Ben stop Oscar.

"He *can't* bring her here!" protests Regina. "You know what John will think. I saw him this afternoon: I had to beg him to come tonight. He doesn't know why Birdie wants him to come, but—Ben, he'll think we meant to do it, planned to insult them—"

"Yes, I'm sure he will." Ben is smiling.

The music has started on the porch. For a moment Ben and Regina stand listening. Regina is still unhappy—

"What's the matter with Papa?" she demands. "Why did he let Oscar—"

"You're going to learn some day about Papa," promises Ben. "It's not as easy as you think, Regina." He continues to look out at the musicians. "He gave those clowns five thousand last month for something they call their music school. Now that they are playing his composition he should be good for another five thousand—"

"Did he really?" Regina shakes her head. "Well, anyway, he's promised me plenty for—"

"To marry Bagtry? Enough to support you the rest of your life, you and your husband? I'm taking a vacation the day he finds out about your marriage plans."

"I don't know what you're talking about." Regina is both angry and nervous. She moves away from Ben, then turns back and says tensely—"Leave me alone, Ben. Leave me alone. Stop making trouble. If you dare say *anything* to Papa about John, I'll—"

"Don't threaten me. I'm sick of threats."

"You'll be much sicker of them if you—" Regina is finding it difficult to control her anger. "Ben, don't! I'm in love with John!"

"But he's not in love with you," softly answers Ben.

Coralee has managed to get Lavinia into her company dress. Lavinia is approaching the concert apprehensively. She can't remember whether people curtsy or just shake hands these days—

". . . I guess it's just about the first guests we had since the suspicion on your papa."

"Now, Mama!" Regina is worried. "Please don't talk about any of that tonight. Don't talk at all about the war, or anything that happened. Please remember, Mama, do you hear?"

It is Coralee who answers. "She won't," she says, protectively. "You all have been teasing her and she's tired."

Marcus and his musicians have finished the preliminaries. Now they are ready to start the regular program. Marcus doesn't see any reason why they should wait for the guests. So they start with a Mozart "divertisement for violin, viola and cello." . . .

Oscar has arrived with Laurette Sincee. "Laurette is about 20, pig-face cute, a little too fashionably dressed." She is standing in the door, greatly admiring the room. Presently she stops to wonder what the noise is. It's Papa's concert, Oscar explains. Papa is playing the violin. Which reminds Laurette of a Frenchman she knew once. He played a violin too.

Oscar doesn't like to have Laurette talk about other men. He is "deeply and sincerely" in love with Laurette, he repeats. He is hoping to ask Papa for a loan. Then he and Laurette will go down to New Orleans and get married. Papa is in a good humor tonight. If Laurette will help things along by flattering him and his music, and telling him how interested she is in reading and things like that—that will help—

"Don't let him worry you, honey," advises Oscar. "Just take it nice and easy. Pretend nobody knows anything about you, pretend you're just as good as them—"

"*Pretend?* Pretend I'm as good as anybody called Hubbard? Why, my pa died at Vicksburg. He didn't stay home bleeding the whole state of Alabama with money tricks, and suspected of worse. You think I been worried for that reason?"

"No, no! I—for God's sake don't talk like that—"

"You may be the rich of this county, but everybody knows how. Why, the Frenchman, I used to eat dinner with and his sister, the Countess— What you mean, boy, your folks—?"

"I didn't mean anything bad. Haven't I just said I wanted to *marry* you? I think you're better than anybody."

"Stop, please!" Oscar has clapped his hand over Laurette's mouth. Outside the company can be heard arriving.

Laurette is quieter now and good-natured again. She even thinks she would like to go to New Orleans. For that Oscar would take her in his arms, kiss her with a considerable show of passion. But Laurette would draw back.

"Now, Oskie, you know this ain't the place or the time for

mush," she says with a giggle. She is still giggling and protesting as the Bagtrys are shown in. Birdie smiles nervously. John stares at Laurette, whom he recognizes.

Lavinia, coming from the porch, doesn't wait for an introduction. She thinks Laurette may be Birdie, and is quick to greet her hospitably. Lavinia is quite flustered before she gets things straightened out. Especially after Oscar has explained that Laurette is a visitor in town—is, in fact, visiting the Hubbards.

As the others settle themselves for the concert, Ben relays the information to Birdie that his father has agreed to the loan. They will settle the details next day—

"You wanted five thousand dollars, Miss Birdie," Ben is saying. "I have asked my father to lend you ten thousand."

"Oh! Mr. Ben, I don't need—"

"You can take five now, but if you should happen to need more, it will be there for you."

"But I won't need ten thousand dollars. No, indeed I won't. It's very kind of you, but—"

"You will get only five," Ben repeats, carefully. "I will keep the rest waiting for you. That's the way these things are done—sometimes."

"But it's bad enough to owe five thousand—not less ten."

"You will only owe five. Now there is nothing more to worry about."

"Well, thank you, sir."

Oscar has come from the porch looking for a drink. "Papa going to play all night?" he exclaims, querulously. "Laurette's getting restless, sitting there."

"She's not accustomed to a sitting position," ventures Ben. "Have another drink. I got a feeling you're going to need it."

The music has stopped. The guests are moving into the living room. Laurette is free to admit that she doesn't think much of the punch. "It don't mean anything," says she. So Ben puts in more brandy to make it mean more.

Now Marcus has met Laurette. She is quick to tell him of her fondness for music. She had an uncle who played. It was the uncle who had taught her to love music. Did Uncle play a violin like Papa? No. Uncle played a small drum. But he sure did like Mozart.

Hearing this, Marcus crosses the room to the Bagtrys. "Miss Sincee pleases me," he tells Birdie. "Her uncle played Mozart on a little drum. Have you ever heard of that, Miss Bagtry?"

"Oh. Well, I haven't, but I'm sure there must be such an arrangement."

The conversation has turned to Europe and travel. Birdie recalls the many countries which John had visited before the war. Marcus has never been to Europe, but he plans to go. He might even settle down there. Would Regina like that?

Regina might, but with Regina Chicago must come first. If Marcus should ever decide to stay in Europe, he thinks he would want to take his residence in Greece. Perhaps Capt. Bagtry would advise him? Capt. Bagtry might, but he has no memory of Europe at all. It is as though he had never been there. In fact, Capt. Bagtry confesses to Marcus, about the only thing that he does remember is the war. Lavinia can believe that, seeing she remembers the day Capt. Bagtry rode away—

"Yes, ma'am," continues John, with interest. "I can't remember the years before, and the years after have just passed like a wasted day. But the morning I rode off, and for three years, three months and eight days after, well, I guess I remember every soldier, every gun, every meal, even every dream I had at night—"

There is a brief interruption and Laurette manages to get in a word. Laurette has been devoting herself rather assiduously to the drinks Ben keeps pouring for her, over Oscar's protests.

"I wouldn't ever name a boy Oscar," announces Laurette. "It's silly."

"I can't remember why we chose the name. Can you, Marcus?"

"Your father's name was Oscar," Marcus reminds her.

"Oh, goodness, yes." Lavinia returns to being worried and crushed.

A moment later Marcus has again forced John Bagtry into a war discussion. ". . . What now seems to you the most important of your battles, Capt. Bagtry."

John is annoyed. "I don't know. But there's no need for us to talk about the war, sir."

"Oh, I'm interested. I know more about the Greek wars than I do of our own."

"Bet you anything there's a good reason for that," ventures the interrupting Laurette. "There's a good reason for everything in this vale of tears." Again Oscar tries to take her glass from her, but she holds on to it and shortly passes it back to Ben for another refilling.

Supper is announced. Marcus is still in an irritable mood and would like to take it out on John—

"People remember what makes them happy, and you were happy in the war, weren't you?" he demands.

JOHN—Yes, sir. I was happy. I thought we would win.

MARCUS—I never did. Never, from the first foolish talk to the last foolish day. (JOHN *turns sharply away.*) I have disturbed you. I'm most sorry. I speak the truth—whenever I can.

BIRDIE (*hastily*)—Oh, John doesn't mind that. He means— well, you see it's hard for us to understand anybody who thought we'd lose—

JOHN (*sharply*)—It's still hard for a soldier to understand.

BIRDIE (*quickly*)—John means once a soldier, always a soldier. He wants to go to Brazil right now. Of course you know, Mr. Hubbard, the radical people down there are trying to abolish slavery, and ruin the country. John wants to fight for his ideals.

MARCUS—Why don't you choose the other side? Every man needs to win once in his life.

JOHN (*angrily*)—I don't like that way of saying it. I don't necessarily fight for slavery. I fight for a way of life. . . . (MARCUS *and* OSCAR *laugh.*)

MARCUS—You disapprove of me, Captain.

JOHN (*in back of the sofa*)—I am in your house, sir, and you forced me into this kind of talk.

MARCUS—Well, I disapprove of you. Your people deserved to lose their war and their world. It was a backward world, getting in the way of history. Appalling that you still don't realize it. Really, people should read more books.

REGINA (*angrily*)—Papa, I didn't ask John here to listen to you lecture and be nasty and insulting.

MARCUS—*You* asked him here? You asked *John?* (*Sharply.*) Come in to supper, Regina.

REGINA (*very sharply*)—When I'm ready, Papa.

Regina has remained behind to explain things to John. She would not have him pay any attention to her father. She will take care of Papa. And she would have John approve her newest plan: Regina is going to Chicago. A month later John will join her and they will be married. Of course Papa will have a fit, but Regina will come home long enough to talk him out of that.

John also has a plan. So has Birdie. Birdie has told John that there will be money enough to run Lionnet and to give him enough to get to Brazil. He wants to be with fighting men again. Regina is disappointed.

"You don't want to come with me? You don't want to marry me?" she charges.

JOHN—No. I don't. I never said I did. I don't want to talk this way. But I don't want to lie, either. Honey, I like you so much. But I shouldn't have let us get like this. You're not in love with me. I'm no good for you—

REGINA—I am in love with you. I've never loved before, and I won't love again.

JOHN—My darling child, everybody thinks that, the first time. You're a lonely girl and I'm the first man you've liked. You can have anybody you want—

REGINA—John. Come away with me. We'll be alone. And after a while, if you still don't want me, then— (*Softly.*) I've never pleaded for anything in my life before. (*Smiles.*) I might hold it against you.

JOHN—Oh, Regina, don't speak of pleading. You go away. By the time you come back, you'll be in love with somebody else, and I'll be gone.

REGINA—Where did you say Miss Birdie was getting this money, this money for you to travel with?

JOHN—I don't know where: she won't tell me. But she says we'll have five thousand dollars this week.

REGINA—Five thousand?

JOHN—I'd guess she's arranged something about the Gilbert Stuart or the West. We haven't anything but the portraits—

REGINA—Is that what you'd guess? Well, I guess different. So she's planning to get you away from me?

JOHN—Nobody's *planning* anything. Oh, look, honey. This isn't any good. We'll go home now—

REGINA—Papa's coming. Please go in to supper now. It will be bad for me if you make any fuss or left now— (*Softly.*) We'll talk tomorrow. I love you.

Marcus is still irritable. Nor does Regina's interest in John serve to cheer him. Of course Marcus will make the Bagtry loan. "It is good for me and bad for them," he says. And he refuses to believe that Ben is scheming to cheat on the deal. Neither does he believe that Birdie Bagtry is trying to make fools of the Hubbards. What he wants to know is why was Regina talking to John Bagtry? Why was John calling her "honey"—

"Ben is sometimes smarter than you are," charges Regina, speaking carefully, "and you are so sure he isn't, that you get

careless about him. Bagtry doesn't know about *your* loan on
Lionnet, but the girl told him she was getting five thousand dollars this week. *Five thousand dollars, not ten.* I'd like to bet the
extra five is for Ben to keep. You're getting older, Papa, and
maybe you're getting a little tired and don't think as fast. I guess
that happens to everybody. You'll have to start watching Ben
even more."

"Regina, I don't want to hear any more." His words follow
Regina, as she goes into the dining room.

The company is coming from supper. Penniman and Jugger,
the musicians, are ready to continue the concert. Lavinia reports
a most interesting talk with Laurette, who, it seems, has a touch
of heart trouble. "She said she was trying to see if good, strong
drink would help," reports Lavinia. "I never heard that, although
I heard Ben said it was a good cure."

Laurette is pretty nervous when she joins the group with
Oscar. In fact, Laurette is inclined to bump into things. Find-
ing herself near the piano, she strikes a note. Then another.
Then a lot of notes. Oscar grabs both her hands and holds them.
But Oskie's papa likes music, protests Laurette, with a grin.

Now she has moved over to Marcus. "Oskie wants to
marry little old Laurette," she informs him.

"Does little old Laurette think that fortunate?"

"Sometimes yes, sometimes no," admits Laurette. "We're going on down to New Orleans."

"That reminds me: I'm told you work for a living. That is
good. Oscar is not a rich man."

"Rich?" Laurette laughs scornfully. "How could he be on
that stinking slave salary you pay him? That's why you're sure
to repent and help us, Oskie says. When you die you're going
to leave it to him anyway, so why not now, Oskie says."

"Oskie is a liar. Always has been. And he steals a little.
Nothing much, not enough to be respectable. But you know all
that, of course. . . . If you want him, Miss Laurette, do have
him."

Oscar is trying to get Laurette away, but she pulls back. She
has a few more things to say to the "old bastard—"

"Everybody in this county knows how you got rich," shrills
Laurette; "bringing in salt and making poor, dying people give
up everything for it. Right in the middle of the war, men dying
for you, and you making their kinfolks give you all their goods
and money—and I heard how they suspected you of worse, and
you only just got out of a hanging rope. (*Points to* OSCAR.) I

didn't even want to talk to him the first night he slept with me. My uncle used to tell me about you and your doings."

"Get that girl out of here!" orders Marcus. "Then come back. And come back quickly."

Lavinia can't quite understand her husband's anger. After all, the girl only told the truth—

The guests are leaving. They do so with every effort at being politely formal. But Marcus is eruptive and John is filled with insults and loathing. It is all Birdie can do to keep them apart. Regina has followed John out. Birdie has stayed behind.

Birdie is sorry John was so upset, but, as Marcus may remember, John's twin brother was killed in the massacre—Marcus can't even remember the massacre. All he remembers is that Birdie's mother hasn't ever bowed to him in the forty years he has lived in that town. He isn't interested in Birdie's simple, though desperate explanation of everything. Or in her self-accusation for having been the cause of it all. . . .

Marcus has decided not to make the loan!

Birdie draws back from the announcement as though she had been struck. The next moment she is pleading with a kind of suppressed hysteria that Marcus change his mind. She has told people. . . . She will do anything . . . give anything. . . . There are still a couple of paintings . . . and a little silver—

"I was going to use the first money to buy molasses and sugar," she sighs. "All that land and cotton and we're starving. It sounds crazy, to need even molasses. . . . I should have known I couldn't do anything right. I never have. I'm sorry to have told you such things about us. You lose your manners when you're poor. (*Goes to* LAVINIA.) Thank you, ma'am."

"Good night, child." Lavinia is smiling gently as she takes Birdie's hand. "You ride over to see me, or come down by the river, and we'll read together."

"Thank you, Mr. Ben. I know you acted as my good friend."

Marcus must laugh at that.

"Goodness, Marcus." Lavinia turns on Marcus as Birdie runs out. "Couldn't you have—it's pig mean, being poor. Takes away your dignity."

"That's correct, Lavinia. And a good reason for staying rich."

The evening is just beginning for Marcus. He quarrels with the musicians, Penniman and Jugger, as he dismisses them, and discovers what Jugger, at least, thinks of him as a musician. He hears Oscar accuse Ben of trying to ruin his life by getting Laurette drunk—

"I told you he had his eye on Birdie and Lionnet, and me getting it for him," cries Oscar, as his father laughs at his threat to beat Ben up. "So I fool him by bringing Laurette here. And then *he* fools *you:* gets Laurette drunk, and you get mad. That's just what he wanted you to do. And you did it for him. I think the joke's kind of on you."

Ben doesn't mind confessing that he did get Laurette drunk and that he had a reason for doing so. "Just as good for Oscar to marry a silly girl who owns cotton, as a silly girl who doesn't even own the mattress on which she—"

Oscar springs at Ben, Ben shakes him off. Before Oscar can charge again Marcus has grabbed him. "Will you stop running about and pulling at people!" he shouts. "Go outside and shoot a passing nigger if your blood is throwing clods into your head."

"I'm going to kill Ben if he doesn't stop—"

"Are you denying the girl makes use of the mattress, or do you expect to go through life killing every man who knows she does."

"Papa, stop it!" screams Oscar. "I am deeply and sincerely in love!"

"In one minute I shall put you out of the room."

Marcus has turned to Ben. Now he understands. "Your tricks are getting nasty and they bore me," he warns his son. "I'm tired of your games, do you hear me? You're a clerk in my store: and that you'll remain. You won't get the chance to try anything like this again: but in case you anger me once more, there won't be the job in the store, and you won't be here. Is that clear?"

"Very clear."

Oscar is pleading again that Laurette be not misunderstood. "Papa, you couldn't condemn a girl for a past that was filled with loathing for what society forced upon her; a woman of inner purity, made to lead a life of outward shame."

"What are you talking about?"

"He's read a book," suggests Regina sarcastically.

"At nine years old I was carrying water for two bits a week," says Marcus, softly. "I took the first dollar I ever had and went to the paying library to buy a card. When I was twelve I was working out in the fields, and that same year I taught myself Latin and French. At fourteen I was driving mules all day and most of the night, and that was the year I learned my Greek, read my classics, taught myself— Think what I must have wanted for sons. And then think what I got. One unsuccessful trickster, one proud illiterate. No, I don't think Oscar's ever read a book." . . .

Marcus has made up his mind about Oscar. If he wants to go away with Laurette, let him go. He (Marcus) will leave a thousand dollars in an envelope on the table at six o'clock in the morning. Let Oscar take it and catch an early train.

Oscar is a bit overcome by this offer. It is kind of strange for him to be saying good-by to them all, after twenty-five years. But there is one thing he means to attend to before he goes. He turns sharply to Ben—

"You've bullied me since the day I was born," he says, fiercely. "But before I leave— You're going to do what I tell you. You're going to be on the station platform tomorrow morning. You're going to be there to apologize to Laurette. . . . And if you're not ready on time, I'll get you out of bed with this. And then you won't apologize to her standing up, but on your knees—"

Marcus has turned quickly to take a revolver away from Oscar. "Put that gun away! How dare you, in this house?"

"You've always been frightened of guns, Papa," taunts Ben. "Ever since that night, wasn't it?"

"That's true: ever since that night," repeats Lavinia, quietly.

"Put that gun away! And get upstairs! Immediately!" orders Marcus, livid with anger.

"See you at the station!" Oscar passes Ben on his way out.

"And they had hot tar and clubs and ropes that night—" Lavinia is still mumbling.

"Stop your crazy talk, Lavinia!"

"I don't like that word, Marcus. No, I don't. I think you use it just to hurt my feelings."

"He's upset, Mama." Ben is smiling. "Old fears come back, strong."

Regina is hoping Ben and his father are not going to have another set-to. They'll have to learn to get along together when she and Mama are gone. Which reminds Marcus that he is going to miss Regina very much. He thinks perhaps he will join her and her mother and take Regina with him to Europe when Lavinia comes home—

"I'm going to be sorry to miss the sight of your face when Regina produces the secret bridegroom," says Ben, insinuatingly. "Oh, you know about it. You guessed tonight. Captain Bagtry. I don't think he wants to marry her. I don't think he even wants to sleep with her any more. But he's a weak man and— (MARCUS *is advancing toward him.*) That won't do any good.

I'm going to finish. Yesterday, if you remember, Regina wanted you to make a loan to the girl. Tonight, when she found out John Bagtry wanted to use a little of the money to leave here, and her, she talked you out of it."

"*Ben, be still! Ben*—" Regina has gone swiftly to her father. "Don't listen, Papa. I have seen John, I told you that. I like him, yes. But don't you see what Ben is doing? He wanted to marry me off to money, he's angry—"

"I'm telling the truth. The whole town's known it for a year. . . . Go up to him, Regina, put your arms around him. Tell him you've never really loved anybody else, and never will. Lie to him, just for tonight. Tell him you'll never get in bed with anybody ever again—"

Marcus slaps Ben sharply across the face. A desperate Lavinia would come between them.

"I won't forget that," promises Ben, softly; "as long as I live!"

Marcus is not frightened. Let Ben get out of the house and out of his life the first thing in the morning.

When Lavinia has pitifully followed her first born through the door, a crushed Marcus turns helplessly to his daughter. How could she let that man touch her? How could she?—

Regina will not deny anything. She is in love, She wants to marry John. After that she is willing to come home and they can all live together.

"*Are you crazy?* Do you think I would stay in this house with you and—"

REGINA—Otherwise I'll go away. I say I will and you know I will. I'm not frightened to go. But if I go that way I won't ever see you again. And you don't want that: I don't think you could stand that. My way, we can be together. You'll get used to it, and John won't worry us. There'll always be you and me. You must have known I'd marry some day, Papa. Why, I've never seen you cry before. It'll just be like going for a little visit, and before you know it I'll be home again, and it will all be over. You know? Maybe next year, or the year after, you and I'll make that trip to Greece, just the two of us. (*Smiles.*) Now it's all settled. Kiss me good night, darling. (*She kisses him. He does not move.*)

LAVINIA (*coming in*)—Ben won't let me talk to him. He'd feel better if he talked, if he spoke out— I'm his mama and I got to take my responsibility for what—

REGINA (*going to door*)—Mama, I think we'll be leaving for Chicago sooner than we thought. We'll start getting ready tomorrow morning. Good night.

LAVINIA (*to* MARCUS)—Did you forget to tell her that I can't go with her? Didn't you tell them all where I'm going? I think you'd better do that, Marcus—

MARCUS (*very tired*)—I don't feel well. Please stop jabbering, Lavinia.

LAVINIA—You tell Regina tomorrow. You tell her how you promised me. (*Desperately—softly.*) Marcus, it's all I've lived for. And it can't wait now. I'm getting old, and I've got to go and do my work.

MARCUS—It isn't easy to live with you, Lavinia. It really isn't. Leave me alone.

LAVINIA (*gently*)—I know. We weren't ever meant to be together. You see, being here gives me—well, I won't use bad words, but it always made me feel like I sinned. And God wants you to make good your sins before you die. That's why I got to go now.

MARCUS—I've stood enough of that. Please—don't ever speak of it again.

LAVINIA—Ever speak of it? But you swore to me, over and over again!

MARCUS—Did you ever think I meant that nonsense?

LAVINIA—But I'm going!

MARCUS—You're never going! Never! Dr. Seckles knows how strange you've been, the whole town knows you're crazy. I try to leave you alone, try to leave me alone. If you worry me any more with it, I'll have to talk to the doctor and ask him to send you away. Now I don't want to listen to any more of that talk—ever. (*Softly, crying.*) Please go to bed now, and don't walk around all night again . . .

LAVINIA (*staring at him*)—Coralee!—Could I—Coralee— He never meant me to go! He says I *can't* go! (*She starts to leave the room slowly, then she begins to run.*) Coralee! Are you in bed . . . could I . . . Coralee. . . . Oh, Coralee. . . .

The curtain falls.

ACT III

It is early the next morning. Lavinia is in the living room, waiting for Ben. As she waits she rocks back and forth, humming a Negro spiritual. Ben is not long in coming. He carries a suitcase. He has left all his things in the ironing room and will send for them.

Lavinia would have Ben take her with him—as far as Altaloosa. There she would get off the boat and there she would stay. And Marcus couldn't bring her back or send her—

"You've got to take me," pleads Lavinia. "Last night he said he'd never ever meant me to go. Last night he said if ever, then he'd have Dr. Seckles, have him, have him . . . Take me away from here. For ten years he swore, for ten years he swore a lie to me. I told God about that last night, and God's message said, 'Go, Lavinia, even if you have to tell the awful truth. If there is no other way, tell the truth.' "

"The truth about what?"

"I think now, I should have told the truth that night. But you don't always know how to do things when they're happening. It's not easy to send your own husband into a hanging rope."

"What do you mean?"

"All night long I been thinking I should go right up those steps (*Pointing to steps.*) and tell him what I know. Then he'd have to let me leave or— (*Puts her hand to her face.*) I've always been afraid of him, because once or twice—"

"Of course. But you're not afraid of me."

"Oh, I been afraid of you, too. I spent a life afraid. And you know that's funny, Benjamin, because deep down I'm a woman wasn't made to be afraid. What are most people afraid of? Well, like your papa, they're afraid to die. But I'm not afraid to die because my colored friends going to be right there to pray me in."

Tensely, angrily, Ben continues his questioning. What has she been saying? What has she meant—

BEN (*carefully*)—Mama. Now listen to me. It's late and there isn't much time. I'm in trouble, bad trouble, and you're in bad trouble. Tell me fast what you're talking about. Maybe I can get us both out of trouble. Maybe. But only if you tell me now. *Now.* And tell me quick and straight. You can go away and I—

LAVINIA—I saw him, like I told you, the night of the massacre, on the well-house roof.

BEN (*rising*)—All right. I understand what you mean. All right. But there's a lot I don't know or understand. I'll ask the questions and you just answer them, don't say anything else—

LAVINIA (*as if she hadn't heard the last sentence*)—One time last night, I thought of getting his envelope of money, bringing it out here, tearing it up and watching his face when he saw it at breakfast time.   But it's not nice to see people grovel on the ground for money—

BEN—The envelope of money?   The little envelope of money or the big envelope?

LAVINIA—And I thought too about giving it to the poor.   But it's evil money and not worthy of the poor.

BEN—No, the poor don't want evil money.   That's not the way.

LAVINIA (*turning to him*)—Oh, I'm glad to hear you say that, but you can see how I have been tempted when I thought what the money could do for my little school.   I want my colored children to have many things.

BEN (*desperately*)—You can have everything for them if—

LAVINIA—Oh, nobody should have everything.   All I want is a nice school place, warm in the winter, and a piano, and books and a good meal every day, hot and fattening.

BEN—Come here, Mama.   (*He takes her by the shoulders.*) He will be awake soon.

LAVINIA—First part of the war I was so silly I thought it was brave of your papa to run the blockade, even though I knew he was dealing with the enemy to do it.   People were dying for salt and I thought it was good to bring it to them.   I didn't know he was getting eight dollars a bag for it, Benjamin, a little bag. Imagine taking money for other people's misery.

BEN (*softly*)—Yes, I know all that, Mama.   Everybody does now.

LAVINIA (*puzzled*)—But I can't tell what you know, Benjamin. You were away in New Orleans in school and it's hard for me to put in place what you know and—   (BEN *moves impatiently.*) So—   Well, there was the camp where our boys were.   It was up the river, across the swamp fork, back behind the old delta fields.

BEN—Yes, I know where it was.   And I know that Union troops crossed the river and killed the twenty-seven boys who were training there.   And I know that Papa was on one of his salt-running trips that day and that every man in the county figured Union troops couldn't have found the camp unless they were led through to it, and I know they figured Papa was the man who did the leading.

LAVINIA—He didn't lead them to the camp.   Not on purpose. No, Benjamin, I am sure of that.

BEN—And he proved to them he wasn't in town so he couldn't have done it. So now where are we?

LAVINIA—They were murder mad the night they found the poor dead boys. They came with hot tar and guns to find your papa.

BEN (*softly*)—But they didn't find him.

LAVINIA—But I found him!

It was four-thirty that morning that Lavinia and Coralee had seen Marcus on the well-house roof. It is so written in Lavinia's Bible. . . . "Twenty minutes to six he climbed down from the roof, unlocked the well-house door, got some money from the envelope, and went on down through the back pines. Coralee and I ran back to the house, shivering and frightened. . . . Three days later—no, two days later, the morning of April 5, 1864, at exactly ten-five—"

"What are you reading?" Ben's tone is tense.

LAVINIA—He rode back into town, coming up the Mobile road. They were waiting for him and they roped him and searched him. But he had two passes proving he had ridden through Confederate lines the day before the massacre, and didn't leave till after it. The passes were signed by Captain Virgil E. McMullen of the 5th Tennessee from Memphis. They were stamped passes, they were good passes, and they had to let him go. But he had no money when he came home. So Coralee and I just knew he paid Capt. Virgil E. McMullen to write those passes. (*Looks down at Bible.*) Virgil E. McMullen, Captain in the 5th Tennessee—

BEN (*tensely, pointing to the Bible*)—It's written down there?

LAVINIA—Coralee and I were half wild with what was the right thing to do and the wrong. So we wrote it all down here in my Bible and we each put our hand on the book and swore to it. That made us feel better—

BEN—I'm sure of it. Give me the Bible, Mama—

LAVINIA (*turning away*)—I think there's one in your room, at least there used to be—

BEN—Oh, Mama. For God's sake. I need it. It's the only proof we've got, and even then he'll—

LAVINIA—You don't need half this proof. That's the trouble with your kind of thinking, Benjamin. My, I could just walk down the street, tell the story to the first people I met. They'd believe me, and they'd believe Coralee. We're religious women, and everybody knows it. (*Smiles.*) And then they'd want to believe us. I think people always believe what they want to believe, don't you? I don't think I'd have any trouble, if you stood behind me, and gave me courage to do the right talking.

BEN (*laughing*)—I'll be behind you. But I'd like the Bible behind me. Come, Mama, give it to me now. I need it for us. (*Slowly she hands the Bible to him.*) All right, now I'd like to have that envelope.

LAVINIA—But what has the money got to do with— I don't understand why the envelope— I'm trying hard to understand everything. But I can't see what it has—

BEN—I can't either. So let's put it this way: it would make me feel better to have it. There's nothing makes you feel better at this hour of the morning than an envelope of money.

LAVINIA (*thinking*)—Oh. Well. It's in the upper small left-hand drawer of your papa's desk. But I don't know where he keeps the key.

BEN (*laughing*)—That's very negligent of you. We won't need the key. Now call Papa. I'll be back in a minute.

Lavinia is hesitant about calling Marcus. She has never dared to do anything like that before. But Ben insists. "You're going to do a lot of things you've never done before," he promises his mother.

Marcus finally appears in his shirt sleeves on the balcony. He is annoyed by Lavinia's shouting, though he can understand her being up early to give her blessings to her departing sons. Has Benjamin gone?

"No, Marcus. He hasn't gone. He's inside knocking off the locks on your desk."

And that is what Ben has done—with the butt end of a pistol. He comes in presently, carrying the pistol in one hand and the large envelope in the other.

The envelope, Ben intimates, contains something like $40,000. The pistol he flourishes modestly when Marcus starts to come quickly down stairs. "I like you better up there," he calls to his father. "So stay there. *Stay there!*"

Ben has taken money from the large envelope, put it in a smaller envelope and called Jake. Jake is to take the small envelope over to the Bagtrys', talk to no one but Birdie Bagtry, give her the envelope and tell her to forget last night. Tell her, too, that Mr. Ben wishes Capt. Bagtry good luck. That done, Jake is to buy two tickets on the sugar boat.

Marcus, beside himself with anger, shouts denials of all these orders, but the threatening revolver in Ben's hands keeps him on the balcony. He'll be getting even in the years to come—

"In the years to come," echoes Ben, "when you think about me, do it this way: (*Sharply.*) You had been buying salt from the Union garrison across the river. On the morning of April 2nd you rode over to get it; early evening of April 3rd you started back with it—"

"Are you writing a book about me? I would not have chosen you as my recorder."

"You were followed back, which is exactly what Union officers had been waiting for, at eleven o'clock that night—"

"Marcus didn't *mean* to lead them back. I explained that to you, Benjamin—"

"*You* explained it to him? What—"

"Eleven o'clock that night twenty-seven boys in the swamp camp were killed. The news reached here, and you, about an hour later."

With occasional promptings from Lavinia, and despite Marcus' interruptions, Ben goes on with his recital of events that fatal night.

He traces the stricken townsfolk's discovery of the massacre and their rightful guess that Marcus was the guilty informant; he follows Marcus from his hiding place on the well-house roof, where Lavinia and Coralee had seen him, to his escape with the money to buy from a certain Capt. Virgil E. McMullen the passes that saved him from hanging sixteen years ago.

Marcus pretends not to be frightened, but his voice is changed and strange when he pleads with Lavinia as a religious woman to remember that not only Dr. Seckles, but a Dr. Hammanond in Mobile, to whom she was taken later, had pronounced her—well, a very, very sick woman. Ben didn't know about Dr. Hammanond, did he?

Ben is not impressed. He would have Lavinia go change her dress and get ready for a walk. She will still have time to get on the sugar boat, but first—

"I figure you can wear the same costume to a lynching as you can on a boat." Ben moves around to where Marcus can see and hear him plainly. "We'll walk around to old Isham first, whose youngest son got killed that night. John Bagtry will be mighty happy to remember that his twin brother also died that night. And Mrs. Mercer's oldest son and the two Sylvan boys and— We won't have to go any further because they'll be glad to fetch their kinfolk and, on their way, all the people who got nothing else to do tonight, or all the people who owe you on cotton or cane or land. Be the biggest, happiest lynching in the history of Roseville county. All right. Go change your clothes—"

"A lynching?" Lavinia protests. *"I don't believe in lynching.* If you lynch a white man, it can lead right into lynching a black man. No human being's got a right to take a life, in the sight of God."

"You're losing your witness," calls Marcus. "What a clown you turned out to be. Only you would think your mother would go through with this, only you would trust her—"

"She won't have to do much. I'm taking her Bible along." He picks the Bible up from the table. "On this page, that night, she wrote it all down. The names, the dates, the hours. Then she and Coralee swore to it. Everybody will like the picture of two lost innocents and a Bible, and if they don't, sixteen-year-old ink will be much nicer proof than your Mobile doctor. Anyway, you won't have time to get him here. Want to finish now?"

But Lavinia never told Ben that she would have anything to do with a lynching. No, she didn't. And she won't. She only said she was going to tell the truth to everybody.

"If there's any nasty talk of lynching, I'm going to plead for your life hard as I can, yes, I am!" Lavinia calls to Marcus.

"Now, that's merciful of you," says Ben, laughing. "I am going to do the same thing. I'm going to plead with them for Papa's life."

"That's the least a son can do for his father."

"Better than that. I'll come tomorrow morning and cut you down from the tree, and bury you with respect. How did the Greeks bury fathers who were murdered? Tell me, and I'll see to it. You'd like that, wouldn't you?"

LAVINIA—Benjamin, don't talk that way—

MARCUS (*starting down the steps*)—You gave him the right to talk that way. You did, Lavinia, and I don't understand anything that's been happening. Do you mean that you actually wrote a lie in your Bible. You who— (*He stands on landing.*)

LAVINIA (*angrily*)—Don't you talk like that. Nobody can say there's a lie in my Bible— You take that back. You take it back right away. I don't tell lies, and I don't swear to them, and I don't swear on my Bible to a false thing, and neither does Coralee. You just apologize to me, and then you apologize to Coralee, that's what you do—

MARCUS (*quickly*)—No, no. I don't mean you knew it was a lie. Of course not, Lavinia. But let me see it, and then tell me—

LAVINIA—Let him see it. Of course.

BEN—Oh, tell him to come down and look at it. I'll put it here, under the gun.

LAVINIA—Bibles are there for all people. For grown people. I'm not going to have any Bibles in my school. That surprise you all? It's the only book in the world, but it's just for grown people, after you know it don't mean what it says. (*She reaches for the Bible.* BEN *restrains her.*) You take Abraham: he sends in his wife, Sarah, to Pharaoh, and he let Pharaoh think Sarah is his sister. And then Pharaoh, he, he, he. Well, he does. And afterward Abraham gets mad at Pharaoh because of Sarah, even though he's played that trick on Pharaoh. Now if you didn't understand, a little child could get mighty mixed up—

MARCUS (*gently*)—You want to go to your school, don't you, Lavinia?

LAVINIA—Or about Jesus. The poor are always with you. Why, I wouldn't have colored people believe a thing like that. That's what's the matter now. You have to be full grown before you know what Jesus meant. Otherwise you could make it seem like people ought to be poor.

BEN—All right. Go upstairs now and start packing. You're going to be on the sugar boat.

Marcus has again changed the note of his pleading with Lavinia. He won't say that theirs had been a good marriage, but they had taken sacred vows. Surely Lavinia wouldn't be wanting to break those? It was wrong, too, Marcus admits, for him to have denied Lavinia her sacred mission, but there is time for him to make up for that. What did she think she would be needing?

Well, Lavinia's message had told her that a thousand dollars a year would make her little colored children very happy, but she is sure ten thousand dollars would make them happier. Marcus agrees that ten thousand dollars would hardly be enough. Then, suggests Lavinia, there's Coralee to be remembered—and Coralee takes care of a lot of relatives right here in town. Probably two hundred dollars a month would take Coralee's mind off worrying. Marcus is sure it would—and Lavinia's friends should have the best.

"You're being mighty nice to me, Marcus," agrees Lavinia. "I wish it had always been that way."

"It started out that way, remember? I suppose little things
happened, as they do with so many people—"

"No, I don't really think it started out well. No, I can't say
I do."

"Oh, come now. You're forgetting. All kinds of pleasant
things. Remember in the little house? The piano! I saved,
and bought it for you and—"

"Bought it for me? No, I don't remember it that way. I always thought you bought it for yourself."

"But perhaps you never understood why I did anything. Perhaps you were a little unforgiving with me."

Ben has picked up the gun and moved nearer Marcus. "Aren't
you getting ashamed of yourself?" he asks.

"For what? For trying to recall to Lavinia's mind that we
were married with sacred vows, that together we had children,
that she swore in church to love, to honor—"

"If I wasn't in a hurry, I'd be very amused."

"I did swear. That's true I—"

"Mama, please go upstairs. Please let me finish here. You
won't get on the boat any other way—"

But Marcus has caught Lavinia's attention with a new plea
now. She doesn't have to go to Altaloosa by boat. It would be
nicer if they were to drive over, and stay overnight in Mobile,
and see the churches and have dinner—

That's the way Lavinia had always dreamed of going back.
And the mention of churches reminds her— She would like to
leave a mahogany pew in the church here in Bowden, with her
name on it—in brass—

"Brass! It shall be writ in gold!" promises Marcus.

"I don't like gold. Brass. Now, what else did I think about
last night?" Lavinia would not like to overlook anything.

"We'll be in constant communication. And if you have more
practical messages from God, we can take care of them later.
Now bring me the envelope and the Bible, and we'll start immediately—"

Ben is growing impatient. As Lavinia starts to pick up the
Bible he quickly goes to her and takes her hand. "Do I really
have to explain it to you?" he demands. "Do I really have to
tell you that unless you go through with it, he's got to take you
to the hospital. You don't really think that he's going to let you
go to Altaloosa with what you know, to tell anybody— Why do
you think he took you to Dr. Hammanond in the first place?
Because he thought you might have seen him, and because it

wouldn't hurt to have a doctor say that you were—"

"That's a lie!" shouts Marcus.

"Maybe it is.   But then you're only sorry you didn't think of it that way."

Again Marcus pleads with Lavinia to reconsider and to believe that he will do for her all the things that he has just promised. But Marcus goes a little too far.   Even Lavinia must protest when he insists that because he, too, had taken the vows she can believe him—

"Oh, now.   I don't believe what you're saying.   One lie, two lies, that's for all of us; but to pile lie upon lie, and sin upon sin, and in the sight of God—"

"Write it to him, Mama," interrupts Ben.   "Or you'll miss your boat."

"Oh, yes, oh!   I wouldn't want to do that."   Lavinia recovers her Bible and goes quickly into the living room.

Now Ben is ready for Marcus.   First he would have Marcus write a piece of paper, he will sell the Hubbard store for one dollar.   Marcus agrees to that, but he would like Ben to turn over the envelope.   Second, Ben suggests that Marcus shall write another piece of paper telling Shannon in Mobile to turn over to Ben immediately "all stocks and bonds, your safety deposit box, all liens, all mortgages, all assets of Marcus Hubbard, Inc."

"I will certainly do no such thing," announces Marcus, angrily. "I will leave you your proper share of things in my will, or perhaps increase it, if you behave—"

"You're making fun of me again."   Ben's anger is also mounting.   "A will?   That you could change tomorrow?   You've made fun of me for enough years.   It's dangerous now.   One more joke —so stop it now.   Stop it!"

"All right.   But I would like to give you a little advice— you're so new at this sort of thing.   If you get greedy, and take everything, there's bound to be a lot of suspicion.   And you shouldn't want that.   Take the store, take half of everything else, half of what's in the envelope.   Give me the rest.   I'll go on living as I always have, and tell everybody that because you're my oldest son, I wanted you to have—"

"You'll tell nobody anything, because you can't, and you'll stop bargaining.   You're giving me everything you've got.   Is that clear?   If I don't have to waste any more time with you, I'll give you enough to live on, here or wherever you want to go.   But if I have to talk to you any longer, you won't get that.   I mean what I'm saying, and you know I do.   And it's the last time I'll

say it. (*Pauses. Smiles.*) All right, now start writing things
down. When you finish, bring them to me."

Marcus goes slowly up the stairs. In front of his door he
pauses. He is trying, he admits, to think of a way out. But, Ben
assures him, he had better remember the past and waste no more
time. He doesn't realize what Ben's temptation has been. For
years he has had ugly dreams. But this, he admits, is better than
anything he had dreamed. "Go in and start writing now," he advises his father. "I consider you a lucky man: you'll die in bed."

Jake is back. He had delivered the message to Miss Birdie.
She was mighty happy. He had got the sugar boat tickets. Now
he'll get Mr. Ben's breakfast.

Oscar appears from indoors in a state of considerable excitement. He has been knocking on his father's bedroom door, but
can't get in. He runs up the porch stairs and tries the outside
door. From the balcony he sees Ben. Why isn't Ben at the station to make his apologies to Laurette. Oscar hasn't changed his
mind. But Ben has. And Oscar's gun has changed hands.

Oscar tries his father's door again and calls. He can't find the
check Papa said he'd leave—and Laurette is waiting for him to
fetch her up! Neither Ben nor Regina, who has appeared in
riding skirt and shirt on the porch, is interested in Oscar's trouble.

Jake has brought in Ben's breakfast and taken it to him at the
table. "You're in Papa's chair, Ben, eating breakfast at Papa's
table on Papa's porch," warns Regina.

"Come on down and have breakfast with me, darling. I'm
lonely for you." There is a note of mockery in Ben's voice.

Oscar has reached the screaming stage. Marcus finally appears on the porch to quiet him. Screaming, he warns, is hard
on the voice of youth. Oscar had not been able to find the money
on the table because Marcus had not put it there—

"An unhappy event interfered," he explains. "I am thus unable to finance your first happy months in the rose-covered
brothel about which you have always dreamed. I assure you I
am most sorry, for many reasons, none of them having anything
to do with you."

"What the hell does all this mean? That you're *not* giving me
the money to leave here—"

"It means that," puts in Ben. "And it means that Papa has
found a new way of postponing for a few minutes an unpleasant
writing job. Go back in, Papa."

Marcus waxes sarcastic. Would Ben like him to have his

breakfast on a tray in his room, on the porch, or in the dining room?

"Any place you like," Ben agrees, generously. "My house is your house." But Ben wants those papers written. That's what he is waiting for.

Regina can't understand. What has happened to Papa? And why isn't Ben getting on the train?

"I can't ever tell you that," laughs Ben. "My lips are sealed in honor."

Regina reports her mother is packing—preparatory to "going to her destiny." Ben, she says, knows what that always means. Ben does. And that's where Lavinia is going. Who said so? Papa? No, Ben said so. And who has Ben become?

"A man who thinks you have handled yourself very badly," answers Ben. "It's a shame about you, Regina: Beautiful, warm outside, and smart. That should have made a brilliant life. Instead, at twenty, you have to start picking up the pieces, and start mighty fast now. . . . You're not going to Chicago. And for a very simple reason. Papa has no money at all—now. No money for you to travel with, or to marry with, or even to go on here with."

"What are you talking about? What happened? What's he done with his money—"

"Given it to me."

"Do you take that new drug I've been reading about? What would make you think he had given it to you?"

"You mean what are his reasons? Oh, I don't know. I'm the eldest son: isn't that the way with royalty? Maybe he could find me a Greek title—go up and talk to him. I think he's been waiting."

Regina starts for the staircase and hurries to Marcus' room. She lets herself in. Shortly Regina reappears. Her father will tell her nothing. She found him crying. What does that mean? What has Ben been doing to Papa?

"A great deal," admits Ben. "Whatever you think of me, honey, you know I'm not given to this kind of joke. So take it this way: what is in your room is yours. Nothing else. And save your time on the talk. No Chicago, honey. No nothing."

"You can't stop my going, and you're not going to stop it—"

"Certainly not. What people want to do, they do. You go ahead, your own way. Ride over to your soldier. Stand close and talk soft; he'll marry you. But do it quickly: he was angry last night and I think he wants to get away from you as fast as he can. Catch him quick. Marry him this morning. Then come back here to pack your nice Chicago clothes, and sell your pearls."

"Do you think I'm going to take your word for what's happening, or believe I can't talk Papa out of whatever you've done to him—"

"Believe me, you can't. Not because your charms have failed, but because there's nothing to talk him out of. I have it now, and your charms won't work on me. Money from the pearls will be plenty to take you to Brazil, and love and war will feed you. People in love should be poor."

Again Regina pleads for an explanation, but there is no answer from Ben. He advises her, if she doesn't want to go to the war in Brazil, she can stay here and starve with the three ninnies dying on the vine at Lionnet—

"I'll find out what happened, and the day I do, I'll pay you back with carnival trimmings," threatens Regina.

Ben would not blame Regina—but meantime she would be wise to learn how to win and how to lose. He's getting tired of loser's talk—

"You can't go away, or at least not on my money, and therefore a willful girl can't have a willful way. You're not in love; I don't think anybody in this family can love. You're not a fool, stop talking like one. The sooner you do, the sooner I'll help you."

A dejected Oscar is back from the station. A determined Laurette has gone to New Orleans without him. She wouldn't wait, and when he tried to carry her off the train she had spit in his face—with everybody staring and laughing. Regina can understand that—

"Your love didn't laugh," Oscar tells her with satisfaction. "Your love, looking like a statue of Robert E. Lee. Dressed up and with all his old medals all over him." Regina's shocked surprise is apparent. "So you didn't know he was going on the train, huh? I thought not. So you're no better off than me, are you, with all your laughing. Sneaked out on you, did he?"

Regina has turned on Ben. "So you arranged that too, did you, so I couldn't—"

"All right. That's enough. I'm sick of love. Both of you: follow the trash you've set your hearts on, or be still about it from now on. I don't want any more of this."

"You don't want any more? What the—" Oscar hasn't heard.

Ben is talking to Regina. "You, early maturing flower, can go any place you want and find what it's like to be without Papa's money." He turns to Oscar: "And you, lover, can follow your spitting heart and get yourself a wharf job loading bananas. Or you can stay, keep your job, settle down. I got a girl picked out for you—make yourself useful." To Regina again: "Now, honey, about you, if you're staying. You're a scandal in this town. Papa's the only person didn't know you'd been sleeping with the warrior. . . . Papa and Horace Giddens in Mobile. How soon he'll find out about it I don't know. Before he does, we're taking you up to see him. You'll get engaged to him by next week, or sooner, and you'll get married in the first church we bump into. Giddens isn't bad off—and if you're lucky it'll be years before he hears about you and the Brazilian General. I don't say it's a brilliant future, but I don't say it's bad. You could have done a lot better, but girls who have been despoiled in this part of the country—"

Marcus is disturbed. "You don't have to marry a man, Regina, just because . . . We can go away, you and I—" She does not answer, but rather, with Oscar, agrees it is time they were having breakfast. Ben is greatly pleased—

"That's my good girl," he says, laughingly. "Nothing for anybody to be so unhappy about. You both going to do all right. I'm going to help you. I got ideas. You'll go to Chicago some day, get everything you want— Then—"

"When I'm too old to want it," mutters Regina.

Marcus repeats his suggestion that he and Regina could go away together, but Regina takes no notice of the suggestion. She can only wonder if Marcus, when he did what Ben made him do, had realized what he was doing to her. And if he did, what good did it do?

Ben is deep in the morning paper. "Big doings on all over the country," he reports. "Railroads going across, oil, coal. I been telling you, Papa, for ten years. Things are opening up."

"That don't mean they're opening up in the South," ventures Oscar.

BEN—But they are. That's what nobody down here sees or understands. Now you take you, Papa. You were smart in your day and figured out what fools you lived among. But ever since the war you been too busy getting cultured, or getting Southern. A few more years and you'd been just like the rest of them.

MARCUS—Bring my breakfast, Jake.

JAKE (*at serving table*)—Belle will have to do it, Mr. Marcus. Last breakfast I can bring. I got the carriage waiting to take Miss Viney.

BEN (*smiling*)—But now we'll do a little quiet investing, nothing big, because, unlike Papa, I don't believe in going outside your class about anything—

OSCAR—Think we've got a chance to be big rich, Ben?

BEN—I think so. All of us. I'm going to make some for you and Regina and—

LAVINIA (*coming in with* CORALEE)—Well, I'm off on my appointed path. I brought you each a little something. This is my pin. (*Kissing* LAVINIA.) Smile, honey, you're such a pretty girl. (*Goes to* OSCAR.) Here's my prayer book, Oscar. I had it since I was five years old. (*She kisses* OSCAR. *To* BEN.) I want you to have my papa's watch, Benjamin.

BEN (*kissing her*)—Thank you, Mama.

LAVINIA—I didn't have anything left, Marcus, except my wedding ring.

MARCUS—That's kind, Lavinia.

LAVINIA—Well, I guess that's all.

BEN—Mama, could I have your Bible instead of Grandpa's watch? (MARCUS *laughs*.) It would make me happier, and I think—

MARCUS—Or perhaps you'd give it to me. I can't tell you how happy it would make me, Lavinia.

LAVINIA—Oh, I wouldn't like to give it up. This Bible's been in my papa's family for a long time. I always keep it next to me, you all know that. But when I die, I'll leave it to you all. Coralee, you hear that? If I die before you, you bring it right back here.

CORALEE—Come on, Miss Viney.

LAVINIA—I'll be hearing from you, Benjamin?

BEN—You will, Mama. Every month. On time.

LAVINIA—Thank you, son. Thank you in the name of my colored children.

CORALEE—Miss Viney, it's late.

LAVINIA (*wistfully*)—Well. Don't be seeing me off, any of you. Coralee and I'll be just fine. I'll be thinking of you, and I'll be praying for you, all of you. Everybody needs somebody to pray for them, and I'm going to pray for you all. (*Turns to* MARCUS.) I hope you feel better, Marcus. We got old, you and me, and— Well, I guess I just mean it's been a long time. Good-by.·

MARCUS—Good-by, Lavinia.

As Lavinia and Coralee leave, Marcus moves over to sit by Regina.

"Pour me a cup of coffee, darling," he says softly.

Regina looks at him, then goes to the serving table and pours the coffee. As she does so Marcus moves forward a chair next to his. Regina hands him the coffee, but ignores the chair. Picking up her own cup, she crosses to the other table and moves a chair down near Ben. Ben looks up and smiles.

THE CURTAIN FALLS

YEARS AGO

A Comedy in Three Acts

By Ruth Gordon

(Digest by John Chapman)

RUTH GORDON, the actress, had written a play for herself to act in titled "Over 21"—a quite successful comedy. Next, in "Years Ago," she wrote a play *about* herself—but one she could not play in because it was about the Ruth Gordon Jones who once was sixteen years old. Producer Max Gordon (no relation) presented it at the Mansfield Theatre December 3, 1946, with young Patricia Kirkland playing the young Ruth Gordon and Fredric March and Florence Eldridge impersonating her parents. For his performance as Clint Jones Mr. March was given one of the first Antoinette Perry Awards by the American Theatre Wing—an honor which capped a season in which Mr. March had also won the "Oscar" of the American Academy of Motion Picture Arts and Sciences for his work in Samuel Goldwyn's film, "The Best Years of Our Lives."

The circumstances under which a successful play came to be written always are a subject of interest, and Miss Gordon's own account of how "Years Ago" came into being is illuminating.

"One fortunate night nearly ten years ago," she relates, "I was to dine with Edward Sheldon. It was fortunate for me because Edward Sheldon was a rare and stimulating companion. But as I dressed for dinner I thought sympathetically of poor Ned—for, this night of all nights, I felt extremely blue. Why, I don't remember. I felt conversationless and empty and doubtful if I should know anything to talk about.

"Troubled, I considered what might take the place of conversation, and it occurred to me that Ned might feel some faint pleasure in hearing my high school diary. (Ed. note: The late Edward Sheldon, playwright, confidant and guide to theatrical people, was bedridden, almost paralyzed and blind.) Only a few days ago the diary had shown up with some dreary odds and ends of my existence which had come out of storage. On reading it over

204

it struck me as an astonishingly lively picture of my days that
had gone by.

"Edward Sheldon had beautiful manners, so when I suggested
reading my diary to him he protested that he would be delighted.
This was in 1937, and the diary was the account of my senior
year at Quincy High School in 1913. Years ago.

"When I had finished Ned asked what I was going to do with
it. I said that I had not thought of doing anything with it further than bringing it back home. This seemed to him amazingly
shiftless.

" 'It is *Atlantic Monthly* material,' he said. I was flattered
but dubious, and thought no more of it. . . .

"The telephone rang and it was Alexander Woollcott. 'What's
all this nonsense Ned tells me about your having kept a high
school diary?' inquired Woollcott, only moderately irritable.
'Why haven't I seen it? Send it up to me at once.'

"Having as good an understanding of Alexander Woollcott as
the next one, I sent for a messenger boy. The diary met with
Mr. Woollcott's pleasure, and he rang up to say that he was
having my illegible scrawls typed at his own considerable expense. He added that he thought it was gracious of him and
hung up.

"A few days passed and Ned sent for me. He had the whole
idea for the diary well in hand: 'The daily entries are too brief
and uninformative as they now stand. Use these entries as the
heading for a story.'

"This seemed interesting, and when I had done one I was so
pleased at *having* done one that I sent it to *The New Yorker*. In
almost no time it came back to me, clipped to a rejection slip. I
had to tell Ned how misjudged his enthusiasm had been.

" 'Nonsense,' he said. 'I told you to send it to the *Atlantic
Monthly.*'

"Mr. Woollcott agreed, and finding himself in Boston, discussed the idea with the editor, Edward Weeks. Mr. Weeks felt
only a mild interest in the record of a Quincy High School senior,
but, goaded on by Woollcott's enthusiasm, he suggested amiably
that I do six sample copies and he would see—

"The six sample copies brought a telephone call of acceptance
and a request to continue on the same. The stories appeared in
four issues of *The Atlantic Monthly* under the rather pretentious
title—my own—'Look in Your Glass.'

"Being an actress as well as an authoress, I could not help but
notice that, though the stories were written in narrative form,

they contained a vast amount of dialogue—and what would be simpler than to rip out the 'I saids' and 'he dids' and shove the whole thing into three acts?

"So I did. The last of the 'I saids' was used on Max Gordon, the theatrical producer. 'Max, why don't you produce my play?' I said. And the last of the 'he dids' I have saved up for the happy ending to this story. He did. Playwriting is so simple provided you have good friends."

Ruth Gordon Jones, age 16, is standing on a chair while her mother pins up the hem of a new dress she is wearing—a brick red creation with a three-tiered skirt, a white net vest and narrow strips of bear fur around the neck and wrists. It is an imposing affair, and Ruth probably copied it from a picture of some actress or from a hasty glance into the Bon Ton or the Elite at the news-dealer's. Ruth's mother wears a white embroidered shirtwaist with a high-boned collar and a gray wool skirt whose dust braid sweeps the floor.

It is not alone the garb of mother and daughter, but also the decor of the room they are in, which indicates the period. It is an evening in January, 1913, in the combination dining room and sitting room of the Clinton Jones home, 14 Elmwood Ave., Wollaston, Mass. It is a small room but there is nothing small in it— a heavy golden oak sideboard, a large oblong dining table with a white damask cloth and a fern basket on it; a rickety bamboo table holds old *Saturday Evening Posts,* and there also is an oval-topped reading table with a green-shaded gasolier. Beside the reading table is Mr. Jones' rattan armchair, which leans toward the gasolier even when he isn't in it. He is in it now.

The front hall door is on the left side of the room, and near it is the stair leading to the second floor. The parlor, with a piano, is out of vision behind the stair. On the other side of the room, at the back, is the door to the kitchen and another one to the cellar. There is a hot-air register under the big sideboard.

While Ruth and her mother are busy with the dressmaking Clint Jones, "who looks like no one in Wollaston," is reading *McClure's Magazine.* His suit is nondescript and too large for him—and so is his stiff collar. He has graying hair and a bushy, graying mustache. Obviously, Ruth has been chattering while her mother has been working on the hemline.

ME—I *hate* Jones for a name. I wish our name was something else.

My Mother (*finishing pinning up the hem*)—Why, Jones is a good name . . . easy to remember . . . short to write.

Me—It's too plain. Papa, do you think our name is *really* Jones? (My Father *makes no reply and I continue my attack.*) I wish you were a changeling, Papa, and our name was somethin' else.

My Father—Don't go through life looking for changelings! Aim to *amount* to something! Then it won't matter if your name is Jones or Finnegan or Andrew J. Forepaugh. Good wine needs no bush.

My Mother (*finished with the hem*)—All right now. You can get down.

Me (*getting down and noticing my skirt*)—*No*, Mama—!

My Mother (*hastily interrupting Me*)—Ruth . . . hand me my hug-me-tight off that chair. . . . (*Indicating it hanging on the back of the dining room armchair.*)

Me (*going to the chair and doing so*)—But, *Mama* . . .

My Mother (*cutting me off*)—Clinton, do you think you could get the furnace to give out a little more heat?

My Father (*takes off his glasses, puts his magazine down and rises*)—It ain't the *furnace!* It's the coal they sent us. We order a ton of half nut and half egg and what we get is a ton full of God damn clinkers. (*The cellar door slams after him.*)

My Mother (*slipping into the hug-me-tight which I'm holding for her; in an exasperated whisper*)—I had to get your father to go *do* that so I could tell you about this skirt.

Me (*in despair*)—It's all *wrong*, Mama!

My Mother—No, it is *not* all wrong. It is the way it's going to *be!* I am *not* going to let you wear any skirt like that actressy picture you showed me.

Me—Oh, Mama . . . slit skirts are all the rage!

My Mother—Well, let them be! But I'm certainly not going to have you walking round Wollaston in a skirt slit halfway up past all decency!

Me—Oh, Mama!

My Mother—You want people to think you live in a harem?

Me—It's how the dress *has* to be. It *has* to, Mama. It's what gives it the *Frenchy* touch.

My Mother—Has to or *not* has to . . . *I will not!* Why, all you'd have to do is walk up Newport Avenue once in that dress and everyone in Wollaston would know you wanted to be an actress. If you don't feel able to tell your own father, then please don't flaunt it out to *everybody else.* You can't go round dressed

like Gaby Deslys. This is Wollaston, Massachusetts, please remember, not Gay Paree!

ME (*in despair*)—It doesn't cost any more to have it stylish,
does it?

MY MOTHER (*near the end of her patience*)—Ruth, do you or
do you not want your father to know you want to be an actress?

ME—*No.*

MY MOTHER—Well, then don't go appearing before him in a
hobble skirt with a slit! You'll not only look like an *actress,*
you'll look downright *fast!*

ME (*unmoved*)—If it wasn't for you and Papa, I'd go in Boston
and be fast right this minute!

MY MOTHER—Oh, Ruth, do try to talk sensible if for only
just *part* of the time. Let me make your skirt *pretty* and I'll talk
to Papa about letting us have a telephone.

ME (*in despair*)—You'll just ruin all my books!

MY MOTHER—No, I won't. Go in the parlor and get on your
other dress.

ME (*reluctantly giving in*)—Well, then, you ask him about the
telephone. You *promised.*

MY MOTHER—I will if the *furnace* hasn't made him mad. (*I
disappear into the parlor.*)

MY FATHER (*coming in*)—Thermometer says four above but a
course ours ain't a reputable thermometer. No-one's is. . . .

MY MOTHER (*enthusiastically*)—Oh, it's warmer in here already. The register's letting out a real heat!

MY FATHER (*returning to his magazine with considerable satisfaction*)—Damn good magazine, *McClure's.*

MY MOTHER—I'm glad you got something to enjoy, Clinton,
and if you say so it *must* be good, because you don't like to read
just any old thing. And I'm sure Mrs. Litchfield will be glad to
lend you next month's, too. (MY MOTHER *picks up her* Unity
Magazine *and sits down at the reading table.*) You know I been
thinking, Clinton, everybody else has got one and we ought to
have a telephone.

MY FATHER (*amiable*)—Wouldn't have one if you gave it
to me!

MY MOTHER—Why, Clinton? What have you got against it?
(MY FATHER *sits still as a statue for a moment, then gives a loud
sneeze.*)

MY FATHER (*indignantly*)—Get that cat off the register! Hot
air comin' up through cat fur'll give me back my old malaria.
(MY MOTHER *hurries over to the sideboard.*)

My Mother—Here, Punk.

My Father—Get him off there! I ain't goin' to have him layin' around warmin' up all his germs!

My Mother—Punk's clean an' healthy an' hasn't any germs! (*She gets him out from under the sideboard and starts for the kitchen.*) Clinton, please try not to be against a telephone. (*She puts* Punk *into the kitchen and closes the door.*)

My Father—I *ain't* against it, so long as we don't have to have one.

Me (*enthusiastically from the parlor*)—The kind of telephone *we* want, Papa, won't cost anythin' at all to speak of except just one old nickel a day.

My Mother—And that's only for when *we* telephone.

Me—When people telephone *us* it's *free!*

My Mother—So what *we* want is to get a coin-in-the-slot one. . . .

Me—All you have to do is every day put in a nickel.

My Mother (*happily*)—And that way makes the bills be all paid. Isn't that lovely? (*A soothing after-thought.*)   And, Clinton, if you don't want to, you don't personally have to have a thing to do with it; it can just be Ruth's and mine.

Ruth's father agrees genially that the telephone can be anybody's, as long as he doesn't have to pay for it. Another sneeze comes upon him and he recommends that Punk be thrown away, but this suggestion only momentarily sidetracks mother and daughter from the subject of a telephone and how handy it would be.

"You'd have felt awful that day President Cleveland died," reminds Ruth, "if you couldn't have called up Mrs. Litchfield to tell Mama to hang out our flag at half mast." And Mama adds that it was a further blessing that Eaton's iceman happened by and hung it out for her.

"That feller," Mr. Jones ruminates, "lashed them ropes to the halliards like he'd took lessons from Corticelli's cat!"

"Well, now, Clinton," soothes his wife, "just because *you* happen to have been a sailor doesn't mean *everyone* can knot a rope right!"

"People don't *happen* to be sailors. There's quite a knack to it."

Irrelevantly, Ruth voices the wish that their name had been Cleveland. And there's a girl in the Quincy Mansion School named Fentress Serene Kerlin. Mr. Jones, unimpressed, goes back to his *McClure's;* Mrs. Jones is deep in her *Unity Magazine.* Ruth surreptitiously takes a large magazine from under some tablecloths in the sideboard drawer and heads quietly for the stair—but her mother, without even looking up, tells her to stay downstairs where it's warm, and besides it will save electricity. Ruth gives in. Cautiously enclosing her magazine in a copy of the *Saturday Evening Post,* she sits down to read.

Saving electricity reminds Mr. Jones of something. "Got your grocery list ready for Pierce's?" he asks his wife. He pronounces Pierce "Perce," as do all good New Englanders in referring to S. S. Pierce & Co., providers of provender. Mrs. Jones rummages for the catalogue, finally finds it; but the order sheet is not with it. More fluttery hunting turns it up in the stein where Mrs. Jones keeps her change purse and receipted bills.

Now another idea strikes Mr. Jones. "Did you have a grocer's bill at Backus' this week?" Reluctantly, his spouse admits she did, for one or two little things she ran short of.

"Well, it beats the Dutch! Every two weeks we get a order of groceries sent out from Boston from S. S. Pierce! I bring home the eggs an' the meat every Saturday from Faneuil Hall Market! Friday I get us a fish at T Wharf! And yet each week comes dribblin' out a damn Backus grocery bill!"

He scans the Backus items. Butter. He thought Ruth had gone to get it from a farmer. Ruth started to, explains her mother, but she says climbing the hill hurts her back.

"She climbs up there all right to go coastin', doesn't she?"

"Well, it's *carrying* butter tired her out."

Mr. Jones studies his offspring morosely. "Lazy as a louse! How old is she anyway? Fourteen? Fifteen?" With displeasure Ruth announces she is sixteen. At that age, snorts her father, he had had nine years before the mast, and one of them was spent sailing under Captain Dermott out of Rockland Harbor.

The name of Dermott brings an eager query from Ruth; can't her father remember just a *little* what Maxine Elliott looked like?

"Why the hell should I? She was just old man Dermott's daughter Jessie, stoppin' off from high school to see her father's ship set sail." Mr. Jones goes back to quarreling over the Backus bill. An item for cat meat infuriates him.

Beneath his furies are the worries of a hard-pressed man. Clint Jones is foreman of the Mellins' Food factory and he gets $37.50 a week. Last week's extra grocery bill was $1.98 and this one is over $2.00. Something has to be paid to Dr. Adams, and the insurance premium is due January 23rd.

MY FATHER—I'm fifty-two years old and I worked at the Mellin's Food Company for twenty-four years . . . And I got sixty dollars in the bank to show for it! If they ever went and laid me off, then runnin' up bills the way we do, how would we live on *that?*

MY MOTHER—Clinton—you exaggerate so! The Mellin's Food Company would *never* lay you off.

MY FATHER—How do you *know?*

MY MOTHER—Why, where could they ever get anyone like you?

MY FATHER—You can always get a foreman.

MY MOTHER—You appreciate your schooling, Ruth. It's what Papa had to do without. . . . But besides the thirty-seven dollars and fifty cents, Clinton, don't forget there's your bonus.

MY FATHER—What the hell's that to count on? There ain't nothin' certain about a bonus till they actually hand it over— A man has to grovel and curtsey 364 days a year, then the 365th day, you might offend Dollaber and a whole damn year's bonus is gone!

MY MOTHER—Oh, well, I guess money isn't everything.

MY FATHER—Well, poverty is! Poverty's everything there is in my whole world!

MY MOTHER (*gently reproving*)—Clinton, you can't call us poverty!

MY FATHER (*vehemently*)—Yes, I can too! I even know what color it is; it's a rotten, dark brown. And it's everywhere I am, every day of the year in every kind of weather. . . . It's in my hair and eyes and nose and ears and feet. It's in my front walk when I come home at night and in the goddam *Saturday Evening Post!*

MY MOTHER (*with a little gasp*)—Clinton, you're just crazy! You're just all tired out!!

MY FATHER (*hollering*)—Yes, and if I'm crazy, I'm crazy because I'm *poor!* Seems like there isn't *anything* you mention, that I can afford! Not one damn anything. I can't even afford to take a *cold!* If Waterhouse, up on the hill, feels like it, he can have one week in, week out! Why, even when I sit down on our furniture, especially the stuff in the parlor, I sit *careful* so it won't wear out! I buy *The Saturday Evening Post* and I wish it was *The Scientific American* but I buy *The Saturday Evening Post!* Why! Because it costs just a damn five cents and *The Scientific*

American . . . Well, what the hell's the use talkin'. . . . I got
the brains and the inclination but I ain't got the thirty-five sou
markees!   (*Bitterly.*)   And we live on hash and stew and
Louisiana cat meat for all I know, when I got a taste for oysters
and curry, like they make it in Bombay ·and bird's nest soup and
cheese fondue the way that French girl fixed it in Wiscasset where
I went with Fred Gee, and a good ripe custard apple they pretty
near give away for nothin', at Mozambique!

MY MOTHER (*distracted*)—Oh, I *don't* know what to do!   I
don't know what to do, Clinton, I *really* don't!

MY FATHER (*with a world of meaning*)—Don't trouble!   I'm
goin' out!

MY MOTHER (*aghast*)—Why, Clinton, you *can't!*   It must be
nine o'clock!

MY ·FATHER (*in a thundering tone*)—Don't try to stop me!   I
been out every hour of the night there is!

MY MOTHER—Oh, Clinton, where are you going?   (*Beseeching
him.*)   Don't do anything rash, Clinton!   *Please,* Clinton, for all
our sakes!

MY FATHER (*filled with determination and high purpose*)—
Nothin' rasher than to just go lay down on the New York, New
Haven and Hartford railroad tracks!

MY MOTHER (*wringing her hands*)—Oh, Clinton, you wouldn't!
(MY FATHER *stops a minute and gives a furious sneeze, his indignation reaches a new high.*)

MY FATHER (*wrathfully*)—And what's more I'm going to take
that cat *with* me!

The demise of Clint Jones and the cat on the New Haven tracks
is postponed, at least, by the doorbell ringing and the arrival of
two school friends of Ruth's, Anna Witham and Katherine Follett.

Ruth makes another break for the stair, explaining that she and
her friends have Latin to do, and again her mother stalls her.   "Sit
down here in the dining room.   Papa and I'll take our things in
the kitchen."   But Papa now has a sudden inclination to talk—
of getting chilblains in the Northern Straits one time. . . .

That was the first voyage out he had his spy glass, he remembers.   Mrs. Jones fetches the glass from the parlor and he proudly
shows it to the nonplused girls.   Finally his wife manages to herd
him, the Pierce catalogue and the order sheet into the kitchen.

His parting words are some genial advice to Katherine: "Don't
never make port in Halifax in wintertime, if you can make some
other arrangements."

Now alone with her friends, Ruth gets her mysterious magazine from inside the *Saturday Evening Post,* and the visitors show intense excitement. Ruth warns them to shush; if Papa saw that magazine he'd kill her, because it cost 35 cents.

It is the *Theatre Magazine,* and the reason for the excitement is that this issue has a whole page of pictures of Hazel Dawn—one from "The Pink Lady" and the others of Miss Dawn in private life.

ME (*proudly*)—Seein' "The Pink Lady" changed my whole life.

ANNA—But did you think right there in the Colonial Theatre you'd go be an actress yourself?

ME—I don't know if I did exactly, I mean at the Matinee. Of course I knew right off I'd rather be like Hazel Dawn than anybody else in the world, but then when I got the letter from her and *you didn't* . . . well . . . I knew then I must be different. *Before* that I thought I was just only peculiar. Katherine, open your Latin book, so if Papa comes in . . .

KATHERINE (*doing as requested*)—Ruth . . . when do you think you're going to ever tell your father?

ANNA—Tell him what?

KATHERINE—About going on the stage.

ANNA (*astonished*)—Ruth, haven't you told your own father you're going to be an actress?

ME (*with a good deal of expression*)—*Mercy . . . No!*

KATHERINE (*placidly turning the pages of her Latin book*)—He'd kill her. (*Guardedly.*) Oh, Mr. Jones has a *terrible* disposition. Why, when Ruth only went and looked in the Waterhouses' window the night Gertrude Waterhouse got married, Mr. Jones grabbed Ruth by the ear when she came home and kept banging her head down *right there* on this dining room table. (KATHERINE *reaches over and designates the exact spot.*)

ANNA—*Golly!*

KATHERINE—And hollering at her, "You old Goat!"

ANNA—Ruth, why should your father get so mad at you rubbering at the Waterhouses'? We were all up there doing it.

KATHERINE—It's just Mr. Jones' *disposition!* . . .

ME—He was mad because he and Mama got invited but he didn't have a dress suit.

ANNA—I suppose he got that way being a sailor.

KATHERINE (*disapprovingly*)—He wants her to be a Physical Culture Instructor!

ME (*briefly*)—I would rather be *dead!*

KATHERINE (*loyal even to handing me the hemlock*)—Oh, Ruth'd just soon kill herself.

ME (*threateningly*)—I certainly *would!*

ANNA—Well, why does your father think you should be a physical . . .

ME—Anna, open *your* Collar and Daniels, too.

KATHERINE (*turning the pages of* The Theatre Magazine)— Here's picture of Edith Wynne Mathison with her own fox terrier.

ANNA (*opening her Latin book as requested*)—Why does he want you to be a physical . . .

ME (*very disgusted, poring through my Latin book*)—Oh, because he goes in Boston to that evenin' gymnastic class at the Y.M.C.A.

KATHERINE (*equally disgusted, turning the pages of magazine*) —To keep from having a cold or something . . .

ME—And he's wild about the director of it, Mr. Bagley, and Mr. Bagley has a friend, Miss Glavin, that's a physical culture instructor.

KATHERINE (*to* ANNA)—Out to Brookline . . .

ME—And she's so healthy, Papa wants *me* to be one . . .

KATHERINE (*admiringly to* ANNA)—Ruth'd rather be dead.

ANNA—But you couldn't be an actress, could you, without telling your father?

KATHERINE—You have to tell him *some* time!

ME—But no matter what he says I'm goin' to be an actress. I'm goin' to be somebody wonderful like you *read* about. I don't want to be just *people.*

ANNA—Well, but . . .

ME—And I want to have everythin' around me gorgeous and no *scrimpin'* and *plannin'.* But have things be all rich and careless. And I want to have stunnin' clothes and travel around in parlor cars and ocean liners. Sometimes in the South Station, when the Merchant's Limited is next track, I see the pink lights on in the dinin'-car and the parlor cars all mahogany and green velvet with fringe and not one person on the whole train looks economical.

KATHERINE—Gosh!

ME—*Everyone* looks extravagant . . . and that's how I want to be. If I have to be rich, I will be, but what I *want* is to be *extravagant!* It's disgustin' to be *normal!* And I want to meet famous people and see what they look like close to. Hazel Dawn and Woodrow Wilson and Willie K. Vanderbilt . . .

KATHERINE—Oh, Ruth, *they* wouldn't want to meet *you!*
ME—They have to if *I* get wonderful. They got to meet *some-body!*

One of the girls wants to see Ruth's *own* Hazel Dawn picture
again, and while Ruth goes upstairs to get it the girls talk her over
a bit. Listening to Ruth, Katherine concludes, is like reading
Green Book Magazine. Such ecstatic observations are interrupted
by Mrs. Jones coming in from the kitchen with a plate of marble
cake. When Ruth reappears and sees her mother she hastily hides
the Hazel Dawn photo behind her back.
"What you got, Ruth?"
"Nothin'."
"Well, put it away where Papa can't see it."
Mother goes back to the kitchen and the girls go after the cake.
Between mouthfuls they wax rapturous over the portrait of Miss
Dawn. Soon, sparked by Ruth, the trio is singing the "Beautiful
Lady" waltz from "The Pink Lady," with Ruth, picture in hand,
waltzing dreamily about the room. The racket, of course, draws
Papa out of the kitchen to inquire if the girls have to *sing* their
lessons. An education, he observes, should be treated with some
respect. Then he notices *Theatre Magazine* on the table by the
cake, and its 35-cent price. It is a tough spot, but Ruth wriggles
out of it by saying she borrowed the periodical from Katherine.
Back to the kitchen goes Papa, and forth comes Ruth with her
biggest surprise—a letter which she has pinned inside her corset
cover. She just got it tonight, down to the Wollaston post office.
"Is it a letter from Hazel Dawn?" queries a breathless Katherine.
Ruth is enjoying the effect she is having. "It's a letter," she
explains in triumph, "from Miss Doris Olsson, leadin' lady of the
whole John Craig Castle Square Stock Company invitin' me to
come see her *tomorrow!*" She won't let anybody touch the missive, because she is going to have it framed; but she reads it and
it *is* a letter from Miss Olsson:
"Dear Miss Jones: Thank you for your letter. I think it is
fine that you want to be an actress. If you ever come to a matinee
perhaps you would like to come to my dressin' room and meet me."
And Ruth is going—to the matinee tomorrow. It's a school
day, but she will say she has a headache, and if that won't work
she will vomit and Miss O'Neill will *have* to let her out of school.
She will wear her new red tango dress, even if it is still partly
basted.

A momentary discouragement comes upon Ruth—maybe she looks funny. Her friends loyally insist that she doesn't. Why, one boy told Gladys Bain and Gladys told Katherine that Ruth had a cute *shape!* And there is another boy who has an eye on Ruth—Fred Whitmarsh, and Fred is older than she is, too. Ruth brushes Fred Whitmarsh off by saying that she probably never will get married. "On the stage you don't have to. Actresses aren't *ever* old maids," she advises.

Just as the factory whistle is heard blowing the 9 P.M. curfew the doorbell rings. Ruth hastily hides her Hazel Dawn picture in her Latin book and her mother and father come in from the kitchen, wondering who it could be at this time of night. Ruth answers the bell—and it is Fred Whitmarsh. He saw the lights still on, so he knew they were sitting up . . .

Anna and Katherine bundle up and head for home, and Mrs. Jones allows that Fred can come in for a minute, but why isn't he at Harvard College? Fred explains that he came out home to supper because it is his sister's birthday. The elder Joneses repair once more to the kitchen, where Mama makes a big fuss over getting the cat off the stove.

Fred's approach is a masterpiece of deviousness, and it isn't helped any by the noise of the capture of Punk, or by Mr. Jones bedding down the furnace in the cellar for the night. Fred touches on the subject of Latin, which never seems to be *about* anything. On the other hand, there is a book about a Roman, Ben Hur, which is a *good* book.

Mother comes in just long enough to offer Fred some cake. Fred is now on the subject of whether Ruth is going to Radcliffe or not, and the young lady says she isn't going to any college, which is rather puzzling to the boy. In comes Mama again, this time to take her best silver off the sideboard and put it in a wooden box. She always puts this box under her bed at night so anyone won't just walk in and help themselves to it.

The elder Joneses make elaborate and meaningful preparations to retire to their daughter's acute embarrassment. Punk is put in the cellar, Papa winds his watch with his key, Mother asks Ruth to get the alarm clock out of the kitchen. After withering New England good-night kisses the parents go aloft—where the slamming of doors, the running of water and Mama's loud inquiry for the right time continue to keep poor Fred from getting to the point.

"It's kind of noisy in here. Would you want to go in the kitchen and maybe make some cocoa?" he suggests.

Ruth is primly and firmly against the hint. She won't even go there for a glass of water. She wouldn't even go there for President Taft. The now-desperate youth comes out with it at last:

FRED—Well, anyway what I came to ask you about—and the reason I came to ask you *tonight* is, the Harvard Class Day Invitations Committee got elected today and I'm on the committee.

ME—Oh, Fred, that's *dandy!*

FRED—And you're the only girl I feel like this about, so would you go to Harvard Class Day with me?

ME—*Fred!*

FRED—Well, would you? It's not till June, of course.

ME—Oh, gee, Fred!!!

FRED—June the *fifteenth.*

ME—Harvard Class Day! . . . Oh, *gorry* . . . Oh, *Fred.* Oh, that's wonderful!!! Harvard Class Day! . . . *Golly!* You know sometimes how you get thinkin' about things? You know? How no fellow will ever send you flowers? Or take you to the Harvard and Yale football game? Or ask you to . . . Well, I just soon say it . . . Ask you to get married? Well, look, Fred, I really never *did* think anyone would ever so long as lived, ask me to Class Day at Harvard College. And here I am and I *did* get invited. . . . Gee, Fred, even if I never *do* go, it's *dandy* bein' invited . . .

FRED—What do you mean if you never *do* go. You're comin' with me!

ME—Well, I'd like to . . . only . . . Only you know what Harvard Class Day sort of means . . . well, *you* know.

FRED (*earnestly*)—Yes, I *do* know and that's what I mean. I don't want you to think I just *said* that . . . I mean without thinking. I *have* thought about it. I've thought about it quite a lot. I didn't know exactly if I'd *say* anything to you about it until after I graduate but since the subject's come up, I'm *glad* it has. I'm kind of glad to get it off my *chest!*

ME—Oh, Fred, I really thought everyone in the whole *world* would get asked but me!!

FRED—I thought I'd wait till day after graduation and then I'd speak to your father about it. . . .

MY FATHER'S VOICE—Has he gone yet?

FRED—I thought I'd maybe write him a *letter.*

Ruth, stalling, says maybe Fred had better go now. Mama and Papa call "good night" from above, and Fred agrees to go if he can drop back tomorrow. He has his coat on, but he returns to the room with a renewal of courage. There is a new song, "Too Much Mustard," which he hums. A song to do the Maxixe to. "Here, let me show you." Still humming, he puts his arm about Ruth and begins a very mild maxixe beside the dining room table.

"Goddam it," roars Mr. Jones from above, "Claflin's gone and got his graphaphone on again!"

Fred suddenly leans down, plants a kiss on Ruth's mouth, jumps as though he's been stung, and bolts straight out through the front door. Ruth just stands, moody and transfixed. She drifts over to the sideboard and smiles bewitchingly at herself in the mirror. She admires her profile, her "cute shape." Softly humming "Too Much Mustard" she does a solo maxixe—a slow one, like a maxixe done under water.

As she floats around the room she catches up the Hazel Dawn picture. Then from her bosom she takes the letter from Miss Olsson . . . and with these two treasures in her hands she changes her song to the "Beautiful Lady" waltz. Ambition has mastered romance. Humming the "Pink Lady" tune, the stage-struck girl waltzes to the gasolier, and turns it out; to the cake platter for the last piece; to the front hall to try the door; to the hall light to put it out—and, still in waltz time, up the stairs to bed.

The curtain falls.

ACT II

Scene 1

Ruth has been to her matinee and has seen Miss Olsson, and now is helping her mother lay the dining room table in great style. Just the day her father chooses to invite company, Ruth has to go and see Miss Doris Olsson. "Ruth, please, try not to look so happy! Your father'll know right off somethin's the matter!"

The guests will be Mr. Bagley and Miss Glavin, who are giving the Baptist Church entertainment and are coming over afterward. Mr. Jones, who won't go inside a church, has gone to meet them at the front walk of the church and bring them home.

Ruth knows what is up and her mind is set against it. "They can't talk me into bein' a physical culture instructress, Mama, and just meetin' Miss Glavin isn't goin' to get me interested." She relapses into rapture: "Oh, Mama, if you had just *seen* Miss Olsson! Her makeup was so *beautiful!* Bright blue paint on her eyelids and little red dots painted in each eye. . . ."

Mother's mind is on more important things as Ruth rambles on.

Papa's spy glass ought to be put on the mantel in case he wants
to show it to the visitors. There's food to be served. And there
is the telephone. She has ordered one and it is going to be put
in tomorrow and there is no telling what Papa will say.

Fred Whitmarsh drops by, and Ruth abruptly warns him he
can't stay long because Papa is having company. Mama goes
upstairs to put on her dotted Swiss apron, and Fred proffers Ruth
a package. "I brought you this. Did you get to think more
about—er—Class Day?"

Ruth didn't. She is more interested in the package, which is two
pounds of Huyler's. Ruth stalls about Class Day: no, it isn't
some*one*, it's some*thing*, which is holding her back from accepting
and thus making a serious commitment of the heart.

The doorbell rings and Fred prepares for flight out the back
door; but it isn't the company. It is Mr. Sparrow, who has
brought Ruth a telegram. Since it is the first telegram she ever
got, just getting it is enough to put her in a flutter and set her
shrieking for her mother. The contents is even more shattering.

It is a wire from Doris Olsson telling Ruth that John Craig, of
the Castle Square Theatre, will see her at his office tomorrow
afternoon.

Fred is forgotten—but still game. By 2:30 tomorrow afternoon Ruth may be an actress, and there is Papa to think of, and
company coming—but Fred still wants to know about his honor-
able Class Day proposal. Fred is bustled out the back way with
an "I'll let you know" from Ruth as Mr. Jones brings his guests
in the front.

Miss Glavin is from Sargent's School of Gymnastics out to
Brookline and Mr. Bagley is from the Y.M.C.A. in Boston. "Miss
Glavin," announces Mr. Jones, "has consented to size Ruth up as
to her chances of gettin' into Sargent's Physical Culture School."
Miss Glavin has brought her Indian clubs.

The visitors talk of the church social and Mr. Jones is expan-
sively genial. He was brought up Episcopalian and he and Mama
were married, he relates, by the Reverend Skinner, father of "this
Otis Skinner, now appearin' on the stage." Ruth has never heard
this before and exclaims excitedly over a new-found reflected
glory.

After a fast bite at some of the cake which has been set forth on
the dining table Miss Glavin gets down to her business. She is a
bear on walking. She won the state championship for ladies'
broad jump year before last. She could have done better only

the judges made her wear shoes, and Miss Glavin is one who believes people should give up shoes. "Best pair of feet I ever saw
belonged to a Carlisle Indian that gave exhibitions so's to put himself through college, jumpin' barefoot on broken glass. It's all in
trainin'!"

Miss Glavin examines Ruth for possible trainin'. "She isn't
made for it, but on the other hand, she hasn't got anything the
matter." Mr. Bagley warns that physical culture is a very demanding career. He is proud of Mr. Jones' work in the evening class
at the "Y."

Miss Glavin now drops the blade of the guillotine on the head
of the suffering Ruth. She has made special arrangements at
Sargent's so that, if Ruth passes muster, she can get into the
Summer term in July instead of having to wait for the autumn
course. Between now and July Ruth can go at her Indian clubs.

Miss Glavin leaves some enrollment papers to be filled out and
she and Mr. Bagley finally make their departure. Mr. Jones
promises that his daughter will be at the physical culture school
tomorrow afternoon, with her papers filled out ready to pass
muster. Without waiting for the dining table to be cleared he gets
out his fountain pen and begins immediately to fill out the blanks
as to Ruth's age, sex, weight, height and schooling.

Ruth manages a last-minute but feeble protest: "I don't want
to be a physical culture teacher."

My Father (*sternly*)—What *do* you want to do?

My Mother (*urgently*)—Tell Papa, Ruth. He wants to know.

Me (*even weaker than before*)—I don't want to be a physical
culture instructress.

My Father—*Why* don't you?

Me (*in a tearful whisper*)—Because I rather be dead.

My Mother (*earnestly*)—Ruth, don't say that. God will hear
you.

My Father—God's listenin' to harps and trumpets and
watchin' sparrows fall.

My Mother—God's listening to *everybody.* . . .

My Father (*turning to* Me *again*)—God's listenin' to everybody but *I'm* listening to *her!* (*I sit tensely, trying to get some
courage.*)

My Mother—Tell Papa!

Me—I have to do my homework.

My Mother—Why, no, you don't, it's Friday night.

ME—Well . . .

MY MOTHER—*Ruth!*

MY FATHER—God damn it, don't sit there like a dyin' calf. If you got somethin' to say, spit it out!

ME (*all the misery in the world in my looks and tone*)—I want to go on the stage. (*This is said in such an agony of emotion, it is little more than a whisper. There is a long pause.* MY FATHER *looks at* ME *doing my best to hold back the tears. He knows, as anyone would to look at me, that this is not some childish whim. Right or wrong, here is a person with his whole heart and soul in a cause. Looking at* ME, *surprised at the violence and depth of my feeling, he finds himself looking at the little boy of eight that he had been, that had needed to do what he had to do. He sits and looks at* ME. *It is a long time before he speaks.*)

MY FATHER (*gravely*)—What makes you think you got the stuff it takes?

ME (*just barely audible*)—I don't know. (*There is another long pause as* MY FATHER *looks at me.*)

MY FATHER—What give you the idea?

ME—I don't know, Papa. Maybe I got to be rovin' like *you* felt.

MY MOTHER—And, Clinton, she has a chance to. Ruth got a telegram today. Well, tell Papa about it, Ruth. He wants to know.

ME—I got a telegram from Miss Doris Olsson, the leadin' lady of the whole Castle Square Theatre Stock Company, sayin' there's part openin' up there and Mr. John Craig will see me *tomorrow.* . . .

MY FATHER (*startled*)—John Craig of the Castle Square Theatre?

ME (*radiantly*)—Yes, Papa.

MY FATHER—He wants *you* to be in the company?

ME (*almost in a state of exaltation*)—There's a *chance!* . . . And Miss Olsson says for me to go see him at two-thirty in the afternoon. Oh, Papa, I *wish* I could be like what you want me to be, but it's like if you asked me to be a giant and I'm *not* a giant and I'm not a Physical Culture person *either!*

MY FATHER (*considers for a moment. Then gravely*)— What makes you think you're a *actress?*

MY MOTHER (*eagerly*)—She's not statuesque, of course, but she looks all right when she remembers to stand up straight. And when she smiles and doesn't look like a thundercloud, Ruth

can be very appealing. She has all *sorts* of artistic leanings.
And *mercy,* Clinton, I guess *some* things, you got to trust in the
Lord.

Papa's sudden softening, the revelation that he once worked as
a stage hand, is an advantage to be pressed to the utmost, and
Mama and Ruth are both aware of it. To prove she is an actress
Ruth volunteers to recite two pieces, one comical and one tragical,
from the stair landing. Papa, the keen critic, can't tell which is
which.

The details of the exciting afternoon are revealed to Mr. Jones—
how Miss Olsson said the best way to become an actress was to
get a job and begin acting. If she went to New York to do it she
could live at the Three Arts Club, which is like the Y.W.C.A., but
maybe she could begin with the Castle Square Theatre Stock Company, because a place is opening up and an appointment with John
Craig has been arranged.

Mr. Jones won't give up the physical culture project too easily.
"Life on the stage isn't anythin' near so benefitin' as bein' a physical culture teacher. . . . Bein' a actress means headin' out on a
rough voyage."

The advantage that Ruth and her mother have gained, sudden
and astonishing though it is, is far from complete. When Mrs.
Jones speculates that John Craig might want Ruth to go to work
right away, Papa puts his foot down. Ruth must finish her
schoolin' first. It makes no difference that Maude Adams went
on the stage at the age of six weeks, or that nobody cares whether
Ethel Barrymore or Booth or Lotta Crabtree ever got a diploma.
An education to Papa is paramount, because he never had one.
When he was eighteen he went to Elmira in up-state New York,
hired a room and put in a whole Winter attemptin' to pick up some
learnin' and they put him in the fourth grade.

"But you got to know Mark Twain there, Clinton," interposes
Mrs. Jones.

"But I missed what I set out to *get!* It was too late for a
education!"

Ruth tries to argue her point further, but Papa ends the discussion by ordering, "Get the cat out and batten down the hatches.
It's time to go to bed." He stamps down cellar to minister to the
furnace.

My Mother—Oh, *why* couldn't you forget all this about being
an actress, Ruth, and settle down with some good man?

ME—*Please don't be disgustin'!* (MY FATHER *stalks through the room, picks up his pen and glasses from the dining room table, and disappears up the stairs.*)

MY MOTHER—Oh, dear, you had to go and be so *different!* (*A thud at the door and it is* PUNK. MY MOTHER *puts him briskly down cellar.*)

ME—Oh, Mama, when two-thirty comes tomorrow afternoon, I'll never live through it.

MY MOTHER—Yes, you will. (*She closes the cellar door.*) I'm not even going to bother with the silver.

MY FATHER'S VOICE—Douse the glim and don't be chewin' the rag all night. Electric light costs money.

MY MOTHER—Come to bed, Ruth, or your father'll have a fit.

ME—I'll go ravin' mad, Mama! If I knew *one single man* that wanted a *mistress,* I'd go in Boston and be *kept!*

MY MOTHER—Oh, dear! When I'm quietly reading my *Unity,* life seems so simple and it's easy to have faith but *Unity* never seems to take into consideration there's people like you and your father! Oh, dear! I suppose it's no use asking you because you know all about *everything,* but for the last time, before I turn out this light, wouldn't you, just for *all* our sakes, Ruth, please *consider* being normal? (*My only answer is to stomp up the stairs.*)

The curtain falls.

SCENE 2

It is late afternoon the next day and the telephone has been installed and is ringing. Papa is in his chair, gloomily sucking an unlit pipe.

"I won't even answer it, Clinton," offers his wife, "and I'll have the telephone company take it right out tomorrow."

"Tomorrow's Sunday."

"Well, Monday, then."

Papa is morose and Mama is trying to work him out of it. He wants to know where Ruth is and she rejoins that Ruth is up to Katherine Follett's. Mrs. Jones thinks that her husband's dour behavior is a hangover from last night's discussion of the stage—but it isn't. It's about Papa this time—about him and the factory.

Dan Weymouth, who has been at the factory even longer than Clint Jones, is going to retire. Maybe he is quitting because he wants to, but on the other hand maybe he is being made to quit—and if so, where is the ax going to fall next? "If I knew Dan went and retired of his own free will and accord, that would be all right," explains Clint. "All right for Dan, I mean. But if they asked me to go do likewise, the only answer I got is to go over and lay down on the New York, New Haven and Hartford railroad tracks! . . . Here I been worryin' if I'm goin' to get my bonus, that ain't even due me, providin' they decide to give it to me, until July, and *now* it turns out it ain't my bonus I have to worry about. It's my whole job!"

Mrs. Jones has a fine and simple suggestion: why doesn't Clint just call up Dan on the new telephone and find out if he retired on purpose or was asked to? Isn't Clint's peace of mind worth a nickel? She finds Dan's number in the book and Clint, speaking carefully as though the telephone were a new and feeble instrument, gives the operator the number. Dan isn't home—he's at a lodge meeting, but will call back. Mrs. Jones, clutching at a straw, opines that this is a good sign—a man who has just been laid off wouldn't go to a lodge meeting.

And Ruth isn't home yet. Her mother thinks she is at Katherine Follett's, but when the phone rings—Mr. Jones thinks it is Dan calling right back—it is Fred on the wire, looking for Ruth, and he has already tried Katherine's and Ruth isn't there. Mr. and Mrs. Jones are talking about Clint's early days as a sailor, when he wore gold hoop earrings and a sash for a belt, when the young lady in question makes a forlorn appearance. She is wearing her "best gear" and her father at once guesses that she has been to see this Craig feller.

Ruth admits the charge. Admits she went when her father told her not to. "I thought if I didn't," she explains, "I'd kill myself." She would like very much to creep up to her room, but Papa prods her with questions until she tells what happened when she saw Mr. Craig: "He just looked at me like he was quite busy . . . And then he said, 'What experience have you had?' . . . So I got all mixed up and said, 'No amateur experience, only professional.' And then I had to go on and say, 'I mean no professional, only amateur.' . . . And then he just said he didn't think I'd fit into the company because it didn't seem like I was suited to hardly any parts."

This crushing confession is too much for Ruth, who slumps into a chair by the dining table and bursts into a long fit of crying. Surprisingly, it is her father who comes up with the first offer of solace. "*He* don't sound like much!" he snorts. "What'd you want to go see *him* for?" Ruth just sobs on, and the telephone rings again. . . .

This time it *is* Dan Weymouth, returning Clint's call with a message of happy relief. Dan has retired from the factory because he wanted to, and Mr. Dollaber, the boss, didn't ask him to do it. With his soul considerably eased, Clint can now bend more attention to the problem of his problem daughter. Gravely he opines, "This Castle Square Company strikes me as kind of a *fresh-water* craft. Next time you try, go after somethin' sea-worthy. . . . A kick in the pants ain't never agreeable, but it don't dislocate your whole life.

"I told you to get a education. *Get it!* Then you're ready for a first-class ship. You better write to that place in New York City. Where was it you said to live at that was like the Y.W.C.A.?"

The conversion of Clint Jones to support of his daughter's ambition is suddenly and touchingly complete. His irritation at John Craig turning down his child results now in his masterful support of the New York plan. If Ruth will go ahead and graduate from high school, he will give her two weeks' board at the Three Arts Club and fifty dollars besides. Clint is indeed a splendid father, as his wife ecstatically tells him.

"I ran away from the people that was in charge of bringin' *me* up. They were awful people!"

MY MOTHER—Only one I ever met was your old Cousin Hartwell.

MY FATHER—They were awful people. They worked me long and *hard*. If I went against their will, they beat me or locked me in the shed, and then when Sunday came, they went to church three times. The Christmas I was eight years old, they wrapped up my good suit I'd been wearin' all winter and hung it on the Sunday School Christmas tree. . . .

MY MOTHER—Oh, Clinton. . . .

MY FATHER—I been to the Fiji Islands and I got along with *them people;* and I been up to the Baltic where I seen men catch fish with their hands and eat 'em raw, but they was pleasant spoken and agreeable . . . and I've ate many a bowl of rice with the heathen Chinee . . . but from one end of the world to the other I ain't never seen no one to equal them psalm singin' *hypocrites,* my great-aunts Jerusha an' Reliance Rogers of Orleans, Mass. So that Christmas night I set off for New Bedford and signed on as a cabin boy. . . . Vessel with a cargo of whale oil bound for Barcelona. I didn't care *where* she was bound for; I was eight and anythin' seemed better than my great-aunts Reliance an' Jerusha, that was in charge of bringin' me up. . . .

My Mother (*gently*)—If only your mother'd been alive, Clinton, everything'd have been different.

My Father (*grimly*)—But she wasn't alive. . . . My mother wasn't alive because she killed herself in a Boston boardin' house. I was two years old and there she was, left with me. My father ran away with a Polish woman. . . .

My Mother—Oh, Clinton . . . (*I just look at* My Father *wide-eyed.*)

My Father—There wasn't nothin' much my mother *could* do but kill herself. She wasn't trained for no kind of labor. And with a small child to look after. *She* knew what mean folks them Rogerses was. . . . And I figure, rather than return to 'em she . . . well, she done what she done.

Me—Gee, Papa. . . . Oh, *gee!* (*It had never occurred to me* My Father *was someone to feel sorry for. I have to wink back the tears.*)

My Mother—Oh, your poor mother! . . . Oh, Clinton, you never told me . . .

My Father—So now you know why I never see none of my people and why I wouldn't talk about 'em none. I'll feel bitter to 'em if I live to be a hundred. They was awful people. Till the day I *die,* I'll feel bitter! So when the time comes *my* child sets out I'd like to try to grease the ways for her, about fifty dollars' worth.

Me (*very near to crying*)—Oh, *Papa!* (*Flinging my arms around him.*) Oh, *Papa!*

My Father—Only thing is I don't know where the hell it's goin' to come from.

My Mother—You'll get it, Clinton. Just *believe* you will. . . .

My Father—Of course there's my bonus. That falls due first week of July. *That's* a hundred. So half of that you *could* consider to be yours. That is, if they'll advance it to me. . . . If it's goin' to be mine July third anyways, then they could, if they wanted, advance it just as well in June. . . .

My Mother—Oh, they *would*, Clinton. I just know they would. . . . Why, what difference would it make to anybody?

My Father—Only difference is, Dollaber's a rich man. Only *poor* people know money is more valuable on certain days than it's ever goin' to be again.

My Mother—You know what fifty dollars means to your father and I, Ruth? In my whole life I never saw fifty dollars together, not even *once.*

Me—Oh, Mama!

My Mother—But money isn't everything. All we *really* need is faith!

My Father—Well, you and Ruth grapple with the faith end of it and I'll tackle D. W. Dollaber. Faith is a wonderful thing all right, but I never was in no situation where havin' money made things any *worse!*

The curtain falls.

ACT III

This is it! It is a June morning, five months later. The dining table is stripped for action, and on one side of it Ruth is making peanut butter sandwiches to take on the train with her, while Fred Whitmarsh sits alongside, watching.

Fred—But I still don't see why you have to go to New York City the very day after your graduation. It doesn't matter if you start to be an actress this week or next, does it? And with Class Day only day after tomorrow. . . .

Me—I *can't* wait till day after tomorrow, Fred. Every minute counts.

Fred—The day after I graduate I don't feel I have to hop right into the Shawmut National Bank just because my uncle's got me an opening there. I'm going to go to Marblehead like always, then in September I'll go to work. (*Shaking his head.*) What's the address of The Three Arts Club?

Me—340 West 85th Street, New York City. My room is number 61. It's reserved beginnin' today! Fred! In New York City, there's a room waitin' for me to just unlock the door an' walk in!

Fred—Gosh! I wonder where 340 West 85th is. I went through New York once on my way to Buffalo. . . .

My Mother (*coming through from the kitchen*)—Why, Fred, I never knew you'd been out West. . . . (*She holds up my gradua-tion dress. It is white ruffled net with short sleeves and a hand-embroidered collar. The skirt is long enough to sweep the floor. She holds it up for my approval.*) Look lovely? I pressed it where you got the ruffles flat last night. I'll get it in the trunk; Mr. Sparrow'll be here any minute to cart it to the station. . . . (*She goes upstairs holding the dress aloft.*)

Fred (*slightly mournful*)—I'm not taking anyone to Class Day. I didn't ask anyone else. . . . Will you miss me? I'm going to miss you. . . .

ME (*thoughtfully*)—I don't *think* I will. It sounds awful, but I want to *go* so, I don't guess I'm goin' to miss *anybody*. I don't mean to *ever* like anybody—a fellow, I mean—that is, not unless they live in New York City, or just outside.

FRED (*surprised*)—Why?

ME—Because New York City is where an actress has to live most of the time.

FRED—Well, but suppose you liked a fellow and he *didn't* live in New York City. Suppose he lived in *Boston*.

ME (*very definite*)—I *couldn't*.

FRED (*doggedly*)—But how could you help it if you *did* like him?

ME—Because I wouldn't let myself get to like him in the *first* place. See, Fred, if I ever got to fallin' in love with a fellow, then I myself might not want to be an actress, that's why, except that *one time*, I never would kiss anybody except of course in games of Post Office. Maybe I'll never kiss anybody, but if I do, it's either got to be Post Office or the fellow *has* to live in New York City.

There is a rattle of wagon wheels in the street, and Mr. Sparrow, the man who brought the fateful telegram, has now come to get Ruth's trunk. He takes a dim view of her going to New York to be an actress. She always was a dabster.

Fred goes upstairs with Mr. Sparrow to help haul the trunk down, and Anna arrives bearing a gift—half for last night's graduation present, half for today's going away. It is a corset cover, wrapped in tissue paper. Katherine, too, arrives, in a state of excitement, bearing a copy of the *Quincy Patriot* with a story about Ruth in it:

"Miss Ruth Gordon Jones, daughter of Mr. and Mrs. Clinton Jones of 14 Elmwood Avenue, is leaving Wollaston shortly to embark on a career of acting in New York City where she hopes to make a name for herself on the Great White Way. She plans to appear under the name of Ruth Gordon."

This is Ruth's first press notice. A true actress, if an untried one, she regards it blissfully.

Katherine has also brought a going-away present—a box of U-All-No After Dinner Mints, which have advertisements in the *Theatre Magazine*.

Fred takes a wan and disconsolate farewell, little cheered by Mrs. Jones' observation that maybe Ruth isn't going to go forever. Ruth consolingly declares that she will think about Fred on Class Day . . . but right now she is thinking more about Papa. He

ought to be here by now. "Do you suppose anything awful's happened, like the bank said he didn't *have* fifty dollars?" she asks
her mother. "Oh, why didn't he just ask Mr. Dollaber like he said
he would, just to advance him his *bonus?*"

"Your father doesn't want to give the impression he's unreliable
and has to borrow past his salary." But Mama does telephone
the factory, and learns that Papa has left there—so he should be
home any minute. Ruth must go upstairs and get ready.

A very grim Clinton Jones arrives. Ruth, he says, can heave
to, and never mind dressing. She isn't going to New York, he
tells his wife, "I can't afford to send no one off to be an actress,"
he explains, "because right this minute I ain't got a job!"

MY MOTHER (*despairingly*)—Oh, how could this happen to us?

MY FATHER—It happened to us because Mr. Dollaber had me
come into his office and asked me did I think Charley Folsom
was entitled to his bonus and I launched out and told him what
I thought of his God damn bonuses!

MY MOTHER—Oh, but, Clinton, you decided not to talk to him
about it.

MY FATHER—How the hell could I help it when he went and
talked to me first?

MY MOTHER—Oh, Clinton! Oh, dear!! Oh, *dear!!!*

MY FATHER—He didn't like it none, and he says to me very
snippy, "Well, how would you propose to remedy that?" And I
let him have it right out, "Pay me what's due me," I says, "and
don't give me no lallygaggin' favors! Pay me like what the damn
bonus would amount to if it was a weekly pay increase. Instead
of you handin' me a hundred simoleons at the end of the fiscal
year, split it up into a weekly raise of two dollars. Then I *got* it
and I *know* I got it and there ain't no *damn worryin' palaver.*"

MY MOTHER (*almost in tears*)—Oh, Clinton, to pick *today* of
all days to say damn to Mr. Dollaber.

MY FATHER (*stubbornly*)—I don't regret it, worked up as I
was.

MY MOTHER—And you mean he went and fired you just because you asked for something you were entitled to?

MY FATHER—I didn't *wait* for him to fire me; I went and fired
myself! He said, "You mean you don't care to continue on, the
way you been goin' for the last twenty-four years?" And I says,
"No," I says. I was kind of surprised myself.

MY MOTHER—Oh, Clinton. . . . Couldn't you have tried to be
just a little more tactful?

My Father—Let *him* be tactful part of the time! For once I had to speak out. So he says they'd hate to lose me but it don't do for a man to try an' run the whole shop, so he'd have to let the matter rest till he thought about it some. "It ain't the two dollars a week I'm begrudgin'," he says, "but the *principle* seems highhanded!" "Well," I says, "think it over, Mr. Dollaber, you can find me at Fourteen Elmwood Avenue, Wollaston!" I'm glad it happened. I'm only askin' for what's mine.

My Mother—But Ruth's *fifty* you were going to give her, Clinton, to go to New York City—

My Father—I can't spare it. She'll have to go some other time. I got sixty-two dollars in the Five Cent Savin's Bank and shellin' out fifty of it'd leave us sailin' too close to the wind.

While the unwitting Ruth sings joyfully upstairs, her mother tries frantically to think of a way out. What about collecting on the insurance—the insurance on her? How about borrowing on her engagement ring? "No, God damn it, no!" roars Clint. "This is a family and Ruth's part of it, she can share the bad with the good."

Down the stair comes Ruth, done up to the nines in her going away outfit—a peacock blue corded silk suit with a narrow and decently slit skirt; a black tulle halo with a gardenia on it for a hat, and high-heeled patent leather pumps. She is every inch an actress, she feels.

She still stands, holding her suitcase and wearing the stupidest smile, after her father has told her, "You can't go. So get them duds off and stow away your gear." He hasn't the do-re-mi, he explains. "So get them duds off and hyper down to the railroad station and turn back your parlor car ticket. . . ."

For a minute Ruth stands there; for one whole awful minute she feels the way she did when the water closed over her head once at Nantasket Beach. Then, just as at Nantasket, she jerks her head up through the breakers. "I will not! I will not take my ticket back! I will *so* go! You said I could be an actress and I *am* goin'!"

Her father tries to explain that she hasn't any money—but she counters that she won't need any. Her room at the Three Arts Club has been paid in advance for two weeks.

Me—Don't you care about the fifty dollars, Papa. I don't need it. I got two dollars an' forty cents of my money and my railroad ticket, so I'll just get a job sooner so's I can look after you and Mama.

MY MOTHER (*beseechingly*)—Oh, Clinton, she can't go be an actress on two dollars and forty cents.

ME—I can so! Where's my box of lunch, Mama? You'll hear from me day after tomorrow!

MY MOTHER—Oh, Clinton, let me give her my engagement ring. *Do* let me, Clinton, *please.*

MY FATHER—I gave you that to *keep.*

MY MOTHER (*pleading*)—She could get some money for it.

ME—Mama! You mean go in a *pawn shop? I'd rather be dead.*

MY FATHER—If you're goin' to be an actress, you'll be in and out of a pawn shop, all the rest of your life!

ME—I'll go see every single manager in New York City to-morrow. I'll go see 'em beginnin' at six o'clock in the mornin'!

MY FATHER—Well, by God, you've got spirit!

ME—I got anythin' I *want* to have; but I'll never have anythin' *at all* if trouble makes me go an' give up! I'm *never* goin' to let trouble stop me! Why, to actresses it's even a *help!* I don't know if it's any use to private people, but actresses have to *have* troubles, so's they can *act!* Why, I bet I can even learn to welcome trouble! I bet I *can* actually enjoy it. I bet—

MY FATHER—Hold on a minute! Hold on! No call to render a solo on the beauties of bein' in the soup. On the other hand if what it takes to be an actress is *gumption,* you at least got that! I know what's goin' on inside you, Snuggy. Your mother says you take after me, and better or worse, I guess you do. Of course, I don't suppose you know what you're tacklin', but I'm willin' to give you a chance to find out. I always staked you up to now, and, by God, I'm willin' to continue on the same. Mama, go look on the parlor mantelpiece and get me down my spy glass.

MY MOTHER (*startled*)—Clinton!—What're you goin' to do?

MY FATHER—I'm goin' to wrap it up in a newspaper if you got a decent one. Give me the *Boston Globe.* When you get to New York City, Ruth, take it down to Cap'n Alex Forbes, Twenty-two South Street, and he'll give you one hundred dollars for it. (MY MOTHER *rushes into the parlor and returns with the spy glass.*)

ME (*dazed*)—Papa!

MY FATHER—And if Forbes is away on a voyage, take her to any ship chandler along the street; there ain't one wouldn't give you a hundred, spot cash.

ME—Papa!—I *can't* take it. I *wouldn't.* It's your *spy* glass!

My Father—Money's for those who need it. A spy glass ain't no further use to me.

Me—But, Papa—I know I can get along!

My Father—Don't be bousin' your jib. You may love your Hazel Dawns and your Doris Olssons, but money's a damn lovin' friend too! (My Mother *rushes back with the* Boston Globe.)

Me (*anxiously*)—But what about you and Mama, if just maybe I didn't get a job right off?

My Father (*starting to wrap up the spy glass*)—Rest easy! I been on a payroll since I was eight, and I been cast over-board before. It ain't like I was lookin' for a job as vice-president; there's always plenty of room at the bottom.

Me—Oh, Papa, I won't only just merely look after you and Mama, but we'll *have* things! And every time we feel like it, we'll throw *away fifty dollars!*

Once again Ruth's departure is imminent—and to the luggage has been added Papa's spy glass. Her father regards her for a minute. "Snuggy," he says, "I ain't talked to you a whole lot and I ain't goin' to start spoutin' out now. If I didn't think you could shift for yourself, I wouldn't let you go. But from my own personal experience of knockin' around the world, there's more temptation when you're rovin' than you're likely to run up against at home. However, I ain't goin' to impose a whole lot of rules on you, nor chart no exact course, but I want you to promise me *one thing,* Snuggy; no matter what you do, nor where you go, don't never act in no place where they serve hard liquor!"

Ruth, radiant again, swears she'll make good. Her mother observes that it is a wonderful thing for a girl to have a father who believes in her a hundred dollars' worth.

"No," says Clint, "you don't have to doff your tops'l and feel beholden. What you're gettin' is what a person's got a right to. You're only gettin' your chance. And on your side of the ledger you can remember your mother and I pleasantly, and that'll make it come out square."

Ruth, father, mother, suitcase, umbrella, spy glass and some carnations from Fred are jumbled in a last loving embrace. They go out the door—Clint last. He locks the door.

THE CURTAIN FALLS

JOHN LOVES MARY

A Farce Comedy in Three Acts

By Norman Krasna

SOME years back in the theatre we made frequent use of the term "farce comedy" as a play classification. It usually connoted a good farce that wasn't quite equal to the strain of being described as a comedy, or a good comedy that slipped occasionally into situations that were frankly, and often a little brazenly, farcical. In fact, almost any comedy that was more dependent upon contrived situations than it was upon developed character for its entertainment values was pretty sure to be called a farce comedy.

Well, this "John Loves Mary" is best described, and most comfortably accepted, as a farce comedy. Its plot foundation is one of those stories that, as Ward Morehouse wrote of it in the New York *Sun*, "is definitely of the manufactured variety, and one for which there would be no second and third acts if the simple truth had been told in the first."

We selected it for this particular collection of best plays because, first, we liked it, and thought it honestly representative of the best theatre entertainment of the season, and second, because we felt the need of a good light comedy to leven the more serious post-war dramas from which we had to make a choice.

Something of the same impulse induced us, a few seasons back, to include Norman Krasna's other frivolously serious (or maybe seriously frivolous) study of a returned GI's involvement in a post-war romance called "Dear Ruth." That choice did not meet with the approval of all our "Best Plays" reviewers, but it did give us a better balanced list of contents for that particular season, and considerable personal satisfaction.

For "John Loves Mary" we probably owe as much thanks to Joshua Logan, who joined Richard Rodgers and Oscar Hammerstein 2d in its production, and also took charge of the play's staging, as we do to Mr. Krasna, who wrote it. The script was first given to Mr. Logan to read. It was he who called it to the Rodgers-Hammerstein attention. And it is he who has had more to do with the building up and projection of the comedy situations than any other of the interested parties. It is, as indicated, definitely a comedy of situation, rather than a comedy of character. The reader will probably be quick to recognize that fact.

Neither the housing shortage nor the OPA disturbed the family of Senator James McKinley. They have had an apartment in the St. Regis Hotel, New York, for twelve years. As we see it now it is an apartment furnished with good antiques, combined with bright fabrics, which "bespeak good taste, good living and a good deal of money." The furniture is arranged for comfortable conversation.

At the moment Mary McKinley is setting the scene for an event. "Mary is twenty-two, eager, alert and sympathetically pretty." She comes from the pantry, which is to the right of the entrance doors from the hall, carrying a bottle of champagne in a bucket too small for it.

Disposing of the champagne by setting the bucket on the coffee table, Mary goes back to the pantry for a tray of crackers and a can of caviar set in a bowl of ice. The arrangements please her.

Now, her anxiety temporarily getting the better of her, she confirms by phone the information that the three o'clock train from Norfolk, Virginia, is on time. She gives orders to Betty, the phone girl, that she would like not to accept any more calls the rest of the day. If anyone persists, let Betty tell them that Mary has gone back to Washington.

Even with everything thus settled, Mary is plainly startled at a sudden buzz of the doorbell. It is only Oscar, the elevator man. Oscar is "fifty, kindly and Irish." He has brought a larger bucket for the champagne. He is also interested in the other preparations. But he certainly doesn't think that any can of caviar is worth twenty-eight dollars. No, ma'am—

"It's the occasion, Oscar," Mary tries to explain. "You associate a good time with spending a lot of money."

Oscar can remember back ten years, when he first knew Mary. She certainly has grown into a fine young lady. "He won't be disappointed in you," Oscar assures her. "You know how absence makes the heart grow."

"Not always," ventures Mary. "Three years apart is awful long for people in love. Awful long. I know a girl who counted the minutes for her soldier to be back, and one day she met him on the street. He'd been back a month."

Another buzz at the doorbell and Mary is practically panic-stricken. This time Oscar is quickly shooed out through the

pantry. Mary hurries to the phonograph, and starts it playing
"If You Were the Only Girl in the World." From there she
dashes back to the center of the room, grips the back of a chair
and closes her eyes. She is standing there with a rapt expression
when the bell buzzes a second time.

"The door is open!" Mary calls, holding her expectant pose.

The door opens and Fred Taylor enters. Fred is a "large,
good-natured fellow of twenty-four, dressed befitting a maintenance man in the telephone company." He is carrying a large
package, and he is greatly puzzled by Mary's pose.

"Shall I open my eyes?" she asks.

That would be okay with Fred, so she does. Then she leaps
back with a start. Who is this? What does he want? Who
asked him to come?

Well, Jack Lawrence asked Fred to come. Jack had telephoned
from Norfolk. Said his train would be in at three, and asked
him to be there. He's Fred Taylor. He and Jack were in the
same company overseas.

Now Mary understands and is properly impressed. Fred
Taylor! Of course she knows Fred Taylor! She goes quickly
to him. Tenderly she bends over and kisses him. That would
be for John!

"John wrote me all about it!" she says, by way of explanation. "You saved his life!"

"It was nothing! He'd've done the same for me," says Fred.

"You carried him in your arms, like a baby, for two hundred
yards. With shells flying all around."

"Mostly thirty-calibre stuff. That's all."

"I'm forever obligated to you."

"You don't have to be."

She is looking at him admiringly. "I guess it seemed odd to
you, my standing there with my eyes closed."

"It did look kind of funny."

"That's how John's supposed to see me for the first time."

"Oh."

"That's how he saw me last. 'If You Were the Only Girl' was
playing on the radio. I bought the record."

"Oh, sure. I get it."

"When he comes through that door again we're going to pretend the last three years never happened."

"Well, it's a good trick if you can do it."

Fred is beginning to feel a little easier now. The McKinley
apartment interests him. To Fred a hotel has always been a

place where you rent a room for the night, and you better have a bag—"I mean a handbag," he is quick to add, fearing he may have said the wrong thing.

The hotel apartment, Mary explains, is more convenient for her father, the Senator, who has to be in Washington most of the time.

"How did John sound to you on the telephone?" she asks. "I thought his voice was deeper than when he left."

"Could be. He was a sergeant," explains Fred.

Would Fred have some caviar? It's fresh. Fred wouldn't mind. He finds a place on the love seat in front of the refreshments and starts in. The first spoonful gives him pause, but not for long. He's never eaten caviar before, but it's all right. He takes another spoonful.

Mary watches him, a little uncertainly. "It's not like ice cream, you know," she says. "You eat it with crackers. I'm sorry I haven't any spreaders. You can spread it on the crackers with the spoon."

"Oh, I don't mind. Spoon's fine." Fred helps himself to more. "You learn something every day," he admits. He is glad to have something, too. He had missed his lunch because he had had to go to the Harvard Club to pick up a suit for Jack. Jack is anxious to get back into civvies.

"One meal of this isn't bad, but I wouldn't like it as a steady diet," Fred admits. He picks up the can and is trying to read the Russian label when it slips out of his hand. The caviar he hasn't had a chance to finish goes on the floor.

Mary is on her hands and knees sopping up the caviar with a napkin when the outer hall door slams. The next instant John Lawrence stands in the doorway, a duffle bag over his shoulder and an expansive grin on his face. "He is a Sergeant, twenty-four, handsome, vital, and immediately likable."

"Mary!" shouts John, dropping the duffle bag and stretching out his arms.

"Oh, no!" groans a stricken Mary, making no effort at getting up or even looking back. "You get out! You turn right around and leave!"

"Mary!"

"You heard me! I planned for three years how you were going to see me, and it wasn't going to be like this! Get out and count to twenty and then come in again!"

"All right, Mary."

Fred moves out of the picture, John goes back to the hall and Mary resets the scene. She has just restarted the phonograph and taken her pose when the door opens. This time it is Oscar with a bowl of ice. That's the end of Mary's posing.

"Eighteen—nineteen—twenty!" John is counting. "Mary! Honey!" He is in with a rush and Mary is in his arms. At first she would push him away a little, but then "the biology sets in" and they are swaying happily.

"Where've you been?" demands Mary, lovingly.

"I was away on a little business trip, honey."

"What took you so long? You promised you'd be back in twenty minutes."

"I over-estimated myself, kid."

After a minute Mary and John unfold. Oscar is sent on his way and Fred and John have a chance to complete their own lightly emotional reunion—

"Mary, I wouldn't be here if it wasn't for him," says John.

"Oh, sure you would," protests Fred, modestly.

"I was leaking like a sieve. They didn't know where I was hit."

"We were both soaked," adds Fred. "At the base hospital they washed *me* off twice looking for where *I* was wounded!"

They both laugh. For a moment they are silent.

"Yeah, that was quite a time!" admits John, forcing himself out of the mood. "Well, enough of that! We've got other things to talk about!"

Now he has put Fred in a chair and drawn Mary to the love seat beside him. As soon as he can get her close enough he is ready to listen to Fred's report.

There isn't a lot to tell. Fred had got his old job back, with the telephone company. Of the other fellows they know who live in New York, one's got a gas station on the Parkway and another's inherited his father's cigar store. As for O'Leary, the louse! The lieutenant—

"We took a solemn oath. No matter where he was—in what jail or insane asylum—we were going to track him down," John explains to Mary.

The lieutenant, it seems, is still in uniform. He's a balcony usher at the Paramount Theatre. This may give them a chance to gang up on him some night and push him into the orchestra. . . .

As the boys go on with their reminiscences, Mary brings the

conversation around to the question of girls—the girls they knew
on the other side. She has seen pictures of them in the news-
reels: " 'Me like American soldiers! Gimme chewing gum.' "

This is a serious matter with John. "Mary," he says, "you've
hit on an unfortunate subject. Many soldiers really fell in love
overseas, and very often there were unhappy endings. Fred here
is one of those cases."

MARY (*quickly crossing to* FRED)—Oh, I'm terribly sorry.
Please forgive me.

FRED—That's all right.

MARY—Is it something you don't care to talk about?

FRED—I was in love with an English girl, and we got separated,
and I couldn't find her again.

MARY—How dreadful!

FRED—She was a wonderful girl.

JOHN—Yes, she was.

FRED (*to* MARY)—I met her in a night club. She was an
acrobatic dancer. She used to walk on her hands, and do a little
dance kind of, and sing a song at the same time. It doesn't
sound like much, but it was cute.

MARY (*sincerely*)—I'm sure it was.

JOHN (*putting his arm around* MARY)—I was there when he
asked her to marry him. During an air raid.

FRED—We went right to the adjutant to fill out the papers.
(*He thinks a moment.*) What the hell did the army do with
all those papers we signed?

MARY—Did you get married?

FRED—We would have but there was a little complication.
The next day was D-Day!

MARY—Oh, no!

FRED—Twenty-four hours later we were in France.

MARY—Couldn't you write to her?

FRED—The only address I had was the night club. We heard
it was blitzed.

MARY—Oh.

FRED—After V-E Day I got a leave, and went looking for her.
Not a trace.

MARY—That's awful.

FRED—I took it pretty bad for a while. Drank a lot. Gave
Jack a hell of a time, I guess.

JOHN—Oh, no.

FRED—I still think of her sometimes. I don't like to go to night clubs.

Getting a signal from John, Mary is quick to excuse herself. This leaves John free to take up the subject of Lily from where Fred left it. John had seen Lily before he left London. He had gone into a little night club and there was a girl walking on her hands. He recognized her from her back—

"She asked about you all night long. When she wasn't crying."
"What was she crying for?"
"I told her how you looked for her, and how you felt. She nearly had hysterics."

FRED—No kidding?
JOHN—In the morning we went to the Embassy, to find out how she could get to America.
FRED—Well?
JOHN—Years, if she was lucky. A lot of people want to come to America.
FRED—I guess so.
JOHN—I took one of the Embassy clerks out to lunch. I tried to bribe him! There was only one way Lily could get into America. One way. Do you know how?
FRED—How?
JOHN (*triumphantly*)—As the wife of an American soldier!
FRED (*unbelieving*)—N-N-No!
JOHN—She's arriving day after tomorrow!
FRED (*pointing to* JOHN)—You married Lily!
JOHN (*grinning*)—You don't mind, do you?
FRED—Holy Mackerel!
JOHN (*coming to* FRED)—It's legal and it's fool-proof. She gets off that boat, you and she take the first train to Reno!
FRED—Holy Mackerel!
JOHN—You said that.
FRED—Jack, I don't know what to say!
JOHN—You don't have to say anything, Fred, not to me! (*Smiling.*) She comes in day after tomorrow, we pick her up at the Red Cross! It takes six weeks to get a divorce in Reno. Twenty minutes after the divorce, you two are married! What's wrong with that? (*He laughs.*) Close your mouth, you look like a flounder!
FRED—Jack, I don't know what to say!
JOHN—Don't you think I owe you that much?

FRED—Holy Mackerel! . . . What about Mary?

JOHN—I'll tell her. And it'll be all right. Mary'll wait six weeks. That's the kind of girl she is.

John calls Mary back from the pantry. Now it will be all right with him if Fred decides to leave them, and Fred, still dazed by the news of Lily, as well as by John's plan, is finally eased out into the hall.

Naturally John is eager for the home news. He gets it—between hugs and kisses. Where are Mary's mother and father? They're in Washington. That's good. How did Mary manage it? She told Mother that Father wasn't looking well—

"Dad doesn't take care of himself when she's not around," Mary explains. "He eats the wrong things and they disagree with him."

"What food would have enough nerve to disagree with your father?" demands John, making another lunge for Mary and gathering her to him with a good deal of enthusiasm. He has pulled her down on the couch—

"This isn't exactly as I planned," protests Mary. "I was going to be more stand-offish."

"Why?"

"I read about it in a magazine. 'How to resume relations with a soldier,' by Doctor W. Zooger. He's supposed to be an authority."

John is not impressed. The hell with Doctor Zooger.

"Doctor Zooger said the reason we're supposed to be reserved is to show you the difference between us and the foreign girls who threw themselves at you."

"Zooger's a German spy. The Germans used to drop leaflets from airplanes saying our girls were being untrue to us with 4Fs. Were you untrue to me with a 4F?"

"You couldn't ask a man to show his draft card."

"That's right, dear."

They are silent and contented for a moment, then Mary has a new idea. She wants to see John's wound.

"I've made up my mind. If you could be shot, the least I can do is to look. . . . I won't get sick, John. I've prepared myself. . . . Tell me when to look."

John has loosened his tie and opened his shirt. "Now!" he says. Mary forces herself to open her eyes. It is an effort. Then she sees—

"Is that all?"

"What do you mean, 'Is that all?' What did you expect? To see through me!"

"It's so tiny!"

"Not to me! That was a thirty-eight-caliber bullet!"

"That couldn't kill anybody," says Mary, hugging her casualty delightedly.

They are remembering now the things they used to do, the places they used to go.

"I used to dream about us at Tony's," says Mary.

"Tony's! Antipasto! Ravioli! Chicken Cacciatore! They don't know how to cook Italian food in Italy."

"Tony always asks about you. And he always gives me our booth, no matter how crowded it is."

That gives them an idea. Why not go to Tony's tonight? They could have a drink or two. And an early dinner. The champagne can wait.

While Mary is putting the champagne back in the pantry John has unpacked the gray suit, a shirt and a tie from the package Fred brought. He starts changing his clothes. When Mary comes from the pantry she is ordered to turn her back. John wants her to get a look at the civilian all at once. She sits on the sofa while he proceeds with the change. He takes off his trousers, revealing his khaki shorts. The conversation has returned to Fred and his English girl. Mary has been thinking about them. Cautiously John tries to get some idea of how she feels. Of course Fred's girl may still be alive—she wasn't on any of the casualty lists. And if she is alive would it, or would it not, be the right thing to let Fred know? If he knows, he's almost sure to try to locate her, and if he should find her what could he do? It might take years to get Lily to America. Maybe it would be kinder to let them forget each other—

"It would not!" explodes Mary. "And I think it's very unfeeling of you."

"You're sure, now?" He is smiling. "Letting them know they are available to each other and then sentencing them to years apart." He watches her carefully. "You still say it's worth it?"

"Yes."

This, John decides, is the appointed time to tell Mary everything. In his excitement he forgets about the exposed shorts and comes around the end of the sofa to sit with her and explain. He has just settled himself and is holding Mary's hand, when the hall doors open and in walk Senator and Mrs. McKinley.

John and Mary jump up from the sofa. The next second John has become aware of the Senator's gaze fixed on his shorts. He quickly moves over behind the arm of the chair.

"I was just showing Mary where I was wounded," offers John, nervously, by way of a quick explanation.

"I understood it was your shoulder," barks the Senator.

"He was shot by a thirty-eight-caliber bullet, Dad. You can be killed by that."

"I was in the first World War! We had bullets then!"

"I know this looks peculiar, sir, but I wouldn't like you to get the wrong impression. There was somebody with us until just a few minutes ago."

"A friend of John's, the one who saved his life."

"I presume *he* was dressed."

"Oh, Dad, this is John. You haven't even said 'Hello' to him!"

"I didn't leave a committee room of the United States Senate, at a time I'm urgently needed, to say 'Hello' to John! (*He approaches* JOHN.) I'll thank you to put your trousers on, if not out of courtesy to my daughter, to my wife!"

"Certainly, sir!"

John recovers his army trousers and starts putting them on. He is still the focus of attention, but he continues bravely. His final gesture with his zipper is definitely defiant. A formal "Thank you!" from the Senator brings the incident to at least a temporary end.

Senator McKinley is "broad in the shoulder, 55, and used to having his own way." Mrs. McKinley "is 50, loves her husband dearly, and considers herself dominated by him, which is not true."

There is still considerable explaining to do. Why did Mrs. McKinley return directly to New York? Because she wasn't asleep when Mary thought she was, and knew of her daughter's conspiring to be alone with John.

Why had Mary tried to deceive her parents, not only this time, but the time she had been discovered seeing John off to camp before he sailed? Because on that occasion John's movements were a military secret—

"I am a member of the Military Affairs Committee!" announces the Senator. "I know more important secrets than an enlisted man getting on a boat!"

With the Senator's permission, John decides it is time for him to speak. He can understand a father's feelings in a situation such as this, but he had taken it for granted that Senator McKin-

ley had accepted his intentions toward Mary as being above
suspicion. Of course he hoped to marry Mary—

"You don't have to marry me, John," Mary interrupts. ". . .
You're a free agent! You do as you please! I've no call on
you to marry me! Absolutely none!"

"Of course I'm going to marry you!" John's excitement mounts.
"Why, no wonder your father feels this way. Why—" He has
turned to the Senator. "Senator McKinley, I love your daughter
very much. I believe she loves me. I have no greater wish in
life than to make her happy. I would consider it a great honor
and privilege if you would give your permission for our marriage. . . . After a suitable engagement, of course."

"Well, you have it!" The Senator's acceptance is curt but he
is plainly touched. Mary too— "John! That was beautiful!
You surprised me!"

The family congratulations are now free and sincere. Mrs.
McKinley confesses that she has always liked John. The Senator,
though he has fought Mary's marrying with all the ammunition
he had, is pleasantly reconciled, and after John and Mary are
married he will do his best to be like a father to John. Right now
he would like to hurry things along—

"I can spend only a limited time in New York," the Senator
explains. "If you apply for your marriage certificate and take
your blood test tomorrow morning— (*He takes a small engagement book from his vest pocket and consults it.*) That's Tues-
day—the three day waiting period will be Wednesday, Thursday,
Friday—you can be married on Saturday, and I can be back in
Washington Sunday."

John is worried. He had counted on some kind of engagement. Six weeks, he had always thought, was the minimum socially. John is not in favor of rushing things, even though the
others are.

"I consider you've been engaged for three years," announces
the Senator. "I give my permission."

To John the room has become unbearably hot. "You're not
used to being in this room with your clothes on," suggests the
Senator, and roars loudly at his own joke.

The hall door is pushed open. Fred Taylor comes in. The
McKinleys are proud to meet the hero and to add their congratulations. To Fred's further embarrassment, John feels the Senator
should hear the story in detail—

"I'd like to tell you about it as it really happened," he says.
"It's important that you get the right picture. Fred here—and I

—were side by side when I got hit. Shells were flying all around. It was worth a man's life to stand up. (*He gets down on one knee, really acting it out.*) Fred looked at me. I looked at him. I knew what was going through his mind. If he kept his head down he was safe. But here was his friend—me—bleeding— what was he to do?"

PHYLLIS (*Mrs. McKinley*)—That was a decision!

JOHN (*snapping his fingers*)—He made up his mind like that! He picked me up in his arms as you do a baby, and carried me not fifty yards, not a hundred yards—but two hundred yards! He brought me in! He saved my life! (*He offers his hand.*) I want to thank you again, Fred.

FRED (*to* MARY)—May I use the phone?

MARY (*pointing*)—Why, certainly.

FRED (*at phone*)—Butterfield 8—5500.

JOHN (*anxious to preserve the mood he's built up*)—Senator McKinley, would you say I owed this man a great deal?

JAMES (*Senator McKinley*)—Yes, I'd say that. I think you're quite obligated to him.

JOHN (*jumping at it*)—That's it, sir! That's the word! I'm obligated to him! There's nothing I could do for him that would be too much! Nothing! That's what you're saying, sir?

JAMES—Well, yes—

FRED (*into telephone*)—Hello. Lenox Hill Hospital? The Maternity Ward, please . . . (*They all look at him. He's looking at* JOHN.) Is this the Maternity Ward? This is Mr. Taylor again. Any news about my wife? Thank you. (*He hangs up. He looks at* JOHN *pathetically.*)

JOHN (*turning his head slowly*)—Maternity Ward?

PHYLLIS—You're not having a—?

MARY (*jumping up*)—Fred! You're married!

FRED (*still to* JOHN)—And I'm having a baby.

JOHN—Oh, no! No, no!

MARY (*to* FRED)—How wonderful! Oh, Fred, I'm so happy for you! (*To her parents.*) You don't know the whole story behind this!

JOHN (*to himself*)—I don't believe it!

MARY—I'm so happy for you, I think I'm going to cry! Oh, Fred.

JOHN (*shaking his head*)—No, no!

PHYLLIS (*to* MARY)—You certainly are excited about this baby!

MARY—It isn't just the baby, but he's married!

JAMES—I should hope so!

MARY—You don't understand! He had a terribly tragic love-affair, and he was able to forget. (*To* FRED.) My, what a strong character you must have.

JOHN (*facing* FRED)—Character! You call that character! You were never going to forget Lily! You were going to remember her to your dying day!

FRED—What did you expect me to do? Join a monastery?

JOHN (*furious*)—Yes! You were so much in love with her! You couldn't live without her!

FRED—What about your advice? Life has to go on! Well, I went on!

MARY (*standing between them*)—John! Shame on you! Are you begrudging him his new happiness?

JOHN—You bet I am!

MARY—This is your best friend! He saved your life!

JOHN—Who asked him to! (*He throws himself face down on the sofa.*)

MARY (*as they all go to him*)—John!

FRED—It's war nerves! He gets them every once in a while!

JAMES—Open his shirt! Get some brandy!

FRED (*bending over him*)—Just don't talk, Jack!

PHYLLIS (*taking his shoes off*)—Oh, the poor boy! He's crying!

JAMES (*rising in wrath*)—This is a hell of a way to release a man from the army! Eisenhower's going to have to do some explaining about this!

The curtain falls.

ACT II

That night the McKinleys gave a small party for the prospective bride and groom at the Stork Club, but it didn't seem to cheer John up perceptibly. All evening he perspired a lot. This worried Mrs. McKinley. It might indicate that her future son-in-law's war nerves were permanent, though the Senator is sure they're not.

It is now 11 o'clock next morning, and presently John and Mary come swinging through the hall doors. At least Mary is swinging. John, still a bit on the droopy side, follows slowly after. They have been for their marriage license and had gotten it without a hitch. Doctor Wilber himself had given them their blood test. . . .

"This ceremony will be in the Mayor's office, Saturday morning at 11 o'clock," the Senator is saying. "The Mayor had a transit commission meeting, but he was kind enough to postpone it. There will be a small reception here after the wedding. Just close friends and family. I've confined myself to Senators Vandenberg, Taft, Pepper, Secretary Harriman and Justice Frankfurter. Not every young man has a Supreme Court Judge at his wedding reception."

"No, sir." John has reached for a cigarette and is smoking nervously.

"Has everyone accepted, Phyllis?"

"Dorothy's little girl has a fever, and she may not come, but the Senator will definitely. (*She looks at her list.*) Our relations are more of a problem. (*To* JAMES.) Your sister and her family will be eight altogether. The Whittakers are three, the Simons, the Lewisohns and their two daughters, and the Hallidays. That's all the relations we have who live within a day of New York. I don't know what I'm going to say to the others."

"Why don't we get married in different cities, Mother, on a tour?"

"I must say I never thought I'd see my only child married off surreptitiously, as though we're trying to avert a scandal."

"Surreptitiously? In the Mayor's office?"

"I wanted a wedding with bridesmaids and organ music, and I expected to cry."

"You'll cry, Mother dear."

"It's not the same, crying in the Mayor's office."

Fred Taylor brings news. Not the news of his expected baby, but a report that when he went to the Harvard Club—thinking he would pick John up there and go with him to the license bureau—he had found an officer—a lieutenant—there looking for John—

"What did he want?" John's surprise is a trifle overdone.

"He didn't say. He just asked for you. I gave him this address. I would've talked to him further, but I called the hospital, and the nurse sounded as though I ought to come right over—so I left him."

He could have been one of the officers of their division, John and Fred are agreed. Probably wants to know how John is getting on, and could he loan him money or something.

"I'm glad to hear you say that," agrees the Senator. "We've had a great deal of talk in the Senate about enlisted men not

having a high regard for their officers. I never believed a word
of it."

"You didn't?" Fred is surprised.

"No. I was in the first World War, and I can tell you, the
enlisted men worshiped their officers."

"What rank were you, sir?"

"I was a Colonel! . . . Would you say the enlisted men didn't
respect and admire their officers in this war?"

"I'd say they had the same feelings toward them as they did in
your day, sir. Exactly."

Incidentally the Senator had made a speech on that very subject. The newlyweds can read it in the Congressional Record,
which he will see is one of their wedding presents. And that's
not all. They are also going to get a wedding trip for a month.
They can go wherever they like—

"And read the Congressional Record," adds Mary, slyly. . . .

Mary and her mother go to check Mary's underthings. The
Senator, deciding that this is an occasion that justifies a drink,
even this early in the day, has disappeared into the pantry. John
and Fred have a chance to compare notes.

John admittedly is worried. Not only about being in Reno
for six weeks with Lily, but about the whole conspiracy. Getting someone to impersonate an officer—they could be court-
martialed for that.

Fred is calmly confident. There have, however, been a few
changes in the plan they had agreed upon the night before. Fred
had been unable to get Lieutenant Harris, who had refused to
take the chance. Neither had he been able to get Bennett. Bennett could have worn his brother's uniform, but unfortunately
brother was wearing it at the gas station, because he found it
was good for business.

"Who did you get?" demands John, anxiously.

"Under the circumstances the man I got is ideal. We need
someone who can lie! A born liar! Who's had practice besides!"

"Out with it! Who is it?" John has grabbed Fred by the
lapels. But before he can answer, Senator McKinley is in with
the drinks.

They have their liquor now, and the Senator thinks they should
also have a toast. What shall it be?

"Well, sir," suggests Fred, with a significant glance at John,
"may the only uniform we see from now on—be the uniform of a
Paramount Theatre usher!"

John doesn't get it at first. When he does he chokes on his drink, and it takes all Fred can do to pull him out of it. As soon as he recovers control, John demands another drink.

There is a buzz at the door and the next they know Lieutenant Victor O'Leary is with them. "I rehearsed it with him ten times," Fred has a chance to whisper to John, after the Senator has gone to the door. "He can do it!"

The Lieutenant "is twenty-five; handsome in a smirking way, and too self-assured. He carries off the deception much better than John and Fred."

"My name is Lieutenant LeRoy," O'Leary is explaining to Senator McKinley, as they come into the room.

JAMES (*offering his hand*)—I'm Senator McKinley. How do you do.

O'LEARY (*shaking hands*)—How do you do, sir. I was told I could find Sergeant Lawrence here.

JAMES (*indicating* JOHN)—You've found him. There he is.

O'LEARY—How do you do, Sergeant.

JOHN (*shaking hands*)—How do you do, sir.

O'LEARY (*smiling*)—I didn't expect to find you in civilian clothes.

JOHN—Enlisted men have terminal leave now, sir. It's optional. Lieutenant, may I present Fred Taylor.

FRED (*not looking him in the eye*)—How do you do, Lieutenant.

O'LEARY—How do you do.

JAMES (*as* MARY *and* PHYLLIS, *attracted by the voices, enter*)—Lieutenant LeRoy, Mrs. McKinley, and my daughter, Mary.

PHYLLIS—How do you do, Lieutenant.

MARY—How do you do.

O'LEARY (*looking too searchingly at* MARY)—I'm pleased to meet you.

JAMES (*to* JOHN)—Something wrong with our sergeant? You're not missing a tank or anything?

O'LEARY—Oh, nothing like that, sir. I—(*He hesitates.*)—hope I'm not disturbing you. I have some business with Lawrence.

JAMES—It's not a military secret?

O'LEARY—Oh, no, sir.

JAMES—We're all in the family. What is it?

O'LEARY—Well, Lawrence, I hope you won't take this as bad news, but—there's a small job the army needs you for—I'm afraid you're in for another sixty days!

MARY—No! No! That's not fair!

FRED—No, it isn't!

JOHN—Sixty days!

JAMES—That's too bad.

FRED (*part of the rehearsal*)—Why do they need him?

O'LEARY—We have a tremendous property disposal job to do.
(FRED *steps back*.) Captured enemy equipment, you know, the
kind of thing Lawrence has been doing overseas, and we're just
short trained men. That's the whole story. Somebody has to
do it.

MARY (*to* O'LEARY)—He's been overseas for three years! He
only came back yesterday!

O'LEARY—I'm in the same boat myself, Ma'm. It's not my decision.

JAMES—Of course, Lieutenant. Sit down. Let's discuss this
calmly.

O'Leary is glad of a chance to explain that he has brought the
news personally because, after all, it is his squad and he doesn't
like to see his men unhappy. It's kind of a rough deal, he admits, but after all—"Ours not to wonder why, ours but to do
and die."

Where will John have to go? Mary is anxious to know. He
will have to go to a storage depot in Nevada, the Lieutenant explains. Both Fred and John are surprised and disappointed—
but there is nothing to do about that.

All right, Mary decides, if John has to go to Nevada she'll go
too. Fred and John are even more surprised by this suggestion,
but the Lieutenant is quick to explain that that can't be. There
are no quarters for women at this storage depot. And the nearest town is quite a ways out. John wouldn't be able to come in
more than one day a week. Mary doesn't care. She's going anyway.

"How much time has Sergeant Lawrence got in New York?"
asks Fred, a little pointedly. "At least a week, hasn't he?"

"Didn't I mention that?" The Lieutenant is chagrined.

"No, you didn't!" Fred is mad.

"Couldn't we have two weeks? We're being married Saturday."

"I don't like to say this. He has to leave tonight!"

This is a bombshell. Consternation is general. It just can't
be that way. Mary won't permit it to be. The Army will have
to come and take John—and she'd like to see them try.

"You go back and tell them he absolutely refuses to consider it and if they're sensible they'll get somebody else!"

"It doesn't work that way, Ma'm," protests O'Leary.

"It's only sixty days, dear," comforts Mrs. McKinley.

"It's a lifetime!" wails Mary. "I've waited three years already! Every girl in my graduating class has been married! Some have been married twice!"

"I'll write you every day," promises John. "And I'll call you regularly."

"I'm tired of letters! I want you! I'll be sixty years old and I'll still be waiting for you to marry me!"

Mary is not to be mollified. Her father could, if he would, do something about it.

"You're a Senator! Call up some of those fancy Generals who are always hinting for promotions! They can get John off!"

"It's hard for me to believe my own ears, Mary. If there was one thing I thought I had accomplished in my lifetime, it was instilling in you the spirit of good citizenship. Would you like to see me use my high office to get John off?"

"You're not asking your father to do that, dear?"

"Yes, I am! The Germans are back to their wives and sweethearts, the Italians are back, the Japs are back—the only woman in the whole world who's being kept apart from the man she loves is me! (*Crying but never missing a beat.*) Who won the damn war anyhow!"

With this Mary runs out of the room. Everyone is distressed. Mrs. McKinley also thinks the Senator could do something if he would. He has done enough for others, why not for his own family?

"I've been criticizing the War Department for two years," explains the Senator. "I can't ask a favor! This is just another instance of their poor management!"

The Senator decides he needs another drink. Perhaps Lieutenant O'Leary will join him. The Lieutenant will, and gladly. The Senator also feels a headache coming on. Perhaps, suggests his wife, if he were to go to a movie and relax he would feel better. Lieutenant O'Leary can help with the suggestion, too. He happens to know that "Blue Moon" with Dorothy Lamour, is playing at the Paramount. Feature at twelve-twenty-two, three-ten and five-forty-eight. In fact it takes considerable maneuvering on Fred's part to get O'Leary off the subject.

When the McKinleys go to send wires to the invited guests,

Lieutenant O'Leary is quick to turn on John and Fred and demand his fee.

"Hand it over!" he says, gleefully.

FRED—We owe him fifty dollars.

JOHN (*getting it out of his pocket*)—Fifty dollars for ten minutes? That's a little more than they're paying at the Paramount, isn't it?

O'LEARY—Stop squawking. If I'd a known it was the Senator, you'd've paid more.

JOHN (*throwing the money on the table*)—Here you are.

FRED—"What's playing at the Paramount? Dorothy Lamour! Twelve-twenty-two!" I thought the jig was up!

O'LEARY—I forgot myself. (*He reaches for the bottle, looking around.*) This is some dump.

JOHN—You haven't much time to get back to the Paramount and change uniforms.

O'LEARY—Relax. What are you two cooking up here?

FRED—Nothing. I explained it all to you.

O'LEARY—You don't think I believed that cock and bull story about mining business in Nevada. (*He drinks.*) What's wrong with that dame?

JOHN—Nothing's wrong with her.

O'LEARY—Then why are you running?

FRED—He's got some business in Nevada. Mining business.

O'LEARY—Malarkey! However, being we're buddies—and for old time's sake—I'm willing to take care of her while you're out of town.

JOHN (*alarmed*)—Don't you try and get in touch with her.

FRED—You're supposed to be going out to Nevada too! We paid you for that!

O'LEARY—Relax! I'm just getting a rise out of you. I wouldn't take that dame on a platter. Not my type. Cold cuts.

JOHN—I remember some of your type!

O'LEARY—Yeah. So do I. Those were the dames. You didn't even have to know the language. Just give 'em their choice—a bar of laundry soap or a bar of chocolate.

FRED—Now that I think of it, it's damn funny our company never had any laundry soap!

O'Leary has reached again for the bottle. It is John's opinion that if the Lieutenant doesn't have a care he will be stumbling around that balcony. O'Leary isn't worried. His men will cover for him. Besides, he's a balcony major, and that means a lot. "There's no nonsense at the Paramount about whether or not you've been to West Point!" he announces—pouring himself another drink.

O'Leary is inclined to irritability as the liquor soaks in. Also he would like them to know that they aren't fooling him a bit. In fact, he's inclined to queer the whole deal. The McKinleys are a fine American family and Mary is a fine American girl—

"Well, I'm marrying her! She's getting more than a bar of laundry soap!" snaps John.

"Don't get so high and mighty with me!" warns O'Leary. "I watched you operate overseas."

JOHN—You watched *me* operate?

O'LEARY—Both you dogfaces! You didn't have any dames, eh? What about Lily! (*This is a shock to* JOHN *and* FRED.)

FRED—Lily?

O'LEARY—Rang the bell, eh? Thought I didn't know about it. And I'll tell you what else I know.

FRED—What?

O'LEARY—You tried to cut me out with her! All the time I was pitching you were giving me the needle. I know about that.

FRED—You're wrong, Lieutenant!

O'LEARY—"You're wrong, Lieutenant!" I trailed you in Piccadilly for an hour one night and lost you in the blackout!

FRED—Lieutenant. Jack. I swear I never touched her.

JOHN—I believe you.

O'LEARY—Let's not get religious about it. The reason you couldn't lay a hand on her was because she wanted to be married and come to America. I got that line. But I got around that.

FRED (*rising*)—That's a damn lie!

O'LEARY—How do you know?

FRED—I was with her every night!

O'LEARY (*archly*)—Not after you went to France you weren't. You went over two weeks ahead of me. Remember?

FRED—Why, you dirty lying no-good skunk!

O'LEARY—Why are you so upset about Lily now?

FRED—Who's upset about Lily?

O'LEARY—What's going on here?

FRED (*scared*)—Nothing. (*The doorbell buzzes.*)

JOHN (*to* O'LEARY)—Be careful what you say, will you? And don't stay too long.

O'LEARY—Who the hell wants to hang around here? (*He looks at his watch.*) I'm late now. Mickey Mouse is on!

They suggest O'Leary's leaving through the kitchen, and he goes out singing. A moment later they have another visitor. He is George Beechwood, "fifty, friendly, competent and a little pedantic." Beechwood represents the Red Cross, and he has brought a surprise for Sergeant John Lawrence. Her name is Lily. The Red Cross knows her as "Mrs. John Lawrence." So do the slightly startled John and Fred. They did not know she had yet arrived in America.

Lily "is a girl who used to walk on her hands in a night club that had one shilling cover charge. She doesn't think she has a cockney accent any more, but she's wrong. She's blond, a little defiant, which passes for being proud, and when she relaxes, sympathetic."

It is a little puzzling to Beechwood that John should act shy before his wife, and even more puzzling to Lily that Fred is not overjoyed to see her. John kisses her on the cheek. Maybe Fred would, too, but Lily "throws her arms around his neck and kisses him ravenously," with a good hair rumpling thrown in.

John had expected to meet Lily at the Red Cross, but she had beaten her schedule two days by crossing on the *Queen Elizabeth.* "We take better care of our brides than our soldiers," boasts Beechwood.

Lily, he reports, had been quite excited when she was not met by John on her arrival at the Red Cross. In her resentment she had struck their Mr. Abernathy with a small suitcase. But that was a mistake. She had thought they were going to send her back to England.

Lily is happy now, and ever so glad she and Fred are going to live in New York, which she finds quite like it is in the cinema. In fact, on the advice of a sailor on the *Queen Elizabeth,* Lily plans never to go west of New Jersey. It isn't easy to explain to her that she will have to go to Reno for six weeks at least to get her divorce. And that she will have to go with John instead of with Fred.

Right now John thinks it would be helpful if Fred would take Lily to some quiet place, and have a couple of drinks, and explain things to her. Fred reluctantly agrees, but before they can get away Senator McKinley is back. He is pleased to meet this Miss Herbish, a friend of Fred's who is just over from England, but he finds it a little hard to understand why Lily should

nudge him familiarly when she tells him about going out West—
"where the deer and the antelope play."

"Tell me, what's it like west of New Jersey?" she asks.

"Republican!" answers the Senator, sharply.

Fred and Lily have gone now, and the Senator turns to John
for a fuller explanation. He and Fred had known Lily's brother
in London, explains John, wiping the perspiration from his face.
Lily was in the neighborhood. . . .

Mary and her mother have come from the lobby, triumphantly
bringing with them no less a person than Brigadier General Harwood Biddle, "fifty, crispy and regular army."

They had spied General Biddle just getting into an elevator.
Mary had yelled lustily to him, and now they had brought him
to meet John, whose case he had agreed to investigate. To the
General, from what he's heard, it seems like a case of undue
hardship—

"Now, look here, General," Senator McKinley is quick to protest, "I don't want anything done that smacks of favoritism."

"Why, Senator, I wouldn't show this boy any more favoritism
than I would expect you to show me."

"The Senator understands perfectly," Mrs. McKinley assures
him.

The phone is ringing. That would probably be in answer to a
call the General has put in to the Pentagon Building. It is.

"General Biddle speaking. I'll hold on." The General is
answering long distance. "May I see a copy of your orders?"
he asks, turning to John.

JOHN—I haven't any. They were oral orders, sir.

PHYLLIS—A very nice young man, a Lieutenant, came here to
tell John where to go.

MARY (*standing beside* JOHN)—Even he thought it was unfair. He felt terribly about it.

BIDDLE—Where did you say you were going?

JOHN (*hardly able to say it*)—A storage depot in Nevada, sir.

BIDDLE (*into phone*)—Colonel McCoy? General Biddle.
Colonel, I'm calling you from Senator McKinley's apartment.
(*Significantly.*) Senator McKinley! It seems the Senator's
prospective son-in-law has just returned from overseas, eligible
for discharge, in fact, on terminal leave, yet he's just been ordered to duty for another sixty days. Now—I don't want any
special consideration given him because of the Senator, you
understand that. (*He nods to the Senator.*) However—it's quite

probable that a mistake has been made and his name is no longer on that roster. I want you to check that roster very—carefully. (*To* JOHN.) Your name, Sergeant?

MARY (*after an effort from* JOHN)—John Lawrence.

BIDDLE—Serial number?

JOHN (*hesitating*)—1—2—

MARY—12783819.

BIDDLE (*into phone*)—Sergeant Lawrence. 127 (MARY *finishes the number for him.*) 83819. The orders were oral. Check the travel roster out of New York to some storage depot in Nevada. I'll hold on. (*He turns.*) We'll have that roster in a minute. You are now in the hands of the world's most efficient organization.

The curtain falls.

ACT III

There has been no lapse of time. The General is still at the phone, and still insisting that the Army is the world's most efficient organization.

Mary and her mother are still a little excited at their good luck running into General Biddle, and General Biddle is delighted to have been of service.

Now General Biddle again has contact with Colonel McCoy in Washington. He listens a moment and again turns to John: Is John sure it is a storage depot in Nevada? Yes, John's sure. It couldn't maybe have been some place that sounded like Nevada? No, sir. Mary also remembers it was in Nevada. And Mrs. McKinley—she also distinctly heard the Lieutenant say Nevada—

"The hell there's no storage depot in Nevada!" The General is glaring into the phone now and he's pretty mad. "Look for it!" He listens for another split second. "Look on Ryan's desk! It's locked? Where's Ryan? His day of exercise! Cancel all exercise on the fourth floor! There'll be a staff meeting in my office at nine o'clock tomorrow morning."

The General has found his handkerchief and is agitatedly mopping his hands and forehead—

JAMES (*quietly*)—Missing something, General?

BIDDLE (*sweating*)—We're reorganizing the department, Senator. There's a little confusion.

JAMES—And you can't locate a whole storage depot?

PHYLLIS—But it's in Nevada!

JAMES—You know it, Phyllis, and I know it, but does the world's most efficient organization know it! How many millions of dollars of taxpayers' money does an installation like that cost, General? In round figures.

MARY—Do you mean to say John still has to go because they can't find a little piece of paper in Washington?

JAMES—A little piece of paper! They can't find a whole depot!

BIDDLE—We'll find it, Senator.

MARY—But when? John's leaving tonight!

JAMES—John, when you get to the depot, wire the War Department you've found it.

PHYLLIS—But if the Army doesn't know where the depot is, how will John know where to go?

BIDDLE (*restraining himself*)—We know where it is, Mrs. Mc-Kinley. It's just a clerical error that the travel roster for that particular day is not on a certain desk. That's all.

MARY (*watching* JOHN)—General Biddle, that's not going to stand in the way of John's being excused?

JOHN—Mary—

MARY—Sending him would still be an undue hardship.

JOHN—Mary, dear!

MARY—It would be unjust for him to be punished for this clerical error, wouldn't it, General Biddle?

JOHN—What has to be, has to be.

BIDDLE—You're right! Absolutely right!

JOHN (*fearfully*)—General!

BIDDLE—I take it upon myself to remove you from the roster!

JOHN—General! SIR!

MARY—Thank you!

BIDDLE (*starting to the telephone*)—There's no reason for you to suffer for the mistakes of idiots even in uniform!

But John isn't prepared to accept this sacrifice on the General's part. It's too much like favoritism. He's going to Nevada, and nobody can stop him! He owes that much to his buddies! It's the only decent thing he can do!

"I didn't enlist for one year, or two years, or three years! I enlisted for as long as my country needs me! They need me in Nevada!"

The General is agreeably impressed. "It's only a storage depot, Sergeant. You'll be packing crates, that's all."

"Oh, no! It must be more than that! Besides, it's the principle of the thing!" insists John. He has turned to Mary: "I have to go to Nevada, Mary. You don't know what it means to me!"

But Mary does know—or thinks she knows. It means that John doesn't want to marry her. His duty is to go to Nevada? Who does he think he is, Nathan Hale? Well, she doesn't want to marry anyone as noble and patriotic as that. Mary has known, she says, from the first ten minutes after John got home that he has a feeling of being trapped. Now he wants to get out of marrying her and doesn't know how to go about it! Mary knows! John's afraid of her father and he's embarrassed for her. Well, he needn't be!

With this Mary runs out of the room in tears. Nor will she pay any attention to their pleading through the door. Not even to John's agonized: "I tell you I'm not embarrassed!" He is knocking on the door. "I love you! Mary! I love you!" He tries to open the door. It's locked.

The situation is too much for the Senator. His predicted headache has developed full force. He will have to go some place and sit down. Maybe the General will go to a movie with him. The General thinks that would be fine.

"You coming, Phyllis?" the Senator calls back, as he and General Biddle are going into the hall.

"I guess it would be the best thing," admits Mrs. McKinley, following them out.

Three hours later Mrs. McKinley is back from the movies and is trying to locate Mary. She's not in her room. She's not, according to Betty, the phone girl, in the beauty parlor. She's not—

About which time Mary walks in. She has been downstairs, in the bar. Drinking? Well, that's what the rest of them were doing.

Mary is disturbed, but calm. She has not heard from John. She waited in her room for two hours, but he did not come back—

"It's a little humiliating to face," admits Mary, "but I'm afraid the young man isn't as much in love with the charming Miss McKinley as the charming Miss McKinley has been imagining. And I'd better damn well realize it."

"Don't make a hasty decision," advises her mother. "You've been in love with John for a long time."

"Not this John."

"What do you mean, not this John?"

"This is not the one I sent overseas. *He* would have dragged me to Nevada. By my hair if necessary."

As to whether or not she is going to marry John, Mary doesn't think she is. Neither does she think she will have to tell him. He will probably tell her.

A moment later John walks in. He is again in uniform. He has been to see about his railroad ticket. His train leaves at nine-thirty, but he should be at the station fifteen minutes earlier.

Mary suggests that he might have dinner there. Then she could drive him to the station. But John doesn't want her to do that. There'll be others at the station, and kissing, and all that. It could be kind of embarrassing.

In that case, if John doesn't mind, Mary will go and lie down. She feels fine, but— And she is gone.

John turns to Mrs. McKinley. "If she's all right, why is she lying down?" he would like to know.

"I don't know. I just came back from the Paramount."

"You—went to the Paramount?"

"Yes. The Senator wanted to see himself in a newsreel."

"When you go to a movie, Mrs. McKinley, where do you sit? Upstairs or down?"

"We always sit upstairs. The Senator likes to smoke."

"You sat upstairs!"

"Yes, why?"

"Nothing. I just think it's interesting where different people sit."

"I wish we'd been in the orchestra. There was a drunkard in the balcony."

"A drunkard?"

"He kept singing at the top of his lungs that he had a jolly, jolly sixpence. I can't understand why the ushers didn't stop him."

"I can't either. Did the Senator do anything about it?"

"Oh, he'd left by then. He and General Biddle excused themselves half way through the picture. I don't know why. I like Dorothy Lamour."

She goes to the door of Mary's room and hesitates. Then she asks John to excuse her and goes out. She is crying a little.

John also is listening at the door of Mary's room when the hall door slams and Fred Taylor, his hair tousled, his manner agitated, comes bursting in. Fred is looking for Lily. He thought she might be there. He had been driving her around in a taxi showing her the city. He told her about the baby. She acted terribly. Oh, the things she said! But after a time she calmed down. Even suggested that they drive to the hospital so he could see his wife—

"I got a baby boy. Seven pounds, six ounces!" boastfully announces Fred.

"Lily! What about Lily?"

"I left Lily in the cab. I told her to wait. I told the driver to wait. I was sure they'd be there when I came out, there was eight dollars on the clock."

JOHN—She tricked you! She didn't want to go to Reno! She's hiding some place!

FRED—Hiding?

JOHN—What am I going to do about the divorce? If you can't find your wife, you have to wait seven years!

FRED—We'll find her sometime before that.

JOHN—You saved my life, and now you've ruined it. We're even.

FRED—Don't say that, Jack.

JOHN—I don't owe you a thing, not a thing.

FRED—I'm naming my kid after you. I'm going to call him John Harold Taylor.

JOHN—He hasn't got a chance.

FRED—Remember what we've been through together. When you were wounded I carried you in my arms like a baby. One of us was crying and it wasn't you!

JOHN—You should have let me stay there!

FRED—I carried you two hundred yards!

JOHN—It wasn't one hundred! Nearer seventy-five!

FRED—It was at least two hundred!

JOHN—Carrying me behind the lines was a nice way to get out of the shooting, don't forget that!

FRED—That's a hell of a thing to say! You're just excited, Jack.

JOHN (after a moment)—I'm sorry, Fred. (FRED dismisses it.) Congratulations. (A pause.) What did Lily say when you left her in the taxi? Did she give you any hint where she'd go?

FRED—Hint? I don't think so.

JOHN—What was the last thing she said?

FRED (thinking)—Good-by.

Suddenly Fred does remember: He had gone in the Seventy-sixth Street side of the hospital, and come out the Seventy-seventh Street side! Lily and the taxi are probably still waiting. They'd better telephone the hospital and ask.

At the door Fred and John practically bump into Senator Mc-

Kinley and General Biddle, but they have no time for explanations.

General Biddle is a little disheveled. His glasses have been tied together with a string—

"I was attacked by a drunken usher in the men's room of the Paramount Theatre!" the General explains to Mrs. McKinley. "He broke my glasses! And look at this hat!"

"Why did he do that?"

"I don't know why! He asked me whether I'd been to West Point and I said I had! He seemed pleasant enough! I thought he was going to ask me about the football team! That's what they usually ask. And then he jumped on me!"

"For heaven's sake! I hope you struck him back!"

"Unfortunately, there's an Article of War entitled 'Conduct Unbecoming an Officer.' I'm not supposed to strike anybody back!"

"Not even in self-defense?"

"An officer's supposed to be able to reason with anybody!" The General is pretty mad. He slams his torn hat down on the sofa. "That's the damnedest rule I ever heard of!" he growls.

Mary has come from the bedroom. She is far from happy. Even when she hears of a grand surprise her father and the General have arranged for her—a surprise which will see her and John happily married by the Mayor within the next hour—she is barely able to speak her thanks for their trouble.

It seems the General had thought of the possibility of his giving John his permission to get married immediately while they were in the movie. He had left the movie and gone immediately to his office, waded through yards of red tape, signed a raft of necessary papers and now everything is set. The Senator can't understand why Mary isn't excitedly throwing her arms around the General's neck—

"I appreciate what you've done, General Biddle, but—marrying and separating immediately isn't exactly love's young dream," says Mary.

"You're not separating," beams the Senator. "You're taking the car, and you'll have your honeymoon on the way to Nevada."

"John's entitled to five days' travel time," adds the General cheerily.

"You can motor nice and leisurely, and stop at night in good hotels. When you get to John's camp, you'll find a place to live, and while John'll only be able to see you once a week, I think you can endure that for two months. I'm not sure that's not an ideal

way to start married life. Teach you restraint." He's laughing
with the General. "What do you think of your old father now?"

"I don't care to get married today, Father," says Mary, simply.
And that's all she will say. She's sorry, but this is something her
father wouldn't understand.

Nor does he understand, even after Mrs. McKinley tries pa-
tiently to explain that Mary has decided not to marry John at
all. She's convinced that John doesn't love her.

Both Mary and her mother are in tears. The Senator considers
the situation and decides Mary needs comforting most. He sits
down beside her on the love seat, puts his arm around her, brings
her head to his shoulder, gives her his handkerchief and bids her,
tenderly, to go ahead and cry. Then she can tell him all about it.

Mary hasn't a very strong case against John, but she has sensed
a change in him. If John really loved her, he would have insisted
that she go to Nevada with him. Even though they're not married, she would have gone anyway, and married him out there.

Well, decides the Senator, there is one easy way to find out if
she is right. Let them see if John backs out when he is told he
can marry Mary immediately.

"I'm not going to find out that way," announces Mary, firmly.
"It'd be too humiliating. . . . Let him go to Nevada. I'll soon
get a letter that he's changed his mind."

Fred and John are back. They have made their phone call,
but the party wasn't there. They're both pretty depressed.

It's four hours until train time, John figures. Perhaps Mary
would like to go some places for a while. They might take a walk
in the park. Mary doesn't think she would be interested in that.

The Senator has been thinking. After all, sixty days isn't a life
time. And with plenty of time to prepare for it, there's no reason
why Mary and John couldn't have a big wedding when he gets
back. John wouldn't mind a big wedding, if it suits Mary.

Suddenly Mary makes up her mind. She will try her father's
test. What's the surprise the Senator had been talking about before John came? The surprise he wouldn't tell her about until
John came?

The Senator is caught a little off balance, but he manages to get
back. The surprise is that the General has fixed everything so the
marriage can take place today, and the happy pair can be on their
way to Nevada within an hour. It won't take Mary any time to
pack, and she's eager to begin.

Of course, if there's anything about that arrangement that John
doesn't approve, the Senator adds, let him feel free to mention it.

After all, it's his wedding—

"I was only looking at it from Mary's angle," stammers John. "Living out there in some room, and my coming in only once a week—"

"Mary doesn't seem to be objecting," observes the Senator.

"I'd love you to do it, Mary—but— . . . If you want a big wedding—your mother does— . . . Maybe the best thing would be to wait until I come back."

Her father has gone to Mary. He knows the jig is up. "I'm sorry, Mary. I was mistaken," he says, sympathetically.

"That's all right, Dad. I guess I was mistaken, too." She turns to John. "Well, John—or is it Sergeant Lawrence? I guess the quicker the good-bys the less embarrassment. So, if you don't mind, good day. It was nice knowing you, I think. It was nice knowing you too, Fred."

John refuses to be dismissed. Even the Senator's threat to throw him out doesn't move him. No matter how things look, protests John, he does love Mary—

"Would you do me this one courtesy? Please leave!" pleads Mary, holding her father back.

A door slam is followed by the appearance of Lily in the doorway. She spies Fred and quickly goes to him—

"Fred! Where did you go to?" she cries. "I've been riding around in a taxi for hours. The cabbie wants me to pay him fourteen dollars! He's downstairs in the lobby waiting."

FRED—I'll go right down!

LILY (*pulling away from him and going to* JAMES)—How do you do, Senator. (JAMES *smiles at her and then looks quickly away.*)

FRED—This is a friend of mine from Europe, that we used to—

JOHN (*turning in wildly*)—No! No! She's not a friend of his. Let me tell you who she is! She's my wife! Mrs. Lawrence! That's who she is!

JAMES—Your wife!

JOHN—Yes, my wife! I married her for Fred! To get her to America! He saved my life and I was going to do *him* a favor! Was that so terrible? I couldn't help it if he had a baby!

FRED—I couldn't help it, either.

JOHN—I only started with one little lie, but with your help, Senator, this damn thing's grown, and grown, with Mayors and Generals, and Pentagon Buildings—and I don't know where it will stop! (*Pleading.*) It's even gotten to where Mary doesn't believe

I love her. I do love you, Mary. I've never stopped loving you for one single minute. Mary, I know this is asking a great deal, but will you come to Reno with this girl and me? Just the three of us? While we get our divorce? Would you please, Mary? (MARY *looks at him.*)

LILY (*going toward* MARY)—I hope you believe he's telling the truth. He only married me to bring me to Fred.

MARY (*never taking her eyes from* JOHN)—I believe you.

LILY—If there's been any hankie-pankie between your John and me, may I drop dead on this very spot! (JAMES *looks at her sternly.*)

JOHN—What did you say, Mary?

MARY (*crossing to him*)—I'll go to Reno with you, John, with both of you.

JOHN—MARY!

MARY—I'll go any place with you. To the ends of the world. (*She falls into his waiting arms. All watch this tableau for a moment.*)

JAMES—Why didn't you explain this to me yesterday?

JOHN—I couldn't!

MARY (*in tears*)—He didn't have his pants on, Father!

LILY (*crying*)—I'm not crying because I'm unhappy! I like to see people in love! Maybe it's because I haven't had much luck in love myself. (*She gestures to* FRED.) Fred here, and then there was my first husband. He died. He was an American too. (JAMES, PHYLLIS *and* FRED *have gathered around her chair.*)

FRED—I didn't know you were married before.

LILY—You knew him. Lieutenant Victor O'Leary.

JOHN—O'Leary? No!

FRED—No!

LILY—As soon as he got a job, he was going to send for me. And then I got a lovely letter from his mother telling me how he passed away. (FRED *nods knowingly.*)—Double pneumonia. And his dying words were, "Send my love to Lily, and tell her I'll see her up there."

FRED—In the balcony! (*He looks down at* LILY.) Lily? Would it cheer you up to see a movie? For instance, "Blue Moon" with Dorothy Lamour?

LILY (*enthusiastically*)—She's one of my favorites!

FRED—Come on, Lily!

BIDDLE—I'd like to see the rest of that picture!

FRED—Come along with us, General! (BIDDLE *picks up his hat and starts to the door.*)

BIDDLE—Good-by, Senator. (*Tips his hat.*)   Mrs. McKinley.

JAMES—Good-by.

PHYLLIS—Good-by.

JOHN (*stopping them*)—Fred!   Be sure you get them good seats, in the right place!

FRED (*at the door*)—Oh, I'm going to introduce them to a friend of mine, the balcony major!   (*He starts out.*)   There's going to be a hell of a show at the Paramount today!

PHYLLIS (*looking after them as they leave . . . picking up engagement book on end table*)—Give me your pencil, James. The Whittakers are three, the Simon's—the Lewisohns and their two daughters, and the Hallidays.   Isn't that right, James?

She looks at James and sees him looking at John and Mary. She smiles at them fondly, looks back at James, who has settled back in the love-seat, then turns her back to the children as—

THE CURTAIN FALLS

THE FATAL WEAKNESS

A Comedy in Three Acts

By George Kelly

(Digest by John Chapman)

WHEN, after more than a year of labor, George Kelly turned over the script of "The Fatal Weakness" to the Theatre Guild, he had nobody in mind for the role of Mrs. Paul Espenshade. He never has an actor in mind, he says, when he writes a play.

But, immediately after she read the script, the Guild's Theresa Helburn had an actress in mind—Ina Claire, who had been living in retirement in San Francisco for five years. The play was air-mailed to her and she immediately accepted the role. The return of so highly skilled a comedienne was one of the events of the season.

The return of so highly skilled a workman as George Kelly was also an event of importance—for, whether his plays succeed or fail, they command attention and respect. "The Fatal Weakness" was a moderate hit in New York, and it finished the season in Chicago after a very successful tour. Before knocking off for the Summer, Miss Claire had promised the Guild to continue touring in 1947-48, and a route to the Pacific Coast was laid out.

Kelly, one of the most meticulous of playwrights, always stages his own works. His completed scripts are, indeed, far more detailed as to stage directions than any other current American dramatist's. In his scripts he puts complete directions for every movement every actor makes, including such minutiae as "she raises her handkerchief to her left eye."

Miss Claire, in addition to being a star of long standing, is an individualist accustomed to making a part her own creation during the weeks of rehearsal and the tryout period. Often, at the beginning of a tryout, she is not letter-perfect in her lines, and bluffs her way through until such time as she gets the feel of the role and the play as a whole.

When the Guild announced Ina Claire for a George Kelly play, intimates of one and the other predicted that there would be a notable clash of personalities—for Kelly would, as always, insist upon being the supreme commander of how his comedy was to be presented. The expected clash failed to come off. Director and star worked smoothly together, confounding the wiseacres.

Nor was "The Fatal Weakness" the only Kelly play to be produced during the season. His prize-winning "Craig's Wife," eighteen years old but still a vigorous drama of a possessive woman, was given a well-praised revival with Judith Evelyn in the title role.

"The Fatal Weakness" opens on a Saturday afternoon early in June.

It is about one o'clock when Mrs. Espenshade nervously enters her apartment living room and picks up the telephone. The living room is smartly appointed and so is she. She is a handsome woman in her middle forties—and obviously a distracted one, for, having dialed her call, she looks out the window, sees something down on the sidewalk which interests her, lays down the phone without making a call and goes over to the hallway to call Anna, the maid.

The telephone begins to buzz and she looks at it curiously, not realizing she has left the receiver off. When Anna appears she instructs, "I just see Mrs. Wentz getting out of a taxicab downstairs. Will you be ready to let her in, please? She'll be up in a minute and I'm waiting for her."

The buzzing of the phone again catches her attention and this time she remembers and goes to pick it up. "Hello— Yes, I see that it is, I'm sorry. I was just going to call my daughter and I saw a friend getting out of a taxicab downstairs here, and I was afraid the maid might not hear the buzzer, and I was particularly anxious to—" As she hangs up and turns to greet Mrs. Wentz she dashes a tear from her eye. Mrs. Espenshade is a great one for dabbing with a handkerchief.

The dutiful Anna has admitted Mrs. Wentz, a sharp-looking woman of middle age. "I expected at least to find you on your deathbed the way you were carrying on on that telephone," announces the visitor.

"I know," replies Mrs. Espenshade. "I must have sounded rather frightening. But I *was* upset."

"What's the matter?"

The matter seems to be a letter, which Mrs. Espenshade removes from the bosom of her dress. "I don't *know*, Mabel, *what* it is, any more than you do. And I'm not even allowing myself to think. Because, of course, there may be nothing to it at all. It simply came in the ten o'clock mail this morning and I called you right away."

While Mrs. Wentz examines the missive and its envelope her friend rambles on: "*He* generally gets home here, you know, about this time on Saturday. And Penny nearly always wanders over right after lunch, while the girl is walking the child. So I *did* want to see you before either of them got here. I was just going to call Penny when I saw you getting out of the taxicab—to see if *she* knew anything about it. I don't suppose she does. And she probably wouldn't admit it even if she did; so I'm glad I didn't get her. She's always defended him, you know—at least where I'm concerned. Poor Papa! That's all you ever *get* out of her. You'd think somebody had been persecuting him all his life. Nothing at all about me. I wonder what she'll think of poor Papa now. But he never fooled my grandmother. Oh, no! She knew him even then; and it's over twenty-five years ago. I remember distinctly what she said the first time I ever introduced him to her. . . ."

Mrs. Espenshade's friend has been only half listening. The subject in hand is the letter.

MRS. WENTZ—Well, what about it?

MRS. ESPENSHADE—I don't *know*, Mabel—*what* about it: that's what I want *you* to tell *me!* Do you think it's genuine? Because, you know, it could quite easily be just some jealous person trying to upset my peace of mind. But you don't think it's that?

MRS. WENTZ—No.

MRS. ESPENSHADE—You mean you think it's perfectly honest?

MRS. WENTZ—Well, I think the fact that she doesn't say that she's telling you "as a friend" is suggestive.

MRS. ESPENSHADE—That's what *I* think.

MRS. WENTZ—I'm always a little suspicious of women that tell you "as a friend" that you're losing your husband.

MRS. ESPENSHADE—But beyond anything that she actually says here, I have a feeling somehow or other that the thing is sincere. I mean, that she's genuinely concerned: and just feels that *somebody* ought to tell me—before this *fool* makes a show of me—and of himself and everybody else.

MRS. WENTZ—Now, calm down, darling, before you make a show of *yourself*.

MRS. ESPENSHADE—No, but the *duplicity* of it, Mabel!

MRS. WENTZ—I know.

MRS. ESPENSHADE—And the cunning of him—that's what hurts

me. A woman doctor! So that he'd always have the excuse, you know, that he was simply a patient of hers, in case I ever heard anything.

MRS. WENTZ—That's the reason I tell you you've got to go slow in this thing, Ollie—or he'll make you look foolish. I mean, you *can't* just accuse him of going to see a woman doctor.

MRS. ESPENSHADE—But she's a woman osteopath, Mabel!

MRS. WENTZ—Even so.

MRS. ESPENSHADE—It says so there in the letter.

MRS. WENTZ—But it also says she's a *medical* doctor.

MRS. ESPENSHADE—But I'll bet her specialty is the osteopathy.

MRS. WENTZ—Well, whether it is or not, she's a doctor. And he can always say that there was something the matter with him, and that *she* was recommended.

MRS. ESPENSHADE—The blatancy of it!

MRS. WENTZ—So sit down there, now, and let's decide what you're going to do about it before he walks in on you.

MRS. ESPENSHADE—What those women doctors have to answer for!

MRS. WENTZ—It's nearly a quarter past one.

MRS. ESPENSHADE—If he should get here before you leave— just say you were over this way on an errand and dropped in.

MRS. WENTZ—All right. Now, listen—it says here that she's a *very* good doctor.

MRS. ESPENSHADE—The better they are the worse they are, my dear, I'm telling you.

MRS. WENTZ—Well, I mean, she must be pretty well known.

MRS. ESPENSHADE—I wouldn't trust one of them any more than I'd trust a trained nurse. And you know what I think of them.

MRS. WENTZ—And I have an idea that this woman lives up there somewhere in your old neighborhood.

MRS. ESPENSHADE—Which woman?

MRS. WENTZ—The woman that wrote this letter. I think that's how she happens to see all this. I think she must live somewhere where she can see this doctor's house or apartment from her windows, and sees *him* coming there.

MRS. ESPENSHADE—You think the doctor lives up that way, too?

MRS. WENTZ—Yes; I think they both live up that way.

MRS. ESPENSHADE—What makes you think so, Mabel? I mean, is there something there in that letter?

MRS. WENTZ—No, I don't think so.

Mrs. Espenshade—Then, what makes you think it?

Mrs. Wentz—I couldn't tell you, darling, *what* makes me think it: it's just something I think.

The two women agree that the letter sounds honest enough, and not gossipy. Obviously, the writer knows the Espenshade family. And evidently the affair has been going on for months; without Mrs. Espenshade ever dreaming of it or Mrs. Wentz ever hearing of it.

Mrs. Wentz is curious about Mr. Espenshade's recent behavior. Has he, for instance, done a lot of looking at himself in the looking glass lately?

"No, I can't say that he has. . . . Of course, he's everlastingly talking about his hair—wondering if it isn't going back further here at the sides. And naturally it's going back further; he'll be 52 the twenty-seventh of next April."

Mrs. Wentz, the detective, still is on the prowl for clues. How about whistling? Here, indeed, is a clue, for Mr. Espenshade has been driving his wife nearly out of her mind with his whistling. And another thing: "But the thing I've noticed about him lately more than anything else is a funny little *skip* he gives occasionally." The skipping, apparently, is for no reason at all; it's just a little leap, as though he'd stepped on a spring or something.

Other clues pile up. Mr. Espenshade isn't home much evenings, and on Saturday afternoons he goes to Brookside for golf, or if the weather is bad to the Riverview to play handball to keep his waist down. "He's always been a great bender and kicker ever since I've known him," his wife explains.

Mrs. Wentz's mind is made up: the sooner her friend finds out about her husband, the better, even if they have had twenty-eight happy years of married life. "I think," declares Mrs. Wentz, "twenty-eight years is too long for any two people to put up with each other. And how they do it is one of the mysteries of my life. And how they go back into it once they're out of it is a bigger mystery."

"Well," pleads Mrs. Espenshade, "how am I ever going to *know* it unless I *do* something?"

Mrs. Wentz has the answer—for the case is now in her hands. "I'll find out something for you—as soon as I can get hold of Minerva Nichols."

Mrs. Espenshade—Listen, Mabel—who is this that you say you're going to get hold of?

Mrs. Wentz—Minerva Nichols. She's a friend of mine that lives up there where *you* used to live.

Mrs. Espenshade—Do *I* know her?

Mrs. Wentz—No; but *she* knows everything that's going on in the world. And if she doesn't, she knows somebody that does.

Mrs. Espenshade—Well, you won't actually *tell* her about this, will you?

Mrs. Wentz—No, of course not.

Mrs. Espenshade—I mean, there's no point in saying anything till we're sure.

Mrs. Wentz—You don't have to tell her anything: you just give her a hint. She has her own car, and she has absolutely *nothing* else to do.

Mrs. Espenshade—And do you think she'll do it for you?

Mrs. Wentz—Of *course* she'll do it for me; she does it for everybody.

Mrs. Espenshade—Well, how will you tell her, Mabel?—I mean, so that she won't know what you're talking about?

Mrs. Wentz—I'm trying to think.

Mrs. Espenshade—Because, of course, I'll simply *die* if anybody finds out about it.

Mrs. Wentz—Oh, don't be silly, Ollie, she probably knows all about it already.

Mrs. Espenshade—She probably does: the wife is always the last one in the world to hear about this kind of thing.

Mrs. Wentz, a woman of action, has formulated a plan and she will call Minerva Nichols right now and get it going. It is an ingenious scheme to start trailing Espenshade immediately. He is due home any minute. Mrs. Wentz will ask him to drop her off at her home on the way to the golf club—and Mrs. Nichols will be parked out in front of Mrs. Wentz's place. When she sees Mrs. Wentz get out of a car she can identify the quarry and set off in pursuit. Espenshade might go to the club, or he might not—but anyhow Mrs. Nichols can phone Mrs. Wentz and tell her where he did go, and Mrs. Wentz can then call Mrs. Espenshade. A devious but workable plan.

"What time will you call me, Mabel?" Mrs. Espenshade wants to know. "I have to go to a wedding at St. Stephen's this afternoon. And I don't think I'll get back here much before six."

"Whose wedding *is* it over there this afternoon?"

"I don't think you know them, Mabel; but they're *very* old

friends of mine. And I think I *should* put in an appearance over there."

Mrs. Wentz agrees to call with whatever information has been obtained some time after six; and now she calls Mrs. Nichols. She knows the number. "It's the same as yours only the exchange is Belmont 3 instead of Arlington 4. And the last two numbers are the same as mine only turned around. I mean, the 6 is a 2, and the 2 is a 6. That's how I always remember it."

Minnie Nichols is home. "I think," Mrs. Wentz informs her, "a friend of mine is giving his wife a bit of a runaround and it's making me mad." The scheme of pursuit is outlined, and Minnie, the bloodhound, is all for it.

There is the toot of a motor horn below—Espenshade's car.

MRS. ESPENSHADE—Do I look as though I've been crying?

MRS. WENTZ—No.

MRS. ESPENSHADE—Because I wouldn't please him to let him see that I'd shed a tear over him.

MRS. WENTZ—You can always say you've been bathing your eyes.

MRS. ESPENSHADE—And I'm *not* shedding any tears over *him*, I can promise you.

MRS. WENTZ—Well, what *are* you shedding them over, Ollie?

MRS. ESPENSHADE—Well, I think a woman's *pride* ought to be of *some* consideration after twenty-eight years. And so do you, Mabel Wentz, if you'd admit it.

MRS. WENTZ—I *do* admit it.

MRS. ESPENSHADE—Paul Espenshade wasn't the only man that ever looked at *me*.

MRS. WENTZ—I think her pride should be so hurt that she would disdain to include him in any of her future arrangements. That's what *I* did in a similar circumstance: and that's why I can tell of many lands. And that's what you'll do if you've got any sense.

MRS. ESPENSHADE—I don't think it's quite the same with you as it is with me.

MRS. WENTZ—I'm more self-sufficient I suppose.

MRS. ESPENSHADE—Well, you know you *are* more capable than I am, Mabel, you know that as well as I do.

MRS. WENTZ—I don't think we know much about *what* we are till something like this happens to us. But you've been saying for years that you wish you could pick up and go the way *I* do whenever you took the notion. But you couldn't leave Paul. Well, according to that letter he's been leaving *you* for some time. And this is your chance to try it on *him*, if you'll only take it.

MRS. ESPENSHADE—I feel just like a ship without a sail.

Mr. Espenshade's appearance is a jaunty one. He is wearing a very becoming light suit, with a white carnation in the lapel. "I knew you were here," he tells Mrs. Wentz, "by the fluttering of my heart as I approached the premises."

"I think," he observes, "you two are up to *something*, sitting in here this afternoon."

The women control their reactions. *"I* was waiting for *you,"* explains Mrs. Wentz. "Your wife says that you generally go out to Brookside on Saturday afternoon if the weather is good, and I thought you might drop me at my house."

Espenshade gallantly falls into the trap. "I can think of nothing more exciting." He'll just go get a glass of milk and a sandwich in the dining room and they'll be off.

Mrs. Wentz, the sleuth, tosses a feeler at her victim. "That's a very good-looking suit," she remarks. He takes the bait, and asks, "You don't think it is too light? You don't think it makes me look heavier?"

Mrs. Wentz reassures him, even remarking that it makes his hair look darker. He preens himself in the glass over the mantel and says that his hair is going back further at the sides by the minute.

Anna announces that his sandwich and milk are ready and he starts for the doorway. Mrs. Espenshade looks after him, and just as she does he executes that funny little skip; and then, breaking into a rather jaunty little whistle, he careens into the hallway.

"Do you see what I mean, Mabel?" asks Mrs. Espenshade.

"The little skip? Yes, I saw it."

"That's been going on for about six months now. And I've been wondering whether there might be something the matter with him."

"I don't think so, dear."

"But, I mean, I've often heard that men that do a lot of exercising the way he does are apt to have what they call concussions that they don't even know about."

Mrs. Wentz doesn't believe it's a concussion. "I think it's his age. A lot of men start skipping that way when they begin to get into the fifties. . . . And the whistling usually goes with the skip. I think they're kind of surprised at themselves that they can still do it."

The hall buzzer sounds. That would be—and is—Penny, the

Espenshades' daughter. Penny's mother goes to her bedroom to fix up a bit, so Mrs. Wentz holds the fort.

MRS. WENTZ—How is your child, Penny?

PENNY—Well, I haven't seen very much *of* him lately, Mrs. Wentz, to tell you the truth. I mean, he's at school every day until noon; and then in the afternoon he's some place else.

MRS. WENTZ—Does he go to school already?

PENNY—Oh, my dear, he's been going since last September.

MRS. WENTZ—Not really?

PENNY—He started the *very* first day of the term.

MRS. WENTZ—He's very young, isn't he, to be going to school?

PENNY—He'll be three in August.

MRS. WENTZ—I *thought* he couldn't be much more than that.

PENNY—I suppose it *was* a bit young to start him. Mother was simply horrified. But, as I told her, I'd been looking at the child since he was born, and I *knew* he was a type that should begin his adjustment as early as possible.

MRS. WENTZ—Where does he *go* to school, Penny?

PENNY—To Doctor Bajarian, in the Zeigler Building, right there beyond the Medical Arts.

MRS. WENTZ—Oh, yes.

PENNY—He's that wonderful Russian child specialist from Russia that I suppose you've been hearing about.

MRS. WENTZ—No, I haven't.

PENNY—Well, he's a perfectly *fascinating* person. I'd heard two of his lectures before I decided to send Punchy over there: and they were absolutely breath-taking. I mean, they were so *sane*.

MRS. WENTZ—How does Punchy *like* going to school? I suppose he hates it, doesn't he?

PENNY—No, I don't think so. At least, I've never heard him *say* that he did. And of course I never ask him; because Doctor Bajarian is rather positive on that score.

MRS. WENTZ—You mean, about asking him how he likes school?

PENNY—Well, about asking him questions generally. He says it's a form of talking *down* to children, that they resent, as a rule—especially little boys. And we *are* expected to co-operate to a certain extent in the school's attitude. I really think that's the reason Punchy and Mother have never been able to hit it off very well; she just *will* not co-operate.

MRS. WENTZ—Doesn't Punchy like your mother?

Penny—Oh, my dear, he loathes her—intensely. You've never seen anything like it. A perfect Oedipus complex in reverse. I've simply given up trying to drag him over here: he just will not walk.

Mrs. Wentz—Doesn't he come over here at all?

Penny—I don't think he's been here since Christmas. Just sits right down on the pavement if he even *suspects* that I'm heading in this direction. And of course it's entirely Mother's fault, for she *will* talk down to him. And he just can't bear it.

Mrs. Wentz—What does she say to him that he dislikes so?

Penny—Well, she asks him if he's been out on his bicycle lately; and how the little dog is, and how he's getting along at school. And, naturally, the child just stands and looks at her as though she'd gone *completely* ga-ga.

When Mrs. Espenshade returns from her bedroom, mother and daughter greet each other with a "Hello."

"I was telling Penny," offers Mrs. Wentz, "that you thought you had something in your eye."

"I thought," says Penny, "that was *my* specialty. Vernon always says that. . . ."

Which brings up another subject for conversation, and Mrs. Wentz dutifully inquires how Vernon, Penny's husband, is.

"He's very well. . . . At least he appeared to be—the last time I heard from him."

"Did you have another fight with Vernon?" asks Penny's mother.

Certainly not, the young matron insists. She never has fights. "We simply had a discussion, that's all."

Vernon, Penny goes on to explain, is a bit naïve about life and marriage, and he sulks for a day or two if she doesn't happen to agree with his particular ideas on faithfulness and moral obligation.

Any revelation of interesting details is interrupted by the sound of Mr. Espenshade whistling in the dining room and his appearance in a few moments. The greeting between father and daughter is of the warmest sort. Penny admires his new suit, tells him he is getting so handsome she can't bear it.

"I think you'd better watch him, Mother. I think he has plans." Penny's joke brings a dry reply from her mother: "He's being watched." Espenshade misses the significance—or is, perhaps, innocent enough.

Mrs. Wentz wishes that she had met so handsome a man down

town this morning—it might have helped her socially. She had gone down town to an old doctor friend to get some tablets for a funny shoulder business she gets once in a while, she explains.

"Why don't you go to a woman osteopath?" suggests Penny.

"I didn't know there was such a thing."

"Oh, yes, I think there are. There are women osteopaths, aren't there, Popsy?"

Popsy, busy hunting some golf tees in a console drawer, answers absently, "I don't know. I never heard of one. Why, has somebody dislocated something?"

He pooh-poohs Mrs. Wentz's shoulder trouble. "If you'll just lean heavily upon me," he offers, "you'll be astounded at what it'll do for you."

When they leave, Mrs. Espenshade eases back into the subject of Penny's husband. Is he figuring on spending the Summer in Maine, as usual?

"He can go up there if he likes. But that doesn't mean that I've got to go. As a matter of fact, that's my principal reason for not wanting to go up there. I think we ought to get away from each other for a while. He's getting terribly edgy."

Mrs. Espenshade wants to know more about the "discussion." Her questions bring the revelation that Vernon hasn't been home since Thursday night. He has left the house, just the way he did twice before—last Thanksgiving and again in February.

"And where is he?"

"I don't know, I didn't ask him."

"Well, after all, I don't think it's a thing you should be too casual about, Penny."

"Well, what do you expect me to do, Mother," flashes Penny, "go running around the city after him?"

The basis of disagreement, Mrs. Espenshade learns, is Vernon's sentimentality.

PENNY—I simply refuse to allow him to *bully* me—into agreeing with *his ideas* about things.

MRS. ESPENSHADE—About *what* things? That's what I'd like to *know*. What was the discussion *about* Thursday night? What were you talking about?

PENNY—About something that he'd *read* somewhere—or someone had *told* him about. Some married man that was having a great romance with somebody. And he was perfectly furious because the man had been married over twenty years. He said if people had stayed together that long he thought they should be

sufficiently adjusted to spend the *rest* of their time together. And
I didn't agree with him. I said I didn't think it was a question
of adjustment at all—that I thought it was a matter of growth.
And that there was no reason why people should stop *growing* just
because they were married. And then he started the old "silver
threads among the gold" business. That he saw no reason why
two people couldn't grow old together. And I said I thought that
was ridiculous: that no two people could *possibly* react in the same
way to a given experience. And then of course he had to person-
alize as usual, and ask me if I thought *I* had outgrown *him* would
I leave him. And I said of *course* I would; that there was nothing else I could *do*. And that was where he began to sulk.

Mrs. Espenshade—You'd be perfectly agreeable of course to
his leaving *you, too,* if he felt that he'd outgrown *you?*

Penny—Of course I'd be perfectly agreeable to it: I'd expect
him to. I certainly wouldn't want to feel that I was hanging on
to a man that didn't want me any more.

Mrs. Espenshade—Vernon may not be the type that outgrows
people.

Penny—Well, that's *his* misfortune, darling: if he wants to be
just a case of arrested development.

Mrs. Espenshade—Did he *know* this married man that was
having the romance?

Penny—*I* don't know whether he did or not. But that
wouldn't make any difference: he can become quite as moralistic
whether he knows the people or not. I think the thing that really
annoys him is that I refuse to take marriage seriously—I mean,
as a permanent relationship in my life. I think it's an interesting
experience; and I think it's an experience that the majority of
women should have. But, like any other experience, I think if it's
persisted in it can become a habit. And I think there are too
many really important things that a person can do in his life to
allow that.

There is a telephone call which Mrs. Espenshade answers. It
is Vernon. Penny quickly says, voicelessly, "I'm not here," so
her mother tells Vernon she doesn't know where his wife is. She,
however, will do, apparently, for Vernon invites himself over.
"Come right over," says Mrs. Espenshade. "I was just sitting
here—reading a letter."

"Well, I'd better go," announces Penny. "I don't want to be
running into him downstairs." "And I," says Mrs. Espenshade,

"must put on a dress."

Penny urges her mother not to try conciliating Vernon, but her
mother is worried. He has walked out twice already, and some
day he might walk out and never come back. "Surely you don't
want that to happen. Vernon is your husband, after all. And
you were certainly crazy enough about him when you married him
six years ago. . . . I'll never forget your wedding day while ever
I live. I don't think I ever saw a more radiantly happy bride."

Besides, Mother continues, think of the child. Children are
always more or less abandoned when their parents are separated.

Penny is unmoved. "Most children see too much of their parents anyway. . . . Doctor Bajarian was only saying on Thursday
that—"

For the first time, Mrs. Espenshade shows real anger. Almost
viciously she cries, "I don't give a damn *what* Doctor Bajarian
was saying on Thursday! For I think he must be as big a fool
as those that go and listen to him. . . . So you'd better go now."

After Penny's departure Mrs. Espenshade rings for Anna to
warn her that Mr. Hassett is coming in a few minutes and she
must not mention Miss Penny having been here.

"Don't forget about your appointment at three o'clock," Anna
reminds her.

"Did I say what it was, do you remember?"

"I think you said it was a wedding, Mrs. Espenshade, over at
St. Stephen's Church."

This reminder throws Mrs. Espenshade into a feminine flurry.
Here it is, a quarter past two, already. And she can't call Vernon
and postpone his visit because he was phoning from a pay station
somewhere. "You'll simply have to tell him," she instructs Anna,
"that I'd completely forgotten about an appointment, but that if
he'll call me any time after six I'll be delighted to make another
appointment.

"And say that I'm frightfully sorry . . . but that this was a
wedding of two very close friends of mine, and that I didn't see
how I could possibly stay away without offending them."

Mrs. Espenshade starts for her bedroom to dress. "Whose wedding *is* this that you're going to this afternoon, Mrs. Espenshade?"

"I don't know *who* they are, Anna, really; but their pictures
were in last Sunday's paper, and *she* is the most *beautiful* thing
you've ever seen in your life." Anna looks at her curiously as she
continues, "And the young man she's marrying is quite as good-
looking. So that's the reason I've been rather anxious about get-

ting over there this afternoon, for I *know* they're going to make the most adorable-looking couple. . . ."

The curtain falls.

ACT II

Mrs. Espenshade comes home, smartly outfitted but looking tearful. It is now about six-thirty, and she has been to the wedding. She looks ruefully at herself in the mantel mirror, dabbing at her eyes. Anna reports that there has been a phone call from Mrs. Wentz, and Mrs. Espenshade is to call as soon as she gets in; Penny also has called, leaving the same message. And Mr. Espenshade has telephoned that he'll have dinner at the club.

And now Vernon Hassett puts in a call. He'd like to see his mother-in-law right away.

MRS. ESPENSHADE—You don't think I look as though I'd been crying, do you, Anna?

ANNA—No, I don't think so.

MRS. ESPENSHADE—I always cry so at a wedding. And it makes my eyes look *so* dreadful.

ANNA—I always thought weddings were sad.

MRS. ESPENSHADE—Oh, they make a perfect wreck of *me*.

ANNA—Especially when you know the way the majority of them are going to turn out.

MRS. ESPENSHADE—Yes, I suppose that's true.

ANNA—I wonder sometimes why people bother.

MRS. ESPENSHADE—But there's always been something so terribly touching to me about two people standing up before all the world and promising to be faithful to each other while ever they live.

ANNA—Yes, it *is* sad.

MRS. ESPENSHADE—I mean, it's so beautifully trusting. And I seemed to sense that this afternoon for some reason or other, more than I ever have in all the countless weddings I've been to. I don't know when I've cried so.

ANNA—Maybe you shouldn't go to so many weddings, Mrs. Espenshade. I mean, when they upset you so.

MRS. ESPENSHADE—But the flowers were so perfectly exquisite: I don't know who ever arranged them. And such wonderful music. The girl that sang "Oh, Promise Me" had one of the most heavenly voices I've ever heard in my life. I must ask Miss Clyde who she was.

ANNA—Isn't it funny, that's a song I've never cared for.

Mrs. Espenshade—"Oh, Promise Me"?

Anna—Yes, Ma'am. Somehow or other I just don't like it.

Mrs. Espenshade—Oh, I think it's a very lovely song, Anna.

Anna—I know. But it always sounds to *me* as though they didn't trust each other. I guess that sounds terrible—but that's the way it always sounds.

Somebody is at the door. It couldn't be Mr. Hassett so soon—and it isn't; it's Mrs. Wentz, who is bursting with news but who holds herself down to polite conversation until the maid retires out of earshot. Mrs. Espenshade, who is bursting to receive news, asks, "Did you hear from this woman?"

"Yes, she called me."

"And what did she say, Mabel?"

"Well, he's not out at the country club."

Minnie Nichols, the volunteer sleuth, has indeed been on the trail. Mrs. Wentz relays Minnie's report to Mrs. Espenshade. As planned, Espenshade dropped Mrs. Wentz off home and Minnie, in her car, took up the scent. He went to the club, all right, but came out again in about fifteen minutes.

"Why," queries Mrs. Espenshade, "do you think he went out to the Country Club at all this afternoon, Mabel, when he didn't intend to stay there?"

"That's part of the trick, Ollie."

"He said he was playing golf out there."

"They *all* say that, darling. . . . Either that or they're going fishing. Minnie says they always say the same thing."

The knowing Minnie, Mrs. Wentz continues, followed them for nearly two hours.

"Followed whom, Mabel?"

"This woman, darling, that he's been going around with."

"Well, she wasn't with him then, was she? I mean when he left you?"

"No, certainly not; he picked her up afterwards at her offices. . . . She has a suite in the Meredith Memorial Building, on the third floor; and her name is Hilton—Dr. Claudia Hilton."

"How do you know?"

"I've just come from there, Ollie," reveals Mrs. Wentz, who is no mean sleuth herself.

When Espenshade stopped at the Meredith Memorial Building, with Minnie Nichols on his tail, he tooted his horn and this woman came out. "And Minnie says," continues Mrs. Wentz, "the minute he saw her he literally *leaped* out of the car and ran around to the other side to help her in. But she says when he jumped out of the car he kind of turned his ankle."

"I'm glad he did," observes Mrs. Espenshade, grasping any consolation, however slight.

"And she says he must have given it quite a twist, for they stood talking about it on the pavement for quite a while."

Mrs. Espenshade is burning to know what the woman looked like. Rather plump, reports Mrs. Wentz, but neat-looking. A navy blue one-piece dress and a white hat—and some kind of light coat on her arm as though they might be going out for the evening somewhere.

This information checks, all right, with Espenshade's phone call that he wouldn't be home for dinner.

Minnie followed the couple until nearly four o'clock. They went across the viaduct and out through Ravenswood toward Cloverton, and then Minnie noticed that her gas was getting low. When she stopped to get some, she lost the trail.

"She says she drove around there for a while," recounts Mrs. Wentz, "but they must have turned off on to a side road some place."

"And parked somewhere, you may be sure," rejoins Mrs. Espenshade. "And that's undoubtedly where they are right now, too."

"But it must have been a pretty lonely road when Minnie couldn't find it," Mrs. Wentz dryly observes.

It wasn't Minnie who found out the woman's name; it was Mrs. Wentz. The minute Minnie called in with her report, Mrs. Wentz hopped aboard a taxicab and went right out to the Meredith Memorial Building and took a look at the directory in the lobby. The directory listed Claudia Hilton, M.D., *and* Osteopath. "And she's the only woman doctor in the building so it couldn't be anybody else."

MRS. ESPENSHADE—Well, what do you think I ought to do, Mabel? Do you think I ought to *say* anything to him?

MRS. WENTZ—What can you *say* to him, Ollie!

MRS. ESPENSHADE—Well, I mean, don't you think it might *frighten* him a little, if he thought I suspected something?

MRS. WENTZ—No, dear, I don't.

MRS. ESPENSHADE—Not even if he thought people were talking about him?

MRS. WENTZ—No.

MRS. ESPENSHADE—Then *I* don't know what to do about it.

MRS. WENTZ—I think the best thing to do is wait till next Saturday afternoon and have Minnie Nichols follow him again.

MRS. ESPENSHADE—I can't *wait* till next Saturday afternoon, Mabel, I've got to *know* something!

MRS. WENTZ—What else can you *do*, darling!

MRS. ESPENSHADE—Can't she follow him some *night*, when he goes out?

MRS. WENTZ—You can't find out anything in the dark, Ollie!

MRS. ESPENSHADE—She can find out where he *goes*, at least.

MRS. WENTZ—And what good would *that* be, if she can't see what he does when he gets there. Besides, you have to have a witness; they won't take just one person's word for anything.

MRS. ESPENSHADE—What do you mean, Mabel, if I ever want to *do* anything about it?

MRS. WENTZ—Well—you'd hardly be satisfied to let it go along this way, would you? I mean, if it's what we think it is?

MRS. ESPENSHADE—You mean, divorce him?

MRS. WENTZ—That depends on what you find out. And how much it means to you.

MRS. ESPENSHADE—Well, it doesn't mean enough to me to be just another of his women, I can promise you that.

MRS. WENTZ—Then you'll have to force him to a decision of some kind.

The hall buzzer sounds—most likely Vernon. Mrs. Wentz declines to join her friend at dinner and makes her getaway through the dining room so she won't encounter Vernon.

At this moment Penny again phones her mother, but is cut off with the hasty information that her husband is at the threshold. Mrs. Espenshade is all apologies for having stood him up this afternoon, and he amiably accepts them. "I was only hanging around down at the club, anyway, till it was time to go over to my aunt's."

Vernon wants to talk about Penny and himself; they don't seem to be hitting it off well lately. "No, I wouldn't exactly say we've been quarreling. As a matter of fact, I'd be a little more optimistic about things if we were. It's just that we don't seem to *agree* about anything. . . . And from the way she talks, I don't think it's going to be any better in the future."

Mrs. Espenshade opines that Penny is just repeating what she hears at those lectures she goes to, but Vernon is not so sure, because she talked that way before she went to the lectures. "I thought she was just trying to sound advanced, but now I think

it's a sort of conviction she has, I mean, something that she believes in—or at least something that she's trying to make herself
think she believes in—and intends to mold her future by."

Mrs. Espenshade makes a small gesture of annoyance, and
Vernon, in a kind of troubled irresolution, continues, "And I've
been wondering lately whether it wouldn't be wiser for me just
to accept it that way—and do something of the same thing myself."

The unhappy Vernon confesses what his mother-in-law already
knows—that he's been down at the club since Thursday.

"But you don't intend to *stay* there, do you?"

He shrugs, significantly.

"Oh, you mustn't do that, Vernon!"

"I feel that I'm wasting my time, Mrs. Espenshade."

"That's simply out of the question."

"That's what *she* intends to do. . . . That's what she *says* all
the time."

"But you mustn't believe her, Vernon! Women don't seriously
want to see their marriages broken up, I assure you."

Vernon won't be convinced, in the case of Penny. "She says
marriage is an arrestment of the spirit. . . . And she absolutely
refuses to have any more children."

"And what," queries Mrs. Espenshade, "does she call that—an
arrestment of something else, I suppose?"

"No—she says she considers having more than one child is a
surrender to the new generation. . . . And if *she* doesn't say
something, the kid does; she's got him almost as nutty as herself."

Mrs. Espenshade earnestly pursues a losing battle to make
Vernon go back and try for an understanding of some kind. He
informs her of his firm intention: "They've got to come to *me*
this time. I like my home, and I like a family. And I'm perfectly willing to do whatever is necessary to keep it going. But
I don't like it well enough to let anybody push me around."

Mrs. Espenshade has heard the ultimatum—but she still doesn't
know, from Vernon, exactly what brought about the recent break,
or "discussion." She wants to know now, but Vernon hedges.

MRS. ESPENSHADE—Well, I simply wanted your *version* of it,
Vernon.

VERNON—Well, I remember starting to tell her about a case
here in town that I've been hearing a lot about for the past year,
of a man that's been married over twenty years, running around

with another woman. He's been married over twenty-*five* years, as a matter of fact. And *I* said I thought that was stupid. I said I thought if he were going to run around that way, he ought to come to some decision about it; and act accordingly. It's *bound* to become known sooner or later: and in the meantime it makes it a little awkward for people. And, of course, *she* didn't agree with me; and started the usual line about the—static of conventional thinking; and people outgrowing each other, and all that stuff. And then, as usual, she starts applying it to *me:* and to *our* marriage. Well, of course, there's no use arguing with her.

Mrs. Espenshade—I know.

Vernon—For she'll only keep going while ever you answer her. So I just stopped talking. And after a while she went out into the back garden to take some kind of breathing exercises that she's been doing lately. But after she'd gone, I began to think it was time that I came to a few conclusions of my own. But I couldn't think anything out there. So I got a few things together, and went down to the Club. And I've *been* there ever since.

Mrs. Espenshade—Was the man that you were telling her about Mr. Espenshade, Vernon? (*There is a beat of physical stillness; then he continues to press the fire out of a cigarette as though he hadn't heard her.*)

Vernon—Which man, Mrs. Espenshade?

Mrs. Espenshade—The man that you say has been married over twenty-five years, and is going around with another woman. Because I think that's who you mean, isn't it?

Vernon—Well, as long as you ask me, Mrs. Espenshade, it is.

Mrs. Espenshade—And that's really what you were trying to tell Penny Thursday night, wasn't it, when she kept interrupting you all the time?

Vernon—I didn't know what else to do about it, to tell you the truth.

Mrs. Espenshade—I understand.

Vernon—I'd been hearing little left-handed references to it from time to time. But I didn't feel it was *my* place to say anything to Mr. Espenshade. And I knew he wouldn't want *you* to know anything about it. So I thought maybe if I said something to Penny. She's always been so close to her father.

Mrs. Espenshade—She'd only have given you an answer, Vernon.

Vernon—Yes, I suppose she would.

Mrs. Espenshade—She's made a perfect idol of her father all

her life. Because he always allowed her to do exactly as she pleased. And thought it was very amusing to hear her insist upon having the last word in every argument with *me:* especially where he was concerned. So I'm rather glad you *didn't* have an opportunity of telling her this the other night; for *I* want to tell her myself. She'll very likely accuse *me* of being responsible for it—but I've got my answer all ready for her if she does. And *she* gave it to me: just as she's given me several others I can use if she comes here about this business between you and her.

VERNON—Well, I hope I haven't *started* anything around here.

MRS. ESPENSHADE—You haven't at all, Vernon, not in the least.

VERNON—I certainly didn't intend to say anything about this business of Mr. Espenshade when I came here this evening.

MRS. ESPENSHADE—I'd heard it before.

VERNON—Well, I imagined you had, when you spoke the way you did.

MRS. ESPENSHADE—I seem to have been hearing it for a long time.

VERNON—It's very unfortunate.

MRS. ESPENSHADE—And it's very curious—the fact that I don't find it nearly so disturbing as I would have imagined I would. I have an idea that my husband and daughter have been teaching me quite a few things these past years, that I'd hardly have realized if something of this kind hadn't happened. And it's surprising, now that it *has* happened, how well their teachings have prepared me to meet it.

VERNON—I'm afraid it isn't going to be easy to make Penny believe a thing like this about her father.

Mrs. Espenshade guilefully asks Vernon's assistance in the matter of making Penny understand. She wants to know all he knows, with names and dates—otherwise Penny won't believe this about her father.

The woman, Vernon informs her, is a doctor. And she lives out near his aunt somewhere. And he has even met her once, about a year ago. "One of the girls down in the office used to do secretarial work for her once in a while. And I was coming back from lunch with her one day and we ran into her. And after she left I happened to say that I thought she was rather a nice little woman. And *she* said, 'I'm glad you like her.' And I said, 'Why?' And she kind of laughed. And I said, 'I don't know what you mean.' 'Well,' she said, 'you never can tell—she might be your mother-in-law some day.' "

At Mrs. Espenshade's behest Vernon describes the woman while she makes notes on a pad. Plump. Kind of little. Neat-looking. Not much past forty. Not pretty, but something rather appealing about her. Had on a blue dress, very plain. And, yes, a white hat. A halo hat, he thinks they're called.

"He can't be spending very much money on her," deduces Mrs. Espenshade. "She's still wearing that outfit, I understand."

With an occasional question from his mother-in-law, Vernon continues the recital of what he knows. Apparently the woman hasn't any family, and has had a pretty hard time of it. She was brought up in an orphanage, and then went to work as a waitress in a medical college. She used to sit in at the various lectures and finally decided she would be a doctor. The college let her work her way through.

"Did this girl in the office tell you how she happened to meet Mr. Espenshade?"

Even this detail is available. He was playing golf one afternoon and his partner wrenched his back making a shot. Espenshade drove him to Dr. Hilton's office.

"This girl," explains Vernon, "was there when they came in. And she said it was just one of those things. It can happen, you know."

"But," interposes Mrs. Espenshade, "don't you think she was probably *flattered* more than anything else? I mean, being a plain little person, as you say, that probably nobody ever looked at; and then suddenly to have some rather attractive man pay attention to her?"

"Well, this girl says that Mr. Espenshade's got it just as bad as *she* has. As a matter of fact, she says that this woman told her that when he first told her he was married, *she* wanted to call the whole thing off; but that *he* took such a sinking spell that she had to give *him* a treatment."

Mrs. Espenshade, the incurable romantic, is bemused by this recital. Her gaze veers from its sharp attention to Vernon toward the window and the far-off hills. He continues:

"And she says she was talking to her again on the street about a month ago, and she said *she* couldn't call it off herself now, either; that she'd rather die."

By now Mrs. Espenshade is wandering in the moonlight among the daffodils, only half-hearing Vernon as he continues, "So it's evidently quite a romance. One of those 'in which we feel the pressure of a hand' things. Do you remember that one?"

Completely transported, she rejoins, " 'One touch of fire'—"
"That's it."
" '—and all the rest is mystery.' "
Vernon laughs, "I didn't think anybody remembered that but me—" But Mrs. Espenshade is still hearing only the laughter of lovers in some far-off glade. A single silvery chime from a French clock on the mantel gives Vernon a convenient cue for departure.

The moment he is gone, Mrs. Espenshade is on the wire to Mrs. Wentz. "Are you listening, Mabel?—Well, my dear, Vernon has just left here, and it's a wonder I'm able to talk to you at all, for he's left me absolutely speechless. Well, darling, he simply *knows* everything. . . ."

Mrs. Espenshade's recital is complete and headlong, and even Anna announcing that dinner is served cannot halt it. "I've never heard anything so romantic in all my life. . . ."

(*The curtain is lowered, denoting the passage of an hour.*)

It is after dinner now, and Mrs. Espenshade is having coffee in front of the mantelpiece, and considering the notes she made from Vernon's testimony. When the buzzer sounds she tears her notes from the pad, folds them and puts them in the bosom of her dress.

The caller is her daughter. "Whose wedding was it that you went to this afternoon? Anna said you went to a wedding at St. Stephen's."

Mrs. Espenshade, studiously arranging the coffee table, evades, "I don't think *you* know them; they're connected with the church over there."

However, Penny has not come just to talk about weddings— nor is Vernon the subject of her visit. "It's about Papa," she whispers, lest Anna be listening. "Somebody telephoned me at home; that's the reason I called you right away."

"You mean your *poor* Papa?"

"Oh, really, Mother! I don't think you'll be nearly so complacent when you hear what it is!"

Mrs. Espenshade invites her daughter to give—but Penny suddenly switches to the subject of her own husband. "I suppose Vernon has been telling you his tale of woe here this evening, hasn't he?"

"Not especially."

Penny makes it clear that her attitude toward Vernon is unchanged, and is derisive at her mother's suggestion that he may have left for good. "I got a distinct impression," her mother says, "that he did *not* intend to allow *you* to draw any pension for breaking up his home."

"I wish you'd tell him for me that I don't think he'll have very much to say whether I'll have a pension or not, after he has walked away from his wife and family."

Mrs. Espenshade applies the crusher: "I think all he'd have to do would be just repeat a few of your observations on marriage in any court, and they'd probably give *him* a pension. . . . And appoint him your guardian, in the bargain."

Penny tartly declares that this is the sort of thing she'd expect from her mother—taking Vernon's side.

MRS. ESPENSHADE—Yes, Vernon and I have quite a few things in common.

PENNY—Well, I think you have your sentimentality in common, at least.

MRS. ESPENSHADE—The only difference between us is that Vernon isn't going to allow himself to be held cheap for as many years as I have. And that's really what you came over here to tell me about tonight, isn't it?

PENNY—What?

MRS. ESPENSHADE—About your father's lady friend? The doctor woman that lives out near Vernon's aunt?

PENNY—Did *he* tell you?

MRS. ESPENSHADE—Don't be naïve, Penny.

PENNY—Well, he *knows* about it; for his aunt told me so. It was she that telephoned me this afternoon.

MRS. ESPENSHADE—I don't have to wait for some *man* to tell me what the entire city has been talking about for years.

PENNY—Well, do you believe it?

MRS. ESPENSHADE—I don't *have* to believe it, I *know* it.

PENNY—Well, who *told* you?

MRS. ESPENSHADE—*He* told me, as a matter of fact!

PENNY—You mean Papa?

MRS. ESPENSHADE—Yes! Your poor Papa!—with his ridiculous skipping and leaping every time he crosses the floor. And dancing in front of every looking glass in the house, trying to make himself believe that his hair isn't going. Whenever you see a man starting that kind of thing, you may be sure there's a lady in the woodpile *somewhere*. And if *you* hadn't been so absurdly sentimental about him all your life, you'd have realized it long ago. And he's always whistling, too; that's another sign. Nobody's so happy that he's got to be whistling all the time: it isn't natural.

PENNY—Well, hasn't anybody ever actually *told* you about him, Mother?

MRS. ESPENSHADE—Oh, don't be tiresome, Penny! I've heard about him from so many sources that I've had to make notes so that I'd remember the details.

PENNY—And haven't you ever *said* anything to him?

MRS. ESPENSHADE—What for?

PENNY—Well, at least to let him know that you know.

MRS. ESPENSHADE—And give him a chance to lie out of it I suppose? No, I haven't. She's a woman doctor, you know. And an osteopath. It'd be a very easy matter for him to insist that he was simply taking a course of treatments from her.

PENNY—Well, it seems to me you could have done *something*, Mother.

MRS. ESPENSHADE—Of course I could have done something. I could have done a great many things. But, as you say, I'm sentimental. Although *I* prefer to call it morally responsible. And I had a child on my hands. And I knew something of what *happens* to children that are deprived of a normal upbringing. How they come to privately despise and resent the parents that are responsible for it. So, like many another woman, I simply closed my eyes; and that's how he's been able to do what he's done.

PENNY—Well, you don't have to *continue* to close your eyes, do you?

MRS. ESPENSHADE—No.

PENNY—Why haven't you done something since I've been married?

MRS. ESPENSHADE—Because he lay very low for a long time after your marriage. I think he suspected that I'd heard something. So I wasn't able to do very much. But he's been emerging again this past year or so—so I've been able to get just about what I need.

PENNY—You mean to talk to him?

MRS. ESPENSHADE—Among other things, yes.

PENNY—What did you do, Mother, get a detective or something.

MRS. ESPENSHADE—I'm my own detective. It's been a little slow; because it has to be facts—that can't be explained away to suit *his* convenience.

PENNY—Well, when are you going to talk to him, Mother? Because I think it's *terribly* important that you do. And I think the sooner you do it the better.

MRS. ESPENSHADE—*I'll* talk to him.

Penny—And what are you going to say? I mean, are you going to show him your notes?

Mrs. Espenshade—I think that's what was worrying Vernon when he was here this evening.

Penny—What?

Mrs. Espenshade—What I was going to say to your father when I talk to him.

Penny—About this, you mean?

Mrs. Espenshade—Yes.

Penny—I thought you said he didn't tell you about Papa.

Mrs. Espenshade—I told *him* about Papa. Only to discover that he knew it long before *I* did. And I told him because I thought he might be a little curious as to just how *you* might fare with a stepmother in the picture. That's probably what he was trying to suggest to *you* Thursday night, when he was telling you about the married man that was going about with another woman, and you kept interrupting him with your views on feminine emancipation. So I think he was rather glad of the opportunity to discuss it with *me*. He knows you have no particular equipment or profession of any kind. And he *certainly* understands how much *my* sympathy with most of your ideas could be counted upon. So I think he was a little troubled. Because *he's* sentimental, too, you know—even about *you*.

Penny—Well, Mother, you don't mean that you would think of *divorcing* Papa, do you?

Mrs. Espenshade—Why not?

The tables have been turned on Penny, who now finds herself defending a marriage—her mother's. She squirms when her mother quotes Penny's own philosophy back at her. The idea of Mrs. Espenshade "outgrowing" Papa is absurd. Her mother parries, "I probably wouldn't have believed it, or even realized it, if I hadn't listened to so many of *your* dissertations."

"Well, Mother, you know the way these things are magnified. All a man in Papa's position would have to do would to be seen out with a woman a few times, and they'd talk about it forever. As a matter of fact, he may not have seen the woman for years."

Quietly, Mrs. Espenshade informs her daughter, "He's with her *now*.—This very night—*parked* in his car, on a lonely road somewhere out beyond Cloverton. And that's where he's *been* parked, every Saturday night, and every Saturday afternoon, too, unless it was raining; and then he was very likely parked somewhere else."

"I thought he played golf," says Penny.

"That's what *I* used to think—till I discovered that that was simply another name for driving out to Meredith Village and picking *her* up at her office. And if you wait around here a while you'll very likely see *him* hobble in and tell us how he turned on his ankle out at Brookside this afternoon. When the fact of the matter is that he turned on his ankle this afternoon out at Meredith Village, leaping out of his car the minute *she* appeared."

Penny thinks something should be done about the woman immediately—that her mother should *say* something to her father. This Mrs. Espenshade promises.

"I haven't told you," Penny admits, "some of the things that Vernon's aunt told me this afternoon— They say this woman and Papa are going to be married." Mrs. Espenshade works calmly at a cigarette.

The information comes, Penny explains, from a nurse in the woman's office, whose sister is Vernon's aunt's hairdresser. Furthermore, the woman is going away for a couple of months in the middle of July—to some lake in Pennsylvania near Eaglesmere—and when she comes back, she is going to marry a Mr. Espenshade.

There is the sound of the outer door opening and closing, and mother and daughter hear Espenshade's greeting to the maid: "Anna, you're just in time to help a poor, crippled old man."

"Oh, did you hurt your foot, Mr. Espenshade?"

"No, just gave my ankle a little turn on the golf course this afternoon."

He limps in and greets his family.

MRS. ESPENSHADE—Did I hear you say something happened to your ankle out there today?

ESPENSHADE—Oh, that was nothing. I just happened to give it a little twist, going to the fourteenth hole. I didn't notice it much till I got out of the car a minute ago.

MRS. ESPENSHADE—How did you happen to do it?

ESPENSHADE—Well, it was a very curious thing. (*Turning and speaking directly to* PENNY.) It'll show you how things can happen. (PENNY *inclines her head knowingly.*) I pulled my drive going to the fourteenth—right into the rough—at least, that's what I *thought* I did. But the rough there is very narrow, and very deceptive. It slopes up into a kind of series of little knolls. And right behind them is one of the worst sand-traps on the course. But *I* didn't think I'd gotten anywhere *near* that far. But there she was—sitting right in the middle of it.

MRS. ESPENSHADE—Who?

ESPENSHADE—The ball, Ollie.

MRS. ESPENSHADE—Oh!

PENNY—He's talking about the golf ball, Mother.

MRS. ESPENSHADE—Yes, I understand.

ESPENSHADE—The golf ball was in the trap.

MRS. ESPENSHADE—I see. I don't know anything about golf.

PENNY—Go on, Papa.

ESPENSHADE—Well, I always play safe in a trap. I think it's
the only thing to do, unless you're a professional. But this looked
like a pretty good lie. And I thought if I just played it regular,
I might be able to get away with it.

PENNY—But you weren't.

ESPENSHADE—Exactly: there's a mental hazard, you know, in
a trap—even when everything's all right. So, of course, the minute I swung full at it, I threw myself off balance. And in trying
to shift my weight quickly, to keep from falling, my right foot
kind of twisted under me.

MRS. ESPENSHADE—It's a wonder to me you haven't turned
on your ankle long before this the way you are always hopping
out of that car of yours.

ESPENSHADE—I wasn't hopping out of the car when I did *this*.

PENNY—He was trying to get out of a trap, Mother.

MRS. ESPENSHADE—Well, he shouldn't get *into* traps; and then
he wouldn't have to be trying to get *out* of them.

Penny is preparing to go home when her father asks her when
she is going to Maine. Penny hasn't decided. "You going to
Meadow Beach again this Summer, Mother?" she asks. Mother
hasn't decided.

Papa chimes in with the opinion that he, personally, is a little
tired of the seashore. It's all right for weekends, but he'd like to
break it up a little this year.

"You mean the country?" asks Penny.

"Well, the country, or the mountains—I don't care, as long as
it's a change. There's a friend of mine out at the club that's
always giving me quite a line about some place up in the mountains; he's got a lodge of some kind up there."

"In the Adirondacks?"

"No, I think it's in Pennsylvania somewhere, as a matter of
fact."

Penny takes her leave, and Mrs. Espenshade returns to business. "Who's the friend that has the place up in the mountains?"

"He's a fellow that makes up our foursome sometimes on Saturdays."

"It's near Eaglesmere, I suppose, isn't it?" Espenshade takes this shot with innocent calm.

Further queries by his wife elicit the information that this fellow hasn't any family at his lodge. He was brought up in an orphanage. Gives the impression of having had a pretty tough time of it. "I often watch him when his face is in repose; and, for some reason or other, he always makes me a little sad. I imagine he's gotten hurt a lot in his life by people; and he very likely wants to get away from them as far as possible."

MRS. ESPENSHADE—It's a wonder he'd ask *you* up there.

ESPENSHADE—I suppose he gets lonesome—like everybody else. He *says* he feels the *remoteness* of the place once in a while; but that it's so wonderful up there that he's never been able to think of not going back there again the next year. He says there's a little mountain road runs past the place; and he says as you walk along it in the evening, it looks exactly like old silver in the moonlight. (MRS. ESPENSHADE *slowly raises her eyes to some far-off moon.*) And he says you hear those little mountain streams at night, just like voices in the darkness. And he says there's always a fragrance up there, like wild honeysuckle. Of course, I may not go up there at all. It's just a small place— a cabin, really; he's shown me a couple of snapshots of it different times: and I think there'd only be room for the two of us. So I don't know. I told him I *might* run up there sometime this Summer.

MRS. ESPENSHADE (*still entranced*)—I think that might be very nice for you.

ESPENSHADE—You don't think you'd mind if I didn't come down to the shore every weekend?

MRS. ESPENSHADE—Not if you prefer it up there.

ESPENSHADE—Of course I'd come down there occasionally. But I've never been to the mountains much—and I think it might be interesting.

MRS. ESPENSHADE—Those sounds at night in the mountains are unearthly.

ESPENSHADE (*with a glance at her*)—That's what *he's* always talking about.

Mrs. Espenshade—And that fragrance of wild honeysuckle.
(Espenshade *rests his elbow on the mantelpiece and looks quiz-
zically at his still apparently entranced wife.*)
The curtain falls.

ACT III

Sunday evening, two months later, Mrs. Espenshade is making
notes from a letter on the desk beside her when Penny arrives.
One gathers that mother and daughter have not seen each other
in some time, for their preliminary conversation is mostly how-
are-you's and remarks about the dreadful heat. Mrs. Espenshade
has been at the shore, but Penny has remained in town with her
son, Punchy.

Penny has a new maid at her house. "I had to get rid of the
other one."

"I just couldn't stand any more of her everlasting whining
about Punchy," she explains. "If she only took him to the corner,
she came back with a whole list of things that he'd done to her—
or to somebody else. And I believe she made up half of them;
because when I'd question him about them, he simply didn't know
what I was talking about.

"She came in in a perfect tantrum the Saturday she left and
said that he'd kicked her—all the way back from the park.
Which was a perfect falsehood, of course—because whatever else
Punchy does, he *does not kick* people. And I told her so. And
she flounced out of the room and up the stairs. And the next
thing I knew I saw her going down the sidewalk of the house
with her things."

Penny learns that Mrs. Espenshade is expecting her father—
and is greatly surprised to be told that her father hasn't been
at the shore. "I haven't *seen* your father since I left here on the
17th of last month," her mother reveals. "And I don't think a
great many other people have seen him, either—at least over the
weekends."

Now it all comes back to Penny—the trouble. "You don't
think he has started that other business again, do you?" she inquires, hoping for a negative answer. "I mean, you talked to
him that night after I left here, didn't you?"

"Really, Penny," chides her mother, "I think you should go
back to your husband with as much haste as possible. I think
you're much too unsuspecting to be going about unattended."

Facts, Mrs. Espenshade explains—facts were what she needed
before talking. And now she has them. And she has a witness.

Papa headed for the mountains the day after his wife left for the shore, and has spent every weekend since up there. "He picked the lady friend up at her offices on the afternoon of Saturday, July 18. And they drove straight to Eaglesmere, to the Clifton Hotel. And he registered there; and then drove her out to the cabin. And he stayed there till they drove back to the hotel on Sunday night to let him check out. . . . And that's been the program the three weekends since."

The detective who has supplied the facts is, Penny learns, a woman. "That's the kind of work she likes, I suppose," says Mrs. Espenshade.

Espenshade usually gets back to town about this time Sunday nights, and his wife has a surprise for him. Penny thinks, and hopes, that it will be just a "talk." "Because I think if he knows you know about it, it'll put a stop to it."

Her mother informs Penny that she is a sham and a fool; that she fears that her parents' divorcing will make her own posturing at the expense of her own husband less secure. Penny denies this, and still believes her mother could have stopped her father's romance had she wanted to.

"I think," says Mrs. Espenshade, "that *you* were more or less responsible for my silence. . . . Oh, it wasn't out of any consideration for you, I assure you. I'd always felt that a certain disillusionment about your father would be about the best thing that could possibly happen to you. But when my own disillusionment about him occurred, I found myself, ironically enough, remembering some of the speeches you'd been making around here —and appreciating their application to my own case.

"But they say we find ourselves in our tribulations. And sure enough, I soon began to discover that I wasn't nearly so heartbroken as I was romantic. And I actually began to follow your father's romance with a certain interest."

Penny snorts, "And I suppose you'll go to his wedding, too, if he ever marries her."

Mrs. Espenshade has had enough talk about her own marriage; now she wants to talk about her daughter's. She has, she informs Penny, had four letters from Vernon and Vernon hasn't changed his mind. He won't come back until there is an understanding.

"On *his* terms, of course," sniffs Penny.

On certain terms, yes, she is informed. Punchy must be taken out of the hot city and delivered to Maine within a week. Penny

can come if she wants to.   Punchy cannot go to Dr. Bajarian's
summer camp, or back to his school in the Fall.

MRS. ESPENSHADE—You don't want to see these letters?

PENNY—No, I do not.   For I know just about what's in them.

MRS. ESPENSHADE—Did you know that he's going to demand
the custody of your child—if you make it necessary for him to
divorce you?   He's genuinely alarmed over that child's upbringing.

PENNY—And I wonder if it's occurred to him that *I* might
divorce *him* first,—on the grounds of desertion.

MRS. ESPENSHADE—He would *still* demand the custody of the
child.

PENNY—On the grounds that I am not a fit person to bring
him up I suppose?

MRS. ESPENSHADE—That's the grounds that such demands are
usually made on.

PENNY—Well, I'm afraid he'll need one of your female
witnesses, Mother, to establish any such claim as that.

MRS. ESPENSHADE (*with ominous steadiness*)—He already has
such a witness, Penny.

PENNY—Really?

MRS. ESPENSHADE—And her testimony against you might be
very conclusive, if you're ever fool enough to let it come to that.
You've held me cheap long enough, through the attitude of that
child: and I'll welcome an opportunity to put a stop to it.

Espenshade has quietly appeared in the doorway.   "What's going on?" he inquires.   "What's the matter?"

"There's nothing at all the matter with *me!*" cries Penny.
"Mother is simply distributing a few divorces here this evening;
so if you wait around a while you may get one of them."   She
storms out of the apartment.

Once again, the preliminaries toward an important conversation
are mere small-talk.   Espenshade gives his wife a kiss and compliments her appearance, and she tells him his hair needs brushing back on the left side.   Did she come up from the shore by
train?   No, Mabel drove her up, and will drive her back tomorrow.

And how about him, in the mountains?   Wonderful!   The place
that fellow has is like something you'd see on a picture postcard.
And never in his life has he played such golf; it must be the

atmosphere up there. "Do you know what I've been doing that course in, Ollie?"

Tonelessly, Mrs. Espenshade launches her harpoon. "Yes—I do."

"Why, how would you know, Ollie?"

"Because I've been keeping your score these past three week-ends. And I know all about the kind of game you've been playing. And whom you've been playing it with; and for how long. So I hope you won't be tiresome now, and start explaining how you've been going to her for a series of osteopathic treatments. For I've lost interest in the game, and Mabel Wentz and I would like to do a bit of traveling."

Espenshade confesses that he doesn't know what to say. "Well," he manages to utter, "I hope it hasn't hurt you too much, that's all."

His wife, maintaining her calm, assures him that he's quite free to stand up again any time he likes and swear to be faithful to death to somebody else. "I don't think you'll have very much difficulty persuading someone else to believe you."

ESPENSHADE—You know, I've often *wondered* whether you knew about this. And sometimes I almost persuaded myself that you didn't. But, as long as you did, I won't be tiresome. And of course, it's got to be whatever way you want it, Ollie. And that's the way *I* want it, too,—it really is. I suppose Penny knows about it, too, doesn't she?

MRS. ESPENSHADE—Of course. I suppose everybody knows about it.

ESPENSHADE—Funny,—the way a man'll get into this kind of thing,—so deep that there's just no getting *out* of it. I used to ask myself once in a while just why I was *letting* myself get into it so deep.

MRS. ESPENSHADE—Were you ever able to find an answer to that?

ESPENSHADE—Well, the only thing I could ascribe it to was the fact that I *needed* someone.

MRS. ESPENSHADE—And I didn't understand you perhaps.

ESPENSHADE—No, I don't think it was so much that, as it was that *I* didn't understand *you*. At least a certain *quality* about you. I don't think I've *ever* understood it, really. And yet I think it was the quality that first attracted me to you. Because you've had it ever since I've known you.

MRS. ESPENSHADE—What is it?

ESPENSHADE—Well,—it's hard to describe, Ollie;—it's an intangible kind of thing—that I doubt *anybody* could describe very well. But I used to reproach myself for even wanting to marry you. Really, I guess it was what they call the self-depreciation of the lover. And yet I don't think it was altogether that, either. But you always seemed a peculiarly innocent kind of woman, for some reason or other. I remember the day we were married,— when we got back from the church, and were standing out under the trees at your Mother's place; and you still had your bridal dress on,—I couldn't get that out of my mind. (*She touches her handkerchief to her eye.*) You looked so unreal to me that day,—so absolutely unphysical. I kept saying to myself, "*I* shouldn't have married this girl; it isn't right. I'm not good enough for her. And *no* man is good enough for her. She should have been allowed to just pass through her life as a kind of symbol of the romance that every man'd like to be worthy of." (*She turns her head slowly and looks off through the lower window to the Phaeacian Glades.*) And I remember some lines of a poem kept coming into my mind,—a poem called "Sibylle" that I had to translate at school one time—something about—

> "I see thee standing in a maiden light,
>   Beyond the stealth of time; and all alone
> The secret quest of ev'ry errant knight,
>   Yet none may ever know thee as his own.

(MRS. ESPENSHADE *has to raise her handkerchief to her eyes again; and the curtain starts to descend very slowly.*)

> Oh, Wisdom's Child, how did'st thou learn that love
>   Fulfilled is but the end thereof!"

It is about 2:30 Saturday afternoon, six weeks later, and Anna hurries in with a small box of flowers. Mrs. Espenshade, in her bedroom, calls to Anna to put them somewhere for a minute; she'll be right out. The buzzer summons Anna to the entrance door, and Mrs. Espenshade appears, wearing a navy blue dress and fastening on some bracelets. From the box Anna has brought she removes an elaborate corsage of white orchids, white sweet peas and lilies-of-the-valley. She tries it out against her dress, looking in the mantel mirror, then returns to her bedroom with it.

The caller, as expected, is Mabel Wentz. She has barely got settled in a chair when her friend reappears, hurriedly, with an open letter in her hand. "I can't *tell* you how much I appreciate your coming right over, Mabel. . . . I was afraid I might not be able to get hold of you at all."

"Where are we going, Ollie?"

Ollie will get to this in her own fashion—but first, about the letter. It's from Penny, and Penny is up in Maine with Vernon having quite a second honeymoon. "But she also says that Vernon had a letter from his aunt telling him that the hairdresser that she goes to was telling her that the nurse that works for Dr. Hilton had been in to have her hair and eyebrows done for Dr. Hilton's wedding. And that she had said that the doctor was back from the mountains and was to be married on the 24th at 5 o'clock in the afternoon, at a little church somewhere out beyond Cloverton, called the Little Church in the Woods."

Mrs. Wentz gazes steadily at her friend, wondering what is coming next. It comes:

"And today is the 24th, Mabel. I mean, it's today."

Mrs. Wentz (*still uncomprehending*)—Well, that isn't where you were thinking of going this afternoon, is it?

Mrs. Espenshade—Yes, and now please don't try to talk me out of it, Mabel, because I've been promising myself this for a long time.

Mrs. Wentz—You've been promising yourself what, Ollie?

Mrs. Espenshade—This—to see it through to the end and I intend to do it.

Mrs. Wentz—And you expect me to drive you out to Paul's wedding?

Mrs. Espenshade—I thought you might—you know I'm not able to drive, myself.

Mrs. Wentz—But I'm not a contributor to delinquency, darling.

Mrs. Espenshade—I have a very good reason for wanting to go out there.

Mrs. Wentz—You want to drain the cup of martyrdom to the dregs, I suppose.

Mrs. Espenshade—You can call it whatever you like but I'm going just the same and if you won't take me I'll go by myself.

Mrs. Wentz—But, Ollie, do you realize what it is that you're asking me to do?

Mrs. Espenshade—Yes, of course I do.

Mrs. Wentz—To drive you out to your own husband's wedding?

MRS. ESPENSHADE—I want to prove to myself that I am completely untouched by the entire thing.

MRS. WENTZ—But, Ollie, you haven't gone so completely out of your mind as not to realize that that isn't the interpretation that'll be put upon such a thing by anybody that sees you out there.

MRS. ESPENSHADE—No one need see me out there at all.

MRS. WENTZ—How can you *avoid* being seen?

MRS. ESPENSHADE—The place is nearly thirty miles from here, Mabel.

MRS. WENTZ—Even so, *somebody* is bound to see you.

MRS. ESPENSHADE—But I'm going to wear a *veil*, darling!

MRS. WENTZ—Oh, well, now, *that's* going *entirely* too far!

MRS. ESPENSHADE—But it's just a little summer veil, Mabel.

MRS. WENTZ—About six yards long I imagine,—and fastened with orange blossoms.

Ollie has called the church and got all the information. It's to be a very private and informal ceremony. She is deaf to Mabel's grim prediction that if she goes she will be the laughing-stock of the entire city. Her plan is to get there early and slip in before anybody else gets there and sit away over to the side at the back.

"Oh, don't be silly, Ollie! You know perfectly well that no woman in the world has ever gone to her husband's wedding."

But the romantic Mrs. Espenshade has rationalized her motives. For one thing, she must prove to herself that she can "let go gracefully." And for another, there is the future Mrs. Espenshade to consider.

"Everybody has told me what a very nice person this woman is that he's taken up with," she explains. "A rather pathetic poor thing, they say, that apparently no one has ever looked at, and that has known nothing all her life but poverty and hard work.

"And this is her first wonder, I suppose, and it's just been too much for her. And he's probably taken advantage of it and deceived her—just as he deceived *me*. And I will *not* let him break her heart, as he's broken mine."

This recital brings on a fit of weeping which leaves Mabel Wentz unmoved. She doesn't believe the broken-heart angle, and anyway Ollie isn't going to stop anything by simply appearing at the wedding.

Mrs. Espenshade's determination is unshaken, and Mabel finally agrees to drive her out to the church. "We'd better get started. It's nearly 3 o'clock and it'll take us nearly an hour to get out there."

Mrs. Espenshade retires to her bedroom for a final fixing-up, while Mabel telephones her maid to say that she will be bringing Mrs. Espenshade home to dinner. When Ollie reappears, she is wearing the corsage and a white halo hat with a detachable veil. Mrs. Wentz, looking up from the telephone and catching the picture, has given in on enough points and now she offers an ultimatum:

"Now listen, Ollie—you are *not* going to wear that veil out there, or I simply will not go with you. You look exactly like an emergency bride, darling, if you know what I mean."

"Well, it's detachable, you know."

"Well, you'd better detach it—unless you want them throwing rice at *you* as you go in the church. . . . And that corsage is a bit suspicious-looking, too."

Mrs. Espenshade objects, "Now you know I always wear white flowers with a dark dress, Mabel."

Mabel is unconvinced. "I know. But that's a little more than just white flowers. I'd like to have been listening when you ordered it."

Mrs. Espenshade accepts defeat, for once, and removes the veil and corsage. "You look a little less *involved* than you did before," approves her friend.

MRS. ESPENSHADE—Do I look as though I'd been crying?

MRS. WENTZ—No, you don't.

MRS. ESPENSHADE—Because my eyes *feel* as though I do. Let me see if I have my key.

MRS. WENTZ—I'm sure you'll look much better than the bride, if that's any satisfaction to you.

MRS. ESPENSHADE—Well, I wonder I look half as good as I do, when I get thinking about all this. (*She starts to weep again.*)

MRS. WENTZ—Well, now, don't start thinking about it; it only upsets you.

MRS. ESPENSHADE—But it *is* fantastic, isn't it, Mabel, that I should be going out there today?

MRS. WENTZ—Well, you don't *have* to go out there, you know!

MRS. ESPENSHADE—But, I mean, that such a thing should happen to me, after all these years. But it is incredible, just the same.

MRS. WENTZ—But it's a wedding, Ollie, and you'll love it, and that's the only reason you're going out there, so stop acting. . . .

Mrs. Espenshade—But Paul *did* idealize me, Mabel.   He really did.

Mrs. Wentz—I'm sure he did, darling, but we'd better get started.

Mrs. Espenshade—I remember the last time I talked to him he said he saw me as a symbol of romance.

Mrs. Wentz—That's very pretty, dear.

Mrs. Espenshade—

> He said he saw me always, standing in a maiden's light—
> Beyond the stealth of time, and all alone—
> The secret quest of every errant knight,
> Yet none may ever claim me as his own.
> Oh, Wisdom's Child—how did'st thou learn
> That love fulfilled is but the end thereof.

THE CURTAIN FALLS

THE STORY OF MARY SURRATT

A Drama in Three Acts

By John Patrick

MANY an author has been puzzled by the failure of his play on Broadway. This takes in the better-known, as well as the lesser-known dramatists. In this instance it takes in specifically John Patrick, who was credited in the record with two failures and one success in New York before "The Story of Mary Surratt" was brought in. The failures were a tragic story of a dirigible crash in the Arctic Circle called "Hell Freezes Over," and a fairly weighty drama, "The Willow and I," which got twenty-eight performances the season of 1941-42. Both these plays were on the depressing side. This fact, with "Mary Surratt" added, may indicate a weight in the scale against Capt. Patrick, so far as popular approval is concerned. His previous success was the appealingly human "The Hasty Heart," which was light, but not too light, and agreeably studded with laughter.

"My own interest in Mary Surratt goes back to the days of enforced study of American history," Capt. Patrick has written. "The apologetic line or two given this disgraceful episode whetted my appetite to know more. I read everything available, from the angry protestations of historian DeWitt to the equally angry excuses of Gen. Harris. Determination was born to write a play about the case one day. The two-volume transcription of the trial was the most valuable primary and unbiased source of data. When my own anger got out of hand I put the play aside. Most of the manuscript was completed just before the outbreak of what we ominously call World War II. This was withheld for the duration for obvious reasons.

"Sins of omission and sins of invention are necessary in historical plays. This is no exception. The chronology of events is conveniently rearranged to accommodate the curtain. But there is no real violation of the essential truth of the story. The trial scene is, for the most part, taken from the records. Actually Mary Surratt was never allowed to testify for herself. All reference to the petition for mercy that might have saved her life (which was withheld from President Johnson) was omitted. Of the sins of invention, there is the character of Father Wiget, who is a composite of several priests who testified in Mary's behalf. And the final cell scene is permissible invention, since no record exists."

It was early February when the play was produced. The first-night audience was more than usually enthusiastic, cheering the actors and granting the company several recalls. The reviews were divided, but less favorable than unfavorable. The producers did not consider it sound business to make a fight for the play and it was shortly withdrawn.

It is the evening of April 14, 1865. In the living room of Mary Surratt's boarding house in Washington, D. C., Anna Surratt, the 16-year-old daughter of the house, is calling to her mother through the door leading to the kitchen and dining room. Anna has just come from upstairs and reports that from her bedroom window she has been able to see the reflection of bonfires still burning in the streets of the city. Anna would like very much to go downtown and get a closer view of the celebration. Her mother, however, is sure it is too late.

"The excitement is about over," Mary says, coming into the room. "We'll stay home and celebrate peace peacefully."

Mrs. Surratt is a smallish, gentle-voiced woman. She expresses the same warmth and friendliness that the furnishing of the living room gives us—a room that "conveys an atmosphere of mellowness and peace," a room in which people have lived.

Anna is inclined to be rebellious. She can't understand why her mother always keeps her in when there is any excitement. In that mood she is quick to resent a picture of President Lincoln she finds on the table. An ugly man. She'd certainly hate to have to kiss him. "He looks like a gorilla!" says Anna.

"Aren't you being rather ugly yourself?"

"I'm only quoting what his political enemies say," Anna insists, holding up a fold of newspaper. "Senator Weldon calls President Lincoln 'That gorilla in the White House.' "

"I never understood why bad manners should be considered good politics," observes Mary. "If the country wants its presidents pretty let them elect a woman."

Mary has picked up her work basket and taken out her knitting. Anna, still irritable, changes tactics. Now she wishes she could have a coral necklace like her mother's. It certainly is getting too tight for Mother. Besides Mother has worn it for years and years. She should be tired of it by this time. Anyway, coral necklaces are getting to be awfully tacky. Where did her 'mother get it?

"I'm not going to give it to you!" declares Mary, firmly, and for the third or fourth time. "Don't be so persistent."

"Nothing ever happens to me," sighs Anna. "I sometimes wonder if tomorrow is worth waking up for. There are so many things I'd admire to have that I'll never have."

Mary continues knitting for several minutes. Anna is standing disconsolately at the window. Then her mother gives in. The necklace is Anna's. "It makes a mark on my neck anyhow," admits Mary.

"I've wanted this ever since I can remember," exclaims Anna, surveying herself in the mirror and beaming happily. "Who gave it to you, Mother? Please—I ought to know about it, since it's mine."

Mary is slow to answer. "It was given to me by a boy who lived on the next plantation when I was a girl; a boy who later went away and became quite famous."

ANNA—And you've worn it all these years. Oh, that's beautiful.

MARY—It's hard to tell now how much has been sentiment and how much habit.

ANNA (*with enthusiasm*)—What was he like? Was he slender and strong? Was he quick to anger and quick to smile?

MARY—You don't expect me to remember all that! I've forgotten.

ANNA—You haven't forgotten, if you have felt his fingers around your throat all these years.

MARY—I haven't felt his fingers around my throat all these years. Don't be giddy.

ANNA—But you haven't forgotten him, have you?

MARY—No.

ANNA—And you do remember everything about him?

MARY—I remember remembering.

ANNA (*leaning forward*)—Were you desperately in love with him?

MARY—As desperate as only first love can be.

ANNA—Why didn't you marry him?

MARY—Your father asked me. Reverdy didn't.

ANNA—Was that his name? Reverdy? What happened to him? Did he die? What's his whole name?

MARY—Reverdy Johnson.

ANNA—Senator Reverdy Johnson?

MARY—Yes.

ANNA—You actually knew Senator Johnson!

MARY—Anna, get up off the floor!

ANNA (*stopping* MARY's *knitting*)—Won't stop now. Why did he go away?

MARY—He was restless and driven with ambition . . . so he left. He was about 19 then. I haven't seen him since.

ANNA—You let him get on his horse and just ride out of your life!

MARY—Should I have thrown myself in front of him?

ANNA (*rising*)—Yes, yes. And he rode off into the night— with your heart on his sword. . . .

MARY—No, he rode off early one morning and it was raining and I couldn't go out to say good-by to him alone. And that was the end.

ANNA—You should have waited for him forever.

MARY—I did wait forever. A year. Then there was your father. So I married. Then there was Johnny and a little later you were born. And I suddenly look in the mirror and find myself a middle-aged widow with a boarding house and much to be thankful for. And the necklace that delighted me as a girl now delights my daughter. That's as it should be.

Mary has put up her knitting to investigate her son's supper, which she is keeping warm in the kitchen. Anna has stretched herself out on the sofa and closed her eyes. She is still day-dreaming about the necklace when Louis Weichmann, "a young man in his early twenties" who suggests "the contradictory quali-ties of being both defiant and subservient," comes down the stairs and into the room. He stands for a moment gazing down at Anna, then leans over and calmly kisses her upon the mouth.

With a cry of protest Anna springs to her feet, grabs a maga-zine from the table and starts pummeling the somewhat befuddled Lothario. She is still pressing her attack, and practically order-ing this "stupid" boarder from the house, when her mother returns and demands that she shall apologize for such an exhibition of rudeness.

Anna dutifully apologizes, but if Louis believes that she is sorry, she calls back from the stairs, that will prove that he is stupid.

Now it is young Weichmann's turn to apologize, and to explain. He is very much in love with Anna, and can't understand why she despises him. Why is it nobody likes him for long? He doesn't

want anyone to be kind to him out of pity, but he is very unhappy.

It is Mary's idea that Louis is not as desperately in love with
Anna as he imagines. He just has a great deal of affection and he
feels the need of giving it to someone, to anyone. Mary wouldn't
have Louis try to change himself—

"There is something very lovable about you as you are," comforts Mary, "whether you believe it or not. But if you are unhappy here, I shan't urge you to stay."

Mary's sympathy leads Louis into the confessional. There is
something he feels that Mary should know. She knows that he
is Johnny's friend, but she doesn't know how worried he is about
Johnny. The other day Louis had found Johnny sitting on the
edge of his bed counting over a lot of money. Another time he
had seen Johnny hiding a dagger under his mattress. Something's
wrong—

"A lot goes on in this house, Mrs. Surratt, that you don't know
anything about," he says. "Ever since Johnny brought Mr.
Payne here to live strange things have been happening." . . .
"If Johnny's got himself into trouble, Mrs. Surratt, you can
blame his new friends. All of them. Including Mr. Booth."

"Before we blame anyone, let's find out a little more about
this," suggests Mary, putting down her knitting and going to her
desk.

"I warned John that he was making a mistake when he waited
at the stage door and introduced himself," Louis is continuing.
"But he wouldn't listen to me. Now he follows Mr. Booth around
like a servant."

Mary has finished her note. She would have Louis take it over
to the National Hotel at once and ask the clerk to be sure and
see that Mr. Booth gets it. No, she will not tell Johnny anything
about what Louis has told her. Louis has done what is right.

With Louis gone, Anna comes down the stairs. Now it is her
turn to enter the confessional. Anna, too, is worried about herself and very unhappy. Anna is convinced that her whole future
is threatened. There is something wrong with her. She knows
now that she will never be able to marry anyone. Why? Well,
Anna's *frigid*—that's why—

"Anna Surratt! Where did you ever hear such an ugly word?"

"Ugly or not, it's true. I'm frigid."

"Will you please stop repeating it?"

"I can't bear to have anyone touch me. That's why I was so
furious with Louis. It isn't that I don't want to be loved. I do.

I want to be worshiped and adored. Only— I don't want anyone to *touch* me."

Again Mary is sympathetic and understanding. She calls her
daughter to her and gently and tenderly tells her there is nothing
to be worried about. Not only does Anna perfectly reflect her
mother's own youth, but when the right man comes along she'll
forget all about worrying.

"Suppose the man God made for me was killed in the war? I'd
go to my grave unawakened."

"Will you *please* stop using such words as frigid and unawakened!"

"Are you afraid of the truth, Mother?"

"They sound indecent on your lips. Besides—they're not true."

"I suppose that's the difference between us—you don't like the
sound of words—and I *don't like the taste of them."*

The front door is heard to open and close. The next moment
three men have entered the room. They are Lewis Payne, a
"tall, robust young animal"; David Herold, "boyish looking, in
his twenties," and George Atzerodt, "a short, heavy-set German."

Mary is surprised to see them back so soon. Do they know
anything about Johnny? He has missed his supper again.

They, too, are disappointed that Johnny has not come. Especially Atzerodt, the German. But, he agrees with Mary, it is
probably the celebration that has kept him—

"Everywhere is soldiers—people singing—carrying in the hands
torches," says Atzerodt, whose accent is heavy.

They have come, Lewis Payne explains, to tell Mary that they
will be leaving her that night. They have all got a chance to go
to work on a place in Virginia. Their board is paid up, but they
would like to leave some of their belongings with Mary until they
can send for them.

That will be all right. Mary will have Johnny store their
things in the basement. And she will send Johnny up to say
good-by to them as soon as he comes. They would not, they insist, like to go without seeing Johnny.

"Mother—don't let Johnny bring any more of *that* kind here
to live," protests Anna, as soon as the men are out of earshot.
. . . Why can't we rent our rooms to really nice people? Young
officers, some young, wounded officers?"

"All right, honey. I'll put a notice in the paper—'young officers
wanted—handsome, and preferably wounded.' "

Mary thinks if Anna had something to occupy her mind it
would be a good thing. If she would get back to the quilt she

has been making. If it's a need of scraps that has been delaying Anna, she will find plenty of those in a white shoe box in the closet under the stairs.

Anna reluctantly goes in search of the scraps. The first thing she stumbles on is a carpet-bag belonging to Johnny. What's that there for? Mary doesn't know. But if Anna will bring it out she will take it back upstairs, where it belongs.

Anna is still looking for the box of scraps when Mary decides to see what's in Johnny's bag. What she finds is startling—a wallet bulging with bills! For a moment she studies the money thoughtfully. Then, dropping the wallet into her sewing basket, she calls to Anna to put the bag back in the closet. Johnny will probably be looking for it later.

John Surratt lets himself in the front door, hangs up his hat and starts upstairs. He is a slight, dark young man of twenty. His coloring is high, his features sensitive. He wears his hair a little too long.

John is late, he explains, because he has been down town watching the city get drunk. One fool had galloped by him and splashed him with mud. Supper? No, he didn't have time for supper. Anna goes to the kitchen to bring in the hot plate.

Mary is anxious about John. She is afraid he got too tired down town. As she passes him she passes her finger tips tenderly across his forehead. He twitches nervously away from her. "Please don't do that!" he says, querulously.

"John, I'm not a stranger. You were born to me," Mary protests.

"I didn't ask to be born," he snaps.

"Every mother since time began has had that hurled at her." Mary smiles. "Cain probably said it to Eve, and Eve must have said it to God—and both God and I are weary of it."

Anna has brought Johnny's supper. His friend, Louis, she reports to him, had tried to kiss her and she slapped him. John is surprised. He didn't think Louis had that much nerve. Neither does his friend, Wilkes.

Mary picks up her work basket and puts it down again. Evidently she decides not to tell John about either the money or the dagger. She does remember to tell him that Mr. Payne and his friends are leaving tonight. They are upstairs now, waiting to say good-by. With an exclamation of irritation, John dashes for the stairs. He had been anxious to see his friends.

Louis Weichmann is back. He had met Mr. Booth just outside the National Hotel. Booth had read Mary's note. A moment later Louis lets him in the front door.

"John Wilkes Booth is a handsome man, slight and graceful. His black hair, worn rather long, has a blue, metallic sheen. He carries himself with assurance and pride." As Mary comes forward to greet him he assures her that, although he is pressed for time, he had come at once. Her note had said urgent. What can he do to help her?

Mary asks Louis Weichmann to excuse them, and as that young man stalks up the stairs she turns anxiously to her visitor.

"I sent for you, Mr. Booth, because—well—because you seem to have more influence with my son than I have."

"I've played many roles, Mrs. Surratt," answers the actor, "but Mephistopheles is not one of them."

MARY—I'm worried about John. Mr. Booth—do you lend my son money?

BOOTH—I never lend money to friends, Mrs. Surratt. I find it too expensive. I simply give it to them and keep their friendship.

MARY—Where does he get the money he spends with you and your friends?

BOOTH—I was not aware that he spent a great deal. Frankly, we don't itemize each other's generosity.

MARY—How well do you know the men John brought here to board?

BOOTH—We met in a bar one night, and they attached themselves to John and me. Not a high recommendation, but I'm sure they're all right. Why do you ask?

MARY—Because I've just made an alarming discovery.

BOOTH—And what have you discovered, Mrs. Surratt?

MARY (*taking dagger out of knitting basket*)—This was found under John's mattress this morning. (*She takes out the money.*) Quite by accident I discovered this in a bag which he had packed and hidden away under the stairs. There is more money here than John or any one of his new friends could have lawfully earned in a year.

BOOTH (*taking money*)—Where do you think he got the money?

MARY—I don't know. I thought you might know.

BOOTH—Mrs. Surratt, there's nothing alarming in your discovery. (*Returns money.*) That money belongs to me.

MARY—It was in John's bag.

BOOTH—Safely hidden.

MARY—Why should John have money of yours?

BOOTH—It's quite simple. I'm buying some oil lands in Pennsylvania. I offered John a commission to go up and act as my agent.

MARY (*holding up the dagger*)—And this is yours, too?

BOOTH—No—my father once used it in "Macbeth." John admired it, and I gave it to him as a souvenir—months ago.

MARY—Why didn't he tell me all this?

BOOTH—Why didn't you ask him, Mrs. Surratt?

MARY—Isn't it a great deal of money to trust him with?

BOOTH (*leaning forward*)—Isn't your son trustworthy?

MARY—It isn't that I distrust John. It's just that I've come to distrust everyone. It's one of the awful things that war has done to me. Shaken my faith in what to expect of people. So I close the door and shut the violence outside. With my two children beside me, I can draw a circle around my happiness. But I find a weapon in my son's possession. My circle is broken. And I'm frightened.

BOOTH—There is no need to be frightened. If you really trust your son. Put the money back under the staircase; allow him to earn his commission.

MARY—Yes, you are quite right, Mr. Booth. (*Puts money and dagger in basket.*) I'll return the money and would you please not mention this to John? It would only antagonize him.

BOOTH—Certainly.

Booth is in a hurry, but he thinks he will have time to say good-by to John. As Mary goes to call her son she passes Payne, Herold and Atzerodt on the stairs. She stops to say good-by to them, and again to assure them their things will be all right left in the house. As she disappears up the stairs there is a flutter of excitement among the men. In a moment they have swarmed on Booth. What has happened? Why is he there? How much does Mrs. Surratt know?

Booth answers them quickly, but warily. He also has orders for them: David Herold, who knows the roads in lower Maryland, is to wait for him at the bridge. Johnny is being sent into Canada to wait for them. Atzerodt doesn't like that. Johnny was to help him. He thinks maybe he'll back out—

"It's too late, George," Booth tells him. "I've left a letter in my room with your name on it. All our names are on it. . . . Why risk this night's work and claim no recognition for our labor? The boy who fired the Ephesian Dome outlived in fame the pious fool who reared it, yet who knows his name?   We'll claim our authorship!"

"You shouldn't have done it!" protests Payne.

"It's done.   Our names are already written.   Let's waste no more time.   Be off, George."

"I'll be caught."

"Not if you play your part.   You will have fame and money for the rest of your life.   Don't wait any longer."

They have all gone now.   Booth, crossing to the work basket, takes out the dagger and puts it in an inside pocket.   John hurries down the stairs.   He had gone to Wilkes' hotel, but did not find him.   Yes, he had the horses, the fastest he could get.   He'll get the bag now, and they'll leave.   But Booth stops him—

"John—I won't need you tonight.   There's less risk if I venture this alone.   I've sent Herold ahead!"

"But I know all the back roads in Maryland—I know them by heart."

"Herold knows them, too."

"You said I could go with you tonight."

"Don't whimper, John.   It doesn't suit you."

"What will happen to me?"

"Take the money you're keeping for us to Montreal.   As soon as I can I'll let you know where I am."

"All right, if that's what you want."

"Good—I'll join you when I can.   You be out of Washington within half an hour."

"I'll leave in a few minutes.   Don't take too many chances, Wilkes."

" 'If it were done, when 'tis done, then it were well that it were done quickly,' " quotes Booth and he is gone.

For a moment John stands staring after him.   He has started for the staircase closet when he hears his mother on the stairs and turns toward the desk.   There is little need of Mary's coming down, he calls.   He will lock up.   Mary hesitates, but decides to come on.   She wants her work basket.   Being down she decides to stay a little and work on her knitting.   Which makes John nervous.   He doesn't see why she should want to stay.   He doesn't see why she should be interested in knowing where he had been all day.   Isn't he old enough to come and go without questioning? Why should she want to spy on him?

Mary protests that she has no intention of spying.   And if she wants to sit there and work for a little—it's her home.

"Well, it's not mine!" declares John, viciously.   He has started for the stair closet. He brings out his bag and takes his coat from a hook. "I'll go. And I won't come back!" he says, starting for the hall.

"You'll not find that money in your bag," Mary calls, without pausing with her knitting.

John has stopped. Putting the bag on the floor he kneels before it and searches it hurriedly. His face turns white with anger as he faces Mary. "Where is it?" he demands, hoarsely.

MARY—I've decided not to give it back to you. If this is what his influence does to you—you're better off without his help. I'll return the money to Mr. Booth instead.

JOHN—Mr. Booth!

MARY—He told me it was his . . . I . . . talked to him.

JOHN—You turned him against me. That's why he left alone. I'll hate you for this as long as I live.

MARY—John. You're angry now but—

JOHN—Where is it?

MARY—I've told you, I shall give it back to Mr. Booth myself.

JOHN—It's too late— WHERE DID YOU PUT IT?

MARY—Don't shout at me, John. (JOHN *turns from her and begins a frantic search of the room. He looks through desk. Then chest.*) Johnny—don't . . . Anna will hear you. (JOHN's *gaze falls on the knitting basket.* MARY *makes no attempt to stop him as he catches it up and dumps the contents on the table.*) Anna found it by accident. If you'd taken me into your confidence this wouldn't have happened. Johnny—listen to me—

JOHN—Not in this my lifetime. If you ever think of me, think of me as dead. (*He exits.*)

MARY—Wait, John. If I've been wrong, I'm sorry.

LOUIS (*coming downstairs as front door slams*)—I heard the door slam. Did Johnny go out again?

MARY—Yes.

LOUIS—Where has he gone to?

MARY—I don't know.   •

LOUIS—Mrs. Surratt—could I speak to you about Anna?

MARY—Louis, go back to your room, please.

LOUIS (*coming into the room*)—You could help me, Mrs. Surratt, if you would talk to her. She'd listen to you. You could make her feel differently about me.

MARY—I shall not talk to her. I'll not tell anyone what to do. I'll not make that mistake again. Louis, please go back to your room. (LOUIS *crosses to hall. He turns to look at* MARY *and then goes upstairs.*)

The curtain falls.

It is three hours later. A green-beaded table lamp casts a dim light over the Surratt living room. Mary is standing at the window. As she returns to the sofa, Anna appears on the stairs in her nightgown and robe. She had been awakened suddenly and is worried about her mother. Has she been waiting for Johnny again? No, she hasn't.

"If you were not waiting for Johnny, what were you waiting for?"

"I don't know, honey. I suppose I thought if I sat very still the world wouldn't move."

Mary would have Anna go back to bed before she catches cold, but Anna refuses to budge until her mother comes, too. With Johnny still out, Anna will lock the kitchen door and leave the front door open. A moment later Anna's scream is heard from the rear of the house. She comes running into the living room to report that there is someone coming up on the porch.

Anna has picked up the lamp and started to investigate when the kitchen doorway is slowly filled with armed men. Others are seen through the shadows to be coming into the front hall.

"What do you want?" Mary demands, backing into the room. "Who are you? Get out! Get out of here!"

They pay no attention to her. Capt. Smith, "a disheveled and belligerent officer," steps through the line of men and faces her.

CAPTAIN—Is this where John Surratt lives?
MARY—Yes.
CAPTAIN—Who are you?
MARY—I'm Mrs. Surratt. What do you want?
CAPTAIN—Where is your son?
MARY—I don't know.
CAPTAIN (*turning to soldiers*)—Search the house. (*He turns back to* MARY *as two of the soldiers start up the stairs.*) Who is she?
MARY—My daughter—Anna. What do you want with John?
CAPTAIN—The President was assassinated at the Ford's Theatre tonight by John Wilkes Booth. . . .
MARY—No!
CAPTAIN—There's a plot to murder the entire cabinet. I am here to place John Surratt under arrest. If you're hiding him,

you better turn him over to us.

MARY—What do you want with John?

CAPTAIN—We have the names of every one of the— (*He reads from a memorandum.*)   Lewis Payne, George Atzerodt and David Herold. Do they live here?

MARY—They . . . did.

CAPTAIN—Where are they now?

MARY—I don't know. They left tonight. You're making a mistake if you think my son is involved. (*A soldier comes downstairs pushing* LOUIS WEICHMANN *ahead of him.*)

SOLDIER—Found this man upstairs, sir.

LOUIS—What's happened? Why are they searching the house?

CAPTAIN—Is this your son?

MARY—This is Louis Weichmann—one of my boarders.

LOUIS—I've got my papers. . . . (*Taking identification papers from his pocket.*) I haven't done anything. I'm Louis Weichmann. (*Turning to* MARY.) What do they want? Why are they doing this?

MARY—Something terrible has happened, Louis. Mr. Lincoln has been killed.

LOUIS—But what are they looking here for?

MARY—They think John had something to do with it.

The Captain turns to Weichmann. Does he know where John Surratt is? No. A soldier comes from upstairs. He has found a coil of rope, a picture of John Wilkes Booth and a rifle hidden in one of the rooms. The picture belonged to her son, Mary admits.

The soldiers have picked up a man outside the house. He had started to enter and then to leave as soon as he saw the soldiers. He had asked for Mrs. Surratt. They drag him into the hallway. He is wearing a brown overcoat, his pants are tucked into boots, his head is covered with a stocking cap and his clothes are splashed with mud.

"Who are you? What's your name?" demands Captain Smith.

"My name is—Wood. I'm a working man."

"Where do you live? What do you want?"

"I don't live any place. I came . . . to see Mrs. Surratt."

"You came to see *Mrs.* Surratt?"

"Yes, sir."

"What for? What do you want with her?"

"Nothing. She sent for me. She wanted me to dig a ditch for her."

"Why, I never . . ." Mary is quick to protest.

"Do you know this man?" demands the Captain, turning on Mary.

"I never saw him before." Mary is trying to peer into the darkness of the hall.

"Are you sure?"

"I don't know the man, nor did I send for anyone."

Captain Smith walks over to the man in the hall and jerks the stocking cap from his head.

"It's Mr. Payne!" exclaims Weichmann.

"Who did you say it was?"

"It's Lewis Payne. He lives here."

"Place him under arrest! He's the man who stabbed the Secretary of State."

The soldiers have drawn their pistols and grabbed Payne. The Captain turns on the captive. Where is Booth? Where is John Surratt? Payne remains contemptuously silent.

"Take him away. If he attempts to escape shoot him!" He turns again to Mary. "Well . . . Madam . . . your lie betrayed you," he sneers.

"I didn't recognize him."

The Captain turns again to Weichmann. "What did she have to do with this murder?" he shouts.

"I don't know."

"What did she have to do with this murder?"

"I don't know," repeats Louis.

The Captain is standing before him, yelling: "What did she have to do with this murder? . . ."

Louis slowly sinks into a chair.

The curtain falls.

It is a few days later. In the Surratt living room Capt. Smith is sitting at the center table, figuring. A soldier guard is across the room.

The soldier reckons that Gen. Hogan must have arrested close to five hundred people the last week, but, as the Captain reminds him, five hundred people don't spell John Surratt. The soldier has also read in the paper that his pursuers had shot Booth in a barn in Virginia—shot him right through the neck! Too bad *they* couldn't have got Booth. It would have fattened their reward money.

"I've just been figurin' it out," says Capt. Smith. "Nabbing Payne and the Surratt woman doubles our shares. But there was ten of us caught them, so that means its divided by ten."

Gen. Holden, Gen. Ekin and Col. Burnett arrive. They have come for a final talk with Mary Surratt before ordering her to prison. While they are waiting to have Mary brought from upstairs a rock is thrown through the window. It is, Capt. Smith explains, a common occurrence. Crowds milling around outside; rocks thrown at windows. If it were not for the guard an angered people would undoubtedly have burned the house down days ago. Col. Burnett orders the guard doubled.

All three of the high officers take part in questioning a pale and nervous Mary. She protests that she has told them all there is to tell, but they persist. Where is her son hiding? She doesn't know. Is he with the rebels in Canada? She doesn't know where he is. Were there more than seven in the plot? She didn't even know there was a plot. If she had known, the President would be alive today—

"I'm telling you the truth. I have nothing to do with this terrible crime."

BURNETT—We would prefer not to prosecute a woman in this case. We would prefer to have you as our own witness.

HOLDEN—There is no sane or laudable reason why you should sacrifice yourself for the confederates who deserted you.

BURNETT (*placing confession on table in front of* MARY)—I have a full confession here. If you sign it, and assist your government in this case against these seven, you will earn your freedom.

HOLDEN—Confess that this crime was planned under your roof and with your full knowledge.

MARY—I don't know where it was planned.

BURNETT—We're offering you a chance to save your own life.

EKIN—You are implicated in one of the blackest crimes in history.

HOLDEN—If we freed you now, you'd be stoned in the streets.

BURNETT—Yet you sit here, protected by the government you've wronged, and hesitate.

MARY—I don't hesitate. How can I sign a confession condemning men whose guilt or innocence I know nothing about?

HOLDEN—Very well, you will be transferred to the prison on the Arsenal Grounds this afternoon.

BURNETT—You will be tried by a military commission under a single charge with the other conspirators held there—as equally guilty with them—as if you had pulled the trigger yourself.

HOLDEN (*turning to soldier in hall*)—Sergeant, hold her here until we send for her.

BURNETT (*to* HOLDEN)—Well, we've done what we could. We've given her a last chance. (*To soldier.*) When she is transferred to the prison, see that a hood is placed over her head.

Anna Surratt, not being under arrest, had been permitted to leave the house. Now she is back. With her is Senator Reverdy Johnson. She had told Capt. Smith that she wanted to see Father Wiget of her church, but she had gone straight for the Senator. Reverdy, it appears, had not recognized the Widow Surratt to whom the newspapers referred as the Mary he had known. If he had he would have been there sooner—

"Mary," he says, "I opened my door this morning and this child stood there twisting that small pink necklace at her throat and looking at me out of the past. Suddenly I was nineteen again. I swear to you, Mary, I knew she was your daughter before she uttered a sound."

Anna has gone to her room. The Sergeant in charge of the guard agrees to wait in the hall. The Senator and Mary are alone and eager with explanations. Why had Mary not sent for her old friend before? Because she did not feel she had the right. Was not their old friendship a claim? Did she not remember that she was his first love? Mary had not forgotten.

REVERDY (*taking her hands*)—I've often thought of you—and wondered what time and people had done to you. But somehow never thought of you with a daughter, or this son. Mary—do you think he had anything to do with this tragic plot?

MARY—I don't really know, Reverdy. He may be guilty, and if he is—do I really want him caught?

REVERDY—You haven't a choice, Mary. I made a few investigations this morning. You've become a political pawn. The Secretary of War is determined to establish the precedent of a military trial in this case. He intends to convict everyone involved.

MARY—But why, Reverdy? I've committed no crime.

REVERDY—Mary—let me explain. Before the war, Congress was dominated by Southern Senators. The present Cabinet doesn't want that to happen again, now that the war is won. If the Secretary of War can establish this precedent, he will then have the power to prevent any Southern leader he disfavors from

returning to Congress simply by trying him for treason before a
Military Commission. This trial opens the way to political control of the country by the Secretary of War.

MARY—I cannot believe that I can be condemned for political
reasons.

REVERDY—That crowd outside have condemned you already,
Mary. The Government has offered 100 thousand dollars reward
for conviction. And the newspapers demand that you be punished
as an example to the South for striking a blow after surrender.
The Cabinet couldn't ask for a more popular case on which to
stake its future. We have everything against us.

MARY—We?

REVERDY—Naturally, I intend to defend you.

MARY—But General Holden is appointing counsel for me.

REVERDY—You've a right to choose your own counsel. You're
going to need the best lawyer in the country. (*Smiling.*) May I
admit that I'm that lawyer?

MARY—I know you are, Reverdy. I can't tell you what your
willingness to defend me means. But if they condemn me already
without knowing the truth, won't they condemn you for defending
me?

REVERDY—That wouldn't prevent me. I would fight for your
life had I never seen you before. (*Takes her hand.*) But I have
seen you before. Mary—allow me the great honor of defending
you.

MARY—Once in everyone's life something so unexpected, so
kind and generous happens that it seems to make up for the unfairness of a lifetime. It can be a single word, spoken at the right
moment. But it's enough. Your kindness is more than a word—
and my gratitude more than—

REVERDY—No, Mary—it is I who am grateful. Nothing gives
me greater pride—than to appear as counsel for Mary Surratt.
And I promise you—no harm shall come to you. (*A rock comes
crashing through the window, another through the door. Outside
voices can be heard shouting.*)

SOLDIER—Burn the house down! (MARY *looks frightened.*
REVERDY *puts his arms around her.*)

The curtain falls.

ACT II

It is a few days later. "A large square room on the third floor
of the Old Penitentiary building has been converted, for the pur-

poses of this trial, into a crudely arranged courtroom. A prisoner's dock has been constructed along one wall. (To the audience
left.) . . . The only door to the room divides this platform into
two sections. Mary Surratt occupies the smaller section. The
seven men prisoners, George Atzerodt, David Herold, Lewis
Payne, Dr. Samuel Mudd, Edward Spangler, Michael O'Laughlin
and Samuel Arnold, occupy the larger section of the dock."

On the opposite side of the room a series of flat tables have been
placed together. Behind these sit the nine solemn members of the
Military Commission in full dress uniform. They are Gens. Harris,
Tompkins, Glendenin, Howe, Hunter, Foster, Kautz, Ekin and
Wallace.

At a table in front of the Commission sit Judge Advocate Gen.
Holden and his assistant, Judge Bennett.

In the center of the room the witness stand is so placed the witnesses must face the Commission while testifying. Between the
witness stand and the prisoners' dock is a table for the use of the
defense counsel.

The prisoners are chained and hooded, their wrists connected
with iron bars manacled to the railing. A detail of six soldiers is
variously deployed at strategic points of the courtroom. Major
General Hunter, a large, aggressive officer, represents the Commission as prosecutor.

At the command of Gen. Hunter the hoods are removed from the
heads of the prisoners, each answering to his name as called by
Col. Burnett.

"Admit counsel for Mary Surratt," orders Hunter. As soon as
Reverdy Johnson has taken his place, Gen. Hunter turns in explanation to the Commission. He has received a note of protest from
one member of the Commission objecting to the admission of
Reverdy Johnson as counsel before that court, and requesting that
he withdraw from the case. The note is from Brig. Gen. Harris.

Asked by Senator Johnson on what grounds his objection is
based, Gen. Harris explains that, in his opinion, "when an active
representative of the government voluntarily takes advantage of
his position to champion a traitor and discredit his country" he
should be stopped.

"May I interrupt to assure the gentleman that I am as filled
with revulsion at this murder of my President as any one of you,"
says Reverdy. "But I am filled with equal revulsion, as Lincoln
himself would be if he were alive, at the idea of sacrificing an innocent woman in place of the guilty."

"I have not finished. I say a man who, unsolicited, offers his services to traitors, violates his oath of loyalty and renders himself unacceptable to this court."

"Gentlemen, I am confused. Am I on trial? Who gives you the jurisdiction to declare me incompetent to appear before you? By what right do you decide my loyalty?"

"We are empowered, by the order constituting this Commission, to establish our own laws and rules of procedure."

Having taken that oath in the Senate of the United States, in the Circuit Court and the Supreme Court, and having the right to appear in all the courts of the country, Reverdy does not see why his right to appear before this Commission should be questioned—

"I do not think that in defending Mary Surratt I am any more disloyal than is any member of this court disloyal in giving her a fair trial."

There is a slight suspicion that that remark conceals an intentional slur, but it is finally overlooked, both by Gen. Holden and by Gen. Harris. Reverdy is permitted to proceed.

The first witness called is Maj. Henry Rathbone. A young officer in full dress uniform takes the stand and repeats the oath. He was, he testifies, in the box with President Lincoln the night of the assassination at Ford's Theatre.

"I was watching the action on the stage very intently when I heard the discharge of a pistol behind me. I looked around and through the smoke I saw a man standing in the back of the President. Mr. Lincoln had slumped down in his chair. The man shouted something which I thought was 'Thus will it ever be with tyrants'—"

" 'Thus will it ever be with tyrants—'?"

"I believe that is what he said. I sprang forward and seized him. He made a violent thrust at my breast with a dagger. I attempted to hold him but my arm was bleeding and he managed to free himself. Then he leaped over the edge of the box to the stage below."

Turned over to Reverdy, Maj. Rathbone admits that he does not know Mary Surratt, nor does he recognize any of the other prisoners. He does, however, identify the dagger as the one he picked up on the floor of the theatre box.

Louis Weichmann is called. Facing the prisoners Louis is positive in his identification of Mary Surratt, Lewis Payne, George Atzerodt and David Herold. The others he had never seen before. He had made the acquaintance of those he recognizes when John

Surratt brought them home to board at his mother's, in March of that year.

HOLDEN—Did Booth frequently meet these men at Mrs. Surratt's?

LOUIS—Yes, sir.

HOLDEN—Did they talk freely in the presence of others?

LOUIS—They usually met in Johnny's room.

HOLDEN—And you were excluded from these meetings?

LOUIS—Always.

HOLDEN—Did Mrs. Surratt know of these secret meetings?

LOUIS—Always.

HOLDEN—Did she encourage her son's friendship with Booth?

LOUIS—Yes, sir.

HOLDEN—When did you last see John Wilkes Booth alive?

LOUIS—About an hour or so before the President was assassinated.

HOLDEN—Where did you see him?

LOUIS—In Mrs. Surratt's living room.

HOLDEN—Do you know why he called?

LOUIS—Mrs. Surratt had sent for him.

HOLDEN—She sent for him?

LOUIS—Yes, sir.

HOLDEN—Do you know what they discussed?

LOUIS—No, sir. Mrs. Surratt asked me to leave them alone.

HOLDEN—Did she state any reason for wanting a private interview?

LOUIS—She said she had important business to discuss.

HOLDEN—She sent for him an hour before the assassination to discuss a private and important matter?

LOUIS—Yes, sir.

HOLDEN (*picking up dagger from table*)—Can you identify this weapon?

LOUIS—Yes, sir.

HOLDEN—Will you state where you first saw it?

LOUIS—I found it hidden under John Surratt's mattress.

HOLDEN—What day was this?

LOUIS—Friday the fourteenth.

HOLDEN—What did you do with it?

LOUIS—I gave it to Mrs. Surratt.

HOLDEN—Did you tell her where you had found it?

LOUIS—Yes, sir.

HOLDEN—Did she take the dagger from you?

Louis—Yes, sir.

Holden—What did she do with it?

Louis—She hid it in some knitting she had.

Weichmann is also quick to admit that he was present when the men had captured Payne, and that he had no difficulty in recognizing him.

On cross-examination Louis explains to Reverdy that he had boarded with Mary Surratt ever since he left school; that he had been a room-mate of John Surratt's both at school and at the boarding house; that they had been friends for seven years—

"You went to school together—you roomed together—you ate together—you slept together. If John Surratt were involved in such a plot, wouldn't you have been more likely to have known about it than his own mother?"

"I object to that question," objects Col. Burnett. "The witness is not on trial for knowledge of a conspiracy."

"If the court pleases—I wish to show that if Louis Weichmann did not suspect the plot—it supports the theory that Mary Surratt had even less opportunity to suspect one."

"The witness' answer at best would be an assumption. I've yet to find assumption constituting evidence."

"Objection sustained," intones Gen. Hunter.

Reverdy takes Louis back to his discovery of the dagger under John's mattress and his bringing it to Mrs. Surratt. Did he see Mrs. Surratt give the dagger to Booth? No. Did he hear any part of her conversation with Booth? No.

"Then, for all you know, they could have talked about anything under the sun?"

"I hardly think she would have sent Booth an urgent message an hour before the assassination to discuss the weather," interposes Col. Burnett.

"Were you offered part of a hundred thousand dollar reward to testify at this trial?" asks Reverdy.

"I offered my services to the government with no thought of reward," answers Louis, "because I considered it a patriotic duty."

"Did you consider your duty to a woman who had befriended you?"

"Mrs. Surratt forfeited my friendship by placing me in this position. If I must choose between friendship and my government, I choose my government." That is all for Louis Weichmann.

Captain William Smith is called. The Captain remembers in

detail the events of the night of April 14, when, following the discovery of a letter left by Booth in his hotel room—the letter containing the names of the conspirators—he and his men had surrounded the Surratt home.

He recounts the capture of Lewis Payne and Mrs. Surratt's positive statement that she did not know him.

"Was he standing in full view of her when she denied knowing him?"

"She was within a few feet of him."

When the witness is turned over to him, Reverdy Johnson takes up first the matter of the Booth letter. Was Mary Surratt's name mentioned in that? The name of Surratt was mentioned, but not Mary Surratt specifically, Capt. Smith admits. And how was Lewis Payne dressed when captured? He wore a gray coat, a cap made out of a shirt sleeve on his head, a sweater and a good pair of boots, with black pants tucked in, as the Captain recalls. Anyone who had ever seen him before would recognize him in such a garb. Yes, there was a light in the hall—a light "turned on at full head." Yes, the Captain is sure the coat was gray—Confederate gray. He knows it could not possibly have been brown, or brown and white.

Reverdy has taken a coat from the table. He crosses to the Commission with it. "I ask the Commission to observe the coat taken from the prisoner Payne, at the time of his arrest—*and so marked*. You will observe that it is a *brown* and *white* coat, and *not* gray. I offer this as defense exhibit A. I wish to repeat a question. If you saw a man who was customarily well-dressed present himself in the night with a sleeve pulled over his head and his pants tucked into his boots—would you immediately recognize him?"

"Certainly I would."

"How?"

"You can always recognize a person after you have seen him once."

"But you couldn't remember the right color of his coat once you'd seen it."

"The light in the hall was dim. I couldn't see as clearly as—"

" '*The light in the hall was dim.*' No more questions."

Henry Von Steinacker is called and sworn. Von Steinacker testifies that he had joined the Confederate forces at the outbreak of the rebellion; that he was stationed at Andersonville, Georgia; that he had seen hundreds of Union soldiers mistreated there—

"The sick and the wounded had their shoes taken from them

and were forced to live in a swamp. They had to sleep in mud without blankets or shelter. They were given very little to eat, and that was rancid."

"I object to this whole line of questioning!" protests Reverdy, with vigor. "It is intended to prejudice a Commission made up of Northern officers and has nothing to do with present testimony. Mary Surratt is *not* on trial to answer for the crimes and offenses of an army of which she was not a member! Nor is she on trial for being born in the South."

"If the court pleases—I will make a single remark," answers Col. Burnett. "History itself attests how kindred are the crimes of rebellion against a nation and the assassination of its chief magistrate."

"According to that reasoning, every man who took up the Southern cause did so to assassinate the President."

"Everybody who entered into the rebellion entered into it to assassinate everybody else that represented the Government, whether it was in the field—the Navy or in the White House."

"But, gentlemen, Mary Surratt did not belong to the Army."

The Commission holds that the testimony is germane. Steinacker is permitted to continue with his lurid description of what happened to Andersonville prisoners. Reverdy objects strenuously, but is told he must either accept or withdraw. He accepts.

Steinacker recalls having met John Wilkes Booth accidentally in a tavern, of falling into conversation with him and of hearing Booth predict that "Old Abe would go up the spout and the Confederacy would gain its independence." Booth had named as two of his confederates "John Surratt and his mother, Mary Surratt."

Taking the witness, Reverdy proceeds to discredit much of his testimony by tricking him into a series of confused statements. Among them is one that he had served at Andersonville under Gen. Jubal Bentley. Granted permission to call a new witness, Reverdy bids the Provost Marshal summon Gen. Jubal Bentley, now being held in the building used for the trial. Bentley, wearing a rather shabby Confederate uniform, takes the stand and is sworn.

In answer to Reverdy's first question the General announces that he is Maj. Gen. Jubal Bentley of the Confederate Army; that he is now a prisoner of war, having been captured at Nashville about the fifteenth of January and held in Washington since that time. Before he can continue Gen. Howe of the Commission presents an objection. It is based on the fact that Jubal

Bentley had been educated at the National Military Academy at the government's expense; that he took the oath of allegiance on receiving his commission, and that at the outbreak of the Civil War he forgot his debt and joined the Confederate forces—

". . . He comes to testify here, his hands red with blood of his Northern countrymen. I consider his presence here an insult to every officer on this Commission."

"And I regard it as a contemptible gesture on the part of the Hon. Mr. Johnson," adds Gen. Harris.

"May I remind the court that the prosecution itself has introduced witnesses who have borne arms against the government. What, then, makes my witness different?"

"He is incompetent to testify."

"I think the Judge Advocate will bear me out on this point of the law: Before a witness can be rendered incompetent he must have been convicted by a judicial proceeding."

"If the witness cannot legally be declared incompetent," suggests Col. Glendenin, "I don't see how we can vote on the motion."

"Let the witness testify—for the sake of this investigation—not out of consideration for the witness," suggests Gen. Wallace.

"I withdraw my objection," mumbles Gen. Howe.

Despite continued objections, Gen. Bentley is finally permitted to insist that he was never at Andersonville, as the Confederate records will show.

"I object to this line of questioning," interrupts Col. Burnett. "Counsel insinuates that Von Steinacker is a perjured witness— that he was either coerced or bribed by the Government to give testimony."

"That is exactly what I am insinuating," snaps Reverdy. "Von Steinacker is a liar coached to perjure himself on the stand. He was not an officer under Gen. Bentley—he was a private—he was not in Andersonville or Richmond and he never heard of Mary Surratt in his whole miserable life."

The court is considerably stirred by this allegation of the witness Von Steinacker's perjury. It is again demanded that Senator Johnson apologize. Reverdy refuses to apologize. If the Generals will not accept his exposure of the Von Steinacker perjury, he demands the recall of the witness. The Commission cannot recall Von Steinacker because he already has been given his freedom, and left the building.

"Gentlemen, I should like to ask a question," pleads Reverdy. "If Mary Surratt is not to be given a fair hearing, why in God's name bring her here in chains to suffer a mock trial! Why not save everyone time and pass sentence now?"

"Mr. Johnson—if you find the manner in which this trial is conducted so offensive, I have suggested before—and I believe I speak for the other officers of the Commission—that you withdraw as counsel for Mary Surratt. We find the manner in which you are conducting your case equally offensive."

"I shall not withdraw."

"Then the court expects your apology."

Reverdy is silent for a moment. "Gentlemen—I offer my apologies," he then submits, with obvious reluctance.

Anna Surratt is called. Failing, through Anna, to establish the nature of the jealous friendship of Weichmann for her brother Johnny, by reason of frequent objections, Reverdy is able to establish the fact of Mary Surratt's impaired eyesight, and of the dimness of the light in the hall in which Lewis Payne was standing when Mary denied that she knew him. When the prosecutors hammer home the damaging charge that Mary had offered to "hide" the belongings of the prisoners in her basement, Anna is reduced to sobbing. Further testimony is unnecessary decides Gen. Hunter.

Father Wiget is called. "He is a small, rotund man with remarkable poise," and he briskly swears to tell nothing but the truth, so help him God. Father Wiget is the president of Gonzaga College. He has known Mary Surratt for about twelve years. Yes, he had seen her the morning of April 14, which was Good Friday. He had seen her as she entered church, though she had not seen him. Yes, indeed, he is acquainted with Mary Surratt's general reputation. Accusing her of so monstrous a crime as the assassination is nonsense . . . pure nonsense.

"Have you ever heard Mary Surratt utter a single loyal sentiment?" demands Gen. Holden.

"Our discussions are never political."

"Then for all you know of her political thoughts her reputation might be that of an intensely disloyal woman?"

"We have never discussed witchcraft. Does it then follow that she must be a witch?"

"But you only know her reputation as a Christian?"

"My dear man, Christianity isn't a one-sided cassock worn before the altar. It's a way of thinking carried *beyond* church walls . . . inseparable from life . . . and I find the absence of it here appalling!"

"That will be all."

"God bless you," murmurs Father Wiget, but through clenched teeth.

Reverdy Johnson has arisen and faced the Commission. "Mr. President and Gentlemen of the Commission: I should like at this time to put Mary Surratt on the stand, and request that she be sworn as a witness."

"Bring the prisoner to the stand," commands Gen. Hunter.

Mary's irons are unlocked and she makes her way to the witness stand. She is still rubbing her wrists as she begins her testimony. She is, she says, under Reverdy's prompting, the sole support of her children, neither of whom is of legal age. She takes in boarders. Occasionally her son John has found work, but it was difficult for a Southern boy to find anything to do during the war. Why did John not join the Confederate Army? Because she had begged him not to. She did not want him killed.

"How did your son meet John Wilkes Booth?"

"Mr. Booth was playing at one of the theatres here. John admired him and waited outside the stage door. When Mr. Booth came out he spoke to him. Mr. Booth liked him. He took him for some supper. They became friends."

REVERDY—Was Booth a man of pleasing manner?

MARY—He was a very handsome man . . . he had great charm.

REVERDY—Was Mr. Booth the type of man who would use this charm to influence an impressionable younger man?

HARRIS—I fail to see what difference it makes whether Booth was as charming as Adonis or repugnant as Medusa.

HUNTER—What is the purpose of these questions?

REVERDY—I wish to show why Mary Surratt sent for Booth on the night of the assassination.

HARRIS—Did she send for him because he was charming?

REVERDY—She sent for him because she knew that Booth's influence over John Surratt was greater than her own.

HUNTER—Let the witness answer your questions.

REVERDY—Mrs. Surratt— Why did you send for Booth that night?

MARY—I felt that my son was in danger. We had found a dagger under his mattress. I sent for Mr. Booth to learn if John was in trouble.

HARRIS—Why didn't you question your son?

MARY (*hesitating*)—He was a strange boy.

HARRIS—I'll not challenge that.

MARY—I don't know if I can make you understand. When he was little he never ran to me when he was hurt. If he was ill or sick with fever he never told me. I had to discover it for myself. He fought affection. I never knew what he thought. I never knew what unimportant thing became important to him. I loved him in a dark house. I only knew that deep down inside he was frightened and despised those who suspected it.

REVERDY—Did you show Booth the dagger you had found?

MARY—Yes. He said he had given it to John as a present.

REVERDY—Did that satisfy you?

MARY—I wanted to be satisfied.

REVERDY—Did you return the dagger to Booth?

MARY—No.

REVERDY—Do you know how he secured possession of it?

MARY—He must have taken it when I was out of the room.

REVERDY—Did you at that time—or at any time—have knowledge of a treasonable purpose or act or conspiracy?

MARY—No.

Mary recalls her experiences with the prisoners Payne, Herold and Atzerodt. They had boarded with her a little under a month. Yes, she had given them permission to leave their belongings in her basement when they claimed to have found employment in Virginia. Her last meeting with Payne was the night of the assassination, when she did not recognize him in the half light of the hall. She could not have known of his attempt on the life of Secretary of State Seward. She thought Payne was in Virginia.

"Were you offered immunity if you would testify against the accused?"

"I object to that question," interrupts Col. Burnett. "Even if such an offer had been made, it doesn't establish the woman's innocence."

"Mary Surratt, are you guilty of the charge for which you face this commission?"

"The only treason in which I have ever taken part has been this trial. And that is against my will." Mary's voice has risen in cold anger. "The only traitors I know as such I have met here."

"Are you speaking of these officers, Madam?" demands Gen. Harris.

"I am. For you betray a trust. You must know that I am innocent."

"We know nothing of the sort."

"Then listen to me: I have committed no crime!   I have committed no crime!   I have committed no crime!"

"We have heard your claim, Madam.   We have also heard the evidence."

"No, you haven't.   Nor do I expect you to."

"Come—come!   That's enough.   Any more questioning, Mr. Johnson?"

"That is all."

In response to Gen. Holden's cross-examination, Mary admits that no one overheard her conversation with Booth.   Nor was there any witness to her claim that she did not give the dagger to Booth.   Why was she sitting up the night of the assassination? Because she was worried.   Not because she feared John would be caught—because she wanted to think.

Holden takes up the point of Mary's poor eyesight.   If it is so hard for her to see, how can she sew—or knit—at night?   Because she can knit without watching what she is doing, says Mary, her nervousness palpably mounting.

"With the court's permission I should like to try an experiment," Gen. Holden is saying.

"Very well."

HOLDEN (*taking a black silk handkerchief from his pocket*)— This woman has based her claim of innocence on poor eyesight. Yet it is well established that she frequently knits.   Her answer for this is that she is able to handle the needles without watching her work.

REVERDY—I object to this demonstration!

HOLDEN—May I ask why?

REVERDY—You are requesting that the Commission accept her entire innocence or guilt on the results of a single experiment that is savage in its unfairness.

HUNTER—I fail to see what is unfair in allowing her to prove her innocence.

REVERDY—The subject is in a highly nervous condition . . . she has been harassed and threatened every day for weeks . . . her wrists are sore and bruised by iron bands she is forced to wear . . . she is in no mental or physical condition for such a test!

HUNTER—Objection overruled.   You may proceed with the demonstration.

HOLDEN (*tying handkerchief over* MARY'S *eyes; takes up knitting*)—I have the scarf here which Mrs. Surratt was knitting on the night the President was murdered. (*Touching* MARY'S *arm.*) Mrs. Surratt, you will take these needles—and show the court how you are able to knit without watching your hands. (MARY *holds knitting for a moment trying to steady herself.*) We are waiting, Mrs. Surratt.

REVERDY—General Hunter—

HUNTER—Your objection has been overruled, Mr. Johnson.

Reverdy grips the table and watches Mary. Her hands are trembling. She holds the needles poised and then begins. Her knees can be seen trembling under the folds of her dress. The needles become hopelessly ensnarled, and in attempting to straighten the yarn, she drops the knitting to the floor. Mary buries her blindfolded eyes in her hands.

MARY (*crying, reaching out trying to find work*)—I'm frightened. I'm frightened. Where is my work? (*Rises.*) Give me my work!

The curtain falls.

ACT III

It is midnight, three weeks later. Members of the Commission are milling about the trial room, some with the collars of their uniforms open, several of them fanning themselves vigorously. There is considerable disorder and a lamp on the table has replaced the gas chandelier as a source of light.

The talk is of the verdict. Gen. Foster can't understand just why Gen. Harris is so determined to hang Mary Surratt. Whatever they say, whatever the evidence may seem to indicate, hanging this woman is in the nature of a vindictive sentence.

"She kept the nest in which the egg was hatched," growls Gen. Harris. "I think Gen. Foster has mercy and weakness confused."

"She's a woman. I think we should consider that," ventures Gen. Kautz.

"It seems to me," says Gen. Hunter, "that if we let the sex of the accused influence our judgment, we are encouraging a dangerous practice. It amounts to an invitation hereafter for assassins to employ women, knowing they would be less severely punished."

Senator Reverdy Johnson has requested that he be admitted. Harris is for refusing the request. Foster and Glendenin would be lenient. "No one will criticize us for generosity," says Foster.

On being admitted, Reverdy explains that he had spent the entire day at the White House trying to see the President. He had tried to see the Secretary of War, but was barred there, too. He has come now to throw himself on the Commission's mercy. He also would like to call their attention to one final injunction. Are they sure they have the right to pass judgment on Mary Surratt? Aren't they denying Mary her constitutional right to a public trial? She has committed no military crime.

"You have no more legal right to try Mrs. Surratt than would nine policemen, sitting in the back room of a police station, have the right to try and to condemn any citizen they happened to suspect."

HARRIS—I am not as learned in constitutional law as eminent counsel, but I do know that civil rights have always been secondary to military law. Especially in time of war.

REVERDY—Do you assume that constitutional guarantees were designed only for a state of peace?

HARRIS—If not—why do we have laws of war?

REVERDY—I have never heard of *laws* of war. War is a negation of law. The rights of the individual are more in peril during a period of war than at any other time. There is no greater threat to personal liberty than war. That is why we must be jealous of the constitutional limitations of power. There can be no exception, or the door is open to tyranny.

HUNTER (*rising*)—Mr. Johnson, we cannot and do not intend to decide upon our authority to try Mrs. Surratt.

REVERDY (*angrily*)—Then if you pass judgment on her—honest as that judgment may be—you are each and every one of you personally responsible for whatever happens to her.

WALLACE—I, for one, should like to say that I have faced death on the battlefield and am not likely to cringe at facing responsibility.

HUNTER—Mr. Johnson—we have already found Mrs. Surratt guilty of treason. Our concern at the moment is to decide what sentence to pass upon her. I must ask you to conclude briefly whatever else you have to say. We have found her guilty.

REVERDY (*gripping the side of the table*)—Gentlemen—if at any time during this long trial I have seemed abrupt—or appeared discourteous—I tender my apologies. What I have said and what I have done in Mary Surratt's defense has not been an

attack upon you or my country. It has been an attack on what
I believe abhorrent to a free people. In this respect, her cause is
the cause of every citizen. (*He pauses.*) We are given but one
life. We are given a world filled with pleasure that makes life
desirable. When you sit down to determine the taking away
of that which you did not give, and which once taken you cannot
restore, you consider a subject as solemn as you will find in the
range of human thought. But there is more to consider. We
have struggled through centuries of ignorance and terror to where
life is made secure and worth living—*by a faith in justice.* Far
greater than anything man has wrought from his surroundings,
is that concept of justice. He may lose his belief in God and
still find life endurable. He can be robbed of his belief in love
and the goodness of man and still survive. But render justice
meaningless and you destroy the last of his faiths. In self-defense
he must turn back to violence for survival. This room is filled
with a million ghosts. The dead and the unborn plead for a just
world. It has been over two thousand years since we were told
that the race is not to the swift nor the battle to the strong nor
justice to the innocent. Is that to be the hopeless law of life?
Surely we have made a little progress in all these years. Surely
justice can be the reward of the innocent. I beg you to pause—
to listen above the cries for vengeance and hear the voices of
these gentle ghosts.

After a moment, he slowly turns and starts to leave as the
curtain falls.

The next day, a few minutes before noon, Father Wiget is with
Mary in her cell. She has not found it easy to find comfort in
his words or in his arguments—

"It isn't courage I ask for," she says, with some resentment.
"I can easily die without it. I ask for some reason or meaning
in what has happened to me. I will not bow my head and say,
'For this unjust death, O Lord, I thank thee.' I ask why. Why?
(*Her voice is softer.*) If I hurt you, Father, I am sorry, but
I am deeply hurt myself."

"There must be times, Mary, when faith is greater than wisdom. God may not intend for you to understand."

"Why should He deny me the meager mercy of understanding?
I've done nothing for which I should be punished. Is He so
vain that He must test me? How ungodlike of God."

"Do you condemn God for not conforming to man-made concepts of law and justice? Surely, that is a great presumption."

"Then what am I to believe? I've broken no law. Should I have fought deceit with deceit? Is hatred the only weapon with which to fight hatred? I have kept faith only to find that life belongs to the arrogant—that goodness and kindness are the virtues of the stupid."

The guard has admitted Anna Surratt. She rushes to her mother's arms in some excitement. Father Wiget has told her that Johnny Surratt has been found. Surely that will make a difference. If Johnny's found will they let Mary come home?

Mary is calm. Her heart is beating fast as the hour of noon approaches. If Johnny is found, let Anna never reproach him.

"Tell him that I didn't mind," says Mary. "Tell him that I felt no bitterness toward him. Tell him that I loved him—my wretched . . . frightened . . . son . . ."

"I can't," protests Anna. A moment later she adds: "I won't listen to you. You're coming home. You can sit in a chair by the window, while I do all the work. We'll make you wear a nice dress. And I'll fix your hair."

Anna has taken the coral necklace off and hooked it around her mother's neck. "We'll make you forget this mean and ugly place. . . . There . . . you look lovelier already."

The guard has opened the door to admit Reverdy Johnson. In answer to Anna's excited question about Johnny, Reverdy speaks with some difficulty. Johnny was never caught—

". . . We traced him to Canada, only to find out that he has fled to Rome," reports Reverdy. "He never intended to come back to help you, Mary. . . . The State Department refuses to extradite him. I demanded a stay of execution. A writ was denied me. I have pleaded and threatened. The War Department is determined to rush this sentence through. . . . There is no one left to whom I can turn."

"If you had found my son and brought him back to me, they might have spared my life but they would have demanded his," says Mary. "There never was much choice. . . ."

Mary's nerves have snapped. "No! No! No! I can't accept it," she cries hysterically, turning to Reverdy. "Nothing in my life prepared me for this. There were many times when I was a child that I was desperately ill. But I lived. I might have died a thousand times before today, but each time I escaped. For what was I saved? Only now to discover that life is without point or purpose? I cannot go to my death bewildered. I cannot die ignored. I cannot! I cannot! It's wrong! It's wrong! It's wrong!"

With utter despair in her voice she has turned to the wall and is clinging to the iron rings embedded in the stone.

"Mary—Mary— Don't let them drag you from your cell!" Reverdy pleads, catching her hands and holding her in his arms. "Mary, an incredible thing has happened to you and no words of mine can make it right." His voice softens as she is quieted. "But I beg you to consider a high purpose that sometimes rises from the grossest wrong. We know—you and I—that injustice has always been a part of life. It's the pattern of the blind weavers. And we know—you and I—that each generation suffers a countless number of heroic men to die for no heroic cause. Men with no names in unmarked graves. But the sum of their lost lives is not all waste. The time comes when the weight of their numbers alone stirs the conscience of the world. (*She looks up at him.*) I can't promise you a martyr's recognition. The story of Mary Surratt may never be known, but I do promise you a place among the mass of men whose needless deaths point to the flaw in our design. You endow us with indignation. You keep small fires burning in the dark corners of history. You send our hatred of injustice flaming. You frighten us into building a safer home."

MARY—Then it's enough. How vain of me to have expected so much from this one life. How ungrateful to the forgotten.

REVERDY—And so we come to the moment that was not yet due. When an unfinished life narrows to a second. This is the moment that lends your life meaning. It is yours to claim for eternity.

WIGET (*entering as door is opened by the Officer*)—It's time, Mary. The guards are here.

REVERDY—I went away from you when we were young. I should like you to know that the heart that was young dies with you.

WIGET—The guards are here, Mary.

MARY (*looking up*)—I shall be ready in a moment.

Father Wiget has stepped out of the cell into the corridor. Mary takes Anna's face in her hands and kisses her. She takes the coral necklace off her neck and puts it on Anna. "It has

taken so long. From the bottom of the sea. Coral upon coral
. . . upon coral . . . How far is the surface?"

Anna has gone to Reverdy as Mary moves toward the cell door
to join Father Wiget.

"How far is the surface?" she is repeating.

THE CURTAIN FALLS

CHRISTOPHER BLAKE

A Drama in Two Acts

By Moss Hart

IT would be pretty difficult to determine just what started the run on fantastic plays this theatre season of 1946-47. It may have been the war, on which so many motivations are being blamed. It may have been the success of previous stories told fantastically, both in the theatre and on the screen. But it was probably due to the familiar situation of authors seeking novel themes and backgrounds—"Something new," "Something different," as they say—plus the restlessness and mystery that have afflicted truth-searching humans from the beginning of time.

In the case of Moss Hart and his "Christopher Blake" it may easily have been his success with that fascinating study of psychoanalysis which resulted in the widely popular "Lady in the Dark," and the triumph of Gertrude Lawrence as the mentally distraught heroine. Or it may have been the result of Mr. Hart's intimacy with and sympathy for a friend during the latter's quite distressing adventure in the divorce court. It could not reasonably have stemmed from the author's personal brooding. He had a happy though short childhood, having been nudged by fate into the workers' world in his early teens. He has never lived much with children, nor had any of his own. It was natural, however, that he should be attracted to the theme of this play, which aims to depict such possible fantasies as might disturb the thought and imagination of a boy who is asked to make a choice between his father and mother as to the one he prefers to live with after they have separated. As a dramatist Mr. Hart is sensitive to human values and the characteristic reactions of people he feels he knows well.

"Christopher Blake" was produced in New York in early December. The first performances followed the form which has been used in making this digest. Later there was a rearrangement of scenes which started the action with the scene in court, in place of beginning with Christopher's highly imaginative and colorful picturing of himself as a national hero.

As this year book is really a historical as well as a factual record of the Broadway season, your editor did not deem it wise to take a hand with Mr. Hart in the rearrangement of the material. Audience interest has undoubtedly been improved and stimulated by the change, but neither the play's subject nor the author's argument has been affected.

In this original version of the drama we first meet Christopher, a lad of twelve years, on the grounds of the White House as they have been decorated in honor of such a medal-presenting ceremony as has been frequently duplicated during the war years.

". . . A warm Spring sunlight streams down over the lawn and back portico of the White House as though it, too, were aware of the occasion and took pleasure in being part of it. Never have the lawns seemed so green, nor have the tall, white columns ever gleamed so whitely. The Portico itself is ablaze with color, as the flags of all nations flutter idly in the breeze."

Beneath the flags radio technicians are fussing with a battery of microphones. Newsreel cameramen are checking their cables, and press photographers are clicking shutters and testing flash bulbs. An Honor Guard including a Soldier, a Sailor and a Marine, is marching back and forth, rifles at their shoulders. From the far distance come the strains of a military band playing patriotic airs, and there is the "subdued rumble of the great crowds lining the streets."

The conversation of the technicians assembled would indicate that the person being honored is certainly popular. "He's a great man all right, but, boy, I'll be relieved when he takes off in the plane tomorrow. I need a rest," declares a photographer.

"What beats me is how the hell *he* stands up under it—but he does. Looks fresh as a daisy. And now he's got to go through the same thing in London, Paris and Moscow. Rather him than me, brother, but I tell you one thing—I'm damn proud he's an American!"

Now there is a great roar from the crowd outside the gates. The Honor Guard takes its station and snaps to attention. A presidential aide appears and lays the President's speech on the speaker's table. Aides of Gen. Eisenhower, Gen. MacArthur and Admiral Nimitz are followed to the stand by the generals themselves. The generals are smiling and waving to the crowd. The band strikes up "Hail to the Chief" and President Truman, his arm linked with that of Christopher Blake, appears on the stand.

Christopher is also smiling and waving to the crowd. He has stopped now to pose with the President and the generals for the photographers. The President glances at his watch and a hush falls over the crowd. The radio man steps forward and announces: "Ladies and Gentlemen—The President of the United States."

The President begins to speak. "My fellow Americans. I speak to you on a day and in a moment in our history when men and women all over the world are lifting up their hearts in thanksgiving to one of your fellow citizens—one of our fellow Americans. It was the privilege of our great country and the splendid destiny of this man to create two instruments of world import. The super Atomic Bomb, and, at the same time, the Blake Plan for Peace. Christopher Blake not only perfected a weapon so shattering that one super Atomic Bomb would wipe out an entire hemisphere, but he offered, along with it, to this country and to the world, A Plan for Peace so profoundly just and right that it has been unanimously adopted as law by all peoples on the face of the globe. Thus, my friends, for the first time in the history of mankind, War is at last permanently outlawed, and World Peace is a living reality. This is the day we celebrate, and this is the man who has made it possible. Ladies and Gentlemen—I give you a great American—Christopher Blake."

Christopher steps up to the microphone, but he is too moved to say much. The crowd is cheering wildly as he manages to squeeze out his compliments to the generals and the President and add: "My Fellow Americans, I have only this to say: I am proud to be of service to my country."

The President again takes over to introduce probably "the proudest parents in the world today," Christopher Blake's father and mother. There is a roar from the crowd, but evidently something has gone wrong. Christopher is passing his hand wearily across his eyes. The aide whispers to the President. The President speaks to the radio man, who steps to the microphone to ask the crowd to stand by momentarily.

The President is irritated. Why was he not told? Because Christopher had asked that nothing be said. On the President's order Christopher explains—

"My mother and father are getting a divorce, sir."

The President is stunned. "Divorce? Your parents—want to divorce?"

"They're in Court now, sir. This is the last day. That's why they're not here. I tried to tell you—but I couldn't."

The President is still stunned. He would talk with Mr. and Mrs. Blake immediately. Let the Judge be told to stop all proceedings until he can have this interview. "Do they understand?"

he demands of Christopher; "do they realize what this means to you? Have they told you why?"

"They told me why—but I don't believe it. I don't. I'd give anything if they . . . Would *you* speak to them? It would mean more to me than all these honors—the Medal—everything."

Mr. and Mrs. Blake are announced. "Christopher meets their eyes for a moment, then turns away." Yes, the Blakes confess, it is true that they are being divorced. Yes, they both want a divorce. They have talked it over with Chris, and they think he understands—

"And you do understand, Christopher, don't you?" pleads Mrs. Blake. "Sometimes people fall out of love, and when they do they get divorced. You understand that, Chris."

"No—no, I don't," wails the unhappy Christopher. "I know I said I did but I don't. I'll never understand it."

"But, Chris . . ."

"Just a moment, Mr. Blake. As President of the United States, I order you to stop this divorce at once."

There is a moment's absolute silence. "It's too late, sir," says Mr. Blake. "The divorce has just been granted!"

A pistol shot rings out. Christopher has placed a revolver to his heart and fired just as his father finishes speaking. Slowly he sinks to the floor. His mother, with a scream of horror, rushes to her son's side, and is quickly followed by Mr. Blake.

"Oh, Chris, why? Why? Why did you do this terrible thing?"

"My work was done, Mother. And without you and Dad—I just didn't want to go on."

The radio man is at the microphone telling the people what has happened. He asks them to stay close to their radios for a later word from the President. Christopher's father and mother are anxiously pleading with him to tell them what they can do to help right the wrong they have done him. Chris knows he hasn't long, but he would like to have them as they were before, just for a little. He would like to have his father kiss his mother as he used to. Seeing that happen, Chris is content.

The President has returned to the microphone. "Fellow Americans," he is saying, "Christopher Blake is dying. It can only be a matter of moments now. His mother and father are at his side. I will not try to express what is in my heart—what I am sure is in all of our hearts. There will be a military funeral with full honors, and a period of national mourning. All flags will be lowered. The body will lie in state in the Lincoln study. I can say no more."

The Soldier and the Sailor begin lowering the flag. From the distance a bugler is blowing "Taps," and there is a faint boom of cannon. It is a twenty-one-gun salute for Chris—

"Everything I did, I did just to make you proud of me . . ." he says, smiling at his parents. Then his eyes close

"He's gone, Evie," says Mr. Blake, brokenly.

"No. . . . Now he belongs to the ages," solemnly declares the President.

The cannon continues to boom. The lights fade.

The clock in Judge Adamson's chambers is striking two. Christopher, deep in the big chair, looks even smaller and younger than his twelve years warrant. The room is formally furnished after the custom in legal circles and is rather forbidding. Christopher, softly whistling "Taps," is draining to the last dregs the solace of his fantasy.

The doors leading into the courtroom open and an attendant, a kindly old fellow, comes in. It will still be a little while before they are ready for Christopher, he reports. There is nothing to worry about. The Judge is a very understanding person. He is as likely to talk to Chris about baseball, or the Boy Scouts, as anything else. The whole thing will be over in no time.

"Suppose I won't talk at all," ventures Chris. "Suppose I make believe I'm sick or something? What does he do then?"

"Now, you wouldn't do that. That'ud just be silly. You're too big a feller for that."

"Oh, sure. I wasn't even thinking about it. I don't care what old questions he asks me. I just wish he'd hurry up, that's all. Are you married?"

Chris is interested to learn that the attendant is not only married, and the father of a son, but also he is a grandfather. Also that he has never been divorced—though a great many people have been. Nearly everyone has been divorced, Chris would like to think. This thing about his father and mother will be in all the papers, but at school only the teachers take the New York papers, so he doesn't have to worry about that. Maybe he won't be going back to school anyway.

But this business of deciding which of his parents he should like to go with, that's pretty troublesome to Chris. Still, the attendant tells him, that's something every person has to decide for himself.

"Oh, it doesn't matter," says Chris, boldly. "I was just wondering on account of maybe changing school, and all my stuff being up there and things like that."

The attendant has gone back into the courtroom when Mr. and Mrs. Blake appear, accompanied by their respective lawyers, Mr. Kurlick and Mr. Caldwell. His mother would straighten Christopher's tie and smooth down his hair. His father, at a nod from Mr. Kurlick, suggests that probably Chris would like to go down to the corner and buy himself a hamburger. He must be getting a little hungry. The suggestion is okay with Chris. . . .

The conference of the Blakes and their attorneys has not progressed very far when Judge Adamson comes in to get some papers. He stops long enough to give the Blakes a bit of advice. He doesn't want them to force him to call Christopher—

"No reason you can't settle this," he advises them. "You've agreed on everything else. I don't want to call the boy, understand? I hate it, and it's no good anyway. Been doing this for thirty years and never felt I made a right decision when I had to call the child. Whole thing's no good anyway. How can I decide rightly who gets a child—its mother or its father! Silly. Shouldn't be asked to. Tell you something else. Every time the parents make me decide, it's bad for everybody. Bitterness all around. No good for them—no good for the child. You settle it between you. No reason you can't. Both sensible people. Can't give you too much time on this. Not my fault. Should have been done before."

The Judge has started for the courtroom. At the door he turns to repeat his admonition. "I don't want to call the boy unless you make me, and don't make me," he says. "It's no good. Don't understand why sensible people like you are here in the first place. Still a good deal I don't understand. Bachelor myself."

The attorneys can't do much with their clients in conference. On one subject neither Mr. Blake nor Mrs. Blake will give an inch. Mr. Blake is willing to confess that he is the aggressor and that the chances of the Judge awarding him more than part time custody of his son is remote—

"I understand I haven't a leg to stand on," Mr. Blake admits. "I also know how unreasonable I'm being—how badly I'm behaving. I want you to know I understand it all and I don't give a damn. There's only one thing I'd like to understand—and I can't. That's the charming lady on my right, gentlemen—the lady I've been married to for sixteen years."

"Oh, for God's sake, Kenneth, stop badgering me!" Mrs. Blake's protest is vehement. "You never wanted this divorce and you still don't! If you're sick of the word 'sensible' I'm sick of hearing *that!* And I'm sick of seeing you try to play the guilty barefoot boy with straw in his hair. It's too shoddy and it's too late."

"I see. I'm still the complete sonofabitch."

"Oh, stop it! It's your fault we're here—not mine! You've been trying to turn it around for weeks, and you're still trying even now. Well, it won't change around. I didn't take a lover. You took a mistress. There's no buck-passing on that."

It is Mr. Blake's suggestion that they ask the lawyers to leave them while they talk things over alone—just for five minutes, but Mrs. Blake will not agree. She's tired and the whole thing has already been gone over too often—

"But you never told me *why*, Evie," protests Mr. Blake, desperately. "I'm reaching—I'm searching—I'm trying to understand. It's not jealousy. It can't be on some silly moral grounds. I don't believe it. Evie, we've had good years together—and we've had Chris. We owe each other something for those years, Evie, don't we? It can't all end like this—you can't be doing this to us both with no reason. I know you too well for that. Why, Evie? Why is it too late even now?"

"Because . . . Kenneth, there isn't always a reason—one specific reason—even one I can give to myself—even you and Ruth. Don't you think I've tried? But when it happened—there was no going back. I knew it. And there isn't now. I can't tell you why. I don't know. It's just—true."

Again the attorneys try their arguments. Mr. Blake cannot expect to get more than six months custody of his son each year. With Mrs. Blake living in California, that will mean yanking Christopher out of school every six months, and they would not want to do that.

"Get this through your heads—all of you," shouts Mr. Blake. "It's not just because my wife's going to live in California that I'm fighting for Christopher—I wouldn't care if she was going to live on the next block. I want my son with me—all the time. I want him to live with me—to be part of my life. I want him."

"Kenneth, you want him now the way you've always wanted him—when it was fun to want him. To take him to that baseball game on Sunday—to see him for that two hours at night when you came home. He's been a part of your life—but he's been most of mine. I've wanted him when it wasn't fun—cooped up in the house with him when he was sick, telling him he couldn't do this and mustn't do that—punishing him when you couldn't and building you up in his eyes. I know you love him but so do I. I can't help that anymore than you can."

"And I don't believe a damn word you're saying. If you had any real feeling for him or for me we wouldn't be here."

"All right. You asked for this. Maybe I do know the reason now. Maybe I did all along—but now you can have it."

This confession is stopped by the return of Christopher. He has had his hamburgers—and some strawberry ice cream—and everything's okay. Then the Judge summons Mrs. Blake and Mr. Caldwell.

It is while they are alone that his father tries to tell Christopher the reason his mother wishes to have a divorce. It is pretty hard to explain, Father admits, but he hopes Chris will understand, even though they had been fully truthful with him before. They had told him that they were going to be divorced because they didn't love each other any more, but there was more to it than that. And it's all Mr. Blake's fault. He had made a friend of another lady. She was a very nice lady, but they had seen so much of each other that Chris' mother was deeply hurt.

But why? Why didn't his father tell his mother about this other lady? What if they had gone to theatres and night clubs together? They had often done this with other friends. Why not this one? And, if his mother were so hurt, wouldn't his father have stopped going out with this lady as soon as he understood?

"You see, Chris, a thing like that hurts a woman very much," Mr. Blake explains, a little lamely. "It isn't easy to forgive. Women are different than men, Chris. A thing like that is a blow to a woman's pride—it goes very deep."

"Why did you do it if you knew it was wrong?"

"I can't answer that, Chris," Mr. Blake admits, slowly. "I don't know. But very often people do wrong things sometimes even without meaning to. I don't mean it wasn't my fault, Chris, it was. It's just—too bad—this is what happened. Now you know."

But Chris doesn't know. He's not mad at his father. Nor his mother. But he still doesn't understand.

"I know," sympathizes Mr. Blake. "It's hard. It was hard for me to tell you this, too. But I wanted to tell you, Chris, because very soon now you'll be asked to decide who you want to stay with—your mother or me. I don't know what you're going to say. I don't want to know."

Mr. Blake has paced his way nervously to the window and back. "Your mother is a very fine woman, Chris," he goes on. "We both love you and we both want you. But if you did choose me, I had to feel you knew the truth. I didn't want you to choose unfairly. I couldn't stand that."

Chris takes command of the quiz. What is his father's lady friend's name? Ruth. Is she as pretty as Mother? In a different way, yes. How old is she? About Mother's age. Does Mother know her? No. Why not? Well, they just never met. He (Mr. B.) had met Ruth at a cocktail party. They had liked each other right away. Why?

"I don't know, exactly," confesses a worried Mr. Blake. "You know you meet somebody and like them and they like you. Like you and Bob, Chris. You were great friends the minute you laid eyes on each other. Remember?"

"Yes, but— Why did you like her so much?"

"Well— We always seemed to have fun together, Chris. She made me laugh and—sort of forget about things. She—well, we both enjoyed being together, Chris."

Ruth, it seems, is a sculptress. She makes statues. Yes, she had made a head of Mr. Blake—like the head of Socrates they (the Blakes) have in the library. How do you make a statue?

"Oh, God!" exclaims Mr. Blake, helplessly. "I mean, I don't know how to explain it, Chris. With a hammer and chisel—at least those are the tools. But it's a talent—like painting a picture or writing music. I can't quite explain it to you."

"Are you still friends?"

"Yes. We haven't seen each other lately, but—she's one of the best friends I ever had, Chris."

"Why did she let you do wrong if she was your friend? Aren't friends supposed to help you?"

"Yes."

"Then why did she? (Mr. Blake doesn't answer.) Didn't she know it was wrong? That it was going to hurt Mother?"

"Yes. We both knew. I can't do anything about that, Chris. It's true. Only . . . no, there it is. It's true."

The appearance of Lawyer Kurlick saves Mr. Blake temporarily. There are some things that his lawyer still has to go over with him, whether he (Blake) likes it or not. The question of the child's maintenance, for instance—

Chris has wandered over to the window and is leaning against the window sill and whistling an indistinguishable fragment of song as the lights begin to dim. The men's voices fade.

As the lights come up they reveal the stage of a theatre. Stage hands are busily getting the stage ready for a rehearsal, lowering scenery, dragging in furniture, etc.

Presently a stage doorman appears piloting Mr. and Mrs. Blake toward the front of the stage. Mr. Upton, the stage director, would stop them, but it seems they bring a letter from Mr. Bascom himself.

Now Mr. Upton is all attention. Of course Mr. and Mrs. Blake may stay. Anywhere they like. But they will have to excuse him. He has started away when Mr. Blake stops him—

"Just a moment. Could you tell us something, please? We're both completely mystified. This is my wife, Mr. Upton. (*They murmur how-do-you-dos.*) You see, we don't *know* Mr. Bascom— either of us. Never set eyes on him in our lives. Of course, we've seen his plays—we know what a famous man he is—but why would he write to us—why should he ask *us* to come here today. Have you any idea?"

"Why, no. That's his handwriting, all right. And the letter certainly says it's most important that you be right here at two o'clock this afternoon."

"But why *us?*" queries Mrs. Blake. "Out of a clear blue sky? Does he often invite perfect strangers to his rehearsals?"

"He certainly doesn't!" says Mr. Upton. "But you've probably read a lot about Mr. Bascom—he's a very great man. I never try to understand him. I've been stage-manager of his plays for ten years—and even I never know what's through that fabulous mind of his. So you'd better wait. Will you excuse me, please."

As Mr. Upton hurries away a great hush falls over the stage. Out of the hush J. Roger Bascom appears. "It is, of course, Christopher—but now he is J. Roger Bascom, the world-famous playwright, complete with black Fedora hat, malacca stick, pearl-gray gloves, and a white silk-lined Inverness cape. He comes slowly down a lane of almost religious 'Hello, Mr. Bascom,' 'Good afternoon, Mr. Bascom,' and benevolently and graciously returns the 'hellos' as he walks to a large desk at one side of the stage, where a chair labeled J. Roger Bascom stands. He hands his hat, stick and gloves to an obviously English man-servant who stands waiting."

MANSERVANT—Top-hole day, Mr. Bascom.

CHRISTOPHER—Thank you, Butts. You needn't lay out my things, tonight, Butts. I'll probably be rehearsing right through tomorrow. Better cancel that dinner I'm giving at the Waldorf, too.

MANSERVANT—Righto, Mr. Bascom.

CHRISTOPHER—That will be all, Butts. (*He turns to a woman standing at the other side of the desk.*) Anything important for me to do before rehearsal, Miss Holly?

MISS HOLLY—The New York *Times* wants a statement, Mr. Bascom, and *Life* wants a picture of you for next week's cover.

CHRISTOPHER—Haven't time for pictures, Miss Holly. What kind of a statement does the New York *Times* want?

MISS HOLLY—They want to know how does it feel to receive the Pulitzer Prize five times in a row.

CHRISTOPHER—Five times? Four, isn't it?

MISS HOLLY—Oh, I forgot to tell you, Mr. Bascom. The prize came in the mail this morning. That makes it five.

CHRISTOPHER—Well, that's quite an honor. This is the first time I ever received the Pulitzer Prize before the play opened, isn't it?

MISS HOLLY—Yes, Mr. Bascom. Shall I send the Prize to the Crippled Children at Bellevue Hospital as usual?

CHRISTOPHER—Yes. No card. Just anonymous. And some flowers. Anything else?

MISS HOLLY—Just the usual Hollywood offers, Mr. Bascom. And can you have a midnight supper with Miss Gertrude Lawrence at the Stork Club, tonight?

CHRISTOPHER—No. You know I always do my best writing at night, Miss Holly. I'm afraid that's all I'll have time for now. Mr. Upton, are we ready to begin?

MR. UPTON—Yes, Mr. Bascom.

Mr. Upton now leans over to whisper something in Mr. Bascom's ear. Of course, Mr. Bascom understands. Let Mr. and Mrs. Blake approach. Let chairs be brought for them. Naturally they must be a little mystified at his summons to them, but he can explain that. If it happens that they have seen any of his plays—

"I'm one of your most ardent admirers, Mr. Bascom," explains Mrs. Blake. "That's why this is so mystifying—and thrilling."

CHRISTOPHER—Thank you. Then you know that all of my plays deal with human passions. And where do the passions come from? Life. Just life. I'll tell you a little secret, Mr. and Mrs. Blake. Do you know where I get all my ideas from? The newspapers. Which brings me to you. I've been reading about your divorce in the newspapers, Mr. and Mrs. Blake.

MR. BLAKE—Oh, I see.

CHRISTOPHER—And I thought you might be very interested in my new play.

MRS. BLAKE—But how would your new play concern us, Mr. Bascom?

CHRISTOPHER—Just an idea of mine, Mrs. Blake—a passing fancy. Sometimes, the smallest chance can change people's lives. I know that from writing plays.

MRS. BLAKE—But it's all decided, Mr. Bascom—nothing can change that now.

CHRISTOPHER—Perhaps. But surely, Mrs. Blake, you can lose nothing by witnessing my play.

MR. BLAKE—Let's watch it, Evie. It's very kind of Mr. Bascom to take all this interest in us. Of course we'll stay, Mr. Bascom. Won't we, Evie?

MRS. BLAKE—Well—all right. I don't think it will make any difference, Mr. Bascom, but thank you, just the same. This is a great privilege.

CHRISTOPHER—You know, Mr. Blake—your wife is a very attractive woman. It seems a pity you two are divorcing. All right, Mr. Upton. Tell everyone to get ready. We will do the third act. That's the one I want Mr. and Mrs. Blake to see. (*He turns to them directly.*) I'll tell you the story of the play up to the third act. It begins when the wife finds out that the husband has made friends with another woman. This hurts the wife very much. You see, women are different than men—they don't forget easily, and a thing like this hurts a woman very much. But the husbands knows he did wrong. He gives up this friend—he doesn't see her any more—but still the wife won't forgive him. So they get divorced. And the last act is all about what happens to their son afterwards. That's the part I want you to see. Is everything set, Mr. Upton?

MR. UPTON—Yes, Mr. Bascom. Ready and waiting.

CHRISTOPHER—All right. The first scene is in the son's room at school. His name is—Christopher. Okay, Mr. Upton.

The lights are raised on the scene the stagehands have been setting. It is a boy's room at school, and presently two boys come bursting in. They have overcoats and hats on. Two suitcases, packed and ready to be closed, are on their respective beds. They go enthusiastically about closing them, talking as they work. Gee, this is certainly going to be a great Christmas vacation! Boy, the things they are going to do!

"My father's taking me to the Ice Show tonight," reports

Johnny. "Then we're going down to the country for Christmas Eve—the whole family—and then . . ."

"Hey, Johnny—your father is downstairs. Hurry up. Mine is, too. Hi, Chris—"

"Hi, Ray. My father or mother there yet, did you notice?"

"Nope. Didn't see 'em. C'mon, Johnny—get a move on."

"Okay, okay. 'By, Chris. Merry Christmas and a sloppy New Year."

" 'By."

There are seasonal salutations echoing up and down the hall outside, accompanied by a great slamming of doors. Chris goes back to trying to get his bag shut. Then the door opens and the Headmaster of the school appears. He has come to report that the last train is in and there is no Mr. or Mrs. Blake on it. No, there can't be any mistake about it—

"Your parents are divorced, aren't they?" demands the Headmaster, accusingly.

"Yes, sir."

"Have they married again?"

"Yes, sir."

"Well, then, it is quite obvious what has happened. They've simply forgotten about you. Christmas season and all that. They always do. I take it, Blake, that your stepfather and stepmother are not overfond of you?"

"No, sir."

"Well, Blake, you can't stay here. The School's closing for ten days. No teachers, no food, there'll be nobody here. You simply can't stay here, Blake."

"Where will I go, sir?"

"Really, Blake, you can't expect us to worry about you when your parents don't. Have you any of your allowance left?"

"No, sir."

"What have you been squandering it on this month, Blake?"

"Nothing, sir. It didn't come this month, sir."

"Forgot that, too, eh? Well, it's most irritating. I've always been against taking children of divorced parents in this school. They're a confounded nuisance. Very well. Here's your train fare to New York. Your father lives in New York, doesn't he?"

"Yes, sir. My mother lives in California."

"Well, go to your father's apartment and tell him to take you in—and ask him please to be a little more considerate of the school, if he expects us to keep you here." He slams the door as he goes out. Christopher picks up his suitcase and disappears through the door. The lights black out.

When the lights go up we see Christopher standing before the door of an apartment house ringing the bell. He explains to the janitor that he would like to get into the Blake apartment. He can't. The Blakes are away.

"Mr. Blake no come back for a long time," explains the janitor. "He go away with new wife to Florida."

"But I'm Mr. Blake's son. I guess my father must have been pretty busy, because he forgot to send me the key or anything. Will you let me into the apartment, please?"

"Please, you don't bother me no more. I got to trim Christmas tree for my family." He slams the door in Christopher's face. It has begun to snow. Christopher turns up his coat collar and walks away, as the lights black out.

When next we see Christopher he is staring through a bakeshop window at the good things inside. Gay Christmas crowds are passing along the street, frequently hailing each other with holiday salutations. Christopher has put his hand in his pocket and drawn it forth again. Three cents is his total capital. A blind beggar passes and Chris drops the three cents into his cap. Then he sits down on the grating in front of the bakery. It's warmer there. Several people hurrying past trip over Christopher and scowl in protest. One particularly irate man threatens to call the police. A copper appears and orders Chris to move on

"I've got no place to go, and it's warm here," protests Chris.

"Oh, you haven't, eh? Well, this'll send you on your way— good and warm." And he raps his club against the soles of Chris' feet. Chris grabs his suitcase and beats it precipitately, just as a crowd gather to watch the sport. The lights fade.

Next, Christopher has found his way to a church. He sinks wearily into a pew, blowing on his hands to warm them. Looking about him, and finding the church deserted, he falls to his knees in prayer—

"Oh, God, why did you do this to me? Why didn't you make my mother forgive my father? Please don't let them forget me— please get them together again somehow. I can't stand it this way. Is it too late—even now? Isn't there some way?"

The sobbing of a woman is heard. It is Mrs. Blake. "Stop it! Stop it!" she cries. "I can't stand it! I can't stand any more!"

With this Chris rises to his feet and resumes his role as Mr. Bascom. "Okay, Mr. Upton," he calls; "tell everybody to smoke a cigarette or something. And bring Mrs. Blake a glass of water. I'm sorry my play upset you, Mrs. Blake."

Mrs. Blake—Oh, Mr. Bascom—I know it's only a play—but is that what happens? Is that what really happens?

Christopher—I'm only a poor writer, Mrs. Blake, but—I know life. There it is.

Mr. Blake (*brokenly*)—We have a son, too, Mr. Bascom.

Mrs. Blake—His name is Christopher, too. Oh, Kenneth, I can't do this—I can't go through with it. Not now.

Mr. Blake—Evie! (*He takes her tenderly in his arms.*)

Christopher—Miss Holly—bring some iced champagne. I think this is a cause for celebration.

Miss Holly (*adoringly—her voice choked with sobs*)—Yes, Mr. Bascom.

Mrs. Blake—How did you know, Mr. Bascom—how can one man's heart be so great?

Christopher (*shrugging his shoulders*)—Just a passing fancy, Mrs. Blake—just one of my little ideas. I believe Shakespeare would have done as much. He was a writer, too. Ah, the champagne. Let me drink to you both. And may you live happily ever after—with the blessings of J. Roger Bascom.

They lift their glasses. Their arms are around each other and their eyes are shining. As the three glasses clink the lights fade.

Now we are back in the Judge's Chambers. Christopher is still leaning on the window sill, softly whistling. The voices of his father and Mr. Kurlick come gradually through the darkness. The attendant comes from the courtroom. This time he summons Mr. Blake and Mr. Kurlick.

Chris is still at the window when his mother appears. The courtroom has been stifling and she is a little faint. Chris gets her some water. If he wants to, she tells him, he can stay over tonight and they will go see "Show Boat"—if she can get tickets. That would be okay with Chris.

Soon they are talking earnestly about the problems that face them. Chris would have his mother know of his talk with his father, and that his father isn't friends with Ruth, any more. Yes, Chris knows about Ruth. His father has told him because he wanted him to know all about everything before he had to say which one he wanted to go with. Couldn't his mother now find it in her heart to forgive his father?

"He knows it was all his fault. He knew it was wrong. He said so. . . . Sometimes people do wrong, Mom, without meaning to. Like the time Bob and I ran away from camp. . . . Don't you think you could forget about it, Mom?"

"Chris, dear, it's different when you're grown up. This isn't like your running away from camp—or anything like that."

"I know that. But—he's sorry. I think he's awful sorry, Mom."

"Oh, darling, don't," pleads Mrs. Blake, painfully. . . . "Chris, I'm sorry, too. I can't help this. I can't." She is pacing the room now. "I wish with all my heart this didn't have to be."

"Then why does it, Mom? Is it something else? Is it something you can't tell me? I understand a lot of things you don't think I do."

"Do you, Chris—do you? Maybe if . . . Chris, I'll try to tell you. I don't know if I can, but I'll try." She is quite still for a moment as though gathering up her courage. "It isn't because I can't forgive Dad, Chris. If it were only that—it would be easy."

"Then what is it?"

"It's something in me—something I should have faced years ago. Oh, darling, this is going to be so hard for you to understand!"

"I will, Mom."

They had met, she and his father, Mrs. Blake tells her son, when they first came to New York and were working in the same office—the only two out-of-towners there. Suddenly they had discovered that they were desperately lonely and turned naturally to each other for understanding and sympathy. They planned to take their vacation at the same time—and then they were married—

"Darling, I told you this would be hard. You're so little yet and this is such a big thing to tell you. You see, I was frightened and lonely—we both were—Dad was kind and sweet and gentle—just as he is now—but it wasn't right. Don't ask me why, Chris—I don't know. It just wasn't right. Something in me. And that's when this should have happened—that's when we should have parted—then—not now. That was the mistake, Chris—the big mistake—that's what I blame myself for. But I didn't have the courage. We were both nice people—I kept thinking it would get better. And then you were going to be born—and I thought somehow that would make everything all right. I was sure of it. . . .

And, whatever else was wrong, darling, I always wanted you and loved you. Remember that. . . . When this happened—about Ruth—I was hurt, yes—but that isn't the most terrible thing. And I think Dad needed something—some deep affection that he missed in me. I even understood it in a way. No, it wasn't that—though I made myself believe it was for a long time. I couldn't face it honestly even then. But now I have. . . . I'm thirty-six years old, Chris. Age doesn't make much sense to you now, but, darling—try and think of me as a person—as a separate human being—I'm your mother and Dad's wife, yes—but I'm me, too. A separate person with separate needs. I'm trying to reach out for a little happiness while there's still time. I don't know how—or even if I will—but there's still time now—and if I wait—there won't be. I don't think you know what that means—but someday you will. And I want the chance. I want it. Do you think I could do this to Dad and to you unless I couldn't help it—unless I had to? Chris, do you understand? Even a little? Look at me, Chris."

He has raised his eyes to hers, but before he can answer a young woman from Mr. Kurlick's office comes through the door. She has brought papers for which the lawyer has telephoned. She will wait until he comes from the courtroom. While she waits she would like to discuss the case of Blake vs. Blake with Mrs. Blake. All the girls in the Kurlick office get terribly interested in divorce cases, despite their monotony. Usually they make bets on them. Just now they are wondering which of his parents Christopher will choose.

When Mrs. Blake excuses herself the young lady would continue her discussion of the Blake problem with Christopher, but Chris is not interested. He is leaning down, re-tying his shoe laces when the lights fade.

The lights are up now, on "a large and dismal institution bedroom. Long rows of straight unpainted iron bedsteads stand facing each other, the floor is uncarpeted, the walls and windows a grim and dirty gray—even the sheets and blankets on the beds have the same gray and hopeless look."

There are several old men and women in the room. The men, with pails and brushes, are scrubbing the floors. The women are bending painfully over to make the beds. Mr. and Mrs. Blake are among them.

The talk is of the misery of life in this institution, and of such relief from it as a few have gained. One old man has filched an extra slice of bread at supper. They are cackling gleefully over his account of that adventure when the door back of them opens quietly and the Superintendent steps in. He listens for a moment and then shouts them back to their places. They emit little screams of terror as they go.

"Well, my friends, was that your morning meeting?" sneers the Superintendent, after an impressive interval. "The Pauper's Parade? How dare you? Two slices of bread! When will you get this through those old skulls? This is a Poorhouse—you're paupers—all of you—wards of the State—charity cases—and you're lucky to have one slice of bread for your supper. Do you hear me?"

They mumble a panic-stricken "Yes" and the Superintendent goes on to inform them that, as they seem ungrateful for what they do get, there will be no supper at all that night. Nor are they to talk to each other. Any who are heard to speak so much as a single word will be put on the water diet for the rest of the week.

The sound of sobbing interrupts the Superintendent's orders. It is Mrs. Blake. "Tears? Tears?" he explodes. "Well, we have a cure for that, too. Suppose you wash the windows on the outside this afternoon, Mrs. Blake. There's a cold wind this afternoon—that will dry those tears. And make that bed properly. Tuck the edges in."

"Wait until our son comes to take us out of this. Just wait." Mrs. Blake is defiant now.

"What's that? Who spoke?"

"I did," answers Mr. Blake, with some spirit. "I don't care what you do to me—it can't be much worse. Just wait till our son comes to take us out of this, that's all."

The Superintendent breaks into peals of laughter. "Oh, it's wonderful! I love it every time I hear it!" he chortles. "I've been Superintendent of this Poorhouse for twenty-five years, and I bet I couldn't count the number of sons that were coming to take their dear parents away. And do you know something? Not one of them—not one son—not one son in twenty-five years has ever showed up. Go ahead. Make me laugh some more."

The Blakes are not discouraged. They know their son. They know their Christopher. He is now the richest man in all South America. They had clipped his picture from a newspaper. He is known now as Juan Fernandes Escolito, but he's Christopher all right. They had written him a letter and told him where they were. He'll be coming.

The Superintendent is still not impressed. With a final order for them to return to their work, he stomps out. One by one the workers finish their jobs. Only the Blakes are still working when the roar of an airplane is heard overhead. They rush to the window. It's Christopher! They're sure. Mrs. Blake knew he'd come. "Thank God!" thankfully exclaims Mr. Blake. For a moment they are in each other's arms. Then, hearing footsteps along the corridor, they straighten up, brush their rumpled clothes, pat their hair and turn to face the door. Now Christopher stands in the doorway. "He wears a Gaucho hat, a kind of South American business suit, and carries a riding crop in his hand."

CHRISTOPHER—Good morning, amigos!

MR. AND MRS. BLAKE—Christopher!

CHRISTOPHER—Well, well. We meet again!

MRS. BLAKE—You look so wonderful, Christopher.

MR. BLAKE—I can hardly believe it—coming out of the sky! Is that your plane, Christopher?

CHRISTOPHER—One of them. I dropped the pilot at Rio Janeiro. Too slow. Flew her up myself. By the way, take a look at tonight's papers. I broke the record from Buenos Aires to New York.

MRS. BLAKE—Think of it, Kenneth! Christopher—that we used to order around!

CHRISTOPHER—Yes, seems mighty far away now, doesn't it? Well, tell me, what seems to be the trouble? This is not exactly the Waldorf-Astoria, is it? (*He looks slowly around the room.*)

MRS. BLAKE (*after a silence*)—You begin, Kenneth. Tell him.

MR. BLAKE—All right. After the divorce, I married Ruth. You remember my telling you about Ruth, Chris?

CHRISTOPHER—Oh, yes. And?

MR. BLAKE—I didn't have a moment's peace. She kept making new friends—other men—just the way she made a friend of me. I began to drink—just to forget. My business failed—and I finally lost it. At last, when all my money was gone, she left me—without even a note to say good-by—just disappeared. I've never seen her since. But I had fallen so low, Christopher, that none of my old friends would even see me. One day I was picked up off a park bench—and they brought me here. It's been bitter, Christopher, bitter.

CHRISTOPHER—I see. (*He turns to his mother.*) And you?

MRS. BLAKE—I wanted a chance—remember, Christopher—while there was still time. (*She laughs harshly.*) Well, I got my chance—only there was too much time. I married a man—I won't even speak his name—I swore that name would never pass my lips again—and the very day of our marriage he beat me unmercifully. He made me go out and work for him—take in washing and sewing—and when I broke down from overwork, he laughed and wouldn't call a doctor. One day, when I was going begging from door to door for work—I came home and the door was locked. I begged him to let me in, but he wouldn't. He said when I could earn my keep I could come back. I never went back—I came here instead. There was no place for me to go. Oh, Christopher—you don't know how glad I am that you've come at last.

They could not have stood what they have been through much longer, Mr. Blake declares. It was only by accident that they had seen their son's picture in the paper. But why the new name? What happened to Christopher Blake?

"I'll tell you what happened to Christopher Blake. Christopher Blake shipped on a cattle boat for South America and wandered across the Pampas—living with the Gauchos—stealing, shooting, keeping alive from day to day. Then one night, Christopher Blake wandered into a small coffee plantation. The Fernandez Plantation. He came to steal—but Mr. and Mrs. Fernandez gave him food and clothing and shelter."

"How good of them!"

"He stayed on to work—they were so good to him. Slowly, they built up the Plantation together—and they bought more and more plantations—until now the name of Fernandez is the greatest name in South America."

"But why did you take their name, Christopher?"

"And why is it, Chris, that since you came into this room, you've never once called us Dad or Mother?"

"Why? I'll show you why!"

With a sweeping gesture Chris goes to the door and calls. "Dad!" "Mother!"

A man and woman, "magnificently dressed," come into the room. They "put their arms around Christopher, smiling at him lovingly."

"This is why!" Chris is saying. "This is my father and mother! Not you! They've been a real father and mother to me! Take a good look and see what a real father and mother look like! And take another look and see what *you* could have had—jewels and money, and cars and yachts and planes—instead of this!"

The Superintendent comes in, bowing and scraping. He is so sorry to have missed Chris. Isn't there something he can do?

Shall he pack the Blakes' things? Shall he have food put up for their journey?

CHRISTOPHER—No, thank you—there is nothing you can do. Because I'm not taking them away. I'm leaving them to what they deserve—*this!*

MRS. BLAKE—Oh, Chris, don't! Don't say that!

MR. BLAKE—Chris—you're joking! This is a joke, isn't it?

CHRISTOPHER—Joke! I wouldn't lift my little finger to save you!

MRS. BLAKE—I don't believe it—I don't. You used to love us, Christopher—I know you did—you loved us both.

CHRISTOPHER—Sure I did, and some thanks I got for it.

MR. BLAKE—But we couldn't help it, Christopher, we couldn't.

MRS. BLAKE—We told you why, Chris—there were reasons why we had to. You know that.

CHRISTOPHER—Sure you told me. You gave me reasons, too. But what are reasons—I don't care about your reasons. I don't care what they were. What about me? I didn't ask to be born, did I? No, you can't answer that, can you? Well, now you know what it feels like to be all alone—to be kicked out. Now you know what it feels like—how do you like it, eh? How do you like it? (MRS. BLAKE *reaches out her hand to him.*) Don't touch me! Don't come near me—either one of you! I hate you—I hate you both. I hope you die! Take 'em away! I never want to see them again! I hate them! I hate them! I hate them!

As the lights begin to dim the Superintendent drags the Blakes from the room. When the lights come up again we are back in the Judge's Chambers. Chris is standing exactly where he was standing before. The door to the Courtroom opens. The attendant appears to motion silently to Chris, who starts toward the Courtroom.

The curtain slowly begins to fall.

ACT II

When the curtain rises a Courtroom of Christopher's fevered imagination is revealed. "It is dimly lit, almost dark, with great shafts of light zigzagging through the barred windows, slanting crazily across the Judge's Bench, the Witness Stand, and the spectators."

Policemen are holding back crowds peering through the windows. These crowds are shoving, pushing and shouting. As Christopher comes through the door he is greeted with yells and catcalls: "That's him!" "That's the kid!" "Boy, I'll bet he's scared stiff!" "Lookit his face!"

Two policemen lead Chris to a table below the Judge's Bench. A couple of bailiffs take his finger prints. The Chief Bailiff, who fancies himself as a humorist, puts him through a series of intimate questions: What's his name? How old is he? What're his parents' names? Has he ever been arrested for breaking windows, stealing apples, setting fires in empty lots? What subjects did he fail in at Mapleton Military Academy?

Christopher admits to failing in "Math," but immediately a jeering crowd of boys adds "Chemistry" and "Geography." "That's why he was kicked off the track team this year!" they shout gleefully.

Now they are taking his photograph. He becomes "Witness Number 42648." He asks if he may speak to his mother? No. Father? No. "You can't speak to anyone. You're a witness. You just answer 'yes' or 'no.'"

"Order in the Court! Order in the Court! Everyone stand up! The Judge is coming in!" growls a bailiff.

The Judge is not the Judge we have seen at all "but the imposing and fearful figure Christopher imagines a Judge to be—shaggy-haired, bulbous-nosed, a large bristling mustache. . . . He goes directly to the Bench and bangs loudly with his gavel."

Christopher is to be sworn. A policeman hands him a book. Yes, Chris knows what happens to him if he swears on the Bible and tells a lie.

"All right," growls the Judge, "repeat this: 'I swear to tell the truth while I am on this stand or God help me.'"

After Christopher repeats the oath, the Judge pounds his gavel three times. Immediately the Courtroom is plunged in darkness. "A blinding white light is turned on Christopher on the witness stand, à la the third degree."

THE JUDGE—Have you, Christopher Blake, son of Mr. and Mrs. Kenneth Blake of this city, made up your mind which one you want to go with? Your mother or your father? Answer "yes" or "no." (CHRIS *is silent*.) Well?—"yes" or "no"?

CHRIS—No. I haven't made up my mind.

THE JUDGE—Well, you know that's what you're here for, don't you? You've got to decide.

CHRIS—Yes, sir. I know that.

THE JUDGE—Well, hurry up. I haven't got all day. I've got other cases besides this. Which is it? Your father or your mother.

CHRIS—I can't—I don't know what to say. (*The* CROWD *laughs.*)

THE JUDGE—You don't know what to say? Why not? Too difficult? Like Arithmetic? I notice you failed in Math. Two terms in a row. (*The* CROWD *laughs again.*) Come on—make up your mind. This is costing the state a lot of money. What's holding you up?

CHRIS—I don't know whose fault it was, sir?

THE JUDGE—The divorce?

CHRIS—Yes, sir.

THE JUDGE—What's that got to do with it—whose fault it was. What's it matter to you?

CHRIS—It does matter. If I knew whose fault it was—if I could get it straight—it would be easier. I wouldn't go with the one who did this. But I'm all mixed up in my mind. They didn't tell me the truth until today—and now I'm all mixed up.

BOY IN CROWD—Like if you had to paper a room 18 x 20 how many rolls of wallpaper would you need, eh, Chris? (*The* CROWD *laughs.*)

THE JUDGE—Well, whose fault do you think it was? If they told you the truth you ought to know. Whose fault was it?

CHRIS—Maybe you could help me—it's so mixed up. I thought it was my father's fault at first. He said it was himself. He—he made friends with another woman.

THE JUDGE—Well, that's simple enough. Sure it's his fault. Go with your mother. All right—you ready to decide? (*He lifts rubber stamp ready to stamp the papers and close the case.*)

CHRIS—But he stopped being friends with her. He doesn't see her any more. Don't grown-up people make mistakes, too?

Stumblingly Christopher tries to explain his mother's position, too; to tell of her long time knowing that she was not happy with his father; that she had always wanted him (Christopher), and loved him, but that she can't help doing what she's doing.

The Judge is confused, or pretends to be. If, as Chris says, his father loves his mother, why did he make a friend of another woman? He knew that was wrong—

"Yes, sir, but he doesn't see her any more," protests Chris.

"Maybe he'll see her again after the divorce, Chris. Maybe

he'll bring her up to school—we can all take a look at her!" yells a boy in the crowd. There is a great laugh at this.

THE JUDGE—And your mother could forgive him for *that*—but it's not that at all, it's something that happened even before you were born! And she can't help doing this! And your father still loves her! And you're all mixed up! (*The* CROWD *roars with laughter.*) And I'm supposed to sit here wasting my time while you make up your mind, am I? While you sit there and decide whose fault it was! Well, do you know whose fault *I* think it was?
CHRIS—No, sir.
THE JUDGE—Your fault! If you hadn't been born they'd have been divorced years ago. Can't you see that? If they loved you— either one of them—they wouldn't be doing this now, would they? Why are they making you decide? Why don't they decide for themselves? Because it's your fault—that's why! Because they never wanted you in the first place! They don't care who gets you!
THE BOYS (*chanting in unison*)—Mr. Blake, Mr. Blake, Mr. Blake had a wife he couldn't take, Up the river, down the lake, Blake had a wife he couldn't take!

Chris can't stand any more. Blazing with anger "he leaps down from the stand and rushes at the boys, his fists flying." Everyone in the room is laughing now and jeering. The lights begin to dim.
For a moment the laughter continues in the darkness. When the lights come up Chris is just coming through the door of the real courtroom. "It is the very opposite of Christopher's fantasy; a bright, cheerful room, empty, except for the two lawyers, Mr. Blake, the Judge on the Bench and the Court attendant. Christopher stands hesitant in the doorway for a moment."
"Hello, Christopher. Come on up and sit down," calls the Judge, cheerily.
"Yes, sir." Chris crosses the room and sits on the edge of the chair.
"We've all been a mighty long time about this, Chris," explains the Judge. "Couldn't be helped, I'm afraid. The minute you start fooling around with lawyers, you're dead."
The Judge offers Chris a life-saver. He prefers gum himself, but of course he can't chew gum on the Bench. The Judge knows all about Boy Scouts, too. Knew Dan Beard in the old days. Fine old fella, Beard. "He could do anything any of the scouts could do," boasts the Judge. Is Christopher a baseball fan? Yes,

sir. A Giant fan? Yes, sir. "You looked like a Giant man to me," admits the Judge, with a smile. "Well, we're both in trouble this year, Chris. I guess you know that."

After a while the Judge seems suddenly to remember the business of the moment. "Well, now, *I* seem to be doing all the talking, here, Chris. I'd kinda like to hear from you."

"Yes, sir."

"No hurry, Chris. We've kept you waiting all day. Just take your time and say anything you want to say. I'm sure you've been doing a lot of thinking about it, haven't you? (CHRISTOPHER *does not answer.*) I'd just like to hear from you yourself, Chris, in your own way. What do you want to do, and why—just anything you've got on your mind, Chris. If you'd like me to ask you some questions, why, I can do that, but why don't you just tell me, Chris."

For a moment there is complete silence. "Christopher sits utterly still—then it comes. Complete hysteria—wave after wave. He puts his arm across his face and his voice comes chokingly through sobs."

"I can't! I can't!" shrieks Chris. "I don't want to say! I don't want to say! I want my mother and I want my father! I want 'em both! I can't say which one! I don't know! I don't know! They don't want me! They don't care! They don't want me!" He can speak no longer. He is sobbing wildly.

"Mr. Blake—Mrs. Blake—I think you had better talk to your son. The Court will recess for fifteen minutes."

Mr. and Mrs. Blake hurry toward Chris as the lights dim out. The stage is in complete darkness, a small light picking out Christopher's face—"panic and anguish writ plain across it."

"They don't want me! They don't care!" he continues to cry out. Now he has covered his face with his hands. "They don't want me! What'll I do? What'll I do?"

Through the blackness a shaft of light is focused on two giant brass-studded doors back of Chris. Becoming aware of them, they suggest to him a way of escape. He charges against them, but they are locked. He hammers with his fists against one and then the other. Suddenly one of the doors opens, revealing the Judge seated at his stand in the real Courtroom.

"You see, Chris," the Judge is saying, "you can't run away from it. There's no way out. There just isn't. You'd better choose, Christopher. You'd better do it."

"All right! All right! I will! I will! I'll go with my mother!"

Immediately Mr. Blake steps from the darkness. "So that's what you're going to do?" he says. "So that's the thanks I get! Who took you to baseball games, Chris? Who bought you your Scout equipment? Who stood up for you against Mom when you got bad marks at school? . . . This is the thanks I get, is it? Well, go ahead and do what you want to—only don't ever come around me. I don't want you—you're not my boy—I don't want any part of you!"

"Oh, no! No! I am your boy! I want to be your boy! I'll go with you! Don't say I'm not your boy! Take it back! I'll go with you!"

Now Mrs. Blake steps out of the darkness. "Then you don't want me?" she says. "Is that right, Chris? You don't want me to kiss you any more—or to be there when you're sick—or have our talks together—I won't be there any more when you're in trouble—or for Christmas—or for your birthday—I won't be there when you bring Bob home—and when Bob talks about his mother you won't have any mother to talk about. . . . If this is the way you feel—you don't want me—you're not my Chris any more. I don't want you this way."

"Mom! Dad!" Chris has turned frantically to the Judge. "Help me! Help me! You're a Judge—why don't you help me! I thought you were going to tell me what to do! Why don't you tell me what to do? You talk to me about baseball—I don't care about baseball now—why don't you help me?"

The Judge can think of nothing but another baseball reminiscence. It's about the big game in Appleton. As he starts to speak the doors open slowly and out of them come baseball players to take their positions in the formation of a diamond. As he continues "all the creatures of Christopher's fantasies pour out of the darkness and mix crazily with the baseball players. President Truman, the Generals, the Newsreel Photographers, the Headmaster, Miss Holly, the People of the Poorhouse, the Bailiffs, the Spectators in the Courtroom and the Judge of Christopher's inner terror. They weave in and out among the ball players as the Judge continues to describe the game, like a silent, nightmare ballet, as Christopher's hysteria reaches its height—"

"Jones dropped a dinky in short left and Smith put him on second with a handle hit that got past the third baseman," the Judge drones on; . . . "The only thing I can do in a place like that is to try to fog it past him. Give it everything right down the middle and trust in God. So that's what I did, Christopher, with everything I had left. He missed it a foot!"

The lights have come up in the Judge's Chambers. "Chris, his hands covering his face, is seated in the big leather chair, his mother kneeling beside him. On the other side of his chair his father kneels also, both of them trying to stem the flood, to comfort him—"

MRS. BLAKE—Chris—Baby—don't—don't! We love you! Don't you know that? We always have and we always will. Baby, don't, please! We want you more than anything else in the world! Both of us! Won't you believe me, darling?

CHRIS (*chokingly*)—I don't believe it. Why are you doing this to me? Why?

MR. BLAKE—Chris, we're not "doing" this to you. Try and listen to me, Chris.

CHRIS—I can't help crying. I'm ashamed, but I can't help it.

MR. BLAKE—I know. Of course you can't. But I want you to listen to this. I want you to get one thing very clear. We both want you very, very much. So much, Chris, that we couldn't decide. We agreed on everything else but we couldn't agree on that. That's why we wanted you to say, Chris. We couldn't help ourselves, Chris.

MRS. BLAKE—Chris, dear, it's true. It's true. You must believe Dad and me about that. Won't you, darling?

CHRIS—But I don't want to choose. What good is that? What good is having a mother and no father—or the other way 'round. What good is it?

MRS. BLAKE—But you'll have us both. Don't you understand, Chris? It doesn't mean you won't ever see one of us again.

CHRIS—Oh, sure. I'll see you once a year or something if I'm lucky. (*Again he breaks into sobs.*)

MR. BLAKE—Satisfied, Evie? It's not a very pretty sight—but maybe you like it! I don't know. What kind of a woman are you, Evie? I don't know that either. What kind of a woman are you? Me—all right—I accept that—I don't understand it—but all right—but to do this to Chris—to know what it's doing to him! What do you want, Evie? Anything I've overlooked—anything I've missed doing? You want me on my knees—you want me to grovel? Go ahead, Evie—tell me. I'll do it! I'm not like you, Evie. I can't see my child suffer. Go ahead! What do you want? Let's hear from you, Evie. I'd like to know how you're able to stand there and take this. I would—I really would!

MRS. BLAKE—What are you trying to do, Ken? Tear me down in front of Chris?

MR. BLAKE—Yes! Yes! Maybe I am! Maybe I'm trying to show you up! It's about time! I've tried every other way! Maybe this is the kind of talk you understand!

MRS. BLAKE—All right! If that's the way you want it you can have it! I never told you this—I told Chris—but I never wanted you to know. It's not Ruth—it never was. It wasn't right fourteen years ago. It wasn't ever right. If that's what you want you've got it.

There is a dead silence for a moment. Then Mr. Blake takes up the argument as he sees it. He sneers at the suggestion that Evie had used Ruth as an excuse to spare him. Certainly she had done pretty well for fourteen years—what with her food, shelter and someone to pay the bills. What had happened? Probably she had got a little bored after she had made full use of him. Well, so long as they are at it, they had better drag everything out. Let Chris know everything. There are a few things Mr. Blake would like to know himself. Was their married life ever right. If so, when did it stop being right? All those years that he had thought they were happy together, was she just grinning and bearing it? No, she protests, that's not right.

"Because I was happy with you—sometimes, Kenneth," Mrs. Blake tries to explain. "Those were the times that would make me try again—make me believe it could work, give me new hope that it would. I kept trying because of those times and because of Chris. And you, too. And myself. That's true whether you believe it or not."

But wherein had he failed? And when? Mr. Blake insists on knowing. Let Chris know, too. It concerns him also, right down to the ground. It was, Mrs. Blake tries to explain, when she saw that her own marriage was turning into just such an unhappy venture as she had seen her mother's become. It was this situation she had come to New York to get away from. She had hoped to avoid "bitterness, and pretense and dishonesty" that she had seen in her own home. Her mother had tried, too, but she had stuck it out and her marriage was a failure—

". . . Ken, I didn't come to this without pain, believe me. I know what this has been for you, and now for Chris—but, Ken, pain isn't always destructive. Maybe this is right for us. Think about it for a minute, Ken, please."

It is a long minute before he answers. "Don't you think most people grow apart after a while? Don't you think every marriage has its own crisis?"

"Yes."

"What do you think most women do, Evie? They get through it somehow. They compromise—they don't destroy it. Why can't you? Don't you think some of these years have been tough sledding for me, too? . . . What are you reaching for? Why can't we try it together? Because no matter what you say now, I know what we once had and I'm willing to fight to make it work again. Why can't you?"

"Because I've faced it, Ken. Why can't you? Part of all this fight you're putting up is not just for me—you may think it is but it isn't—you like the way your life is now—the way it's arranged and run and settled. You don't want it changed—you don't want all this smashed up no matter how we put the pieces together again, but we don't belong together any more, Ken. We haven't anything to share any more, Ken. We haven't anything to share any more."

When they had started out, Mrs. Blake goes on, they at least had their loneliness, their need of someone to cling to, their need for a home and a life together. Now there isn't even that, or anything else—

". . . Our whole life has been a compromise to safety and security and the good-will of people I don't care a damn about. I'm not judging them or you, Ken, but I can't compromise any longer."

The attendant has appeared to warn them that the Judge cannot give them much more time. "Tell him to wait!" snaps Mr. Blake. "Tell him it may be just another case to him, but we're fooling around with our lives in here, that's all. Tell him to wait!"

Mr. Blake has crossed the room and is staring out the window. Now he comes back and drops wearily into a chair. He is bending and rebending a packet of paper matches in his hand. When he speaks it is as though he were "talking aloud into space or to himself."

"I guess I know now, Evie," he is saying. "I guess I've really known for a long time. Funny—it never surprises you about other people—their marriages—but your own—somehow you can't think of it happening to you. It's always somebody else who gets run down by that taxi—not you. How did we come to this, Evie? Where did we go wrong? We have grown apart—terribly—and yet Ruth gave me everything you didn't—and it was no good. I'm afraid it will always be you, Evie? Do you think I can—change, Evie? . . . I'd like to be—the person you want me to be,

Evie. I'd like to try. We've never really faced it like this—together. I'd like to try."

She has come to his side. Her hand drops tenderly on his shoulder. "Ken, oh, Ken, dear—what does this do to us—why isn't your loving me enough? What can I say? I have no answer. I don't know. Oh, Ken, I don't know."

She is weeping openly. The Judge comes from the Courtroom. He pays no attention to Mr. and Mrs. Blake, crossing directly to Chris. If Chris is feeling better he thinks they might go on with their chinning right there. It is okay with Chris. Well, the Judge hopes Chris doesn't feel ashamed of the way he had busted out in the Courtroom. The Judge thinks he did the right thing. A lot better than making believe he didn't care.

"Say, I'd like to ask you something, Chris," the Judge goes on. "You know I go through this thing every day— It isn't always as tough as this, but it's never easy. Been doing it for a long time, too. What do you think goes through my mind when I have to decide about a feller like you?"

"I don't know, sir."

"Well, I'll tell you something, Chris—you're going to learn it yourself after a while, but I think you can see what I mean even now. Y'see, when I was your age I felt just the way you do. Once I grew up—made my own decisions—no one telling me what to do—I'd know all the answers—just get grown-up and the answer would be in the back of the book. Well, it isn't, Chris. Grown-ups get lost, too—just as much as children. I know how you felt inside—lost and alone—not knowing what to do—where to turn—well, grown-ups get that way, too."

This trouble that people have with marriage, the Judge explains, is nothing new. It has been going on as long as marriage has existed. Nowadays people face such troubles more often. "I think it's better to face it openly and honestly. Lots of people come before me and I don't always try and bring them together, Chris. Sometimes I do, because I feel that if they can get over that one jam they're in, they've got a good chance to make it work and they ought to try. . . . And, Chris, the toughest thing in the world that I know of is the relationship between a man and a woman. I tell you, Chris, it's a tribute to the downright courage and decency of men and women that so many do stick it out."

He looks at Chris and smiles. "Yes," he goes on, "I can see you expect me to have the answer. Well, I haven't, Chris. Except that maybe not many human beings are grown-up enough to make good marriages. I don't know what's right, Chris—I just know an awful lot of what's wrong. And that the answer is not in the back of the book, Chris. Grown-ups get lost, too. Listen— I'm going to ask you a big question. You don't have to answer it if you don't want to but I'd like you to. You've heard a good deal now, and I think you're a pretty smart feller. Suppose you were me, Chris, sitting up there on that Bench. What would you decide—not about yourself—not just what's going to happen to you—but about your mother and father—what's good for them?"

Chris takes his time. "You mean—you want me to say?"

"Yes, Chris, I do."

"Oh, I never thought about it this way but—I guess Mom ought to do this. I think maybe it's right. She'll be a lot happier this way. I kinda understand it more now."

"Well, now you know something, Chris? That was a mighty important thing you said. That's the first sign of really growing up when you begin to think of another person's happiness—not just your own. Children are a very selfish people, Chris. Wonderful and terrible. They think the sun rises and sets in them. Nothing usually matters to 'em but what's going to happen to *them*. And sometimes they never get past that—all their lives. Chris—you've just made a big step forward. You're going to be all right. I wish I were as sure of the Giants! I'll be inside when you want me."

For a moment, they stand utterly still. Mr. Blake is first to break the silence. He is a little shocked at Chris' decision. Not that he thinks it's wrong—only—well, he had always hoped Chris had wanted them all to be together—

Chris does—but he has come to see it can't be that way. A moment later, after his father has suggested that perhaps his mother and he should go in and tell the Judge, Chris says, a little plaintively—

"Don't I still have to say which one I'm going with?"

"Yes."

"Yes, Chris," echoes Mrs. Blake.

"I'm—I'm going to stay with Dad."

There is a considerable stillness before they can adjust themselves to the shock. Then Mr. Blake quietly takes Chris in his arms and holds him very close. When he releases him, he looks wildly toward the door and bolts.

Mrs. Blake has dropped into a chair and has begun to cry— softly, quietly, almost without a sound.

"Don't cry, Mom," pleads Chris, softly. "Mom, don't cry, please."

MRS. BLAKE—I have to cry, Chris, for a minute—it hurts. Just give me a moment. I didn't know—how much it was going to hurt. Oh, Chris, it does!

CHRIS—Mom. . . .

MRS. BLAKE—I guess I always thought you'd choose me, Chris —that's how vain—how selfish—I am. And suddenly I feel so empty—so alone. Give me just a moment, Chris.

CHRIS—You all right, Mom?

MRS. BLAKE—Yes, Chris.

CHRIS—You're not—mad at me—are you, Mom?

MRS. BLAKE—No, Chris. I'm very proud of you. (*She takes his face in her hands and looks tenderly at him.*) Darling, you're wiser and stronger than both of us. And Dad needs you very, very much—you felt that, didn't you? You knew it. (CHRISTOPHER *nods.*) The Judge is right, Chris—you're growing up—this is the beginning. Sometimes it happens this way—in an hour or in a day. Suddenly you grow up. You make me feel kind of old, Chris.

CHRIS (*as she smiles and turns her face away*)—I'll be able to come to California to see you, won't I? On a vacation?

MRS. BLAKE—Of course, darling. And I'll be coming back— often. I'll be back for Christmas, certainly.

CHRIS—You won't be lonely, will you, Mom?

MRS. BLAKE—A little. You won't write me those nasty little bits of letters you usually write, will you?

CHRIS—No. I'll write big ones, Mom. I promise.

MRS. BLAKE—Don't forget, Chris. Because I'll be missing you and thinking about you all the time. But I'm going to be all right, Chris, because *you* are—you don't know how much that means!

CHRIS—I'm glad, Mom. (*He leans over and kisses her, and they cling to each other silently until the outer door opens and* MR. BLAKE *returns.*)

MR. BLAKE—Hello. . . . Didn't mean to make such a fool of myself. (*He smiles gently.*) Well—shouldn't we take some steps to get out of here—finally?

MRS. BLAKE—Oh, yes, Ken—let's. I'm ready.

MR. BLAKE—Okay, Chris?

CHRIS—Okay. I can tell the Judge myself. You don't have to come in with me.

MR. BLAKE—No?

CHRIS—Oh, sure. I can do it by myself.

MR. BLAKE—Yes, Chris, I guess you can. Okay, Chris. Go ahead.

His mother and father are standing watching him as Chris walks briskly toward the door to the Courtroom. At the door he turns and smiles back at them—"a proud boyish grin of assurance and reality." They are standing motionless, smiling back as the door closes behind him.

THE CURTAIN FALLS

BRIGADOON

A Musical Fantasy in Two Acts

BOOK BY ALAN JAY LERNER; MUSIC BY FREDERICK LOEWE

ON only two previous occasions have we included plays with music in this annual record of the New York theatre. The season of 1931-32 we headed the play list with the Kaufman-Gershwin "Of Thee I Sing," a timely political satire of such compelling superiority as to demand inclusion. Ten years later we added the Rodgers-Hammerstein "Oklahoma," both because of its outstanding quality as a musical comedy and also because it had been built on the framework of Lynn Riggs' "Green Grow the Lilacs," a "Best Plays" selection of the 1930-31 season.

Our contention has been, quite reasonably we think, that a musical score usually adds so much to the libretto of any musical comedy that it dwarfs the importance of the libretto if it does not practically obliterate it. "The music is excellent (or fair, or good, or average) but the book is frankly disappointing." This long ago became a commonplace comment in eight out of every ten musical comedy reviews. It continues to appear in most critical estimates.

During this season of 1946-47, however, we were witness to a revival of interest in musical plays that happens to have been excited by the unexpected quality and unusual novelty of the works themselves, as you will find more fully reported in the chapter devoted to "The Season in New York."

"Brigadoon" has been chosen to represent this re-emergence of the American music play of quality, and the novelty of the fantasies that have come with it. It was voted by the New York Drama Critics' Circle as the best musical play of the year. This could have come as a pleasant surprise to the Alan Jay Lerner who wrote the book to match a musical score by Frederick Loewe, but probably didn't. The boys had become used to praise by the time the critics met.

It was a general impression at the time "Brigadoon" was shown that Mr. Lerner had accidentally hit upon an old Scottish legend having to do with a disappearing village of the Scottish Highlands

369

and worked it over into a story suitable for staging. He assures me that isn't true—

"I have been a James Barrie lover since I was a wee lad," says he, "and lurking somewhere in the back of my mind the last five years existed the ambition to write something with a Scottish background. . . . One day, while in the throes of writing 'The Day Before Spring' my partner and composer, Frederick Loewe, mentioned something about faith moving mountains.

"This started me thinking. For a while I had a play about faith moving a mountain. From there, as I remember, we went on to all sorts of miracles occurring through faith, and eventually faith moved a town. So, in a way, the last scene of 'Brigadoon' was really the beginning of the idea. The fact that so many people ask me if 'Brigadoon' is a real legend I have always taken as rather a compliment, because we tried to write it in as much a 'legendary' way as possible."

I think Mr. Lerner is to be congratulated upon the skill developed in his search for the legendary atmosphere used in telling the story of "Brigadoon." Also, as editor, I am again seriously conscious of the complete impossibility of doing his story justice without the use of Mr. Loewe's appealing score and more particularly without being able to indicate satisfactorily the very considerable charm that Agnes de Mille has so deftly woven into the text of the whole with her staging of a dozen or so Scottish dances.

However, if we have been able to give some idea of the type of musical novelty that has played so important a part in this Broadway theatre season of 1946-47 we will rest content with that.

Being familiar with various styles of musical comedies, and with many varieties of opera—light, heavy, comic, romantic and grand —you doubtless are also familiar with the opening chorus. You would naturally be more familiar with it if you had ever been able to understand what the smiling choristers were singing.

In the musical fantasy the opening chorus takes on an added importance. In addition to telling the audience what and who the choristers are, and, it may be, something of what the authors hope to state, or to prove, or even merely to suggest, as the evening wears on, the opening chorus should help to set the fantastic scene.

Thus in "Brigadoon," after we have pushed by the more fortunate aisle seaters and found our places, we are conscious that the orchestra is still softly continuing the overture. Now the lights are down and the curtain is up. We are looking upon "a forest in the Highlands of Scotland."

It is about 5 o'clock in the morning, and in the soothing description of our librettist, "The forest is dipped in the deep gray that comes between night and morning," a gray that lightens as the scene progresses.

It is while we are still absorbing this forest scene that the harmonious notes of the overture gradually fade and we hear from somewhere quite near, and yet not too near, a chorus singing. It is quite possible you will again not be able to make out the words. So, here they are—

> "Once in the Highlands, the Highlands of Scotland,
> Deep in the night on a murky brae;
> There in the Highlands, the Highlands of Scotland,
> Two weary hunters lost their way.
> And this is what happened,
> The strange thing that happened
> To two weary hunters who lost their way."

In the forest we meet two young men, Tommy Albright and Jeff Douglas. "Tommy is about thirty. He is of medium height, virile-looking, with an attractive but sensitive face. He is dressed in tweeds. Jeff is about thirty-five. He is retiring, and good-natured primarily because he doesn't care. He is in gray flannels and a tweed jacket."

In the immediate background a kind of curved bridge of a modified oriental design leads into a mystic somewhere—perhaps a little beyond the trees and the clearing in which Tommy and Jeff have stopped. Jeff is sitting on a sort of rucksack. Tommy, nearer the first step of the bridge, is studying a road map, and Tommy, as even the most casual students of road maps will readily understand, is deeply puzzled. He has found Auchintoul, which is on the left, and Braemore, which is on the right, but where the hell are they?

"What's in the middle?" asks Jeff.

"Nothing."

"That's where we are."

"In nothing?"

"Yes. And for a fellow with my potentialities, this is an ideal location. We'll find our way out when the sun comes up."

Tommy is folding up the map. "A fine couple of game hunters we are. We come all the way over here from New York, and the first night out we get lost."

"Maybe we took the high road instead of the low road," suggests Jeff, extracting a flask from his pocket.

Jeff is not given to drinking as heavily as many comedians. In fact there had been a time quite recently, he admits, when he had planned to give up drinking entirely, this in response to a wonderful girl's pleading. Then he discovered that he and the girl had nothing else to talk about, so they broke up.

Tommy, on the other hand, and he not anything of a drinker, is no more at peace with himself than Jeff, and it worries him—

"That's the silliest thing I've ever heard," exclaims Jeff. "You've got a fine job and you're engaged to a fine girl. What more do you want?"

"I don't know. But something seems wrong, especially about Jane and me. And that makes everything seem wrong. Look how I postpone getting married. I just can't get myself to that altar."

"I don't know what could be wrong about it. She's young, attractive, fits smack into your niche in life; and on top of that she loves you. And just the proper amount, too."

"What's the proper amount?"

"Enough to make you happy and not enough to embarrass your friends."

Again the near-distant voices are heard. It is about a place called Brigadoon that they are singing—

> "Brigadoon, Brigadoon,
> Blooming under sable skies,
> Brigadoon, Brigadoon,
> There my heart forever lies.
> Let the world grow cold around us;
> Let the heavens cry above!
> Brigadoon, Brigadoon,
> In thy valley there'll be love."

Gradually the outlines of a village begin to take form just across the bridge. By some magic the lines deepen, the buildings multiply, and the boys' wonder mounts—

Tommy is pointing. "Look over there!"

"It looks like a village," ventures Jeff.

"It is."

"But I thought you said there were no towns listed on the map around here."

"I did. Look! See where that village is? There's a peculiar heavy fog all around it."

"And there's no other mist in the valley."

"Only around that village. Let's walk over to it. It can't be very far from here. Come on!"

Jeff runs back to recover his flask and they disappear over the bridge.

The curtains close.

Scene 2

We are now in MacConnachy Square in Brigadoon. "Physically this is an eighteenth-century-looking community. It was the custom in Scotland then for a fair to be held once a week. At these fairs, the townsfolk engaged in mutual buying, selling and bartering. This, then, is the activity of the moment."

Most of the buying is done at a series of booths and carts very like contest booths at a modern amusement park. There are a half dozen of these around the Square—"a milk and cream booth presided over by a middle-thirtied Scot named Angus MacGuffie. . . . A candy booth run by Sandy Dean. . . . A weaving cart covered with wools, plaids and the like, operated by a kind-looking Scot about fifty named Archie Beaton."

The singing natives of Brigadoon are filling the square in groups of twos and threes and fours. They are gathering, they tell you melodiously, from the hills and the mills, from the looms, from pails and brooms. When there's a fair down on MacConnachy Square you can count on their gathering there from everywhere.

Now Sandy would sell you a bit of the sweetest candy that ever "shook loose a tooth." Or Angus would supply you a glass of the finest milk and cream that "ever came out of a cow." "There's nothin' to do but sell it all," Angus confides. "The cow winna take it back."

There is a good deal of buying and bartering of one sort and another by the tuneful citizenry. Andrew MacLaren is there with his two pretty daughters—Fiona, about twenty-two, "who is bright, has a gentle sense of humor and is completely frank and direct to a point that is often quite disarming," and Jean, about eighteen, who "is also attractive but obviously shy and diffident."

Soon, being attentive, we learn that Fiona has come to the fair hoping to buy a jacket for her father to wear to the wedding, and that at the wedding bonnie Jean will be the bride and young Charlie Dalrymple the groom. The announcement is not pleasing to Archie Beaton. He had hoped Jean would choose his son Harry, and jealous Harry Beaton is prepared to be downright nasty about it.

For a moment Mr. MacLaren stops the activities of the Square, and calls the friends around him. He has brought a parchment on which the dominie, Mr. Lundy, has written a few reminders. Mr. MacLaren will hang it in the Square where they all can read it—

"This is the second day of our blessing," Mr. LacLaren reminds them, "and this is to remind ye of the obligations we have so gratefully accepted." There is a proper stir among the citizens.

Now we meet Meg Brockie, who has also come a-shopping, and largely for men. "Meg is about twenty-five or so. She is a brash, buxom, wide-eyed, impulsive young woman."

Being as she is, Meg finds it hard to understand why Fiona is not envious of her sister, Jean, for being the bride of the day. Marriage is an important business to Meg. She can't understand any girl's looking lightly upon a lack of opportunity to marry, whatever the cause. Fiona is not impressed. She is impelled to state her idea in a song—"Waitin' for My Dearie"—

> "Many a lassie, as everyone knows, 'll
> Try to be married before twenty-five.
> So she'll agree to most any proposal
> All he mus' be is a man an' alive.

> "I hold a dream an' there's no compromisin';
> I know there's one certain laddie for me.
> One day he'll come walking o'er the horizon;
> But should he not then an old maid I'll be.

> "Foolish ye may say.
> Foolish I will stay.
> Waitin' for my dearie
> An' happy am I
> To hold my heart till he comes strollin' by."

Eight of the prettiest Brigadoon heartily agree with Fiona, and are also prepared to assert their understanding by repeating the chorus of her song with her—

> "Though I'll live forty lives
> Till the day he arrives
> I'll not ever, ever grieve.
> For my hopes will be high
> That he'll come strollin' by;
> For ye see, I believe

> "That there's a laddie weary
> An' wanderin' free
> Who's waiting for his dearie;
> Me!"

The music has stopped abruptly. Tommy and Jeff are entering the Square. The citizens have practically been struck dumb. In both amazement and curiosity the boys stroll through the crowd, trading stare for stare, smile for smile. Finally they venture a timid "Hello!" and get another "Hello!" equally uncertain, back—

JEFF—Could you tell us where we are?

ARCHIE—Of course we can tell ye. Ye're in Brigadoon.

TOMMY—Brigadoon?

ARCHIE—Aye.

TOMMY—That's funny. There's no town called Brigadoon on the map.

ARCHIE—I shouldna be surprised.

JEFF—You mean you know it isn't on the map?

ARCHIE—Aye.

JEFF—It's a little snobbish of you, don't you think?

TOMMY—Why isn't it on the map?

ARCHIE—For good and sound reasons.

JEFF (*to* MEG)—What are you all dressed up for? Is this the day you take pictures for post-cards?

MEG—We're not dressed up.

JEFF—You mean you always walk around looking like this?

TOMMY—Now come on. Somebody. What's going on here? What is this?

MEG—We're having a fair.

TOMMY—Oh! (*Seeing the cream booth.*) Is that milk you're selling there?

ANGUS—Aye!

TOMMY—Can I buy some? I'm thirsty. I've been walking all night.

ANGUS—I'll have to see your money first.

TOMMY—What? (*He stops, then shrugs and tosses* ANGUS *a coin.* ANGUS *takes it and before* TOMMY *can move any nearer the booth, a group gathers quickly around* ANGUS *examining the coin. Exclamations of "Oh" and "Ah" and "Look at the date" and "Nineteen hundred and—" come from the group.*)

JEFF (*as he and* TOMMY *look at each other in amazement*)— What did you give him, a small diamond?

Tommy—Just a shilling.

Jeff—It's a good thing you didn't pull out a pound note. They'd've all dropped dead.

Tommy—What a loony lay-out this is!

Angus (*handing* Tommy *the coin*)—'Tis very interesting, sir, but it does me no good.

Tommy (*a little irritated*)—What do you mean it does you no good? Sell me something and it will.

Angus—I'm sorry, but I canna sell ye anythin'. However, if ye're thirsty I'll *give* ye some milk.

Tommy—Never mind. I don't want any favors.

Meg takes over the investigation and discovers that Tommy and Jeff are not English, but American. This intrigues her mightily, but her enthusiasm is not shared completely by Jeff. Meg, he indicates to Tommy, is "obviously the daughter of two first cousins."

Then Fiona steps in with the suggestion that the visitors must not mind the manners of the townspeople. They are naturally a little startled, seeing that people do not come to Brigadoon very often—

"If ye've been walkin' all night, ye must be tired and hungry," suggests Fiona. "Winna ye like somethin' to eat an' perhaps a place to lie down afore ye start back?"

"That's very nice of you," answers Tommy. He turns to Jeff. "What do you think?"

"I could use some refreshments," admits Jeff, tapping his flask pocket. "It's empty."

It is Fiona's suggestion that they go to a little tavern in the next street, where they can get food. Meg is quick to volunteer as guide. She enthusiastically grabs the reluctant Jeff's arm. They are passing the weaver's cart when Archie Beaton leans out—

"Is Miss Meg going to take care of ye, sir?" the weaver asks Jeff.

"I think so. Why?"

"Well, I have some plaid trousers here an' after ye leave the tavern if Miss Meg should take ye some place to rest an' ye should happen to rip your own on a thistle, I'd be more than pleased to replace them for ye."

"Thanks, old man, but I don't expect to get stuck."

Archie begins to chuckle. "Laddie, ye dinna know it, but ye're stuck now!"

"Ye tend to your sellin', Mr. Beaton."

Meg and Jeff have gone on. Tommy lingers to ask Fiona where

he might find a phone, but they know naught of phones in that village.

"Tell me," persists Tommy. "What's so strange about this town?"

"Nothin', sir. You're the one who's strange."

And now Charlie Dalrymple, the bridegroom to be, appears with a group of boisterous fellows. "Charlie is a sandy-haired youth in his early twenties. He has a ruddy, glowing complexion, and a twinkle in his eye."

He is gay, is Charlie, and happy in the thought of his marrying bonnie Jean. He's grateful for Jean, and grateful, too, to Mr. Forsythe "for postponin' the miracle."

Tommy is interested. What would the miracle be? Fiona is evasive. " 'Tis a toast we have," she says. "I'll explain it to ye sometime." Next thing they know Charlie has burst into song— "I'll Go Home with Bonnie Jean—"

> "I used to be a rovin' lad,
> A rovin' an' wanderin' life I had.
> On any lass I'd frown
> Who would try to tie me down
> But then one day I saw a maid
> Who held out her hand an' I stayed an' stayed.
> An' now, across the green,
> I'll go home with bonnie Jean."

The townsfolk know the chorus perfectly and sing it lustily. Charlie continues a series of promises of reform and ends with—

> "Hello to married men I've known.
> I'll soon have a wife an' leave yours alone.
> A bonnie wife indeed,
> And she'll be all I'll ever need.

> "With bonnie Jean my days will fly.
> An' love her I will till the day I die.
> That's why, across the green,
> I'll go home with bonnie Jean."

It is after Charlie Dalrymple has gone home to rest up that Tommy admits to Fiona that "it's wonderfully refreshing to see a fellow so enthusiastic about getting married."

FIONA—Is it so unusual?
TOMMY—I think it is. Look at me. I'm not bubbling over like

Charlie. And next month I'm legalizing my desires.

Fiona—Ye're getting married?

Tommy—Yes.

Fiona—Oh!

Tommy—Oh—what?

Fiona—I'm very surprised. Somehow ye dinna look like the sort of lad who would want to settle down.

Tommy—I didn't say that. I just said I was getting married.

Fiona—If ye feel that way, why are ye?

Tommy—Because the girl wants to.

Fiona—Is that reason enough?

Tommy—Sure. I don't know how it is in the Highlands, but in my neighborhood if you've been going with a woman for a while and she decides she wants to get married, you'd better agree right away and save yourself a lot of trouble.

Fiona—Why?

Tommy—Because if you don't, she'll either torment you so you'll marry her for relief. Or she'll be so sweet about it you'll feel guilty and your conscience will make you do it.

Fiona—I must say it dinna sound like ye love your wife-to-be very much.

Tommy—It doesn't, does it?

Fiona—An' it also sounds like a very peculiar land ye come from.

Tommy—Well, believe me, "lass," this isn't the usual hamlet off the highway either. What was that business about Charlie and the man who postponed the miracle?

Fiona—Oh, that. (*Thinks a moment.*) I'm sorry. I canna say.

Tommy—But you said you'd tell me later.

Fiona—I know. But I canna say.

Tommy—That's fine. You know, if I hang around this town very long I'll probably discover that everybody in it is slightly nutty. Is that possible?

Fiona—I canna say.

Tommy—Why not?

Fiona—I dinna know what "nutty" means.

Tommy—It means slightly insane.

Fiona (*turning on him suddenly*)—Well, then I can assure ye we're all far from insane. We're a most blessed group of people. An' I never realize how fortunate we are until I meet someone from the outside—I mean a stranger to Brigadoon. I dinna know anythin' about ye, but from the little ye've said I'm quite certain that everythin' ye think I think differently about, an' I'm also quite certain that what I think is much more— (*She begins to calm down.*) . . . Well . . . pleasant. An' now I'm sorry I said all that, but ye angered me when ye called us insane.

TOMMY (*quite surprised and a bit sheepish at the outburst*)— Hey, you don't like me very much, do you?

FIONA—That's the odd part. I like ye very much. I jus' dinna like anythin' ye say.

Fiona must be going, she announces, to gather some heather for the wedding. Tommy would like to go along, but she thinks she would work much faster alone.

"I won't bother you. Really," promises Tommy. "Maybe I'm the one who's slightly nutty, but . . ."

As Fiona starts to walk away from him Tommy decides to try a song—"The Heather on the Hill—"

> "Can't we two go walkin' together
> Out beyond the valley of trees.
> Out where there's a hillside of heather
> Curtseyin' gently in the breeze,
> That's what I'd like to do:
> See the heather—but with you.
> The mist of May is in the gloamin'
> And all the clouds are holdin' still.
> So take my hand and let's go roamin'
> Through the heather on the hill."

By the time he has finished a second verse, Fiona is quite impressed. It just goes to show that he "can say nice things when he wants to."

"It almost sounded like I was makin' love to you, didn't it?" ventures Tommy.

"Oh! There's a difference between makin' love and jus' bein' sentimental because ye're tired."

"Is that what I'm being—sentimental because I'm tired?"

"I believe so. But 'tis very agreeable."

With this Fiona decides to do a little singing on her own account. Melodiously she picks up the song where Tommy left it—

> "The mist of May is in the gloamin'
> An' all the clouds are holdin' still;
> So take my hand and we'll go roamin'
> Through the heather on the hill.

The mornin' dew is blinkin' yonder;
There's lazy music in the rill;
An' 'tis a lovely time to wander
Through the heather on the hill."

Now their enthusiasm is joined and they finish the song together. For a moment they stand looking wonderingly at each other. The ringing of many bells breaks the spell.

Suddenly the Square begins to fill with townsfolk. The merchants begin taking in their wares, and the music has hit into the tune of "MacConnachy Square."

"What are the chimes for?" demands Tommy.

"That means 'tis the end of the fair," explains Fiona. "Everybody goes back to work now. I'll get my basket an' we'll be off."

The bells are ringing louder now. Everybody is singing. Hand in hand Fiona and Tommy disappear.

The curtains close.

Scene 3

Meg and Jeff have arrived at an open shed on the Brockie place. It is primitively furnished with a sort of cot and an armless rocking chair. It is a little past noon, and Jeff likes the view of the glen, and he is grateful that Meg has brought him there so he can rest. But he is tired. He would like to take a nap.

"I shouldna think a long walk would fatigue a young lad like ye," protests Meg.

"A young lad?"

"Aye! Ye're very young."

"That is either a deliberate lie or wishful thinking. I am ancient, decrepit, and disintegrating rapidly."

Jeff tries the cot and finds it very hard. Meg can't understand that. Her father used to sleep on it fine. Father used to come frequently from the fields after he had finished his plowin', toss off a jug or two of heather ale and go to sleep on that cot. In fact, it was there that Meg's father and mother met—

"Ye see, my mother was a gypsy," relates Meg. "An' one day she was walkin' past this shed an' she saw my father asleep on the cot. She liked his looks an' she was a wee bit tired anyhow, so she took off her shoes, sat in the rockin' chair an' waited for 'im to wake up. An' it wasn't long after that that I was born."

"That's one of the sweetest bedtime stories I ever heard," admits Jeff, lying back as comfortably as possible, on the rock-like cot. Now, if Meg will only go away—he'd like to go asleep. "There are times in every man's life when all he wants to do is to sleep," protests Jeff.

"But dinna ye see? I'm highly attracted to ye."

"Thank you very much. When I wake up we'll discuss the whole problem. And believe me, you have a problem."

"An' when I look at ye lyin' on the cot, I feel little tadpoles jumpin' on my spine."

"That's about as repulsive an idea as I've heard in years. You know, if sex were a hobby, you'd be a collector's item."

Meg has never been lucky with men, drat 'em. She's suffered ever so many heartbreaks. A half dozen of them she has put into a song, "The Love of My Life," which she proceeds to sing with considerable gusto—

"At sixteen years I was blue and sad.
Then father said I should find a lad.
So I set out to become a wife,
An' found the real love of my life.

"His name it was Chris an' his last was MacGill.
I met him one night pickin' flow'rs on the hill.
He had lots of charm an' a certain kind o' touch
An' a certain kind of eagerness that pleased me very much.
So there 'neath the moon where romance often springs,
I gave him my heart—an' a few other things.
I don't know how long that I stayed up on the hill,
But the moon had disappeared, an' so had Christopher MacGill."

After MacGill there was MacGowan, a friend of MacGill's. After MacGowan came a lad from the lowlands. And was he low! A poet and a soldier also had their day, but they too, got away.

"Now pa said: daughter, there must be one.
Someone who's true or too old to run.
So I'm still lookin' to be a wife,
An' find the real love of my life."

By the time Meg has finished her song Jeff is sound asleep. She nudges him a bit, but he doesn't stir. Resigned, she comes back to the rocker, takes off her shoes and sits down. She begins to rock. She is smiling broadly now.

The curtains close.

SCENE 4

In the sparsely furnished living room of the MacLaren home,
about four o'clock that afternoon, a group of Jean's friends have
gathered to help her pack. They are stretched across the room,
from the door of the bride's bedroom to a crate near the opposite
wall. They are passing bits of feminine Scottish clothing down
the line to the girl next to the crate, and she is doing the packing.
Thus, they are packing the hard way, but singing as they do it
and having a good time—

> "Jeanie's packin' up!
> Jeanie's movin' out. . . .

> "The town all knows
> Tonight away she goes!

> "What with all the clothes
> All these an' those,
> Why do ye suppose
> Jeanie never froze?
> Hankies for her nose!
> Ribbons for her bows!
> Cotton for her hose!
> Slippers for her toes!
> Pack all her clothes!
> Tonight away she goes!"

The eager bridegroom appears. Charles MacPherson Dalrymple has come to sign the family Bible. He knows he is not
supposed to see the bride before the wedding, and is content.
"An' ye better not come out," he calls to Jean, "or all our children
will have the temper of your father. . . ."

Charlie has signed the Bible. Jean would send him on his way,
now, but Charlie is reluctant to leave. He must sing a song of
longing first. And does— It's called "Come to Me, Bend to
Me"—

> "Because they've told me
> I can't behold ye
> Till weddin' music starts playin'.
> To ease my longin'
> There's nothin' wrong in
> Me standin' out here an' sayin':

> "Come to me, bend to me, kiss me good day!
> Darlin', my darlin' 'tis all I can say;
> Jus' come to me, bend to me, kiss me good day!
> Gie me your lips an' don't take 'em away."

Again Jean can be heard begging her lover to go away, but Charlie decides to sing another verse or two. Finally he finishes and is gone. The music, however, continues. There is no use wasting this. Stealthily Jean slips in from her room and, finding her singing swain gone, starts a dance with the girls. A very nice dance it is, too. . . .

Fiona and Tommy are back from their heather gathering, a little late but very happy. Jean is pretty mad. Her sister, she says, should have been there long ago to help her start dressing. Now they must hurry.

"Fiona! I want to ask you something," calls Tommy, as Fiona starts for Jean's room. He has followed to the door, and, without a word, takes her in his arms and kisses her.

"What did ye want to ask me?" asks Fiona.

"If I could kiss you."

"Aye! Ye can!"

Jeff is back from his siesta at Meg's cottage. He is sporting a new pair of trousers. "Not brilliant plaid, but obviously new." The thistles had got him. But, Tommy needn't worry. Jeff's other pair will be ready before they leave—

"And another thing, disregard all that rubbish about Scottish frugality," advises Jeff. "Their generosity is overpowering!"

Taking count of their present feelings, both Tommy and Jeff are highly delighted. In fact, Tommy's new enthusiasm for living impels him to again burst into song—something called "Almost Like Being in Love"—

> "Maybe the sun gave me the power,
> For I could swim Loch Lomond
> And be home in
> Half an hour.
> Maybe the air gave me the drive,
> For I'm all aglow and alive.

> "What a day this has been!
> What a rare mood I'm in!
> Why, it's . . . almost like being in love!

There's a smile on my face
For the whole human race.
Why, it's almost like being in love!

"All the music of life seems to be
Like a bell that is ringin' for me!

"And from the way that I feel
When that bell starts to peal,
I would swear I was falling,
I could swear I was falling,
It's almost like being in love."

Fiona has come from Jean's room. She has heard Tommy singing and joins in as quick as anything. She has come for the
heather they brought from the hills, but she stays to finish the
song with Tommy. Which sets Jeff wondering. Just what does
all this loving mean?

"Well, when do we start back?" Jeff asks sharply.

"There's no hurry. Let's stay for the wedding. After all, how
often do you—"

Tommy pauses abruptly. His eyes have fallen on the open
Bible that Charlie Dalrymple left lying on the crate. He picks it
up, reads it a little excitedly—

JEFF—What's the matter?

TOMMY—I must be a little touched. Read this.

JEFF—Married: Elizabeth Lang to Andrew MacLaren. July
second, seventeen nineteen. What's so amazing? People used to
get married then.

TOMMY—Go on.

JEFF—Children: Fiona, born October tenth, seventeen twenty-
two: Jean, born April eighth, seventeen twenty-eight. Well?

TOMMY—That girl in the next room, the one I spent the day
with, her name is Fiona. She's twenty-four. She's got a sister six
years younger named Jean.

JEFF—Well?

TOMMY—But those are the two sisters in that Bible. The
same ones.

JEFF—Ridiculous, they're probably just named after them.

TOMMY—Jean's getting married today. Did you know that?

JEFF—Yes. . . .

TOMMY—Do you know the name of the guy she's marrying?

JEFF—They told me at the tavern. Someone named Dalrymple.

TOMMY—Well, read on.

JEFF—Married Jean MacLaren to Charles MacPherson Dalrymple, May twenty-fourth, seventeen forty-six. (*He looks at* TOMMY *in blank amazement. Neither says a word for a moment.*)

TOMMY—Now what do you say?

JEFF—I don' know.

TOMMY (*piecing it together*)—No Brigadoon on the map. No phones in the whole town. Thanks to Mr. Dumfaddle for doing something about a miracle. And three or four other things that I passed over when I was out with Fiona.

JEFF—That hyper-thyroid I was with never heard of Haig and Haig.

TOMMY—What do you make of it?

JEFF—I don't know.

TOMMY (*suddenly becoming angry*)—Somebody is trying to make awful damn fools of us around here! (*He goes to the door and bangs on it.*) Fiona! And we're going to find out about this right now! (*Shouts.*) Fiona!

FIONA (*opening the door*)—What, Tommy?

TOMMY (*taking her hand and half pulling her down the steps*) —Come here!

FIONA—Tommy! What is it?

TOMMY (*leading her to the Bible*)—Is this your name here in this Bible?

FIONA—Aye! An' why . . . ? (*She stops herself.*) Oh!

JEFF—Someone seems to have loused up your books.

TOMMY—Are these dates right?

FIONA—Aye!

TOMMY—Well, come on! What does all this mean? And let's have no coy evasions either!

FIONA—I canna tell ye, Tommy.

TOMMY—Is there anybody who can? I'd like to know!

FIONA—Ye must talk with the dominie.

TOMMY—The who?

FIONA—Our school master, Mr. Lundie.

TOMMY—Where does he live?

JEFF—Down the road, in a tree.

TOMMY—You're probably right.

FIONA—I'll take ye to 'im. (*The music of "Come to Me, Bend to Me" starts softly in the orchestra.*) An', Tommy, I was hopin' an' prayin' ye wouldna have to be told everythin'.

TOMMY—Why?

FIONA—'Tis goin' to be so hard for ye to believe what ye'll hear. Ye'll think there *is* somethin' wrong with us an' ye'll leave. An' I wanted so for us to have this day together. Promise me ye wouldna go after ye see 'im.

TOMMY—Maybe I will and maybe I won't. All I want to do now is meet him. Come on, Jeff!

They start for the door.
The curtains close.

SCENE 5

A few minutes later Fiona, Tommy and Jeff arrive at Mr. Lundie's cottage. The dominie is sitting on his porch reading. "He is a quaint Scottish school master in his late fifties. Though his eyes have a genuine kindness and his manner is entirely benign he speaks with little trace of emotion. Running from ear to ear, around under his chin, is a semi-circle of white hair. He wears metal-framed glasses. On his head is a red tam-o'-shanter.

Mr. Lundie is pleased to greet Fiona, and to meet her friends. That they are from New York interests him. Yes, he is willing to tell them the story of Brigadoon, as Fiona asks, though he warns them that they will not believe it. Why? Because what had happened in Brigadoon was a miracle. Miracles require faith, and most folk these days, lacking faith, no longer believe in miracles. If any outsider who might chance to come to Brigadoon should hear the story of the miracle he or she would be almost certain to think the one who told it was daft. For this reason the guardianship of the story was placed in Mr. Lundie's hands.

"And you don't imagine anybody would think you're crazy?" inquires a sarcastic Jeff.

"Ye might very well," the dominie admits. "But it winna hurt me. I'd jus' pity ye."

And now he has begun his story. "Two hundred years ago the Highlands of Scotland were plagued with witches; wicked sorcerers who were takin' the Scottish folk away from the teachin's of God an' puttin' the devil in their souls. They were indeed horrible destructive women. I dinna suppose ye have such women in your world."

TOMMY—Witches?

JEFF—Yes, we still have them. We pronounce it differently.

MR. LUNDIE—It dinna matter they were not *real* sorcerers, because ye an' I know there is no such thing. But their influence was very real indeed. Now here in Brigadoon we had an old minister of the kirk named Mr. Forsythe. An' a good man he was.

FIONA—The kindest man in Scotland.

MR. LUNDIE—I believe he was. No man ever loved his parish as did Mr. Forsythe. But he was growin' old, an' it grieved him that one day soon he would leave all those so dear to him. But most of all, he worried about the witches. They hadna visited Brigadoon yet, but he knew there was a band of them comin' our way. So he began to wonder if there wasn't somethin' he could do to protect the folk of his parish not only from them, but from all the evils that might come to Brigadoon from the outside world after he died.

FIONA—What a kind man!

MR. LUNDIE—He spent days walkin' through the glen, thinkin'. An' if ye had passed his house any hour of the night, ye would have seen the candles lit an' Mr. Forsythe sittin' in his chair thinkin'. Then one day he came to me an' told me he had decided to ask God for a miracle.

FIONA—This part is so nice I cry thinkin' about it.

MR. LUNDIE—He consulted with me about it because he knew I had a highly logical mind, an' he figured as long as he was goin' to ask for a miracle, it might as well be a well-organized miracle. So for many days I walked through the glen with him, an' for many nights I sat with him by candle-light. Finally, Mr. Forsythe decided what he was goin' to pray for. An' on an early Wednesday morn right after midnight Mr. Forsythe went out to a hill beyond Brigadoon an' made his prayer to God. There in the hush of a sleepin' world, he asked God that night to make Brigadoon an' all the people in it vanish into the Highland mist. Vanish, but not for always. It would all return jus' as it was for one day every hundred years. The people would go on leadin' their customary lives; but each day when they awakened it would be a hundred years later. An' when we awoke the next day, it was a hundred years later.

TOMMY (whispering)—My God!

MR. LUNDIE—Ye see, in this way Mr. Forsythe figured there would be no change in the lives of the people. They jus' winna be in any century long enough to be touched by it.

Tommy is quite shaken by the dominie's recital. It is difficult for him to believe that when the folk of Brigadoon go to sleep at night and then wake up next morning it is really a hundred years later.

And what had become of Mr. Forsythe, Jeff would like to know.

The minister had disappeared, Mr. Lundie explains. He had known that to ask for such a miracle some sacrifice would have to be made and he elected to be the one to make it. So, the night of his prayer he went out to a hill beyond Brigadoon, knowing that if the miracle were granted he would never see Brigadoon or his beloved family again.

But suppose someone should get fed up and decide to leave Brigadoon. Then what? Does he (Tommy) have to stay there now?

"No, no, lad," Mr. Lundie is quick to explain. "But accordin' to Mr. Forsythe's contract with God, if anyone *of* Brigadoon leaves, the enchantment is broken for all. That night when the people go to sleep, Brigadoon will disappear forever."

But supposing, for the sake of argument, a stranger should come to Brigadoon and want to stay. Could he?

Yes, he could—providing he loves someone of Brigadoon enough to be willing to give up everything and stay with that person.

"Which is how it should be," concludes Mr. Lundie. " 'Caus after all, lad, if ye love someone deeply, anythin' is possible."

It's that part of the story that Fiona loves the best. She must go now and dress for the wedding. Will Tommy be there?

Tommy thinks he will. He has a notion he would like to stick around and see if Brigadoon does really evaporate.

"Tell me, Mr. Lundie, you're all perfectly happy living here in this little town?"

"Of course, lad. After all, sunshine can peep through a small hole."

"But at night when you go to sleep; what's it like?"

"Well, for me, 'tis like bein' carried on shadowy arms to some far-off cloud an' there I float till mornin'. An' yet, sometimes I think I hear strange voices."

"Voices?"

"Aye. They say no words I can remember. But they're voices filled with a fearful longin'; an' often they seem to be callin' me back. I've pondered it when I'm awake; an' I think—I have a feelin' I'm hearin' the outside world. There mus' be lots of folk out there who'd like a Brigadoon."

The distant choir is heard again, and there is a full ringing of wedding bells. Tommy and Jeff move bewilderedly about, preparing to leave. Mr. Lundie shakes both their hands.

The curtains close.

Scene 6

In the dusk of that same day we are standing before the kirk of Brigadoon, waiting for the gathering of the townsfolk for the wedding of Jean and Charles. It is a colorful little kirk, with a low wooden fence running along back of it.

The chimes are ringing and the tune of "I'll Go Home with Bonnie Jean" is heard faintly. Soon the townsfolk begin to arrive in groups. They are all dressed in their wedding finery and are happily singing.

Presently Mr. Lundie arrives. He goes straight to the steps of the kirk and turns to face the neighbors as the music dies down. "There's goin' to be a weddin'," he announces, just as though no one had thought of that.

Now Charlie enters and stands at Mr. Lundie's left. Tommy has come in and is leaning against the kirk at the right. We see Jeff "working his way through the crowd, with Meg edging after him."

Now Jean and Mr. MacLaren have taken their places before Mr. Lundie. They are followed by Fiona, who stands back a little. The crowd has quieted.

"We have no minister in Brigadoon now," Mr. Lundie is saying. "In most villages this would be a calamitous thing. But we know 'tis a blessin'. When there is no minister present it is perfectly proper accordin' to the laws of Scotland for two people to be wed by sincere mutual consent. There need be nothin' in writing."

(*The townsfolk start humming "Brigadoon" softly.*)

"All that's necessary is the promise of love as long as ye both are on earth."

He pauses briefly, then bids Charlie to go ahead.

"I shall love ye till I die," mumbles Charlie, awkwardly slipping a ring on Jean's finger. "An' I'll make all effort to be a good husband to ye."

"An' . . . an' so much will I try . . . to be a fine . . . an' . . . lovin' wife," adds Jean.

For a moment the newly-weds stand looking at each other uncomfortably. "Well, kiss her, lad!" prompts the dominie. When that ceremony is taken care of he continues: "Mr. Forsythe, I know would have liked to be here. But if ye'll both be good and true to each other then ye canna help but live in the Grace of God. An' Mr. Forsythe could have asked no more than that."

The townsfolk are crowding forward, eagerly and noisily. There is a good deal of embracing, kissing and such. Through the crowd Tommy has made his way to Fiona. They are both near to tears. Tommy's arms are open, and that's where Fiona goes. But not for long. A little desperately, she is pushed away. Tommy doesn't know exactly why, but he feels that he must be going, quickly—

"Look!" he says, sharply. "I still don't know what goes on here. I don't know what to believe and what to let myself believe. But I can' even wait to find out because I'm getting too deeply involved in it. Do you understand?"

"I think so!"

"Thank you. For that as much as anything. And good-by."

For a second Fiona stands amazed. Then she begins to sing a kind of lament—

> "But when the mist is in the gloamin',
> An' all the clouds are holdin' still;
> If ye're not here I won't go roamin'
> Through the heather on the hill;
> The heather on the hill."

The song brings Tommy running back, but just as he is about to take Fiona in his arms again the townsfolk decide to go into the wedding dance. This is led by Jean and Charlie, and is very gay.

Next comes the Sword Dance, led by the jealous one, Harry Beaton, who manages finally to be downright offensive. Bridegroom Charlie has to step in and stop him—

"Why dinna ye go an' leave us alone, Harry?" demands Charlie.

"It isn't fair for one man to have gotten so much of what I wanted," cries Harry Beaton. "It isn't fair, an' I winna let it happen."

With that he pulls a dirk from his stock and lunges at Charlie. Might have struck him, too, if Tommy hadn't grabbed his arm and twisted it until the dirk dropped to the ground.

Seeing this, Fiona runs to Tommy. Sobbing, she throws herself against him. "Oh, Tommy!" she cries. "Ye're all right! I'd die if anythin' happened to ye! I love ye so!! I love ye. . . ."

Harry has broken loose from the men who were holding him and made a dash for the woods. At the kirk he stops and bellows back:

"The miracle's over!   I'm leavin' Brigadoon, and 'tis the end of all of ye!!"

The crowd is stunned.   For a moment no one moves.   Then, as they gradually realize the import of what is happening, they spring into action and also pursuit.   There are cries of "We mus' stop 'im!"   All the men are after Harry!   Tommy just barely has time to kiss Fiona before joining the pursuit.   He motions to Jeff to follow.

The curtain falls.

ACT II

We are deep in the forest now, just at the edge of Brigadoon. It isn't easy to see through the trees and shrubbery, but from the orchestrated agitation and the shouting it is easy to conclude that the chase for jealous, vindictive Harry is on.   "A stream of yellow moonlight cuts across the deep blue of the night."

"Harry Beaton!   Harry Beaton!"   The chorus is crowding in. A disheveled Harry dashes hysterically in and out.   "Run an' get 'im!   Run an' get 'im!   Run, ye men, or ye will never see another mornin'!"

Tommy and Jeff run in and decide to separate.   There's no telling which way Harry went—

"It'll probably be just my luck to run into the nut!" says Jeff.

"If he comes into sight hold him fast," sings Tommy.   "Many lives are depending on it!   This must not end tonight!   They must know that tomorrow is really gonna come!"

Suddenly from the deeper forest comes an ear-splitting yell! There are more orchestrated agitations.   Then a group of the men appear, dragging the body of Harry Beaton.   It is Sandy's idea that they should say a prayer.   Harry is dead!

On the other hand, as Angus MacGuffie points out, there is no sense in being sad about it.   This is clearly God's work.   Nor should they say anything to the neighbors about it—

"They'll find he's dead tomorrow.   Let 'em sing tonight!" advises Charlie.   To which the answer is a vigorous "Aye!"

The darkness closes in.

Scene 2

That night, in a glen in Brigadoon, the townsfolk are celebrating the stopping of Harry Beaton.   The men are secretive about the story, but that Harry has indeed been stopped is admitted. There is great rejoicing and a good deal of community embracing.

"What a blessin'! What a blessin'!" Jean is saying to her bridegroom, as she throws her arms around him.

"Imagine, dearie! He wasn't a stone's throw from the creek when we stopped 'im!"

"Was he hurt bad?"

"Hurt? Jus' scratched a wee bit."

Fiona is there. And Meg. They are searching the crowd for Tommy and Jeff, but neither jointly, nor successfully.

Harry Beaton's father has come looking for his son. "I thank God ye stopped 'im from his terrible intention, but I want to see 'im," says Archie.

"He's all right now," Mr. MacLaren tells the father. "He's in good hands. 'Tis better he be left alone for a while."

Presently Tommy appears. He is quite serious, and very tense. He had tried to go away, he admits to his anxious Fiona, but he couldn't stop remembering that Fiona had confessed her love for him. It was like hearing his own secret told.

"Ye mean—ye think ye're in love with me?" asks an excited Fiona.

"Think? What good does thinking do? If I thought about it, it wouldn't make any more sense than the miracle. But what I feel is something else."

"What do you feel then, Tommy?"

Tommy decides to sing his answer—"There But for You Go I"—

> "This is hard to say,
>   but as I wandered through the lea
>   I felt for just a fleeting moment
>   that I suddenly was free
>   of being lonely;
>   then I closed my eyes and saw
>   the very reason why.
>
> "Lonely men around me,
>   Trying not to cry.
>   Till the day you found me
>   There among them was I.
>
> "I saw a man who had never known
>   A love that was all his own.
>   I thought as I thanked all the stars in the sky,
>   There but for you go I."

Fiona is happy to have Tommy confess his love, even at this last minute. And it *is* the last minute, or soon will be. Brigadoon's day in the sun is about to end. And then—— But Tommy can't leave Fiona. Not now he can't.

"Didn't Lundie say someone could stay if he loved someone enough?"

"Aye."

"Well, that's for me! Where do I go? Who do I talk to? Where do I get a passport to disappear?"

"I think we better go to Mr. Lundie."

They start, but remember Jeff. Tommy should talk to Jeff, but Fiona needn't worry. Nothing can change his mind now.

Meg, too, is anxious to get in touch with Jeff. She is irritated no end when the neighbors would make fun of her. True, she's daft about men. But what of it? There's really nothing like a man. To prove which Meg obliges with a second song declaring the virtues of masculinity. Now Mr. MacLaren calls the townsfolk's attention to the fact that their day is fast drawing toward its close——

"There's not much time left afore the curfew so if there's anythin' ye want to be doin', I'd advise ye to do it. Besides, the weddin' couple jus' left an' there's little need for any more celebratin'."

The crowd starts to drift away. Suddenly Archie Beaton appears from the wood. In his arms he carries the body of his dead son. The women start back in horror as Archie lays the body on the ground. Slowly the crowd gathers round, indicating in pantomime their shock and bewilderment. Bagpipes are heard. The pipers are playing a funeral dirge as they march in. They pause near the body. The townspeople move with dignity through the pattern of a funeral service illustrated by a solemn ballet. At its conclusion the neighbors raise the body of Harry Beaton to their shoulders and move off into the wood.

Jeff, standing at the edge of the crowd, is joined by an excited Tommy, come to tell him that he (Tommy) may not be going back. He's in love with Fiona. If what they have heard is true, this Brigadoon will soon be changed into "a hunk of mist." That means that if he is ever to see Fiona again he will have to stay. That's why he has come back to say good-by to Jeff——

TOMMY—I know you won' believe this, but in one day I feel more a part of her and this place than I've ever felt about Jane or anybody or anything I've known back home.

JEFF—That's because it's one day. But what about from now on? You just can't sit around and be a part of her. What will you do with yourself? Become a weaver? Great. Milk cows? An ideal vocation for you. Become an ale brewer? Why, in one week you'd be so bored you'd be drinking the stuff as fast as you made it.

TOMMY (*shakily*)—*That* kind of practical thinking doesn't count.

JEFF—Why, it's all that counts. It doesn't matter how "beautiful" a thing is, it's either possible or impossible. And this ain't possible. Do you realize if you stay here it's for always?

TOMMY—I know.

JEFF—And do you know how long always is around here? It's one hell of a long time.

TOMMY (*a little frantically*)—I know!

JEFF—It can't be a trial marriage, because you can't change your mind after trying it out for six or seven hundred years.

TOMMY—I won't ever want to.

JEFF—How do you know?

TOMMY—Because—well, there's where I know you'll think I'm crazy—because I believe in her. And what's more I believe in this place.

JEFF—You do? Or do you just want to?

TOMMY—It's the same thing.

JEFF—It is not. This Highland voodoo town makes no more sense to you than it does to me. So how can you believe in it when you don't understand it? When you leave here, in a few weeks or even a few days you'll forget about the whole thing. It's all too unreal to be remembered emotionally. You may think about it, but you won't feel anything. That's the way a dream is.

TOMMY—What do you mean—dream?

JEFF—That's what it is. Leaving here will be like waking up. Why, you're not even really moved or touched by it. You just think you are.

There is something on Jeff's mind that convinces him they are experiencing nothing more than a dream. It was he (Jeff) who had killed Harry Beaton. Jeff was behind a bush in the forest as Harry was rushing by. Jeff put out his foot, tripped Harry and he fell, hitting his head against a stone with a very nasty thud. But, curiously, Jeff is not conscious of any sensation of regret or remorse. He doesn't feel anything at all. Of course he might talk himself into feeling something if he wanted to. But he doesn't want to. So he proposes just to dismiss the whole incident as one of those strange things.

Fiona and Mr. Lundie have come in. Jeff decides to wait for Tommy outside the town.

"Fiona tells me ye want to stay, lad," Mr. Lundie is saying. Tommy does not answer.

"Tommy, what is it?"

"It's no good, Fiona. I'm leaving," Tommy mutters, adding as she is staring at him: "And it isn't because I don't love you. I think I do. But I guess I don't trust my feelings."

"Ye mean ye're not sure ye can accept everythin'?"

"That's about it."

Mr. Lundie starts to leave them and then turns back. "Dinna feel ashamed of yourself, Tommy. 'Tis the hardest thing in the world to give everythin', even though 'tis usually the only way to get everythin'."

"Do you understand at all?" Tommy has turned despairingly to Fiona. In answer she starts to sing—

> "Dinna ye know, Tommy,
>   That ye are all I'm livin' for?
>   So how can ye go, Tommy,
>   When I'll need ye more and more."

"No, Fiona. You won't remember that way. And neither will I." And he, too, breaks into song—"From This Day On"—

> "You and the world we knew
>   Will glow till my life is through;
>   For you're part of me
>   From this day on.

> "And
>   Some day if I should love,
>   It's you I'll be dreaming of;
>   For you're all I'll see
>   From this day on.

> "These hurried hours were all the life we could share
>   Still I will go with not a tear, just a prayer.

> "That
>   When we are far apart
>   You'll find something from your heart
>   Has gone!   Gone with me
>   From this day on."

"You see," concludes Tommy, "we mustn't be sorry about anything."

"I'm not," Fiona agrees. "In fact I shouldna be surprised if
I'll be less lonely now than I was afore ye came."

"Why?"

"I think real loneliness is not bein' in love in vain, but not bein'
in love at all."

"But it'll fade in time."

"No. It winna do that—"

> "Through all the years to come
> An' through all the tears to come
> I know I'll be yours
> From this day on."

The lights have begun to fade. From the near distance the
townsfolk can be heard singing their tribute to Brigadoon. It may
be their song of farewell. The singing grows softer and softer.
The lights continue to dim and a mist is rising.

"Oh, Tommy!" Fiona's voice is tremulous with emotion.

"I'm sorry, Fiona. To stay I had to have no fears and no
doubts. And, well . . . good-by."

He kisses her. Their voices fade. Slowly Fiona moves away.
The mist closes about her. Even after Fiona has disappeared, her
voice comes floating back—

"Good-by, Tommy. . . . An' dinna forget . . . any day . . .
any night . . . that always an' always . . . I love ye . . . I love
ye . . . I love ye . . . I love ye . . . I love ye. . . ."

In the darkness and silence the scene is filled with a misty gray-
yellow light. Tommy stands for a moment gazing into the mist.
As he starts away,

The curtains close.

Scene 3

There is the orchestrated roar of an airplane. Above it, but
softly, the song of Brigadoon can be heard. As the curtains are
drawn we discover that we are back in New York.

At the end of an elliptical bar Frank, the bartender, is talking on
a phone. Jeff Douglas is calling. He wants to know if Tommy
has been there. No, Frank hasn't seen Tommy. He has no more
than hung up when Tommy walks in.

Tommy, it seems, since his return from Scotland, has been out of New York for a month. On a farm in New Hampshire he had made an amazing discovery: He really liked to milk cows. Makes him think he should have been a farmer.

When is Tommy going to marry Jane Ashton? Tommy doesn't know. He is not even sure that he wants to get married. Why? Well, it's none of Frank's business, but: Tommy is in love with someone else. He suspects it's for good, even though he knows he can't have her.

"And the trouble is," Tommy explains a little cryptically, "because I can't be with her, I can't be with anyone else. That's why I went away. So many things remind me of her. When I'm with people and they're talking to me, they might say one little word that opens a door to a memory for me and suddenly I don't hear them talking any more. I'm a few thousand miles away with someone else. Then slowly I come back to the conversation. They ask me a question and I don't know what the hell they're talking about. I haven't heard a word."

Jane Ashton has come into the bar. "She is attractive, though a little severe-looking, extremely chic and in her late twenties."

Jane is surprised to find Tommy. And a little miffed that he had not wired her that he was coming to town, or called her after he arrived.

"I thought the minute you'd get in town you'd call me . . . or come to me. . . ."

Tommy has turned away. The words "come to me" have struck a chord in his heart, revived a scene in his memory. As the lights of the bar dim out a misty vision of Fiona singing appears. Tommy is staring straight ahead of him. Jane takes a cocktail from the bartender and is seen to be talking to Frank in pantomime. Tommy can see only the vision of Fiona, hear nothing but her song—

> "Come to me, bend to me, kiss me good-day!
> Darlin', my darlin', 'tis all I can say;
> Jus' come to me, bend to me, kiss me good-day!
> Gie me your lips an' don't take 'em away."

The vision fades. Tommy returns to the conversation with Jane. She has been telling him of a chance they have to buy a home, if he doesn't mind commuting sixty miles out of New York. Tommy hasn't heard a word. Now he will have to call the real estate man and tell him not to hold the house.

Also Jane would like to know about Jeff. Does Tommy still want Jeff to stand up with him? Yes—if Jeff can. Why?

"Nothing. It's just that he's so impossible these days. Everybody is bored to death with him."

"I'm not interested in everybody, especially the everybody we know."

"You've certainly been anti-social since you returned from Scotland! If you really *want* to avoid everybody, why don't we take Mr. Jackson's house. It's far away and right on the top of a high, beautiful hill. . . ."

Again Tommy can hear Fiona's voice. Again the vision drifts in mistily. This time Fiona is singing "The Heather on the Hill—"

> "The mornin' dew is blinkin' yonder,
> There's lazy music in the rill;
> An' all I want to do is wander
> Through the heather on the hill."

The song is finished. The vision is fading. Tommy has turned sharply to Jane—

TOMMY—No! Jane. No!

JANE—No, what?

TOMMY—I can't go through with it! There's going to be no wedding next month.

JANE—Do you mean you're postponing it again?

TOMMY—No, I'm not postponing it. I'm calling it off for good!

JANE—Calling it off?

TOMMY—I can't do it! Ever.

JANE—You have a nerve. After all this time I've waited for you and tried to be patient and put up with your idiotic whims and temperament?

TOMMY—I'm sorry. It's not your fault. You've been wonderfully kind to me; but something strange happened a few months ago that I can't explain and now I don't fit here any more.

JANE—I think you're going clean out of your mind. But I refuse to stand here and argue with you in this bar! Let's go home and . . .

Tommy is back in his dream. This time he can see and hear Charlie Dalrymple and a group of the townsfolk of Brigadoon singing—

"Go home, go home, go home with bonnie Jean!
Go home, go home, I'll go home with bonnie Jean!"

Jane Ashton's voice comes through the mist. She's evidently just finishing a speech— "Think that over, Mr. Albright, when you're all alone!"

Tommy doesn't hear her, or move to follow her out of the bar. He is again staring into space, standing quite near to Fiona as she says—

"I think real loneliness is not bein' in love in vain but not bein' in love at all."

"You were right. It never faded."

Now they are singing together, as they had sung in Scotland—

> "Through all the years to come
> An' through all the tears to come
> I know I'll be yours
> From this day on."

Tommy picks up the phone on the bar and dials a number. "Jeff? Are you sober? . . . Well, listen to me. . . . I want to go back to Scotland. . . . Never mind what for. . . . Do you want to come with me? . . . Well, get plane reservations right away! . . . I know it isn't there, but I want to see where it was. . . . Who cares if it doesn't make sense. . . . I want to go. . . . I want to go, do you hear? . . . I want to go . . . !"

The lights fade.

Again there is the orchestrated roar of an airplane. A muffled shout is heard: "London!" And, a second later: "Scotland!"

The curtains are drawn.

SCENE 4

It is three nights later. We are back in the forest of Brigadoon. Tommy and Jeff are just coming from the wood into the clearing before the curved bridge that leads into the mystic somewhere. They stand for a moment looking around them in the silence—

TOMMY—It's unbelievable! Awful and unbelievable!
JEFF (*quite drunk*)—What is?
TOMMY—To think that somewhere out there—between the mist and the stars, there's somebody I want so terribly. She's not dead. She's only asleep. And yet I'll never see her again.

JEFF—Did you come all the way over here just to say that? You could have told me that on the phone in New York.

TOMMY—No. I'll tell you why. She became so alive to me that I had to come back and see for myself that the place really wasn't here.

JEFF—It didn't work that way for me. It's so much like a dream now that I'd have to work hard to convince myself that it happened at all.

TOMMY—There's the big difference between us.

JEFF—How so?

TOMMY—I found that sometimes the things you believe in become more real to you than all the tangibles you could explain away or understand. (*He looks around for a moment.*) God! Why do people have to lose things to find out what they mean?

JEFF—Take a last look and let's start walking. I got lost around here once.

TOMMY—Okay.

Singing is heard quite clearly. It is the song of Brigadoon: ". . . Let the world grow cold around us, Let the heavens cry above; Brigadoon, Brigadoon, In thy valley there'll be love!"

The boys are standing looking at each other in bewilderment when Mr. Lundie appears. He is very sleepy as he walks half way over to Tommy—

"Tommy, lad! Ye! My, my! Ye mus' really love her! Ye woke me up! Come, lad!"

He holds out his hand. Tommy, as one in a trance, walks toward him.

"Ye shouldna be too surprised, lad. I told ye when ye love someone deeply anythin' is possible. Even miracles!"

They have started over the bridge. Tommy turns and waves to Jeff, who stands staring after them. Jeff half waves back to them as the singing swells. Tommy and Mr. Lundie have disappeared.

THE CURTAIN FALLS

THE PLAYS AND THEIR AUTHORS

"All My Sons," a drama in three acts by Arthur Miller. Copyright, 1946, by the author. Copyright and published, 1946, by Reynal & Hitchcock, New York.

Arthur Miller, whose "All My Sons" won the Drama Critics' Circle prize as the best play of American authorship of the season, and who critics in and out of the circle selected as the most promising young dramatist of the year, is certainly a writing man who sticks to his job. Since collecting his B.A. from the University of Michigan in 1938, after having had his earlier education from the public schools of Manhattan and Abraham Lincoln High in Brooklyn, Mr. Miller has managed to turn out a couple of plays, a whole raft of radio scripts, a few short stories for the magazines and a novel. During his war years he was assigned to the collection of material for the movie, "GI Joe," issued in 1945. His novel, "Focus," was published in 1946. Two years ago his first play, "The Man Who Had All the Luck," was produced on Broadway. It was a good play, too, albeit a bit muddled. Its sponsors decided, after a week's trial, that it was not worth spending the rest of their bankroll on. Mr. Miller was born in New York City in 1915. He lives in Brooklyn with his wife and growing family. "All My Sons" is already scheduled for production in Germany, Switzerland, Austria and Sweden.

"The Iceman Cometh," a drama in two acts by Eugene Gladstone O'Neill. Copyright, 1940, 1946, by the author. Copyright and published, 1946, by Random House, Inc., New York.

Eugene O'Neill's last appearance in "The Best Plays" was with his "Ah, Wilderness" the season of 1933-34. Before that he had made seven appearances in the first fifteen volumes and had won three Pulitzer awards with "Beyond the Horizon," "Anna Christie" and "Strange Interlude." He was given the Nobel Prize for Literature in 1936. It was twelve years after the appearance of "Ah, Wilderness" before Mr. O'Neill was willing to submit a play script for Broadway production. Poor health had kept him

in the West, and he was unwilling to trust the production of a
play wholly to anyone else. His re-emergence from retirement
with "The Iceman Cometh" was hailed as an event of first importance to the American theatre. It was so confirmed by the early
and consistent popular success of that drama. Mr. O'Neill was
born in New York City in 1888, the son of James O'Neill and Ella
Quinlan O'Neill. His father was a popular American actor of the
eighties and nineties, and, for a couple of decades, the star of "The
Count of Monte Cristo." His early plays, mostly one-act dramas
of the sea, were staged by a semi-professional organization, the
Provincetown Players, in Provincetown, Mass., and later in New
York.

"Joan of Lorraine," a drama in two acts by Maxwell Anderson.
    Copyright, 1946, by the author. Copyright and published,
    1946, by Anderson House, Washington, D. C. Distributed
    by Dodd, Mead & Co., New York.

Mr. Anderson's first appearance in these volumes was made in
the 1924-25 issue, when he collaborated with Laurence Stallings
on "What Price Glory?" His last previous appearances were with
his two war-time dramas, "The Eve of St. Mark" and "Storm
Operation." In the twenty-odd years between Author Anderson
has been represented in "The Best Plays" by a variety of dramas
of both high quality and outstanding literary craftsmanship. He
was born in Atlantic, Pa., in 1888, is the son of a preacher, and
began his writing career in journalism.

"Another Part of the Forest," a drama in three acts by Lillian
    Hellman. Copyright, 1946, 1947, by the author. Copyright
    and published, 1947, by Viking Press, Inc., New York.

Lillian Hellman's record of consistency, both as a dramatist and
a "Best Plays" contributor, is maintained this year with a sort of
dramatic prelude to her previous success, "The Little Foxes"
(1938-39). "Another Part of the Forest" deals with the earlier
life stories of most of the characters the author introduced in
"The Little Foxes." Miss Hellman's contributions to the year
books include also her "The Children's Hour," "Watch on the
Rhine" and "The Searching Wind." She approached the drama
by way of book reviewing and professional play reading. She
was born in New Orleans in 1905.

"Years Ago," a comedy by Ruth Gordon. Copyright, 1946, by
   the author.   Copyright and published, 1946, by Viking
   Press, Inc., New York.

Three years ago Ruth Gordon wrote, helped to stage and played
the heroine in a wartime comedy called "Over 21," a refreshing
opus selected for this dramatic year book as one of the best plays
of the 1943-44 season. The year following she stayed home and
did the dishes, or saw they were done, while her husband and
favorite stage director, Garson Kanin, took over stage matters
with the writing and direction of the still prevalent Broadway hit,
"Born Yesterday." The next year it was Ruth's turn again and
she produced this "Years Ago," which comes right out of her
schoolday diary. Her early successes as an actress were scored in
a series of Booth Tarkington comedies. Later she played in a lot
of more mature dramas, including Owen and Donald Davis'
"Ethan Frome" and Ibsen's "A Doll's House." Wollaston, Mass.,
is Miss Gordon's home town.

"John Loves Mary," a comedy in three acts by Norman Krasna.
   Copyright, 1946, by the author.

This is the second time that Norman Krasna has served the
year books with the leaven of laughter. Last season his "Dear
Ruth" was a bright feature of "The Best Plays." That comedy
did not appeal to all the year book's reviewers, but it pleased the
editor mightily. Mr. Krasna continues as one of the more successful collectors of fantastic salary-and-profit contracts in Hollywood. He was born on Long Island in 1909 and his schools included New York and Columbia Universities and Brooklyn Law
School. He got into newspaper work by accepting a job as copy
boy on the *Morning World* in New York. A year or so later he
was writing motion picture reviews when the *World* died. After
which his rise was a little on the meteoric side. In Hollywood he
began modestly enough, but before practically anyone except
Norman knew it he was being paid $100,000 and up for the writ-
ing and direction of a single picture. His plays have included
"Small Miracle," "The Man with Blonde Hair," "Louder, Please"
and, as mentioned, "Dear Ruth."

"The Fatal Weakness," a comedy in three acts by George Kelly.
   Copyright, 1946, 1947, by the author. Copyright and published, 1947, by Samuel French, Inc., New York and London.

In the nineteen twenties George Kelly appeared four times as a "Best Plays" author—with "The Show-Off," "Craig's Wife," which won him a Pulitzer prize, "Daisy Mayme" and "Behold the Bridegroom." Acquiring something of a disgust for the Broadway theatre, and also a commitment in Hollywood, Mr. Kelly retired to the West. He came back to Broadway infrequently after that. Once, in 1929, with "Maggie the Magnificent," again in 1931 with "Philip Goes Forth," with "Reflected Glory," which Tallulah Bankhead played in 1936, and in 1945 with "The Deep Mrs. Sykes." He was born in Philadelphia in 1890, acted successfully as a juvenile, wrote many vaudeville sketches, playing in most of them, and finally scored a minor success with a Little Theatre satire, "The Torchbearers," his first long play.

"The Story of Mary Surratt," drama in three acts by John Patrick. Copyright, 1947, by the author (revised). Dramatic composition copyright, 1940, by John Patrick (John Patrick Goggen) under the title "This Gentle Ghost."

As Best Play readers we met John Patrick first the season of 1944-45, when his "The Hasty Heart" was included in this series of selected dramas. He is a Kentuckian by birth, a San Franciscan by training, a New Yorker by adoption. His first advancements came through radio scripts, several of which he wrote for the National Broadcasting Company and Helen Hayes. He has also been a successful Hollywood collaborator. He got into World War II by joining the American Field Service, from which he was assigned to a British ambulance unit. After that he saw service on many fronts, including the South African, the Egyptian, and the Syrian, winding up in Burma. He wrote "The Hasty Heart" on his way home, and practically smuggled it ashore as unfinished business. He had his education from Holy Cross in New Orleans and Columbia in New York, in addition to a Summer of learning extracted from Harvard Summer School.

"Christopher Blake," a drama in two acts, by Moss Hart. Copyright, 1946, by the author. Copyright and published, 1946, by Random House, Inc., New York.

Moss Hart made his first appearance in these volumes back in 1930-31 with "Once in a Lifetime," that being his first successful collaboration with George S. Kaufman. It was, however, a Moss

Hart comedy before Mr. K. was called in. During the seventeen years that have followed Mr. Hart has reappeared with a pleasing and usually happy regularity. A half dozen times he was again teamed with Mr. Kaufman, with "Merrily We Roll Along," "You Can't Take It with You," "I'd Rather Be Right," "The American Way," "The Man Who Came to Dinner" and "George Washington Slept Here." After that, the collaborators decided to go their separate ways. Mr. Hart has been a "Best Plays" man with "Lady in the Dark" and "Winged Victory," in addition to this year's "Christopher Blake." He was born in New York in 1904, has been fussing with playwriting ever since he was in high school, though for many years he was obliged to work at other jobs to pay for his copy paper and pencils, as well as his food, clothes and ice cream sodas.

"Brigadoon," a musical fantasy in two acts; book by Alan Jay Lerner; music by Frederick Loewe. Copyright, 1946, by the authors. Copyright and published, 1947, by Coward-McCann, Inc., New York.

The Messrs. Lerner and Loewe, librettist and composer of the popular "Brigadoon," had their first experience as a writing team in Detroit, where Frank McCoy a few years back was trying to establish a musical stock company. It was young Mr. Lerner's first experience, professionally speaking, though he had "perpetrated two Hasty Pudding shows on a group of unsuspecting graduates and alumni" while he was at Harvard, Class of 1940. Later Lerner and Loewe did a revue called "What's Up," which, Mr. Lerner is convinced, was an "inarticulate mess," and he may be right, for all it got 63 performances at the National Theatre in 1943. In 1945 John C. Wilson produced the Lerner-Loewe "The Day Before Spring," which was far from inarticulate and quite the joy of many of its critics and practically all its audiences, for a total of 165 performances.

Mr. Lerner was born in New York City in 1918, and in addition to his stretch at Harvard had the usual prep years at Choate School in Connecticut and several months at a school in England. He has tried a 'prentice hand at writing advertising, radio scripts and a couple of vaudeville sketches.

Mr. Loewe was 20 when he left his native Vienna and came to America. He had some experience as a child prodigy and as a concert pianist, but did not pursue a career in America. Here he did a bit of floating about Greenwich Village and served some time as a fly-weight boxer. He is the author of the popular song, "Katrina." It sold something like 2,000,000 copies, but the composer's take was only $12. His collaborations with Mr. Lerner represent his only stage compositions in this country.

PLAYS PRODUCED IN NEW YORK

June 1, 1946—June 1, 1947

(Plays marked "continued" were still playing June 1, 1947)

SECOND BEST BED

(8 performances)

A comedy in three acts by N. Richard Nash. Produced by Ruth Chatterton and John Huntington at the Barrymore Theatre, New York, June 3, 1946.

Cast of characters—

```
Ballad Seller..............................Richard Dyer-Bennet
Nells Garris...................................Elizabeth Eustis
Fenny Brushell...................................Peter Boyne
Yorick..........................................Ralph Cullinan
Anne Hathaway Shakespeare......................Ruth Chatterton
Lewis Poggs.....................................Ralph Forbes
Squire Simon Lummle...........................Richard Temple
The Beadle.......................................Max Stamm
Will Shakespeare................................Barry Thomson
Master Yarrow....................................John McKee
Farmer Legge....................................Jefferson Coates
Michael, The Tavern Keeper.....................Ralph Sumpter
Harelip Ben.........................................John Gay
```

Acts I, II and III.—Main Room and Parlor in Anne Hathaway's Cottage, Shottery, Parish of Old Stratford-on-Avon, Warwickshire, England. Beginning of Seventeenth Century.

Staged by Ruth Chatterton and N. Richard Nash; setting and costumes by Motley.

William Shakespeare, having achieved success in London, pays one of his rare visits to his wife, Anne Hathaway, in the cottage of the postcard etchings. He finds Anne of a mind to divorce him so she can marry a villager named Poggs. Will is too clever for them. He rekindles Anne's affection for him and, temporarily at least, puts a second marriage out of her mind. Then he returns to London.

(Closed June 8, 1946)

NEW YORK CITY CENTER OF MUSIC AND DRAMA

HAMLET

(16 performances)

A streamlined, GI version in two acts of William Shakespeare's tragedy, by Maurice Evans; music by Roger Adams. Revived by Michael Todd at City Center, New York, June 3, 1946.

Cast of characters—

Bernardo...William Weber
Francisco...Robert Berger
Marcellus....................................Alexander Lockwood
Horatio...Whit Connor
Ghost of Hamlet's Father..........................Victor Thorley
Claudius, King of Denmark.......................Thomas Gomez
Hamlet...Maurice Evans
Gertrude, Queen of Denmark.........................Lili Darvas
Polonius..Harry Sheppard
Laertes...Emmett Rogers
Ophelia...Frances Reid
Reynaldo...Victor Rendina
Rosencrantz......................................Howard Morris
Guildenstern......................................Booth Colman
Player King...............................William Le Massene
Player Queen...................................Blanche Collins
Player Villain...................................Alan Dreeben
Player Prologue.................................Howard Otway
Fortinbras..Leon Shaw
Norwegian Captain..........................William le Massena
Osric..Richard Newton

Act I.—Scenes 1 and 4—Battlements of the Castle at Elsinore, Denmark. 2 and 6—Main Hall of Castle. 3 and 5—Apartment of Polonius. 7—Chapel in the Castle. Act II—Scenes 1 and 9—Open Court in the Castle. 2—Chapel in Castle. 3—The Queen's Apartment. 4—Cellar Room in Castle. 5 and 8—Hall in Castle. 6—Street leading to Port. 7—Main Hall.

Staged by George Schaefer; settings by Frederick Stover; costumes by Irene Sharaff.

This version of "Hamlet" was played frequently by Maj. Evans in the South Pacific during World War II, and subsequently played at the Columbus Circle Theatre in New York for 131 performances from December 13, 1945, to April 6, 1946. The City Center revival was at popular prices, closing June 15, 1946.

The first showing in New York of the Technicolor picture, Shakespeare's "Henry V," in which Laurence Olivier appeared as the King and gained additional laurels for his direction of the production, was made at the City Center under the sponsorship of the New York Theatre Guild in association with Mr. Olivier. After a run extending through the Summer, from June 17 to September 2, "Henry V" was transferred to the Golden Theatre, where it continued through the Winter.

The Ballet Russe de Monte Carlo also opened the New York dance season of 1946-47 at City Center on September 4, continuing until September 15. Details of repertory in Dance Drama chapter.

The New York City Opera Company under the direction of Laszlo Halasz began the 1946-47 season September 19, 1946, at the New York City Center with Puccini's "Madama Butterfly." Camilla Williams sang Cio-Cio-San and Guilio Gari the role of Pinkerton. There were 7 performances.

Other operas presented during the Fall season were Gilbert and Sullivan's "Pirates of Penzance" with 3 performances, Bizet's

"Carmen" (6), Verdi's "La Traviata" (5), Puccini's "La Boheme" (4), Mascagni's "Cavalleria Rusticana" and Leoncavallo's "Pagliacci" (5), Gounod's "Faust" (4), Verdi's "Rigoletto" (4), Puccini's "Tosca" (3), Smetano's "The Bartered Bride" (2), Tchaikovsky's "Eugen Onegin" (7), and Richard Strauss' "Ariadne auf Naxos" (6), a total of 52.

ARIADNE AUF NAXOS

(6 performances)

An opera in prologue and one act; music by Richard Strauss; libretto by Hugo von Hofmannsthal; translation of prologue by Lewis Sydenham. Presented by the New York City Opera Company at City Center, October 10, 1946.

Cast of characters—

PROLOGUE

Major-domo	Gean Greenwell
Music Master	James Pease
Composer	Polyna Stoska
The Tenor	Irwin Dillon

ARIADNE AUF NAXOS

Ariadne	Ella Flesch
Bacchus	Vasso Argyris
Najade	Lillian Fawcett
Dryade	Rosalind Nadell
Echo	Leonore Portnoy
Zerbinetta	Virginia MacWatters
Harlequin	Ralph Herbert
An Officer	Lawrence Harwood
Dancing Master	Allen Stewart
Wigmaker	Grant Garnell
Lackey	Arthur Newman
Zerbinetta	Virginia MacWatters
The Primadonna	Ella Flesch
Harlequin	Ralph Herbert
Scaramuccio	Hubert Norville
Truffaldin	Paul Dennis
Brighella	Nathaniel Sprinzena
Scaramuccio	Hubert Norville
Truffaldin	Paul Dennis
Brighella	Nathaniel Sprinzena

Scene—Private Theatre in Mansion of Wealthy Man, 18th Century.

Staged by Leopold Sachse; setting by H. A. Condell; costumes by Paul Engel.

This was the first professional performance in New York City of the Richard Strauss opera within an opera. It was sung in English December 5, 1934, by students of the Juilliard School's Opera Department. The New York City Opera Company sang the prologue in English and the remainder of the opera in German.

The New York City Opera Company included in its casts during the Fall season Frances Anderson, Vasso Argyris, Rosemarie Brancato, Vera Bryner, Carla Castellani, Eugene Conley, George Doubrovsky, Paul Dennis, Irwin Dillon, Doris Doree, John Dudley, Lydia Edwards, Lucia Evangelista, Lillian Fawcett, Gino Fratesi, Ella Flesch, Guilio Gari, Grant Garnell, Gene Greenwell, William Horne, John Hamill, Ralph Herbert, Julia Horvath, Lawrence Harwood, Winifred Heidt, Neure Jorjorian, Steven Kennedy, Mary Kreste, Beverley Lane, Herva Mariono, Virginia MacWatters, Brenda Miller, Lucille Manners, Margery Mayer, Enzo Mascherini, Arthur Newman, Rosalind Nadell, Hubert Norville, James Pease, Lenore Portnoy, Ivan Petroff, Emile Renan, Hilde Reggiani, Allen Stewart, Dorothy Sarnoff, Nathaniel Sprinzena, Polyna Stoska, Giuseppa Valdengo, Ramon Vinay, Camilla Williams, and Norman Young.

Music conductors included Laszlo Halasz, Jean Morel, Julius Rudel, Thomas Martin, Richard Korn, Ann Kullmer and Lee Shaynen. The stage directors were Eugene Bryden, Theodore Komisarjevsky, Leopold Sachse and director of ballet, Igor Schwezoff. Settings were by H. A. Condell and Richard Rychatrik and costumes by Kate Friedheim and Stivanello.

The season closed November 16, 1946.

The New York City Symphony Orchestra opened the 1946-47 season at City Center, New York, September 23, 1946, under the direction of Leonard Bernstein. The tenth and last program of the series, November 25 and 26, 1946, was devoted to "Oedipus Rex," a choral drama in two acts by Igor Stravinsky; text by Jean Cocteau based on the Sophocles tragedy and translated into Latin by Danielou. The cast included Nell Tangeman as Jocasta, Hans Heinz (Oedipus), Ralph Telesco (Creon), James Pease (Tiresias), James Sprinzena (Shepherd). The Collegiate Chorale was directed by Robert Shaw and Norman Corwin was the narrator.

The Jooss Ballet was presented at City Center December 3 to 23, 1946. (See Dance Drama.)

Paul Draper, tap dancer, and Larry Adler, harmonica specialist, with John Colman as accompanist, presented twelve programs from December 25, 1946, to January 5, 1947, with special holiday matinees for children. The programs included Suzari's Marionettes and Salici Puppets, Bob Williams and his dog act, Gil Maison and his animal act and Richard Du Bois, magician.

BLOOMER GIRL

(48 performances)

A musical comedy in two acts, adapted by Sig Herzig and Fred Saidy from a play by Lilith and Dan James; music by Harold Arlen; lyrics by E. Y. Harburg; orchestrations by Russell Bennett. Revived by John C. Wilson in association with Nat Goldstone at City Center, New York, January 6, 1947.

Cast of characters—

Serena	Mabel Taliaferro
Octavio	Holly Harris
Lydia	Ellen Leslie
Julia ⎬ The Applegate Daughters	Dorothy Cothran
Phoebe	Claire Stevens
Delia	Claire Minter
Daisy	Peggy Campbell
Horatio	Matt Briggs
Gus	John Call
Evelina	Nanette Fabray
Wilfred Thrush	Byron Milligan
Joshua Dingle	Carlos Sherman
Ebenezer Mimms ⎬ The Sons-in-law	Lester Towne
Herman Brasher	Victor Bender
Hiram Crump	Walter Russell
Dolly	Olive Reeves-Smith
Jeff Calhoun	Dick Smart
Paula	Lily Paget
Prudence	Noella Pelloquin
Hetty	Alice Ward
Pompey	Hubert Dilworth
Sheriff Quimby	Joe E. Marks
1st Deputy	Edward Chapel
2nd Deputy	Ralph Sassano
3rd Deputy	Donald Green
Hamilton Calhoun	John Byrd
State Official	John Byrd
Governor Newton	Sidney Bassler
Augustus	Arthur Lawson

Act I.—Scene 1—Conservatory of Applegate Mansion, Cicero Falls, New York, 1861. 2—Bathroom. 3—The Lily. 4—Hedge. 5—The Yellow Pavilion. 6—Garden. Act II.—Scene 1—Village Green. 2—Corridor of Town Jail. 3—Stage of Opera House. 4—Conservatory of Applegate Mansion.

Staged by E. Y. Harburg; book directed by William Schorr; music directed by Jerry Arlen; choreography by Agnes de Mille; settings and lighting by Lemuel Ayers; costumes by Miles White.

"Bloomer Girl" opened on Broadway October 5, 1944, and closed April 27, 1946, after 654 performances. The musical comedy was produced at the Shubert Theatre by John C. Wilson in association with Nat Goldstone. See "Best Plays of 1944-45."

(Closed February 15, 1947)

The Ballet Foundation presented Ballet Russe De Monte Carlo at the City Center, New York, February 16, 1947. (See Dance Drama.)

The New York City Opera Company opened a three-week Spring season April 6, 1947, with "Ariadne auf Naxos." Margit Bokor and Virginia Haskins made their debuts with the company. Ann Ayars was the Najade and Ella Flesch the Ariadne. Other operas and casts were practically the same as in the Fall season.

ANDREA CHENIER

An opera in four acts by Umberto Giordano; libretto by Luigia Mica. Presented by the New York City Opera Company at City Center, New York, April 9, 1947.

Cast of characters—

```
Andrea Chénier...................................Irwin Dillon
Gérard..........................................Enzo Mascherini
Maddallena..........................Vivian Della Chiesa (debut)
Bersi...........................................Rosalind Nadell
Contessa de Coigny.............................Lydia Edwards
Vecchia.........................................Terese Gerson
Mathieu....................................Desire Ligeti (debut)
Roucher..........................................Grant Garnell
Fleville........................................Arthur Newman
L'Abate.........................................Allen Stewart
Incredibile................................Nathaniel Sprinzena
Schmidt..........................................Paul Dennis
Dumas..........................................Arthur Newman
Fouquier...................................Edwin Dunning (debut)
    Dancers: Jane Kiser, Cynthia Tobin, Joan Djorup, Ruth Sabotka,
Eloise Milton, Ted Dragon, Job Sanders.
    Act I.—Hall of Castle of the Contessa de Coigny; Act II.—Square
in Paris outside the Cafe Hottot.  Act III.—Seat of the Revolution-
ary Tribunal.  Act IV.—Prison Yard of Saint Lazare.
    Staged by Theodore Komisarjevsky; music directed by Laszlo
Halasz; choreography by William Dollar; settings by H. A. Condell.
```

A second opera given for the first time during the 1946-47 season was Richard Strauss' "Salome," directed by Leopold Sachse, Laszlo Halasz conducting. Brenda Lewis was the Salome, Frederick Jagel the Herod, Ralph Herbert the Jochanaan, William Horne the Narraboth and Teresa Gerson the Herodias. The set was designed by H. A. Condell.

Among those who appeared for the first time with the company during this season were Luigi Infantino, Italian tenor making his American debut in "La Traviata" as Alfredo; Camille Fischelli as Frasquita in "Carmen," Irra Petina as Carmen and Helen George as Michaela; Willa Steward and Gertrude Ribla as Santuzza in "Cavalleria Rusticana"; Frances Watkins as Nadell, Graciella Rivera as Gilda and Manfred Hecht as Monterone in "Rigoletto"; Donald Richard as Silvio in "Pagliacci"; Ann Ayars who appeared in "Ariadne auf Naxos" and as Violetta in "La Traviata"; Carlos Alexander as Jochanaan in "Salome," Vivian Della Chiesa as Maddallena, Desire Ligeti as Mathieu and Edwin Dunning as Fouquier in "Andrea Chenier"; Margot Bokor as Composer, Ann Ayars as Najade and Virginia Haskins as Zerbinetta in "Ariadne auf Naxos"; John S. White and Edwin Ambros as stage directors and William Dollar as choreographer. The Spring season closed April 27, 1947.

The Ballet Theatre returned to City Center April 28, 1947, for a three weeks' engagement. (See Dance Drama.)

UP IN CENTRAL PARK

(16 performances)

A musical play in two acts by Herbert and Dorothy Fields; music by Sigmund Romberg; orchestrations by Don Walker. Revived by Michael Todd at City Center, New York, May 19, 1947.

Cast of characters—

A Laborer	Oren Dabbs
Danny O'Cahane	Walter Burke
Timothy Moore	Russ Brown
Bessie O'Cahane	Betty Bruce
Rosie Moore	Maureen Cannon
John Matthews, of *The New York Times*	Earle MacVeigh
Thomas Nast, of *Harper's Weekly*	Guy Standing, Jr.
Andrew Munroe	James Judson
William Dutton	James Quigg
Vincent Peters	Paul Reed
Mayor, A. Oakey Hall	Rowan Tudor
Richard Connolly, Comptroller of the City of New York	George Lane
Peter Sweeney, Park Commissioner	Harry Meehan
William Marcey Tweed, Grand Sachem of Tammany Hall	Malcolm Lee Beggs
Butler	Dick Hughes
Maid	Louise Holden
2nd Maid	Eve Harvey
Mildred Wincor	Lillian Withington
Joe Stewart	Jack Stanton
Porter	John Thorne
Lotta Stevens	June MacLaren
Fanny Morris	Janet Roland
Clara Manning	Lilias MacLellan
James Fisk, Jr.	Jack Howard
George	George Bockman
The Gnome	Kenneth Owen
Governess	Louise Holden
1st Child	Joanne Lally
2nd Child	Janet Lally
Head Waiter	John Quigg
Arthur Finch	Wally Coyle
George Jones, Owner of *The New York Times*	Rowan Tudor
Newsboy	Hobart Streiford
Organ Grinders	{ Edward Pate / Kenneth Owen

Act I.—Scene 1—Site in Central Park (June, 1870). 2—Park Commissioner's Office in Central Park. 3—Lounge of Stetson Hotel (formerly McGowan's Pass Tavern). 4—Bird House in Zoo. 5—Central Park Gardens. Act II.—Annual Tammany Hall Outing (July, 1871). 2—Office of George Jones, Owner of *New York Times*. 3—Central Park West. 4—The Stetson Hotel. 5—Mall in Central Park. 6—Bandstand in the Mall.

THE BEST PLAYS OF 1946-47

Staged by John Kennedy and Sammy Lambert; music directed by
William Parson; dances directed by Helen Tamaris; setting and
lighting by Howard Bay; costumes by Grace Houston and Ernest
Schraps.

Michael Todd first produced "Up in Central Park" at the Century Theatre, New York, January 25, 1945. The musical play
closed April 13, 1946, after a run of 504 performances.

(Closed May 31, 1947)

THE DANCER

(5 performances)

A melodrama in three acts by Milton Lewis and Julian Funt;
music by Paul Bowles. Produced by George Abbott at the Biltmore Theatre, New York, June 5, 1946.

Cast of characters—

Henry Wilkins	Edgar Kent
Aubrey Stewart	Colin Keith-Johnston
The Inspector	Luis Van Rooten
Sergei Krainine	Anton Dolin
Madeline Krainine	Bethel Leslie
Catherine Krainine	Helen Flint

Acts I, II and III.—Living Room of Aubrey Stewart's House in
Present-day Paris.
Staged by Everett Sloane; settings by Motley.

Sergei Krainine, famous as a ballet dancer, and for fourteen
years a baffling mental case, is living with and under the protection of Aubrey Stewart, a rich dilettante. Suspected of the murder of a neighborhood prostitute, Sergei is also pursued by his
daughter, who, wanting to marry, is trying to discover whether or
not her father's madness is hereditary. Also by his wife, who has
a key to a vault in which the dancer's fortune is supposed to have
been hidden, but which she cannot locate. The dancer is finally
overcome by the law, but not until he has committed a couple of
additional back-breaking murders.

(Closed June 8, 1946)

ICETIME

(405 performances)

A musical icetravaganza in two acts by James Littlefield and
John Fortis; musical arrangements by Paul Van Loan. Produced
by Sonja Henie and Arthur M. Wirtz at the Center Theatre, New
York, June 20, 1946.

Principals engaged—

Freddie Trenkler	Joan Hyldoft
Paul Castle	Claire Dalton
James Caesar	Helga Brandt
Patrick Kazda	Inge Brandt
Jack Reese	Monte Stott
Buster Grace	Geoffe Stevens
Charlie Slagle	Sid Spalding
Fritz Dietl	Bing Stott
Robert Ballard	Florence Ballard
Jay Martin	Denise Briault
Richard Craig	Shirley Weber

Act I.—1—Overture. 2—Winter Holiday. 3—Ski Lesson. 4—Mary, Mary Quite Contrary. 5—Setting the Pace. 6—Higher and Higher. 7—Ole King Cole. 8—Light and Shadow. 9—Sherwood Forest. 10—The Nutcracker. 11—Candy Fairy. 12—When the Minstrels Come to Town. Act II.—1—Entr'acte. 2—Cossack Lore. 3—Divertisement. 4—Lovable You. 5—Zouaves. 6—Double Vision. 7—Garden of Versailles. 8—Those Good Old Days. 9—The Dream Waltz. 10—Style on Steel. 11—Bouncing Ball of the Ice. 12—Finale.

Staged by Sonart Productions; directed by Arthur Wirtz and William H. Burke; choreography by Catherine and Dorothie Littlefield; skating direction by May Judels; music directed by David Mendoza; settings by Edward Gilbert; costumes by Lou Eisele and Billy Livingston; lighting by Eugene Braun.

(Closed April 12, 1947)

TIDBITS OF 1946

(8 performances)

A vaudeville entertainment based on a Youth Theatre revue; sketches by Sam Locke. Presented by Arthur Klein in association with Henry Schumer at the Plymouth Theatre, New York, July 8, 1946.

Principals engaged—

Joey Faye	Muriel Gaines
Josef Marais	Miranda
Carmen and Rolando	Candido
Robert Marshall	Lee Trent
Joshua Shelley	Josephine Boyer
Jack Diamond	Eddy Manson
The Debonairs	The Mack Triplets

Staged by Arthur Klein; music directed by Phil Romano.

(Closed July 13, 1946)

MAID IN THE OZARKS

(103 performances)

A farce in three acts by Claire Parrish. Produced by Jules Pfeiffer at the Belasco Theatre, New York, July 15, 1946.

Cast of characters—

Gram Calhoun	Ervil Hart
Thad Calhoun	Larry Sherman

Mohawk..Jack Mathiesen
Bart Calvert....................................John Connor
Lydia Tolliver..................................Johnee Williams
Temple Calhoun..................................Jon Dawson
Frances Tolliver................................Gloria Humphreys
Cypress Young...................................Burman Bodel
Amy Young.......................................Evelyn Wells Fargo
Daisy Belle.....................................Cecile De Lucas
Miss Bleeker....................................Marcelle Gaudel
    Acts I, II and III.—Kitchen of the Calhoun Home in the Ozark
Mountains in Northwestern Arkansas.
    Staged by Jules Pfeiffer.

The romance of a moonshiner and a slightly soiled waitress in the hillbilly country. Advertised as "the worst play in the world," it proved a disappointment to the critics. They insisted it was not that good.

(Closed September 29, 1946)

THE FRONT PAGE

(79 performances)

A comedy in three acts by Ben Hecht and Charles MacArthur. Revived by Hunt Stromberg, Jr., and Thomas Spengler at the Royale Theatre, New York, September 4, 1946.

Cast of characters—

Wilson, *American*....................................Roger Clark
Endicott, *Post*......................................Jack Arnold
Murphy, *Journal*.....................................Bruce MacFarlane
McCue, City News Bureau...............................Benny Baker
Schwartz, *Daily News*................................Ray Walston
Kruger, *Journal of Commerce*.........................Pat Harrington
Bensinger, *Tribune*..................................Rolly Beck
Mrs. Schlosser..Isabel Bonner
"Woodenshoes" Eichorn.................................Curtis Karpe
Diamond Louie...Joseph De Santis
Hildy Johnson, *Herald-Examiner*......................Lew Parker
Jennie..Blanche Lytell
Mollie Malloy...Olive Deering
Sheriff Hartman.......................................William Lynn
Peggy Grant...Pat McClarney
Mrs. Grant..Cora Witherspoon
The Mayor...Edward H. Robins
Mr. Pincus..Harold Grau
Earl Williams...George Lyons
Walter Burns..Arnold Moss
Tony..Leonard Yorr
Carl..Fred Bemis
Frank...Vic Whitlock
    Acts I, II and III.—Press Room of Criminal Courts Building, Chicago.
    Staged by Charles MacArthur; setting by Nat Karson; costumes by Irene Aronson.

"The Front Page" was first produced by Jed Harris and directed by George S. Kaufman at the Times Square Theatre, August 14, 1928. It had 276 performances. When first produced it seemed to many people scandalous because of the profanity and gutter argot of the police reporters it was portraying, but after eighteen years, during which the theatre has been steadily acquiring more latitude, the dialogue seemed less shocking in the revival. The original production was famous for its taut, biting performance, and particularly for the acting of the late Osgood Perkins as Walter Burns and of Lee Tracy as Hildy Johnson. Although the revival offered nothing as memorable, it conveyed the humor and excitement of a well-written play and was successful at the box office.

(Closed November 9, 1946)

A FLAG IS BORN

(120 performances)

A dramatic pageant in one act by Ben Hecht with music by Kurt Weill. Produced by the American League for a Free Palestine at the Alvin Theatre, New York, September 5, 1946.

Cast of characters—

Speaker	Quentin Reynolds
Tevya	Paul Muni
Zelda	Celia Adler
David	Marlon Brando
The Singer	Mario Berini
Saul	George David Baxter
Old One	Morris Samuylow
Middle Aged One	David Manning
Young One	John Baragrey
David the King	William Allyn
Solomon	Gregory Morton
American Statesman	Jonathan Harris
Russian Statesman	Yasha Rosenthal
1st English Statesman	Tom Emlyn Williams
2nd English Statesman	Jefferson Coates
French Statesman	Frederick Rudin
1st Soldier	Steve Hill
2nd Soldier	Jonathan Harris
3rd Soldier	Harold Gary

Scene—A Graveyard Somewhere in Europe.

Staged by Luther Adler; in charge of production, Jules J. Leventhal; choreography by Zamira Gon; music directed by Isaac Van Grove; settings by Robert Davison; costumes by John Boyt.

To raise money for and arouse interest in the American League for a Free Palestine, many theatre people co-operatively staged this dramatic pageant by Ben Hecht. It presented an aging Jewish couple, dispossessed in Europe, walking hopefully in the direction of Palestine. In the background other historical, religious and political aspects of Jewish life were represented in pageant form; and to one side a commentator discussed the significance of the narrative. Although designed for a limited engagement, the pageant became conspicuously successful and continued, with Luther Adler in the chief role after Paul Muni had completed a brief engagement and was called to Hollywood.

(Closed December 15, 1946)

YOURS IS MY HEART

(36 performances)

An operetta in three acts based on "Land of Smiles," book and lyrics by Harry Graham, Ira Cobb and Karl Farkas; music by Franz Lehar; musical adaptations and arrangements by Felix Guenther. Produced by Arthur Spitz at the Shubert Theatre, New York, September 5, 1946.

Cast of characters—

Guy	Monroe Manning
Lucille	Helene Whitney
Lou	Jane Mackle
Pierre	Harold Lazaron
Fernand (?)	Alexander D'Arcy
Yvonne	Natalye Greene
Fifi	Dorothy Karrel
Marie	Jean Heisey
Archibald Mascotte	Sammy White
Claudette Vernay	Stella Andreva
Butler	Harvey Kier
Prince Sou Chong	Richard Tauber
Huang Wei	Edward Groag
Tschang	Arnold Spector
Hsi Fueng	Fred Keating
Princess Mi	Lillian Held
Master of Ceremonies	Albert Shoengold
High Priest	Fred Briess
Li Tsi	Beatrice Eden

Guests, Maids and Servants, Dancers, Mandarins, Etc.
Solo Dancers: Trudy Goth, Henry Schwarze, Haydee Morini, Wayne Lamb, Alberto Feliciano.
Act I.—Drawing Room of Claudette Vernay's Paris Apartment. Act II.—Hall in Sou Chong's Palace in Peiping. Act III.—Room in Sou Chong's Palace.
Staged by Theodore Bache; dialogue directed by Monroe Manning; music directed by George Schick; dances by Henry Shwarze; settings and costumes by Hienz Condell; lighting by Milton Lowe.

As an operetta that was already familiar to many Europeans, and also to many Americans in other parts of the country, "Yours Is My Heart" was designed to provide a setting for some melodies by Franz Lehar—notably his famous "Yours Is My Heart, Alone," which was the central point of the evening. The story began in Paris, where a Chinese prince had fallen in love with a Parisian opera singer, and then moved to China where the prince tried to defy Chinese custom by marrying the singer. Richard Tauber, whose singing, especially of the title song, was the main public attraction of the operetta, was afflicted with serious throat trouble before the run had fairly started. When it became apparent that he could not return to the cast for regular performances the production was withdrawn.

(Closed October 5, 1946)

GYPSY LADY

(79 performances)

An operetta by Henry Myers with melodies from the Victor Herbert-Henry B. Smith operettas "The Fortune Teller" and "The Serenade"; musical adaptations by Arthur Kay. Produced by Edwin Lester at the Century Theatre, New York, September 17, 1946.

Cast of characters—

```
Baron Pettibois................................Clarance Derwent
Yvonne.........................................Kaye Connor
Fresco.........................................Jack Goode
Musetta........................................Helena Bliss
Sergeant of Gendarmes..........................Edmund Dorsay
The Great Alvarado.............................John Tyers
Valerie, Marquise of Roncevalle................Doreen Wilson
Imri...........................................Val Valentinoff
Rudolfo........................................William Bauer
Boris..........................................Melville Cooper
Roszika........................................Patricia Sims
Sandor.........................................George Britton
Andre, Marquis of Roncevalle...................Gilbert Russell
Stephan, Duke of Roncevalle....................Joseph Macaulay
The Undecided Mademoiselle.....................Suzette Meredith
M. Guilbert Armand.............................Bert Hillner
Majordomo......................................Harvey Shahan
```

Act I.—Scene 1—Baron Pettibois' Academy of Theatre Arts. France about 1900. 2—The Gypsy Camp. 3—The Baron's Garden. Act II.—Scene 1—Suite in a Paris Hotel. 2—Roof of Hotel Overlooking Montmartre. 3—Terrace of Chateau de Roncevalle. 4—Cupid's Cupola. 5—The Road.

Staged by Robert Wright and George Forrest; vocal numbers staged by Lew Kesler; dances by Aida Broadbent; music directed by Arthur Kay; settings by Boris Aronson; costumes by Miles White; lighting and technical supervision by Adrian Awan.

To make use of Victor Herbert melodies from "The Fortune Teller" and "The Serenade," Henry Myers wrote a new operetta book that mischievously betrothed a gypsy princess (Musetta) to a genuine and snobbish marquis (Andre) under the impression that she was a royal princess. The score included such famous Herbert melodies as the "Gypsy Love Song," "I Love You, I Adore You" and "Springtime."

(Closed November 23, 1946)

HIDDEN HORIZON

(12 performances)

A mystery play in three acts by Agatha Christie, based on her own book, "Murder on the Nile." Produced by the Messrs. Shubert in association with Albert de Courville at the Plymouth Theatre, New York, September 19, 1946.

Cast of characters—

1st Beadseller	Monty Banks, Jr.
2nd Beadseller	David Andrews
Steward	Charles Alexander
Miss Ffoliot-Ffoulkes	Eva Leonard-Boyne
Christina Grant	Joy Ann Page
Smith	David Manners
Louise	Edith Kingdon
Dr. Bessner	Peter Von Zerneck
Simon Mostyn	Blair Davies
Kay Mostyn	Barbara Joyce
Archdeacon Pennyfeather	Halliwell Hobbes
Jacqueline De Severac	Diana Barrymore
McNaught	Winston Ross
Two Egyptian Policemen	{ Leland Hamilton / Damian Nimer }

Act I.—At Shellal—in the Observation Salon of the Paddle Steamer *Lotus* on the Nile. Acts II and III.—By the Temple Abu Simbel.

Staged by Albert de Courville; settings by Charles Elson; costumes by Everett Staples.

Among the passengers on a Nile steamer are a rich young English lady and her new husband, formerly her secretary. The couple is being pursued by the husband's former fiancée, who threatens some sort of revenge. The bride is mysteriously murdered. Before the police arrive a British clergyman, who is one of the passengers and also the uncle of the bride, discovers the murderer.

(Closed September 28, 1946)

THE BEES AND THE FLOWERS

(28 performances)

A comedy in three acts by Frederick Kohner and Albert Mannheimer. Produced by Mort H. Singer, Jr., at the Cort Theatre, New York, September 26, 1946.

Cast of characters—

Louise Morgan	Barbara Robbins
Nancy	Jean Frey
Alix Morgan	Sybil Stocking
Tess Morgan	Rosemary Rice
Ilka Morgan	Joyce Van Patten
Winston Atchison	Michael Dreyfuss

```
Tack  Cooper......................................Russell  Hardie
Dippy  Marshall....................................Sylvia  Lane
Drayman...........................................Maurice  Brenner
Tom...............................................Leonard  Bell
Jerry.............................................Peggy  Romano
     Acts  I,  II  and  III.—Terrace  of  Morgan  Apartment,  New  York
City.
     Staged  by  Albert  Mannheimer;  setting  by  Edward  Gilbert;  cos-
tumes  by  Enid  Gilbert.
```

Louise Morgan, divorced wife of a foreign correspondent and mother of three girls, has, without their knowledge, married Tack Cooper, whom she met in Mexico. Since she lacks the courage immediately to tell her children that Tack is their new stepfather, she invites him to stay in the apartment under the guise of a new friend. Since the girls want their mother to reunite with her former husband, they regard Tack as a threat to family solidarity. The comedy involves their attempts to estrange him from their mother until, in the last scene, they learn that their mother and he are already married.

(Closed October 19, 1946)

OBSESSION

(31 performances)

A drama in three acts adapted by Jane Hinton from Louis Verneuil's French play "Jealousy." Revived by Homer Curran in association with Russell Lewis and Howard Young at the Plymouth Theatre, New York, October 1, 1946.

Cast of characters—

```
Maurice..........................................Basil  Rathbone
Nadya............................................Eugenie  Leontovich
     Acts  I,  II  and  III.—A  Paris  Apartment.
     Staged  by  Reginald  Denham;  setting  and  lighting  by  Stewart
Chaney;  gowns  by  Adrian.
```

The late Eugene Walter's adaptation of the Verneuil play, then entitled "Jealousy," was staged at the Maxine Elliott Theatre, New York, October 22, 1928, by Guthrie McClintic and produced by A. H. Woods. The two characters then were played by John Halliday and Fay Bainter, and the production ran for 136 performances. The Jane Hinton version is more earnestly dramatic than the Walter adaptation, but the story is the same one of two lovers in Paris who marry and settle down in the bride's apartment. Almost immediately the groom becomes jealous and suspicious of the bride's guardian, and later strangles him off stage.

(Closed October 26, 1946)

HEAR THAT TRUMPET

(8 performances)

A drama with jazz overtones in three acts by Orin Jannings.
Produced by Arthur Hopkins at the Playhouse, New York, October 7, 1946.

Cast of characters—

```
Mumford (Clarinet)...............................Sidney Bechet
Alonzo Armonk....................................Frank Conroy
Dinger Richardson (Trumpet)....................Bobby Sherwood
Floyd Amery (Piano)...............................Ray Mayer
Abba (Bass Viol)................................Bart Edwards
Rocco (Drums)..................................Marty Marsala
Erica Marlowe..................................Audra Lindley
Skippy (Trombone)..............................Philip Layton
Sally Belle.....................................Lynne Carter
Cleasy.......................................Raymond Bramley
```
    Acts I, II and III.—Dinger's and Floyd's Rooms, Chicago. 1945.
Staged by Arthur Hopkins; setting by Woodman Thompson.

Dinger Richardson, out of the Army, has reorganized his jazz
band, with his old Army pal, Floyd Amery, heading a group of
other talented youth.   The band has a tough time, partly because
the clarinetist, Mumford, is a colored boy, and thus innocently
brings the race question into the bookings.   Rich Alonzo Armonk,
at the behest of his mistress, Erica Marlowe, agrees to sponsor the
band.   When Erica falls in love with, and marries, Richardson,
Armonk's interest turns to hatred and his thought to revenge.
Erica is forced to poison Armonk's tea with sleeping pellets to be
rid of him in the end.

(Closed October 12, 1946)

CYRANO DE BERGERAC

(193 performances)

A drama in five acts by Edmond Rostand; English version by
Brian Hooker; incidental music by Paul Bowles.   Revived by José
Ferrer at the Alvin Theatre, New York, October 8, 1946.

Cast of characters—

```
Porter.......................................Benedict McQuarrie
A Cavalier...................................Samuel N. Kirkham
A Musketeer.....................................George Oliver
A Lackey.......................................Stewart Long
Another Lackey..................................Ralph Meeker
A Guardsman..................................Charles Summers
Flower Girl.......................................Phyllis Hill
A Citizen....................................Wallace Widdecombe
His Son.........................................Walter Kelly
A Cut Purse......................................Nick Dennis
```

```
Orange Girl......................................Patricia  Wheel
A  Marquis.......................................John  O'Connor
Brissaille..........................................Bert  Whitley
Ligniere.........................................Robert  Carroll
Christian  De  Neuvillette.........................Ernest  Graves
Ragueneau........................................Hiram  Sherman
Le  Bret.........................................William  Woodson
Roxane,  Nee  Madeleine  Robin.....................Frances  Reid
Her  Duenna......................................Paula  Laurence
Comte  De  Guiche................................Ralph  Clanton
Vicomte  De  Valvert............................Anthony  Jordan
Montfleury.......................................Leopold  Badia
Cyrano  de  Bergerac.............................José  Ferrer
Bellrose.........................................Howard  Wierum
Jodelet..........................................Robinson  Stone
A  Meddler......................................Francis  Letton
A  Soubrette...................................Mary  Jane  Kersey
A  Comedienne.................................Jacqueline  Soans
Lise............................................Nan  McFarland
Carbon  De  Castel-Jaloux.......................Francis  Compton
A  Poet.........................................Vincent  Donahue
Another  Poet...................................Leonardo  Cimino
A  Capuchin.....................................Robinson  Stone
A  Cadet...........................................Paul  Wilson
Sister  Marthe.................................Jacqueline  Soans
Mother  Marguerite..............................Nan  McFarland
Sister  Claire....................................Phyllis  Hill
A  Nun..........................................Patricia  Wheel
    Ladies,  Thieves,  Lackeys,  Cadets,  Cooks,  Poets,  Sentries,  Pages,
Children,  Actors,  Nuns,  etc.:  Lee  Baxter,  Anthony  Jordan,  Toni
Brown,  Robert  Carroll,  Leonardo  Cimino,  Marion  Clements,  John
O'Connor,  Nick  Dennis,  Vincent  Donahue,  Walter  Kelly,  Samuel  N.
Kirkham,  Francis  Letton,  Stewart  Long,  Benedict  McQuarrie,  Ralph
Meeker,  George  B.  Oliver,  Mary  Jane  Kersey,  Charles  Summers,
Bert  Whitley,  Howard  Wierum,  Wallace  Widdecombe,  Paul  Wilson.
    Act  I.—A  Performance  at  the  Hotel  de  Bourgogne.  1640.  Act
II.—The  Bakery  of  the  Poets.  Act  III.—Roxane's  Kiss.  Act  IV.—
The  Cadets  of  Gascoyne.  Act  V.—Cyrano's  Gazette.  1655.
    Staged  by  Melchor  Ferrer;  production  supervised  by  Arthur  S.
Friend;  settings  and  costumes  by  Lemuel  Ayers.
```

Constant Coquelin first played Rostand's "Cyrano de Bergerac" in Paris in 1897. The first American production was staged by Richard Mansfield, with Margaret Anglin as his Roxane, at the Garden Theatre, New York, in October, 1928. Two years later Sarah Bernhardt and Coquelin toured America in the play. In November, 1923, Walter Hampden revived "Cyrano," with Carroll McComas as Roxane, at the National Theatre, New York, where it was played for 232 performances. Additional Hampden revivals were staged in 1926, 1928, 1932, and 1936, with Marie Adels, Ingeborg Torrup, and Katherine Warren playing Roxane successively. An operatic version by Walter Damrosch was staged in 1930.

(Closed March 22, 1947)

THE ICEMAN COMETH

(136 performances)

A drama in four acts by Eugene O'Neill. Produced by The Theatre Guild in association with Armina Marshall at the Martin Beck Theatre, New York, October 9, 1946.

Cast of characters—

Harry Hope	Dudley Digges
Ed Mosher	Morton L. Stevens
Pat McGloin	Al McGranary
Willie Oban	E. G. Marshall
Joe Mott	John Marriott
Piet Wetjoen	Frank Tweddell
Cecil Lewis	Nicholas Joy
James Cameron	Russell Collins
Hugo Kalmar	Leo Chalzel
Larry Slade	Carl Benton Reid
Rocky Pioggi	Tom Pedi
Dan Parritt	Paul Crabtree
Pearl	Ruth Gilbert
Margie	Jeanne Cagney
Cora	Marcella Markham
Chuck Morello	Joe Marr
Theodore Hickman	James Barton
Moran	Michael Wyler
Lieb	Charles Hart

Acts I, II and IV.—Back Room and Section of the Bar at Harry Hope's. Act III.—Bar and Section of the Back Room. 1912.

Staged by Eddie Dowling; production supervised by Theresa Helburn and Lawrence Langner; settings and lighting by Robert Edmond Jones.

See page 63.

(Closed March 15, 1947)

MR. PEEBLES AND MR. HOOKER

(4 performances)

A comedy in a prologue and three acts by Edward E. Paramore, Jr., based on a novel by Charles G. Givens. Produced by Joseph M. Hyman at the Music Box, New York, October 10, 1946.

Cast of characters—

Hank	James Robertson
Brother Alf Leland	Paul Huber
Hattie	Juanita Hall
Brother Wally Leland	Tom Coley
Bump Sorrell	Arthur Hunnicutt
Ellen Sorrell	Dorothy Gilchrist
Chauffeur	Van Prince
Mrs. Hatcher Craine	Randee Sanford
Nate Corbett	Grover Burgess
Mr. Hooker	Rhys Williams
Sheriff Todd Blakely	Ralph Stantley
Pete	Arthur Foran
Deputy	Charles Thompson
Mr. Hatcher Craine	Neil McFee Skinner

```
Dr. Phil Jameson.....................................Tom Morgan
Judge Fayette........................................Tom Hoier
Mr. Peebles..........................................Howard Smith
A Stranger...........................................Jeff Morrow
Whigsey..............................................Ken Renard
Joe Greer............................................Dennis Bohan
```
Prologue—A Fallen Tree on a Tennessee Hilltop Overlooking a Lake. Act I.—Scene 1—The Leland House. 2—Exterior of Mr. Hooker's Shack. Act II.—Scene 1—The Leland House. 2—Interior of Mr. Hooker's Shack. Act III.—The Leland House.

Staged by Martin Ritt; settings by Frederick Fox; costumes by Eleanor Goldsmith.

Mr. Peebles, an amiable and friendly visitor to Tennessee, represents the great god Jehovah of the Old Testament. His mission of enlightenment to the quarreling, striking, rebelling natives is crossed by a certain Mr. Hooker, representing his Satanic Majesty. Mr. Peebles' son, a gentle carpenter, protests that his father should discard his old law of an eye for an eye, a tooth for a tooth, and teach mercy and forbearance to the misguided Tennesseeans. Jehovah Peebles can't see it that way, continuing as a god of wrath. His son is jailed as a rabble rouser.

(Closed October 12, 1946)

LADY WINDERMERE'S FAN

(228 performances)

A comedy in four acts by Oscar Wilde; incidental music by Leslie Bridgewater. Revived by Homer Curran in association with Russell Lewis and Howard Young at the Cort Theatre, New York, October 14, 1946.

Cast of characters—
```
Lady Windermere..............................Penelope Ward
Parker.......................................Thomas Louden
Lord Darlington..............................John Buckmaster
Duchess of Berwick...........................Estelle Winwood
Lady Agatha Carlisle.........................Sally Cooper
Lord Windermere..............................Henry Daniell
Mr. Rufford..................................Paul Russell
Miss Rufford.................................Jerri Sauvinet
Lady Paisley.................................Marguerite Gleason
Hon. Paulette Sonning........................Tanagra Thayer
Lady Jedburgh................................Elizabeth Valentine
The Bishop...................................Peter Keyes
Miss Graham..................................Pamela Wright
Sir James Royston............................Jack Merivale
Lady Stutfield...............................Anne Curson
Mr. Dumby....................................Evan Thomas
Mrs. Cowper-Cowper...........................Leonore Elliott
Mr. Hopper...................................Stanley Bell
Lady Plymdale................................Nan Hopkins
Sir Augustus Lorton..........................Rex Evans
Mr. Cecil Graham.............................Cecil Beaton
Mrs. Erlynne.................................Cornelia Otis Skinner
First Footman................................Guy Blake
```

Second Footman..................................Richard Burns
Rosalie...Marjorie Wood
    Act I.—Morning-Room of Lord Windermere's House in Carleton
Terrace, London. Acts II and IV.—Drawing Room in Lord Winder-
mere's House. Act III.—Lord Darlington's Rooms.
    Staged by Jack Minster; settings and lighting by Cecil Beaton.

Julia Arthur was the first American Lady Windermere, playing the role in February, 1893. The comedy was revived by Margaret Anglin in 1914, she electing to play Mrs. Erlynne to the Lady Windermere of Marjorie Maude. In a four-day revival by an organization called Afternoon Theatre in 1932, Ellis Baker played Lady Windermere and Theresa Conover the Mrs. Erlynne. The story of the lady with a past (Mrs. Erlynne) sacrificing her reputation a second time to shield her unsuspecting daughter (Lady Windermere) was considered quite daring forty years ago.

(Closed April 26, 1947)

THE DUCHESS OF MALFI

(38 performances)

A tragedy in three parts by John Webster; adapted by W. H. Auden; incidental music by Benjamin Britten. Revived by Paul Czinner at the Barrymore Theatre, New York, October 15, 1946.

Cast of characters—

Ferdinand, Duke of Calabria......................Donald Eccles
The Cardinal.....................................John Carradine
Giovanna, Duchess of Malfi.....................Elisabeth Bergner
Antonio Bologna...............................Whitfield Connor
Delio..Richard Newton
Daniel de Bosola..................................Canada Lee
Officers Attending on the Duchess.............. { Ben Morse / MichaelBey / Lawrence Ryle / Robin Morse
Castruchio...Guy Spaull
Silvio...Michael Ellis
Roderigo...Rupert Pole
Grisolan...Jack Cook
Cariola..Patricia Calvert
Julia..Sonia Sorel
Old Lady.......................................Michelette Burani
Ladies Attending on the Duchess............... { Diana Kemble / Beth Holland
Chaplain to The Cardinal.......................William Layton
Secretary to The Cardinal......................Frederic Downs
Antonio's Son....................................Maurice Cavell
Madmen { Priest (Singer).......................Walter Peterson / Lawyer...........................Robert Pike / Astrologer......................Frederic Downs / Doctor...........................Guy Spaull
Doctor...Robert Pike
    Scene—Malfi, Rome, Ancona and elsewhere in Italy early in the
sixteenth century.
    Staged by George Rylands; settings by Harry Bennett; costumes by
Miles White.

Giovanna, Duchess of Malfi, being widowed, secretly marries her steward, Antonio. Bearing Antonio's three children (out of wedlock so far as her brothers, the Cardinal, and Ferdinand the Duke, are concerned), the Duchess acquires a bad name in the family. In their lust for revenge, the Cardinal and the Duke, aided by De Bosola, their spy, seek to wipe out the Duchess, the steward and the three children. This they cruelly manage to do, and then fall upon each other and increase the horror deaths of the evening to nine. (The De Bosola role was played in New York by Canada Lee, the Negro actor, in white makeup, which was a record of sorts.)

(Closed November 16, 1946)

LOCO

(37 performances)

A comedy in two acts by Dale Eunson and Katherine Albert based on a story by Dale Eunson. Produced by Jed Harris at the Biltmore Theatre, New York, October 16, 1946.

Cast of characters—

Naomi Brewster	Beverly Bayne
Alma Brewster	Helen Murdoch
McIntyre	Barry Kelley
Waldo Brewster	Jay Fassett
David Skinner	Morgan Wallace
Loco Dempsey	Jean Parker
Ginger	Marlo Dwyer
Matron	Darin Jennings
Eben	Parker Fennelly
Pamela Brewster	Elaine Stritch
Nicky Martinez	Si Vario
Miss White	Ethel Remey

Act I.—Scene 1—The Brewster Library. 2—The Golden Bantam. 3—Powder Room of Golden Bantam. 4—Brewster's Bedroom. 5—Brewster's Hunting Lodge in Maine. Act II.—Scenes 1 and 3—The Lodge. 2 and 4—The Library. 5—Brewster's Office.

Staged by Jed Harris; settings by Donald Oenslager; costumes by Emeline C. Roche.

Waldo Brewster of Wall Street, rich and restless, meets Loco Dempsey, an attractive Conover model, and decides to follow up his first urge for a romantic fling. He takes Loco to his hunting lodge in Maine for a holiday, where she goes to bed with an attack of measles instead of Waldo. Playing nurse, and listening to Loco's homely philosophy, Waldo promptly retreats from sin, forgives an erring daughter and returns to his wife, chastened and renewed.

(Closed November 16, 1946)

LYSISTRATA

(4 performances)

A comedy in two acts by Aristophanes in a modern version by Gilbert Seldes; incidental music by Henry Brant. Revived by James Light and Max J. Jelin at the Belasco Theatre, New York, October 17, 1946.

Cast of characters—

Leader of Old Women's Chorus....................Pearl Gaines
Lysistrata...Etta Moten
Kolonika......................................Fredi Washington
Myrrhina..Mildred Smith
Lampito.......................................Mercedes Gilbert
Spartan Women...................Louise E. Evans, Tica Janine
Theban Women.........Lou Sealia Swarz, Eunice Elenora Miller
Corinthian Women................Margaret Tynes, Valerie Black
Leader of Old Men's Chorus.....................Leigh Whipper
Old Men's Chorus..Wardell Saunders, Cherokee Thornton, James H.
            Dunmore, Louis Sharp, Andrew Ratousheff,
            George Dozier, Larri E. Lauria, Service Bell
President of the Senate.............................Rex Ingram
Spartan Envoy....................................Maurice Ellis
Kinesias...............................Emmett Babe Wallace
Trygeus...John De Battle
Nikias...Larry Williams
Polydorus......................................Sidney Poitier
Senators......Harry Bolden, P. Jay Sidney, Bootsie Davis, Hanson
            Elkins, Milton J. Williams, Wilson Woodbeck
Lykon......................................Emory S. Richardson
Officers.....................Milers Winbush, George F. Carroll
Satyrs............................Archie Savage, Jay Flashe Riley
Dancers......Bill O'Neil, Frank Green, H. Roderick Scott, Albert
            Popwell, George Thomas, Royce Wallace, Marble Hart,
            Erona Harris, Gwyn Hale, Hettie Stephens, Ann Henry
Old Women's Chorus........Beatrice Wade, Phyllis Walker, Hilda
            Offley, Theresa Brooks, Olive Ball, Ethel Purnello,
                Wilhelmina Williams and Edyth Reid
Young Women's Chorus....Lora Pierce, Geneva H. Fitch, Laphfawn
            Gumbs, Marie Cooke, Jean Stovall, Geri Bryan,
            Jackie Greene, Courtenay Olden, Minnie Gentry
    Acts I and II.—Daybreak on the Acropolis, Athens, 411 B.C., in
Twenty-first Year of War Between Athens and Sparta.
    Staged by James Light; setting and lighting by Ralph Alswang;
choreography by Felicia Sorel; costumes by Rose Bogdanoff.

The Gilbert Seldes version of Aristophanes' "Lysistrata" was first produced in New York by the Philadelphia Theatre Association in June, 1930. The principals were Violet Kemble Cooper, Miriam Hopkins and Ernest Truex. The play ran for 252 performances. The 1946 revival was given by an all-Negro cast, headed by Etta Moten, Fredi Washington and "Babe" Wallace. It was withdrawn after four performances.

(Closed October 19, 1946)

NAUGHTY NAUGHT ('00)

(17 performances)

A musical satire in three acts by John Van Antwerp; lyrics by Ted Fetter; music by Richard Lewine. Revived by Paul Killiam in association with Oliver Rea at the Old Knickerbocker Music Hall, New York, October 19, 1946.

Cast of characters—

P. de Quincy Devereux	John Cromwell
Spunky	Teddy Hart
Frank Plover	Leonard Hicks
Jack Granville	Kenneth Forbes
Stub	Shepard Curelop
Fred	King Taylor
Claire Granville	Ottilie Kruger
Jim Pawling	Marshall Jamison
Joe	Roy Wolvin
Tom	Len Smith, Jr.
Bartender	George Spelvin
Cathleen	Virginia Barbour
Pugsy	L. A. Nicoletti

Acts I, II and III.—In and Around New Haven.

Staged by Ted Fetter; music directed by Richard Lewine; orchestra directed by Leroy Anderson; dances by Ray Harrison; settings and lighting by Kermit Love; costumes by Robert Moore.

"Naughty Naught ('00)" was previously seen on Broadway at the American Music Hall. It was produced by John and Jerrold Krimsky for 173 performances, starting January 23, 1937.

(Closed November 2, 1946)

MADE IN HEAVEN!

(92 performances)

A comedy in three acts by Hagar Wilde. Produced by John Golden at the Henry Miller Theatre, New York, October 24, 1946.

Cast of characters—

Nancy Tennant	Katharine Bard
Marian Hunt	Sarah Burton
Laszlo Vertes	Louis Borel
Philip Dunlap	Tony Bickley
Elsa Meredith	Carmen Mathews
Zachary Meredith	Donald Cook
Harry Hunt	Lawrence Fletcher
Dorothy	Marrian Walters
Miss Crowder	Jane Middleton
Hank	Maurice Manson
Man at Bar	Willard L. Thompson
June	Ann Thomas

Act I.—Living Room of the Zachary Merediths', Within Easy Commuting Distance of New York. Act II.—Scene 1—Zachary's Office in New York. 2—Bar in Hotel Revere. 3—Room in Hotel Revere. Act III.—The Merediths' Living Room.

Staged by Martin Manulis; settings by Lawrence Goldwasser.

Zachary Meredith and his young wife, Elsa, ten years married and a little fed up with their cocktail set, fall to quarreling and face a threatened break of marital ties. Zachary tries to find comfort in liquor, and a relief from loneliness with an attractive lady barfly. Elsa considers taking up with a fascinating foreigner. In the end the Merediths agree that it were better to stick to the mates they have than fly to others they know a lot less about.

(Closed January 11, 1947)

THE PLAYBOY OF THE WESTERN WORLD

(81 performances)

A comedy in three acts by J. M. Synge. Revived by Theatre Incorporated (managing director, Richard Aldrich) at the Booth Theatre, New York, October 26, 1946.

Cast of characters—

```
Margaret Flaherty, called Pegeen Mike..............Eithne Dunne
Shawn Keogh...................................Dennis King, Jr.
Michael James Flaherty...........................J. M. Kerrigan
Philly Cullen....................................Barry Macollum
Jimmy Farrell.....................................J. C. Nugent
Christopher Mahon.............................Burgess Meredith
Widow Quin.....................................Mildred Natwick
Susan Brady.......................................Mary Diveny
Honor Blake.......................................Sheila Keddy
Nelly..............................................Julie Harris
Sara Tansey...................................Maureen Stapleton
Old Mahon........................................Fred Johnson
Villagers.....Robin Humphrey, Mary Lou Taylor, Mary T. Walker,
            Paul Anderson, James L. O'Neil, Ford Rainey
    Acts I, II and III.—Flaherty's Public House Near Village on
Wild Coast of County Mayo, Ireland.
    Staged by Guthrie McClintic; setting and costumes by John Boyt.
```

This is the eighth revival of "The Playboy of the Western World" staged in New York. The Synge drama was given its first performance here the season of 1911-12 and started a miniature riot in the audience. Most of these revivals have been staged by the Irish Players from the Abbey Theatre, Dublin, the last of them in 1937.

(Closed January 4, 1947)

BLACKFRIARS' GUILD

DERRYOWEN

(24 performances)

A drama in three acts by Michael O'Hara. Presented by The Blackfriars' Guild at Blackfriars' Theatre, New York, October 28, 1946. The Guild sponsored a total of 93 performances during the season.

Cast of characters—

Michael James O'Callaghan	Seamus Maloney
Moira O'Callaghan	Andrée Wallace
Timothy Aloysius Keough	Gerald Buckley
Dan Kilcoyne	F. X. Donovan
Donagh McNamara	Dennis Harrison
Constable McGovern	Burke McHugh
Anne Travis	Mabel McCallum

Alternate for Mr. McHugh, Edward Gibbons.

Acts I, II and III.—Tap Room of Small Seaside Inn on the West Coast of Ireland.

Staged by Dennis Gurney; setting by Avril Gentles; lighting by Rebecca Jennings.

The story of a spy hunt in Ireland that turns out to be a highly extravagant practical joke.

(Closed November 23, 1946)

IF IN THE GREENWOOD

(28 performances)

A play in blank verse in a prelude and three scenes by Victoria Kuhn. Presented by the Blackfriars' Guild January 16, 1947.

Cast of characters—

Elena	Katherine Hamilton
John Barron Mark	Ray Colcord
David Landor	Edwin Ross
Father Benedict	Joseph Boley
Peter Conrad	John Young
Robert Wilde	Paul Gregory
Anne St. John	Ann Linsley

Prelude—A Rectory in a Foreign Country. Scenes 1, 2 and 3— Seas' Cliff, Mark's Home Overlooking the Atlantic.

Staged by Dennis Gurney; settings by Avril Gentles.

An effort to prove that no nation can reasonably enter the United Nations' struggle for world peace without first seeing that his own country has set its house in order.

(Closed February 16, 1947)

ON THE SEVENTH DAY

(25 performances)

A modern morality play in two parts by Urban Nagle. Presented by the Blackfriars' Guild March 6, 1947.

Cast of characters—

THE ANGELS

Sergeant Theodore	Gordon Hunter
Lieutenant Oriel, archangel	Doug Randall
Lieutenant Raphael, archangel	Joseph Lane
Colonel Advocatus, principality	Robert Hayward
Lieutenant Lilio, former archangel	Allen Stapleton
Colonel Asmodeus, former principality	Robert Cordell

THE HUMANS

John Smith	Paul Melville
Mary	Anne Follmann
Jack	Mel York
Jill	Jo Delle Rundquist

On March 20, 21, 22 and 23 the part of Jill was played by Peggy Ann McCay.

THE GADGETS

Mike	Mike Garrett
Cam	Pauline O'Hare
Mr. Press	Jack Delmonte

Scene—Department of Human Relations in Heaven.
Staged by Dennis Gurney; setting by Blackfriars' Studio under direction of Leo Herbert; lighting by Rebecca Jennings.

Lieutenant Oriel selects episodes in the life of the Smith family, going back as far as Pearl Harbor Day and moving forward until mortals knew about the effects of the atomic bomb.

(Closed April 2, 1947)

RESPECTFULLY YOURS

(16 performances)

A comedy in three acts by Peggy Lamson. Presented by the Blackfriars' Guild May 13, 1947.

Cast of characters—

Lydia Greenleaf	Anne Follmann
Alex Greenleaf	Kevin McCloskey
Doris	Mary Morgan
Carl Greenleaf	Clifford West
Connie Greenleaf	Doris Sward
Alan Walker	Henry Hart
Mrs. McClain	Ethel Kenney
Mr. McClain	Owen Dickson
Photographer	Allen Stapleton
Miss Riggs	May Burkan
William Van Ness	Alfred Reilly
Miss Vinson	Jean Emslie

Acts I, II and III.—Cambridge, Mass., 1912.
Staged by Marjorie Hildreth; setting by David Reppa; lighting by Rebecca Jennings.

Lydia Greenleaf, wife of Carl, a college professor, writes a book entitled "How to Command Respect in the Home." Its unexpected success arouses the faculty resentment and almost costs the professor his job.

(Closed May 28, 1947)

PRESENT LAUGHTER

(158 performances)

A comedy in three acts by Noel Coward. Produced by John C. Wilson at the Plymouth Theatre, New York, October 29, 1946.

Cast of characters—

Daphne Stillington	Jan Sterlin
Miss Erikson	Grace Mills
Fred	Aidan Turner
Monica Reed	Evelyn Varden
Garry Essendine	Clifton Webb
Liz Essendine	Doris Dalton
Roland Maule	Cris Alexander
Morris Dixon	Gordon Mills
Hugo Lyppiatt	Robin Craven
Joanna Lyppiatt	Marta Linden
Lady Saltburn	Leonore Harris

Acts I, II and III.—In Garry Essendine's Studio in London.
Staged by John C. Wilson; setting by Donald Oenslager; costumes designed by Castillo and Sylvia Saal.

Garry Essendine, a London stage favorite, runs into considerable woman trouble with Daphne, a stage-struck ingenue; Liz, a former Mrs. Essendine concentrating upon a renewal of marital relations, and Joanna, a strongly sexed wife of one of Garry's play-producing partners. The actor squirms through a variety of adventures, and is reunited with the former Mrs. Essendine on the eve of an American tour.

(Closed March 15, 1947)

HAPPY BIRTHDAY

(242 performances)
(Continued)

A comedy in two acts by Anita Loos; incidental music by Robert Russell Bennett; songs by Richard Rodgers and Oscar Hammerstein 2nd and James Livingston. Produced by Richard

Rodgers and Oscar Hammerstein 2nd at the Broadhurst Theatre, New York, October 31, 1946.

Cast of characters—

Gail	Margaret Irving
Glorious	Musa Williams
Dad Malone	Thomas Heaphy
Gabe	Charles Gordon
Bella	Florence Sundstrom
Herman	Jack Diamond
Myrtle	Jacqueline Paige
June	Jean Bellows
Addie	Helen Hayes
Maude	Lorraine Miller
Don	Dort Clark
The Judge	Ralph Theadore
Paul	Louis Jean Heydt
Policeman	Philip Dakin
Tot	Enid Markey
Emma	Grace Valentine
Manuel	Philip Gordon
Margot	Eleanor Boleyn
Bert	James Livingston
Mr. Bemis	Robert Burton
Mr. Nanino	Harry Kingston

Acts I and II.—Jersey Mecca Cocktail Bar in Newark, New Jersey. Staged by Joshua Logan; music conducted by Maurice Lefton; setting and lighting by Jo Mielziner; costumes by Lucinda Ballard.

Addie was a meek little librarian in Newark, N. J. On impulse she practically followed a young bank clerk named Paul, with whom she had had some slight acquaintance, and for whom she secretly admitted a considerable longing, into the Jersey Mecca Cocktail Bar, where she knew he frequently stopped to get a drink. Being in a bar, Addie decides to experiment a bit. After trying three or four "pink ladies" and a double Scotch, things begin to happen, not only to Addie, but to all the furnishings of the bar and all the people in the place as well. Before the evening is over Addie has won Paul away from the contriving hussy who was trying to get him, and learned a lot about life and alcohol.

PARK AVENUE

(72 performances)

A musical comedy in two acts by Nunnally Johnson and George S. Kaufman; lyrics by Ira Gershwin; music by Arthur Schwartz; orchestrations by Don Walker. Produced by Max Gordon at the Shubert Theatre, New York, November 4, 1946.

Cast of characters—

Carlton	Byron Russell
Ned Scott	Ray McDonald
Madge Bennett	Martha Stewart
Ogden Bennett	Arthur Margetson
Mrs. Sybil Bennett	Leonora Corbett

```
Charles Crowell...............................Robert  Chisholm
Mrs.  Elsa  Crowell...........................Marthe  Errolle
Reggie  Fox...................................Charles  Purcell
Mrs.  Myra  Fox...............................Ruth  Matteson
Richard  Nelson...............................Raymond  Walburn
Mrs.  Betty  Nelson...........................Mary  Wickes
Ted  Woods....................................Harold  Mattox
Mrs.  Laura  Woods............................Dorothy  Bird
James  Meredith...............................William  Skipper
Mrs.  Beverly  Meredith.......................Joan  Mann
Mr.  Meachem..................................David  Wayne
Freddie  Coleman..............................Wilson  Smith
Carole  Benswanger............................Virginia  Gordon
     Act  I.—The  Terrace,  Mrs.  Ogden  Bennett's  Home,  Long  Island.
Act  II.—The  Drawing  Room.
     Staged  by  George  S.  Kaufman;  production  supervised  by  Arnold
Saint  Subber;  music  directed  by  Charles  Sanford;  dances  by  Helen
Tamiris;  settings  and  lighting  by  Donald  Oenslager.
```

Mrs. Sybil Bennett has a disconcerting way of forgetting most of what she knows about her last two or three husbands. She is also casually curious regarding two or three others she might reasonably have married if the evening had been longer and the multiple marriage joke more resilient.

(Closed January 4, 1947)

AMERICAN REPERTORY THEATRE, INC.

The American Repertory Theatre, Inc., with Cheryl Crawford as managing director, began its 1946-47 season November 6, 1946, at the International Theatre, New York. During the season it achieved a total of 248 performances.

HENRY VIII

(40 performances)

A historical drama by William Shakespeare, rearranged into two acts; music by Lehman Engel. Presented by the Repertory Theatre November 6, 1946.

Cast of characters—

```
The  Prologue..................................Philip  Bourneuf
Duke  of  Buckingham...........................Richard  Waring
Duke  of  Norfolk..............................Raymond  Greenleaf
Lord  Abergavenny..............................Robert  Rawlings
Cardinal  Wolsey...............................Walter  Hampden
Cromwell.......................................Eli  Wallach
Sir  Thomas  Lovell............................Emery  Battis
Sergeant  of  the  Guard.......................William  Windom
Henry  VIII....................................Victor  Jory
Duke  of  Suffolk..............................Efrem  Zimbalist,  Jr.
Katherine  of  Aragon..........................Eva  Le  Gallienne
Surveyor.......................................Angus  Cairns
Lord  Chamberlain..............................Ernest  Truex
Lord  Sands....................................John  Becher
Sir  Harry  Guildford..........................Arthur  Keegan
```

```
Ann Bullen........................................June Duprez
First Chronicler..............................Philip Bourneuf
Second Chronicler.........................Eugene Stuckmann
Sir Nicholas Vaux.............................Donald Keyes
Cardinal Campeius................................John Straub
An Old Lady................................Margaret Webster
Griffith.........................................Donald Keyes
Lady in Waiting to Katherine.......................Ruth Neal
Garter King of Arms............................Angus Cairns
Earl of Surrey.............................William Windom
Archbishop of Canterbury.......................Theodore Tenley
Patience....................................Marion Evensen
A Messenger..................................Robert Rawlings
Capucius......................................Eugene Stuckmann
Duchess of Norfolk...........................Mary Alice Moore
    Ladies of the Court, Crowd, Ladies to Katherine.
    Lords, Bishops, Monks, Guards, Servants, Heralds, Pages, Exe-
cutioner, Sergeant at Arms.
    Act I.—Scene 1—Outside the Council Room, Whitehall Palace,
London.  2—The Council Room.  3—A Street.  4—Wolsey's Palace
at York House.  5—Outside the Tower.  6—The King's Apartments.
7—The Hall at Blackfriars.  Act II.—Scene 1—The Queen's Apart-
ments.  2—The King's Apartments.  3—Westminster Abbey.  4—
Room in Kimbolton Abbey.  5—Ante-Room in the Palace.  6—Out-
side Palace at Greenwich.  1521 to 1533.
    Staged by Margaret Webster; settings and costumes by David
Ffolkes; dances directed by Felecia Sorel.
```

Edwin Booth played Wolsey in an 1878 revival of "Henry VIII" at the Booth Theatre. Sir Herbert Beerbohm Tree, touring America in 1916 during the First World War, revived Henry. He played Wolsey to the King of Lyn Harding and the Queen of Edith Wynn Matthison for a total of 63 performances at the New Amsterdam Theatre, New York.

WHAT EVERY WOMAN KNOWS

(21 performances)

A comedy by James M. Barrie, rearranged into two acts. Presented by the Repertory Theatre November 8, 1946.

Cast of characters—

```
Alick Wylie......................................Ernest Truex
James Wylie.....................................Arthur Keegan
David Wylie....................................Philip Bourneuf
Maggie Wylie......................................June Duprez
John Shand......................................Richard Waring
Comtesse de la Briere.........................Eva Le Gallienne
Lady Sybil Tenterden..........................Mary Alice Moore
A Maid........................................Cavada Humphrey
Charles Venables..............................Walter Hampden
A Butler....................................Efrem Zimbalist, Jr.
    Electors of Glasgow and Members of the Cowcaddens: John
Becher, Angus Cairns, Cavada Humphrey, Ann Jackson, Donald
Keyes, Robert Rawlings, John Straub, Eugene Stuckmann, Theodore
Tenley, Eli Wallach, William Windom, Ed Woodhead, Efrem Zim-
balist, Jr.
    Act I.—Scene 1—The Wylie House in the Village of the Pans,
Scotland, in the early nineteen hundreds.  2—Barber Shop Used as
Shand's Committee Rooms, Glasgow.  Act II.—Scenes 1 and 2—The
Shand House in London.  3—The Comtesse's Cottage in Surrey.
    Staged by Margaret Webster; settings by Paul Morrison; costumes
designed by David Fflokes.
```

Maude Adams first played "What Every Woman Knows" in America the season of 1908-09 with Richard Bennett the John Shand. She opened in Chicago and brought the comedy to New York two months later. The only major revival following Miss Adams' retirement was that made by William A. Brady in April, 1926, with Helen Hayes the Maggie and Kenneth McKenna her John Shand.

JOHN GABRIEL BORKMAN

(21 performances)

A drama by Henrik Ibsen; translated and rearranged into five scenes of continuous action; music arranged by Lehman Engel. Presented by the Repertory Theatre November 12, 1946.

Cast of characters—

Mrs. Borkman	Margaret Webster
Ella Rentheim	Eva Le Gallienne
Malene	Marion Evensen
Erhart Borkman	William Windom
Mrs. Fanny Wilton	Mary Alice Moore
John Gabriel Borkman	Victor Jory
Frida Foldal	Ann Jackson
Vilhelm Foldal	Ernest Truex

The action takes place on a Winter Evening at the Rentheim Estate in the Neighborhood of Christiana (Oslo), about 1896.

Staged by Eva Le Gallienne; settings and costumes by Paul Morrison.

Written in 1896, Ibsen's "John Gabriel Borkman" was first produced in both London and New York the year following. It was revived in New York by a Modern Stage organization in 1915, with Emanuel Reicher in the name part, supported by Alma Kruger and Roland Young. Miss Le Gallienne first played Ella to Egon Brecher's John Gabriel in January, 1926, and later the same season with the Civic Repertory Company.

ANDROCLES AND THE LION

(40 performances)

A comedy in prologue and two acts by George Bernard Shaw; music by Marc Blitzstein. Presented by the Repertory Theatre December 19, 1946.

Cast of characters—

Lion	John Becher
Megaera	Marion Evensen
Androcles	Ernest Truex
Beggar	Arthur Keegan
Centurion	John Straub
Captain	Richard Waring

Lavinia...June Duprez
Lentulus.....................................Eugene Stuckmann
Metellus...Angus Cairns
Ferrovius...Victor Jory
Spintho...Eli Wallach
Ox-driver.....................................Robert Rawlings
Call-boy.......................................Arthur Keegan
Secutor..................................Efrem Zimbalist, Jr.
Retiarius.....................................William Windom
Editor.....................................Raymond Greenleaf
Menagerie Keeper................................Ed Woodhead
Caesar...Philip Bourneuf
    Christians: Emery Battis, Cavada Humphrey, Anne Jackson, Don-
ald Keyes, Mary Alice Moore, Theodore Tenley, Gloria Valborg.
    Soldiers, Slaves, Gladiators, Servant: Don Allen, John Behney,
Michel Corhan, Thomas Grace, Bart Henderson, Frederic Hunter,
Robt. Leser, Gerald McCormack.
    Prologue—A Jungle. Act I.—Outskirts of Rome. Act II.—Scene
1—The Coliseum; Entrance to Arena, Behind Emperor's Box. 2—
The Arena. 3—Entrance to Arena.
    Staged by Margaret Webster; settings and costumes by Wolfgang
Roth; animal heads and masks by Remo Bufano.

Preceded by—

POUND ON DEMAND

(40 performances)

A one-act play by Sean O'Casey.

Cast of characters—

Girl..Cavada Humphrey
Jerry..Philip Bourneuf
Sammy..Ernest Truex
Woman..Margaret Webster
Policeman...................................Eugene Stuckmann
    Scene—A Post Office.
    Staged by Victor Jory; settings and costumes by Wolfgang Roth.

"Androcles and the Lion" was first played in America by the
Granville Barker company in January, 1915. O. P. Heggie, Lionel
Braham, Ernest Cossart, Claude Rains and Lillah McCarthy
were in the cast. In a Theatre Guild revival staged in November,
1925, Henry Travers, Romney Brent, Tom Powers, Edward G.
Robinson and Claire Eames were featured. A WPA Federal Theatre revival in 1938 ran 104 performances with Arthur Wilson
playing Androcles.

YELLOW JACK

(21 performances)

A dramatic history in one act by Sidney Howard in collaboration with Paul de Kruif; music arranged by Lehman Engel. Presented by the Repertory Theatre February 27, 1947.

Cast of characters—

```
O'Hara.......................................Arthur Keegan
McClelland...................................William Windom
Busch.............................................Eli Wallach
Brinkerhof.......................................John Becher
Miss Blake.......................................Anne Jackson
Walter Reed................................Raymond Greenleaf
Aristides Agramonte....................Efrem Zimbalist, Jr.
James Carroll......................................Victor Jory
Colonel Tory......................................John Straub
Wm. Crawford Gorgas......................Eugene Stuckmann
Jesse W. Lazear..................................Alfred Ryder
Roger P. Ames...................................Emery Battis
Major Cartwright...............................Angus Cairns
Dr. Carlos Finlay..............................Philip Bourneuf
William H. Dean..............................Robert Rawlings
An Army Chaplain................................Donald Keyes
A Commissary Sergeant..........................Ed Woodhead
```
Soldiers, Orderlies, etc.: Don Allen, John Behney, Michele Corhan, Will Davis, Thomas Grace, Bart Henderson, Fred Hunter, Robert Leser, Gerald McCormack, Walter Neal, James Rafferty.

The Action takes place in Cuba During Summer and Fall of 1900. Staged by Martin Ritt; setting by Wolfgang Roth.

"Yellow Jack" is a dramatic transcription devoted to Walter Reed's research in Cuba for the yellow fever germ. It is taken from Paul de Kruif's "The Microbe Hunters." It was first produced by Guthrie McClintic at the Martin Beck Theatre, New York, March 6, 1934. See "The Best Plays of 1933-34."

ALICE IN WONDERLAND

(65 performances)

(Continued)

A fantasy in two parts adapted by Eva Le Gallienne and Florida Friebus, based on the Tenniel drawings from "Alice in Wonderland" and "Through a Looking Glass" by Lewis Carroll; music by Richard Addinsell. Presented by Rita Hassan and The American Repertory Theatre at the International Theatre, New York, April 5, 1947.

Cast of characters—

PART I

```
Alice........................................Bambi Linn
White Rabbit.....................William Windom (Julie Harris)
Mouse..........................................Henry Jones
Dodo..........................................John Straub
Lory..........................................Angus Cairns
Eaglet.......................................Arthur Keegan
Crab............................................Don Allen
Duck.............................................Eli Wallach
Caterpillar...................................Theodore Tenley
Fish Footman....................................Ed Woodhead
Frog Footman................................Robert Rawlings
Duchess....................................Raymond Greenleaf
Cook............................................Don Allen
Cheshire Cat................................Margaret Webster
March Hare...................................Arthur Keegan
```

Mad Hatter....................................Richard Waring
Dormouse......................................Theodore Tenley
2 of Spades.......................................Eli Wallach
5 of Spades....................................Robert Rawlings
7 of Spades.....................................Donald Keyes
Queen of Hearts................................John Becher
King of Hearts.............................Eugene Stuckmann
Knave of Hearts.............................Frederic Hunter
Gryphon...Jack Manning
Mock Turtle......................................Angus Cairns
3 of Clubs..John Behney
5 of Clubs.....................................Bart Henderson
7 of Clubs...John Straub
9 of Clubs.......................................Thomas Grace
    Hearts: Don Allen, Robert Carlson, Michel Corhan, Will Davis,
Robert Leser, Gerald McCormack, Walter Neal, James Rafferty, Dan
Scott, Charles Townley.

PART II

Red Chess Queen...........................Margaret Webster
Train Guard..John Straub
Gentleman Dressed in White Paper..............William Windom
Goat...Don Allen
Beetle Voice....................................Donald Keyes
Gnat Voice...................................Cavada Humphrey
Gentle Voice....................................Angus Cairns
Other Voices.....................Mary Alice Moore, Eli Wallach
Tweedledum....................................Robert Rawlings
Tweedledee......................................Jack Manning
White Chess Queen...........................Eva La Gallienne
Sheep...Theodore Tenley
Humpty Dumpty..................................Henry Jones
White Knight................................Philip Bourneuf
Horse—Front Legs..................................Will Davis
Horse—Back Legs..............................Charles Townley
Singers.....................................Eloise Roehm, Rae Len
    Marionettes Worked by: Michel Corhan, Thomas Grace, Bart Hen-
derson, Cavada Humphrey, Robert Leser, Mary Alice Moore, Walter
Neal, James Rafferty, Charles Townley, under the Direction of A.
Spolidoro.
    Part I.—Alice at Home. The Looking Glass House. White Rab-
bit. Pool of Tears. Caucus Race. Caterpillar. Duchess. Cheshire
Cat. Mad Tea Party. Queen's Croquet Ground. By the Sea. The
Trial. Part II.—Red Chess Queen. Railway Carriage. Tweedle-
dum and Tweedledee. White Chess Queen. Wool and Water.
Humpty Dumpty. White Knight. Alice Crowned. Alice with the
Two Queens. The Banquet. Alice at Home Again.
    Staged by Eva Le Gallienne; music directed by Tibor Kozma;
choreography by Ruth Wilton; settings by Robert Rowe Paddock;
costumes by Noel Taylor; masks and marionettes by Remo Bufano.

A version of "Alice," written by Alice Gerstenberg, was produced in March, 1915, at the Booth Theatre in New York. The
first performances of the Eva Le Gallienne-Florida Friebus version were given at the Civic Repertory Theatre in New York in
December, 1932, with Josephine Hutchinson in the name part.

BAL NEGRE

(52 performances)

A dance revue in three acts assembled by Katherine Dunham.
Produced by Nelson L. Gross, in assocaition with Daniel Melnik,
at the Belasco Theatre, New York, November 7, 1946.

Principals engaged—

Katherine Dunham	Lenwood Morris
Lucille Ellis	Wilbert Bradley
La Rosa Estrada	Vanoye Aikens
Gloria Mitchell	Ronnie Aul
Richardena Jackson	Jean Leon Destine
Rosalie King	Eddy Clay
Dolores Harper	Jesse Hawkins
Eartha Kitt	Othello Strozier
Mariam Burton	Lawaune Ingram
Mary Lewis	Candido Vicenty
Sylvilla Fort	Byron Cuttler
Roxie Foster	James Alexander
Eugene Robinson	Gordon Simpson
Ricardo Morrison	Julio Mendez

San Souci Singers

Staged by Katherine Dunham; music directed by Gilberto Valdes; lighting and costumes by John Pratt.

(Closed December 21, 1946)

THE HAVEN

(5 performances)

A drama in two acts by Dennis Hoey, based on a novel by Anthony Gilbert. Produced by Violla Rubber in association with Johnnie Walker at the Playhouse, New York, November 13, 1946.

Cast of characters—

Edmund Durward..................................Dennis Hoey
Agatha Forbes...................................Valerie Cossart
Miss Martin.......................................Viola Roache
Mrs. Hart......................................Queenie Leonard
Arthur Cook....................................Melville Cooper
Grace Knowles.................................Eliza Sutherland
Inspector Ramsey.............................Charles Francis
Constable Miller..............................Darby Summers
Coroner..Ivan Simpson
Reporter...Keith Palmer

Acts I and II.—At "The Haven," a House in the Marshy Fen Country of Cambridge, England.

Staged by Clarence Derwent; setting by William Saulter.

Edmund Durward has a habit of making way with unwanted females. This habit greatly excites Agatha Forbes, a recently acquired mail-order bride, and a Miss Martin, a suspicious land-lady. Miss Martin is done in to put an end to her disturbing curiosity, but before anything happens to Agatha, Durward him-self avoids capture by drinking poison.

(Closed November 16, 1946)

JOAN OF LORRAINE

(199 performances)

A drama in prologue, two acts and epilogue by Maxwell Anderson. Produced by The Playwrights Company at the Alvin Theatre, New York, November 18, 1946.

Cast of characters—

Jimmy Masters, the Director (The Inquisitor).....Sam Wanamaker
Al, the Stage Manager.............................Gilmore Bush
Mary Grey (Joan)................................Ingrid Bergman
Abbey (Jacques D'Arc) Cauchon, Bishop of Beauvais..Lewis Martin
Jo Cordwell (Jean D'Arc)..........................Bruce Hall
Dollner (Pierre D'Arc)..........................Kenneth Tobey
Charles Elling (Durand Laxart)....................Charles Ellis
Farwell (Jean de Metz) (The Executioner).......Arthur L. Sachs
The Electrician (Bertrand de Poulengy)..............Peter Hobbs
Noble (La Hire)...................................Martin Rudy
Sheppard (Alain Chartier)........................Berry Kroeger
Les Ward (The Dauphin)..........................Romney Brent
Tessie, the Assistant Stage Manager (Aurore)..Timothy Lynn Kearse
Jeffson (Georges de Tremoille)...................Roger De Koven
Kipner (Regnault de Chartres, Archbishop of Rheims)..Harry Irvine
Long (Dunois, Bastard of Orleans)...............Kevin McCarthy
Quirke (St. Michael) (D'Estivet)...................Brooks West
Miss Reeves (St. Catherine)........................Ann Coray
Miss Sadler (St. Margaret)........................Joanna Albus
Champlain (Father Massieu)....................Joseph Wiseman
Smith (Thomas de Courcelles)...................Stephen Roberts
Marie, the Costumer.............................Lotte Stavisky
    Acts I and II.—The Stage of a Theatre.
    Staged by Margo Jones; settings, lighting and costumes by Lee Simonson.

See page 120.

(Closed May 10, 1947)

THE FATAL WEAKNESS

(119 performances)

A comedy in three acts by George Kelly. Produced by The Theatre Guild at the Royale Theatre, New York, November 19, 1946.

Cast of characters—

Mrs. Paul Espenshade................................Ina Claire
Anna..Mary Gildea
Mrs. Mabel Wentz.........................Margaret Douglass
Penny...Jennifer Howard
Mr. Paul Espenshade........................Howard St. John
Vernon Hassett....................................John Larson
    Acts I, II and III.—In the Apartment of Mr. and Mrs. Espenshade.
    Staged by George Kelly; supervised by Lawrence Langner and Theresa Hellburn; setting by Donald Oenslager; costumes by Bianca Stroock.

See page 265.

(Closed March 1, 1947)

ANOTHER PART OF THE FOREST

(182 performances)

A drama in three acts by Lillian Hellman; music by Marc Blitzstein. Produced by Kermit Bloomgarden at the Fulton Theatre, New York, November 20, 1946.

Cast of characters—

```
Regina  Hubbard.....................................Patricia  Neal
John  Bagtry.....................................Bartlett  Robinson
Lavinia  Hubbard.............................Mildred  Dunnock
Coralee..................................Beatrice   Thompson
Marcus  Hubbard..................................Percy  Waram
Benjamin  Hubbard..................................Leo  Genn
Jacob.........................................Stanley  Greene
Oscar  Hubbard...................................Scott  McKay
Simon  Isham.......................................Owen  Coll
Birdie  Bagtry................................Margaret  Phillips
Harold  Penniman.................................Paul  Ford
Gilbert  Jugger..............................Gene  O'Donnell
Laurette  Sincee.....................................Jean  Hagen
```

Acts I and III.—The Side Terrace of the Hubbard House in the Alabama Town of Snowden. June 1880. Act II.—Living Room of the Hubbard House.

Staged by Lillian Hellman; settings and lighting by Jo Mielziner; costumes by Lucinda Ballard.

See page 163.

(Closed April 26, 1947)

NO EXIT

(31 performances)

A drama in one act by Jean-Paul Sartre; adapted by Paul Bowles. Produced by Herman Levin and Oliver Smith at the Biltmore Theatre, New York, November 26, 1946.

Cast of characters—

```
Cradeau.........................................Claude  Dauphin
Bellboy...............................................Peter  Kass
Inez ................................................. Annabella
Estelle.............................................Ruth  Ford
```

Scene—A Room.

Staged by John Huston; setting and lighting by Frederick Kiesler.

Cradeau, a pacifist and collaborator; Inez, a Lesbian, and Estelle, an embittered sensualist, find themselves in a single room in Hell. Here they are set bedeviling each other for their earthly sins. It is a terrible Hell. There are no toothbrushes, no mirrors, no windows, no doors, no bells. For over an hour they suffer literally the tortures of the damned, as they reveal their individual crimes one to the other.

(Closed December 21, 1946)

A FAMILY AFFAIR

(6 performances)

A comedy in three acts by Henry R. Misrock. Produced by Jesse Long and Edward S. Hart at the Playhouse, New York, November 27, 1946.

Cast of characters—

Florence McConnel	Emily Ross
Mary	Amelie Barleon
Alice Jones	Jewel Curtis
Julia Wallace	Ann Mason
Walter Wallace	John Williams
Johnny Wallace	Joel Marston
Martha	Lenore Thomas
Mike Cassidy	Allan Stevenson
George Weaver	Robert Smith
Peggy Wallace	Margaret Garland
Dr. Christopher Patterson	Frank Lyon
Gregorin	Anatole Winogradoff

Acts I, II and III.—Wallace Living Room, New York City.
Staged by Alexander Kirkland; setting by Sam Leve.

The Wallaces, Walter and Julia, have for twenty years lived simple, contented married lives and reared one set of twins. Boy twin Johnny becomes a playwright, girl twin Peggy a radio scenarist. Johnny writes a play about his family in which he intimates that his father and mother have discovered that they are mismated. To prove Johnny wrong, Walter and Julia proceed to indulge themselves in certain potentially dangerous, but actually harmless, extramarital affairs. There are further complications when the family's friends begin to recognize themselves in Johnny's characters.

(Closed November 30, 1946)

CHRISTOPHER BLAKE

(114 performances)

A drama in two acts by Moss Hart. Produced by Joseph Hyman and Bernard Hart at the Music Box, New York, November 30, 1946.

Cast of characters—

A Soldier	Ira Cirker
A Marine	Dan Frazer
A Radio Man	Hugh Williamson
A Photographer	Jack Garbutt
Another Photographer	Charles S. Dubin
A Radio Announcer	Kermit Kegley
A Newsreel Man	Frederic De Wilde
Another Newsreel Man	Allen Shaw
A Military Aide	Carl Judd

```
A  General....................................Frank  M.  Thomas
An  Admiral.......................................Tom  Morrison
Another  General..................................Guy  Tano
The  President.....................................Irving  Fisher
Christopher  Blake.............................Richard  Tyler
Mr.  Blake...............................Shepperd  Strudwick
Mrs.  Blake.....................................Martha  Sleeper
Mr.  Kurlick...............................Francis  De  Sales
Mr.  Caldwell..................................Watson  White
Judge  Adamson............................Robert  Harrison
A  Courtroom  Attendant...................Raymond  Van  Sickle
The  Doorman....................................Tom  Morrison
The  Stage  Manager..............................Carl  Judd
Butts....................................Hugh  Williamson
Miss  Holly...............................Peggy  Van  Fleet
An  Actress.....................................Phyllis  Tyler
Johnny........................................Mack  Twamley
Ray..........................................Dickie  Leone
The  Headmaster............................Ronald  Alexander
The  Janitor.............................Maximilian  Schultz
A  Beggar....................................Edward  Pegram
An  Angry  Man....................................Allen  Shaw
A  Policeman..................................Kermit  Kegley
Miss  MacIntyre....................................Kay  Loring
The  Superintendent........................Frank  M.  Thomas
The  Mother..................................Susan  Sanderson
The  Father...............................Hugh  Williamson
The  Bailiff...............................Ronald  Alexander
Photographers...........................Guy  Tano,  Bill  Hoe
Three  Boys...........Charles  Nevil,  Dickie  Leone,  Mack  Twamley
Another  Bailiff....................................Allen  Shaw
A  Judge....................................Frank  M.  Thomas
   Spectators  and  Passersby:  Dorothy  Beauvaire,  Maylah  Bradford,
Eileen  Burns,  Lois  Harmon,  Johann  Kley,  Lillian  Marr,  Jennifer
Moore,  Diane  Parker,  Leslie  Penha.
   Act  I.—Scene  1—The  White  House  in  the  Private  World  of
Christopher  Blake.  2,  4  and  6—Judge  Adamson's  Chambers.  3—
The  stage  of  a  Theatre  in  Private  World  of  Christopher.  5—A  Poor-
house  in  Private  World  of  Christopher.  Act  II.—Scene  1—A  Poor-
house  in  Private  World  of  Christopher.  2—The  Courtroom.
   Staged  by  Moss  Hart;  settings  by  Harry  Horner;  lighting  by
Harry  Horner  and  Leo  Kerz;  costumes  by  Bianca  Strook.
```

See page 336.

(Closed March 8, 1947)

YEARS AGO

(206 performances)

A comedy in three acts by Ruth Gordon. Produced by Max
Gordon at the Mansfield Theatre, New York, December 3, 1946.

Cast of characters—

```
Clinton  Jones....................................Fredric  March
Annie  Jones..................................Florence  Eldridge
Ruth  Gordon  Jones............................Patricia  Kirkland
Katherine  Follett................................Bethel  Leslie
Anna  Witham..................................Jennifer  Bunker
Fred  Whitmarsh................................Richard  Simon
Mr.  Sparrow.....................................Seth  Arnold
Mr.  Bagley..................................Frederic  Persson
Miss  Glavin....................................Judith  Cargill
Punk,  Our  Cat.......................................A  Cat
```

Acts I, II and III.—Sitting-Room, 14 Elmwood Ave., Wollaston, Mass.

Staged by Garson Kanin; setting by Donald Oenslager; costumes by John Boyt.

See page 204.

(Closed May 31, 1947)

IF THE SHOE FITS

(21 performances)

A musical comedy in prologue and two acts by June Carroll and Robert Duke; music by David Raksin. Produced by Leonard Sillman at the Century Theatre, New York, December 5, 1946.

Cast of characters—

Town Crier	Robert Penn
Singing Attendant	Eugene Martin
Dancing Attendant	Billy Vaux
Broderick	Jack Williams
Acrobatic Attendants	Jane Vinson and Paula Dee
Cinderella	Leila Ernst
Mistress Spratt	Jody Gilbert
Delilah	Marilyn Day
Thais	Sherle North
The Butcher Boy	Richard Wentworth
First Undertaker	Don Mayo
Second Undertaker	Walter Kattwinkel
Loreli	Gail Adams
Lilith	Eileen Ayers
First Lawyer	Harvey Braun
Second Lawyer	Stanley Simmonds
Lady Eve	Florence Desmond
Herman	Joe Besser
Four Sprites	Vincent Carbone, Harry Rogers, Allen Knowles, Ferd Bernaski
Major Domo	Youka Troubetzkoy
Lady Guinevere	Eleanor Jones
Lady Persevere	Dorothy Karroll
Dame Crackle	Chloe Owen
The Baker	Ray Cook
Dame Crumple	Joyce White
Dame Crinkle	Jean Olds
Prince Charming	Edward Dew
Widow Willow	Adrienne
Kate	Barbara Perry
King Kindly	Edward Lambert
His Magnificence, The Wizard	Frank Milton
Court Dancer	Vincent Carbone
Sailor	Richard D'Arcy

Acts I and II.—The Fabulous Kingdom of Nicely.

Staged by Eugene Bryden; supervised by Leonard Sillman; choreography by Charles Weidman; settings by Edward Gilbert; costumes by Kathryn Kuhn.

An adaptation of the Cinderella story to a musical comedy book of sorts, with the Fairy Godmother doubling as a matchmaker.

(Closed December 21, 1946)

LAND'S END

(5 performances)

A drama in three acts by Thomas Job, based on a novel by Mary Ellen Chase. Produced by Paul Feigay in association with George Somnes at the Playhouse, New York, December 11, 1946.

Cast of characters—

Susan Pengilly	Shirley Booth
Lize	Amelia Romano
Ellen Pascoe	Helen Craig
Mr. Trevetha	Fred Stewart
Derek Tregonny	Walter Coy
Miss Penrose	Frieda Altman
Mrs. Bond	Mabel Acker
Miss Clark	Diane de Brett
Mr. Brooks	Clement Brace
Mrs. Brooks	Xenia Bank
Mr. Bregstocke	Joseph Foley
Mr. Derby	Sydney Boyd
Mr. Harris	Ross Chetwynd
The Professor	Theodore Newton
Dr. Gregory	Horace Cooper
Kitchen Boy	Michael Feigay
Mrs. Tregonny	Merle Maddern
Grandmother Tregonny	Minnie Dupree
The Rector	Jay Barney
First Fisherman	Joseph Foley
Second Fisherman	Sydney Boyd
Third Fisherman	Ross Chetwynd
Fourth Fisherman	Fred Stewart

Act I.—Scene 1—Mr. Trevetha's Fish Chopping Shelter at St. Ives, Cornwall, England. 2—Dining Room in Tower Hotel. 3—Ellen's and Susan's Room in the Tower Hotel, Tinagel. Act II.—Scene 1—Corner of Dining Room in Tower Hotel. 2—The Men-an-Tol Stone at Land's End. Act III.—Scene 1—Dining Room in Tower Hotel. 2—Living Room of Tregonny's at Land's End. The time is between the Two Wars.

Staged by Robert Lewis; production designed by Donald Oenslager.

Ellen Pascoe and Susan Pengilly are fish choppers in a shelter in the village of St. Ives, which is in the Cornwall country of England. St. Ives is the home of the Tristram and Iseult legend, well known to opera goers. Ellen is in love with and engaged to Derek Tregonny, but Susan takes him away from her. Derek, torn between his two loves, hurls himself off the cliff at Land's End. Ellen and Susan agree to go on being friends.

(Closed December 14, 1946)

LOVELY ME

(37 performances)

A comedy in three acts by Jacqueline Susann and Beatrice Cole; music by Arthur Siegel and Jeff Bailey. Produced by David Lowe at the Adelphi Theatre, New York, December 25, 1946.

Cast of characters—

Irving..Arthur Siegel
Auntie...Barbara Bulgakov
Peggy Smith.......................................June Dayton
Matilda..Joyce Allan
Sonny..Paul Marlin
Natasha Smith.....................................Luba Malina
Mr. Forrest.......................................Houston Richards
Thomas van Stokes................................Reynolds Evans
Stanislaus Stanislavsky...........................Mischa Auer
Mike Shane..Millard Mitchell
    Acts I, II and III.—Living-Room of Natasha Smith's Hotel Apartment on Central Park South, New York City.
    Staged by Jessie Royce Landis; setting by Donald Oenslager; costumes by Eleanor Goldsmith.

Natasha Smith, widely experienced matrimonially, is trying to get another husband rich enough to pay her mounting hotel bill and educate her daughter. Two of her former husbands turn up to complicate matters.

(Closed January 25, 1947)

BURLESQUE

(183 performances)
(Continued)

A comedy in three acts by George Manker Watters and Arthur Hopkins. Revived by Jean Dalrymple at the Belasco Theatre, New York, December 25, 1946.

Cast of characters—

Bonny..Jean Parker
Sammy..Robert Weil
Skid...Bert Lahr
Lefty..Ross Hertz
A Fireman...Norman Morgan
Mazie..Kay Buckley
Gussie...Jerri Blanchard
Sylvia Marco......................................Joyce Mathews
Bozo...Bobby Barry
Harvey Howell.....................................Charles G. Martin
Jerry Evans.......................................Harold Bostwick
A Bell Boy.......................................Norman Morgan
Stage Carpenter...................................Michael Keene
Ecdysiast..Irene Allarie
Tenor..Santo Scudi
Orchestra Leader..................................Milton Merill
Girls of the Chorus:
    Marie..Joan Andre
    Kiki...Carolyn Boyce
    Buster...Millicent Roy
    Sugar..Ronnie Rogers
    Mimi...Gene Gilmour
    Mitsy..Darin Jennings
    Blossom..Ruth Maitland
    Bubbles..Jeri Archer
    Cuddles..Eleanor Prentiss

Act I.—Basement Dressing Room in Mid-West Burlesque Theatre.
Act II.—Living-Room New York Hotel Suite. Act III.—Scene 1—
Stage of Star Theatre, Paterson, N. J. 2—Opening of Lefty's Bur-
lesque Show.

Staged by Arthur Hopkins; choreography by Billy Holbrook; settings by Robert Rowe Paddock; costumes by Grace Houston.

Starting September 1, 1927, "Burlesque" was played for 372
performances at the Plymouth Theatre, New York. Barbara Stanwyck was the heroine and Hal Skelly the burlesquer. This engagement brought Miss Stanwyck to the attention of the Hollywood scouts and led to a highly successful screen career. Ob-
scurely placed in that original cast was Oscar Levant, pianist, later
radio and movie personality. The story is of Skid Johnson's ele-
vation from the burlesque wheel to success on Broadway, largely
through the help of Bonny, his wife. Once arrived, Skid returns
to the drink and, though she has started divorce proceedings,
Bonny suspends her suit to help him back on his feet.

WONDERFUL JOURNEY

(9 performances)

A comedy in three acts by Harry Segall. Produced by Theron
Bamberger in association with Richard Skinner at the Coronet
Theatre, New York, December 25, 1946.

Cast of characters—

1st Escort	Phil Stein
Mr. Jordan	Sidney Blackmer
Joe Pendleton	Donald Murphy
Messenger 7013	Wallace Acton
2nd Escort	Michael Lewin
Ames	Richard Temple
Tony Abbott	Hal Conklin
Julia Farnsworth	Fay Baker
Bette Logan	Jean Gillespie
A Workman	Carmen Costi
Max Levene	Philip Loeb
Susie	Ann Sullivan
Williams	Barry Kelley
Plain-Clothesman	Phil Stein
Radio Announcer	Robert Caldwell
Lefty	Richard Taber
Trainer	Michael Lewin
Handler	Stephen Elliott
Doctor	Robert Caldwell

Act I.—Scene 1—Somewhere in Space. 2—The Farnsworth Drawing Room. Act II.—The Farnsworth Drawing Room. Act III.—
Scene 1—The Farnsworth Drawing Room. 2—Dressing Room Under
the Stadium.

Staged by Frank Emmons Brown; settings by Raymond Sovey;
costumes by Bianca Strook.

Joe Pendleton, box fighter, sent to heaven through error fifty
years before his time, is sent back to complete his earth-life in
other bodies—those of a financier and another ring champion.

His adventures are many and varied. He proceeds under the sponsorship of a celestial agent, one Mr. Jordan. It was Mr. Jordan who presided over the successful film fantasy, "Here Comes Mr. Jordan," in the early nineteen forties. The play was not as successful as the picture had been.

(Closed January 1, 1947)

TOPLITZKY OF NOTRE DAME

(60 performances)

A musical comedy in two acts by George Marion, Jr.; additional dialogue and lyrics by Jack Barnett; music by Sammy Fain. Produced by William Cahn at the Century Theatre, New York, December 26, 1946.

Cast of characters—

Army Angel	Phyllis Lynne
Recording Angel	Candace Montgomery
Lionel	Harry Fleer
Angelo	Warde Donovan
Mrs. Strutt	Doris Patston
Betty	Marion Colby
Dodo	Estelle Sloan
McCormack	Gus Van
Roger	Walter Long
Toplitzky	J. Edward Bromberg
A Girl	Betty Jane Watson
Mailman	Robert Bay
Leary	Frank Marlowe
Patti	Phyllis Lynne
Male Quartet	Oliver Boersma, John Frederick, Eugene Kingsley, Chris Overson

Dancers: Priscilla Callan, Ann Collins, Helen Devlin, Cece Eames, Jessie Fullum, Joan Kavanagh, Pat Marlowe, Mollie Pearson, Frances Wyman, George Andrew, Gene Banks, Charles Dickson, Casse Jaeger, Thomas Kenny, Anthony Starman, Rodney Strong, Joe Wagner, John Wilkins.

Act I.—Prologue—Heaven. Scenes 1 and 3—Toplitzky's Tavern, New York City. 2—A Field on the Jersey Shore. 4—Toplitzky's Terrace. Act II.—Scene 1—Toplitzky's Tavern. 2—Toplitzky's Terrace. 3—Going to the Big Game. 4—Yankee Stadium. Army-Notre Dame Game.

Staged by Jose Ruben; dances and musical numbers staged by Robert Sidney; music directed by Leon Leonardi; settings by Edward Gilbert; costumes by Kenn Barr.

Toplitzky, a New York tavern keeper, is a Notre Dame football rooter. The angels in heaven, as everybody knows, are also rooters. The angels send a former football star named Angelo back to earth on a furlough to help Notre Dame beat Army. Toplitzky adopts Angelo, the game is won, Angelo falls in love with Toplitzky's daughter and is allowed to stay on earth for a spell.

(Closed February 17, 1947)

BEGGAR'S HOLIDAY

(108 performances)

A musical in two acts based on John Gay's "The Beggar's Opera"; book and lyrics by John Latouche; music by Duke Ellington. Produced by Perry Watkins and John R. Sheppard, Jr., at the Broadway Theatre, New York, December 26, 1946.

Cast of characters—

The Pursued	Tommy Gomez
Cop	Archie Savage
Policemen	Herbert Ross, Lucas Hoving
Plainclothesman	Albert Popwell
First Girl	Marjorie Belle
Macheath	Alfred Drake
The Cocoa Girl	Marie Bryant
Jenny	Bernice Parks
Dolly Trull	Lavina Nielsen
Betty Doxy	Leonne Hall
Tawdry Audrey	Tommie Moore
Mrs. Trapes	Doris Goodwin
Annie Coaxer	Royce Wallace
Baby Mildred	Claire Hale
Minute Lou	Nina Korda
Trixy Turner	Malka Farber
Bessie Buns	Elmira Jones-Bey
Flora, the Harpy	Enid Williams
The Horn	Bill Dillard
Highbinder	Jack Bittner
O'Heister	Gordon Nelson
The Foot	Lewis Charles
Gunsel	Archie Savage
Fingersmith	Stanley Carlson
Strip	Lucas Hoving
Mooch	Perry Bruskin
The Eye	Pan Theodore
Wire Boy	Paul Godkin
The Other Eye	Tommy Gomez
Slam	Albert Popwell
The Caser	Douglas Henderson
Two Customers	Gordon Nelson, Hy Anzel
A Drunk	Lewis Charles
Bartender	Herbert Ross
Careless Love	Avon Long
Polly Peachum	Jet MacDonald
Black Marketeer	Gordon Nelson
Mrs. Peachum	Dorothy Johnson
Hamilton Peachum	Zero Mostel
Chief Lockit	Rollin Smith
Lucy Lockit	Mildred Smith
Blenkinsop	Pan Theodore
The Girl	Marjorie Belle
The Boy	Paul Godkin

The Dancers: Paul Godkin and Marjorie Belle, Malka Farber, Doris Goodwin, Claire Hale, Elmira Jones-Bey, Lavina Nielsen, Royce Wallace, Enid Williams, Tommy Gomez, Lucas Hoving, Albert Popwell, Herbert Ross, Archie Savage.

Mac's Gang: Stanley Carlson, Lewis Charles, Gordon Nelson, Bill Dillard, Jack Bittner, Perry Bruskin

Act I.—Scene 1—Exterior of Miss Jenny's. 2—Interior. 3—Outside Miss Jenny's. 4—At Hamilton Peachum's. 5—A Street. 6—A Hobo Jungle. Act II.—Scenes 1 and 4—The Street. 2—Chief Lockit's Office. 3—The Jail. 5—Jenny's Bedroom. 6—Under the Bridge. 7—Finale.

Staged by Nicholas Ray; choreography by Valerie Bettis; music directed by Max Meth; orchestrations under supervision of Billy Strauhorn; settings by Oliver Smith; lighting by Peggy Clark; costumes by Walter Florell.

Macheath, in the adapted version of John Gay's "Beggar's Opera," is a dashing young American gangster who gets into a lot of trouble through two master crooks, Peachum and Lockit. He jilts several attractive young women and is about to be sent to the electric chair when he is pardoned in time for the finale. "Beggar's Opera" was sung in New York's Greenwich Village Theatre the season of 1920-21 and again at the 48th St. Theatre in March, 1928.

(Closed March 29, 1947)

TEMPER THE WIND

(35 performances)

A drama in three acts by Edward Mabley and Leonard Mins. Produced by Barnard Straus and Roland V. Haas at the Playhouse, New York, December 27, 1946.

Cast of characters—

Sophie von Gutzkow	Blanche Yurka
Trudi	Charlotte London
Elisabeth Jaeger	Vilma Kurer
Hugo Benckendorff	Reinhold Schunzel
Theodore Bruce	Walter Greaza
Cpl. Tom Hutchinson	George Mathews
Erich Jaeger	Tonio Selwart
Lt. Col. Richard Woodruff	Thomas Beck
Heinrich Lindau	Martin Brandt
Capt. Karel Palivec	Herbert Berghof
Sgt. Edward Green	Paul Tripp
Lt. James Harris	Albert Patterson
Lt. Frank Daniels	Michael Sivy

Act I.—Living-Room of the Benckendorff House in Small Manufacturing Town of Reitenberg in Northwestern Bavaria. Acts II and III.—Scene 1—American Garrison Headquarters. 2—The Benckendorff House.

Staged by Reginald Denham; settings by Raymond Sovey; costumes by Anna Hill Johnstone.

Lt. Col. Richard Woodruff has been sent to Reitenberg, in northwestern Bavaria, as chief of the American occupational forces. Col. Woodruff is intent on democratizing the town, but meets the sly opposition of Hugo Benckendorff, Reitenberg's chief industrialist, and numerous fanatical Nazi influences. Benckendorff wants to reopen his factory under American sponsorship. Theodore Bruce, a big businessman from Chicago with cartel ambitions, would like to help him. But Col. Woodruff, discovering that the Benckendorff employees are mostly Nazi, refuses his consent at the cost of a town riot.

(Closed January 25, 1947)

LOVE GOES TO PRESS

(5 performances)

A comedy in three acts by Martha Gellhorn and Virginia Cowles. Produced by Warren P. Munsell and Herman Bernstein at the Biltmore Theatre, New York, January 1, 1947.

Cast of characters—

Leonard Lightfoot (International Information Agency)
                                                    Gerald Andersen
Tex Crowder (Union Press).......................David Tyrrell
Hank O'Reilly (Alliance Press)...................Warren Parker
Joe Rogers (San Francisco *Dispatch*)...........William Post, Jr.
Major Phillip Brooke-Jervaux (Public Relations Officer) Ralph Michael
Corporal Cramp...................................Peter Bennett
Daphne Rutherford (E.N.S.A.)................Georgina Cookson
Jane Mason (New York *Bulletin*)...................Joyce Heron
Annabelle Jones (San Francisco *World*)...........Jane Middleton
Major Dick Hawkins (U.S.A.A.F.)...................Don Gibson
Captain Sir Alastair Drake (Conducting Officer)......Nigel Neilson
    Acts I and III.—Allied Press Camp, Poggibonsi, Italy, February,
1944. Act II.—Scene 1—A Bedroom, Press Camp. 2—Press Camp.
    Staged by Wallace Douglas; settings by Raymond Sovey; costumes
by Emeline Roche.

Jane Mason and Annabelle Jones are covering the war as women correspondents in Italy. Jane finds her ex-husband at the front representing a competing newspaper, and also falling for a singer who is entertaining the troops. Her husband beats her on an assignment, but she wins him away from the singer. Annabelle falls in love with a British officer. Then both girls quit their romances for another assignment at the front, this time in Burma.

(Closed January 4, 1947)

THE BIG TWO

(21 performances)

A comedy in three acts by L. Bush-Fekete and Mary Helen Fay. Produced by Elliott Nugent and Robert Montgomery by arrangement with David Bramson at the Booth Theatre, New York, January 8, 1947.

Cast of characters—

Karl..Martin Berliner
Meissl...Eduard Franz

```
Corp. Pat McClure................................Robert Scott
Gwendolyn........................................Wauna Paul
Danielle Forbes.................................Claire Trevor
Moser......................................E. A. Krumschmidt
Wirth............................................John Banner
Platschek......................................Felix Bressart
Captain Nicholai Mosgovoy........................Philip Dorn
Fraulein Berger..................................Olga Fabian
Sergeant Kulikoff...............................Mischa Tonken
Guests.........Phil Miller, Zita Rieth, Kenneth Dobbs, Fred Lorenz
Russian Soldiers..Marc Hamilton, Walter Palance, Charles Boaz, Jr.
    Acts I and II.—Lobby of the Waldhotel in Baden, within Russian
Occupied Zone of Austria Near Vienna.  November, 1945.
    Staged by Robert Montgomery; setting and lighting by Jo Miel-
ziner; costumes by Bianca Stroock.
```

Danielle Forbes, glamorous American war correspondent, has invaded the Russian zone in Austria on the trail of a traitorous American broadcaster. In the Waldhotel in Baden Danielle encounters Capt. Nicholai Mosgovoy of the Russian NKVD, interested in the same search. They are more or less embittered rivals until they discover their love for each other, after which the going is equally exciting but more satisfying.

(Closed January 25, 1947)

STREET SCENE

(148 performances)

A dramatic musical in two acts by Elmer Rice; lyrics by Langston Hughes; music by Kurt Weill; based on the play by Elmer Rice. Produced by Dwight Deere Wiman and The Playwrights' Company at the Adelphi Theatre, New York, January 9, 1947.

Cast of characters—

```
Abraham Kaplan................................Irving Kaufman
Greta Fiorentino..................................Helen Arden
Carl Olsen........................................Wilson Smith
Emma Jones.......................................Hope Emerson
Olga Olsen.........................................Ellen Repp
Shirley Kaplan.................................Norma Chambers
Henry Davis...................................Creighton Thompson
Willie Maurrant.................................Peter Griffith
Anna Maurrant....................................Polyna Stoska
Sam Kaplan......................................Brian Sullivan
Daniel Buchanan....................................Remo Lota
Frank Maurrant...................................Norman Cordon
George Jones....................................David E. Thomas
Steve Sankey.....................................Lauren Gilbert
Lippo Fiorentino.................................Sydney Rayner
Jennie Hildebrand...............................Beverly Janis
Second Graduate.................................Zosia Gruchala
Third Graduate...................................Marion Covey
Mary Hildebrand...............................Juliana Gallagher
Charlie Hildebrand.............................Bennett Burrill
Laura Hildebrand...................................Elen Lane
Grace Davis......................................Helen Ferguson
```

```
First  Policeman.....................................Ernest  Taylor
Rose  Maurrant.....................................Anne  Jeffreys
Harry  Easter........................................Don  Saxon
Mae  Jones.........................................Sheila  Bond
Dick  McGann......................................Danny  Daniels
Vincent  Jones.....................................Robert  Pierson
Dr.  John  Wilson..............................Edwin  G.  O'Connor
Officer  Harry  Murphy...........................Norman  Thomson
A  Milkman.....................................Russell  George
A  Music  Pupil....................................Joyce  Carrol
City  Marshal  James  Henry...................Randolph  Symonette
Fred  Cullen......................................Paul  Lilly
An  Old  Clothes  Man...........................Edward  Reichert
An  Interne.........................................Roy  Munsell
An  Ambulance  Driver.............................John  Sweet
First  Nursemaid.................................Peggy  Turnley
Second  Nursemaid...............................Ellen  Carleen
A  Married  Couple.................Bette  Van,  Joseph  E.  Scandur
     Acts  I  and  II.—A  Sidewalk  in  New  York  City.
     Staged  by  Charles  Friedman;  music  directed  by  Maurice  Abrava-
nel;  dances  directed  by  Anna  Sokolow;  setting  and  lighting  by  Jo
Mielziner;  costumes  by  Lucinda  Ballard.
```

"Street Scene" was produced originally by William A. Brady at the Playhouse, New York, January 10, 1929, and directed by its author, Elmer Rice. Mary Servoss, Beulah Bondi, Robert Kelly and Leo Bulgakov were in the cast. In the version with music the leads were played by Norman Cordon, Polyna Stoska, Anne Jeffreys and Hope Emerson.

(Closed May 17, 1947)

FINIAN'S RAINBOW

(164 performances)

(Continued)

A musical comedy in two acts by E. Y. Harburg and Fred Saidy; music by Burton Lane; orchestrations by Robert Russell Bennett and Don Walker. Produced by Lee Sabinson and William R. Katzell at the 46th Street Theatre, New York, January 10, 1947.

Cast of characters—

```
Sunny  (Harmonica  Player)..........................Sonny  Terry
Buzz  Collins..........................................Eddie  Bruce
Sheriff..............................................Tom  McElhany
1st  Sharecropper...................................Alan  Gilbert
2nd  Sharecropper...........................Robert  Eric  Carlson
Susan  Mahoney.....................................Anita  Alvarez
Henry.........................................Augustus  Smith,  Jr.
Finian  McLonergan...............................Albert  Sharpe
Sharon  McLonergan..................................Ella  Logan
Woody  Mahoney................................Donald  Richards
3rd  Sharecropper........................Ralph  Waldo  Cummings
Og  (A  Leprechaun)...............................David  Wayne
Howard...........................................William  Greaves
Senator  Billboard  Rawkins........................Robert  Pitkin
```

```
1st  Geologist.........................................Lucas  Aco
2nd  Geologist..............................Nathaniel  Dickerson
Diane...............................................Diane  Woods
Jane.................................................Jane  Earle
John  (The  Preacher)............................Roland  Skinner
4th  Sharecropper...............................Maude  Simmons
Mr.  Robust........................................Arthur  Tell
Mr.  Shears.........................................Royal  Dano
1st  Passion  Pilgrim  Gospeler.........................Jerry  Laws
2nd  Passion  Pilgrim  Gospeler.......................Lorenzo  Fuller
3rd  Passion  Pilgrim  Gospeler.......................Louis  Sharp
1st  Deputy.......................................Michael  Ellis
2nd  Deputy................................Robert  Eric  Carlson
3rd  Deputy.........................................Harry  Day
Other  Children............Norma  Jane  Marlowe,  Elayne  Richards
```
Act I.—Scenes 1, 2, 4 and 6—The Meetin' Place, Rainbow Valley, Missitucky. 3—The Colonial Estate of Senator Billboard Rawkins. 5—A Path in the Woods. Act II.—Scene 1—Rainbow Valley. 2—A Wooded Section of the Hills. 3—The Meetin' Place. 4—Just Before Dawn.

Staged by Bretaigne Windust; choreography by Michael Kidd; music directed by Milton Rosenstock; vocal direction by Lyn Murray; settings and lighting by Jo Mielziner; costumes by Eleanor Goldsmith.

Finian McLonergan steals a crock of gold from the leprechauns in Ireland and brings it, with his daughter Sharon, to America, thinking to plant it down Fort Knox way and watch it grow. He is followed by Og, an influential leprechaun, and bedeviled by a "Missitucky" Senator, old Billboard Rawkins, a Negro-hating white. Rawkins turns black himself under the leprechaun's curse. Magical justice is done to all before the finale is reached.

LITTLE A

(21 performances)

A drama in three acts by Hugh White. Produced by Sam Nasser in association with Harry Lambert at the Henry Miller Theatre, New York, January 15, 1947.

Cast of characters—

```
Aaron  Storm......................................Otto  Kruger
Lucinda  Storm.............................Jessie  Royce  Landis
Mary  Howard...................................Ottilie  Kruger
Phoebe  Painter.................................Frances  Bavier
Clyde  Painter..................................Harry  Mehaffey
Dr.  Duncan  Brown...............................Wallis  Clark
Donald  Storm....................................Robert  Wiley
```
Acts I, II and III.—Living-Room of the Storm Home in Rockbridge, a Small Town in Northern California.

Staged by Melville Burke; setting by Watson Barratt; lighting by Leo Kerz; costumes by Ernest Scraps.

Aaron Storm (Little A), the spineless son of a domineering and aggressive father (Big A), has most of the cards stacked against him. He had been practically trapped into a marriage with a household servant who had borne his father an illegitimate son. He is nagged and pestered by his wife, and finds his only satisfactions in his affection for and interest in the musical career of orphaned Mary Howard. In the end his wife, shooting at him, kills her illegitimate son, thus clearing at least two pestering influences from his harassed life.

(Closed February 1, 1947)

SWEETHEARTS

(152 performances)

(Continued)

A musical comedy in two acts by Harry B. Smith and Fred de Gresac; lyrics by Robert B. Smith; book revisions by John Cecil Holm; musical arrangements by Russell Bennett. Revived by Paula Stone and Michael Sloane at the Shubert Theatre, New York, January 21, 1947.

Cast of characters—

Doreen	Marcia James
Corinne	Nony Franklin
Eileen	Janet Medlin
Pauline	Betty Ann Busch
Kathleen	Martha Emma Watson
Nadine	Gloria Lind
Gretchen	Eva Soltesz
Hilda	Muriel Bruenig
Dame Lucy	Marjorie Gateson
Lt. Karl	Robert Shackleton
Peasants	Robert Reeves, Raynor Howell
Liane	June Knight
Mikel Mikeloviz	Bobby Clark
Sylvia	Gloria Story
Prince Franz	Mark Dawson
Peter	Richard Benson
Hans	Ken Arnold
Baron Petrus Von Tromp	Paul Best
Hon. Butterfield A. Slingsby	Anthony Kemble-Cooper
Prima Ballerina	Janice Cioffi
Adolphus	John Anania
Homberg	Cornell MacNeil
Ambassadors	Robert Feyti, Louis De Mangus
Captain Laurent	Tom Perkins

Act I.—Village Square in Zilania. Act II.—The Palace.

Staged by John Kennedy; music directed by Edwin McArthur; vocal direction by Pembroke Davenport; choreography by Theodore Adolphus; ensembles by Katherine Littlefield; settings by Peter Wolf; costumes by Michael Lucyk.

"Sweethearts" was produced originally at the New Amsterdam Theatre, New York, in September, 1913, and ran for 136 performances. Christie Macdonald was the star and the cast included Nellie McCoy and Tom McNaughton. It was revived the season of 1929-30 by the Jolson Theatre Musical Co., Milton Aborn, director. Gladys Baxter was the heroine, Charles Massinger the hero.

ALL MY SONS

(142 performances)
(Continued)

A drama in three acts by Arthur Miller. Produced by Harold Clurman, Elia Kazan and Walter Fried in association with Herbert H. Harris at the Coronet Theatre, New York, January 29, 1947.

Cast of characters—

Joe Keller	Ed Begley
Dr. Jim Bayliss	John McGovern
Frank Lubey	Dudley Sadler
Sue Bayliss	Peggy Meredith
Lydia Lubey	Hope Cameron
Chris Keller	Arthur Kennedy
Bert	Eugene Steiner
Kate Keller	Beth Merrill
Ann Deever	Lois Wheeler
George Deever	Karl Malden

Acts I, II and III.—The Backyard of the Keller Home on Outskirts of an American Town.

Staged by Elia Kazan; setting and lighting by Mordecai Gorelik; costumes by Paul Morrison.

See page 29.

IT TAKES TWO

(8 performances)

A comedy in three acts by Virginia Faulkner and Dana Suesse. Produced by George Abbott and Richard Aldrich at the Biltmore Theatre, New York, February 3, 1947.

Cast of characters—

Connie Frazier	Martha Scott
Mr. Fine	Julius Bing
Mrs. Loosbrock	Reta Shaw
Bee Clark	Vivian Vance
Elevator Boy	Robert Edwin
Todd Frazier	Hugh Marlowe
Monk Rathburn	Anthony Ross
Comfort Gibson	Temple Texas
Bill Renault	John Forsythe

Acts I, II and III.—Living-Room of the Fraziers' Apartment in the Murray Hill Section of New York. 1946.

Staged by George Abbott; setting by John Root.

Todd and Connie Frazier, nerves on edge after moving from one army billet to another, work themselves into a quarrel in a New York apartment. They agree on a separation that they plan is to culminate in divorce, but, because of the housing situation, decide to keep the apartment. They gag their way through a variety of audacious situations until late evening, when they decide to give matrimony another trial.

(Closed February 3, 1947)

JOHN LOVES MARY

(136 performances)
(Continued)

A comedy in three acts by Norman Krasna. Produced by Richard Rodgers and Oscar Hammerstein 2d, in association with Joshua Logan, at the Booth Theatre, New York, February 4, 1947.

Cast of characters—

Mary McKinley	Nina Foch
Oscar Dugan	Ralph Chambers
Fred Taylor	Tom Ewell
John Lawrence	William Prince
Senator James McKinley	Loring Smith
Mrs. Phyllis McKinley	Ann Mason
Lt. Victor O'Leary	Lyle Bettger
George Beechwood	Max Showalter
Lily Herbish	Pamela Gordon
Harwood Biddle	Harry Bannister

Acts I, II and III.—Living-Room of Apartment of Senator James McKinley in the St. Regis Hotel, New York.

Staged by Joshua Logan; setting and lighting by Frederick Fox; costumes by Lucinda Ballard.

See page 233.

THE STORY OF MARY SURRATT

(11 performances)

A drama in three acts by John Patrick. Produced by Russell Lewis and Howard Young at the Henry Miller Theatre, New York, February 8, 1947.

Cast of characters—

Anna Surratt	Elizabeth Ross
Mary Surratt	Dorothy Gish
Louis Weichmann	Bernard Thomas
Lewis Payne	Don Shelton
George Atzerodt	Zachary Berger
David Herold	Michael Fox
John Surratt	John Conway
John Wilkes Booth	James Monks
Captain William Smith	Grahan Denton
Sgt. Day	Larry Johns
Colonel Burnett	Douglas McEachin
General Joshua Holden	Richard Sanders
Brigadier General Ekin	Wallis Roberts
Reverdy Johnson	Kent Smith
Major General Hunter	Edward Harvey

Brigadier General Harris.........................Frank McFarland
Major General Wallace..............................Robert Neff
Major General Kautz............................Thomas Glynn
Brigadier General Howe..........................Robert Morgan
Brigadier General Foster...........................Dallas Boyd
Colonel Tompkins...............................Lee Malbourne
Colonel Glendenin...............................Arthur Stenning
Special Provost Marshal..........................Tom Daly
Major Henry Rathbone..........................Gordon Barnes
Lt. Henry Von Steinacker............................Bill Hitch
General Jubal Bentley............................John Pimley
Father Wiget.....................................Harlan Briggs
W. E. Doster.....................................Hugh Mosher
Dr. Samuel Mudd..............................Tom J. McGivern
Edward Spangler................................Lytton Robinson
Michael O'Laughlin..............................Bill Reynolds
Samuel Arnold.....................................Larry Johns
Guard...Earle Dawson
Soldier...Michael Roane
Soldier...Clyde Cook
    Act I.—Living-Room of Mary Surratt's Boarding House.   Act
II.—Improvised Courtroom in old Penitentiary Building.   Act III.—
Scene 1—Courtroom.   2—Cell in Penitentiary Building on U. S.
Arsenal Grounds at Washington, D. C.
    Staged by John Patrick; settings by Samuel Leve; lighting by
Girvan Higginson; costumes by Jane Edgerton.

See page 302.

See page 302.

(Closed February 15, 1947)

THE EXPERIMENTAL THEATRE, INC.

The Experimental Theatre, Inc., under the sponsorship of The
American National Theatre and Academy, presented five productions at the Princess Theatre, New York, beginning February 9,
1947.

(25 performances)

THE WANHOPE BUILDING

(5 performances)

A fantasy in three acts by John Finch; musical score by Arthur
Kreutz. Produced by Theatre Incorporated, February 9, 1947.

Cast of characters—

4-F...Haskell Coffin
Flashy Page...John Jordan
Maggie..Dorothy Patterson
George..Walter Craig
Eddie...Martin Balsam
Mrs. Mead......................................Octavia Kenmore
Michael.......................................Edmond Le Comte
Sleeping Drunk..............................Courtney Burr, Jr.
Housewife.......................................Winifred Cushing
Guard...Frank Richards
Professor Thorstein............................Frederic Cornell
Interviewer...Clark Howat
Medical Examiner...................................Don Peters
Secretary...Penelope Sack

```
Brown  Hat..........................................Will  Kuluva
Announcer...........................................Robert  Wark
Quiz  Master........................................Blair  Cutting
Baritone...............................................Billy  Rollo
Mr.  10..............................................Walter  Craig
Mr.  11.............................................Anthony  Grey
Mr.  12.........................................Courtney  Burr,  Jr.
1st  Customer........................................Ford  Rainey
2nd  Customer....................................Frederic  Cornell
Attendant........................................Frank  Richards
Felina...........................................Beatrice  Straight
Arnold...............................................Lex  Richards
Young  Lovers.....................Penelope  Sack,  Robert  Wark
Miss  Queen.....................................Margaret  Barker
Pomeroy............................................Anthony  Grey
Madam  Endor.......................................Freda  Altman
Jo  Light...............................................Don  Peters
Max...............................................Robert  Wark
John  B.  Sherman....................................Ford  Rainey
Police  Committee..................Blair  Cutting,  Frank  Richards
Pilot...............................................Clark  Howat
      Scene—Michael's  Bar  and  Wanhope  Building.
      Staged  by  Brett  Warren;  settings  and  lighting  by  Wolfgang  Roth.
```

Flashy Page, sailor, sets out to discover, and to conquer, the mysterious and threatening inventor of a W-bomb, which cannot only destroy the works, but also the will of man. The inventor lives at the top of a 500-story building. The sailor is compelled to fight his way through a variety of obstacles, both real and symbolical, as he makes his way upward. When he arrives he discovers that the defeat of the W-bomb is already inherent in the will of man. So long as men refuse to give in to the defeatist doctrine of "What's the use?" the world will be safe.

(Closed February 16, 1947)

O'DANIEL

(5 performances)

A drama in prologue, three acts and epilogue by Glendon Swarthout and John Savacool; incidental music by Alex North. Produced by The Theatre Guild, February 23, 1947.

Cast of characters—

```
Dan...................................................Walter  Coy
Alex..................................................Anne  Burr
Lee..................................................Jack  Manning
Photographers....................Philip  McEneny,  Norman  Budd
Reporter..........................................William  Munroe
Bellhop..............................................James  Holden
Politicians..........................Rudy  Bond,  Keene  Crockett,
                          Billy  M.  Greene,  Robert  P.  Lieb
Pvt.  Sumian......................................James  Holden
Company  Clerk..................................William  Munroe
Bartender.............................................Rudy  Bond
Ethel ..............................................Isabel  Bishop
Potty..........................................Billy  M.  Greene
Colonel  Basil......................................Robert  P.  Lieb
Technician  4th  Grade............................Norman  Budd
```

```
Corporal...........................................James  Holden
Italian  Girl........................................Isabel  Bishop
Workman............................................Billy  M.  Greene
Cleaning  Woman..................................Georgia  Simmons
Vignati............................................Royal  Raymond
J.  P.  Collins......................................Keene  Crockett
    Prologue  and  Epilogue—Chicago  Hotel  Room,  1952.    Act  I.—
Scene  1—Barracks,  1943.    2—Bar.    3—A  Dugout,  1944.    4—Apart-
ment  Living  Room,  1945.    Act  II.—Scene  1—Lee's  Office,  1947.    2
and  4—Dan's  Office,  1947.    3—Telephone  Booth,  1948.    5—Phila-
delphia,  1951.    Act  III.—Scene  1—Campaign  Headquarters,  1951.
2—An  Airport,  1952.
    Staged  by  Paul  Crabtree;  settings  and  lighting  by  Herbert  Brodkin.
```

Dan, a bad soldier in 1943, is still a bad citizen in 1947. However, he talks loud and long and gets himself nominated for the
Presidency in 1952, largely because his fellow GI's were not
watchful and let a lot of other fellows have too much to do with
the running of their country.

(Closed March 2, 1947)

AS WE FORGIVE OUR DEBTORS

(5 performances)

A drama in three acts by Tillman Breiseth. Produced by José
Ferrer, March 9, 1947.

Cast of characters—

```
Mrs.  Torvik.......................................Mary  Fletcher
Mrs.  Ness..........................................Sara  Floyd
Gullick  Sturkelson................................Somer  Alberg
Molla  Sturkelson.................................Jennette  Dowling
Mr.  Svensrud......................................Cyrus  Staehle
Oscar  Svensrud...................................Kenneth  Tobey
Agnet  Benstad  Foss...............................Sylvia  Stone
Chistina  Benstad..................................Joyce  Ross
Odin  Sturkelson...................................William  Lee
Lars  Foss..........................................Joe  Ashley
Gonda  Sturkelson.............................Dorothea  MacFarland
Pastor  Flaten......................................Paul  Ford
Mr.  Torvik.......................................Graham  Velsey
    Acts  I,  II  and  III.—A  Minnesota  Farmhouse.
    Staged  by  José  Ferrer;  settings  and  costumes  by  Carl  Kent;  light-
ing  by  Herbert  Brodkin.
```

The relatives of Aunt Etta, deceased, gather at her home to hear
her will read and to bury her remains. They are mostly an avaricious lot, and react in character to the discovery that Aunt Etta
knew them a lot better than they suspected, and treated them
better, mostly, than they deserved.

(Closed March 16, 1947)

THE GREAT CAMPAIGN

(5 performances)

A drama in two acts by Arnold Sundgaard; music by Alex North. Produced by T. Edward Hambleton at the Princess Theatre, New York, March 30, 1947.

Cast of characters—

Emily Trellis	Kay Loring
Sam Trellis	Millard Mitchell
Jeff Trellis	Thomas Coley
Trivett	John Eaton
Jane	Clara Cordery
Paula	Ruth Rowen
Wilderness	Philip Robinson
Trumpeter	Howard Brockway
Mr. Cook	John O'Shaughnessy
Kenneth	Ray Boyle
Kenneth's Girl	Mary Lou Taylor
Laneth	Frances Waller
Barber	Glen Tetley
Henry	Alan Manson
John	William Roerick
Wallie P. Hale	Robert P. Lieb
Sidney Gat	Erik Rhodes
Roscoe Dray	Robert Alvin
Hamp	Paul Bain
Laura	Marsh McLeod
Eddie	Gayne Sullivan
Anna	Ann d'Autremont
Avery	Howard Wendell

Dancers: Clara Cordery, Margaret McCallion, Ruth Rowen, Solvet Wiberg, Richard Astor, John Eaton, Glen Tetley.

Acts I and II.—In rural Minnesota, Illinois, Columbus, Zanesville, U. S. A.

Staged by Joseph Losey; choreography by Anna Sokolow; settings by Robert Davison; costumes by Rose Bogdanoff.

A misbegotten majority of so-called upright citizens are tricked into electing Wallie P. Hale, a phony, president. They should have voted for Sam Trellis, a simple and plain man of high integrity.

(Closed April 7, 1947)

VIRGINIA REEL

(5 performances)

A comedy in three acts by John and Harriet Weaver. Produced by Leonard Field at the Princess Theatre, New York, April 13, 1947.

Cast of characters—

Old Man Henry Haskins	Alan MacAteer
Ruth Joy Pomfritt	Jimsey Somers
Creed Haskins	Barbara Leeds
John Larkin	Don MacLaughlin

Hobe Kelvin.....................................James Daly
Keen Sowers..............................Philip Youmans Remer
The Widow Curtis.................................Reta Shaw
Ernie Brunk.......................................Robert Emhardt
May Belle Haskins..........................Jetti Preminger
Tuck Henry.................................Richard Shankland
Two Movers................................. { C. J. Parsons
                                          { William Tregoe

Acts I, II and III.—Rural Postoffice and Country Store of Old
Man Henry Haskins, in Blue Ridge Hill Country, near Royalton,
Virginia.

Staged by Gerald Savory; setting by Richard Bernstein; lighting
by Herbert Brodkin.

Creed Haskins, a storekeeper's daughter in a Blue Ridge community, tries to adjust her life to situations arising from the in-
flation and deflation of a land boom.

(Closed April 20, 1947)

RUTH DRAPER

(42 performances)

A repertory of dramatic sketches. Presented by John C. Wilson
at the Empire Theatre, New York, January 12, 1947.

Sketches—

The Return (Cottage in English Village) June 1945
Viva la France (On a Beach in Brittany) Autumn, 1940
Doctors and Diets
Three Women and Mr. Clifford
Opening a Bazaar
The Italian Lesson
A Scottish Immigrant
Three Generations
A Class in Greek Poise
On a Porch—in a Maine Coast Village
In a Church in Italy

Ruth Draper was last seen in New York in an engagement beginning December 25, 1942, and continuing eleven days at the
New York Times Hall.

(Closed February 22, 1947)

CRAIG'S WIFE

(69 performances)

A drama in three acts by George Kelly. Revived by Gant
Gaither at the Playhouse, New York, February 12, 1947.

Cast of characters—

Miss Austin.......................,..........Kathleen Comegys
Mrs. Harold.......................................Viola Roache

Mazie..Dortha Duckworth
Mrs. Craig..Judith Evelyn
Ethel Landreth.....................................Virginia Dwyer
Walter Craig..Philip Ober
Mrs. Frazier....................................Virginia Hammond
Billy Birkmire..................................Herschel Bentley
Joseph Catelle..Hugh Rennie
Harry...Allan Nourse
Eugene Fredericks...................................John Hudson
    Acts I, II and III.—Reception Room at the Home of the Walter
Craigs.
    Staged by George Kelly; settings by Stewart Chaney; decor by
Jensen's.

"Craig's Wife," Pulitzer Prize play for 1925-26, was first pro-
duced by Rosalie Stewart at the Morosco Theatre, New York,
October 12, 1925. The cast included Chrystal Herne (Mrs.
Craig), Charles Trowbridge (Mr. Craig), Anne Sutherland (Miss
Austin) and Josephine Hull (Mrs. Frazier). It ran for 360 per-
formances. See "Best Plays of 1925-26."

(Closed April 12, 1947)

DONALD WOLFIT REPERTORY COMPANY

A repertory of four Shakesperian plays and "Volpone" by Ben
Jonson, with music arranged by Rosabel Watson. Presented by
Hall Shelton by arrangement with Advance Players Association,
Ltd., of London, at the Century Theatre, New York, February 18,
1947. A total of 23 performances were given.

KING LEAR

(8 performances)

A Shakesperian tragedy presented in two acts, February 18,
1947.

Cast of characters—

Lear, King of Britain............................Donald Wolfit
King of France.................................David Dodimead
Duke of Burgundy.............................George Bradford
Duke of Cornwall....................................Josef Shear
Duke of Albany...................................Robert Algar
Earl of Kent...................................Alexander Gauge
Earl of Gloucester..................................Eric Maxon
Edgar..Kempster Barnes
Edmund..Frederick Horrey
Curan...Malcolm Watson
Oswald..John Wynyard
Tenant to Gloucester...........................George Bradford
Doctor..Malcolm Watson
Fool...Geoffrey Wilkinson
Officer..David Dodimead
Herald...Richard Blythe
Servant to Cornwall.............................Richard Blythe
Goneril.......................................Violet Farebrother
Regan..Ann Chalkley
Cordelia...Rosalind Iden

Acts I and II.—Britain.
Staged by Donald Wolfit and Christopher Ede; settings and costumes by Ernest Stern.

(Closed March 8, 1947)

AS YOU LIKE IT

(4 performances)

A Shakesperian comedy presented in two acts, February 20, 1947.

Cast of characters—

Duke, living in exile............................	Alexander Gauge
Frederick, his brother, usurper of his dominion.....	David Dodimead

Jacques ⎱
Lord   ⎰ Lords attendant upon the banished Duke ⎰ John Wynyard
Amiens   George Bradford
                                                      Robert Algar

Le Beau, a courtier attendant upon Frederick....	Geoffrey Wilkinson
Charles, a wrestler...............................	Josef Shear

Oliver ⎱
Jacques ⎰ Sons of Sir Roland de Bois.......... ⎰ Frederick Horrey
Orlando ⎰   David Dodimead
                                                  Kempster Barnes

Adam   ⎱ Servants to Oliver..................... ⎰ Eric Adeney
Dennis ⎰   Charles Ollington

Touchstone, a clown...............................	Donald Wolfit
Sir Oliver Martext, a Vicar......................	David Dodimead

Corin   ⎱ Shepherds.......................... ⎰ Malcolm Watson
Silvius ⎰   Richard Blythe

William, a country fellow in love with Audrey.........	Josef Shear
Hymen..	Robert Algar
Rosalind, daughter to the banished Duke.............	Rosalind Iden
Celia, daughter to Frederick....................	Penelope Chandler
Phoebe, a shepherdess.............................	Ann Chalkley
Audrey, a country wench.........................	Marion Marshall

Acts I and II.—Oliver's Orchard, the Usurper's Court and the Forest of Arden.
Staged by Donald Wolfit; settings and costumes by Ernest Stern.

(Closed March 8, 1947)

THE MERCHANT OF VENICE

(6 performances)

A Shakesperian comedy presented in three acts, February 22, 1947.

Cast of characters—

Duke of Venice.....................................	Eric Adeney

Prince of Morocco ⎱ Suitors to Portia.......... ⎰ Robert Algar
Prince of Aragon ⎰   David Dodimead

Antonio, a Merchant of Venice..................	Alexander Gauge
Bassanio, his Friend.............................	John Wynyard

Solanio ⎱
Salarino ⎰ Friends to Antonio and Bassanio...... ⎰ Frederick Horrey
Gratiano ⎰   Richard Blythe
                                                    Josef Shear

Lorenzo, in love with Jessica....................	Kempster Barnes
Shylock, a rich Jew...............................	Donald Wolfit

Tubal, a Jew, his friend..............................Eric Maxon
Launcelot Gobbo, a Clown, servant to Shylock...Geoffrey Wilkinson
Old Gobbo, Father to Launcelot..................Malcolm Watson
Balthasar, servant to Portia......................George Bradford
Stephano, servant to Portia....................Margaret Stallard
Clerk to the Court.............................David Dodimead
Portia, a rich Heiress............................Rosalind Iden
Nerissa, her Waiting Maid......................Marion Marshall
Jessica, daughter to Shylock....................Penelope Chandler
  Magnificoes of Venice, Officers of the Court of Justice, Jailers,
Servants and other Attendants.
  Acts I, II and III.—Venice and Portia's House at Belmont.
  Staged by Donald Wolfit; costumes by Sheila Jackson.

(Closed March 6, 1947)

VOLPONE

(3 performances)

A comedy by Ben Jonson presented in two acts, February 24,
1947.

Cast of characters—

Volpone...Donald Wolfit
Mosca...John Wynyard
Voltore...Frederick Horrey
Corbaccio...Eric Maxon
Corvino...Alexander Gauge
Bonario...Kempster Barnes
Sir Politick Would-Be.............................Robert Algar
Peregrine......................................Malcolm Watson
Nano..Richard Blythe
Ca Strone.....................................Geoffrey Wilkinson
Androgyno.......................................David Dodimead
Three Magistrates...Josef Shear, George Bradford, Malcolm Watson
Celia...Rosalind Iden
  Acts I and II.—Venice.
  Staged by Donald Wolfit and Christopher Ede; settings by Donald
Wolfit.

"Volpone," in a Stefan Zweig version translated by Ruth
Langner, was produced by the Theatre Guild in New York the
season of 1927-28. The story is of a miserly money-lender who
tests possible heirs by advertising the making of his will. Many
try to bribe him, one with the loan of a young wife. This gets
Volpone into trouble on a charge of attempted rape. Dudley
Digges, Alfred Lunt, Margalo Gillmore, Henry Travers and Helen
Westley were in the cast. A second Guild revival in 1930 had
Sidney Greenstreet, Earle Larrimore and Sylvia Field featured.

(Closed March 6, 1947)

HAMLET

(2 performances)

A Shakesperian tragedy presented in two acts, February 26, 1947.

Cast of characters—

Hamlet, Prince of Denmark........................Donald Wolfit
Claudius, King of Denmark.....................Alexander Gauge
Horatio, friend to Hamlet........................John Wynyard
Ghost...Eric Adeney
Polonius...Eric Maxon
Rosencrantz ⎫   ⎧ Robert Algar
Guildenstern ⎬ Courtiers......................⎨ David Dodimead
Osric   ⎭   ⎩ Richard Blythe
Marcellus   ⎫   ⎧ George Bradford
Bernardo   ⎬ Soldiers.........................⎨ David Dodimead
Francisco   ⎭   ⎩ Richard Blythe
Laertes, son to Polonius.......................Kempster Barnes
Sailor...Hugh Cross
First Player...................................Josef Shear
Second Player................................Frederick Horrey
Player Queen.................................Marion Marshall
First Gravedigger.............................Malcolm Watson
Second Gravedigger..........................Geoffrey Wilkinson
Priest...Robert Algar
Reynaldo.....................................Geoffrey Wilkinson
Fortinbras, Prince of Norway.................Frederick Horrey
Gertrude, Queen of Denmark...................Violet Farebrother
Ophelia, daughter to Polonius....................Rosalind Iden
      Acts I and II.—Elsinore.
      Staged by Donald Wolfit and Christopher Ede; settings by Donald
Wolfit and Eric Adeney.

(Closed March 7, 1947)

THE IMPORTANCE OF BEING EARNEST

(81 performances)

A comedy in three acts by Oscar Wilde. Revived by The Theatre Guild and John C. Wilson in association with H. M. Tennent, Ltd., of London, presenting John Gielgud and his London company in a season of comedy at the Royale Theatre, New York, March 3, 1947.

Cast of characters—

Lane...Richard Wordsworth
Algernon Moncrieff..............................Robert Flemyng
John Worthing, J.P. ....John Gielgud
Lady Bracknell.............................Margaret Rutherford
Hon. Gwendolen Fairfax..........................Pamela Brown
Cecily Cardew....................................Jane Baxter
Miss Prism.......................................Jean Cadell
Rev. Canon Chasuble, D.D...........................John Kidd
Merriman.......................................Stringer Davis
Footman..Donald Bain

Act I.—Algernon Moncrieff's Rooms in Piccadilly.   Act II.—Garden at the Manor House. Act III.—Morning-Room at the Manor House.
    Staged by John Gielgud; settings by Motley; lighting by William Conway.

First produced in London in February, 1895, and in New York the following April, "The Importance of Being Earnest" has been the most popular in revival of all the Oscar Wilde comedies. It has been repeated many times in both London and New York. Henry Miller was the first local John Worthing, William Faversham the first Algy and Viola Allen the original Gwen. In a 1902 revival Charles Richman, William Courtenay and Margaret Anglin played these roles. A musical comedy version entitled "Oh, Earnest!" music by Robert Hood Bowers and book and lyrics by Francis De Will, was produced in New York, May 9, 1927. Hal Forde and Dorothy Dilley were the principals.

(Closed May 10, 1947)

PARLOR STORY

(23 performances)

A comedy in three acts by William McCleery. Produced by Paul Streger at the Biltmore Theatre, New York, March 4, 1947.

Cast of characters—

Marian Burnett	Edith Atwater
Katy	Joan Vohs
Charles Burnett	Walter Abel
Christine	Carol Wheeler
Eddie West	Richard Noyes
Mike	Frank Wilcox
Lainson	Dennis King, Jr.
Mrs. Bright	Dorothy Eaton
Governor Sam Bright	Paul Huber
Mel Granite	Royal Beal

Acts I, II and III.—Living-Room of a Professor's House in a University Town Somewhere West of the Missouri River.
    Staged by Bretaigne; settings by Raymond Sovey; costumes by Bianca Stroock.

Charles Burnett has quit Mel Granite's newspaper to accept a professorship on the faculty of the local university. His ambition is to get himself appointed president of the university, a gift within the control of the Governor. Granite, the reactionary publisher, brings pressure on the Governor to block the appointment of Burnett, hoping to lure him back to journalism. He uses as a lever an editorial on marriage written by Eddie West, published in the college paper, and labeled communistic by the local red-baiters.

(Closed March 22, 1947)

MAURICE CHEVALIER

(46 performances)

An intimate song recital, with character impressions. Irving Actman accompanist. Presented by Arthur Lesser at the Henry Miller Theatre, New York, March 10, 1947.

Program—

Bonsoir Messieurs Dames
Ah! Qu'Elle Est Belle!
La Lecon de Piano
Vingt Ans
A Barcelone
Weeping Willie
Quai de Bercy
Mandarinades
Place Pigalle
La Symphonie des Smelles de Bois

This was M. Chevalier's first professional visit to America since 1934. His encores included his two outstanding favorites of the old days, "Louise" and "Valentine."

(Closed April 19, 1947)

THE CHOCOLATE SOLDIER

(70 performances)

An operetta in three acts by Rudolph Bernauer and Leopold Jacobson; music by Oscar Straus; based on George Bernard Shaw's "Arms and the Man"; American version by Stanislaus Stangé; revised by Guy Bolton with additional lyrics by Bernard Hanighen. Revived by J. H. Del Bondia and Hans Bartsch for the Delvan Company at the Century Theatre, New York, March 12, 1947.

Cast of characters—

Nadina	Frances McCann
Mascha	Gloria Hamilton
Aurelia	Muriel O'Malley
Bumerli	Keith Andes
Massakroff	Henry Calvin
Popoff	Billy Gilbert
Alexius	Ernest McChesney
Stefan	Michael Mann
Katrina	Anna Wiman
Premiere Danseuse	Mary Ellen Moylan
Premier Dancer	Francisco Moncion

Act I.—Nadina's Bedroom in Popoff's House in a Small Town in Bulgaria. Acts II and III.—Courtyard of Popoff's House.

Staged by Felix Brentano; choreography by George Balanchine; music directed by Jay Blackton; settings by Jo Mielziner; costumes by Lucinda Ballard.

"The Chocolate Soldier," produced originally by F. C. Whitney at the Lyric Theatre, New York, Sept. 13, 1909, has been six times revived in New York: by the Shuberts in 1921, with Tessa Kosta as Nadina and Donald Brian as Bumerli; by the Jolson Light Opera Co. in 1930, with Alice McKenzie and Charles Purcell; by the New York Civic Light Opera Co. in 1931, with Vivienne Segal and Purcell; by the Knickerbocker Light Opera Co. in 1934 with Bernice Claire and Donald Brian and by the Messrs. Tushinsky and Bartsch at Carnegie Hall in 1942 with Helen Gleason and Allan Jones.

(Closed May 10, 1947)

BRIGADOON

(92 performances)

(Continued)

A musical play in two acts by Alan Jay Lerner; music by Frederick Loewe; orchestrations by Ted Royal. Produced by Cheryl Crawford at the Ziegfeld Theatre, New York, March 13, 1947.

Cast of characters—

Tommy Albright	David Brooks
Jeff Douglas	George Keane
Archie Beaton	Elliott Sullivan
Harry Beaton	James Mitchell
Kate MacQueen	Margaret Hunter
Fishmonger	Bunty Kelley
Angus MacGuffie	Walter Scheff
Sandy Dean	Jeff Warren
Andrew MacLaren	Edward Cullen
Fiona MacLaren	Marion Bell
Jean MacLaren	Virginia Bosler
Meg Brockie	Pamela Britton
Charlie Dalrymple	Lee Sullivan
Maggie Anderson	Lidija Franklin
Mr. Lundie	William Hansen
Sword Dancers	Roland Guerard, George Drake
Frank	John Paul
Jane Ashton	Frances Charles
Bagpipers	James MacFadden, Arthur Horn
Stuart Dalrymple	Paul Anderson
MacGregor	Earl Redding

Townsfolk of Brigadoon.

Act I.—Scene 1—Forest in Scottish Highlands. 2—Road in Brigadoon and Macconnachy Square. 3—An Open Shed. 4—The MacLaren House. 5—Outside the House of Mr. Lundie. 6—The Churchyard. Act II.—Scene 1—Forest Inside Brigadoon. 2—Road. 3—Glen. 4—Bar in New York City. 5—Forest in Scottish Bagpipers..........................James MacFadden, Arthur Horn

Staged by Robert Lewis; choreography by Agnes de Mille; music directed by Franz Allers; settings by Oliver Smith; costumes by David Ffolkes; lighting by Peggy Clarke.

See page 369.

THE EAGLE HAS TWO HEADS

(29 performances)

A melodrama in three acts by Jean Cocteau; adapted from the French by Ronald Duncan. Produced by John C. Wilson at the Plymouth Theatre, New York, March 19, 1947.

Cast of characters—

Countess Edith de Berg	Eleanor Wilson
Maxim, Duke of Willenstein	Kendall Clark
The Queen	Tallulah Bankhead
Stanislas	Helmut Dantine
Tony	Cherokee Thornton
Baron Foehn	Clarence Derwent

Act I.—The Queen's Bedroom. Acts II and III.—The Library.
Staged by John C. Wilson; settings by Donald Oenslager; costumes by Aline Bernstein.

The lonely and unhappy Queen of a mythical Graustarkian country has gone veiled and taken little interest in the ruling of her country for fifteen years, following the assassination of her bridegroom on her honeymoon. A young and handsome rebel, bent also on assassination, climbs through the window of her bedroom. He came to slay but remains to love until, at curtain time, the still miserable Queen goads him into shooting her and killing himself.

(Closed April 12, 1947)

BATHSHEBA

(29 performances)

A drama in three acts by Jacques Deval. Produced by Maximilian Becker and Lee K. Holland in association with Sylvia Friedlander at the Ethel Barrymore Theatre, New York, March 26, 1947.

Cast of characters—

Gershoum	Martin Ashe
Hiram	Carleton Scott Young
Joab	Rusty Lane
Manasseh	Paul Donah
Shari	Hildy Parks
Uriah	Phil Arthur
Niziah	Leonore Rae
Aroussia	Blanche Zohar
David	James Mason
Ghazil	Horace Braham
Obram	Michael Sivy
Nathan	Thomas Chalmers
Hanoufati	Maud Scheerer
Agreb	Joseph Tomes
Bathsheba	Pamela Kellino

Sourab..Patricia Robbins
Micale...Jane Middleton
Bahila..Barbara Brooks
Orphie...Lenka Peterson
Lady-in-Waiting.......................................Vega Keane
  Act I.—Scene 1—Joab's Tent Before Rabah. 2, 3 and 4—Top
Terrace of King David's Palace in Jerusalem. Act II.—Scene 1—
Uriah's Tent Before Rabah. 2 and 3—The King's Terrace. Act
III.—The King's Terrace. 1030 b.c.
  Staged by Coby Ruskin; supervised by Sylvia Friedlander; set-
tings, costumes and lighting by Stewart Chaney.

King David, in one of his less attractive moods, is tired of life
and the adventures it has brought him. Surveying a disappointing world from his balcony, he happens to catch Bathsheba, wife
of Uriah, while she is in and out of the swimming pool in Uriah's
yard. David sends for Bathsheba. She responds with practically
no reluctance whatever, and stays on for a protracted visit. When
David learns that Bathsheba is to make him a father, he sends for
Uriah and tells him. Uriah, a worshipful Captain in David's
army, intimates that he thinks his king must be kidding. Anyway, he will not return to Bathsheba until he is victorious in battle.
Fearing that may take too long, David sends Uriah to an exposed
position in the front line, where he is killed.

(Closed April 19, 1947)

THE WHOLE WORLD OVER

(77 performances)
(Continued)

A comedy in two acts by Konstantine Simonov; adapted by
Thelma Schnee. Produced by Walter Fried and Paul F. Moss at
the Biltmore Theatre, New York, March 27, 1947.

Cast of characters—

Feodor Vorontsov..................................Joseph Buloff
Nadya...Beatrice de Neergaard
Olya Vorontsov.....................................Uta Hagen
Sergei Sinitsin..................................Sanford Meisner
Sasha.......................................Elisabeth Neumann
Stepan Cheezov...................................Fred Stewart
Dmitri Savelev...............................Stephen Bekassy
Nicolai Nekin...................................Michael Strong
Vanya Shpolyanski.............................George Bartenieff
Colonel Ivanov......................................Lou Polan
Major Anna Orlov...............................Jo Van Fleet
  Acts I and II.—Apartment of Professor Feodor Vorontsov in Mos-
cow Shortly After the End of the War.
  Staged by Harold Clurman; setting and costumes by Ralph
Alswang.

Feodor, an eccentric army engineer, and Olya, his daughter, have
been assigned living quarters in the home of Dmitri, for three

years a colonel in the Soviet army. Olya has lost her fiancé in the war. Dmitri has lost his wife and daughter. Both are bitter and blue. Through the contriving of Feodor, they are made aware of an awakening love.

TENTING TONIGHT

(46 performances)

A comedy in three acts by Frank Gould. Produced by Saul Fischbein at the Booth Theatre, New York, April 2, 1947.

Cast of characters—

Peter Roberts	Richard Clark
Edna Roberts	June Dayton
Lester Pringle	Michael Road
Leonie Roberts	Jean Muir
Phil Alexander	Dean Harens
Stanley Fowler	Ralph Brooke
Sue Fowler	Betty Caulfield
Theda Henderson	Ethel Remey
Marvin Henderson	William David
Joe Wollinski	Joshua Shelley
Elliot Smollens	Jackie Kelk
Yock Janowski	Henry Lascoe
Sherman	Michael Lewin
Harry Nash	Forrest Taylor, Jr.
Billy Heffernan	Edward de Velde
Sammy Foley	James Fallon

Acts I, II and III.—Combination Living-Room Study of Peter Roberts' Home in a Small College Town.

Staged by Hudson Faussett; setting by John Root; costumes by Robert Moore.

The Peter Robertses, he an ex-serviceman who has become a professor in a small college, decide to do their bit to help ex-GIs get a chance at a higher education. They advertise board and room for an ex-GI for one semester. The first candidate to appear (Phil Alexander) brings two buddies and the wife of one of them. The invasion musses up the Roberts' living-room, and complications mount until curtain time.

(Closed May 10, 1947)

BAREFOOT BOY WITH CHEEK

(68 performances)
(Continued)

A musical comedy in two acts by Max Shulman; lyrics by Sylvia Dee; music by Sidney Lippman; vocal arrangements by Hugh Martin; orchestrations by Philip Lang. Produced by George Abbott at the Martin Beck Theatre, New York, April 3, 1947.

Cast of characters—

Shyster Fiscal.....................................Red Buttons
Roger Hailfellow..................................Jack Williams
Van Varsity......................................Ben Murphy
Charley Convertible..............................Loren Welch
Freshman...Patrick Kingdon
Asa Hearthrug....................................Billy Redfield
Eino Fflliikkiinnenn.............................Benjamin Miller
Noblese Oblige...................................Billie Lou Watt
Clothilde Pfefferkorn............................Ellen Hanley
Yetta Samovar....................................Nancy Walker
Professor Schultz................................Philip Coolidge
Peggy Hepp.......................................Shirley Van
Kermit McDermott.................................Jerry Austen
Boris Fiveyearplan...............................Solen Burry
Playwright.......................................Martin Sameth
Bartender..James Lane
Muskie Pike......................................Tommy Farrell
First Band Member................................Harris Gondell
Second Band Member...............................Nathaniel Frey
    Act I.—Scenes 1 and 10—Alpha Cholera Fraternity House, Campus
of University of Minnesota. 2 and 4—College Corridor. 3—Class
Room. 5—Campus Publications Office. 6—The Sty. 7 and 9—The
Street. 8—The Knoll. Act II.—Scenes 1 and 5—Alpha Cholera
Fraternity House. 2—Street. 3—The Knoll. 4—Polling Place.
    Staged by George Abbott; music directed by Milton Rosenstock;
choreography by Richard Barstow; settings and lighting by Jo
Mielziner; costumes by Alvin Colt.

Yetta Samovar, the reddest of the pinks attending the University of Minnesota, would organize the student body into a society of collegiate radicals. She makes a party line and song-singing hero of Asa Hearthrug, an inquiring but wholesome freshman, but loses both Asa and his fraternity pin to sweet-singing Clothilde Pfefferkorn.

MESSAGE FOR MARGARET

(5 performances)

A drama in three acts by James Parish. Produced by Stanley Gilkey and Barbara Payne in association with Henry Sherek, Ltd., at the Plymouth Theatre, New York, April 16, 1947.

Cast of characters—

Margaret Hayden.................................Mady Christians
Stephen Austin.................................Roger Pryor
Maid...Janice Mars
Adeline Chalcot................................Miriam Hopkins
Robert Chalcot.................................Peter Cookson
    Acts I, II and III.—Margaret Hayden's Apartment in Gramercy
Park, New York City.
    Staged by Elliott Nugent; setting by Donald Oenslager.

Margaret Hayden learns of the accidental death of her husband through his best friend, Stephen Austin. As he was dying the husband had asked Stephen to give Margaret his love and thank her for all she had done for him. However, there was a second Margaret in the husband's life. This would be Adeline Chalcot, his mistress for two years, who is about to bear him a child. He had always called the mistress Margaret, too, possibly as a sleep-talking protection. A contest to determine which Margaret is entitled to the dead man's message follows, with the wife triumphant in the end.

(Closed April 19, 1947)

MIRACLE IN THE MOUNTAINS

(3 performances)

A legend in two acts by Ferenc Molnar. Produced by Archer King and Harrison Woodhull at the Playhouse, New York, April 25, 1947.

Cast of characters—

Clement	Kermit Kegley
Dominic	Norman Wallace
Ambrose	Salem Ludwig
The Prior	John McKee
The Attorney	Victor Kilian
Cicely	Julie Haydon
Simon	E. A. Krumschmidt
Sergeant	John Frederick
Gendarme	Mace Gwyer
Veronica	Consuelo O'Connor
Cornelia	Gloria O'Connor
The Squire	Lawrence Tibbett, Jr.
The Judge	Manart Kippen
The Mayor's Wife	Katherine Anderson
The Doctor	Bernard Randall
The Mayor	Frederic Tozere
The Baron	Len Patrick
Butler	Carl Wallace
Young Woman	Vivi Janiss
Court Attendant	Louis Cruger
Girl	Vivian King
Old Woman	Marjorie Dalton
The Prosecutor	Dayton Lummis
The Schoolmaster	Pitt Herbert

Members of the Elder's Council....Jack Hallen, Harry Miller, Jack O'Brien, Charles Russel, C. E. Smith, Augustus Vaccaro
Little Boy......Maurice Cavell
Townswomen.......Elain Flippen, Banice Winters, Jane Du Frayne
Act I.—Scene 1—A Monastery. Small Mining Town in the Dark Carpathian Mountains. About 100 Years Ago. 2—The Mayor's House. Act II.—Scene 1—Judgment Hall. 2—At the Foot of Lime-tree Hill.
Staged by Ferenc Molnar; settings and costumes by Robert Davison.

Cicely, servant girl in the home of the mayor of a small mining town in the Carpathian Mountains, fathers her employer's child. The mayor denies the parentage. The boy is killed and Cicely charged with the murder. A saintly attorney undertakes her defense, is beaten by circumstantial evidence and the mayor's influence in court, but has his day out of court when he summons the spirit of the dead boy to face the girl's accusers.

(Closed April 26, 1947)

A YOUNG MAN'S FANCY

(39 performances)
(Continued)

A comedy in three acts by Harry Thurschwell and Alfred Golden. Produced by Henry Adrian at the Plymouth Theatre, New York, April 29, 1947.

Cast of characters—

Sylvia Wilson	Lynne Carter
Harold Greenley	Bill Talman
Dr. Spee	Hugh Reilly
Dorothy Bennett	Joan Lawrence
Duvie	Richard Leone
Grilly	Donald Hastings
Jokey Stephen	Roy Sterling
Buddy	Bart Roe
Helen Greenley	Lenore Lonergan
Girl Camper	Colette MacMahon
Dickie Crandell	Ronnie Jacoby
Oliver Crandell	Raymond Bramley
Mrs. Mary Crandell	Lee Carney
Faith	Joan Shepard
Miss Weatherhead	Myrtle Ferguson
Camp Trilby Boy	Mickey Carroll

Acts I, II and III.—Boys' Bunkhouse at Camp Freedom, in Connecticut.

Staged by Robert E. Perry; setting and lighting by Ralph Alswang; costumes by Lou Eisele.

Dickie Crandell had rather read Shakespeare than go in for the rough stuff at a co-ed summer camp. The other boys decide to make a man of Dickie and proceed to haze him. Dickie gets even, at the suggestion of a camp councilor, by erecting a series of booby traps and uncoupling several collapsible cots, tricks that make monkeys of his tormenters. He also helps patch up a lovers' quarrel involving the chief councilors.

THE TELEPHONE

THE MEDIUM

(36 performances)
(Continued)

A curtain raiser and a tragedy in two acts; music, book and lyrics by Gian-Carlo Menotti. Produced by Chandler Cowles and

Efrem Zimbalist in association with Edith Lutyens at the Barrymore Theatre, New York, May 1, 1947.

Cast of characters—

THE TELEPHONE (OR "L'AMOUR A TROIS")

Lucy..Marilyn Cotlow
Ben...Frank Rogier

THE MEDIUM

Monica...Evelyn Keller
Toby, A Mute...Leo Coleman
Madame Flora (Baba)..................................Marie Powers
Mrs. Gobineau..Beverly Dame
Mr. Gobineau...Frank Rogier
Mrs. Nolan...Virginia Beeler
    Acts I and II.—Madame Flora's Parlor, in Our Time.
    Staged by Menotti; music directed by Emanuel Balaban; settings and costumes by Horace Armistead; lighting by Jean Rosenthal; production assistance by the Ballet Society.

Ben has a hard time trying to propose to Lucy before leaving town to take a job. Always she is called to, or is busy with, the telephone. Ben finally overcomes the difficulty by telephoning Lucy from the railway station just before train time.

In "The Medium" Mme. Flora, a charlatan fortune-teller, operates a dingy parlor with the aid of her daughter and a deaf-mute boy. Falling victim to an imagined visit of spirit agents, the business of hoaxing trustful people awakens the conscience of Mme. Flora. She gets drunk and goes mad. She shoots into the cabinet from which her "spirit" messages emanate, thinking to destroy the evil side of herself. The deaf-mute boy tumbles out, dead.

HEADS OR TAILS

(35 performances)

A comedy in three acts by H. J. Lengsfelder and Ervin Drake. Produced by Your Theatre, Inc., at the Cort Theatre, New York, May 2, 1947.

Cast of characters—

Cornelius T. Sheldon.................................Les Tremayne
Amy..Lulu Belle Clarke
Helen Sheldon..Audra Lindley
Burton Snead...Joseph Silver
Frank Jones..Gregory Robbins
Marion Gilmore.......................................Lucie Lancaster
Alice Milford..Jean Cobb
Philip McGill..Jed Prouty
Barney McGill..Ralph Simone
Eric Petersen..Werner Klemperer
Mrs. Warren..Lelah Tyler
Ernest Milford.......................................Joseph Graham
Mr. Green..Anthony Gray
Senor Costamara......................................Frank de Kova

Humperdinck...Richard Barron
McNulty...Paul Lipson
    Act I.—Scene 1—Terrace of the Country Home of Cornelius Sheldon. 2—Barney McGill's Office. Act II.—Scene 1—The Terrace. 2—The Milford Living Room. Act III.—The Terrace, the Thirteenth of the Month, Cornelius' Birthday.
    Staged by Edward F. Cline; settings by Watson Barrett; lighting by Leo Kerz; costumes by Alice Gibson.

Cornelius Sheldon, a career diplomat, and Philip McGill, an insurance man, love the same girl. Sheldon and his current wife are about to get a divorce so that he may pursue the new romance. Proceedings are being held in abeyance until he is assured of an important diplomatic post. He and his rival for the new love toss coins to determine which shall get her—the loser to commit suicide. The ending is happy, with the Sheldons still together and no suicide.

(Closed May 31, 1947)

SAN CARLO OPERA COMPANY

The tenth New York season of the San Carlo Opera Company, under the direction of Fortune Gallo, opened at the Center Theatre in Rockefeller Center April 23, 1947, and closed May 11, after 21 performances. The operas were staged by Mario Valle; musical directors, Anton Coppola and Victor Trucco, guest conductor; leaders of ballet, Lydia Arlova and Lucien Prideaux. The repertory:

CARMEN

Cast of characters—

Carmen...Coe Glade
Don Jose..Taola Civil
Escamillo.......................................Mostyn Thomas
Micaela...Mina Cravi
Zuniga.......................................William Wilderman
Dancairo...Sausto Bozza
Frasquita ....Celia Venditti
    Act I.—Public Square in Seville. Act II.—Tavern. Act III.—Ravine in Mountains. Act IV.—Entrance to Arena.
    Staged by Mario Valle; music directed by Anton Coppola.

MADAMA BUTTERFLY—April 24 and 28, and May 11. Cast—Mmes. Koyke, Calcagno, Dixon, Messrs. Palermo, Valle, Wilderman, Bozza and La Chance.

RIGOLETTO—April 25 and May 8. Cast—Mmes. Reggiani, Kalter, Calcagno, Messrs. Scattolini, Morelli, Wilderman, Tatozzi, Bozza and La Chance.

LA TRAVIATA—April 26, May 3 and 11. Cast—Mmes. Andreva, Dixon, Calcagno, Messrs. Palermo, Ballarini, Tatozzi, Bozza, La Chance.

AIDA—April 26, May 4 and 9. Cast—Mmes. Ercole, Browning, Venditti, Messrs. Pravadeli, Thomas, Wilderman, Tatozzi
and La Chance.

LA BOHEME—April 27 and May 3. Cast— Mmes. Cravi,
Venditti, Messrs. Scattolini, Morelli, Ballarini, Wilderman, Bozza
and La Chance.

IL TROVATORE—April 27. Cast—Mmes. Kaye, Browning,
Calcagno, Messrs. Rayner, Ballarini, Wilderman and La Chance.

CAVALLERIA RUSTICANA—April 29. Cast—Mmes. Kaye,
Kalter, Calcagno, Messrs. Palermo and Fiorella.

PAGLIACCI—April 29. Cast—Miss Cravi, Messrs. Pravadeli,
Thomas, Fiorella and La Chance.

LA TOSCA—April 30. Cast—Mmes. Ercole, Dixon, Messrs.
Civil, Morelli, Wilderman, Tatrozzi, Went and La Chance.

FAUST—May 2. Cast—Mmes. Cravi, Kalter, Calcagno,
Messrs. Palermo, Thomas, Wilderman and Tatozzi.

BARBER OF SEVILLE—May 4. Cast—Mmes. Reggiani,
Calcagno, Messrs. Palermo, Morelli, Patacchi, Valle, Bozza and
La Chance.

(Closed May 11, 1947)

PORTRAIT IN BLACK

(22 performances)
(Continued)

A drama in three acts by Ivan Goff and Ben Roberts. Produced
by David Lowe and Edgar F. Luckenbach at the Booth Theatre,
New York, May 14, 1947.

Cast of characters—

```
Tanis Talbot.........................................Claire Luce
Gracie McPhee.................................. Mary Michael
Peter Talbot...................................David Anderson
Winifred Talbot..............................Dorothea Jackson
Cob O'Brien......................................Barry Kelley
Rupert Marlowe...............................Sidney Blackmer
Dr. Philip Graham.................................Donald Cook
Blake Ritchie....................................Thomas Coley
```
    Acts I, II and III.—Drawing Room of Talbot Home in San Fran-
cisco.
    Staged by Reginald Denham; setting and lighting by Donald Oen-
slager; costumes by Helene Pons.

Tanis Talbot conspires with Dr. Philip Graham to be rid of
her invalid husband. After the husband's death Tanis receives
an anonymous letter accusing her and the doctor of the murder.
They decide the letter is from Rupert Marlowe, an old admirer

of Tanis, and proceed to wipe him out. A second anonymous accusation is received, leading to the discovery of Tanis' own duplicity and the doctor's decision to clean up the whole mess.

LOVE FOR LOVE

(8 performances)

(Continued)

A comedy in two acts by William Congreve; streamlined by John Gielgud; incidental music arranged and songs composed to Congreve's words by Leslie Bridgewater. Revived by The Theatre Guild, John C. Wilson and H. M. Tennent, Ltd., of London at the Royale Theatre, New York, May 26, 1947.

Cast of characters—

```
Valentine..........................................John Gielgud
Jeremy.......................................Richard Wordsworth
Scandal...........................................George Hayes
Tattle............................................Cyril Ritchard
Mrs. Frail.......................................Adrianne Allen
Foresight.............................................John Kidd
Robin...............................................Donald Bain
Nurse.............................................Philippa Gill
Angelica.........................................Pamela Brown
Sir Sampson Legend............................Malcolm Keen
Mrs. Foresight..................................Marian Spencer
Miss Prue..........................................Jessie Evans
Ben.............................................Robert Flemyng
Buckram........................................Sebastian Cabot
Jenny................................................Mary Lynn
    Staged by John Gielgud; settings by Rex Whistler; costumes by
Jeanette Cochrane; lighting by William Conway.
    Act I.—Scene 1—Valentine's Lodgings, London, 1695. 2 and 3—
Foresight's House. Act II.—Scene 1—Valentine's Lodgings. 2—
Foresight's House.
```

The Provincetown Players revived Congreve's "Love for Love" in Greenwich Village, New York, in March, 1925. It had 47 performances with Walter Abel (Sir Sampson), Stanley Howlett, Perry Ivins, Adrienne Morrison and Rosalind Fuller in the cast. It was tried again the following season, under the direction of Kenneth Macgowan, Robert Edmond Jones and Eugene O'Neill, for sixteen performances. The Players selected it for a 1940 revival, with Thomas Chalmers playing Sir Sampson, Barry Jones the Valentine, Leo Carroll the Scandal and Cornelia Otis Skinner the Angelica. Peggy Wood, Violet Heming and Dorothy Gish were also in the cast.

ICETIME OF 1948

(6 performances)
(Continued)

An ice skating revue in 2 acts and 24 scenes assembled by Sonja Henie and Arthur M. Wirtz; lyrics and music by James Littlefield and John Fortis; songs by Al Stillman and Paul Mc-Grane; musical arrangements by Paul Van Loan. Produced by Sonart Productions at the Center Theatre, New York, May 28, 1947.

Principals engaged—

Skippy Baxter	Freddie Trenkler
Joan Hyldoft	Joe Jackson, Jr.
Fritz Dietl	James Caesar
James Carter	Claire Dalton
Paul Castle	Jimmie Sisk
Lou Folds	Nola Fairbanks
Richard Craig	Melba Welch
Lucille Risch	Charles Cavanaugh
Kay Corcoran	John Kasper
Cissy Trenholm	Janet Van Sickle
Helga Brandt	Inge Brandt
John Walsh	Monte Stott
Buster Grace	Charles Slagle
Jean Sakovich	Fred Griffith
Sidney Spalding	Geoffe Stevens

Executive director, Arthur M. Wirtz; production director, William H. Burke; staged by Catherine Littlefield; skating direction by May Judels; music directed by David Mendoza; choreography by Catherine and Dorothie Littlefield; settings by Bruno Maine and Edward Gilbert; costumes by Lou Eisele, Billy Livingston and Katherine Kuhn; lighting by Eugene Braun.

EXPERIMENTAL THEATRE, INC.—EQUITY-LIBRARY THEATRE

By George Freedley

After an absence from Broadway of several years, through the good offices of the American National Theatre and Academy (ANTA) and of Robert Breen, the contract for the Experimental Theatre, Inc., was reactivated by the Dramatists' Guild and Actors' Equity Association. During the four months it took these worthy organizations to iron out the wrinkles in the agreement, a producing committee was set up to function. The four principal producing organizations which joined together to plan the revival of an experimental program at ANTA's instance were the American Repertory Theatre, The Playwrights' Company, the Theatre Guild, and Theatre, Inc. To these organizations which were represented respectively by Cheryl Crawford, Maxwell Anderson, Theresa Helburn, and Norris Houghton were added Clarence Derwent for Equity, Richard Rodgers for the Dramatists' Guild, Robert Breen and Margaret Webster for ANTA and George Freedley for Equity-Library Theatre. Robert C. Schnitzer was executive assistant. After the agreement was signed Equity and the Dramatists' Guild set up a board of ten, five from each group, with Mr. Derwent as chairman. John Beal, Ruth Hammond, Philip Loeb, Myron McCormick and Carol Stone stood for Equity. James Gow, Herbert Kubly, Milton Pascal, Gerald Savory and Victor Wolfson represented the playwrights.

On February 9th, ANTA sponsored the Experimental Theatre's presentation of Theatre Inc.'s production of "The Wanhope Building" by John Finch at the Princess Theatre in West 39th Street. This play opened on a Sunday night, played Monday, Friday and Sunday matinees and the following Sunday night. This five performance pattern was followed throughout.

On February 23rd, the Theatre Guild's production of "O'Daniel" by Glendon Swarthout and John Saracool was seen. On March 9th came José Ferrer's production of "As We Forgive Our Debtors" by Tillman Breiseth. T. Edward Hambleton's presentation of Arnold Sundgaard's "The Great Campaign" had its premiere on the 20th. The final production came on April 13th when

Leonard Field produced "Virginia Reel" by John and Harriet Weaver. As an extra attraction for the Experimental Theatre subscribers to ANTA ($15 a seat for five plays with no free lists, as the critics paid their own way) Gertrude Macy's presentation of Edith King and Dorothy Coit's "Aucassin and Nicolette" was offered for the week of April 21st. The Experimental Theatre plans a 1947-48 season under ANTA sponsorship at a theatre to be announced.

The Equity-Library Theatre, with two small offices on the top floor of Actors' Equity Association, operated its most successful season between November 1, 1946, and June 1, 1947. In those seven months ELT produced, with Sam Jaffe and George Freedley as co-chairmen and John Golden and his Theatre Fund as benevolent angel, some fifty-six productions, eight more than in 1945-46. The number more than equaled the new plays offered by Broadway managers for the paying public.

ELT plays are read and cast at headquarters, but are rehearsed mostly in the five branches of the New York Public Library which were used for performances—Hudson Park, Fort Washington, George Bruce, Hamilton Grange, and 115th Street. ANTA (The American National Theatre and Academy) lent its rehearsal halls for more than sixteen hundred hours. John Golden contributed the very small amount of money requested in return for this service. In January, 1947, Mr. and Mrs. C. V. Erickson donated the use, for two productions a month, of their Greenwich Mews Playhouse. Several of the best productions were offered for special performances at the Central Needles Trades High School.

The plays were produced under the same rules—80 per cent Equity and 20 per cent non-Equity players, which permits a tiny infiltration of new actors coming from the colleges, universities and community theatres throughout the country.

The first production of the season was "Rosmersholm," November 20th at Hudson Park, while "The Milky Way" (a production actually planned during the war in the South Pacific) parted the curtains at the George Bruce. "The Shining Hour," "The Long Goodbye," "Hello Out There" and Carl Shain's excellent production of "Kiss Them for Me" concluded the plays scheduled for that month.

"L'Aiglon" and "The Second Man" were the December openings. They were followed by W. S. Gilbert's seldom-seen "Engaged," "Our Town," splendidly produced by Day Tuttle and well acted by Harrison Dowd and David Bell; Edward Ludlom's ingeniously directed "Abe Lincoln in Illinois," "Angel Street," "Elizabeth the Queen," "The Constant Nymph," which brought Peter Cookson to fame, two Broadway productions, and "Ah, Wilderness!"

The New Year ushered in James Joyce's "Exiles," "Rocket to the Moon," Molnar's "The Good Fairy," "The Petrified Forest," "The Green Goddess," "The Church Mouse" and, for the first time in New York, John Webster's gory 1612 tragedy, "The White Devil." "The Dybbuk" was the opening February attraction, followed by "Tomorrow and Tomorrow," "Beyond the Horizon," "Fata Morgana," "Six Characters in Search of an Author," "Uncle Harry," "The Inspector General," "The Great God Brown," three Chekhov one-act comedies directed by José Ferrer, "The Mistress of the Inn" and "Paths of Glory," which was one of the outstanding successes of the season as directed by John O'Shaughnessy.

A group of Thornton Wilder one-act plays started March off to good effect. Then came "Awake and Sing," "Hotel Universe," "Milestones," "A Sound of Hunting," "Home of the Brave," "The Detour," "Peer Gynt" in a new translation by Dan Dickenson, "Justice" and "The Sabine Women." In April came "Success Story," "Arms and the Man," "The Trojan Women," "The Cenci," "There's Always Juliet," "John Ferguson," "The First Year," "Karl and Anna," and "The Lower Depths."

May brought the season to a close with five unusual productions. First, John Reich's excellently directed "Henry IV" by Pirandello, in a new adaptation by the director and with a fine performance in the title role by Herbert Berghof. Maugham's "The Circle" was extremely well received. Then came "The Three Sisters," "Much Ado About Nothing" (in a good cutting by Henry Jones) and "Hedda Gabler," the 144th ELT production.

The office was manned by the efficient Benne Franklin as executive secretary, as well as by volunteer aid. The Summer is a time for rest, but September will see activity again. By October audiences will again be assembling in New York's basement library theatres, and ELT will be off for a new season.

DANCE DRAMA

A series of dance drama programs, sponsored by Dale Wasserman and David Alexander and called "Barbizon Tuesdays," started June 11, 1946, at Barbizon-Plaza Concert Hall. Maria Teresa Acuna and Frederico Rey appeared in "Spanish Classic," excerpts from Albeniz's "Pepita Juminez," "Sevillanas Populares" and "Jota." Rey de la Torre, guitarist, and Pablo Miguel, pianist, were associate artists.

June 18, 1947, Alice Dudley and her company featured a suite of Kentucky Mountain folklore dance dramas. Kathleen O'Brien and Nathan Kirkpatrick were included in the dance group and Glen Baker and Jeanette Wells were associate artists. The program included "Unfortunate Mrs. Bailey," "Fisherman Tell Me," "Woman Song" and "Mountain Song."

June 25, Valerie Bettis and her ensemble offered three dance dramas, including Garcia Lorca's "Yerma." Miss Bettis was assisted by Duncan Noble and Doris Goodwin.

Pearl Primus and her company, including Jacqueline Hairston and Joe Nash, presented "African Ceremonial," "Te Moana," "Afro-Haitian Play Dance," "Strange Fruit" and other dance drama at the Y.M.H.A. November 10, 1946.

Ragina Devi and her group offered "Dance of the Supreme Goddess," "Krishna and the Gopis," and Kathnak dances of North India at the Indian Dance Theatre, November 10, 1946, and again April 13, 1947, when her guest artists were Carlos Toledo, Daniel Sanchez Reyes and Mario Castillo.

Le Meri and her company presented Ethnological Dance programs during the season, beginning November 14 at the Museum of Natural History.

Ruth Mata and Eugene Hari gave a dance drama program of burlesque at the National Theatre, December 11, 1946, and April 13, 1947, at Y.M.H.A. Vladimir Vilyenski and Thaddeus Sadlowsky assisted with music and Marguerite de Anguere, Bill Bradley and Hal Loman headed the company dancing "The Acrobats," "Fakir Dance" by Sadoff, "Looking for Talent," "Original Chapeaux" and "Street Corner" by Kingsley, "Pas de Deux" (Chopin, Tchaikovsky), "On Display" (Hein), and "Carnegie Hall" (Perl).

Jose Limon with his company made his first Broadway appearance at the Belasco Theatre January 5. Doris Humphrey was artistic director. "Lament for Ignacio Sanchez Mejias," by Doris Humphrey, based on a poem by Federico Garcia Lorca, and with score by Norman Lloyd, was presented for the first time. Letitia Ide and Meg Mundy supported by Mr. Limon in the dance drama. Another Humphrey premiere was a mock-epic called "The Story of Mankind," based on a cartoon by Carl Rose. It was danced by Mr. Limon and Pauline Koner.

Martha Graham and her dance company opened a two weeks' engagement under the management of S. Hurok at the Ziegfeld Theatre, February 24. The orchestra was under the leadership of Louis Horst and settings were by Isamu Noguchi. The premieres were "Stephan Acrobat," by Erick Hawkins, "Cave of the Heart," with music by Samuel Barber, and "Errand into the Maze," with music composed by Gian-Carlo Menotti for Miss Graham, who did the choreography. The season closed with the first presentation in New York of "Letter to the World," danced by May O'Donnell, Angela Kennedy, Mark Ryder in the leading parts. Other dance dramas presented were "Dark Meadow," "Appalachian Spring," "Every Soul Is a Circus," "Deaths and Entrances," "Punch and Judy," "Primitive Mysteries," "El Penitente," "Heradiade" and "John Brown." The company included in the leading parts Yuriko, Pearl Lang, Erick Hawkins, John Butler, May O'Donnell, Angela Kennedy and Mark Ryder.

Trudi Schoop and company presented "Barbara," a two-act dance comedy with music by Nico Kaufman and choreography by Miss Schoop, at the Ziegfeld Theatre, New York, April 20, 1947.

The African Academy of Arts and Research gave a series of dance dramas in their annual festival at Carnegie Hall, April 25, 1947. The program consisted chiefly of "A Tale of Old Africa," by Asadata Dafora, and Etuka C. Okala-Abuta, staged by Herbert Gallendre and Dafora. Dancers were Dafora, Julie Adams, Abdul Essen, Clementine Blount, Princess Orelia, Bernice Samuels and Randolph Scott.

Nataraj Vashi and Pra-Veena, Hindu dancers, made their debut in New York May 26 at the Belasco Theatre, under the sponsorship of the Maharajah of Baroda and the Indian Society of America.

The Ballet Society, a Lincoln Kirstein experiment with lyric theatre, gave ten ballets in four programs of dance drama, closing its season May 18 at the Ziegfeld Theatre. The ballets were "The

Seasons," with John Cage music, Noguchi decor and choreography by Merce Cunningham, and "Blackface," with music by Carter Harman and decor by Robert Drew. Dancers included Betty Nichols, Talley Beatty and Tanaquil le Clercq in leading roles.

AT THE METROPOLITAN

Under the management of S. Hurok the Original Ballet Russe opened the 1946-47 season at the Metropolitan Opera House September 29 with "Swan Lake," "Paganini," "Pas de Deux" and "Graduation Ball." The world premiere of the ballet version of "Camille," by John Taras, to Schubert music in an arrangement by Vittorio Rieti, was presented with scenery designed by Cecil Beaton and costumes by Karinsky. Antal Dorati was guest conductor. The principal roles were danced by Alicia Markova and Anton Dolin. The first performance in New York of David Lichine's "Cain and Abel," with Wagnerian music, had Kenneth McKenzie as Cain and Oleg Tupine as Abel. April Olrich, Carlota Perera and Anna Miltova assisted. Another premiere was "Yara," based on Brazilian folklore, choreographed by Guicherme de Almeida, with music by Francisco Mignone, settings and costumes by Candido Portinari. Tatiana Stepanova danced the title role, Genevieve Moulin, Oleg Tupine, Nina Stroganova, Vladimir Dokoudovsky and Vania Psota assisted. William McDermott conducted.

"Mute Wife," a revised version of the dance drama by Antonia Cobos, taken from the central idea of Anatole France's "The Man Who Married a Dumb Wife," was revived with the choreographer as the Wife, George Skibine as the Husband and Francisco Moncion as the Doctor. The setting and costumes were by Rico Lebrun.

"Sebastain," which had its first production in New York two years ago, had its Ballet Russe premiere October 13 at the Metropolitan. Gian-Carlo Menotti wrote the story and composed the music. Choreography was by Edward Caton; settings by Oliver Smith and costumes by Milena. The ballet was danced by Rosella Hightower, Francisco Moncion, George Skibine, Yvonne and Marjorie Patterson as the Sisters.

Other dance dramas presented during the season were "Blue Danube," "Pas de Quatre Fantastic Symphony," "Les Sylphides," "Scheherazade," "Aurora's Wedding," "Prince Igor," "Nutcracker pas de deux," "Firebird," "Prodigal Son," "Constantia" and "Griselle." Mois Zlatin and William McDermott were the music directors and Antal Dorati, guest conductor. Alicia Markova, Anton Dolin and Andre Egelevsky headed the roster of dancers, which included Sirena Adjemova, Lubov Tchernicheva, Nina Verchinina, Rosella Hightower, Olga Morosova, Genevieve Moulin, Tatiana Stepanova, Nina Stroganova, Vladimir Dokoudovsky, Roman Jasinsky, Marion Ladré, Kenneth Mackenzie, Vania Psota, George Skibine, Oleg Tupine, Kiril Vassilkovsky, Margaret Banks, Tatiana Bechenova, Natalie Conlon, Marilla Franco, Moussia Larkine, Lara Obidenna, April Olrich, Carlotta Perera, Rozsika Sabo, Marjorie Tallchief, Raul Celada and Alpheus Koon.

The season ended November 17. The Spring season began March 20 with a limited engagement of thirteen performances. A novelty of the season was the revival of Bronislava Nijinska's "Pictures at an Exhibition," to the music of Mussorgsky and decor by Boris Aronson. A premiere was "Pas de Trois," choreographed by Jerome Robbins especially for Markova, Dolin and Eglevsky, from Berlioz's "Damnation of Faust." The season ended March 29, 1947.

BALLET THEATRE

At the Broadway Theatre, September 30, Lucia Chase and Oliver Smith presented Ballet Theatre with Max Goberman and Daniel Saidenburg as music directors, Ben Steinberg associate conductor and Antony Tudor artistic administrator. American premieres were "Les Patineurs" by Frederick Ashton, to music of Meyerbeer and decor by Cecil Beaton, Jerome Robbins' "Facsimile," with score by Leonard Bernstein, setting by Oliver Smith, lighting by Peter Lawrence and costumes by Irene Sharaff, and the Keith Lester version of the Victorian Pas de Quatre. Other dance dramas performed were "Apollo," "Fancy Free," "Gala Performance," "Giselle," "Graziana," "Interplay," "Jardin aux Lilas," "On Stage," "Petrouchka," "Pillar of Fire," "Romeo and Juliet," "Swan Lake," "Les Sylphides," "3 Virgins and a Devil," "Tally-Ho," "Undertow," "Waltz Academy," "Helen of Troy," "Judgment of Paris," "Bluebird," and "Nutcracker pas de deux." In the company were Igor Youskevitch, Nora Kaye, Hugh Laing, Alicia Alonso, John Kriza, Lucia Chase, Michael Kidd, Dimitri Romanoff, Muriel Bentley, Barbara Fallis, Diana Adams, Donald Saddler, Shirley Eckl, Stanley Herbertt, Fernando Alonso, Norma Vance, Melissa Hayden, Erik Kristen, Kenneth Davis, Paula Lloyd, Mary Heater, Doreen Oswald, Fernand Nault, Cynthia Riseley, Anna Cheselka, Eric Braun, Enrica Soma, Barbara Cole,

Frances Rainer, Zachary Solov, Ruth Ann Koesun, Jean Dovell, Shellie Farrell, Barbara Steele, Roy Tobias, Tommy Rall, Richard Beard, Patricia Barker.
The season closed November 9, 1946.

AT THE CITY CENTER

The Ballet Russe de Monte Carlo, directed by Sergei Denham, opened what John Martin of the *New York Times* called "the busiest New York dance season on record" at the New York City Center, September 4, 1946, with George Balanchine's "Ballet Imperial." The first premiere of the season's program was "The Bells" (Sept. 8) by Ruth Page, based on the Edgar Allan Poe poem; music by Darius Milhaud; decor by Isamu Noguchi. Miss Page, Nikita Talin and Frederick danced the principal roles. Other dance dramas were "Rodeo," "Serenade," "Baisee de la Fee," "Blue Bird," "Frankie and Johnny," "Le Beau Danube," "Snow Maiden," "Night Shadow," "Le Bourgeois Gentilhomme," "Pas de Deux," "Concerto Barocco," "Gaite Parisienne," "The Nutcracker," "Scheherazade," "Swan Lake," "Mozartiana," "Les Sylphides," "Raymonda," "Comedia Balletico." The principals were Alexandra Danilova, Frederic Franklin, Nathalie Krassovska, Leon Danielian, Ruthanna Boris, Nicolas Magallanes, Maria Tallchief, Michel Katcharoff, Marie-Jeanne, Nikita Talin, Gertrude Tyven, Herbert Bliss, Pauline Goddard, Robert Lindgren, Yvonne Chouteau, Peter Deign, Vida Brown, Stanley Zompakos and Patricia Wilde.
The Fall season closed September 15.
The Spring season opened February 16, 1947, with "Danses Concertantes." The first premiere was "Virginia Sampler," a ballet in one act by Valerie Bettis, inspired by Early American Primitives; music by Leo Smit, setting and costumes by Charles Elson, music conducted by Ivan Boutnikoff. The dancers were Miss Bettis, Marie-Jeanne, Patricia Wilde, Constance Garfield, Leon Danielian and Frederic Franklin. Alexandra Danilova and Frederic Franklin headed the company.
A second premiere, "Madronos," a ballet in one act by Antonia Cobos, with music by Moszkowski, Yradier and others; orchestrated and conducted by Ivan Boutnikoff; costumes designed by Castillo, was presented March 26 with Antonia Cobos, Frederic Franklin and Leon Danielian in the principal roles. Other dance dramas in the early Spring season not included in the Fall repertory were "Le Spectre de la Rose," "Coppelia," "Romeo and

Juliet," "Interplay," "Facsimile," "Pas de Quatre," "Tally-Ho,"
"Apollo," "Pillar of Fire," "Fancy Free," "Dim Lustre," "3 Vir-
gins and a Devil," "Petrouchka," "On Stage," "Peter and the
Wolf," "Les Patineurs" and "Helen of Troy." The season ended
March 30.

Ballet Theatre, presented by Lucia Chase and Oliver Smith,
began a three-week Spring season at City Center April 28, with
"Les Sylphides." The dancers were headed by Alicia Alonso,
Lucia Chase, Barbara Fallis and Igor Youskevitch. "Romeo and
Juliet" by Antony Tudor was headed by Nora Kaye and Hugh
Laing, and Jerome Robbins' "Interplay" was danced by John
Krisa, Tommy Rall, Muriel Bentley, Fernand Nault, Fernando
Alonso, Melissa Hayden, Paula Lord and Anna Cheselka. Agnes
de Mille's "Tally-Ho" had in its cast Shirley Eckl, Muriel Bentley,
Lucia Chase, John Kriza, Dmitri Romanoff dancing the leading
parts. In Michael Kidd's "On Stage" (music by Norman Dello
Joio), Ruth Ann Koesun made her major role debut May 3, with
Erik Kristen. Antony Tudor's "Dark Elegies" was revived May 8
and danced to Gustav Mahler's "Songs on the Death of Children."
Carlos Alexander sang the Mahler songs. Other dance dramas in
the repertory were practically the same as those presented at the
Broadway Theatre, New York, in September, 1946, and are listed
in the chapter under "Ballet Theatre," where there is also a list
of the dancers belonging to the company. In addition to those
enumerated the following names appear: Maria Masalova, Kenneth Peterson, Eleonore Treiber, Harry Asmus, Mary Burr and
Jack Miller. (Closed May 18, 1947.)

The Jooss Ballet, presented by Charles L. Wagner, after a five-
year absence imposed by the war, opened a three-week season at
City Center, December 3, 1946. The first of four American premieres was Hans Zullig's "Le Bosquet" (The Grove), inspired by
a painting by Fragonard, with music by Rameau in arrangement
by Martin Penny and with decor by Doria Zinkeisen. The two
principal dancers were Noelle de Mosa and Hans Zullig. "Pan-
dora" (December 10), a dance allegory by Kurt Jooss, with score
by Roberto Gerhard and costumes and decor by Hein Heckroth,
was the second premiere with Noelle de Mosa in the title role and
Ulla Soederbaum as Psyche. The third premiere was "Company
at the Manor" by Jooss, with Beethoven's Spring sonata arranged
by the choreographer and decor and costumes by Doris Zinkeisen.
"Sailor's Fancy," by Sigurd Leeder with music by Martin Penny
based on sea chanteys and costumes by Hein Heckroth, was the
fourth premiere. Other ballets were "The Seven Heroes," "The

Green Table" revised by Jooss with a musical score by F. A.
Cohen, "The Big City," with costumes and musical score by Alex-
ander Tansman; "Parvane," "A Ball in Old Vienna," "The
Prodigal Son," and "Ballade." In the company were Hans Zullig,
Noelle de Mosa, Rolf Alexander, Ulla Soederbaum, Sigurd Leeder,
Mario Fedro, Jay Bolton-Carter, Jack Skinner, Sybil Spalinger,
Gert Kzolanaas, Simone Genand, Nigel Burke and Frederick
Bucher.

BALLETS IN MUSICAL DRAMA

Ballets presented during the season in musical drama included
"Yours Is My Heart" directed by Henry Swartz; "Gypsy Lady"
by Aida Broadbent, "Lysistrata" by Felicia Sorel, "Park Avenue"
by Helen Tamaris, "Alice in Wonderland" by Ruth Wilton,
"Burlesque" by Billy Holbrook, "Toplitzky" by Robert Sidney,
"Beggar's Holiday" by Valerie Bettis, "Street Scene" by Anna
Sokolow, "Finian's Rainbow" by Michael Kidd, "Sweethearts" by
Theodore Adolphus, "Brigadoon" by Agnes de Mille, "Chocolate
Soldier" by George Balanchine, "Barefoot Boy with Cheek" by
Richard Barstow, and "Up in Central Park" by Helen Tamaris.

OFF BROADWAY

The East Harlem Players, an experimental group sponsored by East Harlem League for Unity with the assistance of Margaret Webster, Fredric March and Cheryl Crawford, presented "Noah," by André Obey, at the Heckscher Theatre, New York, June 7 and 8, 1946. The cast included seven nationalities—Japanese, Irish, Austrian, West Indian, German, Italian and American.

"Barbizon Tuesdays," a series of dance dramas, started June 11 at the Barbizon-Plaza Concert Hall with a program by Maria Teresa Acuna and Francis Rey. Two Argentinita dance dramas, "Miller's Dance" and "The Cookie Vendor," were presented and new versions by Miss Acuna of "Moorish Fantasy," "Corboda" and "Tango Flamenco." Valerie Bettis and her dance company, June 25, presented four new compositions: "Yerma," based on a play by Garcia Lorca with score by Leo Smit, "Rondel for a Young Girl," "Toccata for Three" and "Five Abstractions in Space." The Psychodramatic Theatre presented plays August 12 and 13, and "Pinafore" was given under the auspices of Martha Atwood Baker August 20 and 21. Jacques Cartier presented his "One-man Theatre" October 31 and November 4, playing "The Noble Czar" and "Proud Heritage." The Playcrafters presented "Love Comes First," by Pascal Biancardo and Jeff Kerrigan, early in December, and The Playwrights Theatre presented "Save the Pieces," by Leon Morse, December 14. Modern Art, headed by war veterans, started a season February 7 with "Sauerkraut Seeds" by Erwin Peter Faith. Modern Stage Co. presented "We Will Dream Again," a comedy by Giuseppe di Gioa, April 11. In the cast were Bonnie Lou Barker, Robert Ottaviano and Jerry Solars. Bunny and David Kerman presented "Show Party for Easter Week" for children.

The Lewisohn Stadium opened its 29th season June 17. Puccini's "La Boheme," June 22 and 23, with Grace Moore, Jan Peerce, Enzo Mascherini, Neure Jorjorian, Lodovico Oliviero, George Cehanovsky and Lorenzo Alvary in the cast. Alexander Smallens conducted the music and Désiré Defrere staged the performances.

493

IN GREENWICH VILLAGE

At the Provincetown Playhouse Dean Goodman started a ten-week Summer stock company with "Mr. and Mrs. Phipps," by John Hamilton, June 25. The play was staged by Paul Benard. Other plays were "Molehills" by Muriel Roy Bolton, "It's Your Move" by Jerry Stevens, "The Man Who Never Lived" by Madison Goff and "Personal Island" by Pauline Williams. "It's Your Move" was staged by Paul Benard and Don Briody; Alan Banks provided the choreography.

The Spur, a repertory group of Yale, Penn State and Smith College theatre enthusiasts, revived "Juno and the Paycock," "Awake and Sing," "Dear Brutus" and "Shadow and Substance," starting July 1 at the Cherry Lane Theatre. Carmen Capalbo and Leo Lieberman managed the series, which closed August 11.

The Light Opera Theatre at the Provincetown Playhouse gave week-end performances of Gilbert and Sullivan operas, beginning October 11. The operas performed included "H.M.S. Pinafore," "Yeomen of the Guard," "The Gondoliers," "Patience," "Pirates of Penzance," "The Mikado," "Iolanthe," and "The Sorcerer." In the company were Ray Arlen, Bess Meisler, Ruth Ladd, John Francis, Sally White, Ralph Arnold and Yolanda Robfogel.

STAGE AND WATER THEATRE

"Mr. Winkle's Holiday," a stage and water musical in two acts, based on the Washington Irving legend by Elliott Murphy, with dialogue by Norman Zeno and music by Herbert Kingsley, was produced by Elliott Murphy and John Moses at the Flushing Meadow Park Amphitheatre, June 22, 1946. The production was staged by Al White, Jr. Water sequences were by Richard Bolton, dialogue directed by Marc Daniels, music by Lehman Engel, orchestra conducted by Kel Murray. The principals included Joseph Scandur, Rolly Picket, Jack Riano, Robert Cosden, Dorothy Johnson, Irene Carroll, June Earing, P. Steven Cornell, Helene Whitney, The Mack Triplets, Ted Cappy, Terry Lasky, Fayne and Foster, Lane and Clare.

ICE SHOWS

The "Ice Follies of 1947" was presented at Madison Square Garden November 19 by Eddie and Ray Shipstad and Oscar

Johnson, and continued through December 1. The cast included the McKellen Bros., Evelyn Chandler, Frick and Frack, Mae Ross, Ruby and Bobby Maxson, Harris Legg, Betty Schalow, Marshall Beard, Les Hamilton and the Ice Folliettes.

Sonja Henie brought her Hollywood Ice Revue to Madison Square Garden January 23, 1947, and played through January 30, returning February 3 and closing February 13. Supporting Miss Henie were Freddie Trenkler, Geary Steffen, Harrison Thompson and Gene Theslof.

ASSOCIATED PLAYWRIGHTS INC.

Associated Playwrights Inc., composed of ten authors who attended the Theatre Guild's playwriting seminar last year, under the direction of Kenneth Rowe, gave a series of experimental productions at the Grand Street Playhouse, by arrangement with the Henry Street Settlement. They began February 26 with "Winners and Losers," a play in three acts by Nicholas Biel. The play was staged and settings designed by Edward R. Mitchell. It had 6 performances. "The Deputy of Paris," by Edmund B. Hennefeld, was given 8 performances from March 21 to March 30; staged by Day Tuttle, setting designed by Edward R. Mitchell. The third and last of the series, "Our Lan'" by Theodore Ward, was staged and designed by Edward R. Mitchell, the music arranged and directed by Joshua Lee. Leading parts were played by Muriel Smith, William Veasy, Valerie Black and Chauncey Reynolds. The play began April 18 and closed April 27.

Two revivals, "Home of the Brave" by Arthur Laurents, directed by Edward R. Mitchell and lighted by Richard Brown, with Mark Forbes playing the lead, and "The Time of Your Life" by William Saroyan were staged by settlement workers.

AMERICAN NEGRO THEATRE

At its theatre in Harlem the American Negro Theatre presented two dramas during the season, both of which received friendly critical attention. The plays were "The Peacemaker" by Kurt Unkelbach and "Tin Top Valley" by Walter Carroll, with incidental music by Hattie King-Reeves. Frederick O'Neal was prominent in both casts. The plays were staged by Marjorie Hildreth; settings by Frank Neal. "Tin Top Valley," with settings by Roger Furman, was staged by Abram Hill. "The Peacemaker" was presented twenty, "Tin Top Valley" forty-three times.

The Snarks

The Snarks, Ltd. gave the first performance of a three-act fantasy, "The Showman's Tale," written by Virginia Hathaway Chapman, for two performances April 11 and 12 in the theatre of the Dalton School. In the cast were Carlton Gauld, Ray Colcord, Frederick Bradlee, Lenny Wayland and others. Randell Henderson, Jr., directed. The settings were designed by Richard Burns and the costumes by Elthea Peale.

Foreign Language Plays

Players from Abroad Inc., a group of American actors and actresses of Vienna origin, presented "Is Geraldine an Angel?" by Hans Yaray at the Barbizon-Plaza Theatre November 2, 1946. The cast included Oscar Karlweis, Lili Darvas, John E. Wengraf, Kitty Maltern, Fred Lorenz-Inger, Elinor Ventura, Michaela Stoloff and Julius Bing.

The Chinese Cultural Theatre, in its first visit to New York since 1938-39, presented "Evening in Cathay" at the Belasco Theatre March 2. The entertainment consisted of ritual dramas and folk plays, produced and directed by Avril Tam. Members of the cast included Sung Yue-tuh, Pauline Wong, Gardenia Chang, Mickey Kwan and Chien-fee Ju. Miss Tam narrated the presentation in English. A second performance was given at the Barbizon-Plaza April 18.

"Babushka," a modern Russian comedy in three acts, was presented in the original Russian by the Russian Circle of Columbia University at the McMillin Theatre March 29, directed by Mme. Tatyana Tarydina.

"Shylock '47," a play in three acts by Peter Frye, based on "The Merchant of Venice," was presented in Hebrew at the Juillard Music Hall May 27, by the Pargod Theatre Co., sponsored by the Hebrew Arts Committee. It moved to the Master Institute Theatre for seven additional performances. The company represented many types of world Jewry: French, Russian, German, Lithuanian, Palestinian, Canadian and American. Arthur Frye directed.

The Yiddish Theatre

The 1946-47 season in New York started October 1, when "Three Gifts" was produced at the Yiddish Art Theatre. This drama-fantasy by I. R. Peretz, dramatized by Melach Ravitch and Maurice Schwartz, with music by Joseph Rumshinsky, was staged by Mr. Schwartz. The dances were by Lillian Shapero, settings and costumes by H. A. Condell.

At the same theatre October 25 "The Song of the Dnieper," a drama in two acts by Zalman Shneour with music by Rumshinsky, was given. It was dramatized and directed by David Licht, with settings by Samuel Leve, and ran for 50 performances. "Wandering Stars," a comedy in two acts by Sholem Aleichem with music by Abraham Goldfaden, was presented by Mr. Schwartz December 13. Settings were by Alexander Cheroff. Principal parts were played by Beatrice Kessler, Ola Shlifko, Frances Adler and Jacob Rechtzeit for 98 performances. Revivals included "The Dybbuk," by S. Ansky in December; "Yoshe Kalb," by I. J. Singer in January. "Dr. Herzl," by H. R. Lentz and G. Nilioff, was produced December 28, closing February 17. Luba Kadison, Isador Casher and Berta Gersten were in the cast.

At the Second Ave. Theatre, Menasha Skulnik started the season in November with "I'm in Love," a musical comedy by William Seigel with lyrics by Isador Lillian and Jacob Jacobs, music by Abe Ellstein. Other plays produced at this theatre during the season were "Leave It to Me," by Isadore Friedman, and "Wedding Night."

At the Clinton Theatre "The Jewish King Lear" was produced October 5, with Vera Rosanko in the title role. Other productions included "A Night of Love," a musical comedy; "First Love," "A Night in Kankaz," an operetta by L. Rosenberg; "Eternal Mother," "Children Without a Home," "From the Two Coony Lemels to Lovka Molodetz," a musical cavalcade; "Gypsy Aza," "Sister Against Sister," and "Bar Kochba."

COLLEGES

The New York premiere of "The Flies," a drama in three acts by Jean-Paul Sartre, author of "No Exit," translated by Stuart Gilbert, was presented April 17 at the President Theatre by the Dramatic Workshop of the New School for Social Research. The production was supervised by Erwin Piscator and directed by Paul Ransom. Settings were by Willis Knighton, lighting by Doris S. Einstein, choreography by Trudl Dubsky-Zipper, music composed and conducted by Harold Holden. Leading parts were played by Dan Matthews, Jack Burkhart, Carol Gustafson, Frances Adler and Alfred Linder. "The Flies" was presented first in Paris during the German occupation, and was done first in America at Vassar College Experimental Theatre, April 5, 1947. The Dramatic Workshop staged several revivals in a "March of Drama" program at the President Theatre during the season.

Hunter College students presented "A Midsummer Night's Dream" at the College Playhouse November 15, 16 and 17, directed by Frederick Cohen. Settings were designed by Nina Laboumsky and the choreography was by Elsa Cohen.

In celebration of the 75th anniversary of organized dramatics on the campus, Fordham University presented Ibsen's "Peer Gynt" February 11 to 16 and April 24, 25 and 26 at the Fordham Theatre. Fritz Hochwaelder's German play, "Crown Colony," translated by Richard Conlin, was presented at the Penthouse Theatre.

The City College Theatre Workshop produced Maxim Gorki's "The Lower Depths" at the Pauline Edwards Theatre, New York, December 6 and 7, and at the same theatre March 29 the college produced William Saroyan's "Sweeney in the Trees."

Columbia College presented two one-act operas, "Stratonice" and "L'Irato ou L'Importo" by Etienne Mehul at the Brander Matthews Theatre February 6. The operas were translated by Phyllis Mead, and sung in English with an all-student cast of fifteen. Willard Rhodes was musical director and John Wolmut staged the productions.

"Speak for Yourself," the ninety-ninth show of the Harvard Hasty Pudding Club, was presented in the ballroom of the Waldorf-Astoria April 4.

The Columbia University Players produced "Dead to Rights," a musical comedy in two acts by Edward N. Costikyan, Ernest Kinoy and Andrew J. Lazarus, with music by Richard Hyman, April 25 at the McMillin Theatre. The opera was designed by Joseph H. O'Reilly, directed by Preston K. Munter and choreographed by Tracy Morrison.

"The Mother of Us All," an opera in three acts, with text by Gertrude Stein and music by Virgil Thompson, received its premiere May 7 at Brander Matthews Hall. Columbia Theatre Associates produced the opera, in co-operation with the music department of the University. It was staged by John Taras, music directed by Otto Luening, scenario by Maurice Grosser, sets and costumes by Paul Du Pont. In the cast were Dorothy Dow, Robert Grooters, William Horne, Robert Sprecher, Alice Howland and Carolyn Blakeslee.

SOLO SHOWS

Bella Reine, a European choreographic actress, gave a program of her original mimes in Times Hall, with Jane Sears as assistant pianist, February 14. Her program included "Salome," with music by Charles Richard; "Manhattan Side Street," with music by Humbert Traversi; "The Land of My Heart," with music by Joseph Strimer, and "The Fate of My People," with music by Jacques de Menasce.

Raymond Duncan presented "You with Me," a true life drama, at the Shubert Theatre, Febuary 23.

Jeanne Welty made her New York debut at the National Theatre March 9, 1947, in "The Mystery of Theodosia Burr," a monodrama of her own authorship. The performance was sponsored by the Theatre Chapter of the American Veterans' Committee.

CHILDREN'S THEATRE

"Aucassin and Nicolette," as translated by Andrew Land, was presented at the Princess Theatre by Gertrude Macy and the King-Coit Children's Theatre, April 27. The production was presented five times.

STATISTICAL SUMMARY

Plays	Number Performances	
Anna Lucasta	957	(Closed November 30, 1946)
Are You with It?	267	(Closed June 29, 1946)
Around the World	75	(Closed August 3, 1946)
Billion Dollar Baby	220	(Closed June 29, 1946)
Carousel	890	(Closed May 24, 1947)
Dear Ruth	683	(Closed July 27, 1946)
Deep Are the Roots	477	(Closed November 16, 1946)
Dream Girl	348	(Closed December 14, 1946)
I Remember Mama	714	(Closed June 29, 1945)
Lute Song	142	(Closed June 8, 1946)
Old Vic Company	48	(Closed June 15, 1946)
Henry IV, Part 1	17	
Oedipus and the Critic	15	
Henry IV, Part 2	8	
Uncle Vanya	8	
O Mistress Mine	452	(Closed May 31, 1947)
On Whitman Avenue	150	(Closed September 14, 1946)
Show Boat	418	(Closed January 4, 1947)
Song of Norway	860	(Closed September 7, 1946)
St. Louis Woman	113	(Closed July 6, 1946)
Swan Song	158	(Closed September 28, 1946)
The Glass Menagerie	561	(Closed August 3, 1946)
The Magnificent Yankee	160	(Closed June 8, 1946)
The Red Mill	531	(Closed January 18, 1947)
This Too Shall Pass	63	(Closed June 22, 1946)
Three to Make Ready	327	(Closed December 14, 1946)

LONG RUNS ON BROADWAY

To June 1, 1947

(Plays marked with asterisk were still playing June 1, 1947)

Plays	Number Performances	Plays	Number Performances
Tobacco Road	3,182	Seventh Heaven	704
*Life with Father	3,171	Peg o' My Heart	692
Abie's Irish Rose	2,327	The Children's Hour	691
*Oklahoma!	1,790	Dead End	687
Arsenic and Old Lace	1,444	Dear Ruth	683
Hellzapoppin	1,404	East Is West	680
The Voice of the Turtle	1,310	Chauve Souris	673
Angel Street	1,295	The Doughgirls	671
Lightnin'	1,291	Irene	670
Pins and Needles	1,108	Boy Meets Girl	669
*Harvey	1,094	Blithe Spirit	657
Anna Lucasta	957	The Women	657
Kiss and Tell	956	A Trip to Chinatown	657
Carousel	890	Bloomer Girl	654
Hats Off to Ice	889	*State of the Union	649
Follow the Girls	882	Rain	648
The Bat	867	Janie	642
My Sister Eileen	865	The Green Pastures	640
White Cargo	864	Is Zat So	618
Song of Norway	860	Separate Rooms	613
You Can't Take It with		Star and Garter	609
You	837	Student Prince	608
Three Men on a Horse	835	Broadway	603
Stars on Ice	830	Adonis	603
The Ladder	789	Street Scene	601
The First Year	760	Kiki	600
Sons o' Fun	742	Blossom Time	592
The Man Who Came to		The Two Mrs. Carrolls	585
Dinner	739	Brother Rat	577
Claudia	722	Show Boat	572
I Remember Mama	714	The Show-Off	571
Junior Miss	710	Sally	570

501

Plays	*Number Performances*	*Plays*	*Number Performances*
One Touch of Venus ..	567	Sunny	517
*Born Yesterday	560	Victoria Regina	517
Rose Marie..........	557	The Vagabond King ..	511
Strictly Dishonorable..	557	The New Moon	509
Ziegfeld Follies	553	Shuffle Along	504
Good News	551	Up in Central Park ..	504
Let's Face It	547	Carmen Jones........	503
Within the Law	541	Personal Appearance ..	501
The Music Master	540	Panama Hattie.......	501
What a Life	538	Bird in Hand	500
The Red Mill	531	Sailor, Beware!	500
The Boomerang	522	Room Service........	500
Rosalinda	521	Tomorrow the World..	500
Blackbirds	**518**		

(Stop Press Ed. Note: The night of June 14, 1947, "Life with Father" was given its 3,183d performance, thereby breaking the American theatre Long Run record previously held by "Tobacco Road." Mr. and Mrs. Howard Lindsay (Dorothy Stickney) resumed their original roles of Father and Vinnie Day, and there was a Life with Father party following the last curtain.)

NEW YORK DRAMA CRITICS' CIRCLE AWARD

The New York drama critics who are members of the Critics' Circle, accused last year of a kind of snobbish churlishness when four of its personnel refused to make a selection of the best play of American authorship produced during the season, adopted a voting plan this year that had the effect of forcing a selection.

The twenty-five voting reviewers were asked first to indicate anonymously their individual preferences. This resulted in a vote of 12 for Arthur Miller's "All My Sons," 7 for Eugene O'Neill's "The Iceman Cometh," 4 for Lillian Hellman's "Another Part of the Forest," 1 for Maxwell Anderson's "Joan of Lorraine" and 1 for the Lerner-Loewe musical fantasy, "Brigadoon." Proxy votes were cast for two ailing members.

The second ballot was signed, the proxies were discontinued and the result found "All My Sons" leading with 12, "The Iceman" following with 6, "Another Part of the Forest" 4, "Joan" 2 and "Brigadoon" 1.

On the third, or preferential ballot, each voter was obliged to indicate his preferences in rightful order. First choice would count 5, second 4, third 3, fourth 2, fifth 1. On this ballot, the count gave "All My Sons" 86, "The Iceman" 80, "Forest" 72, "Joan" 55, and "Brigadoon" 53.

Jean-Paul Sartre's "No Exit" was given a citation as the best foreign play of the year, and "Brigadoon" was named the best musical play.

Previous Circle awards have been—

1935-36—Winterset, by Maxwell Anderson.
1936-37—High Tor, by Maxwell Anderson
1937-38—Of Mice and Men, by John Steinbeck
1938-39—No award.
1939-40—The Time of Your Life, by William Saroyan
1940-41—Watch on the Rhine, by Lillian Hellman
1941-42—No award.
1942-43—The Patriots, by Sidney Kingsley
1943-44—No award.
1944-45—The Glass Menagerie, by Tennessee Williams
1945-46—No award.
1946-47—All My Sons, by Arthur Miller

PULITZER PRIZE WINNERS

"For the original American play performed in New York which shall best represent the educational value and power of the stage in raising the standard of good morals, good taste and good manners."—The Will of Joseph Pulitzer, dated April 16, 1904.

In 1929 the advisory board, which, according to the terms of the will, "shall have the power in its discretion to suspend or to change any subject or subjects . . . if in the judgment of the board such suspension, changes or substitutions shall be conducive to the public good," decided to eliminate from the above paragraph relating to the prize-winning play the words "in raising the standard of good morals, good taste and good manners."

The present terms of the Pulitzer award are "for an original American play performed in New York, which shall represent in marked fashion the educational value and power of the stage, preferably dealing with American life."

One senses, it may be without reason, a reluctance on the part of the Pulitzer Prize Committee to endorse the selection of the New York Drama Critics' Circle when it comes to voting for the best play of American authorship produced in New York during the season. Last year, after the Circle had fumbled its opportunity and voted no award, because four of its members refused to vote for the majority selection, the Pulitzer committee was quick to name "State of the Union." This year, it may be because the Circle was forced by a new voting method to make a selection, naming "All My Sons," the Pulitzers retired to the rear of their tent and announced a no-award decision.

The Critics' Circle meets early in April. The Pulitzers the first week in May. If interested playgoers could force them to agree on a date mutually satisfactory to both it should serve to stimulate the competition and add to the seasonal excitement.

Pulitzer Prize selections to date have been—

1917-18—Why Marry? by Jesse Lynch Williams
1918-19—No award.
1919-20—Beyond the Horizon, by Eugene O'Neill
1920-21—Miss Lulu Bett, by Zona Gale
1921-22—Anna Christie, by Eugene O'Neill

1922-23—Icebound, by Owen Davis
1923-24—Hell-bent fer Heaven, by Hatcher Hughes
1924-25—They Knew What They Wanted, by Sidney Howard
1925-26—Craig's Wife, by George Kelly
1926-27—In Abraham's Bosom, by Paul Green
1927-28—Strange Interlude, by Eugene O'Neill
1928-29—Street Scene, by Elmer Rice
1929-30—The Green Pastures, by Marc Connelly
1930-31—Alison's House, by Susan Glaspell
1931-32—Of Thee I Sing, by George S. Kaufman, Morrie
          Ryskind, Ira and George Gershwin
1932-33—Both Your Houses, by Maxwell Anderson
1933-34—Men in White, by Sidney Kingsley
1934-35—The Old Maid, by Zoe Akins
1935-36—Idiot's Delight, by Robert E. Sherwood
1936-37—You Can't Take It with You, by Moss Hart and
          George S. Kaufman
1937-38—Our Town, by Thornton Wilder
1938-39—Abe Lincoln in Illinois, by Robert E. Sherwood
1939-40—The Time of Your Life, by William Saroyan
1940-41—There Shall Be No Night, by Robert E. Sherwood
1941-42—No award.
1942-43—The Skin of Our Teeth, by Thornton Wilder
1943-44—No award.
1944-45—Harvey, by Mary Coyle Chase
1945-46—State of the Union, by Howard Lindsay and Russel
          Crouse
1946-47—No award.

PREVIOUS VOLUMES OF BEST PLAYS

Plays chosen to represent the theatre seasons from 1899 to 1946 are as follows:

1899-1909

"Barbara Frietchie," by Clyde Fitch. Published by Life Publishing Company, New York.

"The Climbers," by Clyde Fitch. Published by the Macmillan Co., New York.

"If I Were King," by Justin Huntly McCarthy. Published by Samuel French, New York and London.

"The Darling of the Gods," by David Belasco. Published by Little, Brown & Co., Boston, Mass.

"The County Chairman," by George Ade. Published by Samuel French, New York and London.

"Leah Kleschna," by C. M. S. McLellan. Published by Samuel French, New York.

"The Squaw Man," by Edwin Milton Royle.

"The Great Divide," by William Vaughn Moody. Published by Samuel French, New York, London and Canada.

"The Witching Hour," by Augustus Thomas. Published by Samuel French, New York and London.

"The Man from Home," by Booth Tarkington and Harry Leon Wilson. Published by Samuel French, New York, London and Canada.

1909-1919

"The Easiest Way," by Eugene Walter. Published by G. W. Dillingham, New York; Houghton Mifflin Co., Boston.

"Mrs. Bumpstead-Leigh," by Harry James Smith. Published by Samuel French, New York.

"Disraeli," by Louis N. Parker. Published by Dodd, Mead and Co., New York.

"Romance," by Edward Sheldon. Published by the Macmillan Co., New York.

"Seven Keys to Baldpate," by George M. Cohan. Published by Bobbs-Merrill Co., Indianapolis, as a novel by Earl Derr Biggers; as a play by Samuel French, New York.

"On Trial," by Elmer Reizenstein. Published by Samuel French, New York.

"The Unchastened Woman," by Louis Kaufman Anspacher. Published by Harcourt, Brace and Howe, Inc., New York.

"Good Gracious Annabelle," by Clare Kummer. Published by Samuel French, New York.

"Why Marry?" by Jesse Lynch Williams. Published by Charles Scribner's Sons, New York.

"John Ferguson," by St. John Ervine. Published by the Macmillan Co., New York.

1919-1920

"Abraham Lincoln," by John Drinkwater. Published by Houghton Mifflin Co., Boston.

"Clarence," by Booth Tarkington. Published by Samuel French, New York.

"Beyond the Horizon," by Eugene G. O'Neill. Published by Boni & Liveright, Inc., New York.

"Déclassée," by Zoe Akins. Published by Liveright, Inc., New York.

"The Famous Mrs. Fair," by James Forbes. Published by Samuel French, New York.

"The Jest," by Sem Benelli. (American adaptation by Edward Sheldon.)

"Jane Clegg," by St. John Ervine. Published by Henry Holt & Co., New York.

"Mamma's Affair," by Rachel Barton Butler. Published by Samuel French, New York.

"Wedding Bells," by Salisbury Field. Published by Samuel French, New York.

"Adam and Eva," by George Middleton and Guy Bolton. Published by Samuel French, New York.

1920-1921

"Deburau," adapted from the French of Sacha Guitry by H. Granville Barker. Published by G. P. Putnam's Sons, New York.

"The First Year," by Frank Craven. Published by Samuel French, New York.

"Enter Madame," by Gilda Varesi and Dolly Byrne. Published by G. P. Putnam's Sons, New York.

"The Green Goddess," by William Archer. Published by Alfred A. Knopf, New York.

"Liliom," by Ferenc Molnar. Published by Boni & Liveright, New York.

"Mary Rose," by James M. Barrie. Published by Charles Scribner's Sons, New York.

"Nice People," by Rachel Crothers. Published by Charles Scribner's Sons, New York.

"The Bad Man," by Porter Emerson Browne. Published by G. P. Putnam's Sons, New York.

"The Emperor Jones," by Eugene G. O'Neill. Published by Boni & Liveright, New York.

"The Skin Game," by John Galsworthy. Published by Charles Scribner's Sons, New York.

1921-1922

"Anna Christie," by Eugene G. O'Neill. Published by Boni & Liveright, New York.

"A Bill of Divorcement," by Clemence Dane. Published by the Macmillan Company, New York.

"Dulcy," by George S. Kaufman and Marc Connelly. Published by G. P. Putnam's Sons, New York.

"He Who Gets Slapped," adapted from the Russian of Leonid Andreyev by Gregory Zilboorg. Published by Brentano's, New York.

"Six Cylinder Love," by William Anthony McGuire.

"The Hero," by Gilbert Emery.

"The Dover Road," by Alan Alexander Milne. Published by Samuel French, New York.

"Ambush," by Arthur Richman.

"The Circle," by William Somerset Maugham.

"The Nest," by Paul Geraldy and Grace George.

1922-1923

"Rain," by John Colton and Clemence Randolph. Published by Liveright, Inc., New York.

"Loyalties," by John Galsworthy. Published by Charles Scribner's Sons, New York.

"Icebound," by Owen Davis. Published by Little, Brown & Company, Boston.

"You and I," by Philip Barry. Published by Brentano's, New York.

"The Fool," by Channing Pollock. Published by Brentano's, New York.

"Merton of the Movies," by George Kaufman and Marc Connelly, based on the novel of the same name by Harry Leon Wilson.

"Why Not?" by Jesse Lynch Williams. Published by Walter H. Baker Co., Boston.

"The Old Soak," by Don Marquis. Published by Doubleday, Page & Company, New York.

"R.U.R.," by Karel Capek. Translated by Paul Selver. Published by Doubleday, Page & Company.

"Mary the 3d," by Rachel Crothers. Published by Brentano's, New York.

1923-1924

"The Swan," translated from the Hungarian of Ferenc Molnar by Melville Baker. Published by Boni & Liveright, New York.

"Outward Bound," by Sutton Vane. Published by Boni & Liveright, New York.

"The Show-Off," by George Kelly. Published by Little, Brown & Company, Boston.

"The Changelings," by Lee Wilson Dodd. Published by E. P. Dutton & Company, New York.

"Chicken Feed," by Guy Bolton. Published by Samuel French, New York and London.

"Sun-Up," by Lula Vollmer. Published by Brentano's, New York.

"Beggar on Horseback," by George Kaufman and Marc Connelly. Published by Boni & Liveright, New York.

"Tarnish," by Gilbert Emery. Published by Brentano's, New York.

"The Goose Hangs High," by Lewis Beach. Published by Little, Brown & Company, Boston.

"Hell-bent fer Heaven," by Hatcher Hughes. Published by Harper Bros., New York.

1924-1925

"What Price Glory?" by Laurence Stallings and Maxwell Anderson. Published by Harcourt, Brace & Co., New York.

"They Knew What They Wanted," by Sidney Howard. Published by Doubleday, Page & Company, New York.

"Desire Under the Elms," by Eugene G. O'Neill. Published by Boni & Liveright, New York.

"The Firebrand," by Edwin Justus Mayer. Published by Boni & Liveright, New York.
"Dancing Mothers," by Edgar Selwyn and Edmund Goulding.
"Mrs. Partridge Presents," by Mary Kennedy and Ruth Warren. Published by Samuel French, New York.
"The Fall Guy," by James Gleason and George Abbott. Published by Samuel French, New York.
"The Youngest," by Philip Barry. Published by Samuel French, New York.
"Minick," by Edna Ferber and George S. Kaufman. Published by Doubleday, Page & Company, New York.
"Wild Birds," by Dan Totheroh. Published by Doubleday, Page & Company, New York.

1925-1926

"Craig's Wife," by George Kelly. Published by Little, Brown & Company, Boston.
"The Great God Brown," by Eugene G. O'Neill. Published by Boni & Liveright, New York.
"The Green Hat," by Michael Arlen.
"The Dybbuk," by S. Ansky, Henry G. Alsberg-Winifred Katzin translation. Published by Boni & Liveright, New York.
"The Enemy," by Channing Pollock. Published by Brentano's, New York.
"The Last of Mrs. Cheyney," by Frederick Lonsdale. Published by Samuel French, New York.
"Bride of the Lamb," by William Hurlbut. Published by Boni & Liveright, New York.
"The Wisdom Tooth," by Marc Connelly. Published by George H. Doran & Company, New York.
"The Butter and Egg Man," by George Kaufman. Published by Boni & Liveright, New York.
"Young Woodley," by John Van Druten. Published by Simon and Schuster, New York.

1926-1927

"Broadway," by Philip Dunning and George Abbott. Published by George H. Doran Company, New York.
"Saturday's Children," by Maxwell Anderson. Published by Longmans, Green & Company, New York.
"Chicago," by Maurine Watkins. Published by Alfred A. Knopf, Inc., New York.

"The Constant Wife," by William Somerset Maugham. Published by George H. Doran Company, New York.

"The Play's the Thing," by Ferenc Molnar and P. G. Wodehouse. Published by Brentano's, New York.

"The Road to Rome," by Robert Emmet Sherwood. Published by Charles Scribner's Sons, New York.

"The Silver Cord," by Sidney Howard. Published by Charles Scribner's Sons, New York.

"The Cradle Song," translated from the Spanish of G. Martinez Sierra by John Garrett Underhill. Published by E. P. Dutton & Company, New York.

"Daisy Mayme," by George Kelly. Published by Little, Brown & Company, Boston.

"In Abraham's Bosom," by Paul Green. Published by Robert M. McBride & Company, New York.

1927-1928

"Strange Interlude," by Eugene G. O'Neill. Published by Boni & Liveright, New York.

"The Royal Family," by Edna Ferber and George Kaufman. Published by Doubleday, Doran & Company, New York.

"Burlesque," by George Manker Watters and Arthur Hopkins. Published by Doubleday, Doran & Company, New York.

"Coquette," by George Abbott and Ann Bridgers. Published by Longmans, Green & Company, New York, London, Toronto.

"Behold the Bridegroom," by George Kelly. Published by Little, Brown & Company, Boston.

"Porgy," by DuBose Heyward. Published by Doubleday, Doran & Company, New York.

"Paris Bound," by Philip Barry. Published by Samuel French, New York.

"Escape," by John Galsworthy. Published by Charles Scribner's Sons, New York.

"The Racket," by Bartlett Cormack. Published by Samuel French, New York.

"The Plough and the Stars," by Sean O'Casey. Published by the Macmillan Company, New York.

1928-1929

"Street Scene," by Elmer Rice. Published by Samuel French, New York.

"Journey's End," by R. C. Sherriff. Published by Brentano's, New York.

"Wings Over Europe," by Robert Nichols and Maurice Browne. Published by Covici-Friede, New York.

"Holiday," by Philip Barry. Published by Samuel French, New York.

"The Front Page," by Ben Hecht and Charles MacArthur. Published by Covici-Friede, New York.

"Let Us Be Gay," by Rachel Crothers. Published by Samuel French, New York.

"Machinal," by Sophie Treadwell.

"Little Accident," by Floyd Dell and Thomas Mitchell.

"Gypsy," by Maxwell Anderson.

"The Kingdom of God," by G. Martinez Sierra; English version by Helen and Harley Granville-Barker. Published by E. P. Dutton & Company, New York.

1929-1930

"The Green Pastures," by Marc Connelly (adapted from "Ol' Man Adam and His Chillun," by Roark Bradford). Published by Farrar & Rinehart, Inc., New York.

"The Criminal Code," by Martin Flavin. Published by Horace Liveright, New York.

"Berkeley Square," by John Balderston. Published by the Macmillan Company, New York.

"Strictly Dishonorable," by Preston Sturges. Published by Horace Liveright, New York.

"The First Mrs. Fraser," by St. John Ervine. Published by the Macmillan Company, New York.

"The Last Mile," by John Wexley. Published by Samuel French, New York.

"June Moon," by Ring W. Lardner and George S. Kaufman. Published by Charles Scribner's Sons, New York.

"Michael and Mary," by A. A. Milne. Published by Chatto & Windus, London.

"Death Takes a Holiday," by Walter Ferris (adapted from the Italian of Alberto Casella). Published by Samuel French, New York.

"Rebound," by Donald Ogden Stewart. Published by Samuel French, New York.

1930-1931

"Elizabeth the Queen," by Maxwell Anderson. Published by Longmans, Green & Co., New York.

"Tomorrow and Tomorrow," by Philip Barry. Published by Samuel French, New York.

"Once in a Lifetime," by George S. Kaufman and Moss Hart. Published by Farrar and Rinehart, New York.

"Green Grow the Lilacs," by Lynn Riggs. Published by Samuel French, New York and London.

"As Husbands Go," by Rachel Crothers. Published by Samuel French, New York.

"Alison's House," by Susan Glaspell. Published by Samuel French, New York.

"Five-Star Final," by Louis Weitzenkorn. Published by Samuel French, New York.

"Overture," by William Bolitho. Published by Simon & Schuster, New York.

"The Barretts of Wimpole Street," by Rudolf Besier. Published by Little, Brown & Company, Boston.

"Grand Hotel," adapted from the German of Vicki Baum by W. A. Drake.

1931-1932

"Of Thee I Sing," by George S. Kaufman and Morrie Ryskind; music and lyrics by George and Ira Gershwin. Published by Alfred Knopf, New York.

"Mourning Becomes Electra," by Eugene G. O'Neill. Published by Horace Liveright, Inc., New York.

"Reunion in Vienna," by Robert Emmet Sherwood. Published by Charles Scribner's Sons, New York.

"The House of Connelly," by Paul Green. Published by Samuel French, New York.

"The Animal Kingdom," by Philip Barry. Published by Samuel French, New York.

"The Left Bank," by Elmer Rice. Published by Samuel French, New York.

"Another Language," by Rose Franken. Published by Samuel French, New York.

"Brief Moment," by S. N. Behrman. Published by Farrar & Rinehart, New York.

"The Devil Passes," by Benn W. Levy. Published by Martin Secker, London.

"Cynara," by H. M. Harwood and R. F. Gore-Browne. Published by Samuel French, New York.

1932-1933

"Both Your Houses," by Maxwell Anderson. Published by Samuel French, New York.

"Dinner at Eight," by George S. Kaufman and Edna Ferber. Published by Doubleday, Doran & Co., Inc., Garden City, New York.

"When Ladies Meet," by Rachel Crothers. Published by Samuel French, New York.

"Design for Living," by Noel Coward. Published by Doubleday, Doran & Co., Inc., Garden City, New York.

"Biography," by S. N. Behrman. Published by Farrar & Rinehart, Inc., New York.

"Alien Corn," by Sidney Howard. Published by Charles Scribner's Sons, New York.

"The Late Christopher Bean," adapted from the French of René Fauchois by Sidney Howard. Published by Samuel French, New York.

"We, the People," by Elmer Rice. Published by Coward-McCann, Inc., New York.

"Pigeons and People," by George M. Cohan.

"One Sunday Afternoon," by James Hagan. Published by Samuel French, New York.

1933-1934

"Mary of Scotland," by Maxwell Anderson. Published by Doubleday, Doran & Co., Inc., Garden City, N. Y.

"Men in White," by Sidney Kingsley. Published by Covici, Friede, Inc., New York.

"Dodsworth," by Sinclair Lewis and Sidney Howard. Published by Harcourt, Brace & Co., New York.

"Ah, Wilderness," by Eugene O'Neill. Published by Random House, New York.

"They Shall Not Die," by John Wexley. Published by Alfred A. Knopf, New York.

"Her Master's Voice," by Clare Kummer. Published by Samuel French, New York.

"No More Ladies," by A. E. Thomas.

"Wednesday's Child," by Leopold Atlas. Published by Samuel French, New York.

"The Shining Hour," by Keith Winter. Published by Double-day, Doran & Co., Inc., Garden City, New York.

"The Green Bay Tree," by Mordaunt Shairp. Published by Baker International Play Bureau, Boston, Mass.

1934-1935

"The Children's Hour," by Lillian Hellman. Published by Alfred Knopf, New York.

"Valley Forge," by Maxwell Anderson. Published by Anderson House, Washington, D. C. Distributed by Dodd, Mead & Co., New York.

"The Petrified Forest," by Robert Sherwood. Published by Charles Scribner's Sons, New York.

"The Old Maid," by Zoe Akins. Published by D. Appleton-Century Co., New York.

"Accent on Youth," by Samson Raphaelson. Published by Samuel French, New York.

"Merrily We Roll Along," by George S. Kaufman and Moss Hart. Published by Random House, New York.

"Awake and Sing," by Clifford Odets. Published by Random House, New York.

"The Farmer Takes a Wife," by Frank B. Elser and Marc Connelly.

"Lost Horizons," by John Hayden.

"The Distaff Side," by John Van Druten. Published by Alfred Knopf, New York.

1935-1936

"Winterset," by Maxwell Anderson. Published by Anderson House, Washington, D. C.

"Idiot's Delight," by Robert Emmet Sherwood. Published by Charles Scribner's Sons, New York.

"End of Summer," by S. N. Behrman. Published by Random House, New York.

"First Lady," by Katharine Dayton and George S. Kaufman. Published by Random House, New York.

"Victoria Regina," by Laurence Housman. Published by Samuel French, Inc., New York and London.

"Boy Meets Girl," by Bella and Samuel Spewack. Published by Random House, New York.

"Dead End," by Sidney Kingsley. Published by Random House, New York.

"Call It a Day," by Dodie Smith. Published by Samuel French, Inc., New York and London.

"Ethan Frome," by Owen Davis and Donald Davis. Published by Charles Scribner's Sons, New York.

"Pride and Prejudice," by Helen Jerome. Published by Doubleday, Doran & Co., Garden City, New York.

1936-1937

"High Tor," by Maxwell Anderson. Published by Anderson House, Washington, D. C.

"You Can't Take It with You," by Moss Hart and George S. Kaufman. Published by Farrar & Rinehart, Inc., New York.

"Johnny Johnson," by Paul Green. Published by Samuel French, Inc., New York.

"Daughters of Atreus," by Robert Turney. Published by Alfred A. Knopf, New York.

"Stage Door," by Edna Ferber and George S. Kaufman. Published by Doubleday, Doran & Co., Garden City, New York.

"The Women," by Clare Boothe. Published by Random House, Inc., New York.

"St. Helena," by R. C. Sherriff and Jeanne de Casalis. Published by Samuel French, Inc., New York and London.

"Yes, My Darling Daughter," by Mark Reed. Published by Samuel French, Inc., New York.

"Excursion," by Victor Wolfson. Published by Random House, New York.

"Tovarich," by Jacques Deval and Robert E. Sherwood. Published by Random House, New York.

1937-1938

"Of Mice and Men," by John Steinbeck. Published by Covici-Friede, New York.

"Our Town," by Thornton Wilder. Published by Coward-McCann, Inc., New York.

"Shadow and Substance," by Paul Vincent Carroll. Published by Random House, Inc., New York.

"On Borrowed Time," by Paul Osborn. Published by Alfred A. Knopf, New York.

"The Star-Wagon," by Maxwell Anderson. Published by Anderson House, Washington, D. C. Distributed by Dodd, Mead & Co., New York.

"Susan and God," by Rachel Crothers. Published by Random House, Inc., New York.

"Prologue to Glory," by E. P. Conkle. Published by Random House, Inc., New York.

"Amphitryon 38," by S. N. Behrman. Published by Random House, Inc., New York.

"Golden Boy," by Clifford Odets. Published by Random House, Inc., New York.

"What a Life," by Clifford Goldsmith. Published by Dramatists' Play Service, Inc., New York.

1938-1939

"Abe Lincoln in Illinois," by Robert E. Sherwood. Published by Charles Scribner's Sons, New York and Charles Scribner's Sons, Ltd., London.

"The Little Foxes," by Lillian Hellman. Published by Random House, Inc., New York.

"Rocket to the Moon," by Clifford Odets. Published by Random House, Inc., New York.

"The American Way," by George S. Kaufman and Moss Hart. Published by Random House, Inc., New York.

"No Time for Comedy," by S. N. Behrman. Published by Random House, Inc., New York.

"The Philadelphia Story," by Philip Barry. Published by Coward-McCann, Inc., New York.

"The White Steed," by Paul Vincent Carroll. Published by Random House, Inc., New York.

"Here Come the Clowns," by Philip Barry. Published by Coward-McCann, Inc., New York.

"Family Portrait," by Lenore Coffee and William Joyce Cowen. Published by Random House, Inc., New York.

"Kiss the Boys Good-bye," by Clare Boothe. Published by Random House, Inc., New York.

1939-1940

"There Shall Be No Night," by Robert E. Sherwood. Published by Charles Scribner's Sons, New York.

"Key Largo," by Maxwell Anderson. Published by Anderson House, Washington, D. C.

"The World We Make," by Sidney Kingsley.

"Life with Father," by Howard Lindsay and Russel Crouse. Published by Alfred A. Knopf, New York.

"The Man Who Came to Dinner," by George S. Kaufman and Moss Hart. Published by Random House, Inc., New York.

"The Male Animal," by James Thurber and Elliott Nugent. Published by Random House, Inc., New York, and MacMillan Co., Canada.

"The Time of Your Life," by William Saroyan. Published by Harcourt, Brace and Company, Inc., New York.

"Skylark," by Samson Raphaelson. Published by Random House, Inc., New York.

"Margin for Error," by Clare Boothe. Published by Random House, Inc., New York.

"Morning's at Seven," by Paul Osborn. Published by Samuel French, New York.

1940-1941

"Native Son," by Paul Green and Richard Wright. Published by Harper & Bros., New York.

"Watch on the Rhine," by Lillian Hellman. Published by Random House, Inc., New York.

"The Corn Is Green," by Emlyn Williams. Published by Random House, Inc., New York.

"Lady in the Dark," by Moss Hart. Published by Random House, Inc., New York.

"Arsenic and Old Lace," by Joseph Kesselring. Published by Random House, Inc., New York.

"My Sister Eileen," by Joseph Fields and Jerome Chodorov. Published by Random House, Inc., New York.

"Flight to the West," by Elmer Rice. Published by Coward, McCann, Inc., New York.

"Claudia," by Rose Franken Meloney. Published by Farrar & Rinehart, Inc., New York and Toronto.

"Mr. and Mrs. North," by Owen Davis. Published by Samuel French, New York.

"George Washington Slept Here," by George S. Kaufman and Moss Hart. Published by Random House, Inc., New York.

1941-1942

"In Time to Come," by Howard Koch. Published by Dramatists' Play Service, Inc., New York.

"The Moon Is Down," by John Steinbeck. Published by The Viking Press, New York.

"Blithe Spirit," by Noel Coward. Published by Doubleday, Doran & Co., Garden City, New York.

"Junior Miss," by Jerome Chodorov and Joseph Fields. Published by Random House, Inc., New York.

"Candle in the Wind," by Maxwell Anderson. Published by Anderson House, Washington, D. C.

"Letters to Lucerne," by Fritz Rotter and Allen Vincent. Published by Samuel French, Inc., New York.

"Jason," by Samson Raphaelson. Published by Random House, Inc., New York.

"Angel Street," by Patrick Hamilton. Published by Constable & Co., Ltd., London, under the title "Gaslight."

"Uncle Harry," by Thomas Job. Published by Samuel French, Inc., New York.

"Hope for a Harvest," by Sophie Treadwell. Published by Samuel French, Inc., New York.

1942-1943

"The Patriots," by Sidney Kingsley. Published by Random House, Inc., New York.

"The Eve of St. Mark," by Maxwell Anderson. Published by Anderson House, Washington, D. C.

"The Skin of Our Teeth," by Thornton Wilder. Published by Harper & Brothers, New York and London.

"Winter Soldiers," by Dan James.

"Tomorrow the World," by James Gow and Arnaud d'Usseau. Published by Charles Scribner's Sons, New York.

"Harriet," by Florence Ryerson and Colin Clements. Published by Charles Scribner's Sons, New York.

"The Doughgirls," by Joseph Fields. Published by Random House, Inc., New York.

"The Damask Cheek," by John Van Druten and Lloyd Morris. Published by Random House, Inc., New York.

"Kiss and Tell," by F. Hugh Herbert. Published by Coward-McCann, Inc., New York.

"Oklahoma!", by Oscar Hammerstein 2nd and Richard Rodgers. Published by Random House, Inc., New York.

1943-1944

"Winged Victory," by Moss Hart. Published by Random House, Inc., New York.

"The Searching Wind," by Lillian Hellman. Published by Viking Press, Inc., New York.

"The Voice of the Turtle," by John Van Druten. Published by Random House, Inc., New York.

"Decision," by Edward Chodorov.

"Over 21," by Ruth Gordon. Published by Random House, Inc., New York.

"Outrageous Fortune," by Rose Franken. Published by Samuel French, New York.

"Jacobowsky and the Colonel," by S. N. Behrman. Published by Random House, Inc., New York.

"Storm Operation," by Maxwell Anderson. Published by Anderson House, Washington, D. C.

"Pick-up Girl," by Elsa Shelley.

"The Innocent Voyage," by Paul Osborn.

1944-1945

"A Bell for Adano," by Paul Osborn. Published by Alfred A. Knopf, New York.

"I Remember Mama," by John Van Druten. Published by Harcourt, Brace and Co., Inc., New York.

"The Hasty Heart," by John Patrick. Published by Random House, Inc., New York.

"The Glass Menagerie," by Tennessee Williams. Published by Random House, Inc., New York.

"Harvey," by Mary Chase.

"The Late George Apley," by John P. Marquand and George S. Kaufman.

"Soldier's Wife," by Rose Franken. Published by Samuel French.

"Anna Lucasta," by Philip Yordan. Published by Random House, Inc., New York.

"Foolish Notion," by Philip Barry.

"Dear Ruth," by Norman Krasna. Published by Random House, Inc., New York.

1945-1946

"State of the Union," by Howard Lindsay and Russel Crouse. Published by Random House, Inc., New York.

"Home of the Brave," by Arthur Laurents. Published by Random House, Inc., New York.

"Deep Are the Roots," by Arnaud d'Usseau and James Gow. Published by Charles Scribner's Sons, New York.

"The Magnificent Yankee," by Emmet Lavery. Published by Samuel French, Inc., New York.

"Antigone," by Lewis Galantiere (from the French of Jean Anouilh). Published by Random House, Inc., New York.

"O Mistress Mine," by Terence Rattigan. Published and revised by the author.

"Born Yesterday," by Garson Kanin. Published by Viking Press, Inc., New York.

"Dream Girl," by Elmer Rice. Published by Coward-McCann, Inc., New York.

"The Rugged Path," by Robert E. Sherwood. Published by Charles Scribner's Sons, New York.

"Lute Song," by Will Irwin and Sidney Howard. Published version by Will Irwin and Leopoldine Howard.

WHERE AND WHEN THEY WERE BORN

(Compiled from the most authentic records available.)

Abbott, George .... Hamburg, N. Y. 1895
Abel, Walter .... St. Paul, Minn. 1898
Adams, Maude .... Salt Lake City, Utah 1872
Addy, Wesley .... Omaha, Neb. 1912
Adler, Luther .... New York City 1903
Adler, Stella .... New York City 1904
Aherne, Brian .... King's Norton, England .. 1902
Anders, Glenn .... Los Angeles, Cal. 1890
Anderson, Judith .... Australia 1898
Anderson, Maxwell .... Atlantic City, Pa. 1888
Andrews, A. G. .... Buffalo, N. Y. 1861
Andrews, Ann .... Los Angeles, Cal. 1895
Arden, Eve .... San Francisco, Cal. 1912
Arling, Joyce .... Memphis, Tenn. 1911
Arliss, George .... London, England 1868
Astaire, Fred .... Omaha, Neb. 1899

Bainter, Fay .... Los Angeles, Cal. 1892
Bankhead, Tallulah .... Huntsville, Ala. 1902
Barbee, Richard .... Lafayette, Ind. 1887
Barry, Philip .... Rochester, N. Y. 1896
Barrymore, Diana .... New York City 1921
Barrymore, Ethel .... Philadelphia, Pa. 1879
Barrymore, John .... Philadelphia, Pa. 1882
Barrymore, Lionel .... Philadelphia, Pa. 1878
Barton, James .... Gloucester, N. J. 1890
Beecher, Janet .... Jefferson City, Mo. 1887
Behrman, S. N. .... Worcester, Mass. 1893
Bell, James .... Suffolk, Va. 1891
Bellamy, Ralph .... Chicago, Ill. 1905
Berghof, Herbert .... Vienna, Austria 1909
Bergman, Ingrid .... Stockholm 1917
Bergner, Elisabeth .... Vienna 1901
Berlin, Irving .... Russia 1888
Blackmer, Sydney .... Salisbury, N. C. 1898
Bolger, Ray .... Dorchester, Mass. 1906

Bondi, Beulah ....Chicago, Ill. 1892
Bordoni, Irene ....Paris, France 1895
Bourneuf, Philip ....Boston, Mass. 1912
Bowman, Patricia ....Washington, D. C. 1912
Brady, William A. ....San Francisco, Cal. 1863
Braham, Horace ....London, England 1896
Brent, Romney ....Saltillo, Mex. 1902
Brice, Fannie ....Brooklyn, N. Y. 1891
Broderick, Helen ....New York 1891
Brotherson, Eric ....Chicago, Ill. 1911
Bruce, Carol ....Great Neck, L. I. 1919
Bruce, Nigel ....San Diego, Cal. 1895
Burke, Billie ....Washington, D. C. 1885
Burr, Ann ....Boston, Mass. 1920
Butterworth, Charles ....South Bend, Ind. 1896
Byington, Spring ....Colorado Springs, Colo. ...1898

Cagney, James ....New York 1904
Cagney, Jeanne ....New York 1920
Cahill, Lily ....Texas 1891
Calhern, Louis ....New York 1895
Cannon, Maureen ....Chicago, Ill. 1927
Cantor, Eddie ....New York 1894
Carlisle, Kitty ....New Orleans, La. 1912
Carnovsky, Morris ....St. Louis, Mo. 1898
Carroll, Leo G. ....Weedon, England 1892
Carroll, Nancy ....New York City 1906
Catlett, Walter ....San Francisco, Cal. 1889
Caulfield, Joan ....New York City 1924
Chandler, Helen ....Charleston, N. C. 1906
Chatterton, Ruth ....New York 1893
Christians, Mady ....Vienna, Austria 1907
Claire, Helen ....Union Springs, Ala. 1908
Claire, Ina ....Washington, D. C. 1892
Clark, Bobby ....Springfield, Ohio 1888
Clayton, Jan ....Alamogordo, N. M. 1921
Clift, Montgomery ....Omaha, Neb. 1921
Clive, Colin ....St. Malo, France 1900
Coburn, Charles ....,.....Macon, Ga. 1877
Cohan, George M. ....Providence, R. I. 1878
Colbert, Claudette ....Paris 1905
Collins, Russell ....New Orleans, La. 1901
Colt, Ethel Barrymore ....Mamaroneck, N. Y. 1911

Fletcher, Bramwell ....Bradford, Yorkshire, Eng. .1904
Fontanne, Lynn ....London, England 1887
Forbes, Brenda ....London, England 1909
Forbes, Ralph ....London, England 1905
Foy, Eddie, Jr. ....New Rochelle, N. Y. 1907
Francis, Arlene ....Boston, Mass. ....˙1908
Fraser, Elizabeth ....Brooklyn, N. Y. 1920

Garrett, Betty ....St. Louis, Mo. 1919
Gaxton, William ....San Francisco, Cal. 1893
Geddes, Barbara Bel ....New York 1922
Geddes, Norman Bel ....Adrian, Mich. 1893
Gershwin, Ira ....New York 1896
Gielgud, John ....London, England 1904
Gillmore, Margalo ....England 1901
Gilmore, Virginia ....El Monte, Cal. 1919
Gish, Dorothy ....Dayton, Ohio 1898
Gish, Lillian ....Springfield, Ohio 1896
Gleason, James ....New York 1885
Golden, John ....New York 1874
Goodner, Carol ....New York City 1904
Gordon, Ruth ....Wollaston, Mass. 1896
Gough, Lloyd ....New York City 1906
Grant, Sydney ....Boston, Mass. 1873
Greaza, Walter ....St. Paul, Minn. 1900
Green, Mitzi ....New York City 1920
Greenstreet, Sydney ....England 1880
Groody, Louise ....Waco, Texas 1897
Gwenn, Edmund ....Glamorgan, Wales 1875

Hampden, Walter ....Brooklyn, N. Y. 1879
Hannen, Nicholas ....London, England 1881
Hardie, Russell ....Griffin Mills, N. Y. 1906
Hardwicke, Sir Cedric ....Lye, Stourbridge, England .1893
Hart, Richard ....Providence, R. I. 1915
Havoc, June ....Seattle, Wash. 1916
Haydon, Julie ....Oak Park, Ill. 1910
Hayes, Helen ....Washington, D. C. 1900
Heflin, Frances ....Oklahoma City, Okla. 1924
Heflin, Van ....Walters, Okla. 1909
Heineman, Eda ....Japan 1891
Heming, Violet ....Leeds, England 1893
Henie, Sonja ....Oslo, Norway 1912

Hepburn, Katharine ....Hartford, Conn. 1907
Henreid, Paul ....Trieste, Italy 1905
Hobbes, Halliwell ....Stratford, England 1877
Hoey, Dennis ....London, England 1893
Holliday, Judy ....New York City 1924
Hopkins, Arthur ....Cleveland, Ohio 1878
Hopkins, Miriam ....Bainbridge, Ga. 1904
Holmes, Taylor ....Newark, N. J. 1872
Hull, Henry ....Louisville, Ky. 1888
Humphreys, Cecil ....Cheltenham, England 1880
Hussey, Ruth ....Providence, R. I. 1917
Huston, Walter ....Toronto 1884

Inescort, Frieda ....Hitchin, Scotland 1905
Ingram, Rex ....Dublin, Ireland 1892
Ives, Burl ....Hunt Township, Ill. 1909

Jagger, Dean ....Columbus Grove, Ohio 1904
Jameson, House ....Austin, Texas 1902
Jolson, Al ....Washington, D. C. 1883
Johnson, Harold J. (Chic) ....Chicago, Ill. 1891
Joy, Nicholas ....Paris, France 1892

Kane, Whitford ....Larne, Ireland 1882
Karloff, Boris ....Dulwich, England 1887
Kaufman, George S. ....Pittsburgh, Pa. 1889
Kaye, Danny ....New York City 1914
Keith, Robert ....Scotland 1899
Kelly, Gene ....Pittsburgh, Pa. 1912
Kerrigan, J. M. ....Dublin, Ireland 1885
Kiepura, Jan ....Warsaw, Poland 1902
Kilbride, Percy ....San Francisco, Cal. 1880
King, Dennis ....Coventry, England 1897
Kingsford, Walter ....England 1876
Kirkland, Patricia ....New York 1927

Lackland, Ben ....Waco, Texas 1901
Landi, Elissa ....Venice, Italy 1904
Landis, Jessie Royce ....Chicago, Ill. 1904
Laughton, Charles ....Scarborough, England 1899
Lawrence, Gertrude ....London 1898
Lee, Canada ....New York City 1907
Le Gallienne, Eva ....London, England 1899

Leighton, Margaret .... Barnt Green, England 1922
Lillie, Beatrice .... Toronto, Canada 1898
Linn, Bambi .... Brooklyn, N. Y. 1926
Loeb, Philip .... Philadelphia, Pa. 1892
Lonergan, Lenore .... Toledo, Ohio 1928
Lord, Pauline .... Hanford, Cal. 1890
Lukas, Paul .... Budapest, Hungary 1895
Lund, John .... Rochester, N. Y. 1916
Lunt, Alfred .... Milwaukee, Wis. 1893
Lytell, Bert .... New York City 1885

MacMahon, Aline .... McKeesport, Pa. 1899
March, Fredric .... Racine, Wis. 1897
Margetson, Arthur .... London, England 1897
Margo .... Mexico 1918
Marshall, Everett .... Worcester, Mass. 1902
Marshall, Herbert .... London, England 1890
Mason, James .... Huddersfield, England 1909
Massey, Raymond .... Toronto, Canada 1896
Matteson, Ruth .... San Jose, Cal. 1905
McClintic, Guthrie .... Seattle, Wash. 1893
McCormick, Myron .... Albany, Ind. 1907
McCracken, Joan .... Philadelphia, Pa. 1923
McGrath, Paul .... Chicago, Ill. 1900
McGuire, Dorothy .... Omaha, Neb. 1918
Menotti, Gian-Carlo .... Italy 1912
Meredith, Burgess .... Cleveland, Ohio 1908
Merivale, Philip .... Rehutia, India 1886
Merman, Ethel .... Astoria, R. I. 1909
Middleton, Ray .... Chicago, Ill. 1907
Miller, Gilbert .... New York 1884
Miranda, Carmen .... Portugal 1912
Mitchell, Grant .... Columbus, Ohio 1874
Mitchell, Thomas .... Elizabeth, N. J. 1892
Moore, Grace .... Del Rio, Tenn. 1901
Moore, Victor .... Hammondton, N. J. 1876
Morgan, Claudia .... New York 1912
Morgan, Ralph .... New York City 1889
Morris, Mary .... Boston 1894
Morris, McKay .... San Antonio, Texas 1890
Moss, Arnold .... Brooklyn, N. Y. 1910
Muni, Paul .... Lemberg, Austria 1895
Myrtil, Odette .... Paris, France 1898

Nagel, Conrad .... Keokuk, Iowa 1897
Natwick, Mildred .... Baltimore, Md. 1908
Nolan, Lloyd .... San Francisco, Cal. 1903
Nugent, Elliott .... Dover, Ohio 1900

O'Brien-Moore, Erin .... Los Angeles, Cal. 1908
Odets, Clifford .... Philadelphia 1906
Olivier, Laurence .... Dorking, Surrey, England .1907
Olsen, John Siguard (Ole) ... Peru, Ind. 1892
O'Malley, Rex .... London, England 1906
O'Neal, Frederick .... Brookville, Miss. 1905
O'Neill, Eugene Gladstone ... New York 1888
Ouspenskaya, Maria .... Tula, Russia 1876

Patterson, Elizabeth .... Savannah, Tenn. 1898
Pemberton, Brock .... Leavenworth, Kansas 1885
Petina, Irra .... Leningrad, Russia 1900
Pickford, Mary .... Toronto 1893
Picon, Molly .... New York City 1898
Pollock, Channing .... Washington, D. C. 1880
Price, Vincent .... St. Louis, Mo. 1914

Rains, Claude .... London, England 1889
Raitt, John .... Santa Ana, Cal. 1917
Rathbone, Basil .... Johannesburg 1892
Raye, Martha .... Butte, Mont. 1916
Redman, Joyce .... Newcastle, Ireland 1918
Reed, Florence .... Philadelphia, Pa. 1883
Rennie, James .... Toronto, Canada 1890
Richardson, Ralph .... Cheltenham, England 1902
Roberts, Joan .... New York City 1918
Robinson, Bill .... Richmond, Va. 1878
Robinson, Edward G. .... Bucharest, Roumania 1893
Ross, Anthony .... New York 1906
Royle, Selena .... New York 1905
Ruben, José .... Belgium 1886

Sands, Dorothy .... Cambridge, Mass. 1900
Sarnoff, Dorothy .... Brooklyn, N. Y. 1919
Scheff, Fritzi .... Vienna, Austria 1879
Scott, Martha .... Jamesport, Mo. 1914
Segal, Vivienne .... Philadelphia, Pa. 1897
Shannon, Effie .... Cambridge, Mass. 1867

NECROLOGY

June 1, 1946—June 1, 1947

Anspacher, Louis Kaufman, dramatist and lecturer, 69. Wrote "All the King's Men," "The Embarrassment of Riches" and "A Woman of Impulse" in which his wife, Kathryn Kidder, starred; other plays were "That Day," "Dagmar" for Nazimova, "The Unchastened Woman" for Emily Stevens, "The Ghost Between," etc.; was awarded Townsend Harris Medal in recognition of notable post-war attainment. Born Cincinnati, Ohio; died Nashville, Tenn., May 10, 1947.

Barthololomae, Philip H., playwright and producer, 67. First play "Over Night" (1911); subsequently formed own producing company; staged his own plays, "Little Miss Brown" and "When Dreams Come True," etc.; wrote librettos for "Very Good Eddy" and first edition of "Greenwich Village Follies." Born Chicago, Ill.; died Winnetka, Ill., January 5, 1947.

Barton, John, actor, 76. Veteran actor and vaudeville star; uncle of James Barton; played Jeeter Lester in "Tobacco Road" over 2,000 times in a period of nine years; in vaudeville with his wife, Anne Ashley, became famous in "Canal Boat Sal"; toured England as team; played music hall circuit in England for 25 years. Born Germantown, Pa.; died New York City, December 23, 1946.

Bowes, Maj. Edward E., manager, promoter, 72. Famous in entertainment world for years; part owner and manager Capitol and Cort Theatres in New York, Park Square in Boston; vice-president Metro-Goldwyn-Mayer Corporation; remembered for his "Amateur Hour" on radio, providing opportunity for thousands of tyro entertainers; married Margaret Illington, actress. Born San Francisco, Calif.; died Rumson, New Jersey, June 13, 1946.

Bragdon, Claude F., author, designer, 80. Best known on Broadway for settings designed for Walter Hampden repertory, especially "Cyrano de Bergerac"; lecturer on architecture and designing at Art Institute, Chicago, and Princeton University; wrote philosophical books; with Nicholas Bessara-

boff translated Ouspensky's "Tertium Organum." Born
Oberlin, Ohio; died New York City, September 17, 1946.

Brecher, Egon, actor and director, 66. Became director Stadts
Theatre in Vienna; assistant producer Civic Repertory Theatre, New York, with Eva Le Gallienne; last Broadway assignment director of "Two Strange Women" (1933). Born
Czechoslovakia; died Hollywood, Calif., August 12, 1946.

Butterworth, Charles E., actor, 46. Stage and screen comedian
for 20 years. New York debut in "Americana" (1926);
played in "Sweet Adeline," "Flying Colors," "Allez Oop";
monologue specialties, "The After Dinner Speaker," "The
Rotary Speech," etc.; toured Pacific Army bases with USO;
appeared in many motion pictures including "This Is the
Army." Born South Bend, Ind.; died Hollywood, Calif.,
June 13, 1946.

Carr, Alexander, actor, 68. Stage and screen comedian; New
York debut in "Wine, Women and Song" (1904); became
famous as Mawruss Perlmutter in "Potash and Perlmutter";
also played in "The Gay White Way," "Louisiana Lou," etc.;
prominent in motion pictures. Born Rumni, Russia; died
Hollywood, Calif., September 7, 1946.

Chambers, Lyster, actor, 71. Forty years on American stage;
debut with Murray Hill Stock Co.; last appearance in "Sig-
nature" (1945); played in support of Mrs. Pat Campbell,
Madame Simone, Bertha Kalisch and others; played in "The
New Henrietta," "The Wild Duck," "The First Year"; director Fox Movietone News. Born Michigan; died New
York City, January 27, 1947.

Colton, John, playwright, 60. Wrote "Rain" (with Clemence
Randolph), "The Shanghai Gesture," "Saint Wench" and
many scenarios. Born Minneapolis, Minn.; died Gaines-
ville, Texas, December 12, 1946.

Corthell, Herbert, actor, 69. Fifty years on stage and screen;
started in Boston (1897); with Robert Edeson in "Strong-
heart"; Lillian Russell in "Wildfire"; last stage appearance
in New York in "Arsenic and Old Lace"; featured comedian
in many musical comedies. Born Boston, Mass.; died Hollywood, Calif., January 23, 1947.

Dunn, J. Malcolm, actor, 70. Well known on London stage before coming to America 43 years ago; New York debut in
"Sweet Kitty Bellairs" (1903); last Broadway appearance
in "The Rock" (1943). Born London, England; died Beech-
urst, Queens, L. I., New York, October 10, 1946.

Dupree, Minnie, actress, 72. On stage 60 years; debut in "The Unknown" (1887); remembered in "The Road to Yesterday," "Held by the Enemy," "The Climbers," "The Music Master," etc.; last appearance in "Land's End" (1946); an organizer of Stage Relief Fund in New York. Born San Francisco, Calif.; died New York City, May 23, 1947.

Fields, W. C. (Dukenfield), actor, 66. World-famous comic on stage and screen, in burlesque and vaudeville; first speaking part with McIntyre and Heath in "The Ham Tree"; with Ziegfeld Follies as featured comedian for seven years; with George White's "Scandals" (1922); ended career in pictures. Born Philadelphia, Pa.; died Pasadena, Calif., December 25, 1946.

Gleason, Lucile Webster, actress, 59. Wife of James Gleason with whom she starred in many plays including "Is Zat So?" and "The Fall Guy"; debut New York (1919) in "The Five Million"; also in "Merton of the Movies," "The Butter and Egg Man," etc.; recently acting in screen plays. Born Pasadena, Calif.; died Brentwood, Calif., May 17, 1947.

Hamilton, Clayton, playwright and critic, 64. Drama critic of *Forum* (1907), *The Bookman* (1910-18), *Everybody's Magazine* and *Vogue;* co-author of "The Love That Blinds," "The Big Idea," and "Thirty Days" (with A. E. Thomas); "Friend in Need" (with Bernard Voight); wrote many books pertaining to the theatre; served on Pulitzer Prize Committee for 16 years; member of National Institute of Arts and Letters; lectured ten years at Columbia University. Born Brooklyn, New York; died New York City, September 17, 1946.

Harris, William, Jr., producer and director, 62. Prominent Broadway producer in the 1920s; produced "East Is West," John Drinkwater's "Abraham Lincoln," "Outward Bound," "The Yellow Jacket," "Twin Beds," "Arms and the Girl," "Mary Stuart," "The Criminal Code," "The Greeks Had a Word for It," etc.; retired 1939. Born Boston, Mass.; died New York City, September 2, 1946.

Hart, William S., actor, producer, 81. Started on stage, ended on screen after 60 years' service; New York debut "Austerlitz" (1889); gained fame in "Ben Hur," "The Virginian," "The Squaw Man"; toured with Ada Rehan in "When Bess Was Queen," with Modjeska in "Camille," with Julia Arthur in "Romeo and Juliet"; started film career in 1914; organized his own studio in Hollywood; wrote autobiography,

"My Life East and West." Born Newburgh, New York;
died Los Angeles, Calif., June 24, 1946.
Henderson, Lucius, actor, author and producer, 99.
Widely known concert pianist; played juvenile roles with Modjeska,
Edwin Booth, Lawrence Barrett and Tomaso Salvini; last
Broadway appearance "My Maryland" (1929); started mo-
tion picture career 1910; radio debut two years ago. Born
Aledo, Ill.; died New York City, February 18, 1947.
Homer, Louise, singer, 76. Contralto opera star who sang 19
consecutive seasons at the Metropolitan Opera House; re-
membered in "Aida," "La Giocondo," "Samson et Dalila,"
"Orfeo et Euridice," etc.; appeared Covent Garden, London,
Royal Opera in Brussels and other European opera houses.
Born Pittsburgh, Pa.; died Winter Park, Fla., May 6, 1947.
Herbert, Henry, actor and producer, 68. Stage debut London
with Ben Greet Players; later managed F. R. Benson company; organized own company playing in British Isles and
Africa; debut New York "Mind the Paint Girl" (1912);
played "Hamlet" more than 500 times; arranged text and
staged revival of "Troilus and Cressida" (1932) for The
Players; last appearance on Broadway in "Arsenic and Old
Lace" (1941); original member of Elizabethan Stage Society
and associate director of Stratford-on-Avon Memorial Theatre. Born England; died Flushing, New York, February
20, 1947.
Hooker, Brian, playwright and composer, 66. Taught English at
Yale and Columbia University; wrote "Fairyland," "Morven
and the Grail" and "Mona" (operas) with Dr. Horatio
Parker; translated "Cyrano de Bergerac," "Ruy Blas,"
etc.; author or collaborator of "Through the Years," "The
O'Flynn," "The Vagabond King," etc. Born New London,
Conn.; died New London, Conn., December 28, 1946.
Intropodi, Ethel, actress, 50. Well known on American stage;
member of theatrical family; stage debut "Mind the Paint
Girl" (1912); last Broadway appearance in "Doctors Dis-
agree" (1943); last theatrical activity in 1945 when she went
to England and Germany with USO production of "Blithe
Spirit." Born New York City; died New York City, De-
cember 18, 1946.
Kaye, Albert Patrick, actor, 68. Veteran of British and American
stage; London debut in "True Blue" (1896); debut New
York in "Man and Superman" (1912); played in "Cynara,"
"Darling of the Gods," "Back to Methuselah," "The Green

Hat," etc.; toured with Katharine Cornell in "The Barretts of Wimpole Street" and "Romeo and Juliet"; last appearance on Broadway in "Uncle Harry" (1942). Born Ringwood, Hampshire, England; died Washingtonville, New York, September 7, 1946.

Lawrence, Vincent, playwright, 56. Started to write plays in 1916 with "Fate Decides"; last play on Broadway, "The Overtons" (1945); other plays included "The Ghost Between," "In Love with Love" and "A Distant Drum"; screen play writer for ten years. Born Roxbury, Mass.; died Corpus Christi, Texas, November 24, 1946.

McCormick, F. J. (Peter Judge), actor, 44. Started stage career in Dublin's Queens Theatre; joined Abbey Theatre 1918; crossed Atlantic five times with the Irish Players; played in "Things That Are Caesar's," "The Far Off Hills," "Juno and the Paycock," "Playboy of the Western World," etc.; married Eileen Crowe, actress. Born Skerries, near Dublin, Ireland; died Dublin, Ireland, April 24, 1947.

McCoy, Frank, producer, 58. In show business 42 years; started as actor in support of Thomas W. Ross in "Checkers"; established stock companies in Milwaukee, Trenton and other cities; stage manager for Comstock and Gest; took "Abie's Irish Rose," "Arsenic and Old Lace," "Stage Door" and other hits on tour. Died New York City, January 16, 1947.

Meek, Donald, actor, 66. On British and Australian stage before coming to U. S. in 1912; played more than 800 roles; started with Sir Henry Irving at 8; first appeared in U. S. at Castle Square Theatre, Boston, 1912; debut New York in "Going Up" (1917). Born Glasgow, Scotland; died Hollywood, Calif., November 18, 1946.

Melville, Rose, actress, 73. First appearance on stage in Zanesville, Ohio, in "Queen's Evidence" (1889); played Sis Hopkins more than 5,000 times; character taken from play called "Zeb"; afterward elaborated and featured in "Little Christopher" in New York (1894). Born Terre Haute, Ind.; died Lake George, New York, October 8, 1946.

Moore, Grace, singer, 45. First appearance on stage in "Hitchy-Koo of 1920"; first appearance at Metropolitan Opera House as Mimi in "La Boheme" (1928); subsequently sang in many operas here and in Europe; commenced film career in 1930; was killed in airliner crash at Danish airport; final concert evening before in Copenhagen. Born Del Rio, Tenn.; died near Copenhagen, Denmark, January 26, 1947.

Nugent, John Charles, actor and playwright, 79. Started long theatre career as a child; toured with repertory and stock companies; headlined with his wife, Grace Fertig, in vaudeville in his own sketches; collaborated with son Elliott on "Kempy," "Dumb-Bell," "The Poor Nut," etc.; last Broadway appearance "Playboy of the Western World" (1946); many years in Hollywood. Born Niles, Ohio; died New York City, April 21, 1947.

Patterson, Joseph Medill, publisher, novelist and playwright, 67. Active in theatre in nineteen hundreds; later co-editor and publisher Chicago *Tribune* and New York *Daily News;* Commissioner Public Works in Chicago; Captain and war correspondent in World War I; with Col. Robert R. McCormick founded *Liberty Magazine;* author of "The Fourth Estate," "A Little Brother of the Rich" and "Rebellion," dramatized in association with Harriett Ford. Born Chicago, Ill.; died New York City, May 26, 1946.

Perry, Antoinette (Frueauff), actress, producer and director, 58. Started theatre career at 16 with David Belasco and David Warfield; debut "Miss Temple's Telegram" (1905); appeared in "Lady Jim," "The Music Master," "The Grand Army Man," "Mr. Pitt"; with Brock Pemberton produced and directed "Strictly Dishonorable," "Personal Appearance," "Ceiling Zero," "Kiss the Boys Goodbye," "Janie," "Harvey," etc.; with Rachel Crothers and Jane Cowl helped organize New York Stage Door Canteen; chairman of board and secretary of American Theatre Wing. Born Denver, Colorado; died New York City, June 28, 1946.

Tanguay, Eva, actress and singer, 68. Started as child actress; toured as Cedric Errol in "Little Lord Fauntleroy" for five years; appeared with Frank Daniels in "The Office Boy" (1903); famous in vaudeville singing "I Don't Care," "I Want Someone to Go Wild with Me," etc. Born Marbleton, Quebec, Canada; died Hollywood, Calif., January 11, 1947.

Toler, Sidney, actor and author, 73. With Corse Payton on road (1901); with Julia Marlowe Company (1902); debut New York "The Office Boy" (1903); starred in "Billy Baxter"; wrote "The Belle of Richmond," "The Dancing Master," "The House on the Sands," etc.; became film actor in 1929 in "Madame X"; on death of Warner Oland fell heir to Charlie Chan role in pictures. Born Warrenburg, Mo.; died Hollywood, Calif., February 12, 1947.

Toohey, John Peter, press representative and author, 66. Newspaper and magazine writer; wrote "Swifty" with W. C. Pritchard (1922), "Jonesy" (with Ann Morrison), "Growing Pains," "Wilbur," "Fresh Every Hour," etc.; general press representative of Sam H. Harris Theatrical Enterprises (1930-1942); represented Max Gordon, George Arliss, John Drew, Emma Calve, William A. Brady; last assignment with "The Late George Apley." Born Binghamton, New York; died New York City, November 7, 1946.

Webster, Ben, actor, 82. Husband of Dame May Whitty and father of Margaret Webster; more than half a century a leading actor of English-speaking stage; started career with Sir Henry Irving; toured with Ellen Terry, Dion Bouccicault, Mrs. Patrick Campbell; first appeared in New York in "The Marriage of William Asche" (1905). Born London, England; died Hollywood, Calif., February 26, 1947.

Welford, Dallas, actor, 74. Gained fame as comedian; debut in England in "The Danites" (1881); debut in New York in "Mr. Hopkinson" (1906); other plays on Broadway included "The Girl from Rector's," "Madame Sherry," "Blossom Time," "The Student Prince," etc.; played with Edna May during long run of "The School Girl." Born Liverpool, England; died Santa Monica, Calif., September 28, 1946.

THE DECADES' TOLL

(Persons of Outstanding Prominence in the Theatre
Who Have Died in Recent Years)

	Born	*Died*
Baker, George Pierce	1866	1935
Barrymore, John	1882	1942
Belasco, David	1856	1931
Bernhardt, Sarah	1845	1923
Campbell, Mrs. Patrick	1865	1940
Cohan, George Michael	1878	1942
De Koven, Reginald	1861	1920
De Reszke, Jean	1850	1925
Drew, John	1853	1927
Drinkwater, John	1883	1937
Du Maurier, Sir Gerald	1873	1934
Duse, Eleanora	1859	1924
Fiske, Minnie Maddern	1865	1932
Frohman, Daniel	1851	1940
Galsworthy, John	1867	1933
Gorky, Maxim	1868	1936
Greet, Sir Philip (Ben)	1858	1936
Herbert, Victor	1859	1924
Patti, Adelina	1843	1919
Pinero, Sir Arthur Wing	1855	1934
Russell, Annie	1864	1936
Schumann-Heink, Ernestine	1861	1936
Skinner, Otis	1858	1942
Sothern, Edwin Hugh	1859	1933
Tarkington, Booth	1862	1946
Terry, Ellen	1848	1928
Thomas, Augustus	1857	1934
Tyler, George C.	1867	1946
Yeats, William Butler	1865	1939

INDEX OF AUTHORS

INDEX OF PLAYS AND CASTS

544

INDEX OF PRODUCERS, DIRECTORS
AND DESIGNERS